JUDITH TURNER

THE HIDDEN WORLD OF
BIRTHDAYS

A FIRESIDE BOOK
PUBLISHED BY SIMON & SCHUSTER

FIRESIDE
Rockefeller Center
1230 Avenues of the Americas
New York, NY 10020

Copyright © 1999 by Judith Turner
FIRESIDE and colophon are registered trademarks
of Simon & Schuster Inc.

Designed by Eve L. Kirch

Manufactured in the United States of America

1   3   5   7   9   10   8   6   4   2

Library of Congress Cataloging-in-Publication Data is available

ISBN 0-684-85798-7

MY WORDS ARE MY FEELINGS, MY FEELINGS ARE MY LIFE
MY GIFT TO YOU MY WORDS.

My parents: Judith Turner and Robert Turner. Thank you for creating such a strong foundation based on love and support and for always continuing to do so.

My siblings: Jeri Turner Sinnig, Andrew Turner, and JoAnne Connelly. For sharing not only in my joys, but trying to change my sorrows.

My children: Briane, Wojo, and Alexandria. You are my world. You are my children. You are what makes the difference in my every day.

My husband: Walter Deptuch. There could never be this fire without the "Spark."

Special People: To some who have touched my life by love and friendship along the way. Ally Walker, Eileen Breen, Susan Frusteri, Kelly Keating, Michael Toback, Robert Metzdorf, Melinda Eppy Daly, Jimmy Behrens, Daniele Gibson, Janice Holden, Miki Taylor, Marguerite Di Donato, Maryanne Colenda, Carol McCracken, Janice Meyer, Debbie Reilly, Bobby, Mike and Joey Tessel, Michele Marsh, Colleen Callaghan, Dr. Howard Adelglass and Susan Adelglass, Timmy Brown, Billy Avon, Patrick Meeuwsissen, Vicki Ullman, Christine Reilly, and Marie Kenny.

YOU HAVE ALL MADE A DIFFERENCE!

ACKNOWLEDGMENTS

Marvin Brown—for having not only an open ear, but an open mind.

Ed Stackler—for encouraging me, even though he knew he was leaving.

Paula Clark—for being kind enough to make a phone call.

Amanda Borghese—for wanting to take a chance.

Robert Metzdorf Esq.—for always believing in me.

Ally Walker—for encouragement from a friend.

Helen Horowitz "Vitamin Shoppe"—for the opportunities to ask all the questions I could.

Joe Ciccio—for the desire to help.

Gladys Callaghan—for the devotion of a friend, that all the money in the world can't buy.

Charles Fortier—"The wiz with the word." Thanks for wanting to help with anything you could.

Janice Holden Meyer—Thanks for always being there—no matter how overwhelming the work.

Pauline Black—Your support and devotion is what helped make this book. Thank you!

Leslie McHale—Your skills are amazing.

Michael Toback, Maryanne Colenda, Marguerite Di Donato "The Tuesday

Night Group"—for creating a night of sanity so I could get through this book.

Debbie Reilly—for being there, being you and always wanting to support me in all I do.

Judy Buonauito—for encouragement along the way and my introduction to astrology.

Terence Sheehan—for continuous help and support with the computer and other tasks.

Jeri Turner Sinnig—for book seeking, stapling, stuffing, collating and everything you did to contribute.

Judith Dunn Turner—for book hunting, stapling, cutting, and reading.

Cape Cod Book Hunters—Noel Keating, Carol McCracken, Judith Dunn Turner, and Jeri Turner Sinnig.

Atlantic City—Helen Schuler, Barbara Tessel, JoAnne Connelly, and Lorraine Jensen.

Miki Taylor—"The chocolate connection."

Jobes and Gertrude—for the dictionary of mythology, folklore, and symbols

Joan Hamburg—Thank you, the woman with all the answers.

Tommy Hilfiger—for your kindness when I needed it.

Pam Bernstein—for being a great agent.

Kate Ford—for wanting this book to happen for me.

Gale Hayman—When the chips were down you were supportive in picking them up.

Mark Weiss—for astrological input.

INTRODUCTION

Who is more important than you? Wouldn't it be interesting to learn important information that could enhance your life, in both large and small ways? Did you know you have a guardian angel? Has anyone explained to you there are different foods that could benefit you? Wouldn't you like to purchase a fragrance that could make others take notice of you? Some types of music should be more relaxing for you than others. You even have your own special flower based on the day you were born. Would you like to know what your lucky numbers are? Which day of the week may be best to ask for a raise? Are you seeking a mate? This book will explain the best bets in selecting a life partner for you. The tiniest things may make a difference, no matter how insignificant they may seem to you. One color may be luckier for you than another, while another color may balance your mood and enhance your environment.

You can use this book to find out all of this information about yourself. Turn to the page with *your* birthday to learn how to have a happier, more productive life. For example, my birthday is July 27. By reading that page I'd learn that I need Orange in my environment when I feel weak, I look great in Plum, and Rubies will help me overcome disappointment in love. Using this book will help you unlock the keys to your personality, needs, motivations, and dreams. You can also look up the birthdays of friends and loved ones to help you understand them better, too.

You may notice that some information repeats itself over several days. That's because there are often similarities between people born around the same time of year. But each person has qualities that are all his or her own, and each day is as special as the person born on it.

Here is a list of the information you'll find in this book:

Gems: These are jewels and precious stones that the ancients felt could be worn to bring the bearer luck, power, and encouragement. Use them carefully, as they can be powerful tools in managing your spiritual life.

Colors: Many studies have shown that the colors we surround ourselves with can change our moods, so it's vital to select the correct combinations. We each have a color that enhances our confidence and calms us when we are troubled. According to research, there are colors that will actually make you feel better, especially if your home or workplace lacks them.

Apparel Colors: There are hues and shades that are better and luckier for you to wear than others. They may give you more charm and charisma.

Astral Colors: These colors are ones you may be naturally drawn to and that may benefit you throughout your life in many subtle ways. Listed is the one that is certain to help you find your place in the universe.

Trees: Trees have the attributes of strength and power. They are full of life and offer individual meaning to each of us. You may be drawn to put a special tree in your yard or even have a memory of a certain tree when you were young. You may just look at one all the time and find that it is talking to you. See what yours might say. Once you know what tree belongs to you, you might look at and relate to your world differently.

Birds: I bet you never realized how much birds and humans really do have in common. When you read the description of birds in this book, you may find in the characterization of the birds a fascinating resemblance to yourself. You may only then recognize that without a doubt you have an attraction to a particular bird.

Health Scents: Besides finding out what to wear to smell good, you'll want to splash on what might make you feel good. There are scents that are relaxing and have better effects on particular sun signs. You may be naturally drawn to a scent because it relaxes you or you just love its smell. These scents have been selected for you for their mystical traits and ingredients.

What's Lucky: What's more fascinating than knowing what "lucky" numbers, times, days, months, and years are yours, particularly if they were picked out according to the day you were born? Do you have a lucky charm? You can now. Each lucky charm has been chosen by either its number or sign and could prove to be more than a little beneficial for you. Picking a mate isn't easy, and neither is picking a partner. Maybe this advice could help.

Spiritual Stones: These small bits of Mother Earth will guide you on your path over her. Use them in broadening your understanding of yourself or nature.

Judith's Insight: I have been a professional psychic for eighteen years and, after much meditation and thought, have developed my own insights for each day of the year. You may notice that the traits of some days are similar to those that surround them; however, each is unique. You may be able to relate to one or two items right away, but—as with the other items—each time you come back to this book you may glimpse a different part of yourself. As the person reading the book changes, the messages will alter and shift. Each insight was written to hold some meaning for you at almost any stage of your life. However, don't expect that everything will make sense right away. For example, careers that may not even interest you today could give you great satisfaction a year or two from now. The insights offer you a peek not just into who you are but who you are capable of becoming. They are crafted to give you encouragement when you may need it. All the listed information is intended to help and guide you in making the right choices for you.

JANUARY

JANUARY 1 CAPRICORN • The goat of the zodiac
December 21 at 10:00 P.M. to January 21 at 3:00 A.M. • NUMEROLOGY 1

Possessions and Desires . . .

Gem: Moonstone—This gem could protect you from danger.
Flower: Oak Geranium—You are constantly open to true friendship.
Astral Color, Color Need, Apparel Color: Your Astral Color is Brown, which helps keep you grounded and stable. Blue in your environment helps you avoid becoming listless and disorganized. In your wardrobe, Green is your power color for overcoming obstacles.
Fragrance: You are stimulated by a combination of greens and flowers, such as white roses, jasmine, and greenery. They give you feelings of elegance, strength, security.
Tree: Walnut—You are unusually helpful and always looking for constant changes in your life.
Instruments: Oboe, flute, clarinet, piano, French horn, organ, piccolo
Composer: Böhm
Bird: Hummingbird—This bird is delicate and graceful. It can remain still for hours, then dart off and be as busy as a bee.
Symbol: Crown—the universal sign of dignity

Harmonious Health and Nutrition . . .

Health Scent: Strawberry—Soothing by nature, the strawberry promotes self-esteem and encourages love.
Favorable Foods: Asparagus, peaches, whole wheat, nuts, buttermilk

What's Lucky . . .

Lucky Numbers: 1, 2, 11
Best Months: March and November
Best Day of the Week: Saturday
Best Month Days: 1, 10, 19, 28
Lucky Charm: A new penny in your shoe.
Harmonious Signs for Relationships and Partnerships: Capricorn, Taurus, Virgo, and anyone born from July 27 to September 27.

Spiritual Guides . . .

Star: Vega—Those with this star can be warriors in search of victory, especially in legal situations.
Angel: Hanaeb—This angel shows us our worldly desires in order to give us strength when we are going through uncertainty.
Guardian Angel: Malachi—"Messenger of Jehovah."
Spiritual Stone: Sardonyx—This stone may cause people to be attracted to you.

✶ JUDITH'S INSIGHT ✶

A determined individual, you do not allow anything to get in your way. You're aggressive when needed, but you like to appear to be the good guy. You can back away from the demands of others; the demands you will put upon yourself are overwhelming.

Family is of key importance, and it is where your loyalty lies. Sometimes you create contradictions in your own life. You build a path on your property for others to cross, only to realize later that your property will become ruined. You are loved by all circles of people, but you need to be cautious with your language. At times your tone may be misunderstood by others.

Look for a career as a comedian, builder, lawyer, or architect. Try to keep in mind that you are creative, inventive, and strong. Look for a working environment that allows you the sense of freedom you desire. A position with growth potential is best for you. Without growth, your desire for work lessens. Be patient. It may take a while to get where you want to go, but once you do, you'll achieve the financial stability and work contentment that you so much need. When all else fails, use that great sense of humor, which is by far your second most appealing trait. Your heart is your first.

With your hands, you're a builder; emotionally, you're the foundation for others. Be cautious of what you carry on those shoulders. On your own, you can be misguided. Learn to protect yourself better. Others find you irresistibly strong.

✶ ✶ ✶

JANUARY 2

CAPRICORN • The goat of the zodiac

December 21 at 10:00 P.M. to January 21 at 3:00 A.M. • NUMEROLOGY 2

Possessions and Desires . . .

Gem: Sapphire—This gem may help you find forgiveness from those you've wronged.

Flower: Multiflora Rose—Grace covers you like a warm blanket.

Astral Color, Color Need, Apparel Color: Your Astral Color is Silver, which stimulates your imagination. Blue in your environment will prevent depression and disappointment. In your wardrobe, Green is your power color for overcoming obstacles.

Fragrance: You are stimulated by a combination of greens and flowers, such as white roses, jasmine, and greenery. They give you feelings of elegance, strength, and security.

Tree: Maple—You have great stability and flashes of intuition.

Instruments: Pipe organ, cymbal, drum

Composers: Handel, Johann Sebastian Bach

Bird: Cuckoo—A good flyer and very seldom a quitter. Some cuckoos seem more independent than they actually are and yearn for more nuturing than one would expect.

Symbol: Cross—The symbol of self-sacrifice and reconciliation.

Harmonious Health and Nutrition . . .

Health Scent: Apple—You are creative, full of joy, and nearly magical. You bring happiness.

Favorable Foods: Brussels sprouts, raspberries, rye, almonds, cottage cheese

What's Lucky . . .

Lucky Numbers: 2, 11, 20

Best Months: March and November

Best Day of the Week: Saturday

Best Month Days: 2, 11, 20, 29

Lucky Charms: Two 50-cent pieces. Give someone else one of them.

Harmonious Signs for Relationships and Partnerships: Capricorn, Taurus, Virgo, and anyone born from July 27 to September 27.

Spiritual Guides . . .

Star: Altair—Those with this star feel compelled to protect the wounded.

Angel: Hanaeb—This angel shows us our worldly desires in order to give us strength when we are going through uncertainty.

Guardian Angel: Uriel—Helps bring the light of God. "God's guidance."

Spiritual Stone: Sardonyx—This stone may cause people to be attracted to you.

✷ JUDITH'S INSIGHT ✷

You look for love in all the right places. You're a natural poet encouraged by your need for laughter. Anything and everything you try, no matter how small or large, will result in success. You're a passionate lover who is willing to work at it. Nobody likes to be without you for very long. Largely because of your capabilities, you can take on too much, too fast, never realizing the size of the burden. Have no fear, workaholics tend to survive. Stamina is your middle name. You sometimes seem to lack compassion, but those feelings are there. Keep this in mind during conflicts with loved ones and especially at work if you hold a supervisory position.

Family members will always be important to you, but check your demanding side and the demands being placed on you by others. One of these areas could pose problems for you. The outside world sees you as smart and sweet, but your loved ones pay for the constant demands you create for yourself. Family can sometimes get underfoot, especially after you've found your "significant other."

Your abilities may lead to teaching or law, but you probably have more romantic aspirations, to be something like an artist, or the head of a movie company. Try to keep your structuring abilities alive while allowing that creative soul to find its passion. Sounds like a conflict of direction, but if you start off early in a structured job, you find creativity later.

As strong as you are, you can be needy. Learn to keep your temper under wraps. The word "stubborn" doesn't begin to describe it: When you are good, you're good, but when you are bad, you're horrid.

✷ ✷ ✷

JANUARY 3   CAPRICORN • The goat of the zodiac
December 21 at 10:00 P.M. to January 21 at 3:00 A.M. • NUMEROLOGY 3

Possessions and Desires . . .

Gem: Moonstone—This gem could protect you from danger.

Flower: Cactus—You have an inner warmth like the sun to those who orbit you.

Astral Color, Color Need, Apparel Color: Your Astral Color is Black, which creates a sense of protection. Blue in your environment helps you avoid becoming listless and disorganized. In your wardrobe, many shades of Green always let you look your best.

Fragrance: You are stimulated by a combination of greens and flowers, such as white roses, jasmine, and greenery. They give you feelings of elegance, strength, and security.

Tree: Elm—You have willpower, strength, and the ability to stand alone.

Instrument: Trombone

Composers: Verdi, Mendelssohn, Schumann

Bird: Swan—Regarded as royal and sacred, this bird has the protective nature of a mother, and can become a furious fighter in the defense of its young.

Symbol: Wreath—You have been crowned with a special personality. You are strong but extremely compassionate.

Harmonious Health and Nutrition . . .

Health Scent: Rose—This scent will lead you to passionate thoughts and make you feel warm inside.

Favorable Foods: Cauliflower, peaches, whole wheat, peanuts, eggs

What's Lucky . . .

Lucky Numbers: 2, 11, 13
Best Months: March and November
Best Day of the Week: Saturday
Best Month Days: 3, 12, 21, 30
Lucky Charm: A pen that someone else has already used.
Harmonious Signs for Relationships and

Partnerships: Capricorn, Taurus, Virgo, and anyone born from July 27 to September 27.

Spiritual Guides . . .

Star: Dabih—The star of the prominent in society.
Angel: Hanaeb—This angel shows our worldly desires in order to give us strength when we are going through uncertainty.
Guardian Angel: Johiel—This angel is a protector of all those with a humble heart.
Spiritual Stone: Sardonyx—This stone may cause people to be attracted to you.

✴ *JUDITH'S INSIGHT* ✴

The more discipline and control you have, the better. Like Tom Sawyer, you have a cunning sense of power over people—they do what you want without realizing they're working so hard. Negative thinkers might call you dictatorial—you're not. A leader, even in the best of circumstances, will encounter many challenges. You have self-control, though you don't always know how to use it.

Applause and appreciation thrill you. Make sure your significant other recognizes this from the beginning. You expect your mate to intuitively know your needs. Learn to communicate better, keeping in mind it takes two to tango. All family will be important to you, especially your children. When children do enter your life, whether they're yours or not, your heart will experience a new love that will open emotional doors.

You can rise to the occasion in any career you choose. You're highly qualified for the medical field, but you thrive in any profession or career that has structure. Uniform jobs, like those of the state or federal government, will be available to you. Since you are extremely conscientious in all that you do, battling with yourself will be one of your biggest downfalls. The next will be battling with others over nothing, especially when you go through times of great frustration. Make sure you keep your mind's doors and windows open to allow the growth in your career that you greatly fear but still want badly. Don't forget to allow your childlike side out once in a while. You're a lover of travel, so stick to those activities where earth's elements are most evident: hiking, camping, boating, and so on.

✴ ✴ ✴

JANUARY 4 CAPRICORN • The goat of the zodiac
December 21 at 10:00 P.M. to January 21 at 3:00 A.M. • NUMEROLOGY 4

Possessions and Desires . . .

Gem: Emerald—Those who carry this stone tend to be lucky in love.
Flower: Aloe—Be sure to guard against religious superstition and grieving too long.
Astral Color, Color Need, Apparel Color: Your Astral Color is Brown, which helps keep you grounded and stable. Blue in your environment helps you avoid becoming listless and disorganized. Your wardrobe should have Black to keep you confident.
Fragrance: You are stimulated by a combination of greens and flowers, such as white roses, jasmine, and greenery. They give you feelings of elegance, strength, and security.
Tree: Cherry—You will find yourself faced with constant new emotional awakenings.
Instruments: Bass, clarinet
Composers: Haydn, Wagner
Bird: Robin—The most sociable of all birds, with the ability to create quick friendships. It also can easily adapt to any home. When it wants something, it has the tendency to try and snatch it.
Symbol: Star—You are full of inner brightness and will stand out in any crowd. You will be seen as special.

Harmonious Health and Nutrition . . .

Health Scents: Vanilla—This scent will fill you with a feeling of cleanliness and stability.
Favorable Foods: String beans, cherries, rye, walnuts, cottage cheese

What's Lucky . . .

Lucky Numbers: 2, 4, 13
Best Months: March and November
Best Day of the Week: Saturday
Best Month Days: 4, 13, 22, 31
Lucky Charm: A piece of material cut from something in your home.
Harmonious Signs for Relationships and

Partnerships: Capricorn, Taurus, Virgo, and anyone born from July 27 to September 27.

Spiritual Guides . . .

Star: Gedi—The star of the best and the brightest.
Angel: Hanaeb—This angel shows us our worldly desires in order to give us strength when we are going through uncertainty.
Guardian angel: Uriel—Helps bring the light of God. "God's guidance."
Spiritual Stone: Sardonyx—This stone may cause people to be attracted to you.

✳ *JUDITH'S INSIGHT* ✳

You are interesting, enjoyable, and a great companion, as long as everything is going your way. Some people never reach that kind of perfection or happiness. Your tendency is to enjoy just about everything, but you need rules and regulations. You love boundaries, but you want to control. Your brains and strength give you many opportunities for relationships. It's okay to be a little cautious in love—just don't confuse caution with fear. Watch out for loneliness. Sometimes you'd rather be funny than romantic, especially when your heart is at stake.

You love your family, but you need a sense of freedom to get along. You're a little bit unconventional with your views and opinions, so you may ruffle the feathers of coworkers; just keep this in mind. You have a great business aptitude and amazing foresight for decision making. This is about the only place you may use your psychic ability and intuition. You can rebel against authority, so stick to jobs that allow you the independence to think and feel: Work in theater or film, or as a mediator, builder, or architect. You have a distinctive character and will conform when you feel safe, so learn to go with where you feel comfort and growth.

You enjoy affection—giving and getting. Try not to let your strong and protective nature get in the way of your getting it. When it comes to relationships, you have more elasticity than a rubber band. You rebound very easily from arguments. Your tendency is to conform to a loved one's needs. That is one of your greatest secrets.

✳ ✳ ✳

JANUARY 5　CAPRICORN • The goat of the zodiac
December 21 at 10:00 P.M. to January 21 at 3:00 A.M. • NUMEROLOGY 5

Possessions and Desires . . .

Gem: Moonstone—This gem could protect you from danger.

Flower: Hydrangea—Beware of being boastful or heartless.

Astral Color, Color Need, Apparel Color: Your Astral Color is Silver, which stimulates your imagination. Blue in your environment will prevent depression and disappointments. In your wardrobe, Green is your power color for overcoming obstacles.

Fragrance: You are stimulated by a combination of greens and flowers, such as white roses, jasmine, and greenery. They give you feelings of elegance, strength, and security.

Tree: Apple—You are creative, full of joy, and nearly magical. You bring happiness.

Instruments: Viola, trumpet

Composer: Liszt

Bird: Flamingo—This beautiful, gregarious bird is always careful of its enemy. It is also a caretaker of the young and tries to keep everyone happy.

Symbol: Triangle—You have the right combination of abilities.

Harmonious Health and Nutrition . . .

Health Scent: Peach—This scent may balance your good qualities so that they equal your charm.

Favorable Foods: String beans, cherries, rye, walnuts, cottage cheese

What's Lucky . . .

Lucky Numbers: 8, 5, 23

Best Months: March and November

Best Day of the Week: Saturday

Best Month Days: 5, 4, 23

Lucky Charm: A rabbit's foot or a white candle.

Harmonious Signs for Relationships and Partnerships: Capricorn, Taurus, Virgo, and anyone born from July 27 to September 27.

Spiritual Guides . . .

Star: Vega—Those with this star can be warriors in search of victory, especially in legal situations.

Angel: Hanaeb—This angel shows us our worldly desires in order to give us strength when we are going through uncertainty.

Guardian angel: Plavwell—The guardian that gives power and strength to one's presence.

Spiritual Stone: Sardonyx—This stone may cause people to be attracted to you.

✳ JUDITH'S INSIGHT ✳

You are as loyal as the day is long. You're a giver, in relationships, friendships, and business. Problems arise when you feel your efforts are not recognized. It's not so much a financial or physical reward you're hoping for, but at the very least, verbal praise for the energy you expend. If you don't feel constant growth, you tend to get bored, and then look for the nearest exit sign.

Decision making can sometimes be difficult for you. Your intuition is often correct. You don't have to be the boss, as long as you are working in an independent environment with continuous growth and new challenges. Keep this in mind when choosing your career. From actor to astronomer, you are good at just about anything. It will be finding your career and staying with it that keeps you challenged. Don't be surprised if you have multiple careers. You're the jack and the master of all trades.

You'll want proof of consistency from your mate before you commit. Doing this earlier rather than later will work better for you. When you do finally commit, you are extremely loyal, but you can be frustrated, because everyone else is aware of your extreme devotion to your mate—except your mate. You tend to keep quiet about your emotions; otherwise you will chatter until the dawn. The problem here is there isn't anyone around to listen.

✳ ✳ ✳

JANUARY 6 CAPRICORN • The goat of the zodiac

December 21 at 10:00 P.M. to January 21 at 3:00 A.M. • NUMEROLOGY 6

Possessions and Desires . . .

Gem: Moonstone—This gem could protect you from danger.

Flower: Ice Plant—Your cold exterior hides a passionate nature.

Astral color, Color Need, Apparel Color: Your Astral Color is Brown, which helps to keep you grounded and stable. Blue in your environment helps you avoid becoming listless and disorganized. In your wardrobe, Emerald Green keeps you confident and always looking great.

Fragrance: You are stimulated by a combination of greens and flowers, such as white roses, jasmine, and greenery. They give you feelings of elegance, strength, and security.

Tree: Palm—You tend to be very healthy and creative.

Instruments: Tambourine, lyre

Composer: Schubert

Bird: Lark—Known for the beauty of its song, which is sometimes very unusual. It is also credited with extraordinary intelligence.

Symbol: Crescent—You are likely to be influenced by the phases of the moon. Your easygoing manner leads you to peaceful situations.

Harmonious Health and Nutrition . . .

Health Scent: Orange Blossom—This scent may balance your body, mind, and soul.

Favorable Foods: Lettuce, blackberries, whole wheat, almonds, buttermilk

What's Lucky . . .

Lucky Numbers: 1, 6, 15

Best Months: March and November

Best Day of the Week: Saturday

Best Month Days: 6, 15, 24

Lucky Charm: A religious token or card from any religion.

Harmonious Signs for Relationships and Partnerships: Capricorn, Taurus, Virgo, and anyone born from July 27 to September 27.

Spiritual Guides . . .

Star: Altair—Those with this star feel compelled to protect the wounded.

Angel: Hanaeb—This angel shows us our worldly desires in order to give us strength when we are going through uncertainty.

Guardian angel: Michael—"Who is like God."

Spiritual Stone: Sardonyx—This stone may cause people to become attracted to you.

✳ JUDITH'S INSIGHT ✳

With your knowledge and understanding, you epitomize common sense. There are downfalls, but as a "naturally smart" person you are quite capable of any number of things. Taking on quite a lot of responsibility at an early age may not have allowed too much room for childhood, so at some point in your life you could rebel and decide you want the childhood you never really had. The problem here is that you could be doing this at fifty.

Sometimes you seem demanding and selfish in love; at other times, you could be content with someone else who behaves that way. You will have no problem attracting a significant other. A weakness could be your lack of participation after the relationship gets underway. Challenges are what you need. If you feel you have trouble with love, then it may be time to open yourself up and stop protecting your heart. One thing you will need to learn about yourself is that balancing your head means balancing your heart. Along the way, you may encounter an unconventional relationship—at first it may be enthralling; later it could be devastating. You're good-looking, which attracts unwanted advances. Remember to keep your distance at the onset of a strong emotional relationship. Don't allow your restlessness to get you into emotionally crazy situations.

Your career can be a little sticky. One of the most beneficial careers for you is working with money: in a bank or as a merchant, accountant, or broker, or in any other job where you handle money. There are other types of careers you could pursue, but keep money in mind as a priority. Somehow money seems to find you in your lifetime.

✳ ✳ ✳

Possessions and Desires . . .

Gem: Ruby—This stone may lead you to energy, friendship, and happiness.

Flower: Japanese Rose—Beauty isn't your only attraction.

Astral Color, Color Need, Apparel Color: Your Astral Color is Black, which creates a sense of protection. Blue in your environment helps you avoid becoming listless and disorganized. Your wardrobe should have many shades of Green to keep you confident and always looking great.

Fragrance: You are stimulated by a combination of greens and flowers such as white roses, jasmine, and greenery. They give you feelings of elegance, strength, and security.

Tree: Sycamore—Yours is the ability to love, communicate honestly with others, and have lasting relationships.

Instrument: Harp

Composers: Gluck, Brahms.

Bird: Skylark—This handsome bird is beautiful when it sings. It always whistles as it works.

Symbol: Heart—You are enthusiastic, empathetic, and full of generosity and love.

Harmonious Health and Nutrition . . .

Health Scent: Jasmine—This scent may make you more easygoing when you are stressed.

Favorable Foods: Celery, strawberries, rye, nuts, cottage cheese

What's Lucky . . .

Lucky Numbers: 1, 7, 16
Best Months: March and November
Best Day of the Week: Saturday
Best Month Days: 6, 15, 24
Lucky Charm: An old key.
Harmonious Signs for Relationships and Partnerships: Capricorn, Taurus, Virgo, and anyone born from July 27 to September 27.

Spiritual Guides . . .

Star: Dabih—The star of the prominent in society.
Angel: Hanaeb—This angel shows us our worldly desires in order to give us strength when we are going through uncertainty.
Guardian angel: Raphael—The angel that attends to all of your needs when you are looking for guidance.
Spiritual Stone: Sardonyx—This stone may cause people to be attracted to you.

✶ JUDITH'S INSIGHT ✶

You are charitable in many ways, yet you are not always recognized for it. With a strong sense of intuition, you understand others without rhyme or reason. You have a magnetic personality, and others are drawn to your strength and humor. Others see abilities in you that you may not necessarily see yourself. Listen to those who give you praise.

You'll have relationships, but be cautious that you don't seem cold when it comes down to intimacy. Learn to set your body free as well as your uninhibited mind. You may be empathetic and understanding, but when it comes to loved ones, it can be hard work. Nobody gets too far without showing their sense of loyalty and devotion. Make sure your family gets to see all the warm and sensible parts of you that others do. Watch out for a tendency to behave insensitively. Love does prevail at least once. Partnerships could work quite well, even if they don't last forever.

With your style and refinement, it will be no wonder that you have strong success in your lifetime. Ready, set, go is the kind of worker you are, as long as the environment remains unstressed. Don't create your own limitations because of fear, or take too long to decide on things. Doctor, lawyer, businessperson: any career will do. You could be a world traveler or maintain a job that requires travel on a regular basis. Plain as day—you add simple pleasures in the lives you touch. Keep your own desires clear for yourself, so you can have the happiness you deserve.

✶ ✶ ✶

JANUARY 8   CAPRICORN • The goat of the zodiac

December 21 at 10:00 P.M. to January 21 at 3:00 A.M. • NUMEROLOGY 8

Possessions and Desires . . .

Gem: Moonstone—This gem could protect you from danger.

Flower: Laburnum—You tend to be pensive and known for your inner beauty.

Astral Color, Color Need, Apparel Color: Your Astral Color is Brown, which helps to keep you grounded and stable. Blue in your environment helps you avoid becoming listless and disorganized. In your wardrobe, many shades of Green keep you confident and always looking great.

Fragrance: You are stimulated by a combination of greens and flowers such as white roses, jasmine, and greenery. They give you feelings of elegance, strength, and security.

Tree: Pine—Your relationships tend to be harmonious and balanced, both emotionally and mentally.

Instrument: Cello

Composer: Mozart

Bird: Bobolink—This charming singer is equally good as a soloist or a member of an orchestra. It is a very romantic bird, useful as an insect destroyer, and elegant, with beautiful feathers and always pleasant to have around.

Symbol: Wings—You are the source of balance in your world—this will bring you contentment.

Harmonious Health and Nutrition . . .

Health Scent: Almond—This scent may revitalize you and open you to greater possibilities.

Favorable Foods: Beans, pineapple, whole wheat, walnuts, eggs

What's Lucky . . .

Lucky Numbers: 8, 17, 26

Best Months: March and November

Best Day of the Week: Saturday

Best Month Days: 8, 17, 26

Lucky Charm: A red ribbon in your wallet or over home entranceway.

Harmonious Signs for Relationships and Partnerships: Capricorn, Taurus, Virgo, and anyone born from July 27 to September 27.

Spiritual Guides . . .

Star: Gedi—The star of the best and the brightest.

Angel: Hanaeb—This angel shows us our worldly desires in order to give us strength when we are going through uncertainty.

Guardian angel: Seraphim—An angel that brings love, light, and passion.

Spiritual Stone: Sardonyx—This stone may cause people to be attracted to you.

✶ JUDITH'S INSIGHT ✶

"Good intentions" could be your first name, and "means well" should be your last. It's a shame you don't get paid for this virtue. Those who don't recognize who you are could describe you as cunning or manipulative. With your strength and perseverance, it's no wonder you always get what you want. You don't, won't, and shouldn't let other opinions interfere with the way you handle your life. You will have the sensitivity to maintain long-lasting relationships, the sensuality to ignite great passion, and the common sense to enjoy them both. You do well when faced with life's challenges. Watch for carelessness with your body. Be careful where and while you walk. How many back, bone, muscle, and neck problems have you had? You are the helping hand for many. Friends count on your love. Just remember, when your shoulders are heavy—it's you who puts all the burdens there.

Business is a great thing; just don't delegate with such coldness. You love many and trust very few. Don't allow this skeptical side to be well known in your career. You need to communicate a bit better. Lawyer, prison warden, inventor, landscaper, or detective are all good career choices. Don't be surprised if later in life you come into a second career, or seek out a hobby that allows you the sense of growth and reward that may be lacking in your career. Strong and stable is fine, but learn to occasionally throw caution to the winds. Family matters are always a priority for you.

✶ ✶ ✶

JANUARY 9 CAPRICORN • The goat of the zodiac

December 21 at 10:00 P.M. to January 21 at 3:00 A.M. • NUMEROLOGY 9

Possessions and Desires . . .

Gem: Moonstone—This gem could protect you from danger.

Flower: Lavender—Be careful of mistrusting others too much.

Astral Color, Color Need, Apparel Color: Your Astral Color is Silver, which stimulates your imagination. Blue in your environment will prevent depression and disappointment. In your wardrobe, Maroon gives you confidence.

Fragrance: You are stimulated by a combination of greens and flowers, such as white roses, jasmine, and greenery. They give you feelings of elegance, strength, and security.

Tree: Holly—Beware that you are not carried away by your passionate nature. The only way to grow is to be open to new experiences.

Instruments: Violin, tympanum

Composer: Gluck

Bird: Mockingbird—The most proficient minstrel in the world's orchestra; graceful and enthusiastic.

Symbol: Anchor—This tranquil symbol signifies stability and strength, and stands for strong commitments in relationships.

Harmonious Health and Nutrition . . .

Health Scent: Lavender—This scent might lead others to trust you and make you patient.

Favorable Foods: Cabbage, watermelon, rye, beechnuts, buttermilk

What's Lucky . . .

Lucky Numbers: 9, 18, 27

Best Months: March and November

Best Day of the Week: Saturday

Best Month Days: 9, 18, 27

Lucky Charm: A U.S. coin or a bill of any amount from the year you were born.

Harmonious Signs for Relationships and Partnerships: Capricorn, Taurus, Virgo, and anyone born from July 27 to September 27.

Spiritual Guides . . .

Star: Vega—Those with this star can be warriors in search of victory, especially in legal situations.

Angel: Hanaeb—This angel shows us our worldly desires in order to give us strength when we are going through uncertainty.

Guardian Angel: Gabriel—"God is my strength."

Spiritual Stone: Sardonyx—This stone may cause people to be attracted to you.

✶ JUDITH'S INSIGHT ✶

Yours is the inquiring mind that always wants to know. Education is not the only way you gain knowledge. With a strong need to investigate things, you get pure enjoyment out of working. Some may say you have natural intelligence, natural intuition, and/or psychic ability.

Success always finds you. Your charm and wit help in finding a mate. Spontaneity can be very attractive, but don't allow your independence to make you seem cold and removed. Family relationships will be a bit erratic. At times, it may seem as if your relations are fine, at other times they will seem pretentious and plastic. Look inside yourself when things seem removed. You have a tendency to be guarded and distant.

In your career, you have all the makings of a born leader and may be drawn to authority. Your resourcefulness and curiosity may lead you down many different career paths. Look for a career in law or research, or with the government or utilities. You can look other places, but these areas may draw you. At some point, you may be wounded or may have a health issue due to stress at work.

Friends will use your ear for your great advice and excellent input. Sometimes, this may be a little more taxing than you think. You may be a thinker, but you're also a dreamer; that's the side that most will never know. That's not such a bad thing.

★ ★ ★

JANUARY 10

CAPRICORN • The goat of the zodiac

December 21 at 10:00 P.M. to January 21 at 3:00 A.M. • NUMEROLOGY 1

Possessions and Desires . . .

Gem: Agate—This stone may promote health and lead you to a long life.

Flower: Withered Leaf—You tend to enjoy feeling blue more than is good for you.

Astral Color, Color Need, Apparel Color: Your Astral Color is Black, which creates a sense of protection. Blue in your environment helps you avoid becoming listless and disorganized. In your wardrobe, Green is your power color for overcoming obstacles.

Fragrance: You are stimulated by a combination of greens and flowers, such as white roses, jasmine, and greenery. They give you feelings of elegance, strength, and security.

Tree: Walnut—You are unusually helpful and always looking for constant changes in your life.

Instruments: Oboe, flute, clarinet, piano, French horn, organ, piccolo

Composer: Böhm

Bird: Bird of paradise—The "bird of the gods." You will shine and love extraordinary form.

Symbol: Crown—The universal sign of dignity.

Harmonious Health and Nutrition . . .

Health Scent: Strawberry—soothing by nature, the strawberry promotes self-esteem and encourages love.

Favorable Foods: Asparagus, cherries, rye, almonds, pressed cheese

What's Lucky . . .

Lucky Numbers: 2, 8, 19
Best Months: March and November
Best Day of the Week: Saturday
Best Month Days: 1, 10, 19, 28
Lucky Charm: A new penny in your shoe.
Harmonious Signs for Relationships and Partnerships: Capricorn, Taurus, Virgo, and anyone born from July 27 to September 27.

Spiritual Guides . . .

Star: Altair—Those with this star feel compelled to protect the wounded.

Angel: Hanaeb—This angel shows us our worldly desires in order to give us strength when we are going through uncertainty.

Guardian Angel: Malachi—"Messenger of Jehovah."

Spiritual Stone: Sardonyx—This stone may cause people to be attracted to you.

✴ JUDITH'S INSIGHT ✴

Precise, organized, and clearly intelligent—this is exactly who you are. Although you do balance the emotional issues very well, be careful when you feel overwhelmed with emotions. You tend to take life too seriously at times.

Devotion will be there with your mate. It takes time for you to get over disappointments from loved ones. You're so strong and easygoing, others may never recognize when you are hurting. Most of the time you will know how and when to be funny. Lucky in love, one way or another don't be surprised if you are one of those late bloomers. Family does tend to take you a little for granted, and vice versa. Just be a little better at recognizing which is which. You seem to wear uniforms—or somewhere through your life people around you could be wearing them.

There is no work ethic better than yours, when your mind is in the right place. Broker, banker, detective, or contractor—it all works for you. As long as you get to take the stage for a moment or two, you will be fine.

Creativity is there, so allow that part of you to shine when you get the courage. Yours are the purest and best intentions. You have a great instinct for cause and effect, but don't be surprised if others see you as complicated.

✴ ✴ ✴

JANUARY 11 CAPRICORN • The goat of the zodiac
December 21 at 10:00 P.M. to January 21 at 3:00 A.M. • NUMEROLOGY 2

Possessions and Desires . . .

Gem: Sapphire—This gem may help you find forgiveness from those you've wronged.
Flower: Lemon—will give you energy and passion.
Astral Color, Color Need, Apparel Color: Your Astral Color is Brown, which helps to keep you grounded and stable. Blue in your environment helps you avoid becoming listless and disorganized. In your wardrobe, many shades of Green always let you look your best.
Fragrance: You are stimulated by a combination of greens and flowers, such as white roses, jasmine, and greenery. They give you feelings of elegance, strength, and security.
Tree: Maple—You have both great stability and flashes of intuition.
Instruments: Pipe organ, cymbal, drum
Composers: Handel, Johann Sebastian Bach
Bird: Cuckoo—a good flyer and very seldom a quitter. Some cuckoos tend to think they favor lonely isolation, but what they really yearn for is a family relationship.
Symbol: Cross—The symbol of self-sacrifice and reconciliation.

Harmonious Health and Nutrition . . .

Health Scent: Apple—You are creative, full of joy, and nearly magical. You bring happiness.
Favorable Foods: Brussels sprouts, blackberries, whole wheat, peanuts, cottage cheese

What's Lucky . . .

Lucky Numbers: 2, 11, 13
Best Months: March and November
Best Day of the Week: Saturday
Best Month Days: 2, 11, 20, 29
Lucky Charms: Two 50-cent pieces. Give someone else one of them.

Harmonious Signs for Relationships and Partnerships: Capricorn, Taurus, Virgo, and anyone born from July 27 to September 27.

Spiritual Guides . . .

Star: Dabih—the star of the prominent in society.
Angel: Hanaeb—This angel shows us our worldly desires in order to give us strength when we are going through uncertainty.
Guardian angel: Uriel—"The light of God."
Spiritual Stone: Sardonyx—This stone may cause people to be attracted to you.

✶ JUDITH'S INSIGHT ✶

They may say that money is the root of all evil, but for ultradetermined you, it just creates the desire for life, and you love it. Eventually it will spell success for you. A generally enthusiastic character makes you quite a desirable catch. Fascinating and charming most of the time, you seem always to draw a bit of a crowd. Somewhere along the way you must watch out for your ego running amok.

You're usually sympathetic, but don't always show it. This can sometimes create problems with friends, family, and relationships. You will do anything for those whom you love and even those you don't. Don't spend too much time helping everyone around you and neglecting those you shouldn't. As a parent, you will be very devoted; beyond, you need to take care with your demands.

Your career can range from top trader to storekeeper to attorney to doctor. You will feel rewarded by people throughout your life, and recognition that boosts your ego may mostly come from complete strangers. You work better with a well-organized plan and can carry out even the tallest of orders. Keep others from pressuring you even half as much as you do yourself.

✳ ✳ ✳

JANUARY 12　CAPRICORN • The goat of the zodiac
December 21 at 10:00 P.M. to January 21 at 3:00 A.M. • NUMEROLOGY 3

Possessions and Desires . . .

Gem: Emerald—Those who carry this stone tend to be lucky in love.

Flower: Lemon Blossom—You are very loyal to those you care for.

Astral Color, Color Need, Apparel Color: Your Astral Color is Silver, which stimulates your imagination. Blue in your environment prevents depression and disappointments. In your wardrobe, Black keeps you confident.

Fragrance: You are stimulated by a combination of greens and flowers, such as white roses, jasmine, and greenery. They give you feelings of elegance, strength, and security.

Tree: Elm—You have willpower, strength, and the ability to stand alone.

Instrument: Trombone

Composers: Verdi, Mendelssohn, Schumann

Bird: Swan—Regarded as royal and sacred, this bird has the protective nature of a mother and can become a furious fighter in the defense of its young.

Symbol: Wreath—You have been crowned with a special personality. You are strong but extremely compassionate.

Harmonious Health and Nutrition . . .

Health Scent: Rose—This scent will lead you to passionate thoughts and make you feel warm inside.

Favorable Foods: Cauliflower, peaches, rye, peanuts, buttermilk

What's Lucky . . .

Lucky Numbers: 3, 8, 21
Best Months: March and November
Best Day of the Week: Saturday
Best Month Days: 3, 12, 21, 30
Lucky Charm: A pen that someone else has already used.
Harmonious Signs for Relationships and

Partnerships: Capricorn, Taurus, Virgo, and anyone born from July 27 to September 27.

Spiritual Guides . . .

Star: Gedi—The star of the best and the brightest.

Angel: Hanaeb—This angel shows us our worldly desires in order to give us strength when we are going through uncertainty.

Guardian angel: Johiel—This angel is a protector of all those with a humble heart.

Spiritual Stone: Sardonyx—This stone may cause people to be attracted to you.

✶ JUDITH'S INSIGHT ✶

You are distinctly ambitious and readily open to just about anything. You have the ability to get in there and make wheels spin and heads turn and bring to life what has long been dead. With a special knack for being in the right place at the right time, you see things clearly in just about any business situation. Your problems will arise in love, if you don't keep a balance of home and work.

Getting relationships will never be your problem—keeping them will take all your attention. Passion you have, and charm you'll provide. You imagine yourself as the great communicator, but in reality that is what you are here to learn. You have the habit of assuming that everybody has the same mind as you. This can cause problems. You may sometimes need to keep your opinions just a little under wraps. Friends and family always adore you.

You are often brilliant, which allows you to succeed in almost any career. You will have to be careful not to get bored, otherwise you may find yourself going from workaholic to another addiction not as attractive. You can be anything from a computer whiz to a Broadway star, a professor or a philosopher. When you finally reach the right track, there won't be any stopping you.

With character and presence as outgoing as yours, one would think you would like praise and compliments, but that is where you can be seen as shy. A final reward you will welcome. Verbally you will be shy.

✶ ✶ ✶

JANUARY 13 CAPRICORN • The goat of the zodiac

December 21 at 10:00 P.M. to January 21 at 3:00 A.M. • NUMEROLOGY 4

Possessions and Desires . . .

Gem: Emerald—Those who carry this stone tend to be lucky in love.

Flower: Imperial lily—You are in utter awe of all your life can offer you.

Astral Color, Color Need, Apparel Color: Your Astral Color is Black, which creates a sense of protection. Blue in your environment helps you avoid becoming listless and disorganized. In your wardrobe, many shades of Green always let you look your best.

Fragrance: You are stimulated by a combination of greens and flowers, such as white roses, jasmine, and greenery. They give you feelings of elegance, strength, and security.

Tree: Cherry—You will find yourself faced with constant new emotional awakenings.

Instruments: Bass, clarinet

Composers: Haydn, Wagner

Bird: Robin—The most sociable of all birds, with the ability to create quick friendships. It also can easily adapt to any home. When it wants something, it has the tendency to try and snatch it.

Symbol: Star—You are full of inner brightness and will stand out in any crowd. You will be seen as special.

Harmonious Health and Nutrition . . .

Health Scent: Vanilla—This scent will fill you with a feeling of cleanliness and stability.

Favorable Foods: Watercress, prunes, whole wheat, almonds, cottage cheese

What's Lucky . . .

Lucky Numbers: 4,13,14
Best Months: March and November
Best Day of the Week: Saturday
Best Month Days: 4, 13, 22, 31
Lucky Charm: A piece of material cut from something in your home.

Harmonious Signs for Relationships and Partnerships: Capricorn, Taurus, Virgo, and anyone born from July 27 to September 27.

Spiritual Guides . . .

Star: Vega—Those with this star can be warriors in search of victory, especially in legal situations.

Angel: Hanaeb—This angel shows us our worldly desires in order to give us strength when we are going through uncertainty.

Guardian Angel: Uriel—This angel brings the light of God's guidance.

Spiritual Stone: Sardonyx—This stone may cause people to be attracted to you.

✳ JUDITH'S INSIGHT ✳

You're inventive and creative, and have lots of initiative—you have the right mix for a perfect businessperson. You have many friends. You are easily bored by old war stories, unless they're your own. You are impeccable in your dress, even with the most casual clothes, and your physical presence is striking.

Home means a lot, and the order in which it is kept means more. You're direct with your love; sometimes a little too direct. With a flirtatious style all your own, you remain devoted to a significant other when you find one. To family, you stand as the king even if you are the queen. Understanding and kind, make sure you have time to hear others out. Generosity can be a good characteristic, so long as you hold the checkbook and write the check.

You would make a great prosecutor, debater, or even a civil rights activist. You love a fight for the underdog; you don't mind the recognition for your "wins." As much as you will be fond of sports and recreational activities, you never let fun interfere with work. You will be a hard worker, making a bit of room for Sunday relaxation. Just remember: to some fun is play, to you it may be building a house, or reorganizing the kitchen.

✳ ✳ ✳

JANUARY 14　CAPRICORN • The goat of the zodiac

December 21 at 10:00 P.M. to January 21 at 3:00 A.M. • NUMEROLOGY 5

Possessions and Desires . . .

Gem: Moonstone—This gem could protect you from danger.
Flower: Hyssop—You like your surroundings and relationships to be neat and orderly.
Astral Color, Color Need, Apparel Color: Your Astral Color is Black, which creates a sense of protection. Blue in your environment helps you avoid becoming listless and disorganized. In your wardrobe, many shades of Green always let you look your best.
Fragrance: You are stimulated by a combination of greens and flowers, such as white roses, jasmine, and greenery. They give you feelings of elegance, strength, and security.
Tree: Apple—You are creative, full of joy, and nearly magical. You bring happiness.
Instruments: Viola, trumpet
Composer: Liszt
Bird: Flamingo—This beautiful, gregarious bird is always careful of its enemy. It is also a caretaker of the young and tries to keep everyone happy.
Symbol: Triangle—You have the right combination of abilities.

Harmonious Health and Nutrition . . .

Health Scent: Peach—This scent may balance your good qualities so that they equal your charm.
Favorable Foods: String beans, raspberries, rye, beechnuts, pressed cheese

What's Lucky . . .

Lucky Numbers: 5, 8, 23
Best Months: March and November
Best Day of the Week: Saturday
Best Month Days: 4, 5, 23
Lucky Charms: A rabbit's foot or a white candle.

Harmonious Signs for Relationships and Partnerships: Capricorn, Taurus, Virgo, and anyone born from July 27 to September 27.

Spiritual Guides . . .

Star: Altair—Those with this star feel compelled to protect the wounded.
Angel: Hanaeb—This angel shows us our worldly desires in order to give us strength when we are going through uncertainty.
Guardian angel: Plavwell—"Strength in presence."
Spiritual Stone: Sardonyx—This stone may cause people to be attracted to you.

✶ JUDITH'S INSIGHT ✶

Friendship and loyalty mean the world to you. Since you have a protective nature, it is no wonder everyone depends on you. You're strong, willing, and able. You're dependable for all that you love, and for even those that you merely like. Two wonderful traits are your sense of humor and good sense.

For some you will seem like the perfect mate. To others you will act remote and pretentiously humorous, afraid of having your heart stolen. It will be a hint you're definitely in love when you start to back up and run. Scared until caught, you're great in the beginning and great at the end; it is definitely the middle that gives you all the trouble. You love many and trust very few.

You need to have a career that will create a sense of fun and freedom. You could be the kind of person who could find fun and freedom in careers such as law or retail, whereas others may consider them too structured.

You crave excitement, even with that serious look about you. You rebound from just about anything. Just allow yourself a little room for emotional issues. You don't have to worry about others being hard on you. That you do on your own.

✶ ✶ ✶

Possessions and Desires . . .

Gem: Topaz—An excellent gift to be exchanged between very loyal friends.

Flower: Marigold—You may try hard to protect yourself from sorrow.

Astral Color, Color Need, Apparel Color: Your Astral Color is Brown, which helps to keep you grounded and stable. Blue in your environment helps you avoid becoming listless and disorganized. In your wardrobe, many shades of Green always let you look your best.

Fragrance: You are stimulated by a combination of greens and flowers, such as white roses, jasmine, and greenery. They give you feelings of elegance, strength, and security.

Tree: Palm—You tend to be very healthy and creative.

Instruments: Tambourine, lyre

Composer: Schubert

Bird: Goldfinch—These gentle creatures can be quite moody, according to the weather. Otherwise they are quite charming.

Symbol: Crescent—You are more likely to be influenced by the phases of the moon. Your easy-going manner leads you to peaceful situations.

Harmonious Health and Nutrition . . .

Health Scent: Orange Blossom—This scent may balance your body, mind, and soul.

Favorable Foods: Cauliflower, peaches, whole wheat, nuts, buttermilk

What's Lucky . . .

Lucky Numbers: 2, 15, 24
Best Months: March and November
Best Day of the Week: Saturday
Best Month Days: 6, 15, 24
Lucky Charms: A religious token or card from any religion.

Harmonious Signs for Relationships and Partnerships: Capricorn, Taurus, Virgo, and those born between July 27 and September 27.

Spiritual Guides . . .

Star: Dabih—The star of the prominent in society.
Angel: Hanaeb—This angel shows us our worldly desires in order to give us strength when we are going through uncertainty.
Guardian angel: Michael—"Who is like God."
Spiritual Stone: Sardonyx—This stone may cause people to be attracted to you.

✷ JUDITH'S INSIGHT ✷

Responsible? You're almost too responsible for your own good. You learned right from wrong much too early in life. This allowed you no freedom to be the bad child; you knew better. Somewhere along the way you could claim responsibility, but you blame everyone else, even when you're the one to blame.

You desire a little spontaneity in your love life. If your significant other recognizes this and supplies the fun and frolic, you may be able to maintain happiness. If not, you go find it for yourself. No, it doesn't mean an affair. But you can put that extra energy to work in other facets of your life by becoming consumed with sports, exercise, spas, shopping, clothes, or entertainment. Allow the freedom and allow the fun; there are fantasies in there, and it's all right to have them. Leave Mom and Dad, the church, and society behind when in the bedroom.

Legal matters will find you—just make sure you're on the right side of the law. Your determination and strength make you a good worker. Earlier in your life you'll have a serious job, then later you'll have more fun, like a lawyer who turns politician. Just stay away from being anyone's therapist until you have seen your own. Give yourself a break; leave the pressure behind as much as you can.

✷ ✷ ✷

JANUARY 16 CAPRICORN • The goat of the zodiac
December 21 at 10:00 P.M. to January 21 at 3:00 A.M. • NUMEROLOGY 7

Possessions and Desires . . .

Gem: Ruby—This stone may lead you to energy, friendship, and happiness.
Flower: Yarrow—You can usually trust in your own abilities.
Astral Color, Color Need, Apparel Color: Your Astral Color is Silver, which stimulates your imagination. Blue in your environment prevents depression and disappointments. In your wardrobe, Maroon will give you confidence.
Fragrance: You are stimulated by a combination of greens and flowers, such as white roses, jasmine, and greenery. They give you feelings of elegance, strength, and security.
Tree: Sycamore—Yours is the ability to love, communicate honestly with others, and have lasting relationships.
Instrument: Harp.
Composers: Gluck, Brahms
Bird: Warbling Parakeet—The most beautiful of all birds, known as the love bird. It does seem to have the powers of imitation.
Symbol: Heart—You are enthusiastic, empathetic, and full of generosity and love.

Harmonious Health and Nutrition . . .

Health Scent: Jasmine—This scent may make you more easygoing when you are stressed.
Favorable Foods: Cabbage, prunes, rye, peanuts, eggs

What's Lucky . . .

Lucky Numbers: 1, 6, 24
Best Months: March and November
Best Day of the Week: Saturday
Best Month Days: 6, 15, 24.
Lucky Charm: An old key.
Harmonious Signs for Relationships and Partnerships: Capricorn, Taurus, Virgo, and persons born from July 27 to September 27.

Spiritual Guides . . .

Star: Gedi—The star of the best and the brightest.
Angel: Hanaeb—This angel shows us our worldly desires in order to give us strength when we are going through uncertainty.
Guardian angel: Raphael—This angel attends to all of your needs when you are looking for guidance.
Spiritual Stone: Sardonyx—This stone may cause people to be attracted to you.

✶ JUDITH'S INSIGHT ✶

A philosopher to some, a judge to others—you will wear different hats throughout your life. You have executive ability with a spiritual charm. Trust your gut feelings—you have an uncanny ability to see through situations and people. This will give others a strong desire to reach out to you. You may find people you hardly know just pouring out their hearts to you. Your quick wit and intelligence will attract others for even more advice. Lovers, family, and friends will always seem to overwhelm you because of your distinct capabilities. This will warm your ego. At other times you will be the one complaining and feeling sorry for yourself, and there's the contradiction.

Love does prevail for you several times in your lifetime. Whether or not you live it out is up to you. Opportunity will always be there. Family members and siblings will be close, but be aware of who is doing all of the work and who is reaping all of the benefits. Aim for more balance and equality in family situations.

You could be an artist, decorator, clergy-person, or therapist. Loving at times, you possess an artistic and poetic nature. You can be charitable in your own way, but have expectations of others. You tend to be on the more cautious side when it comes to spending money, and you love a bargain. Others must win your trust and respect. Move slowly with new undertakings and learn to allow yourself room for making mistakes—even though you are perfect.

✶ ✶ ✶

Possessions and Desires . . .

Gem: Chrysolite—This gem may help you clear your mind of sadness and worry.

Flower: Rosemary—You tend to have an excellent memory.

Astral Color, Color Need, Apparel Color: Your Astral Color is Brown, which helps to keep you grounded and stable. Blue in your environment helps you avoid becoming listless and disorganized. In your wardrobe, many shades of Green always let you look your best.

Fragrance: You are stimulated by a combination of greens and flowers, such as white roses, jasmine, and greenery. They give you feelings of elegance, strength, and security.

Tree: Pine—Your relationships tend to be harmonious, both emotionally and mentally.

Instrument: Cello

Composer: Mozart

Bird: Bobolink—This charming singer is equally good as a soloist or a member of an orchestra. It is a very romantic bird, useful as an insect destroyer, elegant, with beautiful feathers, and always pleasant to have around.

Symbol: Wings—You are the source of balance in your world; this will bring you contentment.

Harmonious Health and Nutrition . . .

Health Scent: Almond—This scent may revitalize you and open you to greater possibilities.

Favorable Foods: Peas, pineapple, whole wheat, almonds, cottage cheese

What's Lucky . . .

Lucky Numbers: 8, 17, 35
Best Months: March and November
Best Day of the Week: Saturday
Best Month Days: 8, 17, 26
Lucky Charm: Red ribbon in your wallet or doorway.
Harmonious Signs for Relationships and

Partnerships: Capricorn, Taurus, Virgo, and anyone born from July 27 to September 27.

Spiritual Guides . . .

Star: Vega—Those with this star can be warriors in search of victory, especially in legal situations.

Angel: Hanaeb—This angel shows us our worldly desires in order to give us strength when we are going through uncertainty.

Guardian angel: Seraphim—love, light, and passion.

Spiritual Stone: Sardonyx—This stone may cause people to be attracted to you.

✴ JUDITH'S INSIGHT ✴

Dreamer that you are, you work to hide that side of yourself. You play the protector of yourself and of others. Cautious by nature, distrusting at times, you exude love only to those you allow to get close, yet you believe you're very open. Patient, honest, and earnest—you're classic when it comes to personal ethics. Be cautious of your fears causing depression. Release yourself from times when you have a desire to be reclusive. Don't analyze so much, especially beyond the age of 35.

Tender person that you are, you will have no problem seeking a mate. Your problems will sometimes be choosing among them. Use caution and good sense when selecting. You get into relationships easily; getting out will be problematic. Sudden and strange experiences will pepper your life, but will generally be uplifting, though at a later time. Others doubt your sensitivity. Let them. In time, they come to know who you are. The strength you display confuses others.

You could do well at a number of different careers, such as banker, merchant, journalist, artist, or psychic. Trust that you'll find more than one title throughout your work life. At times you can be considered cheap, but you're really not, you're just conservative with cash. Friendly to all, cautious with most, you are somewhat dogmatic, a ready and sound reasoner with strong convictions, honest and sincere. Just watch your temper at times. Learn to relax and be happy.

✴ ✴ ✴

JANUARY 18 CAPRICORN • The goat of the zodiac

December 21 at 10:00 P.M. to January 21 at 3:00 A.M. • NUMEROLOGY 9

Possessions and Desires . . .

Gem: Moonstone—This gem could protect you from danger.

Flower: Rue—If you look too often for faults in others, you may overlook those you need to correct in yourself.

Astral Color, Color Need, Apparel Color: Your Astral Color is Brown, which helps to keep you grounded and stable. Blue in your environment helps you avoid becoming listless and disorganized. In your wardrobe, Green is your power color for overcoming obstacles.

Fragrance: You are stimulated by a combination of greens and flowers, such as white roses, jasmine, and greenery. They give you feelings of elegance, strength, and security.

Tree: Holly—Beware that you are not carried away by your passionate nature. The only way to grow is to be open to new experiences.

Instruments: Violin, tympanum

Composer: Gluck

Bird: Mockingbird—the most proficient minstrel in the world's orchestra; graceful and enthusiastic.

Symbol: Anchor—This tranquil symbol signifies stability and strength, and stands for strong commitments in relationships.

Harmonious Health and Nutrition . . .

Health Scent: Lavender—This scent might lead others to trust you and make you patient.

Favorable Foods: Beans, strawberries, rye, walnuts, buttermilk

What's Lucky . . .

Lucky Numbers: 2, 7, 9, 27
Best Months: March and November
Best Day of the Week: Saturday
Preferential Month Days: 9, 18, 27
Lucky Charm: A U.S. coin or a bill of any amount from the year you were born.
Harmonious Signs for Relationships and

Partnerships: Capricorn, Taurus, Virgo, and anyone born from July 27 to September 27.

Spiritual Guides . . .

Star: Altair—Those with this star feel compelled to protect the wounded.

Angel: Hanaeb—This angel shows us our worldly desires in order to give us strength when we are going through uncertainty.

Guardian angel: Gabriel—"God is my strength."

Spiritual Stone: Sardonyx—This stone may cause people to be attracted to you.

✭ JUDITH'S INSIGHT ✭

You have great executive ability, acute reasoning powers, and a fine intellect. You have a keen and discriminating mind and are always leaping to new heights with ideas. You are an honest person. You respect honor of any kind. You're powerful in your presentation of yourself or anything you touch. You're tough at work, but at home you are a teddy bear, kind, sweet, and affectionate.

You're fussy in love, and can be judgmental at first. Marrying you will probably be better than dating you. You're cynical in the early years, but you grow spiritual as you get older. Love will find you even when you aren't looking. Your sex appeal, the trait you don't think you have, is your magnet. Once you have that significant other, it would probably take a bomb to change this. But if that bomb hits, it will be hard to get you to change back.

You were born to lead. Success finds you whether it be in politics, law, or construction. And the list just goes on. How about president of the PTA, head of the little league or scout troop? You'll find who you are sooner or later. It will find you, if you eat when you're hungry, drink when you're thirsty, and take time to enjoy the jokes that you tell. You will be happy. You're easy and fascinating; but when things don't go your way, you become self-absorbed. Just remember, what gets absorbed becomes all dried up.

✭ ✭ ✭

Possessions and Desires . . .

Gem: Moonstone—This gem could protect you from danger.

Flower: Sage—You tend to have a great gift for things relating to the home.

Astral Color, Color Need, Apparel Color: Your Astral Color is Brown, which helps to keep you grounded and stable. Have Blue in your environment to avoid becoming listless and disorganized. In your wardrobe, Emerald Green keeps you confident and always looking great.

Fragrance: You are stimulated by a combination of greens and flowers, such as white roses, jasmine, and greenery. They give you feelings of elegance, strength, and security.

Tree: Walnut—You are unusually helpful and always looking for new beginnings.

Instruments: Oboe, flute, clarinet, piano, French horn, organ, and piccolo

Composer: Böhm

Bird: Hummingbird—This bird is delicate and graceful. It can remain still for hours, then dart off and be as busy as a bee.

Symbol: Crown—The universal sign of a dignified person.

Harmonious Health and Nutrition . . .

Health Scent: Strawberry—soothing by nature, the strawberry promotes self-esteem and encourages love.

Favorable Foods: Brussels sprouts, raspberries, whole wheat, beechnuts

What's Lucky . . .

Lucky Numbers: 1, 2, 8, 37
Best Months: March and November
Best Day of the Week: Saturday

Best Month Days: 1, 10,19, 28
Lucky Charm: A new penny in your shoe.
Harmonious Signs for Relationships and Partnerships: Capricorn, Taurus, Virgo, and anyone born from July 27 to September 27.

Spiritual Guides . . .

Star: Dabih—the star of the prominent in society.
Angel: Hanaeb—This angel shows us our worldly desires in order to give us strength when we are going through uncertainty.
Guardian angel: Malachi—"Messenger of Jehovah."
Spiritual Stone: Sardonyx—This stone may cause people to be attracted to you.

✴ JUDITH'S INSIGHT ✴

Spontaneity isn't the only great quality about you; you have a brilliant mind, broad intuition, and a wit that keeps everyone laughing. You are the truest of friends as long as others are true to you; otherwise, a bit of the tiger appears. Listen to yourself more often.

Another strong trait is your versatility. You have little difficulty in love, family, or work. Your willingness to accommodate attracts many significant others. Your devotion to family may be your best attribute or your worst, and at times it will be hard to tell.

Actor, dressmaker, cook, and artist are good professions for you. You can do just about anything as long as it allows you creativity. If not, you will be prone to depressions and won't know why. Your desire and ability for work are outrageous.

As thoughtful as you are, you tend to get grumpy when your thoughtful gestures are not taken the way you intend them. Just remember, life is not a movie script, and if it is, sometimes others are not on the same page. Every once in a while your mood will get just enough of a twist to it to keep others guessing.

✴ ✴ ✴

Possessions and Desires . . .

Gem: Sapphire—This gem may help you find forgiveness from those you've wronged.

Flower: Snowdrop—Your life is most often filled with hopes realized.

Astral Color, Color Need, Apparel Color: Your Astral Color is Silver, which stimulates your imagination. Blue in your environment will prevent depression and disappointments. In your wardrobe, Maroon gives you confidence.

Fragrance: You are stimulated by a combination of greens and flowers, such as white roses, jasmine, and greenery. They give you feelings of elegance, strength, and security.

Tree: Maple—You have great stability and flashes of intuition.

Instruments: Pipe organ, cymbal, drum

Composers: Handel, Johann Sebastian Bach

Bird: Stork—Turkish bird, held in high esteem the world over. This bird is intelligent but may have strange tendencies.

Symbol: Cross—the symbol of self-sacrifice and reconciliation.

Harmonious Health and Nutrition . . .

Health Scent: Apple—You are creative, full of joy, and nearly magical. You bring happiness.

Favorable Foods: Watercress, peaches, rye, beechnuts, eggs

What's Lucky . . .

Lucky Numbers: 2, 8, 11
Best Months: March and November
Best Day of the Week: Saturday
Best Month Days: 2, 11, 20, 29
Lucky Charms: Two 50-cent pieces. Give someone else one of them.

Harmonious Signs for Relationships and Partnerships: Capricorn, Taurus, Virgo, and anyone born from July 27 to September 27.

Spiritual Guides . . .

Star: Gedi—the star of the best and the brightest.

Angel: Hanaeb—This angel shows us our worldly desires in order to give us strength when we are going through uncertainty.

Guardian angel: Uriel—Helps bring the light of God's guidance.

Spiritual Stone: Sardonyx—This stone may cause people to be attracted to you.

✴ JUDITH'S INSIGHT ✴

You have only the purest of hearts and a loving nature. You enjoy being the good guy. Others sometimes think you overdo it. So what, let them! They are the ones in the doctor's office trying to figure you out. The intuition you have allows you to know the right things to do at the right moment; so if you are getting it wrong, you are not paying attention to yourself.

Relationships will come and go. You do not like to be without a partner, so watch your moodiness at these times. You do tend to be a bit of a dreamer and love to fantasize. This will help when relationships aren't going well. Family, for you, will sometimes get under your skin. That's only because you want to help so much. Watch out for the monster you create; you give and demand love without limits.

Successful you are, patient you are not. Great executive ability will allow you a career as any one of the following: journalist, banker, lawyer, mediator, decorator—the list is endless. Just keep in mind that you always need and desire a sense of freedom in any job you do, along with constant growth.

Remember to allow yourself enough fun so you don't resent others for knowing how to enjoy themselves.

✴ ✴ ✴

JANUARY 21 CAPRICORN • The goat of the zodiac

December 21 at 10:00 P.M. to January 21 at 3:00 A.M. • NUMEROLOGY 3

Possessions and Desires . . .

Gem: Sapphire—This gem may help you find forgiveness from those you've wronged.
Flower: Southernwood—You tend to enjoy bantering as a means of expressing your deepest feelings.
Astral Color, Color Need, Apparel Color: Your Astral Color is Blue, which creates calmness and brings promise. Blue in your environment helps stabilize your mood. In your wardrobe, many shades of Green always let you look your best.
Fragrance: You are stimulated by a combination of greens and flowers, such as white roses, jasmine, and greenery. They give you feelings of elegance, strength, and security.
Tree: Elm—You have willpower, strength, and the ability to stand alone.
Instrument: Trombone
Composers: Verdi, Mendelssohn, Schumann
Bird: Eagle—This bird is quick to use its powers of flight. It can see immeasurable distances in a single glance, and can sometimes appear to be indifferent.
Symbol: Wreath—You have been crowned with a special personality. You are strong but extremely compassionate.

Harmonious Health and Nutrition . . .

Health Scent: Rose—This scent will lead you to passionate thoughts and make you feel warm inside.
Favorable Foods: Celery, grapes, rye, almonds, buttermilk

What's Lucky . . .

Lucky Numbers: 3, 8, 21
Best Months: March and November
Best Day of the Week: Saturday
Best Month Days: 3, 12, 21, 30
Lucky Charm: A pen that someone else has already used.
Harmonious Signs for Relationships and

Partnerships: Capricorn, Taurus, Virgo, and anyone born from July 27 to September 27.

Spiritual Guides . . .

Star: Vega—Those with this star can be warriors in search of victory, especially in legal situations.
Angel: Hanaeb—This angel shows us our worldly desires in order to give us strength when we are going through uncertainty.
Guardian Angel: Phanuel—Protection against the negative.
Spiritual Stone: Sardonyx—This stone may cause people to be attracted to you.

✶ JUDITH'S INSIGHT ✶

You are a cute, cuddly teddy bear. Your strength will allure others; your sweet personality will keep them. Although you're generally truthful, you aren't always direct. Watch out while looking through those rose-colored glasses. Most times it will not hurt you, but sometimes it could be devastating. You will have strong bouts with low self-esteem, though your looks aren't the problem. Taking what others say too personally could hurt you. Try to eliminate this behavior.

You love strong, attractive, funny, flirtatious people. Remember, sometimes we get what we wish for. Your fickle nature won't help your love life. Learn to be comfortable with yourself first, then look for the significant other. You can be protective to a fault, so remember, we don't own our loved ones, friends, or family. They may consider you overbearing sometimes, even though others know your intentions are only positive. There is nobody more devoted than you. Rejection from loved ones is hurtful.

As a natural psychic, you should do well as a stockbroker, schoolteacher, insurance agent, artist of any kind, or in business. Decide whether you want to be liked as the boss or not. Others may see you as moody.

Promises aren't made to be broken; so don't make them unless you intend to keep them. Trust in yourself first; the rest will come easily. Allow your strengths to be used in the right places and recognize your weaknesses. These are the keys to happiness and success, which, for you, are not necessarily the same thing.

✶ ✶ ✶

JANUARY 22 AQUARIUS • The sign of the son of man
January 21 at 3:00 A.M. to February 19 at 5:00 P.M. • NUMEROLOGY 4

Possessions and Desires . . .

Gem: Sapphire—This gem may help you find forgiveness from those you've wronged.
Flower: Mullein—Your good nature may take you as far as you want to go.
Astral Color, Color Need, Apparel Color: Your Astral Color is Blue, which creates calmness and brings promise. Blue in your environment helps stabilize your mood. In your wardrobe, Rose brings you balance and harmony.
Fragrance: Put together a collection of orange blossoms and jasmine with touches of greenery. Always pick scents that are straight from nature instead of manufactured or processed when searching for a scent. This will keep you as unique as you wish to be.
Tree: Cherry—You will find yourself faced with constant new emotional awakenings.
Instrument: Bass
Composer: Haydn
Bird: Robin—the most sociable of all birds, with the ability to create quick friendships. It also can easily adapt to any home. When it wants something, it has the tendency to try and snatch it.
Symbol: Star—You are full of inner brightness and will stand out in any crowd. You will be seen as special.

Harmonious Health and Nutrition . . .

Health Scent: Vanilla—This scent will fill you with a feeling of cleanliness and stability.
Favorable Foods: Lentils, bananas, sugar, chicken, eggs

What's Lucky . . .

Lucky Numbers: 1, 4, 22
Best Months: April and August
Best Days of the Week: Wednesday, Saturday
Best Month Days: 4, 13, 22, 31
Lucky Charm: A piece of material cut from something in your home.
Harmonious Signs for Relationships and

Partnerships: Gemini, Aquarius, Libra, and anyone born from July 30 to August 31.

Spiritual Guides . . .

Star: Deneb Algiedi—This star gives strong spiritual guidance and sound judgment.
Angel: Gambiel—This angel governs health issues. He teaches us the mystery of life, both on earth and in the heavens.
Guardian Angel: Gabriel—"God is my strength."
Spiritual Stone: Sardius (Ruby)—This stone may drive you to make positive changes in your life.

✳ JUDITH'S INSIGHT ✳

Sensitive is not how most would see you, nor would they use words like shy, intimidated, or even humble. However, that side of your personality does exist. You put on a strong, capable, and independent face. You feel the need to protect yourself.

Ironically, your most wonderful attributes cause your downfalls: your family and your desire to be overly generous. But have no fear; as you mature, this will change—or perhaps you'll just hide it better. Learn to trust your intuition when choosing a mate. Attracting others will not pose a problem, but keeping them will. You send mixed signals. Love will prevail at least once for you. This doesn't always mean a formal commitment either—keep that in mind. Unique things will happen to you in your lifetime. You'll realize this when it happens, or years later when you look back on the crazy life you have led.

You are full of ideas but don't always have the energy to go with them. You have a strong sense of intuition and are a dreamer, so you need to be in a creative field. Perhaps being a computer whiz could do for a while; that would also depend on the kind of working environment and whether it allows freedom and growth. You could be boss or manager, though this may take time to manifest itself, so allow time. At the very least, you will retire successfully.

Stop having so many expectations of life. Guess what? You will be happy! Do not depend on others too much and vice versa. Just when you think it can't get any better, it does.

✳ ✳ ✳

JANUARY 23

AQUARIUS • The sign of the son of man

January 21 at 3:00 A.M. to February 19 at 5:00 P.M. • NUMEROLOGY 5

Possessions and Desires . . .

Gem: Sardius—this stone could give the wearer unusual insights into his or her own heart.

Flower: Nightshade—What you know is true will always stay true.

Astral Color, Color Need, Apparel Color: Your Astral Color is Blue, which creates calmness and brings promise. Blue in your environment helps stabilize your mood. In your wardrobe, many shades of Green always let you look your best.

Fragrance: Put together a collection of orange blossoms and jasmine with touches of greenery. Always pick scents that are straight from nature instead of manufactured or processed when searching for a scent. This will keep you as unique as you wish to be.

Tree: Apple—You are creative, full of joy, and nearly magical. You bring happiness.

Instrument: Viola

Composer: Liszt

Bird: Flamingo—This beautiful, gregarious bird is always careful of its enemy. It is also a caretaker of the young and tries to keep everyone happy.

Symbol: Triangle—You have the right combination of abilities.

Harmonious Health and Nutrition . . .

Health Scent: Peach—this scent may balance your good qualities so that they equal your charm.

Favorable Foods: Beets, strawberries, honey, oysters, pressed cheese

What's Lucky . . .

Lucky Numbers: 7, 14, 23

Best Months: April and August

Best Days of the Week: Wednesday, Saturday

Best Month Days: 4, 5, 23

Lucky Charms: A rabbit's foot or a white candle.

Harmonious Signs for Relationships and Partnerships: Gemini, Aquarius, Libra, and anyone born from July 30 to August 31.

Spiritual Guides

Star: Markab—Those with this star often receive more than they give.

Angel: Gambiel—This angel governs health issues. He teaches us the mystery of life, both on earth and in the heavens.

Guardian Angel: Gabriel—"God is my strength."

Spiritual Stone: Sardius (Ruby)—This stone may drive you to make positive changes in your life.

✴ JUDITH'S INSIGHT ✴

You're extremely inventive with a mathematical mind, and have the ability to do amazing things. Do not ever underestimate the power and the know-how that are yours naturally. You are distinctive, cute, and somewhat cunning. Your mind goes where others wish to. Just don't fear your capabilities; this could hinder you. You seem a little different to most who know you, strange to those who don't. You'll have an interesting life if you choose to take the high road. Otherwise, you could find yourself depressed, fighting feelings, always searching for and never really finding that inner peace.

You will have problems with those you love, but none that you will not be able to handle. Your grandest love will probably be your children, if you choose to have them. If not, it will be with things that make you feel like a child. One way or another, the relationship makes you feel young, that will mean the most to you. Make time to spend with family so you don't become overwhelmed. Enjoy the moment and stop obsessing about the next time. Allow the true reality of things to prevail, and you will feel true happiness.

You could be an architect, computer analyst, financial advisor, poet, actor, or director. Bring all the things you do well together, without pushing tomorrow onto today. Allow yourself mental growth, constant stimulation, and an occasional pat on the back.

Good things come to those who wait, and sometimes it may seem like the wait is forever. But don't worry—love, work, money, and friends do come your way. Just remember that sometimes the delivery person is not who we might expect.

✴ ✴ ✴

JANUARY 24 AQUARIUS • The sign of the son of man

January 21 at 3:00 A.M. to February 19 at 5:00 P.M. • NUMEROLOGY 6

Possessions and Desires . . .

Gem: Topaz—This is an excellent gift to be exchanged between very loyal friends.

Flower: Oak—You should always be able to rely on yourself.

Astral Color, Color Need, Apparel Color: Your Astral Color is Blue, which creates calmness and brings promise. Blue in your environment helps stabilize your mood. In your wardrobe, Rose gives you balance and harmony.

Fragrance: Put together a collection of orange blossoms and jasmine with touches of greenery. Always pick scents that are straight from nature instead of manufactured or processed when searching for a scent. This will keep you as unique as you wish to be.

Tree: Palm—You tend to be very healthy and creative.

Instrument: Tambourine

Composer: Schubert

Bird: Falcon—an expert hunter. When well-trained, it can adapt to many tasks and is usually obedient.

Symbol: Crescent—You are more likely to be influenced by the phases of the moon. Your easygoing manner leads you to peaceful situations.

Harmonious Health and Nutrition . . .

Health Scent: Orange Blossom—This scent may balance your body, mind, and soul.

Favorable Foods: Carrots, grapes, sugar, liver, buttermilk

What's Lucky . . .

Lucky Numbers: 1, 15, 24

Best Months: April and August

Best Days of the Week: Wednesday, Saturday

Best Month Days: 6, 15, 24

Lucky Charms: A religious token or card from any religion.

Harmonious Signs for Relationships and

Partnerships: Gemini, Aquarius, Libra, and anyone born from July 30 to August 31.

Spiritual Guides . . .

Star: Sa'ad Melik—This star hangs over those who are generous.

Angel: Gambiel—This angel governs health issues. He teaches us the mystery of life, both on earth and in the heavens.

Guardian Angel: Michael—"Who is like God."

Spiritual Stone: Sardius (Ruby)—This stone may drive you to make positive changes in your life.

✴ JUDITH'S INSIGHT ✴

You will make your statement. Allow yourself time to grow the way you would allow anyone else. Rome wasn't built in a day. You are a perfectionist, especially with yourself. At times you will project this onto others, so be cautious. You will be successful in more than one career. You tend to take on the grandest of responsibilities no matter what the cause, especially when it comes to family and children.

Relationships, in general, are your specialty. You could be a therapist. Seeing things clearly comes easily for you, especially when it comes to others. Be prepared to be a bit more humble. Love will bring you your greatest happiness and your greatest sadness. Family will play a big role in your life; if not in your early years, then later. You can be the one that keeps it all together.

Careers for you could get a little sticky: you want so much. You tend to idealize situations and stay in them too long. Be careful to recognize this. One minute your ego is running high, the next it is searching for your self-esteem at the pit's bottom. You do have that authority, along with a bit of creativity. At times this can be a complicated combination.

Being universally loved helps in almost every way of your life. Stay the good person that you are; all else will eventually fall right into place. Stop looking so hard for happiness; watched pots never seem to boil.

✴ ✴ ✴

Possessions and Desires . . .

Gem: Garnet—This gem might show you how to find faith and emotional stability.

Flower: Motherwort—You may find to your dismay that love unexpressed is love lost.

Astral Color, Color Need, Apparel Color: Your Astral Color is Blue, which creates calmness and brings promise. Blue in your environment helps stabilize your mood. In your wardrobe, Purple reflects your giving personality and brings you luck.

Fragrance: Put together a collection of orange blossoms and jasmine with touches of greenery. Always pick scents that are straight from nature instead of manufactured or processed when searching for a scent. This will keep you as unique as you wish to be.

Tree: Sycamore—Yours is the ability to love, communicate honestly with others, and have lasting relationships.

Instrument: Harp

Composer: Gluck

Bird: Mockingbird—the most proficient minstrel in the world's orchestra; graceful and enthusiastic.

Symbol: Heart—You are enthusiastic, empathetic, and full of generosity and love.

Harmonious Health and Nutrition . . .

Health Scent: Jasmine—This scent may make you more easygoing when you are stressed.

Favorable Foods: Spinach, bananas, sugar, salmon, eggs

What's Lucky . . .

Lucky Numbers: 1, 25, 34
Best Months: April and August
Best Days of the Week: Wednesday, Saturday
Best Month Days: 7, 15, 34
Lucky Charm: An old key.

Harmonious Signs for Relationships and Partnerships: Gemini, Aquarius, Libra, and anyone born from July 30 to August 31.

Spiritual Guides . . .

Star: Sa'ad al Su'ud—The star of hope.

Angel: Gambiel—This angel governs health issues. He teaches us the mystery of life, both on earth and in the heavens

Guardian Angel: Raphael—This angel attends to all of your needs when you are looking for guidance.

Spiritual Stone: Sardius (Ruby)—This stone may drive you to make positive changes in your life.

✳ JUDITH'S INSIGHT ✳

You are intellectual but inclined to work at something in the arts. Your intelligence should lead you into a significant position. Socializing is important to you, you like to be a part of a group or in the midst of a lot of friends. You will desire a long-term relationship, and you will have one. You can put too many expectations on others, so watch that. Relationships of any kind will not be hard for you to obtain; your talk is alluring all on its own. You're a natural beauty. Communication within relationships could be your downfall—you'll always think it's the other person's fault. It isn't.

Family is important to you, but you seem to allow them freedom to pressure you. When they don't, you find ways of doing it yourself. Listen to your own intuition a bit more often. You tend to be extremely enthusiastic in the beginning of a new relationship or a new job. You can get bored easily, so make sure there is enough to keep you going.

In choosing a career, look for opportunities to wear many different hats, whether as office manager, insurance agent, broker, computer whiz, actor, or even psychic. It may take time, but you will find your niche. You sometimes have big ideas that aren't entirely realistic, but at some point at least one of those big ideas will pay off.

✳ ✳ ✳

JANUARY 26

AQUARIUS • The sign of the son of man

January 21 at 3:00 A.M. to February 19 at 5:00 P.M. • NUMEROLOGY 8

Possessions and Desires . . .

Gem: Chrysolite—This gem may help you clear your mind of sadness and worry.

Flower: Orange blossom—Your fairness equals your loveliness.

Astral Color, Color Need, Apparel Color: Your Astral Color is Blue, which creates calmness and brings promise. Blue in your environment helps stabilize your mood. In your wardrobe, Gray gives you encouragement.

Fragrance: Put together a collection of orange blossoms and jasmine with touches of greenery. Always pick scents that are straight from nature instead of manufactured or processed when searching for a scent. This will keep you as unique as you wish to be.

Tree: Pine—Your relationships tend to be harmonious, both emotionally and mentally.

Instrument: Cello

Composer: Mozart

Bird: Bobolink—This charming singer is equally good as a soloist or a member of an orchestra. It is a very romantic bird, useful as an insect destroyer, and elegant, with beautiful feathers, and always pleasant to have around.

Symbol: Wings—You are the source of balance in your world. This will bring you contentment.

Harmonious Health and Nutrition . . .

Health Scent: Almond—This scent may revitalize you and open you to greater possibilities.

Favorable Foods: Okra, apples, honey, chicken, buttermilk

What's Lucky . . .

Lucky Numbers: 7, 8, 26

Best Months: April and August

Best Days of the Week: Wednesday, Saturday

Best Month Days: 8, 17, 26

Lucky Charm: A red ribbon in your wallet or doorway.

Harmonious Signs for Relationships and Partnerships: Gemini, Aquarius, Libra, and anyone born from July 30 to August 31.

Spiritual Guides . . .

Star: Deneb Algiedi—This star gives strong spiritual guidance and sound judgment.

Angel: Gambiel—This angel governs health issues. He teaches us the mysteries of life, both on earth and in the heavens.

Guardian Angel: Seraphim—the angel that brings love, light, and passion.

Spiritual Stone: Sardius (Ruby)—This stone may drive you to make positive changes in your life.

✶ JUDITH'S INSIGHT ✶

You are conscientious and possess great reasoning abilities. You can carry out any order from beginning to end with no complications. You tend to be very ambitious, so don't listen to negativity from the outside world. Others around you can sometimes bring you down. Your greatest problem will be learning to recognize the difference between good input and bad.

Learn to deal more with gut feelings and common sense. You have it: just trust it more often. Significant others will be there. Stop anticipating disaster in love, even though you feel you've had your share. Those of you who have stability with your mate could be overwhelmed by family members and issues.

Artist, musician, healer, social worker, or teacher: any one of these positions would be great for you. You may have to clear a lot of hurdles to feel stable in your job. Once you do, you'll be fine. Money will be there. Have faith and patience.

With your great reasoning powers, you could also be a mediator. You are sensible and have a changeable disposition. You must learn patience; in time your dreams do come true. Unfortunately, some of your life's nightmares will be in there, too. You do survive. You will do much better when you don't sit around feeling sorry for yourself. Think about doing more, and you will get more.

✶ ✶ ✶

JANUARY 27 AQUARIUS • The sign of the son of man
January 21 at 3:00 A.M. to February 19 at 5:00 P.M. • NUMEROLOGY 9

Possessions and Desires . . .

Gem: Opal—Holding this stone may help you discover enough hope to go on.

Flower: Burning Nettle—You can be too quick to put others down.

Astral Color, Color Need, Apparel Color: Your Astral Color is Blue, which creates calmness and brings promise. Blue in your environment helps stabilize your mood. In your wardrobe, Rose gives you balance and harmony.

Fragrance: Put together a collection of orange blossoms and jasmine with touches of greenery. Always pick scents that are straight from nature instead of manufactured or processed when searching for a scent. This will keep you as unique as you wish to be.

Tree: Holly—Beware that you are not carried away by your passionate nature. The only way to grow is to be open to new experiences.

Instrument: Violin

Composer: Gluck

Bird: Mockingbird—The most proficient minstrel in the world's orchestra; graceful and enthusiastic.

Symbol: Anchor—This tranquil symbol signifies stability and strength, and stands for strong commitments in relationships.

Harmonious Health and Nutrition . . .

Health Scent: Lavender—This scent might lead others to trust you and make you patient.

Favorable Foods: Cucumbers, cherries, sugar, oysters, pressed cheese

What's Lucky . . .

Lucky Numbers: 2, 7, 9, 36
Best Months: April and August
Best Days of the Week: Wednesday, Saturday
Best Month Days: 9, 18, 27
Lucky Charms: A U.S. coin or a bill of any amount, from the year you were born.
Harmonious Signs for Relationships and

Partnerships: Gemini, Aquarius, Libra, and anyone born from July 30 to August 31.

Spiritual Guides . . .

Star: Markab—Those with this star often receive more than they give.

Angel: Gambiel—This angel governs health issues. He teaches us the mystery of life, both on earth and in the heavens.

Guardian Angel: Gabriel—"God is my strength."

Spiritual Stone: Sardius (Ruby)—This stone may drive you to make positive changes in your life.

✶ JUDITH'S INSIGHT ✶

You are ambitious and conscientious. Your nature is warm and loving. You have a higher sense of spirituality than most, although this may not be something everyone knows about you. Most think of you as an open book. There is indeed a much more mysterious nature about you than most people see. You have the ability to accomplish much more in life than you can ever imagine. Keep that self-esteem intact and you will be very successful. You have a calming effect on people—when people are drawn to you, remember this.

If you are a woman, you will be a devoted wife and mother. Instinctively you will find the right answers for your family. If you are a man, not only will you be devoted to your wife and children, but also there is a very special place in your heart for your mother and sisters, if you have them. Either gender will have strong psychic abilities.

You're a bit idealistic, poetic, and artistic by nature, so many career doors are open. Just be aware that you sometimes lack endurance. Nevertheless, you will have great achievements within your lifetime. Creative writing, healing, or even working in the garment or beauty industry could work for you. Allow yourself a constant creativity and freedom in anything you do. This will enhance your degree of success.

Don't take life's difficulties too personally. This can be your worst downfall. Keep away from the "poor me" syndrome when the going is rough. When things do get overwhelming, remember to put one good day in front of the other, and soon you will have had a great year.

✶ ✶ ✶

JANUARY 28 AQUARIUS • The sign of the son of man

January 21 at 3:00 A.M. to February 19 at 5:00 P.M. • NUMEROLOGY 1

Possessions and Desires . . .

Gem: Agate—This stone may promote health and lead you to a long life.

Flower: Narcissus—You must be careful not to be so focused on your life that you ignore the needs of those around you.

Astral Color, Color Need, Apparel Color: Your Astral Color is Blue, which creates calmness and brings promise. Blue in your environment helps stabilize your mood. In your wardrobe, Purple reflects your giving personality and brings you luck.

Fragrance: Put together a collection of orange blossoms and jasmine with touches of greenery. Always pick scents that are straight from nature instead of manufactured or processed when searching for a scent. This will keep you as unique as you wish to be.

Tree: Walnut—You are unusually helpful and always looking for constant changes in your life.

Instruments: Flute, clarinet

Composer: Böhm

Bird: Hummingbird—This bird is delicate and graceful. It can remain still for hours, then dart off and be as busy as a bee.

Symbol: Crown—the universal sign of dignity.

Harmonious Health and Nutrition . . .

Health Scent: Strawberry—Soothing by nature, the strawberry promotes self-esteem and encourages love.

Favorable Foods: Carrots, figs, honey, liver, eggs

What's Lucky . . .

Lucky Numbers: 1, 19, 28
Best Months: April and August
Best Days of the Week: Wednesday, Saturday
Best Month Days: 1, 10, 19, 28
Lucky Charm: New penny in your shoe.
Harmonious Signs for Relationships and

Partnerships: Gemini, Aquarius, Libra, and anyone born from July 30 to August 31.

Spiritual Guides . . .

Star: Sa'ad Melik—This star hangs over those who are generous.

Angel: Gambiel—This angel governs health issues. He teaches us the mystery of life, both on earth and in the heavens.

Guardian Angel: Malachi—"Messenger of Jehovah."

Spiritual Stone: Sardius (Ruby)—This stone may drive you to make positive changes in your life.

✴ JUDITH'S INSIGHT ✴

You are an artist by nature with a flair for all kinds of design. You're emotional, sensitive, and enthusiastic. It doesn't take a lot to make you happy or to keep you that way. When the kind of devotion you give is given back, life for you is complete. As you get older, you can become disillusioned and things are less easy, although you try to keep things going smoothly.

Allow others to be closer. Life's downfalls may be difficult for you to adapt to—not because of selfishness, but because of your tendency toward idealism. Family and friends, lovers and mates, and even your children will always make you feel a sense of guilt. Don't let them—except, of course, for the few times when they will be right.

Music may be the right career, or even just a great hobby. You will probably have a strong desire to be a caretaker of some kind. If you don't select this as a career, it will find you somewhere else in your life. Your idealism will draw you to the realm of teaching, or art director, or owner of a photography studio. Make sure structure exists in your life along with the creativity.

You're known to take the long road, but you do get there eventually. Try to listen to your intuition more. Unlike most, you have it naturally. Learn to go with it. Expect the unexpected throughout your life.

✴ ✴ ✴

JANUARY 29
AQUARIUS • The sign of the son of man

January 21 at 3:00 A.M. to February 19 at 5:00 P.M. • NUMEROLOGY 2

Possessions and Desires . . .

Gem: Sapphire—This gem may help you find forgiveness from those you've wronged.

Flower: Liverwort—You are very confident in your ability to succeed.

Astral Color, Color Need, Apparel Color: Your Astral Color is Blue, which creates calmness and brings promise. Blue in your environment helps stabilize your mood. In your wardrobe, Green is your power color for overcoming obstacles.

Fragrance: Put together a collection of orange blossoms and jasmine with touches of greenery. Always pick scents that are straight from nature instead of manufactured or processed when searching for a scent. This will keep you as unique as you wish to be.

Tree: Maple—You have great stability and flashes of intuition.

Instrument: Pipe organ

Composer: Handel

Bird: Cuckoo—a good flyer and very seldom a quitter. Some cuckoos tend to think they favor lonely isolation, but what they really yearn for is a family relationship.

Symbol: Cross—the symbol of self-sacrifice and reconciliation.

Harmonious Health and Nutrition . . .

Health Scents: Apple—You are creative, full of joy, and nearly magical. You bring happiness. .

Favorable Foods: Lima beans, cherries, sugar, salmon, buttermilk

What's Lucky . . .

Lucky Numbers: 1, 2, 29, 36

Best Months: April and August

Best Days of the Week: Wednesday, Saturday

Best Month Days: 2, 11, 20, 29

Lucky Charms: Two 50-cent pieces. Give someone else one of them.

Harmonious Signs for Relationships and

Partnerships: Gemini, Aquarius, Libra, and anyone born from July 30 to August 31.

Spiritual Guides . . .

Star: Sa'ad al Su'ud—This star is the harbinger of the outpouring of hopes.

Angel: Gambiel—This angel governs health issues. He teaches us the mystery of life, both on earth and in the heavens.

Guardian Angel: St. John—This angel simplifies that which is complicated.

Spiritual Stone: Sardius (Ruby)—This stone may drive you to make positive changes in your life.

✶ JUDITH'S INSIGHT ✶

You could be a saint if you just followed your instincts. You're sensible, warm, and witty, with a gentle disposition. You're sensitive to others' feelings, and patience is your most valuable asset. A dreamer by nature, you believe almost anything can happen, and it does! You handle most of life's pitfalls well.

Your kind, compassionate nature leads many to your door. You love to be around people. Contentment comes in the form of a longtime mate, a marriage partner or otherwise. Partnerships in business can work for you as well. You always know how to settle an argument. With your diplomacy and tact, you have no problem being humble.

You're intellectual and artistic, which can lead you to dual careers. Success in more than one career would not be surprising. Somewhere throughout your lifetime, you will be recognized for your contributions—even if it's head of the PTA or coach of the year. You may want to protect your finances by taking on a very stable position, yet you should continue to pursue a more artistic or spiritual career. Sooner or later, you do find work you love. It will come. You have high hopes; higher than you show.

It's all right to keep your favorite toys hidden. Just don't spend too much of your life protecting your heart. Let people in and allow them to help fulfill your dreams.

✶ ✶ ✶

JANUARY 30
AQUARIUS • The sign of the son of man
January 21 at 3:00 A.M. to February 19 at 5:00 P.M. • NUMEROLOGY 3

Possession and Desires . . .

Gem: Ruby—This stone may lead you to energy, friendship, and happiness.

Flower: Mignonette—Your best qualities tend to be overlooked.

Astral Color, Color Need, Apparel Color: Your Astral Color is Blue, which creates calmness and brings promise. Blue in your environment helps stabilize your mood. In your wardrobe, many shades of Green keep you confident and always looking great.

Fragrance: Put together a collection of orange blossoms and jasmine with touches of greenery. Always pick scents that are straight from nature instead of manufactured or processed when searching for a scent. This will keep you as unique as you wish to be.

Tree: Elm—You have willpower, strength, and the ability to stand alone.

Instrument: Trombone

Composer: Verdi

Bird: Swan—Regarded as royal and sacred, this bird has the protective nature of a mother, and can become a furious fighter in the defense of its young.

Symbol: Wreath—You have been crowned with a special personality. You are strong but extremely compassionate.

Harmonious Health and Nutrition . . .

Health Scent: Rose—This scent will lead you to passionate thoughts and make you feel warm inside.

Favorable Foods: String beans, gooseberries, honey, chicken, pressed cheese

What's Lucky . . .

Lucky Numbers: 7, 21, 30

Best Months: April and August

Best Days of the Week: Wednesday, Saturday

Best Month Days: 3, 12, 21, and 30

Lucky Charm: A pen that someone else has already used.

Harmonious Signs for Relationships and Partnerships: Gemini, Aquarius, Libra, and anyone born from July 30 to August 31.

Spiritual Guides . . .

Star: Deneb Algiedi—This star gives strong spiritual guidance and sound judgment.

Angel: Gambiel—This angel governs health issues. He teaches us the mystery of life, both on earth and in the heavens.

Guardian Angel: Johiel—This angel is a protector of all those with a humble heart.

Spiritual Stone: Sardius (Ruby)—This stone may tend to drive you to make positive changes in your life.

✷ JUDITH'S INSIGHT ✷

Faithful, loving, and loyal all describe you. You're not perfect, but with your traits, it sometimes seems that way. Unfortunately, you can be a little impatient, stubborn, and idealistic to the point of frustration. All in all, you always try to put your best foot forward, although your parents, teachers, and bosses may not always see it that way. In time, they know you better and become more understanding.

Relationships for you are like wine: they get better with age. You like to keep busy, and your mate must learn this from the get-go—or the relationship won't last. You may seem lazy sometimes—this is far from the truth; you have the energy to do what you want. Love doesn't come easy, so make sure when you're pushing potential partners out the door that it's what you really want. You tend to change your mind once they are gone. But love will prevail. Just have patience.

You're the perfect employee, except for your tardiness. Allow a sense of creativity in your work, or else you won't be there too long. Long-term jobs appeal to you. In fact, all your relationships benefit with time. Watch out for drops in endurance, especially when you're bored or tired. Routine tasks just aren't for you. You could be a consultant of any kind, head of a department, troubleshooter, physician, social worker, actor, or even a producer or director.

Nothing in love, family, friends, work, or money is out of your reach. Keep this in mind when you're struggling with yourself. Remember, everyone gets a turn at happiness, but only some of us recognize it.

✷ ✷ ✷

JANUARY 31 AQUARIUS • The sign of the son of man
January 21 at 3:00 A.M. to February 19 at 5:00 P.M. • NUMEROLOGY 4

Possessions and Desires . . .

Gem: Emerald—Those who carry this stone tend to be lucky in love.
Flower: Periwinkle—You tend to live your life so as to have many fond memories.
Astral Color, Color Need, Apparel Color: Your Astral Color is Blue, which creates calmness and brings promise. Blue in your environment helps stabilize your mood. In your wardrobe, Purple reflects your giving personality and brings you luck.
Fragrance: Put together a collection of orange blossoms and jasmine with touches of greenery. Always pick scents that are straight from nature instead of manufactured or processed when searching for a scent. This will keep you as unique as you wish to be.
Tree: Cherry—You will find yourself faced with constant new emotional awakenings.
Instrument: Bass
Composer: Haydn
Bird: Robin—is the most sociable of all birds, with the ability to create quick friendships. It also can easily adapt to any home. When it wants something, it has the tendency to try to snatch it.
Symbol: Star—You are full of inner brightness and will stand out in any crowd. You will be seen as special.

Harmonious Health and Nutrition . . .

Health Scent: Vanilla—This scent will fill you with a feeling of cleanliness and stability.
Favorable Foods: Lentils, cherries, sugar, salmon, eggs

What's Lucky . . .

Lucky Numbers: 1, 4, 22, 31
Best Months: April and August
Best Days of the Week: Wednesday, Saturday
Best Month Days: 4, 13, 22, 31
Lucky Charm: A piece of material cut from something in your home.
Harmonious Signs for Relationships and Partnerships: Gemini, Aquarius, Libra, and anyone born from July 30 to August 31.

Spiritual Guides . . .

Star: Markab—Those with this star often receive more than they give.
Angel: Gambiel—This angel governs health issues. He teaches us the mystery of life, both on earth and in the heavens.
Guardian Angel: St. Thomas—This angel brings affection from others and encourages you in all that you do.
Spiritual Stone: Sardius (Ruby)—This stone may drive you to make positive changes in your life.

✷ JUDITH'S INSIGHT ✷

You are practical and very intuitive; some view this as a contradiction. Actually, nothing could be better than someone with psychic inclinations who is practical about it. Your vivid imagination remains grounded. You will feel blessed or guided—others may say protected. Your gentle ways will open a lot of doors in your lifetime. Strong intuitive skills bring things that may make you feel very lucky. This could take years to recognize. Let time pass, and then look back. People are drawn to you.

Home life, although you might not know it, is very important to you, as are friends. The friendships you cultivate will serve as a second family for you. Your comfortable home life may become a haven for others—don't overdo this. Loved ones are important, but don't lose yourself in other people. When your significant others have trouble, they usually have something valid to complain about.

Work as a philosopher, teacher, preacher, healer, or even scientist may be enticing. You could have many careers. You're great at instilling confidence in others—make sure to keep your own confidence up. A long-term position helps boost your faith in yourself. Watch out for sudden changes—don't let the ship sink. Success may come in many ways: in your career, as a volunteer, or in a hobby or sport.

Be cautious about keeping secrets. Stay away from the desire for drugs or alcohol, and be aware of those around you and their dependencies. No, you are not your brother's keeper, but you are your own. Temptations will present themselves; make sure you are doubly aware of your own.

✷ ✷ ✷

FEBRUARY

FEBRUARY 1

AQUARIUS • The sign of the son of man

January 21 at 3:00 A.M. to February 19 at 5:00 P.M. • NUMEROLOGY 1

Possessions and Desires . . .

Gem: Agate—This stone may promote health and lead you to a long life.

Flower: Sweet Pea—Delicate pleasures await you in every season.

Astral Color, Color Need, Apparel Color: Your Astral Color is Blue, which creates calmness and brings promise. Blue in your environment helps stabilize your mood. In your wardrobe, Rose gives you balance and harmony.

Fragrance: Put together a collection of orange blossoms and jasmine with touches of greenery. Always pick scents that are straight from nature instead of manufactured or processed when searching for a scent. This will keep you as unique as you wish to be.

Tree: Walnut—You are unusually helpful and always looking for constant changes in your life.

Instruments: Oboe, flute, clarinet, piano, French horn, organ, piccolo

Composer: Böhm

Bird: Hummingbird—This bird is delicate and graceful. It can remain still for hours, then dart off and be as busy as a bee.

Symbol: Crown—the universal sign of dignity.

Harmonious Health and Nutrition . . .

Health Scent: Jasmine—This scent may make you more easygoing when you are stressed.

Favorable Foods: Lima beans, bananas, honey, liver, buttermilk

What's Lucky . . .

Lucky Numbers: 1, 7, 19, 28
Best Months: April and August
Best Days of the Week: Wednesday, Saturday
Best Month Days: 1, 10, 19, 28
Lucky Charm: A new penny in your shoe.

Harmonious Signs for Relationships and Partnerships: Gemini, Aquarius, Libra, and anyone born from July 30 to August 31.

Spiritual Guides . . .

Star: Sa'ad Melik—This star hangs over those who are generous.

Angel: Gambiel—This angel governs health issues. He teaches us the mystery of life, both on earth and in the heavens.

Guardian Angel: Malachi—"Messenger of Jehovah."

Spiritual Stone: Sardius (Ruby)—This stone may drive you to make positive changes in your life.

✷ _JUDITH'S INSIGHT_ ✷

You are naturally alluring, a powerful, positive presence. Your appealing personality will attract many. Others may be just drawn to you even though they may not necessarily like you. Your name appears on everybody's party list. People find you fascinating, and your sense of humor could have something to do with it. One way or another, you'll step into the limelight.

Family and friends are very important to you. Watch out with love affairs; you crave attention, the romance, the challenge. But poor judgment could lead to many heartaches. Some will just be affairs of the mind that you keep to yourself. Work with what you know; use your intuition in love; it may be hard, but it works. Eventually, you do find the one and only in your life.

Actor, politician, leader, counselor, teacher, professor, or writer: you can do one or you can do them all. And you just might. You are a jack of all trades and definitely a master of some of them. All in all, there is work to be done, and you will do more than your share in more than one career.

You just might get what you wish for. Allow time for things to manifest themselves. Happiness is at your doorstep more than once—open the door and enjoy.

✶ ✶ ✶

FEBRUARY 2

AQUARIUS • The sign of the son of man

January 21 at 3:00 A.M. to February 19 at 5:00 P.M. • NUMEROLOGY 2

Possessions and Desires . . .

Gem: Sapphire—This gem may help you find forgiveness from those you've wronged.

Flower: Yellow Rose—You usually hate any hint of falsehood.

Astral Color, Color Need, Apparel Color: Your Astral Color is Blue, which creates calmness and brings promise. Blue in your environment helps stabilize your mood. In your wardrobe, Rose gives you balance and harmony.

Fragrance: Put together a collection of orange blossoms and jasmine with touches of greenery. Always pick scents that are straight from nature instead of manufactured or processed when searching for a scent. This will keep you as unique as you wish to be.

Tree: Maple—You have great stability and flashes of intuition.

Instruments: Pipe organ, cymbal, drum

Composers: Handel, Johann Sebastian Bach

Bird: Cuckoo—A good flyer and very seldom a quitter. Some cuckoos tend to think they favor lonely isolation, but what they really yearn for is a family relationship.

Symbol: Cross—the symbol of self-sacrifice and reconciliation.

Harmonious Health and Nutrition . . .

Health Scent: Apple—You are creative, full of joy, and nearly magical. You bring happiness.

Favorable Foods: Spinach, strawberries, sugar, salmon, pressed cheese

What's Lucky . . .

Lucky Numbers: 2, 7, 11, 20
Best Months: April and August
Best Days of the Week: Wednesday, Saturday
Best Month Days: 2, 11, 20, 29
Lucky Charms: Two 50-cent pieces. Give someone else one of them.
Harmonious Signs for Relationships and

Partnerships: Gemini, Aquarius, Libra, and anyone born from July 30 to August 31.

Spiritual Guides . . .

Star: Sa'ad al Su'ud—This star is the harbinger of the outpouring of hopes.

Angel: Gambiel—This angel governs health issues. He teaches us the mystery of life, both on earth and in the heavens.

Guardian Angel: St. John—This angel simplifies that which is complicated.

Spiritual Stone: Sardius (Ruby)—This stone may drive you to make positive changes in your life.

✶ JUDITH'S INSIGHT ✶

Proud and capable, you are fascinated by just about everything in life, especially in your youth. You're open to all things and especially easy to get along with. When you start something, you never give up. Be careful of your tenacity; you could get too comfortable and not look for growth. Self-respect is important, too—as long as there are plenty of pats on the back, you won't worry too much about titles.

Should you have children, your opinions will run strong. Protect the family. You will probably find a love mate with a strong personality. You love feeling needed. When you don't, you think something is lacking. If you are neglected or abused in any way, you're out the door. Issues with women in the family may result in some egos clashing.

A career involving mysticism should intrigue you. Teacher would be all right; a decorator or nutritionist could work. You're artistic by nature, so use this ability in some unusual way. You may not be a designer, but the seamstress who does all the beautiful handiwork. Opportunities present themselves throughout your life. Learn to recognize them. Trust your knowledge and your art. Allow time for growth in the career you choose. Check your opinion, particularly with the boss—being a bit humble can come in handy.

You love to spend money, and when depressions hit, you tend to overspend. Those who say money can't buy happiness have never met you.

✶ ✶ ✶

FEBRUARY 3

AQUARIUS • The sign of the son of man

January 21 at 3:00 A.M to February 19 at 5:00 P.M. • NUMEROLOGY 3

Possessions and Desires . . .

Gem: Ruby—This stone may lead you to energy, friendship, and happiness.

Flower: Saffron—You should beware of excess emotions in the early morning.

Astral Color, Color Need, Apparel Color: Your Astral Color is Blue, which creates calmness and brings promise. Blue in your environment helps stabilize your mood. In your wardrobe, Purple reflects your giving personality and brings you luck.

Fragrance: Put together a collection of orange blossoms and jasmine with touches of greenery. Always pick scents that are straight from nature instead of manufactured or processed when searching for a scent. This will keep you as unique as you wish to be.

Tree: Elm—You have willpower, strength, and the ability to stand alone.

Instrument: Trombone

Composers: Verdi, Mendelssohn, Schumann

Bird: Swan—Regarded as royal and sacred, this bird has the protective nature of a mother, and can become a furious fighter in the defense of its young.

Symbol: Wreath—You have been crowned with a special personality. You are strong but extremely compassionate.

Harmonious Health and Nutrition . . .

Health Scent: Rose—This scent will lead you to passionate thoughts and make you feel warm inside.

Favorable Foods: Lentils, grapes, sugar, oysters, eggs

What's Lucky . . .

Lucky Numbers: 3, 7, 21
Best Months: April and August
Best Days of the Week: Wednesday, Saturday
Best Month Days: 3, 12, 21, 30
Lucky Charm: A pen that someone else has already used.

Harmonious Signs for Relationships and Partnerships: Gemini, Aquarius, Libra, and anyone born from July 30 to August 31.

Spiritual Guides . . .

Star: Deneb Algiedi—This star gives strong spiritual guidance and sound judgment.

Angel: Gambiel—This angel governs health issues. He teaches us the mystery of life, both on earth and in the heavens.

Guardian Angel: Johiel—This angel is a protector of all those with a humble heart.

Spiritual Stone: Sardius (Ruby)—This stone may drive you to make positive changes in your life.

✴ JUDITH'S INSIGHT ✴

You can be a showoff and love every minute of it. You have looks, smarts, sensuality, sensitivity, and a desire to be noticed—and you will be! Your ego can run high, and when it does, you're the best. Rejections hurt, and picking yourself up afterward can be work. You're exceptionally resilient, so you eventually bounce back. You do like to hold on to things for sentimental reasons. Friends hold on to you like you hold on to money; you're still friends with your nursery schoolmates. You'll have a million crushes—some good, some bad. Heartstrings break here and there, but you do find that devoted mate; it just takes awhile. You'll pine and pine for the "one that got away," only to thank your lucky stars later in life.

A career in which you give advice is best for you. You could be a politician, teacher, preacher, camp counselor, healer, psychic—the list is endless. You may seem quiet to some, but you need to have a place to speak out and be creative. Patience is not your strong point, but you get by. Success comes and goes because you like to start anew. Strive for balance at work—sooner or later it comes.

If all else fails, start recording some of your fantastic ideas, your daydreaming schemes. You're cunning and cute; it's a great combination. Remember that you don't have to keep both feet on the ground; one foot will help you maintain and the other sustain. Learning which is which is the trick.

✴ ✴ ✴

FEBRUARY 4
AQUARIUS • The sign of the son of man
January 21 at 3:00 A.M. to February 19 at 5:00 P.M. • NUMEROLOGY 4

Possessions and Desires . . .

Gem: Emerald—Those who carry this stone tend to be lucky in love.

Flower: Pansy—You shouldn't do anything unless you clearly think things through.

Astral Color, Color Need, Apparel Color: Your Astral Color is Blue, creating calmness and bringing promise. Keep Blue in your environment to help stabilize your mood. In your wardrobe, Rose gives you balance and harmony.

Fragrance: Put together a collection of orange blossoms and jasmine with touches of greenery. Always pick scents that are straight from nature instead of manufactured or processed when searching for a scent. This will keep you as unique as you wish to be.

Tree: Cherry—You will find yourself faced with constant new emotional awakenings.

Instruments: Bass, clarinet

Composers: Haydn, Wagner

Bird: Robin—The most sociable of all birds, with the ability to create quick friendships. It also can easily adapt to any home. When it wants something, it has the tendency to try to snatch it.

Symbol: Star—You are full of inner brightness and will stand out in any crowd. You will be seen as special.

Harmonious Health and Nutrition . . .

Health Scent: Vanilla—This scent will fill you with a feeling of cleanliness and stability.

Favorable Foods: Romaine lettuce, figs, honey, chicken, buttermilk

What's Lucky . . .

Lucky Numbers: 1, 4, 13, 22

Best Months: April and August

Best Days of the Week: Wednesday, Saturday

Best Month Days: 4, 13, 22, 31

Lucky Charm: A piece of material cut from something in your home.

Harmonious Signs for Relationships and

Partnerships: Gemini, Aquarius, Libra, and anyone born from July 30 to August 31.

Spiritual Guides . . .

Star: Markab—Those with this star often receive more than they give.

Angel: Gambiel—This angel governs health issues. He teaches us the mystery of life, both on earth and in the heavens.

Guardian Angel: St. Thomas—This angel brings affection from others and encourages you in all that you do.

Spiritual Stone: Sardius (Ruby)—This stone may drive you to make positive changes in your life.

✷ JUDITH'S INSIGHT ✷

You have an awesome sense of concentration. With focus like yours, you could master anything. Do you recognize that you see life much clearer than most? You are kind and considerate by nature, and others are fascinated by you. The fact that your looks are quite good doesn't hurt. Frequently throughout your life you'll encounter strange situations: some really good, some not. You know the difference.

You may not think it, but ask others around you: you're a flirt. Family relationships are what you make of them; at times you will need to be tolerant, but mostly it's the other way around. Love mates are usually the ones in the public eye. That's what you want, so don't feel sorry for yourself if they receive all the attention.

You will do great in just about any career having to do with people and creativity. You'd be happy as a clothing designer for the movies or theater. You will love working in an environment that will eventually lead you to glory and glamour. Fear not—you get it. Just keep in mind that opportunities that aren't here today could be here tomorrow. When your biggest dreams seem to be on hold, have patience, your day does come.

Feeling sorry for yourself never helps; it only creates more anxiety. Learn to trust your instincts more often, and temper that vivid imagination. You can have a positive impact on a lot of people's lives; make sure you are as positive for yourself.

✷ ✷ ✷

FEBRUARY 5

AQUARIUS • The sign of the son of man

January 21 at 3:00 A.M. to February 19 at 5:00 P.M. • **NUMEROLOGY 5**

Possessions and Desires . . .

Gem: Sapphire—This gem may help you find forgiveness from those you've wronged.
Flower: Marsh Mallow—The course of your life will tend to surprise you.
Astral Color, Color Need, Apparel Color: Your Astral Color is Blue, which creates calmness and brings promise. Blue in your environment helps stabilize your mood. In your wardrobe, Green is your power color for overcoming obstacles.
Fragrance: Put together a collection of orange blossoms and jasmine with touches of greenery. Always pick scents that are straight from nature instead of manufactured or processed when searching for a scent. This will keep you as unique as you wish to be.
Tree: Apple—You are creative, full of joy, and nearly magical. You bring happiness.
Instruments: Viola, trumpet
Composer: Liszt
Bird: Flamingo—This beautiful and gregarious bird is always careful of its enemy. It is also a caretaker of the young and tries to keep everyone happy.
Symbol: Triangle—You have the right combination of abilities.

Harmonious Health and Nutrition . . .

Health Scent: Peach—this scent may balance your good qualities so that they equal your charm.
Favorable Foods: Carrots, cherries, honey, salmon, eggs

What's Lucky . . .

Lucky Numbers: 5, 7, 14, 23
Best Months: April and August
Best Days of the Week: Wednesday, Saturday
Best Month Days: 4, 5, 23
Lucky Charms: A rabbit's foot or a white candle.
Harmonious Signs for Relationships and

Partnerships: Gemini, Aquarius, Libra, and anyone born from July 30 to August 31.

Spiritual Guides . . .

Star: Markab—Those with this star often receive more than they give.
Angel: Gambiel—This angel governs health issues. He teaches us the mystery of life, both on earth and in the heavens.
Guardian Angel: Gabriel—"God is my strength."
Spiritual Stone: Sardius (Ruby)—This stone may drive you to make positive changes in your life.

✳ JUDITH'S INSIGHT ✳

Creativity is the main word that describes you. You present yourself as perfect; most will think of you as unique. You can seem mysterious, yet you are warm and loving with a fascination for things unknown or off-color. You can be temperamental.

All your relationships border on the unusual. You root for the underdog. At the same time, you have a strong desire to be needed, so you may find yourself the caretaker of family, friends, and any other stranger that wanders across your path. You have a sweet soul and a nurturing quality. Because of your fun-loving attitude, your children may wonder who's the parent and who's the child.

You're a caretaker by nature, and this could open career doors in such fields as medicine or education. With all your other talents, a career in the arts, film, or design is recommended. One way or another, you'll be successful. But just when you think your career is set, you'll be daydreaming. All of a sudden you'll find yourself in a new career, even if it is at age 65.

Intuitive and imaginative as you are, try to maintain some balance, even if it means keeping a journal. You see the world differently from most. It would be interesting to see how you would explain all the journeys of your life and the detours you've taken to get there. You do it with kindness, love, and laughter. Who would believe it? Time to go get the pen and write!

✳ ✳ ✳

FEBRUARY 6

AQUARIUS • The sign of the son of man

January 21 at 3:00 A.M. to February 19 at 5:00 P.M. • NUMEROLOGY 6

Possessions and Desires . . .

Gem: Topaz—This is an excellent gift to be exchanged between very loyal friends.

Flower: Mistletoe—You may need to discover that you are your best ally in surmounting difficulties.

Astral Color, Color Need, Apparel Color: Your Astral Color is Blue, which creates calmness and brings promise. Blue in your environment helps stabilize your mood. In your wardrobe, Purple reflects your giving personality and brings you luck.

Fragrance: Put together a collection of orange blossoms and jasmine with touches of greenery. Always pick scents that are straight from nature instead of manufactured or processed when searching for a scent. This will keep you as unique as you wish to be.

Tree: Palm—You tend to be very healthy and creative.

Instruments: Tambourine, lyre

Composer: Schubert

Symbol: Crescent—You are more likely to be influenced by the phases of the moon. Your easygoing manner leads you to peaceful situations.

Bird: Falcon—an expert hunter. When well-trained, it can adapt to many tasks and is usually obedient.

Harmonious Health and Nutrition . . .

Health Scent: Orange Blossom—This scent may balance your body, mind, and soul.

Favorable Foods: Beets, strawberries, sugar, oysters, pressed cheese

What's Lucky . . .

Lucky Numbers: 1, 6, 15, 24

Best Months: April and August

Best Days of the Week: Wednesday, Saturday

Best Month Days: 6, 15, 24

Lucky Charms: A religious token or card from any religion.

Harmonious Signs for Relationships and Partnerships: Gemini, Aquarius, Libra, and anyone born from July 30 to August 31.

Spiritual Guides . . .

Star: Sa'ad Melik—This star hangs over those who are generous.

Angel: Gambiel—This angel governs health issues. He teaches us the mystery of life, both on earth and in the heavens.

Guardian Angel: Michael—"Who is like God."

Spiritual Stone: Sardius (Ruby)—This stone may drive you to make positive changes in your life.

✳ JUDITH'S INSIGHT ✳

Resourceful and creative by nature, you do wonders with leftovers. You can build shelves from coffee cans or make quilts from scraps. You're thoughtful when it comes to others, not so when it comes to yourself. A lack of spare time and unrealistic expectations can drain you.

You'll want challenge in relationships, especially in love. Your warmth and sensitivity captivate people; your unusual personality can scare them. But that personality is exactly what they're attracted to in the first place. Don't underestimate your power. Passion comes in several unconventional connections in your life, especially in the beginning of relationships. Your love mate has style, and may be in the public eye.

It may take a few jobs to get you settled—not because you're fickle, but because of your diversity. Be patient. With your passion for art, you should look to that field. You could also find satisfaction as a social worker, therapist, or doctor or working with children. You can be team leader or team player. You have no problem with criticism or authority. Others may find you lazy, but it may be simple boredom. You need constant stimulation at work and, perhaps, a bit of freedom. You may be more interested in hobbies than in your job. You may find yourself in the limelight somewhere along the way. You are luckier than you think, and as you mature, you recognize this. Early years are more difficult than later ones—you think others have it better than you. Stop feeling sorry for yourself. As you grow, you learn you have it better than most.

✳ ✳ ✳

FEBRUARY 7 AQUARIUS • The sign of the son of man
January 21 at 3:00 A.M. to February 19 at 5:00 P.M. • NUMEROLOGY 7

Possessions and Desires . . .

Gem: Garnet—This gem might show you how to find faith and emotional stabilty.

Flower: Linden—You don't tend to need much help in seducing someone you care for.

Astral Color, Color Need, Apparel Color: Your Astral Color is Blue, which creates calmness and brings promise. Blue in your environment helps stabilize your mood. In your wardrobe, Purple reflects your giving personality and brings you luck.

Fragrance: Put together a collection of orange blossoms and jasmine with touches of greenery. Always pick scents that are straight from nature instead of manufactured or processed when searching for a scent. This will keep you as unique as you wish to be.

Tree: Sycamore—Yours is the ability to love, communicate honestly with others, and have lasting relationships.

Instrument: Harp

Composers: Gluck, Brahms

Bird: Mockingbird—the most proficient minstrel in the world's orchestra; graceful and enthusiastic.

Symbol: Heart—You are enthusiastic, empathetic, and full of generosity and love.

Harmonious Health and Nutrition . . .

Health Scent: Jasmine—This scent may make you more easygoing when you are stressed.

Favorable Foods: Spinach, grapes, honey, liver, buttermilk

What's Lucky . . .

Lucky Numbers: 7, 25, 43
Best Months: April and August
Best Days of the Week: Wednesday, Saturday
Best Month Days: 6, 15, 24
Lucky Charm: An old key.
Harmonious Signs for Relationships and

Partnerships: Gemini, Aquarius, Libra, and anyone born from July 30 to August 31.

Spiritual Guides . . .

Star: Sa'ad al Su'ud—The star of hope.

Angel: Gambiel—This angel governs health issues. He teaches us the mystery of life, both on earth and in the heavens.

Guardian Angel: Raphael—This angel attends to all of your needs when you are looking for guidance.

Spiritual Stone: Sardius (Ruby)—This stone may drive you to make positive changes in your life.

✶ JUDITH'S INSIGHT ✶

A collector by nature, you love to shop. You love to have fun and you enjoy parties. There simply aren't enough dances to dance for you. If you don't have a career or hobby in the arts, theater, or communication, it would be surprising.

Relationships come and go—many you will keep to yourself—until, of course, you meet that devoted, significant other. Spontaneity and style will keep you coming back for more. Your family grows to know you and appreciate your unique ways and talents. Tolerate each other. You have your own, intuitive ideas in the raising and managing of children, and most of the time you're correct.

Your friendly nature and theatrical mind attract many friends. You'd be a great artist, musician, educator, or scientist. Follow your artistic desires, but watch that possessive nature. Tension in the workplace should be avoided. You're mostly funny and original, but moods will swing. Think before you speak, especially under the age of 28. Afterward, you're less anxious.

Learn to look at the pretty colors and breathe the fresh air around you. You're a very pleasant person to have around. Others like to feel that they have your attention. Learn to enjoy the moment a little more. When you "stop and smell the roses," enjoy the colors as well as the fragrance.

✶ ✶ ✶

FEBRUARY 8

AQUARIUS • The sign of the son of man

January 21 at 3:00 A.M. to February 19 at 5:00 P.M. • NUMEROLOGY 8

Possessions and Desires . . .

Gem: Garnet—This gem might show you how to find faith and emotional stability.
Flower: Pineapple—You are considered by many to be well-mannered.
Astral Color, Color Need, Apparel Color: Your Astral Color is Blue, which creates calmness and brings promise. Blue in your environment helps stabilize your mood. In your wardrobe, Purple reflects your giving personality and brings you luck.
Fragrance: Put together a collection of orange blossoms and jasmine with touches of greenery. Always pick scents that are straight from nature instead of manufactured or processed when searching for a scent. This will keep you as unique as you wish to be.
Tree: Pine—Your relationships tend to be harmonious, both emotionally and mentally.
Instrument: Cello
Composer: Mozart
Bird: Bobolink—This charming singer is equally good as a soloist or a member of an orchestra. It is a very romantic bird, useful as an insect destroyer, and elegant, with beautiful feathers, and always pleasant to have around.
Symbol: Wings—You are the source of balance in your world; this will bring you contentment.

Harmonious Health and Nutrition . . .

Health Scent: Almond—This scent may revitalize you and open you to greater possibilities.
Favorable Foods: Lentils, gooseberries, sugar, chicken, eggs

What's Lucky . . .

Lucky Numbers: 17, 26, 44
Best Months: April and August
Best Days of the Week: Wednesday, Saturday
Best Month Days: 8, 17, 26
Lucky Charm: A red ribbon in your wallet, or doorway.

Harmonious Signs for Relationships and Partnerships: Gemini, Aquarius, Libra, and anyone born from July 30 to August 31.

Spiritual Guides . . .

Star: Deneb Algiedi—This star gives strong spiritual guidance and sound judgment.
Angel: Gambiel—This angel governs health issues. He teaches us the mystery of life, both on earth and in the heavens.
Guardian Angel: Seraphim—This angel brings love, light and passion.
Spiritual Stone: Sardius (Ruby)—This stone may drive you to make positive changes in your life.

✷ JUDITH'S INSIGHT ✷

You are unusual in many ways: the way you live, dress, and even the way you make a living. Some may see you as strange, but I will call you the unique child. One can find you in a dream state about 15 times a day. You are spiritual with or without religion. You're easily misunderstood, and can feel quite sorry for yourself if things don't go your way.

Your significant other is in the media or the limelight, hopefully for good reasons. You're drawn to the artist and the underdog, which could lead to a relationship with a person of poor character. Don't fret, you'll wind up with someone sane and look back upon your earlier relationships as funny. Family members will be patient, and in turn, you learn to be patient with them. Devotion to your friends brings you much harmony.

With your artistic nature, you may have a career so unique that a title hasn't been created for you, and you will probably be very successful at it. Watch out for becoming bored—it may hinder your rise to the top. Make sure you choose a diverse career.

Generosity is a great trait to have just as long as your pocketbook allows it. You tend to rob Peter to pay Paul. You have the ability to meditate and dream. Use this as a positive trait to learn patience. In time you do prevail.

✷ ✷ ✷

FEBRUARY 9 AQUARIUS • The sign of the son of man
January 21 at 3:00 A.M. to February 19 at 5:00 P.M. • NUMEROLOGY 9

Possessions and Desires . . .

Gem: Turquoise—This stone might help you find material gain.

Flower: Leek—You should practice charity whenever possible.

Astral Color, Color Need, Apparel Color: Your Astral Color is Blue, which creates calmness and brings promise. Blue in your environment helps stabilize your mood. In your wardrobe, Purple reflects your giving personality and brings you luck.

Fragrance: Put together a collection of orange blossoms and jasmine with touches of greenery. Always pick scents that are straight from nature instead of manufactured or processed when searching for a scent. This will keep you as unique as you wish to be.

Tree: Holly—Beware that you are not carried away by your passionate nature. The only way to grow is to be open to new experiences.

Instruments: Violin, tympanum

Composer: Gluck

Bird: Mockingbird—the most proficient minstrel in the world's orchestra; graceful and enthusiastic.

Symbol: Anchor—This tranquil symbol signifyies stability and strength, and stands for strong commitments in relationships.

Harmonious Health and Nutrition . . .

Health Scent: Lavender—This scent might lead others to trust you and make you patient.

Favorable Foods: Okra, bananas, honey, liver, pressed cheese

What's Lucky . . .

Lucky Numbers: 9, 26, 36
Best Months: April and August
Best Days of the Week: Wednesday, Saturday
Best Month Days: 9, 18, 27
Lucky Charms: A U.S. coin or a bill of any amount from the year you were born.
Harmonious Sign for Relationships and Part-nerships: Gemini, Aquarius, Libra, and anyone born from July 30 to August 31.

Spiritual Guides . . .

Star: Markab—Those with this star often receive more than they give.

Angel: Gambiel—This angel governs health issues. He teaches us the mystery of life, both on earth and in the heavens.

Guardian Angel: Gabriel—"God is my strength."

Spiritual Stone: Sardius (Ruby)—This stone may drive you to make positive changes in your life.

✴ JUDITH'S INSIGHT ✴

You have a highly evolved mind. You're a teacher by nature, but you may or may not choose that career. You're dependable and honorable and have great organizational skills. Your greatest trait of all is philanthropy—you have a heart. Good reasoning powers allow you continuity with all relationships. People are drawn to you, and you take on relationships thinking they are filling a need, later to realize they provided a need to another. This may pose problems: it's hard for you to get away from old flames; you probably want to keep them as friends. If not, they want to be friends with you. You give so much, you sometimes get restless in relationships. Beware of that complication.

Your multifaceted personality leads to your involvement in more than one career and hobby. Science would allow you freedom and growth. Educator, architect, musician, therapist, or technocrat are other possible career choices. You can raise money with the best of them, and your intuitive nature reveals psychic abilities.

With a heart as big as the ocean, you allow many people in your life. As you get older, this may become overwhelming—allow yourself a mental timeout from others. One way or another, you may find yourself in the role of messenger or teacher. Your natural intelligence and common sense will bring you success in your lifetime. Still, hard lessons are there to learn. At the time you may not believe them, but as time goes on you will. You'll make your mark, and it may be surprising just how you do.

✴ ✴ ✴

FEBRUARY 10 AQUARIUS • The sign of the son of man

January 21 at 3:00 A.M. to February 19 at 5:00 P.M. • NUMEROLOGY 1

Possessions and Desires . . .

Gem: Agate—This stone may promote health and lead you to a long life.

Flower: Hawthorn—You may have an unconquerable belief in yourself.

Astral Color, Color Need, Apparel Color: Your Astral Color is Blue, which creates calmness and brings promise. Blue in your environment helps stabilize your mood. In wardrobe, Purple reflects your giving personality and brings you luck.

Fragrance: Put together a collection of orange blossoms and jasmine with touches of greenery. Always pick scents that are straight from nature instead of manufactured or processed when searching for a scent. This will keep you as unique as you wish to be.

Tree: Walnut—You are unusually helpful and always looking for constant changes in your life.

Instruments: Oboe, flute, clarinet, piano, French horn, organ, piccolo

Composer: Böhm

Bird: Bird of paradise—the "bird of the gods." You will shine and love extraordinary circumstances.

Symbol: Crown—the universal sign of dignity.

Harmonious Health and Nutrition . . .

Health Scent: Strawberry—Soothing by nature, the strawberry promotes self-esteem and encourages love.

Favorable Foods: Lima beans, cherries, sugar, salmon, buttermilk

What's Lucky . . .

Lucky Numbers: 1, 19, 37
Best Months: April and August
Best Days of the Week: Wednesday, Saturday
Best Month Days: 1, 10, 19, and 28
Lucky Charm: A new penny in your shoe.

Harmonious Signs for Relationships and Partnerships: Gemini, Aquarius, Libra, and anyone born from July 30 to August 31.

Spiritual Guides . . .

Star: Sa'ad Melik—This star hangs over those who are generous.

Angel: Gambiel—This angel governs health issues. He teaches us the mystery of life, both on earth and in the heavens.

Guardian Angel: Malachi—"Messenger of Jehovah."

Spiritual Stone: Sardius (Ruby)—This stone may drive you to make positive changes in your life.

✳ JUDITH'S INSIGHT ✳

You are affectionate, tolerant, and truthful; you're also strong-willed and obstinate. Keeping your good and bad traits in balance is the hard part. Your restlessness may create heartaches for you and others. Appearance is important to you, and your neat, though funky, style of dress shows this. To some extent you are materialistic. Your skepticism makes you unpredictable.

Stay away from moody people—they don't blend with your need for affection. At first you appear too nurturing—until others get to know you; then they love it. Be careful with ending relationships; old flames want to hang on. Family grows more important as you mature. It's easier for you to handle constant obligations when you're older.

You could be a marine architect, sculptor, lawyer, actor, or director. How about two or three of them? You may have multiple careers, hobbies, and, certainly, interests. As a collector, you find treasures in the trash. You're motivated by creativity, diversity, and cash, and success will come. Use sports to unleash all your exuberance. Constantly look to stimulate your super-abundant mental energy. Depression and laziness are the worst for you. Aim high and have great expectations, and you'll love every minute of it.

★ ★ ★

FEBRUARY 11

AQUARIUS • The sign of the son of man

January 21 at 3:00 A.M. to February 19 at 5:00 P.M. • NUMEROLOGY 2

Possessions and Desires . . .

Gem: Sapphire—This gem may help you find forgiveness from those you've wronged.

Flower: Cypress Vine—You are happiest when facing new beginnings.

Astral Color, Color Need, Apparel Color: Your Astral Color is Blue, creating calm, bringing promise. Blue in your environment helps stabilize your mood. In your wardrobe, Purple reflects your giving personality and brings luck.

Fragrance: Put together a collection of orange blossoms and jasmine with touches of greenery. Always pick scents that are straight from nature instead of manufactured or processed when searching for a scent. This will keep you as unique as you wish to be.

Tree: Maple—You have both great stability and flashes of intuition.

Instruments: Pipe organ, cymbal, drum

Composers: Handel, Johann Sebastian Bach

Bird: Stork—Turkish bird, held in high esteem the world over. This bird is intelligent but may have strange tendencies.

Symbol: Cross—the symbol of self-sacrifice and reconciliation.

Harmonious Health and Nutrition . . .

Health Scent: Apple—You are creative, full of joy, and nearly magical. You bring happiness.

Favorable Foods: Beets, apples, honey, chicken, eggs

What's Lucky . . .

Lucky Numbers: 2, 7, 38

Best Months: April and August

Best Days of the Week: Wednesday, Saturday

Best Month Days: 2, 11, 20, 29

Lucky Charms: Two 50-cent pieces. Give someone else one of them.

Harmonious Signs for Relationships and Partnerships: Gemini, Aquarius, Libra, and anyone born from July 30 to August 31.

Spiritual Guides . . .

Star: Sa'ad al Su'ud—This star is the harbinger of the outpouring of hopes.

Angel: Gambiel—This angel governs health issues. He teaches us the mystery of life, both on earth and in the heavens.

Guardian Angel: St. John—This angel simplifies that which is complicated.

Spiritual Stone: Sardius (Ruby)—This stone may drive you to make positive changes in your life.

✶ JUDITH'S INSIGHT ✶

Some may see you as strong and ambitious, others as gentle and imaginative. You have all these qualities, depending on the situation. One may be your home personality, the other your work side. In relationships, you can be fickle, or drawn to the underdog—but you know better! Depending on where you are in life, you could be the late bloomer or the early riser. Either way, mates are strong and loyal; it just may take awhile to find the right fit. Don't allow friends and family to overburden you—they will—though you place your share of burdens upon them.

Partnerships in business work well for you. You may work with your significant other or just meet that person at work. You do things better in teams than most and may have more than one career before you find the right one. Listen to the good advice of others. As a partner in a law firm, you do well. As an actor, you could have both a partnership and relationship with the producer. Think partnership!

Team leader or teammate, you'll find your way to the top in life. It infuriates you to be seen as the bad guy—you're not. You're very strong and capable, and this creates a lot of pressure. You make it your own way in life. Others may not always see it that way—they only see what you have, not what it took for you to get it. Your spiritual side will get you through.

✶ ✶ ✶

47

FEBRUARY 12

AQUARIUS • The sign of the son of man

January 21 at 3:00 A.M. to February 19 at 5:00 P.M. • NUMEROLOGY 3

Possessions and Desires . . .

Gem: Ruby—This stone may lead you to energy, friendship, and happiness.

Flower: Dew Plant—You always seem to have a song in your heart.

Astral Color, Color Need, Apparel Color: Your Astral Color is Blue, which creates calmness and brings promise. Blue in your environment helps stabilize your mood. In your wardrobe, Gray gives you encouragement.

Fragrance: Put together a collection of orange blossoms and jasmine with touches of greenery. Always pick scents that are straight from nature instead of manufactured or processed when searching for a scent. This will keep you as unique as you wish to be.

Tree: Elm—You have willpower, strength, and the ability to stand alone.

Instrument: Trombone

Composers: Verdi, Mendelssohn, Schumann

Bird: Swan—Regarded as royal and sacred, this bird has the protective nature of a mother, and can become a furious fighter in the defense of its young.

Symbol: Wreath—You have been crowned with a special personality. You are strong but extremely compassionate.

Harmonious Health and Nutrition . . .

Health Scent: Rose—This scent will lead you to passionate thoughts and make you feel warm inside.

Favorable Foods: Cucumbers, figs, sugar, salmon, pressed cheese

What's Lucky . . .

Lucky Numbers: 1, 7, 12, 32
Best Months: April and August
Best Days of the Week: Wednesday, Saturday
Best Month Days: 3, 12, 21, 30

Lucky Charm: A pen that someone else has already used.

Harmonious Signs for Relationships and Partnerships: Gemini, Aquarius, Libra, and anyone born from July 30 to August 31.

Spiritual Guides . . .

Star: Deneb Algiedi—This star gives strong spiritual guidance and sound judgment.

Angel: Gambiel—This angel governs health issues. He teaches us the mystery of life, both on earth and in the heavens.

Guardian Angel: Johiel—This angel is a protector of all those with a humble heart.

Spiritual Stone: Sardius (Ruby)—This stone may drive you to make positive changes in your life.

✴ JUDITH'S INSIGHT ✴

Why do you show others your bad side? There are so many good things about you. Why do you insist on being negative, selfish, and domineering when you know you're caring and loving when it really counts? When you don't get your way, you're pesky; when you're tired, you get cranky. You're always doing everything for everybody. Well, have no fear . . . your devoted mate sees you for who you really are. With few words, your wit and charm get all the attention. Loyalty is your strong suit, no matter in what kind of relationship. As the devoted child, you pick up the slack for other family members. If they take you for granted, however, you will rebel. You can raise hell if need be.

Have you considered politics? You could be the head of something somewhere along the way, perhaps the principal of a school or a scout leader. You show great strength, devotion, and character. You will be successful—but when?

You love many but trust few, at least until they prove themselves. Since you're a hard worker, your stamina keeps you at the task longer than most. You're generous with your time and money, and you want and expect that generosity in return. Those around you learn this in order to keep you happy.

✶ ✶ ✶

FEBRUARY 13 AQUARIUS • The sign of the son of man
January 21 at 3:00 A.M. to February 19 at 5:00 P.M. • NUMEROLOGY 4

Possessions and Desires . . .

Gem: Emerald—Those who carry this stone tend to be lucky in love.

Flower: Clematis—You are more drawn to mental beauty than the physical kind.

Astral Color, Color Need, Apparel Color: Your Astral Color is Blue, which creates calmness and brings promise. Blue in your environment helps stabilize your mood. In your wardrobe, Rose gives you balance and harmony.

Fragrance: Put together a collection of orange blossoms and jasmine with touches of greenery. Always pick scents that are straight from nature instead of manufactured or processed when searching for a scent. This will keep you as unique as you wish to be.

Tree: Cherry—You will find yourself faced with constant new emotional awakenings.

Instruments: Bass, Clarinet

Composers: Haydn, Wagner

Bird: Robin—the most sociable of all birds, with the ability to create quick friendships. It also can easily adapt to any home. When it wants something, it has the tendency to try to snatch it.

Symbol: Star—You are full of inner brightness and will stand out in any crowd. You will be seen as special.

Harmonious Health and Nutrition . . .

Health Scent: Vanilla—This scent will fill you with a feeling of cleanliness and stability.

Favorable Foods: Lima beans, strawberries, sugar, salmon, eggs

What's Lucky . . .

Lucky Numbers: 1, 4, 22, 31

Best Months: April and August

Best Days of the Week: Wednesday, Saturday

Best Month Days: 4, 13, 22, 31

Lucky Charm: A piece of material cut from something in your home.

Harmonious Signs for Relationships and

Partnerships: Gemini, Aquarius, Libra, and anyone born from July 30 to August 31.

Spiritual Guides . . .

Star: Markab—Those with this star often receive more than they give.

Angel: Gambiel—This angel governs health issues. He teaches us the mystery of life, both on earth and in the heavens.

Guardian Angel: St. Thomas—This angel brings affection from others and encourages you in all that you do.

Spiritual Stone: Sardius (Ruby)—This stone may drive you to make positive changes in your life.

✶ JUDITH'S INSIGHT ✶

You see things differently from the rest of us. You may be an expert in one field or another, considered a genius by some and lucky by others, without even trying. Sudden and inexplicable things happen that will later benefit you. Your life has an "unexpected" quality about it. Because of your quick mind, you find fault in others, which could create heartache for you.

You're happy with home and family, and are affectionate to those in your life. Your strong, protective nature can be misread—keep this in mind. You will debate your position vehemently. The success of relationships actually has more to do with your mate's patience and tolerance than your own. Once you fall, there usually is no turning back, except if you are deceived in any way. Then the tables will turn, and your extreme devotion could change to extreme anger.

Your intuitive nature allows you a role as great caretaker. Many possible careers await you with your creativity. Your ability to defend an issue could lead you right into the courtroom. No matter what career you choose, there are several successful moments in it for you. You are one of those rare creatures who can succeed in more than one way and be recognized for it. Look to develop programs in the area of communications. Advertising may showcase your many talents.

You are driven in all that you do, but recognize that others lack your endurance. Give yourself a break and others, too!

✶ ✶ ✶

FEBRUARY 14

AQUARIUS • The sign of the son of man

January 21 at 3:00 A.M. to February 19 at 5:00 P.M. • **NUMEROLOGY 5**

Possessions and Desires . . .

Gem: Sapphires—This gem may help you find forgiveness from those you've wronged.
Flower: Carnation—Your heart's fulfillment is your only destination.
Astral Color, Color Need, Apparel Color: Your Astral Color is Blue, which creates calmness and brings promise. Blue in your environment helps stabilize your mood. In your wardrobe, Purple reflects your giving personality and brings you luck.
Fragrance: Put together a collection of orange blossoms and jasmine with touches of greenery. Always pick scents that are straight from nature instead of manufactured or processed when searching for a scent. This will keep you as unique as you wish to be.
Tree: Apple—You are creative, full of joy, and nearly magical. You bring happiness.
Instruments: Viola, Trumpet
Composer: Liszt
Bird: Flamingo—This beautiful, gregarious bird is always careful of its enemy. It is also a caretaker of the young and tries to keep everyone happy.
Symbol: Triangle—You have the right combination of abilities.

Harmonious Health and Nutrition . . .

Health Scent: Peach—This scent may balance your good qualities so that they equal your charm.
Favorable Foods: Lima beans, strawberries, sugar, salmon, eggs

What's Lucky . . .

Lucky Numbers: 5, 14, 23
Best Months: April and August
Best Days of the Week: Wednesday, Saturday
Best Month Days: 4, 5, 23
Lucky Charms: A rabbit's foot or a white candle
Harmonious Signs for Relationships and

Partnerships: Gemini, Aquarius, Libra and anyone born from July 30 to August 31.

Spiritual Guides . . .

Star: Markab—Those with this star often receive more than they give.
Angel: Gambiel—This angel governs health issues. He teaches us the mystery of life, both on earth and in the heavens.
Guardian Angel: Gabriel—"God is my strength."
Spiritual Stone: Sardius (Ruby)—This stone may drive you to make positive changes in your life.

✶ JUDITH'S INSIGHT ✶

You are a romantic soul. Full of fun and fantasy, you enjoy a good time. You're smart and hard-working, yet you love to play. Your penetrating knowledge of human nature is uncanny. You're inventive and creative and look at the world differently from the rest of us. Family and children are important, but you expect them to be closer to you than you are to them. You only let people see what you want them to see. Devotion plays a large part in all your relationships. Romance is ongoing—through reality or fantasy. Love prevails at least once in your lifetime. You make it happen.

Your energy and enthusiasm could allow you a career in the theater. Your playful ways will get you anywhere. With style and class, you can accomplish more than most in a short amount of time. Keep it interesting and make sure there's growth, otherwise you'll take off. The combination of structure and creativity in photography may interest you.

You're fun to be with (though you don't know it), but your ego can be big, especially in competition. You may love to gamble, or experiment in playlike careers: horse racing, for example. Be careful of overdoing it financially—you're a spender. Money will come and it will definitely go. Eventually the small coins you save will add up. When your ship finally comes in, it won't be a dinghy.

✶ ✶ ✶

FEBRUARY 15

AQUARIUS • The sign of the son of man

January 21 at 3:00 A.M. to February 19 at 5:00 P.M. • NUMEROLOGY 6

Possessions and Desires . . .

Gem: Sapphire—This gem may help you find forgiveness from those you've wronged.

Flower: Hemlock—The bad things in life are there to teach us the value of the good.

Astral Color, Color Need, Apparel Color: Your Astral Color is Blue, which creates calmness and brings promise. Blue in your environment helps stabilize your mood. In your wardrobe, Green is your power color for overcoming obstacles.

Fragrance: Put together a collection of orange blossoms and jasmine with touches of greenery. Always pick scents that are straight from nature instead of manufactured or processed when searching for a scent. This will keep you as unique as you wish to be.

Tree: Palm—You tend to be very healthy and creative.

Instruments: Tambourine, lyre

Composer: Schubert

Bird: Falcon—an expert hunter. When well-trained, it can adapt to many tasks and is usually obedient.

Symbol: Crescent—You are more likely to be influenced by the phases of the moon. Your easygoing manner leads you to peaceful situations.

Harmonious Health and Nutrition . . .

Health Scent: Orange Blossom—This scent may balance your body, mind, and soul.

Favorable Foods: Cucumbers, apples, honey, chicken, pressed cheese

What's Lucky . . .

Lucky Numbers: 1, 6, 15, 33
Best Months: April and August
Best Days of the Week: Wednesday, Saturday
Best Month Days: 6, 15, 24

Lucky Charms: A religious token or card from any religion.

Harmonious Signs for Relationships and Partnerships: Gemini, Aquarius, Libra, and anyone born from July 30 to August 31.

Spiritual Guides . . .

Star: Sa'ad Melik—This star hangs over those who are generous.

Angel: Gambiel—This angel governs health issues. He teaches us the mystery of life, both on earth and in the heavens.

Guardian Angel: Michael—"Who is like God."

Spiritual Stone: Sardius (Ruby)—This stone may drive you to make positive changes in your life.

✴ JUDITH'S INSIGHT ✴

You are faithful and earnest. Although you're practical by nature, you also have psychic abilities, though you may not admit it. You see beauty in everything. You're quick with your thoughts, but less so in your actions. You're highly intelligent, with a strong desire for reading and learning. Animals and kids love you.

You are often the favorite in the family and love it, but you work at it. Your self-sufficiency delays finding the perfect mate. Be patient. Watch out where your own children are concerned—it may take time to recognize problems.

Any company would be happy to have you. Your inventiveness and creativity should allow you many career possibilities. You could easily be an artist or involved in photography. The media and communications could entice you.

You're saddened by disappointments, no matter how small, but you're also hopelessly optimistic, so negative emotions don't linger for long. Find a sympathetic ear—though most of the time, you're the listener. Be thankful and try to enjoy all the wonderful things in life. You were born with the "happy gene."

✴ ✴ ✴

Possessions and Desires . . .

Gem: Garnet—This gem might show you how to find faith and emotional stability.

Flower: Moss—You often love others with parental fervor.

Astral Color, Color Need, Apparel Color: Your Astral Color is Blue, which creates calmness and brings promise. Blue in your environment helps stabilize your mood. In your wardrobe, Green is your power color for overcoming obstacles.

Fragrance: Put together a collection of orange blossoms and jasmine with touches of greenery. Always pick scents that are straight from nature instead of manufactured or processed when searching for a scent. This will keep you as unique as you wish to be.

Tree: Sycamore—Yours is the ability to love, communicate honestly with others, and have lasting relationships.

Instrument: Harp

Composers: Gluck, Brahms

Bird: Mockingbird—the most proficient minstrel in the world's orchestra; graceful and enthusiastic.

Symbol: Heart—You are enthusiastic, empathetic, and full of generosity and love.

Harmonious Health and Nutrition . . .

Health Scent: Jasmine—This scent may make you more easygoing when you are stressed.

Favorable Foods: Spinach, figs, sugar, salmon, buttermilk

What's Lucky . . .

Lucky Numbers: 7, 25, 34

Best Months: April and August

Best Days of the Week: Wednesday, Saturday

Best Month Days: 7, 14, 21

Lucky Charm: An old key.

Harmonious Signs for Relationships and Partnerships: Gemini, Aquarius, Libra, and anyone born from July 30 to August 31.

Spiritual Guides . . .

Star: Sa'ad al Su'ud—This star is the harbinger of the outpouring of hopes.

Angel: Gambiel—This angel governs health issues. He teaches us the mystery of life, both on earth and in the heavens.

Guardian Angel: Raphael—This angel attends to all of your needs when you are looking for guidance.

Spiritual Stone: Sardius (Ruby)—This stone may drive you to make positive changes in your life.

✶ JUDITH'S INSIGHT ✶

You're curious by nature, so you need to explore anything and everything unique and different. You are often the teacher's pet or favorite child. You're faithful and loyal. A dreamer, you tend see things through rose-colored glasses. But when it comes to disappointments, you aren't too resilient. Change bothers you.

Your affectionate and tender nature leads you into relationships. You look for energy and fire in a partner. You may be with someone in the public eye, or you could wind up there yourself. You're romantic to a fault; watch out for idealizing your mate in relationships. In love, you desire fantasy and may look to a past love to get it. Don't spend too much time living in the past or acting out your fantasies.

Your imaginative gifts give you many career choices, whether it be writer, painter, teacher, musician, dancer, cartoonist, or comedian, for those of you who feel comfortable showing their humor. You lean toward low self-esteem, but you have the determination to make it to the top.

Since you're extremely sensitive to the environment and the vibrations of others, be careful with your surroundings, where you live, and the people you associate with. Your calling will come in this life. You just have to learn to open the door to opportunity when it is knocking.

✶ ✶ ✶

FEBRUARY 17   AQUARIUS • The sign of the son of man
January 21 at 3:00 A.M. to February 19 at 5:00 P.M. • NUMEROLOGY 8

Possessions and Desires . . .

Gem: Garnet—This gem might show you how to find faith and emotional stability.

Flower: Pea—You are someone who can really enjoy what life offers.

Astral Color, Color Need, Apparel Color: Your Astral Color is Blue, which creates calmness and brings promise. Blue in your environment helps stabilize your mood. In your wardrobe, Rose gives you balance and harmony.

Fragrance: Put together a collection of orange blossoms and jasmine with touches of greenery. Always pick scents that are straight from nature instead of manufactured or processed when searching for a scent. This will keep you as unique as you wish to be.

Tree: Pine—Your relationships tend to be harmonious, both emotionally and mentally.

Instrument: Cello

Composer: Mozart

Bird: Bobolink—This charming singer is equally good as a soloist or a member of an orchestra. It is a very romantic bird, most useful as an insect destroyer, and elegant, with beautiful feathers, and always pleasant to have around.

Symbol: Wings—You are the source of balance in your world; this will bring you contentment.

Harmonious Health and Nutrition . . .

Health Scent: Almond—This scent may revitalize you and open you to greater possibilities.

Favorable Foods: Cabbage, cherries, sugar, oysters, pressed cheese

What's Lucky . . .

Lucky Numbers: 8, 26, 35
Best Months: April and August
Best Days of the Week: Wednesday, Saturday
Best Month Days: 8, 17, 26
Lucky Charm: A red ribbon in your wallet or doorway.
Harmonious Signs for Relationships and

Partnerships: Gemini, Aquarius, Libra, and anyone born from July 30 to August 31.

Spiritual Guides . . .

Star: Deneb Algiedi—This star gives strong spiritual guidance and sound judgment.

Angel: Gambiel—This angel governs health issues. He teaches us the mystery of life, both on earth and in the heavens

Guardian Angel: Seraphim—Brings love, light, and passion.

Spiritual Stone: Sardius (Ruby)—This stone may drive you to make positive changes in your life.

✦ JUDITH'S INSIGHT ✦

Conscientious, intuitive, and beautiful—you are the general favorite around the house and easily loved by all. Using your well-balanced mind and strong artistic talents, you may be attracted to the sciences and nature. You have an eye for all that is beautiful. You're slow to start things, but you do learn to move steadily. You desire great things and eventually achieve them.

Your family simply adores you. At times this could be more like a burden than a blessing. Learn to balance the family scale better. With your charm and allure, relationships will appear at your feet. Even your naiveté intrigues people. Try to notice when people are good to you. Don't feel sorry for yourself when things don't go your way

Artist, psychic, schoolteacher, movie director, or editor: any one of these careers could indeed work for you. Time and patience is the key. At times you will quit too easily when things don't move fast enough. No one around you will ever do as good a job as you. You must show them how it should be done. When you finally learn to stick to it, you prevail and make it to the top. How long this takes is entirely up to you.

You have a good and sensitive soul. Make sure you learn to laugh along the way and enjoy yourself. Generosity is truly one of your greatest attributes, and many people will be drawn to your good nature. It's easy to love you. Trust your intuition. Stay optimistic, and good things will happen.

✦ ✦ ✦

FEBRUARY 18 AQUARIUS • The sign of the son of man

January 21 at 3:00 A.M. to February 19 at 5:00 P.M. • NUMEROLOGY 9

Possessions and Desires . . .

Gem: Opal—Holding this stone may help you discover enough hope to go on.

Flower: Rye Grass—You may have a very changeable disposition.

Astral Color, Color Need, Apparel Color: Your Astral Color is Blue, which creates calmness and brings promise. Blue in your environment helps stabilize your mood. In your wardrobe, Purple reflects your giving personality and brings you luck.

Fragrance: Put together a collection of orange blossoms and jasmine with touches of greenery. Always pick scents that are straight from nature instead of manufactured or processed when searching for a scent. This will keep you as unique as you wish to be.

Tree: Holly—Beware that you are not carried away by your passionate nature. The only way to grow is to be open to new experiences.

Instruments: Violin, tympanum

Composer: Gluck

Bird: Mockingbird—the most proficient minstrel in the world's orchestra; graceful and enthusiastic.

Symbol: Anchor—This tranquil symbol signifies stability and strength, and stands for strong commitments in relationships.

Harmonious Health and Nutrition . . .

Health Scent: Lavender—This scent might lead others to trust you and make you patient.

Favorable Foods: Carrots, strawberries, honey, chicken, eggs

What's Lucky . . .

Lucky Numbers: 9, 27, 36

Best Months: April and August

Best Days of the Week: Wednesday, Saturday

Best Month Days: 9, 18, 27

Lucky Charms: A U.S. coin or a bill of any amount from the year you were born.

Harmonious Signs for Relationships and Partnerships: Gemini, Aquarius, Libra, and anyone born from July 30 to August 31.

Spiritual Guides . . .

Star: Markab—Those with this star often receive more than they give.

Angel: Gambiel—This angel governs health issues. He teaches us the mystery of life, both on earth and in the heavens.

Guardian Angel: Gabriel—"God is my strength."

Spiritual Stone: Sardius (Ruby)—This stone may drive you to make positive changes in your life.

✳ JUDITH'S INSIGHT ✳

Beautiful deserves beautiful things. You will have them—if not today, then tomorrow. Kindness brings good things, and your great intuition helps your sense of timing in life. You have your own style of doing things. Others will adjust and later respect you for it. You have strong convictions; others are drawn to you and fascinated by this, usually in a positive way.

You will be the envy of your friends and family. Lovers will be drawn and but are sometimes intimidated by your almost pure nature. Once they get to know you better they will just adore you even more. Relationships can be great or not: timing will determine that. Sometimes family can be a burden. If you don't have any, this in itself could be troublesome.

Artistic and psychic only begin to describe you. You could have any business you choose. Your inner sense of what is right lures customers. You could be a star as a computer programmer, graphic designer, architect, writer, filmmaker, or actor.

Great reasoning powers help you in your career and throughout your lifetime. You have many hidden talents and carry the mark of excellence. It's time you showed it.

✳ ✳ ✳

FEBRUARY 19
AQUARIUS • The sign of the son of man
January 21 at 3:00 A.M. to February 19 at 5:00 P.M. • NUMEROLOGY 1

Possessions and Desires . . .

Gem: Turquoise—You may find this stone helps you gain material wealth.

Flower: Spruce—You should have many reasons to celebrate during your life.

Astral Color, Color Need, Apparel Color: Your Astral Color is Emerald Green, which gives you confidence. Violet in your environment keeps you empathetic toward others. In your wardrobe, Green is your power color for overcoming obstacles.

Fragrance: Put together a collection of orange blossoms and jasmine with touches of greenery. Always pick scents that are straight from nature instead of manufactured or processed when searching for a scent. This will keep you as unique as you wish to be.

Tree: Walnut—You are unusually helpful and always looking for constant changes in your life.

Instruments: Oboe, flute, clarinet, piano, French horn, piccolo

Composer: Böhm

Bird: Bird of paradise—the "bird of the gods." You will shine and love extraordinary circumstances.

Symbol: Crown—the universal sign of dignity.

Harmonious Health and Nutrition . . .

Health Scent: Strawberry—Soothing by nature, the strawberry promotes self-esteem and encourages love.

Favorable Foods: Beets, apples, sugar, salmon, buttermilk

What's Lucky . . .

Lucky Numbers: 1, 19, 28
Best Months: April and August
Best Days of the Week: Wednesday, Saturday
Best Month Days: 1, 10, 19, 28
Lucky Charm: A new penny in your shoe.
Harmonious Signs for Relationships and

Partnerships: Gemini, Aquarius, Libra, and anyone born from July 30 to August 31.

Spiritual Guides . . .

Star: Sa'ad Melik—This star hangs over those who are generous.

Angel: Gambiel—This angel governs health issues. He teaches us the mystery of life, both on earth and in the heavens.

Guardian Angel: Malachi—"Messenger of Jehovah."

Spiritual Stone: Sardius (Ruby)—This stone may drive you to make positive changes in your life.

✴ JUDITH'S INSIGHT ✴

Versatile and full of great ideas, you have the ambition and determination to carry out anything. Good opportunities will come out of nowhere. Others bring you luck, and your kindness and tact come through in all situations.

You want commitment, but you may run away before it happens. Eventually you will find that commitment is what makes relationships work. When you end relationships, you act unaffected. You hide your emotions, though not very well. You love your family and they you. Learn to communicate better in relationships.

With your determination and independence, you should own your own business. You have a unique style and could invent or create things never done before. You should avoid gambling or speculation when it comes to other people's money. A career as a stockbroker is not advisable. You take on responsibility early on in life, either working at a young age or caretaking of some kind.

Your share of family crises hurt you. Your youth may not necessarily be an easy one. You may take on adult responsibility at an early age. Make your own way and create the path for yourself and others. Life can be an obstacle course. You will get exhausted and often drained. Determination does win out, so keep reaching for that big brass ring. It will look great on you!

✴ ✴ ✴

FEBRUARY 20

PISCES • The fish that swim in the pure sea

February 19 at 5:00 P.M. to March 20 at 5:00 P.M. • NUMEROLOGY 2

Possessions and Desires . . .

Gem: Moonstone—This gem could protect you from danger.

Flower: Carnation—Your heart fulfillment is your only destination.

Astral Color, Color Need, Apparel Color: Your Astral Color is Pink, reflecting your compassion. Violet in your environment keeps you empathetic toward others. In your wardrobe, Maroon gives you confidence.

Fragrance: Sandalwood or other rare spices are the scents you need to have on hand. You crave attention, and your perfume or cologne should be your most powerful ally. It will enhance your irresistible charm.

Tree: Maple—You have both great stability and flashes of intuition.

Composers: Handel, Johann Sebastian Bach

Instruments: Pipe organ, cymbal, drum

Bird: Flamingo—This beautiful, gregarious bird is always careful of its enemy. It is also a caretaker of the young and tries to keep everyone happy.

Symbol: Cross—the symbol of self-sacrifice and reconciliation.

Harmonious Health and Nutrition . . .

Health Scent: Apple—You are creative, full of joy, and nearly magical. You bring happiness.

Favorable Foods: Raw beets, prunes, rice, brown sugar, egg yolks

What's Lucky . . .

Lucky Numbers: 6, 11, 20

Best Months: May and June

Best Day of the Week: Saturday

Best Month Days: 2, 4, 11

Lucky Charms: Two 50-cent pieces. Give someone else one of them.

Harmonious Signs for Relationships and Partnerships: Cancer, Scorpio, Virgo

Spiritual Guides . . .

Star: Al Phergal Muachher—Those with this star often cling too long to fond memories.

Angel: Barchiel—This angel shows us right from wrong, encourages us in good decision making, and teaches us to protect ourselves and others.

Guardian Angel: Uriel—This angel brings the light of God's guidance.

Spiritual Stone: Chrysolite—This stone might help you keep things together when you feel frayed.

✶ JUDITH'S INSIGHT ✶

You're faithful and devoted, and a loyal employee. You never shirk your duty—when you give your word, you keep it. Considerable ambition will get you where you want to go. You have a keen way of expressing yourself, and you may be mystical in some way.

Idealism and romanticism bring you some interesting relationships. Drawn to the unusual, you may have many long-term unconventional associations. You may be attracted to foreigners or desire to live in another country at some point—foreigners fit into your life somewhere along the line. Marriage or commitment is good for you, for personal growth and the self-confidence you hope for. Of course, that depends on the partners you pick. It could be just the opposite, if you are not careful

You have many talents but are inclined to develop your gift of imagination. You want to express yourself in art, literature, music, or drama. A career in fashion may be yours. You may become quite wealthy in later years. Keep this in mind if you are struggling now.

Honors could enter into your life, perhaps, also in an unconventional way. Travel is important to you. You may own property in another country. Many challenges and opportunities will come your way, and you find your way to those of influence. Success will find you. At times it won't seem possible, so keep on plugging away.

✶ ✶ ✶

FEBRUARY 21

PISCES • The fish that swim in the pure sea

February 19 at 5:00 P.M. to March 20 at 5:00 P.M. • NUMEROLOGY 3

Possessions and Desires . . .

Gem: Crystallite—You tend to be able to free yourself from unwanted passions and sadness.

Flower: Veronica—You are very loyal.

Astral Color, Color Need, Apparel Color: Your Astral Color is White, which gives you clarity. Violet in your environment keeps you empathetic toward others. In your wardrobe, Cinnamon gives you encouragement and stamina.

Fragrance: Sandalwood or other rare spices are the scents you need to have on hand. You crave attention, and your perfume or cologne should be your most powerful ally. It will enhance your irresistible charm.

Tree: Elm—You have willpower, strength, and the ability to stand alone.

Instrument: Trombone

Composers: Verdi, Mendelssohn, Schumann

Bird: Flamingo—This beautiful, gregarious bird is always careful of its enemy. It is also a caretaker of the young and tries to keep everyone happy.

Symbol: Wreath—You have been crowned with a special personality. You are strong but extremely compassionate.

Harmonious Health and Nutrition . . .

Health Scent: Rose—encourages passion and creates an inner warmth.

Favorable Foods: Sorrel, plums, barley, honey, cottage cheese

What's Lucky . . .

Lucky Numbers: 3, 12, 21

Best Months: May and June

Best Day of the Week: Saturday

Best Month Days: 3, 12, 21, 30

Lucky Charm: A pen that someone else has already used.

Harmonious Signs for Relationships and Partnerships: Cancer, Scorpio, Virgo

Spiritual Guides . . .

Star: Al Risha—Those who have this band of stars as theirs will be happiest as part of a family.

Angel: Barchiel—This angel shows us right from wrong, encourages us in good decision making, and teaches us to protect ourselves and others.

Guardian Angel: Johiel—This angel is a protector of all those with a humble heart.

Spiritual Stone: Chrysolite—This stone might help you keep things together when you feel frayed.

✦ JUDITH'S INSIGHT ✦

Although you are very self-contained, you deeply appreciate encouragement and pats on the back from those around you. You have an open mind and an ability to see things clearly. Use your independence in positive ways, otherwise you may be perceived as domineering.

You seem to attract people out of nowhere. You may not keep these relationships, but you have a knack for getting attention, and you love every minute of it. All your relationships have an element of romance. You are a social butterfly—if not in younger years, then later in life. You're on everybody's "A" list, and your generous ways put you at the center of things.

With your desire for fun and keen insight, critic might be a good career. Food critic could also work; you are so precise, you could probably spot the herbs by taste. Musician, physician, mechanic, journalist, or public relations are also good options, though it's advisable to stick to the arts. You may have more than one career or, perhaps, change careers suddenly midlife.

Remember to keep control of your own money, no matter how much you may trust your stockbroker, wife, husband, or accountant. Others will not do you justice when it comes to money—you will do much better on your own. You sometimes have serious mood swings and can learn to control this. Then again, you may not want to.

✱ ✱ ✱

FEBRUARY 22

PISCES • The fish that swim in the pure sea

February 19 at 5:00 P.M. to March 20 at 5:00 P.M. • NUMEROLOGY 4

Possessions and Desires . . .

Gem: Chrysolite—This gem may help you clear your mind of sadness and worry.

Flower: Amaryllis—You should beware of continually swinging between the extremes of arrogance and shyness.

Astral Color, Color Need, Apparel Color: Your Astral Color is Emerald, which gives you confidence. Violet in your environment keeps you empathetic toward others. In your wardrobe, Green is your power color for overcoming obstacles.

Fragrance: Sandalwood or other rare spices are the scents you need to have on hand. You crave attention, and your perfume or cologne should be your most powerful ally. It will enhance your irresistible charm.

Tree: Cherry—You will find yourself faced with constant new emotional awakenings.

Instruments: Bass, clarinet

Composers: Haydn, Wagner

Bird: Robin—the most sociable of all birds, with the ability to create quick friendships. It also can easily adapt to any home. When it wants something, it has the tendency to try to snatch it.

Symbol: Star—You are full of inner brightness and will stand out in any crowd. You will be seen as special.

Harmonious Health and Nutrition . . .

Health Scent: Vanilla—This scent will fill you with a feeling of cleanliness and stability.

Favorable Foods: Leeks, Concord grapes, bran, brown sugar, egg yolks

What's Lucky . . .

Lucky Numbers: 4, 13, 31
Best Months: May and June
Best Day of the Week: Saturday
Best Month Days: 4, 13, 22, 31
Lucky Charm: A piece of material cut from something in your home.

Harmonious Signs for Relationships and Partnerships: Cancer, Scorpio, Virgo

Spiritual Guides . . .

Star: Al Phergal Muachher—Those with this star often cling too long to fond memories.

Angel: Barchiel—This angel shows us right from wrong, encourages us in good decision making, and teaches us to protect ourselves and others.

Guardian Angel: Uriel—This angel brings the light of God's guidance.

Spiritual Stone: Chrysolite—This stone might help you keep things together when you feel frayed.

✳ JUDITH'S INSIGHT ✳

You are generally honest, sincere, and reliable, not only in your work but with friends and family. You can be a worry wart and create imaginary disasters that never happen. Slow down with your imagination, unless of course you are being paid for it. Your views can sometimes be a little unconventional. This is not a bad thing—it's what gets you noticed. Your appearance is almost perfect, and you like it that way.

You love a nice home. You may be drawn to water. Attracted to outgoing as well as quiet types, you may seek out someone very successful or perhaps someone who seems to be, someone from another country or, possibly, with an unusual career or lifestyle. Family matters to you, but be wary of those who are dependent—on you and on substances. You can easily be misread as uncaring, so make sure your signals are clear.

A plumber or doctor—sound confusing? You would be great at either. You could also be a photographer, scientist, mechanic, philanthropist, social worker, school counselor, or artist. When you find a good working environment, stick with it. It may be hard for you to find serenity, but you work circles around everyone when the atmosphere is right.

Your sweetness and adoring charm will win awards for you. To know you is to love you; those who don't could have a hard time.

✳ ✳ ✳

FEBRUARY 23

PISCES • The fish that swim in the pure sea

February 19 at 5:00 P.M. to March 20 at 5:00 P.M. • NUMEROLOGY 5

Possessions and Desires . . .

Gem: Moonstone—This gem could protect you from danger.

Flower: Pansy—You may incorrectly feel that others are declaring war against you.

Astral Color, Color Need, Apparel Color: Your Astral Color is Pink, reflecting your compassion. Violet in your environment keeps you empathetic toward others. In your wardrobe, Maroon gives you confidence.

Fragrance: Sandalwood or other rare spices are the scents you need to have on hand. You crave attention, and your perfume or cologne should be your most powerful ally. It will enhance your irresistible charm.

Tree: Apple—You are creative, full of joy, and nearly magical. You bring happiness.

Instruments: Viola, trumpet

Composer: Liszt

Bird: Flamingo—This beautiful, gregarious bird is always careful of its enemy. It is also a caretaker of the young and tries to keep everyone happy.

Symbol: Triangle—You have the right combination of abilities.

Harmonious Health and Nutrition . . .

Health Scent: Peach—This scent may balance your good qualities so that they equal your charm.

Favorable Foods: Raw beets, prunes, whole grains, honey, cottage cheese

What's Lucky . . .

Lucky Numbers: 6, 14, 23

Best Months: May and June

Best Day of the Week: Saturday

Best Month Days: 5, 4, 23

Lucky Charms: A rabbit's foot or a white candle.

Harmonious Signs for Relationships and Partnerships: Cancer, Scorpio, Virgo

Spiritual Guides . . .

Star: Al Phergal Muachher—Those with this star often cling too long to fond memories.

Angel: Barchiel—This angel shows us right from wrong, encourages us in good decision making, and teaches us to protect ourselves and others.

Guardian Angel: Plavwell—"Strength in presence."

Spiritual Stone: Chrysolite—This stone might help you keep things together when you feel frayed.

✶ JUDITH'S INSIGHT ✶

You have a sensitive but changeable disposition. You are naturally intuitive and learn how to use your intuition more and more each day. You try to understand everyone around you, but others find you difficult to know. You can accomplish many things if you put your energies in the right place at the right time. You're quite ambitious. You're a good listener and know how to help others.

The more romantic the situation, the more devoted you become. Funny as anything, you don't take criticism well. Your good nature makes you the one who takes on the responsibility of your spouse's family. You seem strong, and others don't recognize when you are hurt—they think you're moody.

Artistic, intelligent, and intuitive, you may take on one career for love and another for money. You would make a fine chemist, inventor, professor, composer, or family physician. Since you are physically fit most of your life, you should be active in sports. You would make a great sports agent.

When it comes to money, you may do better giving advice than taking it. You keep a keen eye on money, especially other people's money, that is, your wife's or husband's. The second half of your life may be better than the first: keep it in mind. You may feel the people around you are takers and want to give very little in return. Have no fear—the angels keep score, and when you're in need, they'll be there.

✶ ✶ ✶

FEBRUARY 24

PISCES • The fish that swim in the pure sea

February 19 at 5:00 P.M. to March 20 at 5:00 P.M. • NUMEROLOGY 6

Possessions and Desires . . .

Gem: Topaz—This is an excellent gift to be exchanged between very loyal friends.

Flower: Straw—You tend to form strong unions with others.

Astral Color, Color Need, Apparel Color: Your Astral Color is Pink, reflecting your compassion. Violet in your environment keeps you empathetic toward others. In your wardrobe, Maroon gives you confidence.

Fragrance: Sandalwood or other rare spices are the scents you need to have on hand. You crave attention, and your perfume or cologne should be your most powerful ally. It will enhance your irresistible charm.

Tree: Palm—You tend to be very healthy and creative.

Instruments: Tambourine, lyre

Composer: Schubert

Bird: Goldfinch—These gentle creatures can seem moody especially in unsettled weather.

Symbol: Crescent—You are more likely to be influenced by the phases of the moon. Your easygoing manner leads you to peaceful situations.

Harmonious Health and Nutrition . . .

Health Scent: Orange Blossom—This scent may balance your body, mind, and soul.

Favorable Foods: Unhulled barley, peaches, rice, brown sugar, egg yolks

What's Lucky . . .

Lucky Numbers: 6, 17, 24

Best Months: May and June

Best Day of the Week: Saturday

Best Month Days: 6, 15, 24

Lucky Charms: A religious card or token from any religion.

Harmonious Signs for Relationships and Partnerships: Cancer, Scorpio, Virgo

Spiritual Guides . . .

Star: Al Phergal Muachher—Those with this star often cling too long to fond memories.

Angel: Barchiel—This angel shows us right from wrong, encourages us in good decision making, and teaches us to protect ourselves and others.

Guardian Angel: Michael—"Who is like God."

Spiritual Stone: Chrysolite—This stone might help you keep things together when you feel frayed.

✳ JUDITH'S INSIGHT ✳

Why are you totally misunderstood? Your overprotective personality sends out the wrong vibes. Don't make yourself an example of love and self-sacrifice. You have a strong and commanding nature with a heart of gold. You may think of yourself as unlucky, especially in love, but in time this proves untrue.

You can attract mates who are beneath your social status or inferior in some way. Several heartbreaks will plague you before you become content in a relationship. Family relationships can sometimes be a task, but you manage to keep things together. You can be the most devoted child. Take extra care with the in-laws. There may be "words" exchanged. You can be moody; so depending on when you're asked something, you may give different responses.

Disappointments come too often in your career. You will most definitely have more than one. You can become a workaholic—this will be the only way you can get where you want to go. You may make your mark in reading, writing, or arithmetic—in other words, you could be a teacher, actor, agent, artist, or professor; maybe even a therapist. Unfortunately, your lucky years come later. Your unique mind may create successful schemes or slogans.

You like nice things, and at times you can be materialistic. Making a good impression and "appearances" are important to you, so you're absolutely driven to success.

✳ ✳ ✳

FEBRUARY 25

PISCES • The fish that swim in the pure sea

February 19 at 5:00 P.M. to March 20 at 5:00 P.M. • NUMEROLOGY 7

Possessions and Desires . . .

Gem: Moonstone—This gem could protect you from danger.

Flower: Spearmint—The spice in your life happens when you shake it up.

Astral Color, Color Need, Apparel Color: Your Astral Color is Pink, reflecting your compassion. Violet in your environment keeps you empathetic toward others. In your wardrobe, Maroon gives you confidence.

Fragrance: Sandalwood or other rare spices are the scents you need to have on hand. You crave attention, and your perfume or cologne should be your most powerful ally. It will enhance your irresistible charm.

Tree: Sycamore—Yours is the ability to love, communicate honestly with others, and have lasting relationships.

Instrument: Harp

Composers: Gluck, Brahms

Bird: Warbling Parakeet—the most beautiful of all birds, known as the love bird. It does seem to have the powers of imitation.

Symbol: Heart—You are enthusiastic, empathetic, and full of generosity and love.

Harmonious Health and Nutrition . . .

Health Scent: Jasmine—This scent may make you more easygoing when you are stressed.

Favorable Foods: Cucumbers, apples, bran, honey, cottage cheese

What's Lucky . . .

Lucky Numbers: 7, 17, 27
Best Months: May and June
Best Day of the Week: Saturday
Best Month Days: 7, 14, 21
Lucky Charm: An old key.
Harmonious Signs for Relationships and Partnerships: Cancer, Scorpio, Virgo

Spiritual Guides . . .

Star: Al Phergal Muachher—Those with this star often cling too long to fond memories.

Angel: Barchiel—This angel shows us right from wrong, encourages us in good decision making, and teaches us to protect ourselves and others.

Guardian Angel: Raphael—This angel attends to all of your needs when you are looking for guidance.

Spiritual Stone: Chrysolite—This stone might help you keep things together when you feel frayed.

✳ JUDITH'S INSIGHT ✳

Oh, cautious one: everything needs to be in its place. Be careful that this doesn't cause anxiety. You feel better keeping things to yourself. You don't like conflict; you have a vivid imagination and strong hope. Although a natural artist, you have great business abilities.

Your devotion runs deep—from friends and family to coworkers and employer. Your unusually sympathetic ear and sensitivity can cause your feelings to be hurt very easily. You may come across as needy and melodramatic. Unhappy when not in a relationship, you gravitate to romance and extravagance. Love prevails for you, including the possibility of a great long-term relationship.

You will be an author of one kind or another, whether it is in books, film, music, or education. You should have something published, even if it is your picture in the paper. Make sure you stay on the right side of the law. Motion pictures, a screen career—anything is in the cards for you. You may be born to money or earn it later in life.

Not one to run away from fear, you're more likely to investigate it. You have a gleam in your eyes when things are going well, and this enhances your good looks. But if things aren't going your way, your eyes won't lie, and the world will know of your sadness.

✳ ✳ ✳

FEBRUARY 26

PISCES • The fish that swim in the pure sea

February 19 at 5:00 P.M. to March 20 at 5:00 P.M. • NUMEROLOGY 8

Possessions and Desires . . .

Gem: Chrysolite—This gem may help you clear your mind of sadness and worry.
Flower: Lady's Delight—You have rigid ideas of what you find beautiful.
Astral Color, Color Need, Apparel Colors: Your Astral Color is Pink, reflecting your compassion. Violet in your environment keeps you empathetic toward others. In your wardrobe, Green is your power color for overcoming obstacles.
Fragrance: Sandalwood or other rare spices are the scents you need to have on hand. You crave attention, and your perfume or cologne should be your most powerful ally. It will enhance your irresistible charm.
Tree: Pine—Your relationships tend to be harmonious, both emotionally and mentally.
Instrument: Cello
Composer: Mozart
Bird: Bobolink—This charming singer is equally good as a soloist or a member of an orchestra. It is a very romantic bird, most useful as an insect destroyer, and elegant, with beautiful feathers, and always pleasant to have around.
Symbol: Wings—You are the source of balance in your world; this will bring you contentment.

Harmonious Health and Nutrition . . .

Health Scent: Almond—This scent may revitalize you and open you to greater possibilities.
Favorable Foods: Spinach, cherries, barley, brown sugar, egg yolks.

What's Lucky . . .

Lucky Numbers: 8, 17, 35
Best Months: May and June.
Best Day of the Week: Saturday.
Best Month Days: 8, 17, 26.
Lucky Charm: A red ribbon in your wallet or doorway.
Harmonious Signs for Relationships and Partnerships: Cancer, Scorpio, Virgo

Spiritual Guides . . .

Star: Al Risha—Those who have this band of stars as theirs will be happiest as part of a family.
Angel: Barchiel—This angel shows us right from wrong, encourages us in good decision making, and teaches us to protect ourselves and others.
Guardian Angel: Seraphim—Brings love, light and passion.
Spiritual Stone: Chrysolite—This stone might help you keep things together when you feel frayed.

✳ JUDITH'S INSIGHT ✳

You are a deep thinker who takes life too seriously at times. People will tend to think of you as "hard." You have a strong and commanding nature and a deep sensitivity—others don't always recognize when you are hurting. You're resourceful, and have great organizational skills that can help or hurt. You take on responsibilities. There is caution in what you wish for in your life.

Earlier in life, you may find it difficult to find the perfect mate. Later, it gets easier as your confidence grows. Marriage or a significant relationship may bring unusual circumstances to your life, both good and bad. Family may bring you sorrow in one way or another, but in time should bring you great joy. The dutiful child, you walk around guilty a lot of the time. Just remember, it's you who jumps into the pressure cooker.

You are great at so many things; the problem is your battle with ego and self-esteem. It may take time to find your niche in life, but you have many great qualities. You can be an artist, photographer, journalist, critic, media person, nutritionist, dietitian, and more. You'll strive for great accomplishment, and when you finally achieve it, you may still feel unsatisfied.

Once you recognize that you are content, a sense of freedom and a world of happiness will open. You have no enemies except yourself, that is more than you need. Take more time for self-exploration—this will bring you the greatest peace.

✱ ✱ ✱

62

FEBRUARY 27   PISCES • The fish that swim in the pure sea
February 19 at 5:00 P.M. to March 20 at 5:00 P.M. • NUMEROLOGY 9

Possessions and Desires . . .

Gem: Chrysolite—This gem may help you clear your mind of sadness and worry.
Flower: Bachelor's Button—Be careful not to spend too much time alone.
Astral Color, Color Need, Apparel Colors: Your Astral Color is White, which gives you clarity. Violet in your environment keeps you empathetic toward others. In your wardrobe, Maroon gives you confidence.
Fragrance: Sandalwood or other rare spices are the scents you need to have on hand. You crave attention, and your perfume or cologne should be your most powerful ally. It will enhance your irresistible charm.
Tree: Holly—Beware that you are not carried away by your passionate nature. The only way to grow is to be open to new experiences.
Instruments: Violin, tympanum
Composer: Gluck
Bird: Flamingo—This beautiful, gregarious bird is always careful of its enemy. It is also a caretaker of the young and tries to keep everyone happy.
Symbol: Wings—You are the source of balance in your world; this will bring you contentment.

Harmonious Health and Nutrition . . .

Health Scent: Lavender—This scent might lead others to trust you and make you patient.
Favorable Foods: Red cabbage, cranberry, bran, honey, cottage cheese

What's Lucky . . .

Lucky Numbers: 9, 27, 36
Best Months: May and June
Best Day of the Week: Saturday
Best Month Days: 2, 9, 18
Lucky Charms: A U.S. coin or a bill of any amount from the year you were born.
Harmonious Signs for Relationships and Partnerships: Cancer, Scorpio, Virgo

Spiritual Guides . . .

Star: Al Risha—Those who have this band of stars as theirs will be happiest as part of a family.
Angel: Barchiel—This angel shows us right from wrong, encourages us in good decision making, and teaches us to protect ourselves and others.
Guardian angel: Gabriel—"God is my strength."
Spiritual Stone: Chrysolite—This stone might help you keep things together when you feel frayed.

✳ JUDITH'S INSIGHT ✳

You should be in the limelight, and sooner or later, you will be. You're good-looking, funny, charming—a star in your own right. You're fickle in just about everything you do, except work. You are in harmony with those around you—but only if that's what you want. Watch your moody side. You are spiritual and psychic beyond your years, and it may take time for you to recognize this. You're imaginative and optimistic. You need a constant flow of mental and physical stimulation.

There isn't enough romance in the world for you. You will have many significant others and a few more insignificant others. You may find yourself alone for a portion of your life, although this is not your style. When you really, really want that special someone, you'll just go and find them. You are a good family member and are deeply devoted, though not necessarily on a daily basis.

You should be in the psychic field. If not, you should be a health care worker—hospital environments will work well for you, at least for a while. Without the public eye, you feel depressed and restless. You'll enjoy some success in your younger years, but much more as you mature. You never feel older—something to keep in mind as you approach the second half of your life. Watch for a new beginning after a dry spell. This may bring you into the limelight. One way or another, you will be a star.

You're criticized for your directness, but still win people over with your magnetic personality. Don't overlook your humanitarian qualities—they may help your dreams prevail.

✳ ✳ ✳

Possessions and Desires . . .

Gem: Moonstone—This gem could protect you from danger.

Flower: Calla Lily—You may be seen as a magnificent beauty if you surround yourself with these.

Astral Color, Color Need, Apparel Colors: Your Astral Color is Emerald, which gives you confidence. Violet in your environment keeps you empathetic toward others. In your wardrobe, Blue Green enhances your luck and makes you feel secure.

Fragrance: Sandalwood or other rare spices are the scents you need to have on hand. You crave attention, and your perfume or cologne should be your most powerful ally. It will enhance your irresistible charm.

Tree: Walnut—You are unusually helpful and aways looking for new beginnings.

Instruments: Oboe, flute, clarinet, piano, French horn, organ, piccolo

Composer: Böhm

Bird: Flamingo—This beautiful, gregarious bird is always careful of its enemy. It is also a caretaker of the young and tries to keep everyone happy.

Symbol: Crown—the universal sign of dignity.

Harmonious Health and Nutrition . . .

Health Scent: Strawberry—soothing by nature, the strawberry promotes self-esteem and encourages love.

Favorable Foods: Artichokes, raisins, rice, brown sugar, egg yolks

What's Lucky . . .

Lucky Numbers: 2, 6, 10
Best Months: May and June
Best Day of the Week: Saturday
Best Month Days: 1, 10, 19, 28
Lucky Charm: A new penny in your shoe.
Harmonious Signs for Relationships and Partnerships: Cancer, Scorpio, Virgo

Spiritual Guides . . .

Star: Al Phergal Muachher: Those with this star often cling too long to fond memories.

Angel: Barchiel—This angel shows us right from wrong, encourages us in good decision making, and teaches us to protect ourselves and others.

Guardian Angel: Malachi—"Messenger of Jehovah."

Spiritual Stone: Chrysolite—This stone might help you keep things together when you feel frayed.

✳ *JUDITH'S INSIGHT* ✳

You are the good guy/girl on the block. Warm, sensitive, and mild-mannered, you are loved by all. Adorable and giving, in time you will learn unfortunate lessons that, hopefully, allow you to grow. You take on responsibilities like a champ while limiting your ability to enjoy life. You'll gain more confidence as you mature. Use your wit more often—it helps get you by. Taking on the world way too early has forced you to think "old." Problems arise from negative and fatalistic thinking. Don't be so quick to blame others when things go wrong.

Charm and sensitivity will bring you love as long as you work to keep it. Stay clear of passive-aggressive types. Communicate with your significant other, and all will work nicely. You make a wonderful, devoted parent. Family can be overwhelming at times—so find time for yourself, but don't pull away entirely. It may take you time to realize how much family life means to you.

You may have a few careers, but you will find your way. If you find yourself on the unemployment line, remember to try to be more forthright about your career desires. You can be anything from a healer or builder to a caterer to a plumber. You could run a business. If all else fails, check out a career in the health care field or government or a unionized job.

You are a late bloomer; the second half of your life is better. You may wish to live near the water. You are a person with a heart of gold. In your later years the gold will not only be in your heart but in your pockets.

★ ★ ★

FEBRUARY 29

PISCES • The fish that swim in the pure sea

February 19 at 5:00 P.M. to March 20 at 5:00 P.M. • NUMEROLOGY 2

Possessions and Desires . . .

Gem: Chrysolite—This gem may help you clear your mind of sadness and worry.

Flower: Grass—You may give in too easily.

Astral Color, Color Need, Apparel Colors: Your Astral Color is Emerald, which gives you confidence. Violet in your environment keeps you empathetic toward others. In your wardrobe, Blue Green enhances your luck and makes you feel secure.

Fragrance: Sandalwood or other rare spices are the scents you need to have on hand. You crave attention, and your perfume or cologne should be your most powerful ally. It will enhance your irresistible charm.

Tree: Maple—You have both great stability and flashes of intuition.

Instruments: Pipe organ, cymbal, drum

Composers: Handel, Johann Sebastian Bach

Bird: Cuckoo—a good flyer and very seldom a quitter. Some cuckoos tend to think they favor lonely isolation, but what they really yearn for is a family relationship.

Symbol: Cross—This is the symbol of self-sacrifice and reconciliation.

Harmonious Health and Nutrition . . .

Health Scent: Apple—You are creative, full of joy, and nearly magical. You bring happiness.

Favorable Foods: Leeks, cherries, honey, cottage cheese

What's Lucky . . .

Lucky Numbers: 2, 11, 20

Best Months: May and June

Best Day of the Week: Saturday

Best Month Days: 2, 11, 20, 29

Lucky Charms: Two 50-cent pieces. Give someone else one of them.

Harmonious Signs for Relationships and Partnerships: Cancer, Scorpio, Virgo

Spiritual Guides . . .

Star: Al Risha—Those who have this band of stars as theirs will be happiest as part of a family.

Angel: Barchiel—This angel shows us right from wrong, encourages us in good decision making, and teaches us to protect ourselves and others.

Guardian Angel: Uriel—This angel brings the light of God's guidance.

Spiritual Stone: Chrysolite—This stone might help you keep things together when you feel frayed.

✸ JUDITH'S INSIGHT ✸

Special as the day you were born—you were born for unique reasons; even if it takes a lifetime to figure it out. You have a soft, sweet, sensitive style and will be recognized for it. Strong intelligence, dry wit, and good common sense allow you to be very inventive or creative. Drawn to the unknown, somewhere along the way you make a statement. The strange and unusual can also happen to you—good and not so good.

Relationships can be easy or hard, depending on where you are in life. You are likely to have an adoring soul mate or significant other. Not everyone is lucky enough to have both in one relationship—you are. Your originality may attract some interesting mates, and you could probably write a book on unusual incidents and people. You are dedicated to family, but they could bring you heartache at times. Trust that the love and dedication are there.

You are creative and arty; look for a career as a writer, scientist or professor. Take care to stay on the right side of the law. You may even have the desire to fly a plane or head a large organization. Poet, philosopher, even astrologer would be great careers for you. You will make a mark one way or another. Sports, particularly water sports, may appeal to you, either as a hobby or career.

You're intriguing, smart, and sometimes very intense; try to enjoy life. Partnerships will flourish if you let them. You may make a strong mark on your generation, or your generation could make a strong impact on you.

✸ ✸ ✸

MARCH

MARCH 1

PISCES • The fish that swim in the pure sea

February 19 at 5:00 P.M. to March 20 at 5:00 P.M. • NUMEROLOGY 1

Possessions and Desires . . .

Gem: Turquoise—This stone may help you find material wealth.

Flower: Heliotrope—You are faithful and devoted.

Astral Color, Color Need, Apparel Color: Your Astral Color is Pink, which reflects your compassion. Violet in your environment keeps you empathetic toward others. In your wardrobe, Cinnamon gives you encouragement and stamina.

Fragrance: Sandalwood or other rare spices are the scents you need to have on hand. You crave attention and your perfume or cologne should be your most powerful ally. It will enhance your irresistible charm.

Tree: Walnut—You are unusually helpful and always looking for new beginnings.

Instruments: Oboe, flute, clarinet, piano, French horn, organ, piccolo

Composer: Böhm

Bird: Flamingo—This beautiful, gregarious bird is always careful of its enemy. It is also a caretaker of the young and tries to keep everyone happy.

Symbol: Crown—The universal sign of a dignified person.

Harmonious Health and Nutrition . . .

Health Scent: Strawberry—Soothing by nature, the strawberry promotes self-esteem and encourages love.

Favorable Foods: Spinach, raisins, barley, honey, cottage cheese

What's Lucky . . .

Lucky Numbers: 1, 10, 37
Best Months: May and June
Best Day of the Week: Saturday
Best Month Days: 1, 10, 19, 28
Lucky Charm: A new penny in your shoe.

Harmonious Signs for Relationships and Partnerships: Cancer, Scorpio, Virgo

Spiritual Guides . . .

Star: Al Phergal Muachher—Those with this star often cling too long to fond memories.

Angel: Barchiel—This angel shows us right from wrong, encourages us in good decision making, and teaches us to protect ourselves and others.

Guardian Angel: Malachi—"Messenger of Jehovah."

Spiritual Stone: Chrysolite—This stone might help you keep things together when you feel frayed.

✳ JUDITH'S INSIGHT ✳

You have more faith and confidence in your abilities than the average person. Your application of life experience creates many positive outcomes. Your sense of concentration and focus is strong. You are true and loyal to your friends, bitter and spiteful to enemies. You work hard to obtain the better things in life.

You make new friends but do not always maintain friendships because you can be fickle, and easily dissatisfied and disillusioned with them. You have a self-protective nature, and it may take some time to connect with the right mate. In time you do, but you will go through many variable relationships first. You will find yourself frustrated by the demands of some people around you. Your intense personality makes it hard for others to always understand you. You may already be aware that you are the responsible child.

A career in nutrition, holistic medicine, or social work would work for you. You may go back and forth for a while before finally settling on one career. Your artistic abilities or creativity could also play a role either in career or extracurricular activity.

Although this may not be the first thing people notice about you, you really are good-natured. You are honest and pure, and with your determination, you will find not only success but also happiness.

✳ ✳ ✳

MARCH 2

PISCES • The fish that swim in the pure sea

February 19 at 5:00 P.M. to March 20 at 5:00 P.M. • NUMEROLOGY 2

Possessions and Desires . . .

Gem: Sapphire—This gem may help you find forgiveness from those you've wronged.

Flower: Thorn—You may be too severe in your judgements.

Astral Color, Color Need, Apparel Color: Your Astral Color is White, which gives clarity. Violet in your environment keeps you empathetic toward others. In your wardrobe, Green is your power color for overcoming obstacles.

Fragrance: Sandalwood or other rare spices are the scents you need to have on hand. You crave attention and your perfume or cologne should be your most powerful ally. It will enhance your irresistible charm.

Tree: Maple—You have both great stability and flashes of intuition.

Instruments: Pipe organ, cymbal, drum

Composers: Handel, Johann Sebastian Bach

Bird: Stork—Turkish bird, held in high esteem the world over. This bird is intelligent but may have strange tendencies.

Symbol: Cross—the symbol of self-sacrifice and reconciliation.

Harmonious Health and Nutrition . . .

Health Scent: Apple—You are creative, full of joy, and nearly magical. You bring happiness.

Favorable Foods: Spinach, raisins, barley, honey, cottage cheese

What's Lucky . . .

Lucky Numbers: 2, 11, 22

Best Months: May and June

Best Day of the Week: Saturday

Best Month Days: 2, 11, 20, 29

Lucky Charms: Two 50-cent pieces. Give someone else one of them.

Harmonious Signs for Relationships and Partnerships: Cancer, Scorpio, Virgo

Spiritual Guides . . .

Star: Al Risha—Those who have this band of stars as theirs will be happiest as part of a family.

Angel: Barchiel—This angel shows us right from wrong, encourages us in good decision making, and teaches us to protect ourselves and others.

Guardian Angel: Uriel—This angel brings the light of God's guidance.

Spiritual Stone: Chrysolite—This stone might help you keep things together when you feel frayed.

✴ JUDITH'S INSIGHT ✴

Sensitive and nurturing by nature, others may see you as weaker than you are. You have strong convictions, but you know better than to push your opinions onto others. Early in life you may have difficulty making ends meet because of your views about money and your nonmaterialistic tendencies. This changes later on. You deeply appreciate and are moved by beautiful scenery, nuances of color, and the harmony of sound. You have not only a dry sense of humor but a warm and witty way with words.

You're a devoted partner. It's not that your mate is difficult, you'll just be doing most of the bending, at least early in the relationship. Tact and style draw others to you easily. Unfortunately, you'll have your share of heartaches (even after the perfect mate is found). Your trusting nature allows others a sense of freedom. Don't become overconfident in your mate, or problems are bound to arise.

You make a sensitive and devoted parent. Through your children (if you have them), you experience the fun childhood you may have missed as a youngster. You have nicer toys now, too.

Your love of sports such as hunting or fishing could lead you into a career, but they'll more likely be a hobby. You're interested in many careers when you are young. After you finally settle on a career, you may still find yourself there twenty years later. Your work environment can't be too serious or intense. You would make a great superintendent, manager, utilities specialist, or graphics designer. You can be secretive, holding your cards close to your chest.

✴ ✴ ✴

MARCH 3

PISCES • The fish that swim in the pure sea

February 19 at 5:00 P.M. to March 20 at 5:00 P.M. • NUMEROLOGY 3

Possessions and Desires . . .

Gem: Ruby—This stone may lead you to energy, friendship and happiness.

Flower: Red Pink—You are pure with your emotions no matter what kind of relationship you're in.

Astral Color, Color Need, Apparel Color: Your Astral Color is Emerald, which gives you confidence. Violet in your environment keeps you empathetic toward others. In your wardrobe, Maroon gives you confidence.

Fragrance: Sandalwood or other rare spices are the scents you need to have on hand. You crave attention and your perfume or cologne should be your most powerful ally. It will enhance your irresistible charm.

Tree: Elm—You have willpower, strength, and the ability to stand alone.

Instrument: Trombone

Composers: Verdi, Mendelssohn, Schumann

Bird: Flamingo—This beautiful, gregarious bird is always careful of its enemy. It is also a caretaker of the young who tries to keep everyone happy.

Symbol: Wreath—You have been crowned with a special personality. You are strong but extremely compassionate.

Harmonious Health and Nutrition . . .

Health Scent: Rose—This scent will lead you to passionate thoughts and make you feel warm inside.

Favorable Foods: Artichokes, peaches, bran, honey, cottage cheese

What's Lucky . . .

Lucky Numbers: 3, 12, 30
Best Months: May and June
Best Day of the Week: Saturday
Best Month Days: 3, 12, 21, 30
Lucky Charm: A pen that someone else has already used.

Harmonious Signs for Relationships and Partnerships: Cancer, Scorpio, Virgo

Spiritual Guides . . .

Star: Al Phergal Muachher—Those with this star often cling too long to fond memories.

Angel: Barchiel—This angel shows us right from wrong, encourages us in good decision making, and teaches us to protect ourselves and others.

Guardian Angel: Johiel—This angel is a protector of all those with a humble heart.

Spiritual Stone: Chrysolite—This stone might help you keep things together when you feel frayed.

✶ JUDITH'S INSIGHT ✶

You have a strong, clear mind and great abilities to go along with it. You usually mean what you say.

If others are loyal, you're loyal back. You become outrageously angry and hold a grudge if you are humiliated. Recognize your mate's point of view, or you could end up alone. You like to be the more controlling partner, although you may never recognize that part of yourself. You have a warm heart and are usually harmless, but when you need to defend yourself, you can be ruthless. You do not make many close friends, but are reliable and worthy of the confidence that people generally have in you.

Your fondness for water could lead to an ideal career. You may have talents in music or poetry. You're also very organized. So working for the government, a large institution, or other structural company might satisfy you. The arts and theater hold a special interest for you. You will achieve success, and your accomplishments will be billboards for all the world to see.

You seem cranky and moody to some. Fearful and protective is more like it. You can jump right out of your skin when things go wrong. You are equally practical, idealistic, and altruistic. You should look forward to earning honors from the community. You have the elements to be a success in whatever you do. So do it all!

✶ ✶ ✶

MARCH 4

PISCES • The fish that swim in the pure sea

February 19 at 5:00 P.M. to March 20 at 5:00 P.M. • NUMEROLOGY 4

Possessions and Desires . . .

Gem: Emerald—Those who carry this stone tend to be lucky in love.

Flower: Rose Geranium—You have a strong desire for life.

Astral Color, Color Need, Apparel Color: Your Astral Color is Pink, which reflects your compassion. Violet in your environment keeps you empathetic toward others. In your wardrobe, Blue-Green enhances your luck and makes you feel secure.

Fragrance: Sandalwood or other rare spices are the scents you need to have on hand. You crave attention and your perfume or cologne should be your most powerful ally. It will enhance your irresistible charm.

Tree: Cherry—You will find yourself faced with constant new emotional awakenings.

Instruments: Bass, clarinet

Composers: Haydn, Wagner

Bird: Killdeer—This bird is usually found consorting with other species, and can adapt to any environment.

Symbol: Star—You are full of inner brightness and will stand out in any crowd. You will be seen as special.

Harmonious Health and Nutrition . . .

Health Scent: Vanilla—This scent will fill you with a feeling of cleanliness and stability.

Favorable Foods: Raw beets, Concord grapes, rice, brown sugar, egg yolks

What's Lucky . . .

Lucky Numbers: 4, 22, 31

Best Months: May and June

Best Day of the Week: Saturday

Best Month Days: 4, 13, 22, 31

Lucky Charm: A piece of material cut from something in your home.

Harmonious Signs for Relationships and Partnerships: Cancer, Scorpio, Virgo

Spiritual Guides . . .

Star: Al Phergal Muachher—Those with this star often cling too long to fond memories.

Angel: Barchiel—This angel shows us right from wrong, encourages us in good decision making, and teaches us to protect ourselves and others.

Guardian Angel: Uriel—Individual archangel meaning "The Light of God."

Spiritual Stone: Chrysolite—This stone might help you keep things together when you feel frayed.

✶ _JUDITH'S INSIGHT_ ✶

You can be unconventional. You have lots of style and love beautiful things. You maintain a neat home as well as a neat appearance. Your early years may be filled with sorrows, or you just may tend to feel sad. As you get older, life blossoms and develops into more fun and less heartache. Your independence is striking. Others may find the need to criticize because of the style in which you handle your life. Once in a while, they're right. You have a style that will leave people with their mouths open.

On occasion, you let people get to you. This may cause some bumpy relationships. You're drawn to unusual people or, perhaps, foreigners, and you like unconventional relationships. Your family life will be decent enough, but you complain about it from time to time. Love prevails, and you settle in for a while, but may become restless in the relationship.

Painting and art may be part of your career. You could also be involved in architecture, teaching, metaphysical counseling, or working for a large corporation or government. You will have visions, dreams, and keen intuition about people and things and may be drawn to mysticism and psychic research. Unusual experiences will pepper your life. You may try to express your "soul nature" in art, literature and music, but you will do well in the collecting of fine art, antiques, and so on. Some call you a bit of an eccentric.

Because your style is considered different, you sometimes create turmoil at work. You may sometimes feel others are laughing at you. In time, when you're on top, you'll laugh all the way to the bank.

✶ ✶ ✶

MARCH 5

PISCES • The fish that swim in the pure sea

February 19 at 5:00 P.M. to March 20 at 5:00 P.M. • NUMEROLOGY 5

Possessions and Desires . . .

Gem: Sardius—This stone could give the wearer unusual insights into his or her own heart.
Flower: Holly—You usually are wise when you plan ahead.
Astral Color, Color Need, Apparel Color: Your Astral Color is White, which gives you clarity. Violet in your environment keeps you empathetic toward others. In your wardrobe, Cinnamon gives you encouragement and stamina.
Fragrance: Sandalwood or other rare spices are the scents you need to have on hand. You crave attention and your perfume or cologne should be your most powerful ally. It will enhance your irresistible charm.
Tree: Apple—You are creative, full of joy, and nearly magical. You bring happiness.
Instruments: Viola, trumpet
Composer: Liszt
Bird: Flamingo—This beautiful, gregarious bird is always careful of its enemy. It is also a caretaker of the young who tries to keep everyone happy.
Symbol: Triangle—You have the right combination of abilities.

Harmonious Health and Nutrition . . .

Health Scents: Peach—this scent may balance your good qualities so that they equal your charm.
Favorable Foods: Leeks, raisins, barley, honey, cottage cheese

What's Lucky . . .

Lucky Numbers: 5, 15, 25
Best Months: May and June
Best Day of the Week: Saturday
Best Month Days: 5, 14, 23
Lucky Charms: A rabbit's foot or a white candle.
Harmonious Signs for Relationships and Partnerships: Cancer, Scorpio, Virgo

Spiritual Guides . . .

Star: Al Phergal Muachher—Those with this star often cling too long to fond memories.
Angel: Barchiel—This angel shows us right from wrong, encourages us in good decision making, and teaches us to protect ourselves and others.
Guardian Angel: Plavwell—Gives power and strength to one's presence.
Spiritual Stone: Chrysolite—This stone might help you keep things together when you feel frayed.

✶ JUDITH'S INSIGHT ✶

You have uncommon intellectual gifts, great adaptability, and can understand just about anything. Your ready wit enables you to turn difficult things around and make them easy. You can be very ingenious and inventive.

You really hate being tied down, so having a mate who allows you freedom would work. You don't like living in the same environment for long periods of time and may have to move often. Perhaps you will just change the furniture and join the "couch of the month club." Maybe you just have a need for a lot of people in your life. You create friendships easily, and this makes life eventful. You are not the kind who ends old friendships, and your network reaches far and wide.

You will have many great ideas that could lead you to a career as an inventor, designer, or journalist, or a job in the movies. You could work with computers, or as a manager, builder, or building manager. Give in to your desire for unusual career options. Be sure to take care of money matters in order to ensure financial stability later on.

You are inclined to self-indulgence of all kinds. Have a little more perseverance, and you will do well. Your life isn't one that starts easily and at times feels as if it is only getting harder. But soon you'll see your happiness grow to your satisfaction.

✶ ✶ ✶

MARCH 6

PISCES • The fish that swim in the pure sea

February 19 at 5:00 P.M. to March 20 at 5:00 P.M. • NUMEROLOGY 6

Possessions and Desires . . .

Gem: Topaz—This is an excellent gift to be exchanged between very loyal friends.

Flower: Dogbane—You may want to guard against your tendency to let your little white lies veer into shady hues of gray.

Astral Color, Color Need, Apparel Color: Your Astral Color is Emerald, which gives you confidence. Violet in your environment keeps you empathetic toward others. In your wardrobe, Maroon gives you confidence.

Fragrance: Sandalwood or other rare spices are the scents you need to have on hand. You crave attention and your perfume or cologne should be your most powerful ally. It will enhance your irresistible charm.

Tree: Palm—You tend to be very healthy and creative.

Instruments: Tambourine, lyre

Composer: Schubert

Bird: Falcon—an expert hunter. When well-trained, it can adapt to many tasks and is usually obedient.

Symbol: Crescent—You are more likely to be influenced by the phases of the moon. Your easy-going manner leads you to peaceful situations.

Harmonious Health and Nutrition . . .

Health Scent: Orange Blossom—This scent may balance your body, mind, and soul.

Favorable Foods: Raw beets, apples, rice, brown sugar, egg yolks

What's Lucky

Lucky Numbers: 6, 16, 26
Best Months: May and June
Best Day of the Week: Saturday
Best Month Days: 6, 15, 24
Lucky Charms: A religious token or card from any religion.

Harmonious Signs for Relationships and Partnerships: Cancer, Scorpio, Virgo

Spiritual Guides . . .

Star: Al Risha—Those who have this band of stars as theirs will be happiest as part of a family.

Angel: Barchiel—This angel shows us right from wrong, encourages us in good decision making, and teaches us to protect ourselves and others.

Guardian Angel: Michael—"Who is like God."

Spiritual Stone: Chrysolite—This stone might help you keep things together when you feel frayed.

✳ JUDITH'S INSIGHT ✳

You have executive ability and a keen, active mind. You often show good, solid judgment. You demand reasons for every thought and action. Your personality is quite consistent to some, while those close to you may see you as more changeable. You're friendly to all, but you are easily hurt. Others see you as strong, but you are quite the sensitive one.

You are a devoted mate and parent. As a child you feel you take on more than your share of family responsibility. With a longtime mate you will have trials and tribulations all along the way. You do the most to maintain the relationship. Try learning to take advice, even though you're better at giving it. You love beautiful things, and the older you get, the more beautiful your surroundings. You love entertaining in your home.

Music, art, poetry, literature, and sculpture all fascinate you, but your career choice may be more structured. To start with, you could work at any level of government. You will be drawn to authority and religion. Careers in art, film, construction, music, or public service are all possibilities. It may take time for you to learn to balance your structured side with your more artistic side. All in all, you eventually find the right path and succeed at work. Your devote yourself to all you do.

Allow yourself a little more fun. When you're unhappy, you shut down your mind and mouth! Give yourself a break and allow yourself more emotional freedom.

✳ ✳ ✳

MARCH 7

PISCES • The fish that swim in the pure sea

February 19 at 5:00 P.M. to March 20 at 5:00 P.M. • NUMEROLOGY 7

Possessions and Desires . . .

Gem: Ruby—This stone may lead you to energy, friendship, and happiness.

Flower: Hyacinth—You usually see the beauty that other people miss.

Astral Color, Color Need, Apparel Color: Your Astral Color is Pink, which reflects your compassion. Violet in your environment keeps you empathetic toward others. In your wardrobe, Blue-green enhances your luck and makes you feel secure.

Fragrance: Sandalwood or other rare spices are the scents you need to have on hand. You crave attention and your perfume or cologne should be your most powerful ally. It will enhance your irresistible charm.

Tree: Sycamore—Yours is the ability to love, communicate honestly with others, and have lasting relationships.

Instrument: Harp

Composers: Gluck, Brahms

Bird: Warbling Parakeet—the most beautiful of all birds, known as the love bird. It does seem to have the powers of imitation.

Symbol: Heart—You are enthusiastic, empathetic, and full of generosity and love.

Harmonious Health and Nutrition . . .

Health Scent: Jasmine—This scent may make you more easygoing when you are stressed.

Favorable Foods: Cucumber, raspberry, bran, honey, cottage cheese

What's Lucky . . .

Lucky Numbers: 7, 17, 34
Best Months: May and June
Best Day of the Week: Saturday
Best Month Days: 7, 16, 25
Harmonious Signs for Relationships and Partnerships: Cancer, Scorpio, Virgo
Lucky Charm: An old key.

Spiritual Guides . . .

Star: Al Risha—Those who have this band of stars as theirs will be happiest as part of a family.

Angel: Barchiel—This angel shows us right from wrong, encourages us in good decision making, and teaches us to protect ourselves and others.

Guardian Angel: Raphael—This angel attends to all of your needs when you are looking for guidance.

Spiritual Stone: Chrysolite—This stone might help you keep things together when you feel frayed.

✶ JUDITH'S INSIGHT ✶

Beauty in any form moves you. You have a taste for the good things in life. High ideals and great ambitions make you inclined to live an independent and unconventional life. You're broad minded and curious, so the mystical or psychic world intrigues you. Vivid dreams and unusual images lead you in your work.

In romantic relationships, you may start out as the weaker partner, only to prove to be stronger later on. Eventually, you take the bull by the horns and either make or break any relationship you are in. Others may see you as quiet, though this is not the case. If handled correctly, you can be the most devoted child ever to your parents. Be careful of overwhelming family dynamics. Family is important, especially your children, if you have them. They become a driving force in your life.

These may be the most natural career choices for you: beautician, fashion consultant, artist, creator, or designer. Stick to what you know instinctively, beauty and the arts. You can find a job either behind the scenes or in front of a camera. You'd also be a perfect model or spokesperson for beauty products.

You are much less complex than people seem to think. Money is important to you and you acquire great things, especially fine jewelry. So now you that know what road to take—drive!

✶ ✶ ✶

MARCH 8

PISCES • The fish that swim in the pure sea

February 19 at 5:00 P.M. to March 20 at 5:00 P.M. • NUMEROLOGY 8

Possessions and Desires . . .

Gem: Chrysolite—This gem may help you clear your mind of sadness and worry.
Flower: Olive—You tend to hope more for peace than happiness.
Astral Color, Color Need, Apparel Color: Your Astral Color is White, which gives you clarity. Violet in your environment keeps you empathetic toward others. In your wardrobe, Cinnamon gives you encouragement and stamina.
Fragrance: Sandalwood or other rare spices are the scents you need to have on hand. You crave attention and your perfume or cologne should be your most powerful ally. It will enhance your irresistible charm.
Tree: Pine—Your relationships tend to be harmonious, both emotionally and mentally.
Instrument: Cello
Composer: Mozart
Bird: Bobolink—This charming singer is equally good as a soloist or a member of an orchestra. It is a very romantic bird, useful as an insect destroyer, and elegant, with beautiful feathers, and always pleasant to have around.
Symbol: Wings—You are the source of balance in your world—this will bring you contentment.

Harmonious Health and Nutrition . . .

Health Scent: Almond—This scent may revitalize you and open you to greater possibilities.
Favorable Foods: Red cabbage, cherries, rice, brown sugar, egg yolks

What's Lucky . . .

Lucky Numbers: 8, 18, 28
Best Months: May and June
Best Day of the Week: Saturday
Best Month Days: 8, 17, 26
Lucky Charm: Red ribbon in your wallet or doorway.
Harmonious Signs for Relationships and Partnerships: Cancer, Scorpio, Virgo

Spiritual Guides . . .

Star: Al Phergal Muachher—Those with this star often cling too long to fond memories.
Angel: Barchiel—This angel shows us right from wrong, encourages us in good decision making, and teaches us to protect ourselves and others.
Guardian Angel: Seraphim—Angel that brings love light and passion.
Spiritual Stone: Chrysolite—This stone might help you keep things together when you feel frayed.

✶ JUDITH'S INSIGHT ✶

You have an active mind and a lot of determination, and that's what keeps you going. A kind nature and sensitive soul are great characteristics, but, sadly, these qualities don't always get you through the hard times. It is your tenacity and principles that ease you through.

Heavy family responsibilities dominate your life, and you take them very seriously. At times, you feel overwhelmed. Conflict about decisions causes you to question your choice of partners. Most of us go through that in our lifetime—you just may have a tougher time with it. You want freedom from time to time because you may not get out often enough. Others will not restrict you—you restrict yourself and then blame others.

Career choices for you could vary a lot. You're a natural caretaker, so health care or education are perfect. You're open to others' needs, so you'd make a great social worker or member of the clergy. Your visual sense could lead you to photography. Your desire for beauty may bring you to the cosmetics industry. You could be a plumber, nurse, or doctor. Talk about diversity! Your mind is your power, it doesn't matter what career. You will be successful, but your life will be like a roller coaster ride.

Responsibility is the key to your life, and you willingly take it on. Sure, it becomes burdensome and feels too heavy. But you are a winner and a survivor. Look forward to your future. It'll all be worth it!

✶ ✶ ✶

MARCH 9

PISCES • The fish that swim in the pure sea

February 19 at 5:00 P.M. to March 20 at 5:00 P.M. • NUMEROLOGY 9

Possessions and Desires . . .

Gem: Moonstone—This gem could protect you from danger.

Flower: Anemone—Be sure to not set your expectations too high.

Astral Color, Color Need, Apparel Color: Your Astral Color is Emerald, which gives you confidence. Violet in your environment keeps you empathetic toward others. In your wardrobe, Green is your power color for overcoming obstacles.

Fragrance: Sandalwood or other rare spices are the scents you need to have on hand. You crave attention and your perfume or cologne should be your most powerful ally. It will enhance your irresistible charm.

Tree: Holly—Beware that you are not carried away by your passionate nature. The only way to grow is to be open to new experiences.

Instruments: Violin, Tympanum

Composer: Gluck

Bird: Mockingbird—The most proficient minstrel in the world's orchestra; graceful and enthusiastic.

Symbol: Anchor—This tranquil symbol signifies stability and strength, and stands for strong commitments in relationships.

Harmonious Health and Nutrition . . .

Health Scent: Lavender—This scent might lead others to trust you and make you patient.

Favorable Foods: Sorrel, prunes, whole grains, honey, cottage cheese

What's Lucky . . .

Lucky Numbers: 9, 19, 29

Best Months: May and June

Best Day of the Week: Saturday

Best Month Days: 9, 18, 27

Lucky Charms: A U.S. coin or a bill of any amount from the year you were born.

Harmonious Signs for Relationships and Partnerships: Cancer, Scorpio, Virgo

Spiritual Guides . . .

Star: Al Phergal Muachher—Those with this star often cling too long to fond memories.

Angel: Barchiel—This angel shows us right from wrong, encourages us in good decision making, and teaches us to protect ourselves and others.

Guardian Angel: Gabriel—"God is my strength."

Spiritual Stone: Chrysolite—This stone might help you keep things together when you feel frayed.

✳ JUDITH'S INSIGHT ✳

You have zest and ambition—what desirable qualities! When you sit with things long enough, you can accomplish anything. Your great mental abilities, combined with an unstoppable energy, will earn you recognition. Curb your tendency to be impulsive. Neighbors may not always be aware of your temper.

Family can be your strongest asset or your greatest downfall. Sometime throughout your life you will feel both extremes, but with different family members. Yes, conflicts may even arise with the same person. You need time away from the family to maintain a healthy balance. At the same time, you need constant reassurance from them. You tend to waffle a bit, and although you're emotionally intelligent, it may be difficult to maintain this balance with regard to intimacy.

Look to your career to bring you into the public eye in one way or another. You do a better job of it when you're in control, because that's when you're at your happiest. Learn to use your terrific intuition—don't be such a skeptic. You could be good at several careers, including movie star, movie writer, police officer, or head of an undercover operation.

You always have the best of intentions, though you may seem selfish. Believe it or not, that is your protection. You dream the dream and then make it happen!

✳ ✳ ✳

MARCH 10

PISCES • The fish that swim in the pure sea

February 19 at 5:00 P.M. to March 20 at 5:00 P.M. • NUMEROLOGY 1

Possessions and Desires . . .

Gem: Turquoise—This stone may help you find material wealth.

Flower: Marsh Mallow—The course of your life will tend to often surprise you.

Astral Color, Color Need, Apparel Color: Your Astral Color is Pink, which emanates compassion. Violet in your environment keeps you empathetic toward others. In your wardrobe, Maroon gives you confidence.

Fragrance: Sandalwood or other rare spices are the scents you need to have on hand. You crave attention and your perfume or cologne should be your most powerful ally. It will enhance your irresistible charm.

Tree: Walnut—You are unusually helpful and always looking for new beginnings.

Instruments: Oboe, flute, clarinet, piano, French horn, organ, piccolo

Composer: Böhm

Bird: Flamingo—This beautiful, gregarious bird is always careful of its enemy. It is also a caretaker of the young who tries to keep everyone happy.

Symbol: Crown—the universal sign of dignity.

Harmonious Health and Nutrition . . .

Health Scent: Jasmine—This scent may make you more easygoing when you are stressed.

Favorable Foods: Spinach, plums, rice, brown sugar, egg yolks

What's Lucky . . .

Lucky Numbers: 10, 20, 28
Best Months: May and June
Best Day of the Week: Saturday
Best Month Days: 1, 10, 19, 28
Lucky Charm: A new penny in your shoe.
Harmonious Signs for Relationships and Partnerships: Cancer, Scorpio, Virgo

Spiritual Guides . . .

Star: Al Risha—Those who have this band of stars as theirs will be happiest as part of a family.

Angel: Barchiel—This angel shows us right from wrong, encourages us in good decision making, and teaches us to protect ourselves and others.

Guardian Angel: Malachi—"Messenger of Jehovah."

Spiritual Stone: Chrysolite—This stone might help you keep things together when you feel frayed.

✶ JUDITH'S INSIGHT ✶

You have strong convictions, a strong mind, and a strong will. You know exactly what you want. Early on in life and the hard way, you learn to be tactful. You like nice things and intend to have them. Don't worry if you don't come into this world with money—you find a way to make it. You have a style all your own and are capable of doing just about anything.

You're a sympathetic ear to some, but you won't give the time of day to others. If you like someone, you move mountains. Dedication to those you love brings you happiness along the way. People try to rattle your cage: your strength threatens them, and they want to know it's genuine. Your love life may be a rocky road, but with your sensuality and charm, romance will come knocking at your door (and more than once). Check your flippant comments and learn patience with others.

Motivated as you are, don't be surprised if you balance two careers at once. Fashion designer, beauty consultant, doctor, lawyer, writer, or movie star—you'll find your niche. As you're inclined to be impetuous and headstrong, you will be enterprising and original in all that you do.

You will encounter long journeys in your life and may be drawn to international things. Overly optimistic at times, you usually bounce back quite well after a temper tantrum. Slowly, you develop the sense of power and self-confidence that are missing in your early years. Then the world will be yours.

✶ ✶ ✶

MARCH 11

PISCES • The fish that swim in the pure sea

February 19 at 5:00 P.M. to March 20 at 5:00 P.M. • NUMEROLOGY 2

Possessions and Desires . . .

Gem: Sapphire—This gem may help you find forgiveness from those you've wronged.

Flower: Blue Violet—You are loyal and faithful in relationships.

Astral Color, Color Need, Apparel Color: Your Astral Color is Pink, which reflects your compassion. Violet in your environment keeps you empathetic toward others. In your wardrobe, Maroon gives you confidence.

Fragrance: Sandalwood or other rare spices are the scents you need to have on hand. You crave attention and your perfume or cologne should be your most powerful ally. It will enhance your irresistible charm.

Tree: Maple—You have both great stability and flashes of intuition.

Instruments: Pipe organ, cymbal, drum

Composers: Handel, Johann Sebastian Bach

Bird: Cuckoo—a good flyer and very seldom a quitter. Some cuckoos do tend to think they favor lonely isolation, but what they really yearn for is a family relationship.

Symbol: Cross—the symbol of self-sacrifice and reconciliation.

Harmonious Health and Nutrition . . .

Health Scent: Apple—You are creative, full of joy, and nearly magical. You bring happiness.

Favorable Foods: Spinach, apple, barley, honey, cottage cheese

What's Lucky . . .

Lucky Numbers: 2, 11, 22
Best Months: May and June
Best Day of the Week: Saturday
Best Month Days: 2, 11, 20, 29
Lucky Charms: Two 50-cent pieces. Give someone else one of them.
Harmonious Signs for Relationships and Partnerships: Cancer, Scorpio, Virgo

Spiritual Guides . . .

Star: Al Risha—Those who have this band of stars as theirs will be happiest as part of a family.

Angel: Barchiel—This angel shows us right from wrong, encourages us in good decision making, and teaches us to protect ourselves and others.

Guardian Angel: Uriel—This angel brings the light of God's guidance.

Spiritual Stone: Chrysolite—This stone might help you keep things together when you feel frayed.

✴ JUDITH'S INSIGHT ✴

Your ambition and enthusiasm inspire those around you. A great drive for accomplishment colors every thing you do. You have extremely good taste in the fine arts and in beauty. You keep your poetic side under wraps. Your dreamlike nature will bring you luck.

Most of the time your family doesn't quite understand you, but that could work in your favor. Early in your life you are needy, and as a youth you may have fantasized about being adopted (or maybe you were). Once you're in touch with your own style, you'll feel less the outsider. Relationships with friends and family undergo a metamorphosis, taking on a whole different dynamic.

When your relationships don't work, your imagination does. You will fill your life with fantasy and romance, and later you will live them out. Communication with your mate may be a problem. You will find people popping back into your life out of nowhere, and you welcome them with open arms.

Musician, scientist, doctor, woodworker, fashion consultant, machinist, computer whiz: you are capable of doing it all. You could also be a police officer or commissioner, screenwriter or movie star. Your career may be difficult at times, but don't worry. You get through it and take it as an opportunity to grow. Staring into space or the closest pond, you can think about nothing for hours. With your visual imagination, reading a book for you is like watching a movie.

✴ ✴ ✴

MARCH 12

PISCES • The fish that swim in the pure sea

February 19 at 5:00 P.M. to March 20 at 5:00 P.M. • NUMEROLOGY 3

Possessions and Desires . . .

Gem: Ruby—This stone may lead you to energy, friendship, and happiness.

Flower: Maple—You are very reserved emotionally.

Astral Color, Color Need, Apparel Color: Your Astral Color is White, which gives you clarity. Violet in your environment keeps you empathetic toward others. In your wardrobe, Blue-green enhances your luck and makes you feel secure.

Fragrance: Sandalwood or other rare spices are the scents you need to have on hand. You crave attention and your perfume or cologne should be your most powerful ally. It will enhance your irresistible charm.

Tree: Elm—You have willpower, strength, and the ability to stand alone.

Instrument: Trombone

Composers: Verdi, Mendelssohn, Schumann

Bird: Swan—Regarded as royal and sacred, this bird has the protective nature of a mother, and can become a furious fighter in the defense of its young.

Symbol: Wreath—You have been crowned with a special personality. You are strong but extremely compassionate.

Harmonious Health and Nutrition . . .

Health Scent: Rose—This scent will lead you to passionate thoughts and make you feel warm inside.

Favorable Foods: Artichokes, prunes, whole grains, brown sugar, egg yolks

What's Lucky . . .

Lucky Numbers: 3, 6, 12, 21
Best Months: May and June.
Best Day of the Week: Saturday
Best Month Days: 3, 12, 21, 30
Lucky Charm: A pen that someone else has already used.

Harmonious Signs for Relationships and Partnerships: Cancer, Scorpio, Virgo

Spiritual Guides . . .

Star: Al Phergal Muachher—Those with this star often cling too long to fond memories.

Angel: Barchiel—This angel shows us right from wrong, encourages us in good decision making, and teaches us to protect ourselves and others.

Guardian Angel: Johiel—This angel is a protector of all those with a humble heart.

Spiritual Stone: Chrysolite—This stone might help you keep things together when you feel frayed.

✦ JUDITH'S INSIGHT ✦

A natural caretaker, always ready to help, you always lend a hand, even when you don't have an extra. Good-natured, pure, practical, and idealistic—what a combination! Your friends are devoted to you. You love to travel, and you make a delightful travel companion. You try to understand others, but when disappointments occur, you don't bounce back so easily.

A long-term mate (or two) should be in your future. The second relationship is better. Family and friends adore you because you work at being a good person and keep their feelings in mind. You have a natural instinct for what is right. You are fond of your home but exceedingly sensitive to the emotional environment, especially when there's discord. Old treasures and toys fascinate you, and as you mature, you grow even more sentimental.

It may take you a little time to find your career because many things interest you. You could be a fisherman, hunter, nurse, doctor, or therapist. Try writing, if not early in life, perhaps later on—even if you write for a town newsletter or keep a journal. Look to your younger years to tap into those old dreams and goals. You may find you have hidden talent that you haven't been in touch with in years. Your need to communicate may draw you to a career involving the theater.

A born ham, you love to have a good time. You may like to play too much at times—some may see that as lazy. You have the makings of a good soul, and you have good karma.

★ ★ ★

MARCH 13

PISCES • The fish that swim in the pure sea

February 19 at 5:00 P.M. to March 20 at 5:00 P.M. • NUMEROLOGY 4

Possessions and Desires . . .

Gem: Emerald—Those who carry this stone tend to be lucky in love.

Flower: Ivy—You are more faithful to your ideals than to other people.

Astral Color, Color Need, Apparel Color: Your Astral Color is Emerald, which gives you confidence. Violet in your environment keeps you empathetic toward others. In your wardrobe, Cinnamon gives you encouragement and stamina.

Fragrance: Sandalwood or other rare spices are the scents you need to have on hand. You crave attention and your perfume or cologne should be your most powerful ally. It will enhance your irresistible charm.

Tree: Cherry—You will find yourself faced with constant new emotional awakenings.

Instruments: Bass, clarinet

Composers: Haydn, Wagner

Bird: Robin—the most sociable of all birds, with the ability to create quick friendships. It also can easily adapt to any home. When it wants something, it has the tendency to try to snatch it.

Symbol: Star—You are full of inner brightness and will stand out in any crowd. You will be seen as special.

Harmonious Health and Nutrition . . .

Health Scent: Vanilla—This scent will fill you with a feeling of cleanliness and stability.

Favorable Foods: Leeks, cherries, bran, honey, cottage cheese

What's Lucky . . .

Lucky Numbers: 4, 13, 26

Best Months: May and June

Best Day of the Week: Saturday

Best Month Days: 4, 13, 22, 31

Lucky Charm: A piece of material cut from something in your home.

Harmonious Signs for Relationships and Partnerships: Cancer, Scorpio, Virgo

Spiritual Guides . . .

Star: Al Phergal Muachher—Those with this star often cling too long to fond memories.

Angel: Barchiel—This angel shows us right from wrong, encourages us in good decision making, and teaches us to protect ourselves and others.

Guardian Angel: Uriel—This angel brings the light of God's guidance.

Spiritual Stone: Chrysolite—This stone might help you keep things together when you feel frayed.

✶ JUDITH'S INSIGHT ✶

You love to play sports and have a good time expending that energy. Unconventional or eccentric qualities emerge after a considerable amount of sorrow. At these low times, your strong will and desire to enjoy life will pull you out of the depths. Later in life, you are drawn to the mystical or psychic.

A nice home is vital to you. When it comes to family, things may not be so easy, but your drive and determination will smooth things over. You're an eternal optimist. Love brings the greatest joy and some heartache, too. You can lean toward the selfish side until you have a family or meet the right mate. You find that special mate in the second part of your life.

You are a good egg, so a career in health care or nonprofit could work well. You may be drawn to volunteerism. Until your forties, you may dabble in many careers. After that, you'll find your love. If you are in a secure career until forty, you may wake up one morning and want something new. You would also do well as a designer, author, or editor. Research may be a profitable option.

You like things crisp and new. You must have variety, especially when it comes to fashion. Your home and furniture may change over the years, or you may decide to trade last year's car for this year's model. Maybe you just want to paint the house a different color? No, you are not fickle, but you like environmental changes. Maybe it's because you don't like emotional ones.

✶ ✶ ✶

MARCH 14

PISCES • The fish that swim in the pure sea

February 19 at 5:00 P.M. to March 20 at 5:00 P.M. • NUMEROLOGY 5

Possessions and Desires . . .

Gem: Sardius—this stone could give the wearer unusual insights into his or her own heart.
Flower: White Violet—You tend to be drawn to creative expression.
Astral Color, Color Need, Apparel Color: Your Astral Color is Pink, which reflects your compassion. Violet in your environment keeps you empathetic toward others. In your wardrobe, Green is your power color for overcoming obstacles.
Fragrance: Sandalwood or other rare spices are the scents you need to have on hand. You crave attention and your perfume or cologne should be your most powerful ally. It will enhance your irresistible charm.
Instruments: Viola, trumpet
Composer: Liszt
Tree: Apple—You are creative, full of joy, and nearly magical. You bring happiness.
Bird: Flamingo—This beautiful, gregarious bird is always careful of its enemy. It is also a caretaker of the young who tries to keep everyone happy.
Symbol: Triangle—You have the right combination of abilities.

Harmonious Health and Nutrition . . .

Health Scent: Peach—this scent may balance your good qualities so that they equal your charm.
Favorable Foods: Red cabbage, apple, barley, brown sugar, egg yolks

What's Lucky . . .

Lucky Numbers: 15, 5, 23
Best Months: May and June
Best Day of the Week: Saturday
Best Month Days: 5, 14, 23
Lucky Charms: A rabbit's foot or a white candle.
Harmonious Signs for Relationships and Partnerships: Cancer, Scorpio, Virgo

Spiritual Guides . . .

Star: Al Risha—Those who have this band of stars as theirs will be happiest as part of a family.
Angel: Barchiel—This angel shows us right from wrong, encourages us in good decision making, and teaches us to protect ourselves and others.
Guardian Angel: Phanuel—protection against the negative.
Spiritual Stone: Chrysolite—This stone might help you keep things together when you feel frayed.

✶ JUDITH'S INSIGHT ✶

You're on everyone's party list. Your presence is truly joyful, and you pick good presents, too. You are generally creative and may have many hidden talents that come about later in life. You were born with uncommon intellectual gifts and a great adaptability to any type of interesting, ingenious, inventive work.

In love, there may be some disappointments, but some day, you will definitely be lucky in love. You allow no interference in your relationships. As long as your mate understands your sense of freedom, you two will do just fine. With the right partner, children may be your greatest accomplishment. Be careful not to compete with the kids—you so love being a child yourself. As long as you are getting the attention you need, you will be in a good place.

You are a great employee and would be a better employer. You do like the occasional pat on the back. As you mature, intuition will manifest itself. See what career you start off having and which one you wind up in.

You are here to have fun and to be entertained. With that need met, you're a happy camper. If you do become depressed, it's usually because the fun has been absent from your life. You need constant mental stimulation. While your serious youth may not have been a joyful one, as an adult you want to have fun!

✶ ✶ ✶

MARCH 15

PISCES • The fish that swim in the pure sea

February 19 at 5:00 P.M. to March 20 at 5:00 P.M. • NUMEROLOGY 6

Possessions and Desires . . .

Gem: Topaz—This is an excellent gift to be exchanged between very loyal friends.

Flower: Walnut—You tend to have a very clear mind and bright intellect.

Astral Color, Color Need, Apparel Color: Your Astral Color is White, which gives you clarity. Violet in your environment keeps you empathetic toward others. In your wardrobe, Maroon gives you confidence.

Fragrance: Sandalwood or other rare spices are the scents you need to have on hand. You crave attention and your perfume or cologne should be your most powerful ally. It will enhance your irresistible charm.

Tree: Palm—You tend to be very healthy and creative.

Instruments: Tambourine, lyre

Composer: Schubert

Bird: Lark—known for the beauty of its song, which is sometimes very unusual. It is also credited with extraordinary intelligence.

Symbol: Crescent—You are more likely to be influenced by the phases of the moon. Your easygoing manner leads you to peaceful situations.

Harmonious Health and Nutrition . . .

Health Scent: Orange Blossom—This scent may balance your body, mind, and soul.

Favorable Foods: Unhulled barley, figs, bran, honey, cottage cheese

What's Lucky . . .

Lucky Numbers: 6, 16, 24

Best Months: May and June

Best Day of the Week: Saturday

Best Month Days: 6, 15, 24

Lucky Charms: A religious token or card from any religion.

Harmonious Signs for Relationships and Partnerships: Cancer, Scorpio, Virgo

Spiritual Guides . . .

Star: Al Risha—Those who have this band of stars as theirs will be happiest as part of a family.

Angel: Barchiel—This angel shows us right from wrong, encourages us in good decision making, and teaches us to protect ourselves and others.

Guardian Angel: Michael—"Who is like God."

Spiritual Stone: Chrysolite—This stone might help you keep things together when you feel frayed.

✶ JUDITH'S INSIGHT ✶

You were born under a "lucky star" and good things will come your way. If you don't succeed careerwise, it will be your own fault. The potential to lead a fascinating life is there. Opportunities will present themselves all the time. You make many friends who will be devoted to you. You're attracted to beauty and order, and have great organizational skills.

You were born to be loved. Most are lucky if they get that once in a lifetime love; you get it twice. Your children, if you have them, will bring you great joy. Your home environment will be warm and nurturing. You check your selfish ways at the door once you find a home. At times you can be difficult to get along with, but your family and friends put up with you.

Although you will have to work hard for a living, you rise to a secure position. You could wind up in your own business as a designer, or decorator, and be very successful. You have a tendency to work too hard, but you may have to in order to achieve your goals. Science may interest you or writing as a career should intrigue you as well.

You love being on the water or maybe living there. A strong constitution will help ward off fits of overindulgence. You can be very extravagant. Save some money for retirement. Your energy wanes later in life. You are not the one who finds success: it will find you! Learn to manage it well.

✶ ✶ ✶

MARCH 16

PISCES • The fish that swim in the pure sea

February 19 at 5:00 P.M. to March 20 at 5:00 P.M. • NUMEROLOGY 7

Possessions and Desires . . .

Gem: Agate—This stone may promote health and lead you to a long life.

Flower: Valerian—You may be very easy to get along with.

Astral Color, Color Need, Apparel Color: Your Astral Color is Emerald, which gives you confidence. Violet in your environment keeps you empathetic toward others. In your wardrobe, Blue-Green enhances your luck and makes you feel secure.

Fragrance: Sandalwood or other rare spices are the scents you need to have on hand. You crave attention and your perfume or cologne should be your most powerful ally. It will enhance your irresistible charm.

Tree: Sycamore—Yours is the ability to love, communicate honestly with others, and have lasting relationships.

Instrument: Harp

Composers: Gluck, Brahms

Bird: Skylark—This handsome bird is beautiful when it sings. It always whistles as it works.

Symbol: Heart—You are enthusiastic, empathetic, and full of generosity and love.

Harmonious Health and Nutrition . . .

Health Scent: Jasmine—This scent may make you more easygoing when you are stressed.

Favorable Foods: Artichokes, cherries, rice, brown sugar, egg yolks

What's Lucky . . .

Lucky Numbers: 7, 27, 17
Best Months: May and June
Best Day of the Week: Saturday
Best Month Days: 7, 16, 25
Lucky Charm: An old key.
Harmonious Signs for Relationships and Partnerships: Cancer, Scorpio, Virgo

Spiritual Guides . . .

Star: Al Phergal Muachher—Those with this star often cling too long to fond memories.

Angel: Barchiel—This angel shows us right from wrong, encourages us in good decision making, and teaches us to protect ourselves and others.

Guardian Angel: Raphael—This angel attends to all of your needs when you are looking for guidance.

Spiritual Stone: Chrysolite—This stone might help you keep things together when you feel frayed.

✶ JUDITH'S INSIGHT ✶

You have a head for business and the determination to succeed. To some, you seem materialistic. You can be a bit impractical. Working with others is easy, provided they give you space. You are as kind and considerate as you are treated, and you adapt to almost any atmosphere. Your persistence enables you to succeed.

You're a bundle of contradictions, and can be strong and weak all at once. Watch for this in relationships. Somehow you know better, but you still encounter traps when it comes to falling in love. It should stop once you decide to get your act together. Family matters may trip you up—here, allow yourself more freedom. You're a good humanitarian most of the time, but you may tire of this. But your giving nature always returns.

You are creative, but will probably end up in a company or office. Structured environments calm you, as long as they allow you freedom. The more restrictive and controlling the environment, the more you rebel and want out. Marketing or advertising may be a good fit, and you're drawn to the beauty industry. You may surprise yourself by how "corporate" you become, either with your own company or someone else's.

Although you achieve your career goals, your vision and desire could change very easily. You make your mark on this world through altruism, even if it is by supporting your local school district or a family on your block. You can be misunderstood, but sooner or later, the smoke clears.

✶ ✶ ✶

MARCH 17   PISCES • The fish that swim in the pure sea

February 19 at 5:00 P.M. to March 20 at 5:00 P.M. • NUMEROLOGY 8

Possessions and Desires . . .

Gem: Chrysolite—This gem may help you clear your mind of sadness and worry.

Flower: Sorrel—You are very affectionate to others.

Astral Color, Color Need, Apparel Color: Your Astral Color is Pink, which reflects your compassion. Violet in your environment keeps you empathetic toward others. In your wardrobe, Cinnamon gives you encouragement and stamina.

Fragrance: Sandalwood or other rare spices are the scents you need to have on hand. You crave attention and your perfume or cologne should be your most powerful ally. It will enhance your irresistible charm.

Tree: Pine—Your relationships tend to be harmonious, both emotionally and mentally.

Instrument: Cello

Composer: Mozart

Bird: Bobolink—This charming singer is equally good as a soloist or a member of an orchestra. It is a very romantic bird, useful as an insect destroyer, and elegant, with beautiful feathers, and always pleasant to have around.

Symbol: Wings—You are the source of balance in your world—this will bring you contentment.

Harmonious Health and Nutrition . . .

Health Scent: Almond—This scent may revitalize you and open you to greater possibilities.

Favorable Foods: Beets, grapes, barley, honey, cottage cheese

What's Lucky . . .

Lucky Numbers: 8, 26, 28

Best Months: May and June

Best Day of the Week: Saturday

Best Month Days: 8, 17, 26

Lucky Charm: Red ribbon in your wallet or doorway.

Harmonious Signs for Relationships and Partnerships: Cancer, Scorpio, Virgo

Spiritual Guides . . .

Star: Al Phergal Muachher—Those with this star often cling too long to fond memories.

Angel: Barchiel—This angel shows us right from wrong, encourages us in good decision making, and teaches us to protect ourselves and others.

Guardian Angel: Seraphim—An angel that brings love, light and passion.

Spiritual Stone: Chrysolite—This stone might help you keep things together when you feel frayed.

✶ JUDITH'S INSIGHT ✶

Showing off your serious side first makes you more comfortable, especially early in life. Although you were very intelligent, you had low self-esteem as a child. You feel misunderstood most of the time, even though you mean well. You try not to show your sadness and need to learn to express your emotions better. Your confidence grows as you mature. You love it when others recognize your humor.

It seems as though your love life takes forever to take off. When it finally does, you scare easily. You relationships take forever to unfold. You could date someone for years before a commitment is mentioned. The longer you put off marriage, the better. But no matter how long you wait, you'll still have second thoughts. You love family; you use them and drive them crazy. If you weren't born with a silver spoon in your mouth, someone will put one there.

Look for a career in communications. You may end up on stage. If you do, stick with comedy: you are a great storyteller. Work is important because you love spending money. You're very inventive. If all else fails, tap into your intuition. Stop laughing and start listening.

Yours is a life far from charmed, though it may look that way to others. You can be quite selective about what you choose to reveal about yourself and what you don't. Ups and downs trouble you during your thirties and forties. Once your confidence grows and reality sets in, you may have that chance to live on Easy Street.

✶ ✶ ✶

MARCH 18

PISCES • The fish that swim in the pure sea

February 19 at 5:00 P.M. to March 20 at 5:00 P.M. • NUMEROLOGY 9

Possessions and Desires . . .

Gem: Moonstone—This gem could protect you from danger.

Flower: Shamrock—You may find that a light heart floats over the highest troubles.

Astral Color, Color Need, Apparel Color: Your Astral Color is White, which gives you clarity. Violet in your environment keeps you empathetic toward others. In your wardrobe, Green is your power color for overcoming obstacles.

Fragrance: Sandalwood or other rare spices are the scents you need to have on hand. You crave attention and your perfume or cologne should be your most powerful ally. It will enhance your irresistible charm.

Tree: Holly—Beware that you are not carried away by your passionate nature. The only way to grow is to be open to new experiences.

Instruments: Violin, tympanum

Composer: Gluck

Bird: Mockingbird—the most proficient minstrel in the world's orchestra; graceful and enthusiastic.

Symbol: Anchor—This tranquil symbol signifies stability and strength, and stands for strong commitments in relationships.

Harmonious Health and Nutrition . . .

Health Scent: Lavender—This scent might lead others to trust you and make you patient.

Favorable Foods: Artichokes, watermelon, bran, brown sugar, egg yolks

What's Lucky . . .

Lucky Numbers: 9, 29, 19

Best Months: May and June

Best Day of the Week: Saturday

Best Month Days: 9, 18, 27

Lucky Charm: A U.S. coin or a bill of any amount from the year you were born.

Harmonious Signs for Relationships and Partnerships: Cancer, Scorpio, Virgo

Spiritual Guides . . .

Star: Al Phergal Muachher—Those with this star often cling too long to fond memories.

Angel: Barchiel—This angel shows us right from wrong, encourages us in good decision making, and teaches us to protect ourselves and others.

Guardian Angel: Gabriel—"God is my strength."

Spiritual Stone: Chrysolite—This stone might help you keep things together when you feel frayed.

✶ JUDITH'S INSIGHT ✶

You were born with power and presence. The lives you touch will be changed forever. You have the gift of gab and the smarts to go with it. You have a strong spiritual nature and are known as "one of a kind." You are gentle when need be, but your strength puts you in the right place at the right time. Others think you are blessed. Enthusiasm and playfulness keep you sane during difficult times. You can overcome depression and sadness with your perseverance and joyful personality.

Devotion and kindness bring the love of your life, and it may be someone you considered "just a friend." An independent soul, you do require a sense of freedom, and your mate understands this. Your relationships are sprinkled with fun and fantasy, and that's what helps keep them interesting. Family can be both your strength and your weakness. Be sure to keep this in mind on life's roller coaster.

You could have more than one career. Your creativity is enhanced with the passing years. Consider the role of caretaker early in life. Try something more creative later on. Success can come from anywhere, but you are recognized publicly at some point in your life. As you get older, intuitive gifts manifest themselves.

As an adult, you learn to enjoy life. Bad moments turn to good. Your mind is more highly evolved than you think, and you'll learn to recognize this as you mature. You take risks along the way that seem easy for you. The older you get, the better life gets! Ambition colors your life, so money is not likely to be much of a problem. You do enjoy good things and are happy to work for them.

✶ ✶ ✶

MARCH 19

PISCES • The fish that swim in the pure sea

February 19 at 5:00 P.M. to March 20 at 5:00 P.M. • NUMEROLOGY 1

Possessions and Desires . . .

Gem: Agate—This stone may promote health and lead you to a long life.

Flower: Cohosh—You must learn to wait for life to bestow its lessons and its gifts.

Astral Color, Color Need, Apparel Color: Your Astral Color is Pink, which reflects your compassion. Violet in your environment keeps you empathetic toward others. In your wardrobe, Blue-Green enhances your luck and makes you feel secure.

Fragrance: Sandalwood or other rare spices are the scents you need to have on hand. You crave attention and your perfume or cologne should be your most powerful ally. It will enhance your irresistible charm.

Tree: Walnut—You are unusually helpful and always looking for new beginnings.

Instruments: Viola, trumpet

Composer: Liszt

Bird: Hummingbird—This birds is delicate and graceful. It can remain still for hours, then dart off and be as busy as a bee.

Symbol: Crown—the universal sign of dignity.

Harmonious Health and Nutrition . . .

Health Scent: Strawberry—Soothing by nature, the strawberry promotes self-esteem and encourages love.

Favorable Foods: Raw beets, raisins, barley, honey, cottage cheese

What's Lucky . . .

Lucky Numbers: 1, 11, 28
Best Months: May and June
Best Day of the Week: Saturday
Best Month Days: 1, 10, 19, 28
Lucky Charm: A new penny in your shoe.

Harmonious Signs for Relationships and Partnerships: Cancer, Scorpio, Virgo

Spiritual Guides . . .

Star: Al Risha—Those who have this band of stars as theirs will be happiest as part of a family.

Angel: Barchiel—This angel shows us right from wrong, encourages us in good decision making, and teaches us to protect ourselves and others.

Guardian Angel: Malachi—"Messenger of Jehovah."

Spiritual Stone: Chrysolite—This stone might help you keep things together when you feel frayed.

✴ JUDITH'S INSIGHT ✴

You respect law and order. Knowledge flows to and from you, especially history. You love to explore and invent. Friends remain loyal, no matter how long you know them. You take on responsibility quite easily, although you're not usually inclined to take the initiative. Take extra care with self-indulgence.

You do well in marriage, partnerships, or unions. Fickle early in life, you later want a well-grounded, stable family life. You need your freedom; avoid smothering relationships. You may wander off emotionally or physically if needs and desires aren't met.

Enterprising and original, you become successful at one longstanding job. You would work well as a teacher, professor, caretaker, or in computers. Just don't limit yourself to these! Your artistic nature may draw you to the fine arts. Sooner or later you'll take on multiple titles and careers.

You mean well, but can be misunderstood. You can be impetuous and headstrong, and your actions may be misinterpreted by others. Others may not understand because you walk around with a smile, even when there is sadness in your eyes.

✴ ✴ ✴

MARCH 20

PISCES • The fish that swim in the pure sea

February 19 at 5:00 P.M. to March 20 at 5:00 P.M. • NUMEROLOGY 2

Possessions and Desires . . .

Gem: Sapphire—This gem may help you find forgiveness from those you've wronged.

Flower: Lettuce—You tend to think that love is an emotion that you can keep on leash.

Astral Color, Color Need, Apparel Color: Your Astral Color is White, which gives you clarity. Red in your environment gives you energy and stamina. In your wardrobe, Green is your power color for overcoming obstacles.

Fragrance: Sandalwood or other rare spices are the scents you need to have on hand. You crave attention and your perfume or cologne should be your most powerful ally. It will enhance your irresistible charm.

Tree: Maple—You have both great stability and flashes of intuition.

Instruments: Pipe organ, cymbal, drum

Composers: Handel, Johann Sebastian Bach

Bird: Cuckoo—a good flyer, and very seldom a quitter. Some cuckoos tend to think they favor lonely isolation, but what they really yearn for is a family relationship.

Symbol: Cross—the symbol of self-sacrifice and reconciliation.

Harmonious Health and Nutrition . . .

Health Scent: Apple—You are creative, full of joy, and nearly magical. You bring happiness.

Favorable Foods: Parsley, gooseberries, rye crisps, chocolate, buttermilk

What's Lucky . . .

Lucky Numbers: 2, 22, 29

Best Months: May and June

Best Day of the Week: Saturday

Best Month Days: 2, 11, 20, 29

Lucky Charms: Two 50-cent pieces. Give someone else one of them.

Harmonious Signs for Relationships and Partnerships: Cancer, Scorpio, Virgo

Spiritual Guides . . .

Star: Al Phergal Muachher—Those with this star often cling too long to fond memories.

Angel: Barchiel—This angel shows us right from wrong, encourages us in good decision making, and teaches us to protect ourselves and others.

Guardian Angel: Uriel—This angel brings the light of God's guidance.

Spiritual Stone: Chrysolite—This stone might help you keep things together when you feel frayed.

✷ JUDITH'S INSIGHT ✷

You can be rather judgmental, thinking others don't notice. Your affectionate nature is strong, but you are masterful, dictatorial, and sometimes impatient. Sometimes you lack common sense. You can be inconsistent with others, which makes you seem flighty. Childhood is tough, and you carry that around until your forties. You're a good humanitarian and usually good-natured.

You desire a stable home life. Some day, you get it and keep it that way. "Long-term relationship" spells S-E-C-U-R-I-T-Y to you. Your home will be difficult to let go of. Children's themes appear over and over in your lifetime. You can be the most devoted and the most difficult child. Your tendency to feel sorry for yourself is valid—you do most of the work. But learn to recognize that doesn't mean nobody else is doing anything.

Careers in law or government, education or health care could easily sustain your interest. Whatever the job, make sure there is enough of a creative outlet. You have great enthusiasm for your work, and may be very social in the workplace. Since you're a workaholic, some would think you are very materialistic—you're not. Sometimes you should treat yourself to something nice.

You are extremely talented, and at times seem to have all the confidence in the world, but low self-esteem will plague you all your life. Your view of life is romantic. As you get older your willpower gets stronger, as does your self-image. As you learn to know yourself better, so will others around you.

✷ ✷ ✷

MARCH 21 ARIES • The lamb of god

March 20 at 5:00 P.M. to April 20 at 4:00 A.M. • NUMEROLOGY 3

Possessions and Desires . . .

Gem: Amethyst—This stone could be good for meditation and concentration.

Flower: Pine—You may find that those you pity are really better off than you are.

Astral Color, Color Need, Apparel Color: Your Astral Color is Pink, which reflects your compassion. Red in your environment gives you energy and stamina. In your wardrobe, Maroon gives you confidence.

Fragrance: Use the subtlest hints of lemon or other citrus fruits to bring freshness into your surroundings. These scents will give you the energy to make things happen in your life.

Tree: Elm—You have willpower, strength, and the ability to stand alone.

Instrument: Trombone

Composers: Verdi, Mendelssohn, and Schumann

Bird: Warbling Parakeet—the most beautiful of all birds. It is known as the love bird. It does seem to have the powers of imitation.

Symbol: Wreath—You have been crowned with a special personality. You are strong but extremely compassionate.

Harmonious Health and Nutrition . . .

Health Scent: Rose—This scent will lead you to passionate thoughts and make you feel warm inside.

Favorable Foods: Endive, strawberries, caraway seeds, molasses, cottage cheese

What's Lucky . . .

Lucky Numbers: 3, 9, 30
Best Months: June and July
Best Day of the Week: Tuesday
Best Month Days: 3, 12, 21, 30

Lucky Charm: A pen that someone else has already used.

Harmonious Signs for Relationships and Partnerships: Sagittarius and Leo

Spiritual Guides . . .

Star: Al Botein—Those with this star often feel that they are under lots of pressure.

Angel: Malchidiel—This is the angel of new beginnings and innovative ideas.

Guardian Angel: Johiel—This angel is a protector of all those with a humble heart.

Spiritual Stone: Beryl—This stone is good for meditation and concentration.

✳ JUDITH'S INSIGHT ✳

Because of your wit and charm, you attract friends easily. You take life too seriously, especially in your early years. You can be practical and idealistic all at once. You have that powerful combination of endless mental energy along with great ambition. If you were paid for your thoughts, you would be a millionaire and that is at a penny a thought.

You look and talk as if you have it all together, and most of the time you do. This is key in attracting a mate—your mind pulls in people like a magnet. You are neat in your appearance, and your manners would make any mother proud. You're top banana in all social situations. Your family will rely on you for constant support. Unfortunately, you have no real communication skills when the conversation turns emotional.

You will be drawn to the sea either for career or pleasure. Athletics play a big role in your life. Look for a career in a large institution, such as a school, college, hospital, or charity. Eventually, you earn a lot.

Partnerships are equally lucky for you. Marriage or marriagelike arrangements bring you happiness and success. You have what it takes to get there. So go ahead and do it!

✳ ✳ ✳

MARCH 22
ARIES • The lamb of god
March 20 at 5:00 P.M. to April 20 at 4:00 A.M. • NUMEROLOGY 4

Possessions and Desires . . .

Gem: Ruby—This stone may lead you to energy, friendship, and happiness.

Flower: Maidenhair—You may have an ability to create great beauty.

Astral Color, Color Need, Apparel Color: Your Astral Color is White, which gives you clarity. Red in your environment gives you energy and stamina. In your wardrobe, Raspberry gives you power and stimulation.

Fragrance: Use the subtlest hints of lemon or other citrus fruits to bring freshness into your surroundings. These scents will give you the energy to make things happen in your life.

Tree: Cherry—You will find yourself faced with constant new emotional awakenings.

Instruments: Bass, Clarinet

Composers: Haydn, Wagner

Bird: Killdeer—This bird is usually found consorting with other species, and can adapt to any environment.

Symbol: Star—You are full of inner brightness and will stand out in any crowd. You will be seen as special.

Harmonious Health and Nutrition . . .

Health Scent: Vanilla—This scent will fill you with a feeling of cleanliness and stability.

Favorable Foods: Swiss chard, prunes, rye crisps, raw sugar, eggs

What's Lucky . . .

Lucky Numbers: 2, 11, 22
Best Months: June and July
Best Day of the Week: Tuesday
Best Month Days: 4, 13, 22, 31
Lucky Charm: A piece of material cut from something in your home.

Harmonious Signs for Relationships and Partnerships: Sagittarius and Leo

Spiritual Guides . . .

Star: Al Thurauya—Woe to the enemies of those with this star!

Angel: Malchidiel—This is the angel of new beginnings and innovative ideas.

Guardian Angel: Uriel—This angel brings the light of God's guidance.

Spiritual Stone: Beryl—This stone is good for meditation and concentration.

✷ JUDITH'S INSIGHT ✷

Your determination, drive, and faithfulness inspire others around you. Since you're enthusiastic and kind, you take on projects and work and handle them with great care, right down to the tiniest detail. You may be criticized for your independence.

If you are a woman, you will have many admirers, but you will not be drawn into marriage unless the man wins your affection and desires by his own worthiness—then he becomes your king.

If you are a man, you will be apt to "shop around" before settling down. You are not a creature of impulse. You will wait to be sure your mate is loyal before commitment. For either gender: once you make a commitment, you are generous and sharing. Stability and love at home are vital.

You can be a judge, lawyer, teacher, business manager, or financier. You have great mental ability, but you may at times overdo it at work. You may have your hand in more than one business venture. You'll own quite a bit of real estate. Your mind is mathematical, peaceful, and shrewd.

You enjoy life most when your loved ones enjoy themselves—even if it is at your expense. You are quite fair when it comes to the rights of others. Just remember that success is at your feet, because you know how to use your head!

✷ ✷ ✷

MARCH 23 ARIES • The lamb of god
March 20 at 5:00 P.M. to April 20 at 4:00 A.M. • NUMEROLOGY 5

Possessions and Desires . . .

Gem: Sardius—This stone could give the wearer unusual insights into his or her own heart.

Flower: Woodbine—You may see everyone as your brothers and sisters.

Astral Color, Color Need, Apparel Color: Your Astral Color is Pink, which reflects your compassion. Red in your environment gives you energy and stamina. In your wardrobe, Copper gives you confidence and a sharp appearance.

Fragrance: Use the subtlest hints of lemon or other citrus fruits to bring freshness into your surroundings. These scents will give you the energy to make things happen in your life.

Tree: Apple—You are creative, full of joy, and nearly magical. You bring happiness.

Instruments: Viola, trumpet

Composer: Liszt

Bird: Flamingo—This beautiful, gregarious bird is always careful of its enemy. It is also a caretaker of the young who tries to keep everyone happy.

Symbol: Triangle—You have the right combination of abilities.

Harmonious Health and Nutrition . . .

Health Scent: Peach—this scent may balance your good qualities so that they equal your charm.

Favorable Foods: Eggplant, apricots, caraway seeds, maple sugar, cottage cheese

What's Lucky . . .

Lucky Numbers: 5, 23, 32
Best Months: June and July
Best Day of the Week: Tuesday
Best Month Days: 5, 23, 25
Lucky Charms: A rabbit's foot or a white candle.
Harmonious Signs for Relationships and Partnerships: Sagittarius and Leo

Spiritual Guides . . .

Star: Al Botein—Those with this star often feel that they are under lots of pressure.

Angel: Malchidiel—This is the angel of new beginnings and innovative ideas.

Guardian Angel: Plavwell—gives power and strength to one's presence.

Spiritual Stone: Beryl—This stone is good for meditation and concentration.

✶ JUDITH'S INSIGHT ✶

You're enterprising, refined, subtle, ambitious, and enthusiastic; if you're not successful, it is your own fault. Some will call you lucky. You're often in the right place at the right time. This is not to say you won't have your share of struggle or heartache—you just sail through it so well. The power of positive thinking is your philosophy.

You want commitment but will test the waters over and over until you are absolutely one hundred percent sure. Then you'll test them again. A romantic, devoted mate who understands your sense of humor is essential to you. You're a harmless flirt, but when you get caught, you tend to stay loyal. You are solid as a rock, and family members look to you for your intelligence as well as your support emotionally. Watch out for impulsiveness.

You love secrets and living on the edge. A career in law may satisfy these proclivities. You do have a flair for theater and performing, even if you don't want to act. A career that would bring you into the limelight will work just fine.

You have many talents and, along the way, you discover some of them. You may jump from one career to another, or you may just do them all. At some point you will have your hand in more than one basket—for charity, that is. As you get older, you'll tap into your spiritual side, not something you thus far feel at home with. You enjoy a party as much as the next guy, but you are usually the host.

✶ ✶ ✶

MARCH 24 ARIES • The lamb of god

March 20 at 5:00 P.M. to April 20 at 4:00 A.M. • NUMEROLOGY 6

Possessions and Desires . . .

Gem: Topaz—This is an excellent gift to be exchanged between very loyal friends.

Flower: Fern—You are fascinated with all the beauty that life offers you.

Astral Color, Color Need, Apparel Color: Your Astral Color is Pink, which reflects your compassion. Red in your environment gives you energy and stamina. In your wardrobe, Copper gives you confidence and a sharp appearance.

Fragrance: Use the subtlest hints of lemon or other citrus fruits to bring freshness into your surroundings. These scents will give you the energy to make things happen in your life.

Tree: Palm—You tend to be very healthy and creative.

Instruments: Tambourine, lyre

Composer: Schubert

Bird: Falcon—an expert hunter. When well-trained it can adapt to many tasks and is usually obedient.

Symbol: Crescent—You are more likely to be influenced by the phases of the moon. Your easy-going manner leads you to peaceful situations.

Harmonious Health and Nutrition . . .

Health Scent: Orange Blossom—This scent may balance your body, mind, and soul.

Favorable Foods: Mustard greens, pomegranates, rye crisps, molasses, eggs

What's Lucky . . .

Lucky Numbers: 6, 16, 26
Best Months: June and July
Best Day of the Week: Tuesday
Best Month Days: 6, 15, 24
Lucky Charms: A religious token or card from any religion.

Harmonious Signs for Relationships and Partnerships: Sagittarius and Leo

Spiritual Guides . . .

Star: Al Sheratan—Those with this star hide their pain from those who could help them.

Angel: Malchidiel—This is the angel of new beginnings and innovative ideas.

Guardian Angel: Michael—"Who is like God."

Spiritual Stone: Beryl—This stone is good for meditation and concentration.

✶ JUDITH'S INSIGHT ✶

Hosting parties is your strong suit, and you enjoy every minute of it. You have a knack of handling and juggling. You love beautiful things and will work hard to acquire them. You don't look for a handout unless you put your hand in. Generosity, kindness, and charity are themes that run through your life.

You tend to have unusual relationships, maybe even an unusual marriage. Relatives of your significant other may be a problem—maybe there are too many of them. Be careful about letting your partner's family's and friends' problems become your own; you take on responsibility so well. In love, balance takes time, and patience is not one of your virtues. Generosity is, and this may be a blessing or a downfall.

As a general rule, you are lucky with money matters and careers. If you want to own a business, you could. Likewise, if you prefer government or real estate, these might make you happy. You get a natural high from new beginnings in business. You may find a longtime career and then moonlight or own a business on the side. Or you may just retire early and do something on your own then.

One way or another you'll have money, even if it comes after age fifty. Your magnanimous personality attracts friends from all walks of life. Childhood friends stick it out. You have the ability to create great things in your life—with or without a paintbrush.

✶ ✶ ✶

MARCH 25 ARIES • The lamb of god

March 20 at 5:00 P.M. to April 20 at 4:00 A.M. • NUMEROLOGY 7

Possessions and Desires . . .

Gem: Ruby—This stone may lead you to energy, friendship, and happiness.
Flower: Allspice—You have compassion for every living thing.
Astral Color, Color Need, Apparel Color: Your Astral Color is White, which gives you clarity. Red in your environment gives you energy and stamina. In your wardrobe, Rose gives you balance and harmony.
Fragrance: Use the subtlest hints of lemon or other citrus fruits to bring freshness into your surroundings. These scents will give you the energy to make things happen in your life.
Tree: Sycamore—Yours is the ability to love, communicate honestly with others, and have lasting relationships.
Composers: Gluck, Brahms
Instrument: Harp
Bird: Warbling Parakeet—the most beautiful of all birds, known as the love bird. It does seem to have the powers of imitation.
Symbol: Heart—You are enthusiastic, empathetic, and full of generosity and love.

Harmonious Health and Nutrition . . .

Health Scent: Jasmine—This scent may make you more easygoing when you are stressed.
Favorable Foods: Spinach, apples, chocolate, buttermilk

What's Lucky . . .

Lucky Numbers: 7, 17, 27
Best Months: June and July
Best Day of the Week: Tuesday
Best Month Days: 6, 15, 24
Lucky Charm: An old key.

Harmonious Signs for Relationships and Partnerships: Sagittarius and Leo

Spiritual Guides . . .

Star: Al Botein—Those with this star often feel that they are under lots of pressure.
Angel: Malchidiel—This is the angel of new beginnings and innovative ideas.
Guardian Angel: Raphael—This angel attends to all of your needs when you are looking for guidance.
Spiritual Stone: Beryl—This stone is good for meditation and concentration.

✶ JUDITH'S INSIGHT ✶

You have a mathematical mind, high ideals, and great ambition. Because you're inclined to be extremely independent, you may lead a rather unconventional life. You are broadminded, with a very curious nature. You love to flirt, but you display a sense of purity. No one will ever know what you're thinking—you hide your secrets well.

Drawn to unusual environments and relationships, you may desire to live in an unconventional place. You may desire wooded areas instead of cleared properties. And your home is a palace, no matter where you live. In time, you will make a devoted mate.

Your career may be anything connected with government, law, state institutions, or schools, and you should advance early on. Do not rule out a more creative position either. You may aspire to paint, compose music, or write screenplays.

People will be drawn to you, especially for business advice. The most eventful, unexpected things seem to happen to you all the time. You have high ideals and great aspirations. Once you figure which one you really want, you'll go out and get it!

✶ ✶ ✶

MARCH 26 ARIES • The lamb of god

March 20 at 5:00 P.M. to April 20 at 4:00 A.M. • Numerology 8

Possessions and Desires . . .

Gem: Chrysolite—This gem may help you clear your mind of sadness and worry.

Flower: Pitch Pine—You can be very philosophical.

Astral Color, Color Need, Apparel Color: Your Astral Color is Pink, which reflects your compassion. Red in your environment gives you energy and stamina. In your wardrobe, Green is your power color for overcoming obstacles.

Fragrance: Use the subtlest hints of lemon or other citrus fruits to bring freshness into your surroundings. These scents will give you the energy to make things happen in your life.

Tree: Pine—Your relationships tend to be harmonious, both emotionally and mentally.

Instrument: Cello

Composer: Mozart

Bird: Bobolink—This charming singer is equally good as a soloist or a member of an orchestra. It is a very romantic bird, useful as an insect destroyer, elegant, with beautiful feathers, and is always pleasant to have around.

Symbol: Wings—You are the source of balance in your world—this will bring you contentment.

Harmonious Health and Nutrition . . .

Health Scent: Raspberry—This scent might bring you a feeling of harmony with the universe.

Favorable Foods: Spinach, apples, chocolate, buttermilk

What's Lucky . . .

Lucky Numbers: 8, 17, 26
Best Months: June and July
Best Day of the Week: Tuesday
Best Month Days: 8, 17, 26
Lucky Charm: Red ribbon in your wallet or doorway.
Harmonious Signs for Relationships and Partnerships: Sagittarius and Leo

Spiritual Guides . . .

Star: Al Thurauya—Woe to the enemies of those with this star!

Angel: Malchidiel—This is the angel of new beginnings and innovative ideas.

Guardian Angel: Seraphim—An angel that brings love, light, and passion

Spiritual Stone: Beryl—This stone is good for meditation and concentration.

✶ JUDITH'S INSIGHT ✶

Obstacles don't faze you. You meet life's sorrow and disappointment head on. Early on in life, heavy responsibility follows you, and this is where you develop your strength of character and sheer will. You may work early or marry early. Groups and teams cramp your style. You do better working alone.

You may desire children early in life. You can be the big kid or the mature adult, depending on the situation. Although you're usually extremely loyal, you may need to pull away sometimes. You are everyone's rock and always make the best of everything. Make sure you don't let the needs of others overshadow your own. You tend to have strong influence over friends, family, and significant others.

You have the ability to take on more than one career. A business you start will succeed. State or government jobs might appeal to you; your investigative nature lends itself to police work. The desire for a stable work environment and long-term employment is there. Your jobs tend to last forever. At one time or another, you may be involved with a family business. Longevity combined with talent make you an ideal worker.

Aim for as much fun as responsibility, or you may feel resentment along the way. Because of your strength, you can be misread and misunderstood. You may be the head of the class, and you love and desire the finer things. Don't worry; you'll have them. Slow down and smell the roses. While you're there, take time to enjoy the pretty colors.

✶ ✶ ✶

MARCH 27
ARIES • The lamb of god

March 20 at 5:00 P.M. to April 20 at 4:00 A.M. • NUMEROLOGY 9

Possessions and Desires . . .

Gem: Diamond—This stone is thought to encourage harmony in relationships and gives strength to the troubled.

Flower: Fir—You may need to take more time for yourself in order to discover who you are.

Astral Color, Color Need, Apparel Color: Your Astral Color is White, which gives you clarity. Red in your environment gives you energy and stamina. In your wardrobe, Maroon gives you confidence.

Fragrance: Use the subtlest hints of lemon or other citrus fruits to bring freshness into your surroundings. These scents will give you the energy to make things happen in your life.

Tree: Holly—Beware that you are not carried away by your passionate nature. The only way to grow is to be open to new experiences.

Instruments: Violin, tympanum

Composer: Gluck

Bird: Mockingbird—the most proficient minstral in the world's orchestra; graceful and enthusiastic.

Symbol: Anchor—This tranquil symbol signifies stability and strength, and stands for strong commitments in relationships.

Harmonious Health and Nutrition . . .

Health Scents: Almond—This scent may revitalize you and open you to greater possibilities.

Favorable Foods: Watercress, gooseberries, caraway seeds, maple sugar, pressed cheese

What's Lucky . . .

Lucky Numbers: 9, 19, 29
Best Months: June and July
Best Day of the Week: Tuesday
Best Month Days: 9, 18, 27
Lucky Charms: A U.S. coin or a bill of any amount from the year you were born.

Harmonious Signs for Relationships and Partnerships: Sagittarius and Leo

Spiritual Guides . . .

Star: Al Thurauya—Woe to the enemies of those with this star!

Angel: Malchidiel—This is the angel of new beginnings and innovative ideas.

Guardian Angel: Gabriel—"God is my strength."

Spiritual Stone: Beryl—This stone is good for meditation and concentration.

✴ JUDITH'S INSIGHT ✴

You have a great spirit and strong desire for life. Enthusiasm alone will take you places. You're easygoing and friendly no matter what the situation and people will recognize this. Your ambitious style may lead you in many different directions, not necessarily connected to your work. Sports, extracurricular activities, and even volunteer work should all satisfy you. You have many good ideas and may find yourself throwing parties at the last minute.

The ideal mate for you is out there. Family life can get overwhelming, but probably because you're making it that way. You draw your strength from nurturing relationships. Although you may be the domineering partner, you do it with class and style, so it doesn't appear that way.

You should engage in business or industry. Counseling or metaphysics may be attractive to you. You would do very well as an artist, architect, judge, or jewelry maker. You find your niche after a few emotional battles. Do not rule out all areas of professional sports. You have high energy and great endurance.

Avoid mood-altering substances as much as possible. You have a tendency to become addicted. However, when habits do form, you recognize you have the willpower to overcome anything. You will enjoy friends in high places. The odds are that you can be there yourself eventually.

★ ★ ★

MARCH 28 ARIES • The lamb of god
March 20 at 5:00 P.M. to April 20 at 4:00 A.M. • NUMEROLOGY 1

Possessions and Desires . . .

Gem: Amethyst—This stone is said to give calmness and peace.

Flower: Sweetbriar—The simpler you keep things the more settled you'll be.

Astral Color, Color Need, Apparel Color: Your Astral Color is Pink, which reflects your compassion. Red in your environment gives you energy and stamina. In your wardrobe, Raspberry gives power and stimulation.

Fragrance: Use the subtlest hints of lemon or other citrus fruits to bring freshness into your surroundings. These scents will give you the energy to make things happen in your life.

Tree: Walnut—You are unusually helpful and always looking for new beginnings.

Instruments: Oboe, flute, clarinet, piano, French horn, organ, piccolo

Composer: Böhm

Bird: Bird of paradise—the "bird of the gods." You will shine and love extraordinary form.

Symbol: Crown—the universal sign of dignity.

Harmonious Health and Nutrition . . .

Health Scent: Jasmine—This scent may make you more easygoing when you are stressed.

Favorable Foods: Watercress, gooseberries, caraway seeds, maple sugar, pressed cheese

What's Lucky . . .

Lucky Numbers: 1, 10, 11
Best Months: June and July
Best Day of the Week: Tuesday
Best Month Days: 1, 10, 19, and 28
Lucky Charm: A new penny in your shoe

Harmonious Signs for Relationships and Partnerships: Sagittarius and Leo

Spiritual Guides . . .

Star: Al Sheratan—Those with this star hide their pain from those who could thelp them.

Angel: Malchidiel—This is the angel of new beginnings and innovative ideas.

Guardian Angel: Malachi—"Messenger of Jehovah."

Spiritual Stone: Beryl—This stone is good for meditation and concentration.

✷ JUDITH'S INSIGHT ✷

You have organizational skills and much executive ability. A quick study, you have an unusually long attention span. You love to live high on the hog. You will lead an eventful life. Anything can happen, with you around. You possess strength and strong will, and your independent character is well recognized and respected.

Stable home life and strong family ties dominate your life. Your bark can be worse than your bite: you can get into arguments but retain close connections. Love does prevail. Your presence and charm and sense of humor are noticed. You can flirt but are unlikely to stray unless living under extreme circumstances for a long period of time.

In your career, you're the initiator, or the boss. If not, you're unhappy. You need recognition and high rank. You will do well in whatever career you choose. You could be a car mechanic, salesperson, lawyer, detective, or even surgeon. Whatever the career, you shoot for the moon and don't settle until you get it.

You are faithful, smart, and sympathetic, surprisingly domestic, and desirous of an orderly home life. Sounds stuffy, but no! For you, every day will have a certain element of surprise.

✷ ✷ ✷

MARCH 29

ARIES • The lamb of god

March 20 at 5:00 P.M. to April 20 at 4:00 A.M. • NUMEROLOGY 2

Possessions and Desires . . .

Gem: Sapphire—This gem may help you find forgiveness from those you've wronged.

Flower: Elder—You can be overzealous when faced with what should be small problems.

Astral Color, Color Need, Apparel Color: Your Astral Color is Pink, which reflects your compassion. Red in your environment gives you energy and stamina. In your wardrobe, Maroon gives you confidence

Fragrance: Use the subtlest hints of lemon or other citrus fruits to bring freshness into your surroundings. These scents will give you the energy to make things happen in your life.

Tree: Maple—You have both great stability and flashes of intuition.

Instruments: Pipe organ, cymbal, drum

Composers: Handel, Johann Sebastian Bach

Bird: Cuckoo—a good flyer and very seldom a quitter. Some cuckoos tend to think they favor lonely isolation, but what they really yearn for is a family relationship.

Symbol: Cross—the symbol of self-sacrifice and reconciliation.

Harmonious Health and Nutrition . . .

Health Scents: Apple—You are creative, full of joy, and nearly magical. You bring happiness.

Favorable Foods: Dill, prunes, rye crisps, raw sugar, cottage cheese

What's Lucky . . .

Lucky Numbers: 2, 20, 22
Best Months: June and July
Best Day of the Week: Tuesday
Best Month Days: 2, 11, 20, 29
Lucky Charms: Two 50-cent pieces. Give someone else one of them.

Harmonious Signs for Relationships and Partnerships: Sagittarius and Leo

Spiritual Guides . . .

Star: Al Botein—Those with this star often feel that they are under lots of pressure.

Angel: Malchidiel—This is the angel of new beginnings and innovative ideas.

Guardian Angel: Uriel—This angel brings the light of God's guidance.

Spiritual Stone: Beryl—This stone is good for meditation and concentration.

✴ JUDITH'S INSIGHT ✴

You have a presence that demands attention and a smile that can change the world. You are faithful, just, sympathetic, and kind—sometimes to a fault. You grasp things very easily, and are strong and ambitious. Even when others step on your toes, you stay out of their way. You can endure just about any situation that arises.

You're loyal and devoted to family, which may not always be to your best advantage. You attract friends easily. You're a good friend, and you occasionally check that friends are as devoted as you. You make a great parent or guardian and seem to understand children better that most. Much love and devotion comes your way, especially as you get older.

You start off with one longstanding career that will keep you grounded, only later to desire a sense of freedom. This may come after retirement! You may never get the total career recognition you wish, but you do gain the respect of others in your chosen field. Whether you are a police officer, police commissioner, politician, decorator, or CEO of a large corporation, your greatest satisfaction comes when you're in love.

You have a way with words and may aspire to use it. You have many hidden talents. Your greatest attribute, however, is your joie de vive. You know how to enjoy life and bring others along for the ride.

✴ ✴ ✴

MARCH 30

ARIES • The lamb of god

March 20 at 5:00 P.M. to April 20 at 4:00 A.M. • NUMEROLOGY 3

Possessions and Desires . . .

Gem: Ruby—This stone may lead you to energy, friendship, and happiness.

Flower: Horehound—You usually see beyond the surface of things.

Astral Color, Color Need, Apparel Color: Your Astral Color is White, which gives you clarity. Red in your environment gives you energy and stamina. In your wardrobe, Raspberry gives power and stimulation.

Fragrance: Use the subtlest hints of lemon or other citrus fruits to bring freshness into your surroundings. These scents will give you the energy to make things happen in your life.

Tree: Elm—You have willpower, strength, and the ability to stand alone.

Instrument: Trombone

Composers: Verdi, Mendelssohn, Schumann

Bird: Swan—Regarded as royal and sacred, this bird has the protective nature of a mother and can become a furious fighter in the defense of its young.

Symbol: Wreath—You have been crowned with a special personality. You are strong but extremely compassionate.

Harmonious Health and Nutrition . . .

Health Scent: Rose—This scent will lead you to passionate thoughts and make you feel warm inside.

Favorable Foods: Eggplant, tomatoes, maple sugar, pressed cheese

What's Lucky . . .

Lucky Numbers: 3, 12, 30
Best Months: June and July
Best Day of the Week: Tuesday
Best Month Days: 3, 12, 21, 30
Lucky Charm: A pen that someone else has already used.

Harmonious Signs for Relationships and Partnerships: Sagittarius and Leo

Spiritual Guides . . .

Star: Al Thurauya—Woe to the enemies of those with this star!

Angel: Malchidiel—This is the angel of new beginnings and innovative ideas.

Guardian Angel: Johiel—This angel is a protector of all those with a humble heart.

Spiritual Stone: Beryl—This stone is good for meditation and concentration.

✶ JUDITH'S INSIGHT ✶

You have great ideas and you know how to put them to good use. A gentle person with a strong exterior, you are loving and nurturing with ambition and enthusiasm to boot. Hidden charms abound, and you are noticed for your high energy. People are drawn to you, even the ones who don't like you. You have great organizational abilities.

Family is your greatest love, and sometimes your greatest pain in the neck. You like a smoothly running household. Sometimes you may go a bit overboard. If mates are consistent with their affection, you will have a harmonious partnership. If not, you may feel indifferent. You have distinct needs and tendencies when it comes to a love relationship. This may be the only area of your life where you follow instead of lead.

You are the top banana in whatever you do. Any one of these careers would work well for you and bring you success and recognition: architect, building contractor, lawyer, writer, or artist.

Your wit and charm attract crowds of onlookers. You have a strong will and are far from lazy. Sometimes your opinions can be taken wrong, but you're willing to back down, especially when nobody's listening. The older you get, the less challenged you feel by your environment. Eventually, you learn to stop challenging it.

✶ ✶ ✶

MARCH 31 ARIES • The lamb of god
March 20 at 5:00 P.M. to April 20 at 4:00 A.M. • NUMEROLOGY 4

Possessions and Desires . . .

Gem: Emerald—Those who carry this stone tend to be lucky in love.

Flower: Love-lies-bleeding—It tends to take a long time for you to fall in love.

Astral Color, Color Need, Apparel Color: Your Astral Color is Pink, which reflects your compassion. Red in your environment gives you energy and stamina. In your wardrobe, green is your power color for overcoming obstacles.

Fragrance: Use the subtlest hints of lemon or other citrus fruits to bring freshness into your surroundings. These scents will give you the energy to make things happen in your life.

Tree: Cherry—You will find yourself faced with constant new emotional awakenings.

Instruments: Bass, clarinet

Composers: Haydn, Wagner

Bird: Robin—the most sociable of all birds, with the ability to create quick friendships. It also can easily adapt to any home. When it wants something, it has the tendency to try to snatch it.

Symbol: Star—You are full of inner brightness and will stand out in any crowd. You will be seen as special.

Harmonious Health and Nutrition . . .

Health Scent: Vanilla—This scent will fill you with a feeling of cleanliness and stability.

Favorable Foods: Parsley, apples, caraway seeds, chocolate

What's Lucky . . .

Lucky Numbers: 4, 14, 24

Best Months: June and July

Best Day of the Week: Tuesday

Best Month Days: 4, 13, 22, 3

Lucky Charm: A piece of material cut from something in your home.

Harmonious Signs for Relationships and Partnerships: Sagittarius and Leo

Spiritual Guides . . .

Star: Al Thurauya—Woe to the enemies of those with this star!

Angel: Malchidiel—This is the angel of new beginnings and innovative ideas.

Guardian Angel: Uriel—This angel brings the light of God's guidance.

Spiritual Stone: Beryl—This stone is good for meditation and concentration.

✶ JUDITH'S INSIGHT ✶

You are a strong thinker and reasoner, somewhat opinionated, and you distrust everything people tell you. You enjoy a good time and the good life. When you get nervous, you get cranky. Although you aren't lazy, you can go through some unproductive stages. Strange and unusual events seem to find you.

You adapt to things quite easily and enjoy harmony at home. Your home must be neat and organized. You command respect throughout the family. Try to dwell less on things that go wrong in your love life. An unconventional marriage or relationship may alleviate this. You make a devoted parent and child.

You could own your own clothing company or be president of someone else's. You take on responsibility with ease. You may also be attracted to law or government. Be careful to stay on the right side of the law. Work around cars may be appealing, or you may be a collector. A knack with mechanical things lends itself to a hands-on career. You have great expectations and the karma to achieve even greater ones. Try to be fair with all those around you, even when your instincts tell you not to.

You may be strong in a hobby or take on outside interests. You'll accomplish many things. Some may consider you a bit eccentric, and you know what? You like it that way!

✶ ✶ ✶

APRIL

APRIL 1
ARIES • The lamb of god
March 20 at 5:00 P.M. to April 20 at 4:00 A.M. • NUMEROLOGY 1

Possessions and Desires . . .

Gem: Turquoise—This stone may help you find material wealth.
Flower: Columbine—You can be seen as foolish in some of your more passionate quests.
Astral Color, Color Need, Apparel Color: Your Astral Color is White, which gives you clarity. Red in your environment gives you energy and stamina. In your wardrobe, Maroon gives you confidence.
Fragrance: Use the subtlest hints of lemon or other citrus fruits to bring freshness into your surroundings. These scents will give you the energy to make things happen in your life.
Tree: Walnut—You are unusually helpful and always looking for new beginnings.
Instruments: Oboe, flute, piano, French horn, organ, piccolo
Composer: Böhm
Bird: Skylark—This handsome bird is beautiful when it sings. It always whistles as it works.
Symbol: Crown the universal sign of dignity.

Harmonious Health and Nutrition . . .

Health Scent: Strawberry—soothing by nature, the strawberry promotes self-esteem and encourages love.
Favorable Foods: Dried beans, prunes, raw sugar, pressed cheese

What's Lucky . . .

Lucky Numbers: 1, 9, 18
Best Months: June and July
Best Day of the Week: Tuesday
Best Month Days: 1, 10, 19, 28
Lucky Charm: A new penny in your shoe.
Harmonious Signs for Relationships and Partnerships: Sagittarius and Leo

Spiritual Guides . . .

Star: Al Thurauya—Woe to the enemies of those with this star!
Angel: Malchidiel—This is the angel of new beginnings and innovative ideas.
Guardian Angel: Malachi—"Messenger of Jehovah."
Spiritual Stone: Beryl—This stone is good for meditation and concentration.

✷ JUDITH'S INSIGHT ✷

You have great ideas. You adapt to and grasp things easily and are generally good with details. Oddly, you're either bursting with energy or lacking it, depending on whether something sparks your fancy. Known for your philosophical mind and sympathetic nature, you can achieve great heights. You like having friends in high places. You love to learn. You can be belligerent on occasion and should keep your guard up, or your aggression could be destructive.

Home is important as long as you have chosen it for yourself. You desire order and live by the phrase "A place for everything and everything in its place." Your friends are your family. Friends are important to you; sometimes so important that they may cloud your thinking. You are faithful and loyal as long as you feel the same in return from your partner. In the early years of life, you may have a roving eye or perhaps just be flirtatious.

Careerwise, you are talented enough to do anything you desire—be it architect or psychologist. Your success may lie in building and/or designing. You're intensely independent, especially at work, and you have great organizational skills. Let no dust collect on things you get involved in, or you will get bored. You set hard goals for yourself, but you achieve them. Beware of going to extremes. Think first—you can be frank and outspoken. Most often, you throw caution to the wind and are impulsive. You are accustomed to overcoming obstacles, but you should carefully evaluate which obstacles you really want to remove. Be cautious of overzealousness in resolving problems.

✷ ✷ ✷

APRIL 2

ARIES • The lamb of god
March 20 at 5:00 P.M. to April 20 at 4:00 A.M. • NUMEROLOGY 2

Possessions and Desires . . .

Gem: Diamond—This stone is thought to encourage harmony in relationships and gives strength to the troubled.

Flower: Rush—You may be too anxious to adhere to other people's opinions of you.

Astral Color, Color Need, Apparel Color: Your Astral Color is Pink, which reflects your compassion. Red in your environment gives you energy and stamina. In your wardrobe, Gray brings out the best in your looks.

Fragrance: Use the subtlest hints of lemon or other citrus fruits to bring freshness into your surroundings. These scents will give you the energy to make things happen in your life.

Tree: Maple—You have both great stability and flashes of intuition.

Instruments: Pipe organ, cymbal, drum

Composers: Handel, Johann Sebastian Bach

Bird: Warbling Parakeet—the most beautiful of all birds, known as the love bird. It does seem to have the powers of imitation.

Symbol: Cross—the symbol of self-sacrifice and reconciliation.

Harmonious Health and Nutrition . . .

Health Scent: Apple—You are creative, full of joy, and nearly magical. You bring happiness.

Favorable Foods: Asparagus, apricots, rye crisps, maple sugar, buttermilk

What's Lucky . . .

Lucky Numbers: 1, 9, 27
Best Months: June and July
Best Day of the Week: Tuesday
Best Month Days: 2, 11, 20, 29
Lucky Charms: Two 50-cent pieces. Give someone else one of them.

Harmonious Signs for Relationships and Partnerships: Sagittarius and Leo

Spiritual Guides . . .

Star: Al Botein—Those with this star often feel that they are under lots of pressure.

Angel: Malchidiel—This is the angel of new beginnings and innovative ideas.

Guardian Angel: Uriel—This angel brings the light of God's guidance.

Spiritual Stone: Beryl—This stone is good for meditation and concentration.

✶ JUDITH'S INSIGHT ✶

You are energetic, impulsive, and sensuous, with lots of creativity, imagination, and common sense. If one were to say you were psychic, you'd probably respond that you have natural intelligence and insight. You could be an inventor, doctor, creator, or producer, combining your creativity and intelligence. You're a jack-of-all trades. You have artistic talent, and if art is not your career, pursue it as a hobby for personal fulfillment. Golf, cars, and sports all appeal to you, as do antiques.

You need attention and get it. If those around you are inattentive, you become cranky. You are sympathetic and kind, a true, faithful friend. Your aspirations and impulsiveness make you a most intriguing and alluring companion. You want a long-term mate. You often bite off more than you can chew and may have problems interacting in unfamiliar groups. You're comfortable as a social butterfly and as a caterpillar in the cocoon. Society accepts you at work or play, and you may find yourself with people in high places. When you get bored, find a good book or great movie, and you'll soon be climbing mountains with the cast, or fighting the bad guys. Such escapism is therapeutic for you. Although you may think you are escaping into the darkness, you are, in reality, finding the light.

✶ ✶ ✶

APRIL 3

ARIES • The lamb of god

March 20 at 5:00 P.M. to April 20 at 4:00 A.M. • NUMEROLOGY 3

Possessions and Desires . . .

Gem: Ruby—This stone may lead you to energy, friendship, and happiness.

Flower: Meadow Saffron—You tend to dwell too much on past experiences.

Astral Color, Color Need, Apparel Color: Your Astral Color is White, which gives you clarity. Red in your environment gives you energy and stamina. In your wardrobe, Raspberry brings you power and stimulation.

Fragrance: Use the subtlest hints of lemon or other citrus fruits to bring freshness into your surroundings. These scents will give you the energy to make things happen in your life.

Tree: Elm—You have willpower, strength, and the ability to stand alone.

Instrument: Trombone

Composers: Verdi, Mendelssohn, Schumann

Bird: Swan—Regarded as royal and sacred, this bird has the protective nature of a mother, and can become a furious fighter in the defense of its young.

Symbol: Wreath—You have been crowned with a special personality. You are strong but extremely compassionate.

Harmonious Health and Nutrition . . .

Health Scent: Raspberry—This scent might bring you a feeling of harmony with the universe.

Favorable Foods: Mustard greens, strawberries, caraway seeds, chocolate, eggs

What's Lucky . . .

Lucky Numbers: 1, 9, 19

Best Months: June and July

Best Day of the Week: Tuesday

Best Month Days: 3, 12, 21, 30

Lucky Charm: A pen that someone else has already used.

Harmonious Signs for Relationships and Partnerships: Sagittarius and Leo

Spiritual Guides . . .

Star: Al Thurauya—Woe to the enemies of those with this star!

Angel: Malchidiel—This is the angel of new beginnings and innovative ideas.

Guardian Angel: Johiel—This angel is a protector of all those with a humble heart.

Spiritual Stone: Beryl—This stone is good for meditation and concentration.

✶ JUDITH'S INSIGHT ✶

You are gifted with great mental energy, innovative schemes, and original plans for interesting things. Since you're strong and self-willed, you make things happen. There is nothing you cannot accomplish. You're candid, positive, forceful, even heroic. You're a natural leader, with many followers. Your leadership ability could enhance or injure a relationship.

Much depends on your mate. Your enterprising and venturesome ways are attractive, and your mate appreciates your spontaneity. Pure energy and ambition will carry you far, even in relationships. In all likelihood your significant other adores you year after year. If a love relationship does fail, another will appear in its place. You are the responsible one—serene yet caring—the one who picks up the pieces for the family. You gain respect from friends in social situations. Children and family mean the world to you, but be on guard—you do not own them. Distinguish between favor and obligation. You will have powerful friends but could make powerful enemies. Most definitely you will be head of the house and possibly even the Senate. Friends and family think you live a charmed life because you make things look easy. What throws others doesn't faze you. You conquer major obstacles as if you were tying your shoes.

When it comes to your life's work, your capabilities are endless and your choices inexhaustible. You could be anything from critic to editor, banker, accountant, police officer and very possibly lawyer, or judge, and you have no problem maintaining dual careers. If not, one career and many hobbies may be for you. You are at your best when your energy is up; just be careful to watch your blood pressure. Your toughness is complemented by your warmth—you are a true diamond in the rough.

APRIL 4
ARIES • The lamb of god
March 20 at 5:00 P.M. to April 20 at 4:00 A.M. • NUMEROLOGY 4

Possessions and Desires . . .

Gem: Emerald—Those who carry this stone tend to be lucky in love.
Flower: Reed—You tend to love music and may be very gifted in that art.
Astral Color, Color Need, Apparel Color: Your Astral Color is Pink, which reflects your compassion. Red in your environment gives you energy and stamina. In your wardrobe, Copper brings you confidence and a sharp appearance.
Fragrance: Use the subtlest hints of lemon or other citrus fruits to bring freshness into your surroundings. These scents will give you the energy to make things happen in your life.
Tree: Cherry—You will find yourself faced with constant new emotional awakenings.
Instruments: Bass, clarinet
Composers: Haydn, Wagner
Bird: Robin—the most sociable of all birds with the ability to create quick friendships. It also can easily adapt to any home. When it wants something, it has the tendency to try to snatch it.
Symbol: Star—You are full of inner brightness and will stand out in any crowd. You will be seen as special.

Harmonious Health and Nutrition . . .

Health Scent: Vanilla—This scent will fill you with a feeling of cleanliness and stability.
Favorable Foods: Lentils, apples, rye crisps, molasses, cottage cheese

What's Lucky . . .

Lucky Numbers: 1, 4, 9
Best Months: June and July
Best Day of the Week: Tuesday
Best Month Days: 4, 13, 22, 31
Lucky Charm: A piece of material cut from something in your home.
Harmonious Signs for Relationships and Partnerships: Sagittarius and Leo

Spiritual Guides . . .

Star: Al Thurauya—Woe to the enemies of those with this star!
Angel: Malchidiel—This is the angel of new beginnings and innovative ideas.
Guardian Angel: Uriel—This angel brings the light of God's guidance.
Spiritual Stone: Beryl—This stone is good for meditation and concentration.

✶ JUDITH'S INSIGHT ✶

Your place is at the bargaining table or in a debate. The skills you have could be fine-tuned for the White House. You are a thinker, a reasoner, and the one with imagination. To top it off, you possess an endearing sense of humor. You have the admiration of friends and family, since you not only bring home the bacon, you fry it up and present it to your neighbor so she can feed her man. Others view you as nice and kindhearted, but you're terrible if someone double-crosses you. You lean toward unconventional relationships. You welcome responsibility but must guard against taking on more than you want to handle.

Your mate sees you as challenging and steadfast. Be careful that others don't misread you. Poor communication on your part could pose relationship problems. Sometimes you seem demanding and must soften your approach. Your relationships improve tremendously when you listen. Your charm and wit bring many to you, and your social calendar will be full. The pressures of trying to balance friends and family may feel burdensome, but you can do it.

You're inventive and creative with many ideas, and you also know how to implement them. Your efforts could mean a novel yet lucrative career for you. In this computer age, programming or analysis could work well for you. Develop those original ideas, keep your hands busy stirring more than one pot, and you can have a very good income. Lucky in financial affairs and capable of adapting quickly, you can respond favorably to sudden, unexpected changes. For such a conventional person with a conventional lifestyle, you can expect very unconventional things to happen.

✶ ✶ ✶

APRIL 5

ARIES • The lamb of god

March 20 at 5:00 P.M. to April 20 at 4:00 A.M. • NUMEROLOGY 5

Possessions and Desires . . .

Gem: Amethyst—This stone is said to give calmness and peace.

Flower: Mouse-ear Chickweed—You are usually clever enough to see that keeping life simple works best for you.

Astral Color, Color Need, Apparel Color: Your Astral Color is White, which gives you clarity. Red in your environment gives you energy and stamina. In your wardrobe, Green is your power color for overcoming obstacles.

Fragrance: Use the subtlest hints of lemon or other citrus fruits to bring freshness into your surroundings. These scents will give you the energy to make things happen in your life.

Tree: Apple—You are creative, full of joy, and nearly magical. You bring happiness.

Instruments: viola, trumpet

Composer: Liszt

Bird: Flamingo—This beautiful, gregarious bird is always careful of its enemy. It is also a caretaker of the young who tries to keep everyone happy.

Symbol: Triangle—You have the right combination of abilities.

Harmonious Health and Nutrition . . .

Health Scents: Peach—This scent may balance your good qualities so that they equal your charm.

Favorable Foods: Endive, prunes, caraway seeds, chocolate, buttermilk

What's Lucky . . .

Lucky Numbers: 1, 5, 9
Best Months: June and July
Best Day of the Week: Tuesday
Best Month Days: 4, 5, 23
Lucky Charms: A rabbit's foot or a white candle
Harmonious Signs for Relationships and Partnerships: Sagittarius and Leo

Spiritual Guides . . .

Star: Al Botein—Those with this star often feel that they are under lots of pressure.

Angel: Malchidiel—This is the angel of new beginnings and innovative ideas.

Guardian Angel: Phanuel—protection against the negative.

Spiritual Stone: Beryl—This stone is good for meditation and concentration.

✶ JUDITH'S INSIGHT ✶

Confident, courageous, convinced, impulsive, stubborn, and strong-willed are all terms that could describe you. These traits usually complement each other, but occasionally they collide. Confidence in your own judgment carries you far, but watch out whose feathers you may ruffle. Generally, to know you is to like you. But sometimes knowing you is loving you, and sometimes those who love you most have a tough time liking you. Anything you devote yourself to can be achieved. Your intuition is good and the outcome is usually always right, but you are not always satisfied with the results. Trust your intuitions more. As you age, relationships improve as more people learn that everything you do comes first from the heart. You have a roving eye, but when you get into a monogamous relationship, you are dedicated.

Your diligence at work and at play brings success. Your employer is satisfied with your performance. You, the employee, are not so satisfied. You demand much of yourself. When your turn comes, you are a terrific manager and a great boss. By not overdelegating to others, you share the workload, and everyone benefits by your teaching. Talented with things mechanical, you like to build, create, and sometimes critique. This could lead to one of many different careers for you. You must work from the bottom up, whether it be funding a foundation or building an empire. You'll be successful—it just may take time. This poses problems for you; patience is not your strongest virtue.

You love money and enjoy being the breadwinner. You could be less demanding, more easygoing. You can be all work and no play, or all play and no work at all. You must somehow learn to balance the two.

✶ ✶ ✶

APRIL 6   ARIES • The lamb of god
March 20 at 5:00 P.M. to April 20 at 4:00 A.M. • NUMEROLOGY 6

Possessions and Desires . . .

Gem: Topaz—This is an excellent gift to be exchanged between very loyal friends.

Flower: Myrrh—You have many reasons to be glad just to be alive.

Astral Color, Color Need, Apparel Color: Your Astral Color is Pink, which reflects your compassion. Red in your environment gives you energy and stamina. In your wardrobe, Maroon gives you confidence.

Fragrance: Use the subtlest hints of lemon or other citrus fruits to bring freshness into your surroundings. These scents will give you the energy to make things happen in your life.

Tree: Palm—You tend to be very healthy and creative.

Instruments: Tambourine, lyre

Composer: Schubert

Bird: Falcon—an expert hunter. When well-trained, it can adapt to many tasks and is usually obedient.

Symbol: Crescent—You are more likely to be influenced by the phases of the moon. Your easy-going manner leads you to peaceful situations.

Harmonious Health and Nutrition . . .

Health Scent: Orange Blossom—This scent may balance your body, mind, and soul.

Favorable Foods: Asparagus, apricots, rye crisps, maple sugar, pressed cheese

What's Lucky . . .

Lucky Numbers: 1, 9, 24, 33

Best Months: June and July

Best Day of the Week: Tuesday

Best Month Days: 6, 15, 24

Lucky Charms: A religious token or card from any religion.

Harmonious Signs for Relationships and Partnerships: Sagittarius and Leo

Spiritual Guides . . .

Star: Al Sheratan—Those with this star hide their pain from those who could help them.

Angel: Malchidiel—This is the angel of new beginnings and innovative ideas.

Guardian Angel: Michael—"Who is like God."

Spiritual Stone: Beryl—This stone is good for meditation and concentration.

✶ JUDITH'S INSIGHT ✶

The key to your happiness is to stop taking life so seriously. You work hard and play hard, and take things to extremes. It's not that your expectations are too high, just that you don't always allow yourself enough time to achieve them. You will be successful, no doubt; you just need to get out of your own way and pay less attention to those who get in your way. Live more in the present and enjoy your dreams as you have them. You are harder on yourself than anyone else.

You're affectionate, demonstrative and warm-hearted. Passionate, too—you are especially attractive to the opposite sex. You are popular socially and make friends wherever you go. Make sure low self-esteem doesn't interfere with letting relationships happen. A satisfying love relationship generally comes later in life. You love to spend money and show off your home and surroundings. You insist on having nice things. Be careful, though, and curb your generosity so it doesn't impoverish you.

Success awaits in artistic circles, such as painting, music, sculpture, poetry, or literature. Your fondness of theater and opera can also result in professional possibilities. You are a caretaker by nature, so if an artistic career doesn't develop, be sure to utilize your nurturing qualities in caring for others. Because you are so emotional, you empathize with others' needs. Pursuing a profession in psychiatry, nursing, or teaching would work well for you.

In money matters, you're lucky during the early part of your life, but less so as the years pass. After forty, you will again enjoy financial success. Remember, opening the palm of your hand makes it more likely that another will place something in it, including his or her hand.

✶ ✶ ✶

APRIL 7 ARIES • The lamb of god
March 20 at 5:00 P.M. to April 20 at 4:00 A.M. • NUMEROLOGY 7

Possessions and Desires . . .

Gem: Diamond—This stone is thought to encourage harmony in relationships and gives strength to the troubled.

Flower: Hop—You tend to loathe injustice.

Astral Color, Color Need, Apparel Color: Your Astral Color is White, which gives you clarity. Red in your environment gives you energy and stamina. In your wardrobe, Raspberry gives you power and stimulation.

Fragrance: Use the subtlest hints of lemon or other citrus fruits to bring freshness into your surroundings. These scents will give you the energy to make things happen in your life.

Tree: Sycamore—Yours is the ability to love, communicate honestly with others, and have lasting relationships.

Instrument: Harp

Composers: Gluck, Brahms

Bird: Warbling Parakeet—the most beautiful of all birds, known as the love bird. It does seem to have the powers of imitation.

Symbol: Heart—You are enthusiastic, empathetic, and full of generosity and love.

Harmonious Health and Nutrition . . .

Health Scent: Jasmine—This scent may make you more easygoing when you are stressed.

Favorable Foods: Asparagus, apricots, rye crisps, maple sugar, pressed cheese

What's Lucky . . .

Lucky Numbers: 1, 7, 9
Best Months: June and July
Best Day of the Week: Tuesday
Best Month Days: 6, 15, 24
Lucky Charm: An old key.
Harmonious Signs for Relationships and Partnerships: Sagittarius and Leo

Spiritual Guides . . .

Star: Al Thurauya—Woe to the enemies of those with this star!

Angel: Malchidiel—This is the angel of new beginnings and innovative ideas.

Guardian Angel: Raphael—This angel attends to all of your needs when you are looking for guidance.

Spiritual Stone: Beryl—This stone is good for meditation and concentration.

✳ JUDITH'S INSIGHT ✳

You are cautious by nature; sometimes your prudence prevents you from doing the things you really want. You are a shining star—the only one that doesn't know the brightness of your shining is you. Others see you in a completely different light from how you see yourself. Unfortunately, your keen intuition benefits others more than yourself. Your heart is made of gold, but be careful where you spend it. You like to explore the unknown, and would make a fine detective. Develop your deep love for music and your hidden love for the theatre. Passion couples well with your original ideas. You are likely to be considered a crank or eccentric by those who don't understand you. You will always have an intense desire for travel away from your birthplace and experience a restlessness because of it. You are always looking to change your surroundings.

You will not be happy with a commonplace job. I wouldn't be surprised to find you racing cars, or inventing new parts for them. More inventive and creative than you give yourself credit for, you will feel more satisfied once you recognize your own skills. Your home is where your heart will be, and a place you create for yourself. You're inclined to live in the land of dreams and illusions regarding the opposite sex, so expect some disappointments. Fear not, though, for you will meet your soul mate and feel at last you have found someone who really understands you, even if you don't yet fully understand yourself.

✳ ✳ ✳

APRIL 8

ARIES • The lamb of god

March 20 at 5:00 P.M. to April 20 at 4:00 A.M. • NUMEROLOGY 8

Possessions and Desires . . .

Gem: Diamond—This stone is thought to encourage harmony in relationships and gives strength to the troubled.

Flower: Almond Tree—You always have hope in your heart that things will get better.

Astral Color, Color Need, Apparel Color: Your Astral Color is Pink, which reflects your compassion. Red in your environment gives you energy and stamina. In your wardrobe, Gray brings out the best in your looks.

Fragrance: Use the subtlest hints of lemon or other citrus fruits to bring freshness into your surroundings. These scents will give you the energy to make things happen in your life.

Tree: Pine—Your relationships tend to be balanced, both emotionally and mentally.

Instrument: Cello

Composer: Mozart

Bird: Bobolink—This charming singer is equally good as a soloist or a member of an orchestra. It is a very romantic bird, most useful as an insect destroyer, and elegant, with beautiful feathers, and always pleasant to have around.

Symbol: Wings—You are the source of balance in your world—this will bring you contentment.

Harmonious Health and Nutrition . . .

Health Scent: Almond—This scent may revitalize you and open you to greater possibilities.

Favorable Foods: Endive, strawberries, caraway seeds, molasses, buttermilk

What's Lucky . . .

Lucky Numbers: 1, 8, 9
Best Months: June and July
Best Day of the Week: Tuesday
Best Month Days: 8, 17, 26
Lucky Charm: Red ribbon in your wallet or doorway
Harmonious Signs for Relationships and Partnerships: Sagittarius and Leo

Spiritual Guides . . .

Star: Al Sheratan—Those with this star hide their pain from those who could help them.

Angel: Malchidiel—This is the angel of new beginnings and innovative ideas.

Guardian Angel: Seraphim—An angel that brings love, light, and passion.

Spiritual Stone: Beryl—This stone is good for meditation and concentration

✶ JUDITH'S INSIGHT ✶

Suspicious, inquisitive, and skeptical by nature, you are extremely reserved and distrustful of people, but you become devoted to those who do pass your test. You are very patient and kind, and ultraconsiderate, in a relationship—once you get there. Although you will do anything for your family, there are times when family overwhelms you. You would make a good government official, detective or investigator. Your tenacity can persevere to the end. You are dedicated and productive no matter what job you take on: attorney, judge, critic, journalist, supervisor, or machinist. You will get the job done and do it well. Remarkable ideas and plans for starting new industries or developing business on any scale, large or small, start with you. They say money does not make the man or woman, but you are the man or woman that will make the money.

Your greatest difficulty will be in finding others who see eye to eye with you. With your perseverance, personal power, and determination, you are likely to carry anything through to the end. Eventually you will enjoy the financial fruit of your labor. Your life, however, brims with contradictions. You want to make your mark and will be confronted with much opposition in carrying out your plans. You can overcome the hurdles, easily or not, and achieve your goals. When it comes to hobby or work, look for things that enlarge your life. Developing or marketing perfumes or cultivating or selling flowers, plants, or trees will bring you satisfaction. If you are unable to work in these or other such fields, your creativity will be expanded through your fondness for music and the decorative arts.

✶ ✶ ✶

APRIL 9
ARIES • The lamb of god

March 20 at 5:00 P.M. to April 20 at 4:00 A.M. • NUMEROLOGY 9

Possessions and Desires . . .

Gem: Amethyst—This stone is said to give calmness and peace.

Flower: Balsam—You are a very sympathetic person.

Astral Color, Color Need, Apparel Color: Your Astral Color is White, which gives you clarity. Red in your environment gives you energy and stamina. In your wardrobe, Copper gives you confidence and a sharp appearance.

Fragrance: Use the subtlest hints of lemon or other citrus fruits to bring freshness into your surroundings. These scents will give you the energy to make things happen in your life.

Tree: Holly—Beware that you are not carried away by your passionate nature. The only way to grow is to be open to new experiences.

Instruments: Violin, tympanum

Composer: Gluck

Bird: Warbling Parakeet—the most beautiful of all birds, known as the love bird. It does seem to have the powers of imitation.

Symbol: Anchor—This tranquil symbol signifies stability and strength, and stands for strong commitments in relationships.

Harmonious Health and Nutrition . . .

Health Scent: Lavender—This scent might lead others to trust you and make you patient.

Favorable Foods: Dried beans, watermelon, rye crisps, raw sugar, pressed cheese

What's Lucky . . .

Lucky Numbers: 1, 9, 10

Best Months: June and July

Best Day of the Week: Tuesday

Best Month Days: 9, 18, 27

Lucky Charms: A U.S. coin or a bill of any amount from the year you were born.

Harmonious Signs for Relationships and Partnerships: Sagittarius and Leo

Spiritual Guides . . .

Star: Al Botein—Those with this star often feel that they are under lots of pressure.

Angel: Malchidiel—This is the angel of new beginnings and innovative ideas.

Guardian Angel: Gabriel—"God is my strength."

Spiritual Stone: Beryl—This stone is good for meditation and concentration.

✳ JUDITH'S INSIGHT ✳

You're extremely independent in thought and action, and have a strong dislike for restrictions and limitations of any kind. You are inclined to candidly express your opinions, sometimes too frankly, while disregarding the feelings of others. You are sometimes combative, and you rush into quarrels or arguments simply because of your impulsive nature. You love running risks and are fearless in the face of danger. At the same time, you can be very nurturing, and are a good volunteer, caretaker, or listener, anxious to lend a helping hand. Be careful of minor accidents: you may slip and fall on ice, crash the car, or trip down the stairs. Don't worry, there won't be any permanent damage, but you are a lawyer's dream. You will have more than your share of love affairs, even if no one in your family knows about them. You are flirtatious by nature, but in a naive way. You are blessed with endless vitality and recover quickly from illness.

You are likely to be more fortunate in money matters after midlife, but you will still be comfortable in earlier years. You'll have to work hard for your money. Your friends admire you. Remember to look for a career that allows independence and creativity, like a computer specialist or graphic artist. Do not be surprised if you find yourself searching for a new career after a few years, even if it is within the same company. You desire authority and would like that at work. Somewhere along the way, your creativity has to come in to play.

✳ ✳ ✳

APRIL 10 ARIES • The lamb of god
March 20 at 5:00 P.M. to April 20 at 4:00 A.M. • NUMEROLOGY 1

Possessions and Desires . . .

Gem: Beryl—This gem could be good for meditation and concentration.
Flower: Barberry—You can have very black moods sometimes.
Astral Color, Color Need, Apparel Color: Your Astral Color is Pink, which emanates compassion. Red in your environment gives you energy and stamina. In your wardrobe, Green is your power color for overcoming obstacles.
Fragrance: Use the subtlest hints of lemon or other citrus fruits to bring freshness into your surroundings. These scents will give you the energy to make things happen in your life.
Tree: Walnut—You are unusually helpful and always looking for new beginnings.
Instruments: Oboe, flute, clarinet, piano, French horn, organ, and piccolo
Composer: Böhm
Bird: Hummingbird—This bird is delicate and graceful. It can remain still for hours, then dart off and be as busy as a bee.
Symbol: Crown—the universal sign of dignity.

Harmonious Health and Nutrition . . .

Health Scent: Strawberry—soothing by nature, the strawberry promotes self-esteem and encourages love.
Favorable Foods: Endive, strawberries, caraway seeds, molasses, buttermilk

What's Lucky . . .

Lucky Numbers: 10, 19, 20
Best Months: June and July
Best Day of the Week: Tuesday
Best Month Days: 1, 10, 19, 28
Lucky Charm: A new penny in your shoe.
Harmonious Signs for Relationships and Partnerships: Sagittarius and Leo

Spiritual Guides . . .

Star: Al Botein—Those with this star often feel that they are under lots of pressure.
Angel: Malchidiel—This is the angel of new beginnings and innovative ideas.
Guardian Angel: Malachi—"Messenger of Jehovah."
Spiritual Stone: Beryl—This stone is good for meditation and concentration.

✶ JUDITH'S INSIGHT ✶

Energetic and courageous, for you honesty is not just the best policy . . . it's the *only* one. Life must be full of problem-solving and challenges to keep you happy. You are well spoken, especially when talking of something about which you care deeply. Sometimes you let difficulties cloud your sparkling zest for life. Don't allow others to sabotage your energy.

Your fiery and forceful nature may sometimes complicate relationships, but because of your smooth, cunning way, you win more hearts than you lose. If you actually caught the person who is your romantic ideal, you'd more than likely be miserable, for what you want and what you need are two different things. Family and friends mean everything to you even though you rarely express this aloud.

Your drive and determination are powerful propellers. The only time "vice" is mentioned in connection with you is when it's paired with "president." Careers in law, finance, or sales are best for you. Working or just dabbling in real estate could bring big rewards. A property inheritance may turn up in your lifetime.

Fun to be with, you have a terrific sense of humor, except when the joke's on you. Your gift for mixing things up makes your parties amusing and diverse. Don't be surprised if you find yourself in the public eye. You make a loyal friend as long as you receive loyalty in return. Seemingly reckless, make sure those around you realize you know exactly what you're doing.

✶ ✶ ✶

APRIL 11 ARIES • The lamb of god

March 20 at 5:00 P.M. to April 20 at 4:00 A.M. • NUMEROLOGY 2

Possessions and Desires . . .

Gem: Sapphire—This gem may help you find forgiveness from those you've wronged.

Flower: Beech Tree—You will have a life of emotional prosperity.

Astral Color, Color Need, Apparel Color: Your Astral Color is White, which gives you clarity. Red in your environment gives you energy and stamina. In your wardrobe, Maroon gives you confidence.

Fragrance: Use the subtlest hints of lemon or other citrus fruits to bring freshness into your surroundings. These scents will give you the energy to make things happen in your life.

Tree: Maple—You have both great stability and flashes of intuition.

Instruments: Pipe organ, cymbal, drum

Composers: Handel, Johann Sebastian Bach

Bird: Stork—Turkish bird, held in high esteem the world over. This bird is intelligent but may have strange tendencies.

Symbol: Cross—the symbol of self-sacrifice and reconciliation.

Harmonious Health and Nutrition . . .

Health Scent: Apple—You are creative, full of joy, and nearly magical. You bring happiness.

Favorable Foods: Parsley, prunes, caraway seeds, buttermilk

What's Lucky . . .

Lucky Numbers: 1, 2, 9

Best Months: June and July

Best Day of the Week: Tuesday

Best Month Days: 2, 11, 20, 29

Lucky Charms: Two 50-cent pieces. Give someone else one of them.

Harmonious Signs for Relationships and Partnerships: Sagittarius and Leo

Spiritual Guides . . .

Star: Al Sheratan—Those with this star hide their pain from those who could help them

Angel: Malchidiel—This is the angel of new beginnings and innovative ideas.

Guardian Angel: Uriel—This angel brings the light of God's guidance.

Spiritual Stone: Beryl—This stone is good for meditation and concentration.

✶ JUDITH'S INSIGHT ✶

You have original, unconventional ideas with an imagination beyond compare. You are a pleasure to be around, and your genuine enthusiasm even makes work pleasurable for coworkers. You not only accomplish just about everything you attempt, but you often exceed your expectations. You work well in partnerships. You may often change your occupation simply because you tire of things if you are tied down too long at one job. With enough diversity, however, you find it easier to remain in one position longer.

Your restlessness could be detrimental at home. You need someone who understands your desire for spontaneity and constant adventure. Marriage can work if it has unconventional overtones in a conventional life setting.

A wide choice of occupations awaits you—there are few things you cannot accomplish. Your inventive nature draws you to creative jobs, although you possess the ability to maintain and sustain just about any career. You may be particularly attracted to jobs that utilize your mechanical aptitude, from fixing computers to repairing airplane engines. You'd also be a dedicated teacher or police officer. You are exceptionally self-reliant and decisive and seek authority over others, even when there is no authority to be had. Watch your sarcasm and criticism. Your forcefulness will make you friends or stir up enemies.

You stick like glue to a friend who is good to you. Through thick and thin, you will always be there to offer support. You know how to keep a promise. Fond of fun and frolic, you show devotion to those devoted to you, and you go to great lengths to ensure their good time.

✶ ✶ ✶

APRIL 12

ARIES • The lamb of god

March 20 at 5:00 P.M. to April 20 at 4:00 A.M. • NUMEROLOGY 3

Possessions and Desires . . .

Gem: Ruby—This stone may lead you to energy, friendship, and happiness.
Flower: Bindweed—You are usually too humble.
Astral Color, Color Need, Apparel Color: Your Astral Color is Pink, which reflects your compassion. Red in your environment gives you energy and stamina. In your wardrobe, Copper gives you confidence and a sharp appearance.
Fragrance: Use the subtlest hints of lemon or other citrus fruits to bring freshness into your surroundings. These scents will give you the energy to make things happen in your life.
Tree: Elm—You have willpower, strength, and the ability to stand alone.
Instrument: Trombone
Composers: Verdi, Mendelssohn, Schumann
Bird: Swan—Regarded as royal and sacred, this bird has the protective nature of a mother and can become a furious fighter in the defense of its young.
Symbol: Wreath—You have been crowned with a special personality. You are strong but extremely compassionate.

Harmonious Health and Nutrition . . .

Health Scent: Rose—This scent will lead you to passionate thoughts and make you feel warm inside.
Favorable Foods: Asparagus, strawberries, raw sugar, cottage cheese

What's Lucky . . .

Lucky Numbers: 1, 3, 6, 9
Best Months: June and July
Best Day of the Week: Tuesday
Best Month Days: 3, 12, 21, 30
Lucky Charm: A pen that someone else has already used.
Harmonious Signs for Relationships and Partnerships: Sagittarius and Leo

Spiritual Guides . . .

Star: Al Botein—Those with this star often feel that they are under lots of pressure.
Angel: Malchidiel—This is the angel of new beginnings and innovative ideas.
Guardian Angel: Johiel—This angel is a protector of all those with a humble heart.
Spiritual Stone: Beryl—This stone is good for meditation and concentration.

✴ JUDITH'S INSIGHT ✴

You are viewed as leading an enchanted life, and for the most part, you do. You're a good person and a caring friend, and are much more independent than you think. Your ambition takes you to great heights, and you appreciate the prestige and the company of high-achieving friends. You have a more philosophical mind and sympathetic nature than most get to see. Part of you is always hidden behind a door—very few get to see what you are all about. You're protective by nature and fearful of hurting yourself. Somewhere along the way, someone hurt you and never apologized. It may seem to take forever, but love does prevail. Be sure you don't sacrifice yourself for your mate. Happiness could be yours if your courage is as strong as your honor.

Your executive skills should bring you to the top, but unfortunately this does not mean overnight. Give it time. Don't be alarmed should you switch careers in midlife and delve into something you never dreamed possible. Your talents are varied and many. You would make a great psychologist, stockbroker, lawyer, or master of ceremonies. Lose the fear of committing to your own business now, and later in life you'll see that's where you should be. Prepare yourself for an entirely independent situation. You are endowed with a strong sense of responsibility and along the way will assume the obligations of others. Just remember to smile—laughter and happiness are truly your best medicine.

✶ ✶ ✶

APRIL 13 ARIES • The lamb of god
March 20 at 5:00 P.M. to April 20 at 4:00 A.M. • NUMEROLOGY 4

Possessions and Desires . . .

Gem: Emerald—Those who carry this stone tend to be lucky in love.
Flower: Cinquefoil—You tend be the advisor to friends and family.
Astral Color, Color Need, Apparel Color: Your Astral Color is White, which gives you clarity. Red in your environment gives you energy and stamina. In your wardrobe, Raspberry gives you power and stimulation.
Fragrance: Use the subtlest hints of lemon or other citrus fruits to bring freshness into your surroundings. These scents will give you the energy to make things happen in your life.
Tree: Cherry—You will find yourself faced with constant new emotional awakenings.
Instruments: Bass, clarinet
Composers: Haydn, Wagner
Bird: Skylark—This handsome bird is beautiful when it sings. It always whistles as it works.
Symbol: Star—You are full of inner brightness and will stand out in any crowd. You will be seen as special.

Harmonious Health and Nutrition . . .

Health Scent: Vanilla—This scent will fill you with a feeling of cleanliness and stability.
Favorable Foods: Lentils, apples, maple sugar, eggs

What's Lucky . . .

Lucky Numbers: 1, 4, 8, 9
Best Months: June and July
Best Day of the Week: Tuesday
Best Month Days: 4, 13, 22, 31
Lucky Charm: A piece of material cut from something in your home.

Harmonious Signs for Relationships and Partnerships: Sagittarius and Leo

Spiritual Guides . . .

Star: Al Sheratan—Those with this star hide their pain from those who could help them
Angel: Malchidiel—This is the angel of new beginnings and innovative ideas.
Guardian Angel: Uriel—This angel brings the light of God's guidance.
Spiritual Stone: Beryl—This stone is good for meditation and concentration.

✷ JUDITH'S INSIGHT ✷

Anticipate the unexpected and go with the flow in making changes in your life, career, home, and family. Feelings of restlessness will resonate through your life. A great reader with a deep love for literature, you possess intense mental energy and activity. You want to be successful and your trump card may be in writing or graphic arts. Perhaps you'll run your own company. You work easily with others but are wary of tense atmospheres. Don't let these moments rattle you. You may become a schoolteacher or work with children in another capacity. You know how to interact with young people, and you reap the rewards as they respond to you. When you look for a job, disregard monotonous positions. You could be an attorney, financier, or salesperson. You simply thrive on change and spontaneity. You are idealistic, with strong personal ethics; when it comes to devotion to a mate or a friend, there is none better than you. While you generate much power and energy, take care to prevent others from draining you. Don't expend more than you can give. Many times you stick to an undertaking long after you should. You love your home and environment but are not averse to relocating if necessary. No matter where you build your nest, it will be a true home.

✷ ✷ ✷

APRIL 14 ARIES • The lamb of god
March 20 at 5:00 P.M. to April 20 at 4:00 A.M. • NUMEROLOGY 5

Possessions and Desires . . .

Gem: Diamond—This stone is thought to encourage harmony in relationships and gives strength to the troubled.

Flower: Birch—Your meekness disguises a vibrant fantasy life.

Astral Color, Color Need, Apparel Color: Your Astral Color is Pink, which emanates confidence. Red in your environment gives you energy and stamina. In your wardrobe, Gray brings out the best in your looks.

Fragrance: Use the subtlest hints of lemon or other citrus fruits to bring freshness into your surroundings. These scents will give you the energy to make things happen in your life.

Tree: Apple—You are creative, full of joy, and nearly magical. You bring happiness.

Instruments: Viola, trumpet

Composer: Liszt

Bird: Flamingo—this beautiful, gregarious bird is always careful of its enemy. It is also a caretaker of the young who tries to keep everyone happy.

Symbol: Triangle—You have the right combination of abilities.

Harmonious Health and Nutrition . . .

Health Scent: Peach—This scent may balance your good qualities so that they equal your charm.

Favorable Foods: Peas, apricots, caraway seeds, chocolate, pressed cheese

What's Lucky . . .

Lucky Numbers: 1, 5, 9, 10
Best Months: June and July
Best Day of the Week: Tuesday
Best Month Days: 4, 5, 23
Lucky Charms: A rabbit's foot or a white candle

Harmonious Signs for Relationships and Partnerships: Sagittarius and Leo

Spiritual Guides . . .

Star: Al Thurauya—Woe to the enemies of those with this star!

Angel: Malchidiel—This is the angel of new beginnings and innovative ideas.

Guardian Angel: Plavwell—gives power and strength to one's presence.

Spiritual Stone: Beryl—This stone is good for meditation and concentration.

✷ JUDITH'S INSIGHT ✷

You're admired by friends and family, and you welcome their company. You can make anything happen. The only person to get in your way is you. Because you're clever, intelligent, and versatile, accomplishments come easily to you. You never shun hard work. Your contagious smile endears you to others. Quick wit and good reasoning enable you to adapt to anything. Your generosity of pocket and self is far better received than your generosity with advice. You will be most comfortable with the way you handle gifts, but do withhold the advice unless you're specifically asked for it. You're a good listener. You're one of the lucky ones, who seem to find a mate that you want to stick to and wants to stick to you. To know you is to love you so keep this in mind.

Authoritative careers beckon. You feel drawn to government careers. With your intense mind, however, big business is not far behind. You have many dreams and will attempt to follow them all. Remember to allow time for things to happen. Heavy responsibilities will burden you at an early age, and you take them seriously. Resolved responsibilities will be repeatedly replaced with new ones. You would make a great detective with your inherent curiosity and investigative qualities. You are an honorable friend and devoted parent. Loyalty is your best quality.

★ ★ ★

APRIL 15   ARIES • The lamb of god

March 20 at 5:00 P.M. to April 20 at 4:00 A.M. • NUMEROLOGY 6

Possessions and Desires . . .

Gem: Topaz—This is an excellent gift to be exchanged between very loyal friends.

Flower: China Aster—You like a lot of variety in your life.

Astral Color, Color Need, Apparel Color: Your Astral Color is Pink, which reflects your compassion. Red in your environment gives you energy and stamina. In your wardrobe, Maroon gives you confidence.

Fragrance: Use the subtlest hints of lemon or other citrus fruits to bring freshness into your surroundings. These scents will give you the energy to make things happen in your life.

Tree: Palm—You tend to be very healthy and creative.

Instruments: Tambourine, lyre

Composer: Schubert

Bird: Lark—known for the beauty of its song, which is sometimes very unusual. It is also credited with extraordinary intelligence.

Symbol: Crescent—You are more likely to be influenced by the phases of the moon. Your easygoing manner leads you to peaceful situations.

Harmonious Health and Nutrition . . .

Health Scent: Orange Blossom—This scent may balance your body, mind, and soul.

Favorable Foods: Spinach, prunes, rye crisps, molasses, buttermilk

What's Lucky . . .

Lucky Numbers: 1, 6, 9, 18
Best Months: June and July
Best Day of the Week: Tuesday
Best Month Days: 6, 15, 24
Lucky Charms: A religious token or card from any religion.

Harmonious Signs for Relationships and Partnerships: Sagittarius and Leo

Spiritual Guides . . .

Star: Al Botein—Those with this star often feel that they are under lots of pressure.

Angel: Malchidiel—This is the angel of new beginnings and innovative ideas.

Guardian Angel: Michael—"Who is like God,"

Spiritual Stone: Beryl—This stone is good for meditation and concentration.

✷ JUDITH'S INSIGHT ✷

A challenge here, a challenge there, you seek challenge everywhere. Develop that power of yours to resolve conflict, and you will rise to the top. Your overabundance of energy, however, must be contained and redirected. Freedom of mind, body, and soul is important to you. Your sense of freedom permeates your life, and you are denied little. Powerful within the family and much respected by friends, you love a homey atmosphere and need a settled haven. But you can stir the pot if things don't go your way. On occasion, you may be overbearing, but your good intentions prevail when a matter concerns your loved ones. These traits may both hinder and help you and your loved ones. Your task is recognizing what works for you and when. Have patience with yourself when it comes to finding a mate. It will take time.

Activity careers offer the best for you. Always include physical work for yourself, even if you are the boss. You could make a successful salesperson, as well as find satisfaction in police work or as an artist or medical assistant. You have a great scientific ability, whether you use it at work or play. You are diligent and principled and finish what you attempt. You take your responsibilities very seriously. You enjoy a battle of wits.

✷ ✷ ✷

APRIL 16   ARIES • The lamb of god
March 20 at 5:00 P.M. to April 20 at 4:00 A.M. • NUMEROLOGY 7

Possessions and Desires . . .

Gem: Amethyst—This stone is said to give calmness and peace.

Flower: Crocus—You may spend too much time stewing over those who have innocently harmed you.

Astral Color, Color Need, Apparel Color: Your Astral Color is White, giving you clarity. Red in your environment gives you energy and stamina. In your wardrobe, Copper gives you confidence and a sharp appearance.

Fragrance: Use the subtlest hints of lemon or other citrus fruits to bring freshness into your surroundings. These scents will give you the energy to make things happen in your life.

Tree: Sycamore—Yours is the ability to love, communicate honestly with others, and have lasting relationships.

Instrument: Harp

Composers: Gluck, Brahms

Bird: Skylark—This handsome bird is beautiful when it sings. It always whistles as it works.

Symbol: Heart—You are enthusiastic, empathetic, and full of generosity and love.

Harmonious Health and Nutrition . . .

Health Scent: Jasmine—This scent may make you more easygoing when you are stressed.

Favorable Foods: Spinach, watermelon, caraway seeds, maple sugar, cottage cheese

What's Lucky . . .

Lucky Numbers: 1, 7, 9, 21
Best Months: June and July
Best Day of the Week: Tuesday
Best Month Days: 6, 15, 24
Lucky Charm: An old key.

Harmonious Signs for Relationships and Partnerships: Sagittarius and Leo

Spiritual Guides . . .

Star: Al Sheratan—Those with this star hide their pain from those who could help them.

Angel: Malchidiel—This is the angel of new beginnings and innovative ideas.

Guardian Angel: Raphael—This angel attends to all of your needs when you are looking for guidance.

Spiritual Stone: Beryl—This stone is good for meditation and concentration.

✶ JUDITH'S INSIGHT ✶

You have a great spiritual side, but you may need more maturity to recognize it. You let caution rule your life. Out of fear and sensitivity, you allow yourself more disappointments than you should. You are naturally intelligent, but you tend to hide this from others and even yourself.

You have to put family in its place at times. Family cohesion will come in time, as does balance. Friends are occasionally almost too important to you, and you place far too much stock in what others say. All others are not smarter than you. Harmony in relationships is surfacing—allow it to be seen. When you want to, you can be a delightful, insightful soul. Let yourself be inspired by positive thoughts, and don't hide behind a cranky, negative exterior. If you want more out of life, go after it. The one you lie to most is yourself. Set yourself free! Decide you want happiness and you will find it.

In your career you will need time to reach the top. You could be a painter, sculptor, or you could also be a hospital administrator, law officer, or executive secretary. You're held back by thinking you don't want to go to the top. Believe it or not, that's where you belong. When you get there, you realize this.

✶ ✶ ✶

APRIL 17 ARIES • The lamb of god
March 20 at 5:00 P.M. to April 20 at 4:00 A.M. • NUMEROLOGY 8

Possessions and Desires . . .

Gem: Amethyst—This stone is said to give calmness and peace.

Flower: Daisy—You are probably very naïve.

Astral Color, Color Need, Apparel Color: Your Astral Color is Pink, which reflects your compassion. Red in your environment gives you energy and stamina. In your wardrobe, Raspberry gives you power and stimulation.

Fragrance: Use the subtlest hints of lemon or other citrus fruits to bring freshness into your surroundings. These scents will give you the energy to make things happen in your life.

Tree: Pine—Your relationships tend to be balanced, both emotionally and mentally.

Instrument: Cello

Composer: Mozart

Bird: Skylark—This handsome bird is beautiful when it sings. It always whistles as it works.

Symbol: Wings—You are the source of balance in your world—this will bring you contentment.

Harmonious Health and Nutrition . . .

Health Scent: Almond—This scent may revitalize you and open you to greater possibilities.

Favorable Foods: Parsley, strawberries, chocolate, buttermilk

What's Lucky . . .

Lucky Numbers: 1, 8, 9, 24
Best Months: June and July
Best Day of the Week: Tuesday
Best Month Days: 8, 17, 26
Lucky Charm: Red ribbon in your wallet or doorway.

Harmonious Signs for Relationships and Partnerships: Sagittarius and Leo

Spiritual Guides . . .

Star: Al Sheratan—Those with this star hide their pain from those who could help them.

Angel: Malchidiel—This is the angel of new beginnings and innovative ideas.

Guardian angel: Seraphim—An Angel that brings love, light, and passion.

Spiritual Stone: Beryl—This stone is good for meditation and concentration.

✷ JUDITH'S INSIGHT ✷

You're very sweet, very kind—almost to a fault. You give until there is no more to give. If only others could recognize your needs. You want everyone to be happy, because you deeply feel if those around you are happy, you'll be happy, too. Responsibility rests on your shoulders; sometimes you must learn to knock it off. Family can be your greatest love and your greatest detractor. Children often get the best of you in there younger years, but later they will give their best to you.

Be more selective in relationships because you're inclined to pick critical, controlling lovers. Choose the not-so-needy, and you'll get more out of the relationship. Don't be misled by your tendency to want to settle down. What you are doing is settling to avoid having to make decisions. Since you're the one that mends everybody's heart, it is hard for you to break anyone's heart.

You could be a lawyer but one with a nurturing and caring personality. You will probably find yourself doing a lot of pro bono work. You'll be a terrific parent. You will succeed.

✷ ✷ ✷

APRIL 18
ARIES • The lamb of god

March 20 at 5:00 P.M. to April 20 at 4:00 A.M. • NUMEROLOGY 9

Possessions and Desires . . .

Gem: Ruby—This stone may lead you to energy, friendship, and happiness.

Flower: Wild Grape—You tend to be charitable to those you feel deserve your help.

Astral Color, Color Need, Apparel Color: Your Astral Color is White, which gives you clarity. Red in your environment gives you energy and stamina. In your wardrobe, Gray brings out the best in your looks.

Fragrance: Use the subtlest hints of lemon or other citrus fruits to bring freshness into your surroundings. These scents will give you the energy to make things happen in your life.

Tree: Holly—Beware that you are not carried away by your passionate nature. The only way to grow is to be open to new experiences.

Instruments: Violin, tympanum

Composer: Gluck

Bird: Mockingbird—the most proficient minstrel in the world's orchestra; graceful and enthusiastic.

Symbol: Anchor—This tranquil symbol signifies stability and strength, and stands for strong commitments in relationships.

Harmonious Health and Nutrition . . .

Health Scent: Lavender—This scent might lead others to trust you and make you patient.

Favorable Foods: Mustard greens, apples, caraway seeds, molasses, eggs

What's Lucky . . .

Lucky Numbers: 1, 9, 18, 27
Best Months: June and July
Best Day of the Week: Tuesday
Best Month Days: 9, 18, 27
Lucky Charms: A U.S. coin or bill of any amount from the year you were born.

Harmonious Signs for Relationships and Partnerships: Sagittarius and Leo

Spiritual Guides . . .

Star: Al Botein—Those with this star often feel that they are under lots of pressure.

Angel: Malchidiel—This is the angel of new beginnings and innovative ideas.

Guardian Angel: Gabriel—"God is my strength."

Spiritual Stone: Beryl—This stone is good for meditation and concentration.

✶ JUDITH'S INSIGHT ✶

Because you're determined and focused, you should get anywhere you want to go. Though you will encounter obstacles, they need not deter you, and in time you will arrive at the destination you desire. It's entirely up to you. Some may think you pushy and anxious at times, but you do get the job done. You accomplish what you set out to do. Since you can be quick-tempered, you sometimes encumber your relationships. In time you will find a tolerant mate who doesn't take you so seriously and helps you to lighten up. You enjoy taking risks, but be forewarned—you could head right into the danger zone if you are not careful. You can use this risk taking to your advantage by choosing a career in law enforcement. Should you not be so inclined, your slot will be in a government institution, perhaps the post office, or a medical office or large company.

You must learn to balance your personality as well as your checkbook. You have the ability to make money, and you will do so, but you must curb your fondness for extravagant things and the desire to spend like mad. You are drawn to the extraordinary or unconventional and may find that you are only satisfied if you are driving an exotic sports car. You see life as a game—just remember, in games you can't always win; with every win there is a loss.

✶ ✶ ✶

APRIL 19 ARIES • The lamb of god

March 20 at 5:00 P.M. to April 20 at 4:00 A.M. • NUMEROLOGY 1

Possessions and Desires . . .

Gem: Turquoise—This stone may help you find material wealth.

Flower: Honey Flower—Your life tends to be sweet and sincere.

Astral Color, Color Need, Apparel Color: Your Astral Color is White, which gives you clarity. Red in your environment gives you energy and stamina. In your wardrobe, Gray brings out the best in your looks.

Fragrance: Use the subtlest hints of lemon or other citrus fruits to bring freshness into your surroundings. These scents will give you the energy to make things happen in your life.

Tree: Walnut—You are unusually helpful and always looking for new beginnings

Instruments: Oboe, flute, clarinet, piano, French horn, organ, piccolo

Composer: Böhm

Bird: Hummingbird—This bird is delicate and graceful. It can remain still for hours, then dart off and be as busy as a bee.

Symbol: Crown—the universal sign of dignity.

Harmonious Health and Nutrition . . .

Health Scent: Strawberry—soothing by nature, the strawberry promotes self-esteem and encourages love.

Favorable Foods: Beans, prunes, rye crisps, maple sugar, cottage cheese

What's Lucky . . .

Lucky Numbers: 1, 9, 20
Best Months: June and July
Best Day of the Week: Tuesday
Best Month Days: 1, 10, 19, 28

Lucky Charm: A new penny in your shoe.
Harmonious Signs for Relationships and Partnerships: Sagittarius and Leo

Spiritual Guides . . .

Star: Al Thurauya—Woe to the enemies of those with this star!

Angel: Malchidiel—This is the angel of new beginnings and innovative ideas.

Guardian Angel: Malachi—"Messenger of Jehovah."

Spiritual Stone: Beryl—This stone is good for meditation and concentration.

✶ JUDITH'S INSIGHT ✶

Generosity is only one of your fine traits. You are decidedly ambitious and will surpass those around you. You are likely to be the most successful and prominent member of your immediate family, eclipsing all your relations as well. Keep this in mind: you find more success with partners than without. This is where you need to develop patience. You're very creative. Your fearlessness and determination prompt success in whatever you decide to do. Lean toward careers that offer steady advancement. Take a job in the mail room at a Fortune 500 company; you will likely advance near the top even if it takes awhile. You would do well running a non-profit organization. You may end up in the public eye as a politician or actor.

You need romance as much as love. You need to be with a sentimental person who will not only adore you, but allow you freedom to have an unconventional home atmosphere. Children will definitely create and foster disputes in your life, but later on, children and family bring you harmony. Those around you require tolerance. As you learn to better communicate, you will be able to have and hold an enduring love.

✶ ✶ ✶

APRIL 20   ARIES • The lamb of god
March 20 at 5:00 P.M. to April 20 at 4:00 A.M. • NUMEROLOGY 2

Possessions and Desires . . .

Gem: Sapphire—This gem may help you find forgiveness from those you've wronged.
Flower: Withered Rose—Your love tends to last forever.
Astral Color, Color Need, Apparel Color: Your Astral Color is Pink, which reflects your compassion. Red in your environment gives you energy and stamina. In your wardrobe, Green is your power color for overcoming obstacles.
Fragrance: Use the subtlest hints of lemon or other citrus fruits to bring freshness into your surroundings. These scents will give you the energy to make things happen in your life.
Tree: Maple—You have both great stability and flashes of intuition.
Instruments: Pipe organ, cymbal, drum
Composers: Handel, Johann Sebastian Bach
Bird: Stork—Turkish bird, held in high esteem the world over. This bird is intelligent but may have strange tendencies.
Symbol: Cross—the symbol of self-sacrifice and reconciliation.

Harmonious Health and Nutrition . . .

Health Scent: Apple—You are creative, full of joy, and nearly magical. You bring happiness.
Favorable Foods: Dill, gooseberries, raw sugar, pressed cheese

What's Lucky . . .

Lucky Numbers: 1, 2, 4, 9
Best Months: June and July
Best Day of the Week: Tuesday
Best Month Days: 2, 11, 20, 29
Lucky Charms: Two 50-cent pieces. Give someone else one of them.

Harmonious Signs for Relationships and Partnerships: Sagittarius and Leo

Spiritual Guides . . .

Star: Al Botein—Those with this star often feel that they are under lots of pressure.
Angel: Malchidiel—This is the angel of new beginnings and innovative ideas.
Guardian Angel: Uriel—This angel brings the light of God's guidance.
Spiritual Stone: Beryl—This stone is good for meditation and concentration.

✶ JUDITH'S INSIGHT ✶

Tenacity is one of your most evident traits. You are also independent, ambitious, and determined. Be on guard, as your loved ones and others around you may feel neglected at times. Occupational changes may occur frequently, unless the atmosphere around you offers constant change. Although your desire for independence is strong, your desire to be with someone is even stronger. You like to be waited on hand and foot and on occasion are inclined to put your foot in your mouth. Relationships will work if you learn to better manage your emotions. Recognize that others may feel you don't want to let them in. All things considered, you have to be alert to recognize red flags' matters of love. Definitely admired by your friends and family and well-respected in the community, you will remember many fond flirtations along the way.

You will work hard for that high standing in the community, but once you get there, don't sit down. You must work at maintaining that status, for it can be fleeting. You love beautiful things and beautiful people. Working in the beauty or fashion industry would work well for you. You have plenty of talent, but you need a constant challenge.

✶ ✶ ✶

APRIL 21 TAURUS • The winged bull of the zodiac
April 20 at 4:00 A.M. to May 21 at 4:00 A.M. • NUMEROLOGY 3

Possessions and Desires . . .

Gem: Emerald—Those who carry this stone tend to be lucky in love.
Flower: Honeysuckle—You are a person filled with generous and devoted affections.
Astral Color, Color Need, Apparel Color: Your Astral Color is Red, which enhances passion, power, excitement, and strength. Yellow in your environment stimulates and exhilarates you. In your wardrobe, Blue-green enhances your luck and makes you feel secure.
Fragrance: You are devoted to the scent of roses. Choose the buds that have the strongest fragrance to create the special emotions you need.
Tree: Elm—You have willpower, strength, and the ability to stand alone.
Instrument: Trombone
Composers: Verdi, Mendelssohn, Schumann
Bird: Eagle—this bird is quick to use its powers of flight. It can see immeasurable distances in a single glance, and can sometimes appear to be indifferent.
Symbol: Wreath—You have been crowned with a special personality. You are strong but extremely compassionate.

Harmonious Health and Nutrition . . .

Health Scent: Rose—This scent will lead you to passionate thoughts and make you feel warm inside.
Favorable Foods: Kale, peaches, eggs, beef

What's Lucky . . .

Lucky Numbers: 3, 4, 5, 6
Best Months: May and July
Best Day of the Week: Friday
Best Month Days: 3, 12, 21, 30
Lucky Charm: A pen that someone else has already used.

Harmonious Signs for Relationships and Partnerships: Virgo, Capricorn, and sometimes Libra.

Spiritual Guides . . .

Star: Al Heka—Those with this star are driven to succeed.
Angel: Asmodel—This angel governs business and other transactions and aids in negotiations.
Guardian Angel: Johiel—This angel is a protector of all those with a humble heart.
Spiritual Stone: Topaz—This stone may protect the bearer from the effects of allergies.

✷ JUDITH'S INSIGHT ✷

Success awaits you in positions of authority, even if you don't think so now. Ambition gets you where you want to go. You are exceptionally capable, independent, and energized. In many areas, you lead a charmed life. Your mate is enamored with you and thrives on the spontaneity in your relationship. You are the romantic, however. Cultivate your sensibilities and let others touch your heart. You may wander through the school of hard knocks occasionally or even accept a few subliminal hard punches from time to time, but this growth can only help you become a better person.

You are best at delegating rather than undertaking matters yourself. This is true even in emotional situations, especially when it comes to family. If you have children, let them enjoy themselves even if you never had that opportunity as a child. You remain a child at heart but shield it well with your ultraresponsible nature. Strive for balance between being an adult and a child. Learn to take the best from both worlds.

Enjoying your friends is high on your list. Don't be surprised if they have relocated once or twice since you last called them. You are definitely a contradiction in every sense of the word. But that keeps them all guessing—even you.

✷ ✷ ✷

APRIL 22 TAURUS • The winged bull of the zodiac
April 20 at 4:00 A.M. to May 21 at 4:00 A.M. • NUMEROLOGY 4

Possessions and Desires . . .

Gem: Sapphire—This gem may help you find forgiveness from those you've wronged.

Flower: Yellow Jasmine—You are most often graceful and elegant.

Astral Color, Color Need, Apparel Color: Your Astral Color is Red, which enhances passion, power, excitement, and strength. Yellow in your environment stimulates and exhilarates you. In your wardrobe, Cream gives you encouragement and style.

Fragrance: You are devoted to the scent of roses. Choose the buds that have the strongest fragrance to create the special emotions you need.

Tree: Cherry—You will find yourself faced with constant new emotional awakenings.

Instruments: Bass, clarinet

Composers: Haydn and Wagner

Bird: Robin—the most sociable of all birds, with the ability to create quick friendships. It also can easily adapt to any home. When it wants something, it has the tendency to try to snatch it.

Symbol: Star—You are full of inner brightness and will stand out in any crowd. You will be seen as special.

Harmonious Health and Nutrition . . .

Health Scents: Vanilla—This scent will fill you with a feeling of cleanliness and stability.

Favorable Foods: Cabbage, bananas, cheese, salmon

What's Lucky . . .

Lucky Numbers: 4, 6, 8, 12
Best Months: May and July
Best Day of the Week: Friday
Best Month Days: 4, 13, 22, 31
Lucky Charm: A piece of material cut from something in your home.
Harmonious Signs for Relationships and Partnerships: Virgo, Capricorn, and sometimes Libra.

Spiritual Guides . . .

Star: Al Debaran—Those with this star are born leaders.

Angel: Asmodel—This angel governs business and other transactions and aids in negotiations.

Guardian Angel: Uriel—This angel brings the light of God's guidance.

Spiritual Stone: Topaz—This stone may protect the bearer from the effects of allergies.

✶ JUDITH'S INSIGHT ✶

Strong yet sensitive describes you. Although you are fond of the arts and drawn to creative things, you feel awkward with them. You are uncomfortable with your creative nature, but that's because you haven't found your niche. You think you would be most satisfied with a structured career, but undoubtedly you'll have a career that's both creative and structured, such as entertainment lawyer, an actress-turned-agent, a doctor who writes a book, an artist who becomes a museum curator. The balance of structure and creativity will be most rewarding for you.

You do like a nice home, and you fear an empty nest—you want someone in it with you. This can be really up to you, but be sure you choose the proper mate. Friends are true, but you are truer. You have an open-door policy with friends and family alike and should not be dismayed when you become overwrought from having so many demands put on you. Learn when to say yes and no. Aware that you're less than perfect, you take great strides to create the opposite impression. This false superiority incites enemies from time to time, and you know it. You are also smart enough to recognize your enemies and deal appropriately with them.

To be imperfect is to be human. The ability to laugh at yourself will bring much satisfaction. You can be pretentious; it would be better if you could just let it all hang out. With your philosophical nature, it is safe to say that still waters run deep, and your depth runs for miles.

✶ ✶ ✶

APRIL 23

TAURUS • The winged bull of the zodiac

April 20 at 4:00 A.M. to May 21 at 4:00 A.M. • NUMEROLOGY 5

Possessions and Desires . . .

Gem: Amethyst—This stone is said to give calmness and peace.

Flower: Lady's Slipper—What you find beautiful may change as swiftly as the pages of the calendar.

Astral Color, Color Need, Apparel Color: Your Astral Color is Red, which enhances passion, power, excitement, and strength. Yellow in your environment stimulates and exhilarates you. In your wardrobe, Blue-green enhances your luck and makes you feel secure.

Fragrance: You are devoted to the scent of roses. Choose the buds that have the strongest fragrance to create the special emotions you need.

Tree: Apple—You are creative, full of joy, and nearly magical. You bring happiness.

Instruments: Viola, trumpet

Composer: Liszt

Bird: Flamingo—This beautiful, gregarious bird is always careful of its enemy. It is also a caretaker of the young who tries to keep everyone happy.

Symbol: Triangle—You have the right combination of abilities.

Harmonious Health and Nutrition . . .

Health Scent: Peach—This scent may balance your good qualities so that they equal your charm.

Favorable Foods: Romaine lettuce, grapes, buttermilk, beef

What's Lucky . . .

Lucky Numbers: 4, 5, 6, 15
Best Months: May and July
Best Day of the Week: Friday
Best Month Days: 4, 5, 23
Lucky Charms: A rabbit's foot or a white candle.
Harmonious Signs for Relationships and Partnerships: Virgo, Capricorn, and sometimes Libra.

Spiritual Guides . . .

Star: Al Debaran—Those with this star are born leaders.

Angel: Asmodel—This angel governs business and other transactions and aids in negotiations.

Guardian Angel: Plavwell—This angel gives power and strength to one's presence.

Spiritual Stone: Topaz—This stone may protect the bearer from the effects of allergies.

✴ JUDITH'S INSIGHT ✴

You are alluring, charming and witty; you attract the passionate—just like you. What a salesperson you would make with your wonderful gift of gab! It is uncanny how you can prepare a gourmet meal from leftovers and attractively decorate the house from the neighbor's discarded trash. Challenges become you, except when the challenge is in sustaining a relationship. You could use some help here. You see things through your eyes only and rarely accept the views of others. At times your imagination and uninhibited nature can run amok—and it's not necessarily a bad thing. Taking action is not your strong point, but in the midst of a traumatic situation your levelheaded understanding and warmth save the day.

You are a valued worker and an asset and fun to have around. You have a tendency to be somewhat scattered; this might be beneficial if you are pursuing an acting career. Your deep-seated yearning for success is undermined by your lack of dedication to do what it takes to achieve the goal. It may take as many as twenty jobs to find the place where you belong. Don't be discouraged; you will eventually find your vocation and avocation while you have fun along the way. Hospital administrator, public relations, or marketing are jobs that you could do well. You handle problems well, so a troubleshooter in any business would be a good career choice for you. Time and space will shower you with harmony; it's just unclear whether the harmony evolves sooner or later.

✴ ✴ ✴

APRIL 24

TAURUS • The winged bull of the zodiac

April 20 at 4:00 A.M. to May 21 at 4:00 A.M. • NUMEROLOGY 6

Possessions and Desires . . .

Gem: Topaz—This is an excellent gift to be exchanged between very loyal friends.

Flower: Musk Plant—Knowing your weakness can be your greatest strength.

Astral Color, Color Need, Apparel Color: Your Astral Color is Red, which enhances passion, power, excitement, and strength. Yellow in your environment stimulates and exhilarates you. In your wardrobe, Rose gives you balance and harmony.

Fragrance: You are devoted to the scent of roses. Choose the buds that have the strongest fragrance to create the special emotions you need.

Tree: Palm—You tend to be very healthy and creative.

Instruments: Tambourine, lyre

Composer: Schubert

Bird: Falcon—an expert hunter. When well-trained, it can adapt to many tasks and is usually obedient.

Symbol: Crescent—You are more likely to be influenced by the phases of the moon. Your easy-going manner leads you to peaceful situations.

Harmonious Health and Nutrition . . .

Health Scent: Orange Blossom—This scent may balance your body, mind, and soul.

Favorable Foods: Kale, black figs, cheese, oysters

What's Lucky . . .

Lucky Numbers: 4, 6, 12, 24

Best Months: May and July

Best Day of the Week: Friday

Best Month Days: 6, 15, 24

Lucky Charms: A religious token or card from any religion.

Harmonious Signs for Relationships and Partnerships: Virgo, Capricorn, and sometimes Libra.

Spiritual Guides . . .

Star: Al Debaran—Those with this star are born leaders.

Angel: Asmodel—This angel governs business and other transactions and aids in negotiations.

Guardian Angel: Michael—"Who is like God."

Spiritual Stone: Topaz—This stone may protect the bearer from the effects of allergies.

✷ JUDITH'S INSIGHT ✷

You are passionate about all things in your life. Unfortunately, you tend to listen to others too much and take on their burdens. You wear your heart on your sleeve. You're vulnerable in your early years. You are not necessarily persuaded by others, but you're susceptible to their ideas. You're in love with love—the true romantic. Your fantasies make it unlikely that real life can measure up to your dreams. You swim with the tides of love and drift much more toward realism with each passing year. In fact, the scales of love and friendship do balance. In one way or another, family will cause a crisis. Many times you could be overwhelmed with family, but only if you allow it. Keep things in perspective, for you tend to be dependent on family members and blame your disappointments on them. Be aware that your expectations may sometimes be out of reach.

Look for a career in health or beauty or perhaps upholstery or tailoring. You have a knack for fixing things and may even utilize your skills as a physician or therapist. As long as you feel needed and confront different problems on a daily basis, you do very well. Many hidden talents will evolve. Eventually you will fall in love with what you do and derive much satisfaction from it. It shouldn't surprise you to find yourself doing what you always wanted to do, but you might be held back by your own inhibitions. You tend to pull away from your own psychic intuition and spiritual desires. When feeling depressed, do something! Keep yourself busy and stay focused.

✷ ✷ ✷

APRIL 25
TAURUS • The winged bull of the zodiac
April 20 at 4:00 A.M. to May 21 at 4:00 A.M. • NUMEROLOGY 7

Possessions and Desires . . .

Gem: Ruby—This stone may lead you to energy, friendship, and happiness.
Flower: Peach Blossom—You tend to want to own those you love instead of having a relationship of equality.
Astral Color, Color Need, Apparel Color: Your Astral Color is Red, which enhances passion, power, excitement, and strength. Yellow in your environment stimulates and exhilarates you. In your wardrobe, Cream gives you encouragement and style.
Fragrance: You are devoted to the scent of roses. Choose the buds that have the strongest fragrance to create the special emotions you need.
Tree: Sycamore—Yours is the ability to love, communicate honestly with others, and have lasting relationships.
Instrument: Harp
Composers: Gluck, Brahms
Bird: Warbling Parakeet—the most beautiful of all birds, known as the love bird. It does seem to have the powers of imitation.
Symbol: Heart—You are enthusiastic, empathetic, and full of generosity and love.

Harmonious Health and Nutrition . . .

Health Scents: Jasmine—This scent may make you more easygoing when you are stressed.
Favorable Foods: Carrots, lime, eggs, chicken

What's Lucky . . .

Lucky Numbers: 4, 6, 7, 21
Best Months: May and July
Best Day of the Week: Friday
Best Month Days: 6, 15, 24
Lucky Charm: An old key.
Harmonious Signs for Relationships and Partnerships: Virgo, Capricorn, and sometimes Libra.

Spiritual Guides . . .

Star: Al Heka—Those with this star are driven to succeed.
Angel: Asmodel—This angel governs business and other transactions and aids in negotiations.
Guardian Angel: Raphael—This angel attends to all of your needs when you are looking for guidance.
Spiritual Stone: Topaz—This stone may protect the bearer from the effects of allergies.

✶ JUDITH'S INSIGHT ✶

You are a caretaker of fine things, and this attribute will contribute to your financial success. Alas, it also means you often take on too much responsibility. You take life much too seriously. Learn to laugh a little more; laugh from the pit of your stomach. You will feel such relief. Try enjoying some moments without analyzing them, and go with the flow. As you lighten up the whole world lightens, too. You have a strong will. Your common sense and your intelligence put you over the top. You believe others think you are stupid; just remember, you do that to yourself. You can get defensive in a working environment, and you certainly don't like your work to be criticized. You will be rather successful, despite this negativity. You're sympathetic and kind when you want to be. Family values are important, particularly when you have your own family. You feel good if catered to, and, more important, you are ready and willing to do some catering of your own. You will be a professional one way or another. You might be a doctor, dentist, or attorney.

You love the niceties in life—the more designer labels, the better. Cut up those credit cards, though, or you could become a candidate for bankruptcy. You will experiment in varied positions before you find satisfaction and success—and dollars. You want to be a landowner and should forget some of the designer labels and work toward owning your own property.

✶ ✶ ✶

APRIL 26
TAURUS • The winged bull of the zodiac
April 20 at 4:00 A.M. to May 21 at 4:00 A.M. • NUMEROLOGY 8

Possessions and Desires . . .

Gem: Sardonyx—A gift of this stone might help in keeping relationships faithful.

Flower: Bridal Rose—You should be very happy in love.

Astral Color, Color Need, Apparel Color: Your Astral Color is Red, which enhances passion, power, excitement, and strength. Yellow in your environment stimulates and exhilarates you. In your wardrobe, Blue-green enhances your luck and makes you feel secure.

Fragrance: You are devoted to the scent of roses. Choose the buds that have the strongest fragrance to create the special emotions you need.

Tree: Pine—Your relationships tend to be balanced, both emotionally and mentally.

Instrument: Cello

Composer: Mozart

Bird: Bobolink—This charming singer is equally good as a soloist or a member of an orchestra. It is a very romantic bird, most useful as an insect destroyer, and elegant, with beautiful feathers and always pleasant to have around.

Symbol: Wings—You are the source of balance in your world—this will bring you contentment.

Harmonious Health and Nutrition . . .

Health Scents: Almond—This scent may revitalize you and open you to greater possibilities.

Favorable Foods: Celery, apples, buttermilk, salmon

What's Lucky . . .

Lucky Numbers: 4, 6, 8, 16
Best Months: May and July
Best Day of the Week: Friday
Best Month Days: 8, 17, 26
Lucky Charm: Red ribbon in your wallet or doorway.

Harmonious Signs for Relationships and Partnerships: Virgo, Capricorn, and sometimes Libra.

Spiritual Guides . . .

Star: Al Debaran—Those with this star are born leaders.

Angel: Asmodel—This angel governs business and other transactions and aids in negotiations.

Guardian Angel: Seraphim—An angel that brings love, light, and passion.

Spiritual Stone: Topaz—This stone may protect the bearer from the effects of allergies.

✶ JUDITH'S INSIGHT ✶

Mistakes happen; learn from them instead of dwelling on them. You are at home before large audiences. Your wit and charm are enticing. You give family matters top priority, so much so that when they move down your list, family members don't always understand. Your refreshing style and presence attract others, but your intensity and stubbornness often drive them away.

Your tendency to jump to conclusions quickly may make your companion feel overwhelmed by you. Only when a relationship is over do you begin to realize how good it was. Your mom or another motherlike figure, at some point, will be the apple of your eye who holds the key to your heart. If you are already a parent, it could be your child who holds that position in your heart. You do tend to hold onto things and not let them go. This may not work in a conflict, but when it comes to being the devoted mate that you are, it is definitely a desired trait.

You do know how to give a party and impress everyone with your decorations. Explore using these talents as your life's work. Your impeccable taste and organizational aptitude suggest success for you in designing or catering. You could also be a great showperson or entertainer. Your strong desire to see that others have a good time will ensure many a success, now and later.

✶ ✶ ✶

APRIL 27 TAURUS • The winged bull of the zodiac
April 20 at 4:00 A.M. to May 21 at 4:00 A.M. • NUMEROLOGY 9

Possessions and Desires . . .

Gem: Emerald—Those who carry this stone tend to be lucky in love.

Flower: Broken Straw—You tend to want to quickly leave unpleasant situations instead of staying to deal with them.

Astral Color, Color Need, Apparel Color: Your Astral Color is Red, which enhances passion, power, excitement, and strength. Yellow in your environment stimulates and exhilarates you. In your wardrobe, Rose gives you balance and harmony.

Fragrance: You are devoted to the scent of roses. Choose the buds that have the strongest fragrance to create the special emotions you need.

Tree: Holly—Beware that you are not carried away by your passionate nature. The only way to grow is to be open to new experiences.

Instruments: Violin, tympanum

Composer: Gluck

Bird: Mockingbird—the most proficient minstrel in the world's orchestra; graceful and enthusiastic.

Symbol: Anchor—This tranquil symbol signifies stability and strength, and stands for strong commitments in relationships.

Harmonious Health and Nutrition . . .

Health Scents: Lavender—This scent might lead others to trust you and make you patient.

Favorable Foods: Celery, apples, buttermilk, salmon

What's Lucky . . .

Lucky Numbers: 4, 6, 9, 18
Best Months: May and July.
Best Day of the Week: Friday
Best Month Days: 9, 18, 27
Lucky Charms: A U. S. coin or bill of any amount from the year you were born.
Harmonious Signs for Relationships and Partnerships: Virgo, Capricorn, and sometimes Libra.

Spiritual Guides . . .

Star: Al Debaran—Those with this star are born leaders.

Angel: Asmodel—This angel governs business and other transactions and aids in negotiations.

Guardian Angel: Gabriel—"God is my strength."

Spiritual Stone: Topaz—This stone may protect the bearer from the effects of allergies.

✳ JUDITH'S INSIGHT ✳

Generous and kind, you frequently do not hesitate to inform others of your self-sacrifices. Alternatively, you can be very secretive about your own affairs. A teacher at heart, you could take teaching to different dimensions, conventional and unconventional. You are very perceptive, and you inspire those around you. You may consider careers in psychology, or work as a writer, doctor, or counselor. You absorb knowledge from every possible source and have great recall for things you read about or see on television. You are multitalented, with the gift of gab; so working with people is for you. Beautician or makeup artist could also be occupations you'd do well. You do have a dab of drama, so acting could be a consideration. Stocks and finance also intrigue you, as long as you are not the one dotting the i's or crossing the t's. You prefer to distance yourself from paperwork.

Avoid the extremes, especially when it comes to relationships. You may be comfortable with one now, but eventually you'll be challenged by the intricacies of many different relationships. You strive to have a truly beautiful home for your family that will mean everything to you. Resist the temptation to refurbish and redecorate your home at every whim. Antiques and oddities will permeate throughout, as somehow you have identified these as feeling like nature. You are here to seek and find answers. Answers may surface for you when you reach that particular chapter in that particular book.

✳ ✳ ✳

APRIL 28   TAURUS • The winged bull of the zodiac
April 20 at 4:00 A.M. to May 21 at 4:00 A.M. • NUMEROLOGY 1

Possessions and Desires . . .

Gem: Emerald—Those who carry this stone tend to be lucky in love.

Flower: Yellow Violet—You tend to be happiest surrounded by nature.

Astral Color, Color Need, Apparel Color: Your Astral Color is Red, which enhances passion, power, excitement, and strength. Yellow in your environment stimulates and exhilarates you. In your wardrobe, Rose gives you balance and harmony.

Fragrance: You are devoted to the scent of roses. Choose the buds that have the strongest fragrance to create the special emotions you need.

Tree: Walnut—You are unusually helpful and always looking for new beginnings.

Instruments: Oboe, flute, clarinet, piano, French horn, organ, and piccolo

Composer: Böhm

Bird: Bird of paradise—the "bird of the gods." You will shine and love extraordinary circumstances.

Symbol: Crown—the universal sign of dignity.

Harmonious Health and Nutrition . . .

Health Scent: Strawberry—soothing by nature, the strawberry promotes self-esteem and encourages love.

Favorable Foods: Celery, grapes, cheese, beef

What's Lucky . . .

Lucky Numbers: 4, 6, 10, 20
Best Months: May and July
Best Day of the Week: Friday
Best Month Days: 1, 10, 19, 28
Lucky Charm: A new penny in your shoe.
Harmonious Signs for Relationships and Partnerships: Virgo, Capricorn, and sometimes Libra.

Spiritual Guides . . .

Star: Al Heka—Those with this star are driven to succeed.

Angel: Asmodel—This angel governs business and other transactions and aids in negotiations.

Guardian Angel: Malachi—"Messenger of Jehovah."

Spiritual Stone: Topaz—This stone may protect the bearer from the effects of allergies.

✳ JUDITH'S INSIGHT ✳

Enthusiastic by nature, you reach out to the people in your life. Sometimes perfectionism makes you too choosy for your own good. You are the epitome of independence and rarely feel needy. Though you are an unconventional person, you will be most content with conventional relationships. You're afraid to be bored and will become dissatisfied if your relationship doesn't bring you a certain amount of excitement. Unfortunately, you may feel lonely even while you have a partner. Remember, you must be the one to make things stimulating. Ordinarily you face and solve problems as they arise. You are forceful and, some might say, dictatorial. This is definitely a deterrent to business partnerships, and you should try to be more diplomatic. Tact will enhance all your relationships; it brings out your other good aspects. You always give 110 percent to every commitment, be it work or love. You welcome change, however, and must guard against jumping out of relationships too quickly.

Strong aggressions surface to put you at the top. Use caution at play and with entertainment. Obstacles will present themselves, but you overcome them easily. You may desire a career in government or business and could do well in both. Either way, take precautions with the legalities. No matter what you take on, you'll rise to the top. Most others recognize your wit and charm; they appreciate your sense of humor. You love to be popular, and your laughter is infectious. You do your best work before a hand-picked audience. You believe less means more when it comes to friends. You prefer having a few close friends and spending quality time with them. Your devotion to your friends will come back to you tenfold.

✳ ✳ ✳

APRIL 29

TAURUS • The winged bull of the zodiac

April 20 at 4:00 A.M. to May 21 at 4:00 A.M. • NUMEROLOGY 2

Possessions and Desires . . .

Gem: Amethyst—This stone is said to give calmness and peace.

Flower: Wormwood—You tend to focus on what you left behind instead of where you could be going.

Astral Color, Color Need, Apparel Color: Your Astral Color is Red, which enhances passion, power, excitement, and strength. Yellow in your environment stimulates and exhilarates you. In your wardrobe, Rose gives you balance and harmony.

Fragrance: You are devoted to the scent of roses. Choose the buds that have the strongest fragrance to create the special emotions you need.

Tree: Maple—You have both great stability and flashes of intuition.

Instrument: Pipe organ, cymbal, drum

Composers: Handel, Johann Sebastian Bach

Bird: Cuckoo—a good flyer and very seldom a quitter. Some cuckoos tend to think they favor lonely isolation, but what they really yearn for is a family relationship.

Symbol: Cross—the symbol of self-sacrifice and reconciliation.

Harmonious Health and Nutrition . . .

Health Scent: Apple—You are creative, full of joy, and nearly magical. You bring happiness.

Favorable Foods: Watercress, peaches, eggs, salmon

What's Lucky . . .

Lucky Numbers: 4, 6, 11, 22
Best Months: May and July
Best Day of the Week: Friday
Best Month Days: 2, 11, 20, 29
Lucky Charms: Two 50-cent pieces. Give someone else one of them.

Harmonious Signs for Relationships and Partnerships: Virgo, Capricorn, and sometimes Libra.

Spiritual Guides . . .

Star: Al Heka—Those with this star are driven to succeed.

Angel: Asmodel—This angel governs business and other transactions and aids in negotiations.

Guardian Angel: Uriel—This angel brings the light of God's guidance.

Spiritual Stone: Topaz—This stone may protect the bearer from the effects of allergies.

✶ JUDITH'S INSIGHT ✶

Although you definitely have the ability to go it alone, the possibilities are enhanced when you join your efforts with another's. Determination and ambition will take you where you want to go in due course. Unfortunately, in this area, you're a little impatient, and it will seem at times like your life is taking you the long way around to your goals. You are beholden to family members and sometimes give too much importance to those relationships. Your frankness gets you into trouble occasionally, but you will have the respect of those around you. Witty and charming, you're welcome in everyone's circle. You flit through relationships at first, but as you mature you won't want to let go. This may pose a problem, but awareness of this tendency to stretch things out will help you make better choices. Your strong presence makes you stand out in the crowd, even when your inner self would rather hide against the wall. You're very honorable, and this attribute will bring you much contentment and happiness, although it may seem like it takes forever.

Money will come and go, but along the way the worries of finance will dissipate. A large windfall will be bestowed upon you more than once during your life. Although you insist on looking good now, as you mature your looks matter even more. Vanity will eventually play a bigger part in your life than your anticipate.

✶ ✶ ✶

APRIL 30 TAURUS • The winged bull of the zodiac
April 20 at 4:00 A.M. to May 21 at 4:00 A.M. • NUMEROLOGY 3

Possessions and Desires . . .

Gem: Ruby—this stone may lead you to energy, friendship, and happiness.

Flower: Vernal Grass—It usually doesn't take a whole lot to make you happy.

Astral Color, Color Need, Apparel Color: Your Astral Color is Red, which enhances passion, power, excitement, and strength. Yellow in your environment stimulates and exhilarates you. In your wardrobe, Rose gives you balance and harmony.

Fragrance: You are devoted to the scent of roses. Choose the buds that have the strongest fragrance to create the special emotions you need.

Tree: Elm—You have willpower, strength, and the ability to stand alone.

Instrument: Trombone

Composers: Verdi, Mendelssohn, Schumann

Bird: Eagle—This bird is quick to use its powers of flight. It can see immeasurable distances in a single glance, and can sometimes appear to be indifferent.

Symbol: Wreath—You have been crowned with a special personality. You are strong but extremely compassionate.

Harmonious Health and Nutrition . . .

Health Scent: Rose—This scent will lead you to passionate thoughts and make you feel warm inside.

Favorable Foods: Turnips, raspberries, buttermilk, beef

What's Lucky . . .

Lucky Numbers: 3, 4, 6, 9
Best Months: May and July
Best Day of the Week: Friday
Best Month Days: 3, 12, 21, 30
Lucky Charm: A pen that someone else has already used.

Harmonious Signs for Relationships and Partnerships: Virgo, Capricorn, and sometimes Libra.

Spiritual Guides . . .

Star: Al Debaran—Those with this star are born leaders.

Angel: Asmodel—This angel governs business and other transactions and aids in negotiations.

Guardian Angel: Johiel—This angel is a protector of all those with a humble heart.

Spiritual Stone: Topaz—This stone may protect the bearer from the effects of allergies.

✷ JUDITH'S INSIGHT ✷

"Strong as a bull" describes both your physical and emotional strength. You can handle just about anything. While others will view your life as charmed, that's not the case. You work hard at building on your strengths, which will always serve you and others. You enjoy overcoming obstacles, and you do this well.

Children, yours and others, are very important in your life. You shine through and around them. You may kiss some toads before you find your prince or princess. After being disillusioned a few times, you will find an appreciative mate. You are somewhat idealistic, but you will eventually balance that tendency with your materialism. You love spending money—it makes you feel good. Disregard those negative thoughts about not accomplishing enough financially; you do climb up the financial ladder.

Your appreciation of others tends to make you the caretaker in most situations, regardless of whether another is outwardly taking care of you or vice versa. Your sense of humor develops little by little. Peace of mind comes in time. Don't watch the clock.

★ ★ ★

MAY

MAY 1   TAURUS • The winged bull of the zodiac
April 20 at 4:00 A.M. to May 21 at 4:00 A.M. • NUMEROLOGY 1

Possessions and Desires . . .

Gem: Turquoise—This stone may help you find material wealth.

Flower: American Aster—You are always thoughtful of others.

Astral Color, Color Need, Apparel Color: Your Astral Color is Red, which enhances passion, power, excitement, and strength. Yellow in your environment stimulates and exhilarates you. In your wardrobe, Rose gives you balance and harmony.

Fragrance: You are devoted to the scent of roses. Choose the buds that have the strongest fragrance to create the special emotions you need.

Tree: Walnut—You are unusually helpful and aways looking for new beginnings.

Instruments: Oboe, flute, clarinet, piano, French horn, organ, piccolo

Composer: Böhm

Bird: Hummingbird—This birds is delicate and graceful. It can remain still for hours, then dart off and be as busy as a bee.

Symbol: Crown—the universal sign of dignity.

Harmonious Health and Nutrition . . .

Health Scent: Strawberry—Soothing by nature, the strawberry promotes self-esteem and encourages love.

Favorable Foods: Romaine lettuce, black figs, eggs, chicken

What's Lucky . . .

Lucky Numbers: 1, 2, 4, 6
Best Months: May and July
Best Day of the Week: Friday
Best Month Days: 1, 10, 19, 28
Lucky Charm: A new penny in your shoe.
Harmonious Signs for Relationships and

Partnerships: Virgo, Capricorn, and sometimes Libra.

Spiritual Guides . . .

Star: Al Debaran—Those with this star are born leaders.

Angel: Asmodel—This angel governs business and other transactions and aids in negotiations.

Guardian Angel: Malachi—"Messenger of Jehovah."

Spiritual Stone: Topaz—This stone may protect the bearer from the effects of allergies.

✶ JUDITH'S INSIGHT ✶

Creativity, originality, and self-reliance bring you an independence that carries you through just about every situation. A good head on your shoulders and a sensitive nature ensure that doors open for you. You can develop your career utilizing either or both your artistic and counseling talents. Follow your larger vision enthusiastically. Whether you crawl or leap up the ladder of success depends on your devotion to the task.

You dislike being alone and thrive on the attention of others. Eat it up while others are interested—there will be lonely spells in your life. Keep it all in perspective. Try not to see the quiet times as lonely—view them as rest and recuperation, and you won't make mistakes in your love life based on loneliness. Your friends and family know you need the occasional pat on the back, and they offer it instinctively. You attract more flies with honey than with vinegar.

Success awaits you, but you must make it happen, and it could take awhile. Fashion and beauty, or perhaps the theater, could offer the most to you. You will not only meet your own burdens in life but also help carry the burdens of others. Because of who and what you are, you probably wouldn't want it any other way. This is your forte.

✶ ✶ ✶

MAY 2   TAURUS • The winged bull of the zodiac
April 20 at 4:00 A.M. to May 21 at 4:00 A.M. • NUMEROLOGY 2

Possessions and Desires . . .

Gem: Amethyst—This stone is said to give calmness and peace.

Flower: Chickweed—You will find your way in life is a very curvy road.

Astral Color, Color Need, Apparel Color: Your Astral Color is Red, which enhances passion, power, excitement, and strength. Yellow in your environment stimulates and exhilarates you. In your wardrobe, Rose gives you balance and harmony.

Fragrance: You are devoted to the scent of roses. Choose the buds that have the strongest fragrance to create the special emotions you need.

Tree: Maple—You have both great stability and flashes of intuition.

Instruments: Pipe organ, cymbal, drum

Composers: Handel, Johann Sebastian Bach

Bird: Stork—Turkish bird, held in high esteem the world over. This bird is intelligent but may have strange tendencies.

Symbol: Cross—the symbol of self-sacrifice and reconciliation.

Harmonious Health and Nutrition . . .

Health Scents: Apple—You are creative, full of joy, and nearly magical. You bring happiness.

Favorable Foods: Turnips, cranberries, buttermilk, salmon

What's Lucky . . .

Lucky Numbers: 2, 4, 6, 11

Best Months: May and July

Best Day of the Week: Friday

Best Month Days: 2, 11, 20, 29

Lucky Charms: Two 50-cent pieces. Give someone else one of them.

Harmonious Signs for Relationships and Partnerships: Virgo, Capricorn, and sometimes Libra.

Spiritual Guides . . .

Star: Al Heka—Those with this star are driven to succeed.

Angel: Asmodel—This angel governs business and other transactions and aids in negotiations.

Guardian Angel: St. John—This angel simplifies that which is complicated.

Spiritual Stone: Topaz—This stone may protect the bearer from the effects of allergies.

✴ JUDITH'S INSIGHT ✴

A diehard romantic, you have a great capacity for love and all that goes with it. You could write compelling love stories drawn from your dreams and imagination. Fear not—your logical side keeps you rooted to earth. To no one's surprise, you may be that lucky one who experiences the love of a lifetime, but it's more likely you'll find love in many places along the way. Love brings happiness, at least once, for you. You will be able to act out some of those romantic fantasies of yours.

Your life's work should involve the arts, beauty, or spirituality, and you'd be an asset and find fulfillment in the theater. Be cognizant of keeping both feet planted on the ground. Your hobbies should also be associated with literature, art, or theater. You may find mystical studies alluring, as well. Follow your need to express yourself. Someday you may find yourself in the public eye, or the public may eventually find you.

You have other hidden talents and a certain style about you. You're put together well, and could easily be a decorator, personal dresser, or personal shopper.

You are most sympathetic to the needs of others and often lean toward helping the underdog. Be wary of your stubbornness. Catch yourself when you are tempted to complain about others—think twice about your own behavior. Let any negative stubbornness give way to a gentler, more positive diligence.

✴ ✴ ✴

MAY 3
TAURUS • The winged bull of the zodiac
April 20 at 4:00 A.M. to May 21 at 4:00 A.M. • NUMEROLOGY 3

Possessions and Desires . . .

Gem: Ruby—This stone may lead you to energy, friendship, and happiness.

Flower: May Rose—Your life will be filled with love and warmth.

Astral Color, Color Need, Apparel Color: Your Astral Color is Red, which enhances passion, power, excitement, and strength. Yellow in your environment stimulates and exhilarates you. In your wardrobe, Rose gives you balance and harmony.

Fragrance: You are devoted to the scent of roses. Choose the buds that have the strongest fragrance to create the special emotions you need.

Tree: Elm—You have willpower, strength, and the ability to stand alone.

Instrument: Trombone

Composers: Verdi, Mendelssohn, Schumann

Bird: Swan—Regarded as royal and sacred, this bird has the protective nature of a mother, and can become a furious fighter in the defense of its young.

Symbol: Wreath—You have been crowned with a special personality. You are strong but extremely compassionate.

Harmonious Health and Nutrition . . .

Health Scents: Rose—This scent will lead you to passionate thoughts and make you feel warm inside.

Favorable Foods: Tomatoes, raspberries, cheese, oysters

What's Lucky . . .

Lucky Numbers: 4, 6, 8
Best Month: May and July
Best Day of the Week: Friday
Best Month Days: 3, 12, 21, 30
Lucky Charm: A pen that someone else has already used.
Harmonious Signs for Relationships and

Partnerships: Virgo, Capricorn, and sometimes Libra.

Spiritual Guides . . .

Star: Al Debaran—Those with this star are born leaders.

Angel: Asmodel—This angel governs business and other transactions and aids in negotiations.

Guardian Angel: Johiel—This angel is a protector of all those with a humble heart.

Spiritual Stone: Topaz—This stone may protect the bearer from the effects of allergies.

✶ JUDITH'S INSIGHT ✶

The best kind of contradiction shines through your personality. You are creative, talented, enthusiastic, and energetic, yet down to earth, logical, and loyal. It's a dynamic combination that you struggle with, but you will eventually fall into step. Your compassion and kindness bring you many friends. Your feisty side will work to your advantage in defense of your ideas. Quite possibly you will find yourself resolving legal issues. Once angered, however, you find it difficult to let go. Time and the persuasion of others usually alter your stance. You crave attention, particularly in your younger years. Good or bad, any attention bodes well for you. It is indifference you cannot tolerate.

Be selective when it comes to romance. You love attractive things and looking good. Sometimes we ought not judge a book by its cover, but merely gaze without being judgmental. Your looks entice others to flirt with you or get closer. But you're very loyal, and you won't find yourself in hot water too often.

Creativity will shine through everything you do. Make laughter your best medicine. Learn to appreciate those funny moments. Simply lighten up and enjoy.

Money is a high priority, and you will be preoccupied with your financial status as you mature. You can be generous as well as miserly. You should seek the middle ground, when it comes to your checkbook, to ensure financial stability.

✶ ✶ ✶

MAY 4 TAURUS • The winged bull of the zodiac
April 20 at 4:00 A.M. to May 21 at 4:00 A.M. • NUMEROLOGY 4

Possessions and Desires . . .

Gem: Emerald—Those who carry this stone tend to be lucky in love.

Flower: Myrtle—Love is yours if you pay close attention to your heartbeat.

Astral Color, Color Need, Apparel Color: Your Astral Color is Red, which enhances passion, power, excitement, and strength. Yellow in your environment stimulates and exhilarates you. In your wardrobe, Rose gives you balance and harmony.

Fragrance: You are devoted to the scent of roses. Choose the buds that have the strongest fragrance to create the special emotions you need.

Tree: Cherry—You will find yourself faced with constant new emotional awakenings.

Instruments: Bass, clarinet

Composers: Haydn, Wagner

Bird: Robin—the most sociable of all birds, with the ability to create quick friendships. It also can easily adapt to any home. When it wants something, it has the tendency to try to snatch it.

Symbol: Star—You are full of inner brightness and will stand out in any crowd. You will be seen as special.

Harmonious Health and Nutrition . . .

Health Scents: Vanilla—This scent will fill you with a feeling of cleanliness and stability.

Favorable Foods: Peaches, eggs, beef, carrots

What's Lucky . . .

Lucky Numbers: 4, 6, 8

Best Months: May and July

Best Day of the Week: Friday

Best Month Days: 4, 13, 22, 31

Lucky Charm: A piece of material cut from something in your home.

Harmonious Signs for Relationships and

Partnerships: Virgo, Capricorn, and sometimes Libra.

Spiritual Guides . . .

Star: Al Heka—Those with this star are driven to succeed.

Angel: Asmodel—This angel governs business and other transactions and aids in negotiations.

Guardian Angel: Uriel—This angel brings the light of God's guidance.

Spiritual Stone: Topaz—This stone may protect the bearer from the effects of allergies.

✷ JUDITH'S INSIGHT ✷

Versatility and flexibility ensure many successes for you. Your adaptability and independent spirit leads others to reach out for you. You remain influential all your life. Friends and family most often relate to you but occasionally back away because you project your high expectations of yourself onto them. They fear you will demand more of them and thus they back off. Nonetheless, your circle of friends will continue to grow, as does the love and understanding of your beloved ones. One minute you welcome your family's dependence on you, the next you urge them to exercise more independence. It all comes together when you take it less seriously.

Success is very much in the picture, particularly if you are self-employed. A natural leader, you can achieve much when coupled with the right partners. Be choosy and take care. Life will reward your efforts financially. Good things develop when you give it your best. You may find a comfortable slot in big business, a home business, or in the public eye—say, in politics. Your creativity ensures retail success.

In matters of the heart, learn patience. Your goodness as a person shines through, and others clamor to share that goodness. You will find stability in your mate, and your mate will support your pursuits.

✷ ✷ ✷

MAY 5 TAURUS • The winged bull of the zodiac
April 20 at 4:00 A.M. to May 21 at 4:00 A.M. • NUMEROLOGY 5

Possessions and Desires . . .

Gem: Sardius—this stone could give the wearer unusual insights into his or her own heart.

Flower: Ophrys—You usually are a delight to be with.

Astral Color, Color Need, Apparel Color: Your Astral Color is Red, which enhances passion, power, excitement, and strength. Yellow in your environment stimulates and exhilarates you. In your wardrobe, Rose gives you balance and harmony.

Fragrance: You are devoted to the scent of roses. Choose the buds that have the strongest fragrance to create the special emotions you need.

Tree: Apple—You are creative, full of joy, and nearly magical. You bring happiness.

Instruments: Viola, trumpet

Composer: Liszt

Bird: Flamingo—This beautiful, gregarious bird is always careful of its enemy. It is also a caretaker of the young who tries to keep everyone happy.

Symbol: Triangle—You have the right combination of abilities.

Harmonious Health and Nutrition . . .

Health Scent: Peach—This scent may balance your good qualities so they equal your charm.

Favorable Foods: Carrots, apples, cheese, chicken

What's Lucky . . .

Lucky Numbers: 4, 5, 6, 10
Best Months: May and July
Best Day of the Week: Friday
Best Month Days: 4, 5, 23
Lucky Charms: A rabbit's foot or a white candle
Harmonious Signs for Relationships and Partnerships: Virgo, Capricorn, and sometimes Libra.

Spiritual Guides . . .

Star: Al Debaran—Those with this star are born leaders.

Angel: Asmodel—This angel governs business and other transactions and aids in negotiations.

Guardian Angel: Plavwell—This angel gives power and strength to one's presence.

Spiritual Stone: Topaz—This stone may protect the bearer from the effects of allergies.

✴ JUDITH'S INSIGHT ✴

You are so special—unusually keen—an original in all you do. You have far-reaching reasoning powers. You are perceptive, analytical, and observant. An independent spirit, you approach situations amiably. You are a master of creativity and you enjoy everything from carpentry to counseling. You're great at anything you try, and you will aspire for more. To no one's surprise, a company of your own would definitely succeed. More than you care to admit, you desire fame. Although you are successful in what you do, you may seek other interests, perhaps a hobby with more guts and glamour. Even if you don't actively seek it, it may find you. You could get involved in golf, boating, organizational writing, or heading the PTA.

Family holds a strong connection for you. Although you're influenced by your mate in a strong way, you remain comfortably independent. Hopefully your youthful love affairs will help anchor your shifting affections. It is wiser for you to marry later rather than sooner. Your mate will understand you.

Financially, you may not win the lottery, but you will be comfortable. With the passing years, you become less spiritual and more materialistic. You appear to be a strong presence, your gentle heart will embrace a chosen few who will be lucky to have been touched by you.

✴ ✴ ✴

MAY 6 TAURUS • The winged bull of the zodiac

April 20 at 4:00 A.M. to May 21 at 4:00 A.M. • NUMEROLOGY 6

Possessions and Desires . . .

Gem: Topaz—This is an excellent gift to be exchanged between very loyal friends.

Flower: Quince—You enjoy the excitement life has to offer.

Astral Color, Color Need, Apparel Color: Your Astral Color is Red, which enhances passion, power, excitement, and strength. Yellow in your environment stimulates and exhilarates you. In your wardrobe, Rose gives you balance and harmony.

Fragrance: You are devoted to the scent of roses. Choose the buds that have the strongest fragrance to create the special emotions you need.

Tree: Palm—You tend to be very healthy and creative.

Instruments: Tambourine, lyre

Composer: Schubert

Bird: Lark—known for the beauty of its song, which is sometimes very unusual. It is also credited with extraordinary intelligence.

Symbol: Crescent—You are more likely to be influenced by the phases of the moon. Your easygoing manner leads you to peaceful situations.

Harmonious Health and Nutrition . . .

Health Scent: Orange Blossom—This scent may balance your body, mind, and soul.

Favorable Foods: Carrots, apples, cheese, chicken

What's Lucky . . .

Lucky Numbers: 4, 6, 12, 16

Best Months: May and July

Best Day of the Week: Friday

Best Month Days: 6, 15, 24

Lucky Charms: A religious token or card from any religion.

Harmonious Signs for Relationships and Partnerships: Virgo, Capricorn, and sometimes Libra.

Spiritual Guides . . .

Star: Al Debaran—Those with this star are born leaders.

Angel: Asmodel—This angel governs business and other transactions and aids in negotiations.

Guardian Angel: Michael—"Who is like God."

Spiritual Stone: Topaz—This stone may protect the bearer from the effects of allergies.

✷ JUDITH'S INSIGHT ✷

Sharing is where your heart is—you have such an intense desire to give of yourself. The kindness of friends tends to overwhelm you. You are very decisive and do not appreciate being diverted from your chosen path. Your enthusiasm for life and your many skills open up many different careers to you.

You can be both angel and devil. Your emotional contradictions may seem unfortunate to you, but to others they're fascinating. Your random acts of kindness come from the heart with no strings attached. You may take many small steps before you arrive at your ultimate career, but you'll derive success from what you've accomplished along the way.

As you reach various plateaus in life, you will in all likelihood seek change. Each plateau represents a period of growth. Family will be your strongest foundation, and you will, despite your career, find the way to have a solid family of your own. You will expand your immediate circle and thrive on the enjoyment of not only yourself but others, particularly in social events. You're certainly equipped to be a politician, but more likely an activist for children, the infirm, or the homeless. The legal arena may have possibilities for you.

Because of your compassion, people are always around you. Although your creativity is strong, your compassion is stronger. Once your career taps into your emotional side you will be happy. Stylish, with some vanity, you'll always try to improve your appearance, and you'll retain your stylish looks as though you'd found the fountain of youth.

✷ ✷ ✷

MAY 7 TAURUS • The winged bull of the zodiac

April 20 at 4:00 A.M. to May 21 at 4:00 A.M. • NUMEROLOGY 7

Possessions and Desires . . .

Gem: Agate—This stone may promote health and lead you to a long life.

Flower: Primrose—You never lose sight of the simple pleasures of childhood.

Astral Color, Color Need, Apparel Color: Your Astral Color is Red, which enhances passion, power, excitement, and strength. Yellow in your environment stimulates and exhilarates you. In your wardrobe, Rose gives you balance and harmony.

Fragrance: You are devoted to the scent of roses. Choose the buds that have the strongest fragrance to create the special emotions you need.

Tree: Sycamore—Yours is the ability to love, communicate honestly with others, and have lasting relationships.

Instrument: Harp

Composers: Gluck, Brahms

Bird: Warbling Parakeet—the most beautiful of all birds, known as the love bird. It does seem to have the powers of imitation.

Symbol: Heart—You are enthusiastic, empathetic, and full of generosity and love.

Harmonious Health and Nutrition . . .

Health Scent: Jasmine—This scent may make you more easygoing when you are stressed.

Favorable Foods: Carrots, cherries, cheese, liver

What's Lucky . . .

Lucky Numbers: 4, 6, 7, 15
Best Months: May and July
Best Day of the Week: Friday
Best Month Days: 6, 15, 24
Lucky Charm: An old key.
Harmonious Signs for Relationships and Partnerships: Virgo, Capricorn, and sometimes Libra.

Spiritual Guides . . .

Star: Al Debaran—Those with this star are born leaders.

Angel: Asmodel—This angel governs business and other transactions and aids in negotiations.

Guardian Angel: Raphael—This angel attends to all of your needs when you are looking for guidance.

Spiritual Stone: Topaz—This stone may protect the bearer from the effects of allergies.

✶ JUDITH'S INSIGHT ✶

You are a dreamer with extraordinary curiosity about nature. With encouragement and support, you could succeed as an inventor, author, or designer, or in almost anything that you originate. Your hands will serve you well, but your heart works best. You are strong mentally which complements your intuitiveness, common sense, and natural intelligence. You search for the unknown. Natural kindness makes you generous, but not foolish. You tend to have predetermined views when it comes to managing money or giving it away. Some may think you eccentric because of your desire for the unusual. You would be likely to collect antiques, especially dolls, games, and toys. It could be you searching for buried treasure or mining for gold.

Perhaps a career as a writer, poet, painter, musician, or inventor would bring you success and happiness. Financial rewards should find you early in life, but most assuredly in your later years. You will share your money to benefit others. Friends and family appreciate your generosity, as will a favorite charity or the local hospital. Public welfare permeates your life in one way or another, whether you will be receiving help or, on a more positive note, being the one who helps others. At first any love commitment would be difficult, but once you have made some minor adjustments, the relationship will do well. You are the mule in the relationship most of the time so keep this in mind.

✶ ✶ ✶

MAY 8 TAURUS • The winged bull of the zodiac
April 20 at 4:00 A.M. to May 21 at 4:00 A.M. • NUMEROLOGY 8

Possessions and Desires . . .

Gem: Emerald—Those who carry this stone tend to be lucky in love.

Flower: White Poppy—You may need more sleep than other people you know.

Astral Color, Color Need, Apparel Color: Your Astral Color is Red, which enhances passion, power, excitement, and strength. Yellow in your environment stimulates and exhilarates you. In your wardrobe, Rose gives you balance and harmony.

Fragrance: You are devoted to the scent of roses. Choose the buds that have the strongest fragrance to create the special emotions you need.

Tree: Pine—Your relationships tend to be harmonious, both emotionally and mentally.

Instrument: Cello

Composer: Mozart

Bird: Bobolink—This charming singer is equally good as a soloist or a member of an orchestra. It is a very romantic bird, useful as an insect destroyer, and elegant, with beautiful feathers, and is always pleasant to have around.

Symbol: Wings—You are the source of balance in your world—this will bring you contentment.

Harmonious Health and Nutrition . . .

Health Scent: Almond—This scent may revitalize you and open you to greater possibilities.

Favorable Foods: Celery, apples, buttermilk, beef

What's Lucky . . .

Lucky Numbers: 4, 6, 8
Best Months: May and July
Best Day of the Week: Friday
Best Month Days: 8, 17, 26

Lucky Charm: Red ribbon in your wallet or doorway.

Harmonious Signs for Relationships and Partnerships: Virgo, Capricorn, and sometimes Libra.

Spiritual Guides . . .

Star: Al Debaran—Those with this star are born leaders.

Angel: Asmodel—This angel governs business and other transactions and aids in negotiations.

Guardian Angel: Seraphim—This angel brings love, light, and passion.

Spiritual Stone: Topaz—this stone may protect the bearer from the effects of allergies.

✶ JUDITH'S INSIGHT ✶

In the early years, nagging loneliness makes you crave attention, sometimes more than others are prepared to give. Be not dismayed or distracted, as you eventually find yourself in a loving and nurturing relationship. Restrictive relationships smother, and you thrive on freely exploring your world. There's a natural glow about you that will brighten as you mature. Your innate sense of responsibility ensures that you'll carry out any task before you. You enthusiasm for life makes things happen around you. You will maintain a high position in such areas as the theater, the arts, decorating, or consulting in beauty.

You are a pleasure to love, and the more amenities in life for you, the better. Love mates will praise you; there will seldom be times when attention is lacking. Your attractiveness lures many, but be watchful to not become complacent about your relationships.

You will succeed financially and will be surrounded with the niceties in life: a wonderful home and family and, eventually, after all the hurdles, a good life.

✶ ✶ ✶

MAY 9

TAURUS • The winged bull of the zodiac

April 20 at 4:00 A.M. to May 21 at 4:00 A.M. • NUMEROLOGY 9

Possessions and Desires

Gem: Emerald—Those who carry this stone tend to be lucky in love.

Flower: Snowball—You tend to bounce back from times of distress.

Astral Color, Color Need, Apparel Color: Your Astral Color is Red, which enhances passion, power, excitement, and strength. Yellow in your environment stimulates and exhilarates you. In your wardrobe, Rose gives you balance and harmony.

Fragrance: You are devoted to the scent of roses. Choose the buds that have the strongest fragrance to create the special emotions you need.

Tree: Holly—Beware that you are not carried away by your passionate nature. The only way to grow is to be open to new experiences.

Instruments: Violin, tympanum

Composer: Gluck

Bird: Mockingbird—the most proficient minstrel in the world's orchestra; graceful and enthusiastic.

Symbol: Anchor—This tranquil symbol signifies stability and strength, and stands for strong commitments in relationships.

Harmonious Health and Nutrition . . .

Health Scent: Lavender—This scent might lead others to trust you and make you patient.

Favorable Foods: Turnips, raspberries, cheese, chicken

What's Lucky . . .

Lucky Numbers: 4, 6, 9, 18
Best Months: May and July
Best Day of the Week: Friday
Best Month Days: 9, 18, 27
Lucky Charms: A U.S. coin or a bill of any amount from the year you were born.
Harmonious Signs for Relationships and

Partnerships: Virgo, Capricorn, and sometimes Libra.

Spiritual Guides . . .

Star: Al Heka—Those with this star are driven to succeed.

Angel: Asmodel—This angel governs business and other transactions and aids in negotiations.

Guardian Angel: Gabriel—"God is my strength."

Spiritual Stone: Topaz—This stone may protect the bearer from the effects of allergies.

✳ JUDITH'S INSIGHT ✳

Persistence and consistency are the key to who you are, perhaps even the key to your heart. You maintain a steady course, though unexpected changes rock your boat. You are confident in your own abilities and have a strong, but not inflated, opinion of yourself. Your self-confidence attracts others.

Your abilities and talents, which are many, add to your charm. Though not surrounded by a fan club, others respect and admire you. If you choose, you will be at the head of the class or department, in whatever career you desire. You manage people well, despite your stubborn nature. Your fun-loving, playful side keeps the balance.

You have exquisite taste and love beautiful ornaments. Not only do you know how to decorate, you know how to conceal the blemishes. You accentuate what is already attractive and make good things better. These skills and experience may foster a career from construction to beauty consulting and everything in between. Any career that would utilize your style and creativity will bring contentment to you. Anything you put your handprint on is unique.

Love gives you a run for your money early in life, when you're really not ready to settle. The powerful person you are seeks powerful mates. You can escape the few tangled webs along the way. You love your mate and are a loyal soul.

✳ ✳ ✳

MAY 10 TAURUS • The winged bull of the zodiac
April 20 at 4:00 A.M. to May 21 at 4:00 A.M. • NUMEROLOGY 1

Possessions and Desires . . .

Gem: Turquoise—This stone may help you find material wealth.
Flower: Red Poppy—You usually are a source of consolation to others.
Astral Color, Color Need, Apparel Colors: Your Astral Color is Red, which enhances passion, power, excitement, and strength. Yellow in your environment stimulates and exhilarates you. In your wardrobe, Rose gives you balance and harmony.
Fragrance: You are devoted to the scent of roses. Choose the buds that have the strongest fragrance to create the special emotions you need.
Tree: Walnut—You are unusually helpful and aways looking for new beginnings.
Instruments: Oboe, flute, clarinet, piano, French horn, organ, piccolo
Composer: Böhm
Bird: Bird of Paradise—the "birds of the Gods." You will shine and love extraordinary circumstances.
Symbol: Crown—the universal sign of dignity.

Harmonious Health and Nutrition . . .

Health Scent: Strawberry—soothing by nature, the strawberry promotes self-esteem and encourages love.
Favorable Foods: Kale, peaches, eggs, salmon

What's Lucky . . .

Lucky Numbers: 2, 4, 6
Best Months: May and July
Best Day of the Week: Friday
Best Month Days: 1, 10, 19, 28
Lucky Charm: A new penny in your shoe.
Harmonious Signs for Relationships and Partnerships: Virgo, Capricorn, and sometimes Libra.

Spiritual Guides . . .

Star: Al Debaran—Those with this star are born leaders.
Angel: Asmodel—This angel governs business and other transactions and aids in negotiations.
Guardian Angel: Malachi—"Messenger of Jehovah."
Spiritual Stone: Topaz—This stone may protect the bearer from the effects of allergies.

✴ JUDITH'S INSIGHT ✴

Faithful and loyal, you stand up for yourself and those around you. You are not to be messed with when angry. Ultraresponsible in all undertakings, you succeed at work, school, or play. When it comes to love and sex, you are generous to the nth degree. You consider no sacrifice too great for your loved one and often end a crisis with openness, honesty, and fair dealing.

You have all the makings of an excellent public servant and could attain a high government position. You may work around uniformed people one way or another. This caretaker personality of yours may lead you down another path: medicine or teaching may be your niche. A lover of animals and gardening, you could be a veterinarian or a landscaper. Lo and behold, you find one way or another to help out your fellow man! This desire is strong, and this is how your humanity shines.

Your creative nature leaves you desirous of a little fame and a bit of fortune, too. Willing to work endlessly and tirelessly, you find yourself in the limelight from time to time. Your personal integrity exposes you to many a splendid thing.

✴ ✴ ✴

MAY 11 TAURUS • The winged bull of the zodiac
April 20 at 4:00 A.M. to May 21 at 4:00 A.M. • NUMEROLOGY 2

Possessions and Desires . . .

Gem: Sapphire—This gem may help you find forgiveness from those you've wronged.

Flower: Sensitive Plant—You may be oversensitive to imagined slights.

Astral Color, Color Need, Apparel Color: Your Astral Color is Red, which enhances passion, power, excitement, and strength. Yellow in your environment stimulates and exhilarates you. In your wardrobe, Rose gives you balance and harmony.

Fragrance: You are devoted to the scent of roses. Choose the buds that have the strongest fragrance to create the special emotions you need.

Tree: Maple—You have both great stability and flashes of intuition.

Instruments: Pipe organ, cymbal, drum

Composers: Handel, Johann Sebastian Bach

Bird: Stork—Turkish bird, held in high esteem the world over. This bird is intelligent but may have strange tendencies.

Symbol: Cross—the symbol of self-sacrifice and reconciliation.

Harmonious Health and Nutrition . . .

Health Scent: Apple—You are creative, full of joy, and nearly magical. You bring happiness.

Favorable Foods: Radishes, watermelon, buttermilk, salmon

What's Lucky . . .

Lucky Numbers: 2, 4, 6, 11

Best Months: May and July

Best Day of the Week: Friday

Best Month Days: 2, 11, 20, 29

Lucky Charms: Two 50-cent pieces. Give someone else one of them.

Harmonious Signs for Relationships and

Partnerships: Virgo, Capricorn, and sometimes Libra.

Spiritual Guides . . .

Star: Al Heka—Those with this star are driven to succeed.

Angel: Asmodel—This angel governs business and other transactions and aids in negotiations.

Guardian Angel: St. John—This angel simplifies that which is complicated.

Spiritual Stone: Topaz—This stone may protect the bearer from the effects of allergies.

✳ JUDITH'S INSIGHT ✳

You become increasingly versatile each day. You like reading and writing and can baffle those around you with your sharp knowledge of history and science. You can be the great observer, you know how to play any kind of game. You enjoy debating, whether it's serious or just for the fun of it.

Fond of travel, you are very likely to relocate often. Should you remain in one place, you will probably vacation frequently. You would make a great florist, designer, landscaper, or developer. You simply love improving, creating, or designing. You have a knack for producing beauty and should pursue a career that showcases that talent. You will find the arts very appealing, whether as part of your life's work or your hobby. Sarcastic and unpredictable is quite a combination, but you will catch many fish with your lures and flirtations. Your undying loyalty ensures the best for you but be aware there will be times when you will be in conflict. Your word is your bond. You like to make those around you happy. Often, you deliver before the recipient is even aware of a need.

As you mature, you learn to accept criticism with more grace and see that it doesn't always have to be destructive.

✳ ✳ ✳

MAY 12   TAURUS • The winged bull of the zodiac

April 20 at 4:00 A.M. to May 21 at 4:00 A.M. • NUMEROLOGY 3

Possessions and Desires . . .

Gem: Ruby—This stone may lead you to energy, friendship, and happiness.

Flower: Star of Bethlehem—You tend not be happy when things are even a little messy.

Astral Color, Color Need, Apparel Color: Your Astral Color is Red, which enhances passion, power, excitement, and strength. Yellow in your environment stimulates and exhilarates you. In your wardrobe, Rose gives you balance and harmony.

Fragrance: You are devoted to the scent of roses. Choose the buds that have the strongest fragrance to create the special emotions you need.

Tree: Elm—You have willpower, strength, and the ability to stand alone.

Instrument: Trombone

Composers: Verdi, Mendelssohn, Schumann

Bird: Eagle—This bird is quick to use its powers of flight. It can see immeasurable distances in a single glance, and can sometimes appear to be indifferent.

Symbol: Wreath—You have been crowned with a special personality. You are strong but extremely compassionate.

Harmonious Health and Nutrition . . .

Health Scent: Rose—This scent will lead you to passionate thoughts and make you feel warm inside.

Favorable Foods: Celery, grapes, cheese, liver

What's Lucky . . .

Lucky Numbers: 3, 4, 6, 12
Best Months: May and July
Best Day of the Week: Friday
Best Month Days: 3, 12, 21, 30
Lucky Charm: A pen that someone else has already used.
Harmonious Signs for Relationships and

Partnerships: Virgo, Capricorn, and sometimes Libra.

Spiritual Guides . . .

Star: Al Debaran—Those with this star are born leaders.

Angel: Asmodel—This angel governs business and other transactions and aids in negotiations.

Guardian Angel: Johiel—This angel is a protector of all those with a humble heart.

Spiritual Stone: Topaz—This stone may protect the bearer from the effects of allergies.

✶ JUDITH'S INSIGHT ✶

You inspire those around you with your love and devotion, despite some displays of bullheadedness. Your charm and wit make it hard for people to turn away. Relationships with friends and family improve steadily through the second half of your life. You are a philosopher in your own right; someday you'll understand just how intuitive you really are. The more you're drawn to the unknown, the more mysteries you unravel and conquer.

You're very versatile and develop talents and then take them for granted. Explore and build on those everyday skills, and eventually you will use them for both pleasure and profit. A career in painting, art, music, or literature brings harmony, although somewhere along the way you may desire something in the public life such as politics or law. You have an inborn sense of justice and believe in standing up for principles.

It's very likely that you will find "the one" easily and marry early. You can also expect to have a minimum of three loves during your lifetime. You seek beauty and are most content when you are surrounded by it. You are equally impressed with natural beauty and man-made creations. Generosity is your most honorable trait. As a highly respected member of the community, you will teach and touch others. Your kindness will be felt by many along your trail of life.

✶ ✶ ✶

MAY 13   TAURUS • The winged bull of the zodiac

April 20 at 4:00 A.M. to May 21 at 4:00 A.M. • NUMEROLOGY 4

Possessions and Desires . . .

Gem: Emerald—Those who carry this stone tend to be lucky in love.

Flower: Strawberry—You may not be able to love what you don't first respect.

Astral Color, Color Need, Apparel Color: Your Astral Color is Red, which enhances passion, power, excitement, and strength. Yellow in your environment stimulates and exhilarates you. In your wardrobe, Rose gives you balance and harmony.

Fragrance: You are devoted to the scent of roses. Choose the buds that have the strongest fragrance to create the special emotions you need.

Tree: Cherry—You will find yourself faced with constant new emotional awakenings.

Instruments: Bass, clarinet

Composers: Haydn, Wagner

Bird: Swan—Regarded as royal and sacred, this bird has the protective nature of a mother, and can become a furious fighter in the defense of its young.

Symbol: Star—You are full of inner brightness and will stand out in any crowd. You will be seen as special.

Harmonious Health and Nutrition . . .

Health Scent: Vanilla—This scent will fill you with a feeling of cleanliness and stability.

Favorable Foods: Brussels sprouts, apples, eggs, chicken

What's Lucky . . .

Lucky Numbers: 4, 6, 8, 13

Best Months: May and July

Best Day of the Week: Friday

Best Month Days: 4, 13, 22, 31

Lucky Charm: A piece of material cut from something in your home.

Harmonious Signs for Relationships and Partnerships: Virgo, Capricorn, and sometimes Libra.

Spiritual Guides . . .

Star: Al Debaran—Those with this star are born leaders.

Angel: Asmodel—This angel governs business and other transactions and aids in negotiations.

Guardian Angel: Uriel—This angel brings the light of God's guidance.

Spiritual Stone: Topaz—This stone may protect the bearer from the effects of allergies.

✶ JUDITH'S INSIGHT ✶

Set boundaries for yourself; balancing the world on your shoulders will become so much easier if you were to take baby steps instead of giant steps. Your strong desires lead you to many accomplishments, along with a barrel-full of struggles. These same desires, accomplishments, and struggles provide you with a foundation to build multiple careers and/or hobbies. Your dedication to achieving the goals you set for yourself ensures success for you. You seldom fail—you are very good at overcoming obstacles and responding to emergencies of every kind. You handle stress like a champ. Your independent approach to life makes you somewhat of a loner, but you very much enjoy the company of others and generally prefer companionship.

Peculiar circumstances surround your family and loved ones. The unusual is commonplace in your life, and the unexpected is most likely to happen around you. Somewhere along the way, you will be impressed with one or two foreign-born mates who come into your life. It appears you may have unusual living situations, or it may just be that you live in unusual living quarters. You work best alone but are comfortable with teamwork. Your performance continues to improve at a steady pace.

You expect the unexpected, and you often resort to stirring the pot merely to create challenges. Writing books or short stories or poetry would suit you, but you might also be content working in a car wash or as a chef.

Very possibly you'll support yourself in one thing while you concentrate on another. You may feel like a puddle-jumper when it comes to career, but you'll find your niche and have a story to tell. Very likely, this is how you become that renowned writer or poet. Hang in there!

✶ ✶ ✶

MAY 14

TAURUS • The winged bull of the zodiac

April 20 at 4:00 A.M. to May 21 at 4:00 A.M. • NUMEROLOGY 5

Possessions and Desires . . .

Gem: Amethyst—This stone is said to give calmness and peace.

Flower: Sumac—You may need to have things perfect before you can enjoy them.

Astral Color, Color Need, Apparel Color: Your Astral Color is Red, which enhances passion, power, excitement, and strength. Yellow in your environment stimulates and exhilarates you. In your wardrobe, Rose gives you balance and harmony.

Fragrance: You are devoted to the scent of roses. Choose the buds that have the strongest fragrance to create the special emotions you need.

Tree: Apple—You are creative, full of joy, and nearly magical. You bring happiness.

Instruments: Viola, trumpet

Composer: Liszt

Bird: Flamingo—This beautiful, gregarious bird is always careful of its enemy. It is also a caretaker of the young who tries to keep everyone happy.

Symbol: Triangle—You have the right combination of abilities.

Harmonious Health and Nutrition . . .

Health Scents: Peach—This scent may balance your good qualities so they equal your charm.

Favorable Foods: Radishes, peaches, eggs, beef

What's Lucky . . .

Lucky Numbers: 4, 5, 6, 14

Best Months: May and July

Best Day of the Week: Friday

Best Month Days: 4, 5, 23

Lucky Charms: A rabbit's foot or a white candle.

Harmonious Signs for Relationships and Partnerships: Virgo, Capricorn, and sometimes Libra.

Spiritual Guides . . .

Star: Al Heka—Those with this star are driven to succeed.

Angel: Asmodel—This angel governs business and other transactions and aids in negotiations.

Guardian Angel: Plavwell—This angel gives power and strength to one's presence.

Spiritual Stone: Topaz—This stone may protect the bearer from the effects of allergies.

✦ JUDITH'S INSIGHT ✦

You have the gift of gab and are quite the talker. Others feel close to you. You somehow manage to keep your left hand from knowing what your right hand is doing. Talk about being complicated! You have a marvelous look and are so appealing to the eye, you'll have no problem in attracting a mate. You do have to be cautious of that occasional sharp tongue, as this could create havoc in any relationship. You can take a lot and are slow to anger, but when you finally lose it, the steam that has been building bursts forth. Passionate to a fault, you have a tendency to avoid too much conversational intimacy.

You should strive for more independence when it comes to your career. Your exceptionally fine brain works well for you, no matter what the demands. Your decision that you are better off working on your own is delayed because you work so well with others. You eventually recognize your capability to take charge. You expect others to pull their own weight, like you, and are intolerant of lazy people.

Working along with others is fine for you, but needing them bothers you. Whether you become the butcher, the baker, or the television producer, you will have many opportunities to use your various talents. You underestimate your own skills, and it's hard for you to realize that others aren't as skilled as you and may lack your keen eye or strong sense of originality.

Be patient with others, and you learn to tolerate yourself better.

✶ ✶ ✶

MAY 15

TAURUS • The winged bull of the zodiac

April 20 at 4:00 A.M. to May 21 at 4:00 A.M. • NUMEROLOGY 6

Possessions and Desires . . .

Gem: Topaz—This is an excellent gift to be exchanged between very loyal friends.

Flower: Sweet William—You love gallantry above all other virtues.

Astral Color, Color Need, Apparel Color: Your Astral Color is Red, which enhances passion, power, excitement, and strength. Yellow in your environment stimulates and exhilarates you. In your wardrobe, Rose gives you balance and harmony.

Fragrance: You are devoted to the scent of roses. Choose the buds that have the strongest fragrance to create the special emotions you need.

Tree: Palm—You tend to be very healthy and creative.

Instruments: Tambourine, lyre

Composer: Schubert

Bird: Lark—known for the beauty of its song, which is sometimes very unusual. It is also credited with extraordinary intelligence.

Symbol: Crescent—You are more likely to be influenced by the phases of the moon. Your easygoing manner leads you to peaceful situations.

Harmonious Health and Nutrition . . .

Health Scent: Orange Blossom—This scent may balance your body, mind, and soul.

Favorable Foods: Turnips, lime, cheese, oysters

What's Lucky . . .

Lucky Numbers: 4, 6, 12, 15

Best Months: May and July

Best Day of the Week: Friday

Best Month Days: 6, 15, 24

Lucky Charms: A religious token or card from any religion.

Harmonious Signs for Relationships and

Partnerships: Virgo, Capricorn, and sometimes Libra.

Spiritual Guides . . .

Star: Al Debaran—Those with this star are born leaders.

Angel: Asmodel—This angel governs business and other transactions and aids in negotiations.

Guardian Angel: Michael—"Who is like God."

Spiritual Stone: Topaz—This stone may protect the bearer from the effects of allergies.

✷ JUDITH'S INSIGHT ✷

You love entertaining friends and family, especially the children. Often considered intense and meticulous, you appreciate a grand home and a designer office. You're always willing to go all out to make things happen, not only for yourself but also for others.

You must be cautious when it comes to finding the right partner. Your ability to idealize relationships also puts strain on them. Your romantic desires sometimes can be more important than simply maintaining a good relationship or keeping harmony within it. You can be both angel or devil with trident in hand, depending on the situation. Most often the angel is readily apparent, but look out when that devil surfaces!

You should seek to work with beauty one way or another. Some options you should consider: architect, landscaper, builder, designer, or florist. The possibilities are endless. You may find your most fulfilling role as a physician, perhaps a plastic surgeon. Beauty is everywhere!

You have a weak spot for animals or the underdogs in life. Keep these emotions and this enthusiasm burning in your heart and devote yourself to a good cause. Try volunteering your time and services or become a caretaker in some other way. Your good nature will inevitably ensure that your kindness will be noticed by others, even if you don't know it at the time.

✷ ✷ ✷

MAY 16

TAURUS • The winged bull of the zodiac

April 20 at 4:00 A.M. to May 21 at 4:00 A.M. • NUMEROLOGY 7

Possessions and Desires . . .

Gem: Agate—This stone may promote health and lead you to a long life.
Flower: Lilac—You may have a phenomenal memory.
Astral Color, Color Need, Apparel Color: Your Astral Color is Red, which enhances passion, power, excitement, and strength. Yellow in your environment stimulates and exhilarates you. In your wardrobe, Rose gives you balance and harmony.
Fragrance: You are devoted to the scent of roses. Choose the buds that have the strongest fragrance to create the special emotions you need.
Tree: Sycamore—Yours is the ability to love, communicate honestly with others, and have lasting relationships.
Instrument: Harp
Composers: Gluck, Brahms
Bird: Skylark—This handsome bird is beautiful when it sings. It always whistles as it works.
Symbol: Heart—You are enthusiastic, empathetic, and full of generosity and love.

Harmonious Health and Nutrition . . .

Health Scent: Jasmine—This scent may make you more easygoing when you are stressed.
Favorable Foods: Spinach, strawberries, liver, eggs

What's Lucky . . .

Lucky Numbers: 4, 6, 7, 16
Best Months: May and July
Best Day of the Week: Friday
Best Month Days: 6, 15, 24
Lucky Charm: An old key.
Harmonious Signs for Relationships and Partnerships: Virgo, Capricorn, and sometimes Libra.

Spiritual Guides . . .

Star: Al Heka—Those with this star are driven to succeed.
Angel: Asmodel—This angel governs business and other transactions and aids in negotiations.
Guardian Angel: Raphael—This angel attends to all of your needs when you are looking for guidance.
Spiritual Stone: Topaz—This stone may protect the bearer from the effects of allergies.

✶ JUDITH'S INSIGHT ✶

Your very presence gives encouragement to others. Friends and family are loyal throughout your life. They know your devotion to them. You are good-natured, kind, and honorable. You are a giver by nature. This benevolence may be detrimental to you, because you give of yourself and your pocketbook to the utmost. You are self-indulgent at times, especially as you pursue the quality things. A nonconformist, you may appear eccentric, and others may view you as peculiar.

Monetary rewards manifest themselves one way or another during your lifetime. You may be successful in the legal issues of your life; maybe an inheritance ensures your fortune. You are better at expressing your feelings through writing rather than speaking. There are many opportunities in which to invest your skills. You may have a career as a nurse or teacher. You will also find much satisfaction as a devoted guardian or parent. Family members residing with you will benefit from your caring ways. This leads to other acts of good will, such as being responsible for getting a new wing on the local hospital, or devoting your time as a volunteer to local charities. Your humanitarian efforts will go far.

Listen to yourself and learn to follow your dreams. Unusual events in life help you and guide you. Let your dreams give you the answers you seek. You count on that guardian angel looking out for you, and in turn you provide great protection to many others.

✶ ✶ ✶

MAY 17 TAURUS • The winged bull of the zodiac
April 20 at 4:00 A.M. to May 21 at 4:00 A.M. • NUMEROLOGY 8

Possessions and Desires . . .

Gem: Sapphire—This gem may help you find forgiveness from those you've wronged.

Flower: Thistle—You tend to feel that to avoid excess is the way to success.

Astral Color, Color Need, Apparel Color: Your Astral Color is Red, which enhances passion, power, excitement, and strength. Yellow in your environment stimulates and exhilarates you. In your wardrobe, Rose gives you balance and harmony.

Fragrance: You are devoted to the scent of roses. Choose the buds that have the strongest fragrance to create the special emotions you need.

Tree: Pine—Your relationships tend to be harmonious, both emotionally and mentally.

Instrument: Cello

Composer: Mozart

Bird: Bobolink—This charming singer is equally good as a soloist or a member of an orchestra. It is a very romantic bird, most useful as an insect destroyer, and elegant, with beautiful feathers, and always pleasant to have around.

Symbol: Wings—You are the source of balance in your world—this will bring you contentment.

Harmonious Health and Nutrition . . .

Health Scent: Almond—This scent may revitalize you and open you to greater possibilities.

Favorable Foods: Spinach, raspberries, cheese, salmon

What's Lucky . . .

Lucky Numbers: 4, 6, 8, 17
Best Months: May and July
Best Day of the Week: Friday
Best Month Days: 8, 17, 26
Lucky Charm: Red ribbon in your wallet or doorway.
Harmonious Signs for Relationships and

Partnerships: Virgo, Capricorn, and sometimes Libra.

Spiritual Guides . . .

Star: Al Heka—Those with this star are driven to succeed.

Angel: Asmodel—This angel governs business and other transactions and aids in negotiations.

Guardian Angel: Seraphim—An angel that brings love, light, and passion.

Spiritual Stone: Topaz—This stone may protect the bearer from the effects of allergies.

✶ JUDITH'S INSIGHT ✶

Craving love and affection the way you do could take you down the wrong paths. So keep this in mind; be cautious about taking unnecessary chances or letting yourself be careless in these matters. You are called the child of fate. This stems from the numerous changes in your surroundings from the time of your birth. Being strong-willed makes it difficult for you to express your emotions. Throughout your life, this will be a challenge all its own. You sacrifice yourself often for others, especially family members, but all the while you are seeking their approval.

The search is on when it comes to love matters—it will indeed take time and patience, yet the outcome is ultimately worth waiting for. Watch out for feelings of loneliness, even when you are in a good, loving relationship. Friendships, however, may be your greatest source of support and contentment, although you tend to underestimate the power of your friends.

Your financial gains come not only from hard work but also through careful investments in solid, grounded companies. You would be good at developing land or landscape architecture. Your talent for innovative ideas is best put to use there, or in the arts, as long as it's in a hands-on situation. Most others must follow their hearts. You, however, must follow your gut. You have great intuition and great instincts. These attributes will enable you to succeed in business.

✶ ✶ ✶

MAY 18　TAURUS • The winged bull of the zodiac
April 20 at 4:00 A.M. to May 21 at 4:00 A.M. • NUMEROLOGY 9

Possessions and Desires . . .

Gem: Emerald—Those who carry this stone tend to be lucky in love.

Flower: Vervain—You usually seem extremely charming to those around you.

Astral Color, Color Need, Apparel Color: Your Astral Color is Red, which enhances passion, power, excitement, and strength. Yellow in your environment stimulates and exhilarates you. In your wardrobe, Rose gives you balance and harmony.

Fragrance: You are devoted to the scent of roses. Choose the buds that have the strongest fragrance to create the special emotions you need.

Tree: Holly—Beware that you are not carried away by your passionate nature. The only way to grow is to be open to new experiences.

Instruments: Violin, tympanum

Composer: Gluck

Bird: Mockingbird—the most proficient minstrel in the world's orchestra; graceful and enthusiastic.

Symbol: Anchor—This tranquil symbol signifies stability and strength, and stands for strong commitments in relationships.

Harmonious Health and Nutrition . . .

Health Scent: Lavender—This scent might lead others to trust you and make you patient.

Favorable Foods: Watercress, bananas, eggs, chicken

What's Lucky . . .

Lucky Numbers: 4, 6, 9, 18
Best Months: May and July
Best Day of the Week: Friday
Best Month Days: 9, 18, 27
Lucky Charms: A U.S. coin or a bill of any amount from the year you were born.
Harmonious Signs for Relationships and

Partnerships: Virgo, Capricorn, and sometimes Libra.

Spiritual Guides . . .

Star: Al Debaran—Those with this star are born leaders.

Angel: Asmodel—This angel governs business and other transactions and aids in negotiations.

Guardian Angel: Gabriel—"God is my strength."

Spiritual Stone: Topaz—This stone may protect the bearer from the effects of allergies.

✴ JUDITH'S INSIGHT ✴

Organization? Nobody does it better than you. You enjoy working and are capable of producing almost anything. In time, and with your natural talents, you will be quite successful. Unfortunately, you get in your own way. Learn to step around yourself, and don't hold back. Competitive by nature, you can debate most topics. A challenge whets your appetite and will be what drives you to get the job done. Just remember, be careful of what you wish for; in time and after skirting many obstacles, you get the golden ring.

The emotional part isn't as easy for you. Your strong will and impatience can sometimes ruin relationships because of your inability to allow them time to work. People can get to you and ruffle your feathers with their indecisiveness. You tend to have more successes in business than you do with love, but inevitably you do find mates who understand and appreciate you.

Your practicality will take you far. It would not be surprising if you sought structure in your career, perhaps with the military or the police force or in a position in government or politics. You may be in charge. You yearn for intrigue and some action, and it is likely you will have dual careers and/or hobbies.

Family members play a big role in your life. You do, however, pull away from time to time because of the pressures on you. Self-confidence will bring you to the door of success and provide the key to open it.

✴ ✴ ✴

MAY 19
TAURUS • The winged bull of the zodiac
April 20 at 4:00 A.M. to May 21 at 4:00 A.M. • NUMEROLOGY 1

Possessions and Desires . . .

Gem: Turquoise—This stone may help you find material wealth.

Flower: Trillium—You are usually very modest about your many gifts.

Astral Color, Color Need, Apparel Color: Your Astral Color is Red, which enhances passion, power, excitement, and strength. Yellow in your environment stimulates and exhilarates you. In your wardrobe, Rose gives you balance and harmony.

Fragrance: You are devoted to the scent of roses. Choose the buds that have the strongest fragrance to create the special emotions you need.

Tree: Walnut—You are unusually helpful and always looking for new beginnings.

Instruments: Oboe, flute, clarinet, piano, French horn, organ, piccolo

Composer: Böhm

Bird: Bird of Paradise—the "bird of the Gods." You will shine and love extraordinary circumstances.

Symbol: Crown—the universal sign of dignity.

Harmonious Health and Nutrition . . .

Health Scent: Strawberry—Soothing by nature, the strawberry promotes self-esteem and encourages love.

Favorable Foods: Watercress, bananas, eggs, chicken

What's Lucky . . .

Lucky Numbers: 1, 4, 6, 10
Best Months: May and July
Best Day of the Week: Friday
Best Month Days: 1, 10, 19, 28
Lucky Charm: A new penny in your shoe.
Harmonious Signs for Relationships and

Partnerships: Virgo, Capricorn, and sometimes Libra.

Spiritual Guides . . .

Star: Al Heka—Those with this star are driven to succeed.

Angel: Asmodel—This angel governs business and other transactions and aids in negotiations.

Guardian Angel: Malachi—"Messenger of Jehovah."

Spiritual Stone: Topaz—This stone may protect the bearer from the effects of allergies.

✴ JUDITH'S INSIGHT ✴

Self-reliance and creativity are your foundation, and you also have a compassionate and nurturing nature. You recoil from criticism, but do not discount everything; some criticism is constructive. Your kindness may be misunderstood by those not as nice as you. You could work well in a hospital either volunteering your services or pursuing a career. Your keen eye and delightful bedside manner would be most appreciated. You stand tall in such a setting. You are happiest with a specific goal, but do not narrow your options when fixing goals. You are likely to aspire to many, and accomplish much.

How you view yourself is far more important than how others see you. You can be your own worst enemy, especially when it comes to love. An adoring mate doesn't ruffle your feathers easily, but that independent companion puts you through many a hurdle. Your tolerance here pays off when your independent companion becomes your adoring mate.

Give yourself a break. It's okay not to extend your helping hand every time. Learn to sit back, enjoy the music, and watch the show, even if you are worrying about your neighbor's needs. The kindness you provide comes back to you.

✴ ✴ ✴

MAY 20

TAURUS • The winged bull of the zodiac

April 20 at 4:00 A.M. to May 21 at 4:00 A.M. • NUMEROLOGY 2

Possessions and Desires . . .

Gem: Sapphire—This gem may help you find forgiveness from those you've wronged.
Flower: Wallflower—You usually have the strength to get through any adversity.
Astral Color, Color Need, Apparel Color: Your Astral Color is Red, which enhances passion, power, excitement, and strength. Yellow in your environment stimulates and exhilarates you. In your wardrobe, Rose gives you balance and harmony.
Fragrance: You are devoted to the scent of roses. Choose the buds that have the strongest fragrance to create the special emotions you need.
Tree: Maple—You have both great stability and flashes of intuition.
Instruments: Pipe organ, cymbal, drum
Composers: Handel, Johann Sebastian Bach
Bird: Stork—Turkish bird, held in high esteem the world over. This bird is intelligent but may have strange tendencies.
Symbol: Cross—the symbol of self-sacrifice and reconciliation.

Harmonious Health and Nutrition . . .

Health Scent: Apple—You are creative, full of joy, and nearly magical. You bring happiness.
Favorable Foods: Turnips, grapes, buttermilk, oysters

What's Lucky . . .

Lucky Numbers: 2, 4, 6
Best Months: May and July
Best Day of the Week: Friday
Best Month Days: 2, 11, 20, 29
Lucky Charms: Two 50-cent pieces. Give someone else one of them.
Harmonious Signs for Relationships and

Partnerships: Virgo, Capricorn, and sometimes Libra.

Spiritual Guides . . .

Star: Al Heka—Those with this star are driven to succeed.
Angel: Asmodel—This angel governs business and other transactions and aids in negotiations.
Guardian Angel: St. John—This angel simplifies that which is complicated.
Spiritual Stone: Topaz—This stone may protect the bearer from the effects of allergies.

✷ JUDITH'S INSIGHT ✷

Community-minded and sociable, you simply love to entertain. You seek that perfect appearance at all times. Your well-balanced mind brings much peace. You can be rather shrewd, but you keep that hidden. Your inquisitive, inventive nature, coupled with your wit, ensures a good future as a counselor, teacher, police detective, or even an incredibly successful politician. You are a leader; you can do anything from being the president of the PTA to being the president of the United States. You'll probably be in government. Somewhere along the way, the law enters your lifestyle. With your questioning mind, you may find yourself taking on some great attorneys or defending renowned criminals.

Early in life your vanity contributes to your condescending attitude toward your love mate. Maturity brings balance and after some emotional bumps and bruises, you become comfortable with close relationships and are very much better at working on those alliances.

Entertainment simply intrigues you; don't be surprised if you occasionally seek a bit of excess. Your fondness for fine art and music may enhance a career or provide a satisfying hobby that consumes all your spare time.

✷ ✷ ✷

MAY 21 TAURUS • The winged bull of the zodiac

April 20 at 4:00 A.M. to May 21 at 4:00 A.M. • NUMEROLOGY 3

Possessions and Desires . . .

Gem: Ruby—This stone may lead you to energy, friendship, and happiness.

Flower: Weeping Willow—You may spend too much time focusing on what you've lost instead of what you have to gain.

Astral Color, Color Need, Apparel Color: Your Astral Color is Red, which enhances passion, power, excitement, and strength. Yellow in your environment stimulates and exhilarates you. In your wardrobe, Rose gives you balance and harmony.

Fragrance: You are devoted to the scent of roses. Choose the buds that have the strongest fragrance to create the special emotions you need.

Tree: Elm—You have willpower, strength, and the ability to stand alone.

Instrument: Trombone

Composers: Verdi, Mendelssohn, Schumann

Bird: Swan—Regarded as royal and sacred, this bird has the protective nature of a mother, and can become a furious fighter in the defense of its young.

Symbol: Wreath—You have been crowned with a special personality. You are strong but extremely compassionate.

Harmonious Health and Nutrition . . .

Health Scent: Rose—This scent will lead you to passionate thoughts and make you feel warm inside.

Favorable Foods: Tomatoes, black figs, eggs, beef

What's Lucky . . .

Lucky Numbers: 3, 4, 6
Best Months: May and July
Best Day of the Week: Friday
Best Month Days: 3, 12, 21, 30
Lucky Charm: A pen that someone else has already used.
Harmonious Signs for Relationships and Partnerships: Virgo, Capricorn, and sometimes Libra.

Spiritual Guides . . .

Star: Al Debaran—Those with this star are born leaders.

Angel: Asmodel—This angel governs business and other transactions and aids in negotiations.

Guardian Angel: Johiel—This angel is a protector of all those with a humble heart.

Spiritual Stone: Topaz—This stone may protect the bearer from the effects of allergies.

✳ JUDITH'S INSIGHT ✳

Your sense of freedom dictates your actions and reactions. It is not surprising if you follow through with those unexpected urges to change your lifestyle by redoing your house or relocating out of state. You are meticulous about your appearance to friends, relatives, and strangers alike. You seek the social environment and everything it has to offer. You rebel against injustice in any form and tend to fight for the underdog. Your artistic nature draws you to the arts one way or another, whether through music, poetry, or the ballet, or merely as a frequent patron of the theater. Staying up late watching movies, you project yourself into nearly every scene.

That strong, devoted love of friends and family makes you more than willing to take on the responsibilities of others, be it giving of yourself or slipping some dollars into pockets. Don't permit your inherent love of home to blind you to the manipulations of some undeserving characters. Although fiercely loyal to your family, you can be fickle with your friends. You enjoy having children around you, and you play a strong role in children's lives. This could be as a loving parent, but more than likely you will be a Dutch uncle, the godmother/godfather, or just the neighbor willing to listen.

You love receiving invitations, whether or not you go where you're invited. You are anxious to be more of a socialite than you are. As time passes, you get to that desired place in society. You can seem eccentric. You like unusual decorations in your home or office. It's possible you will deal in antiques. Whatever path you take, your career takes off, and in time, success means money.

✳ ✳ ✳

MAY 22

GEMINI • The twins of the zodiac
May 21 at 4:00 A.M. to June 21 at 12:00 P.M. • NUMEROLOGY 4

Possessions and Desires . . .

Gem: Topaz—This is an excellent gift to be exchanged between very loyal friends.
Flower: Willow—You love to be free so much that any boundary feels like a prison.
Astral Color, Color Need, Apparel Color: Your Astral Color is Red, which enhances passion, power, excitement, and strength. Violet in your environment will keep you empathetic toward others. In your wardrobe, Green is your power color for overcoming obstacles.
Fragrance: You should flood your living space with the scent of distilled floral bouquet or freshly cut wood. This will give your ever-curious mind a rest from its constant search for new experiences.
Tree: Cherry—You will find yourself faced with constant new emotional awakenings.
Instrument: Bass, clarinet
Composers: Haydn, Wagner
Bird: Robin—the most sociable of all birds, with the ability to create quick friendships. It also can easily adapt to any home. When it wants something, it has the tendency to try to snatch it.
Symbol: Star—You are full of inner brightness and will stand out in any crowd. You will be seen as special.

Harmonious Health and Nutrition . . .

Health Scent: Vanilla—This scent will fill you with a feeling of cleanliness and stability.
Favorable Foods: Kale, grapes, whole-wheat breads, molasses, goat's milk

What's Lucky . . .

Lucky Numbers: 4, 5, 8, 9
Best Months: April and August
Best Day of the Week: Wednesday
Best Month Days: 4, 13, 22, 31
Lucky Charm: A piece of material cut from something in your home.

Harmonious Signs for Relationships and Partnerships: Aquarius and Libra

Spiritual Guides . . .

Star: Al Divah—Those with this star could feel that they are mistreated by relatives.
Angel: Ambriel—This angel governs travel and transportation, particularly over water, and helps to create love and good communication.
Guardian Angel: Uriel—This angel brings the light of God's guidance.
Spiritual Stone: Chrysoprasus—This stone aids in relaxation.

✶ JUDITH'S INSIGHT ✶

You are magnetic. Others are drawn to you and they don't know why. You can hypnotize with your charm. You are loved by all. Your innate desire to be conscientious attracts people. You have a style of your own; you enjoy music and science. It's possible that at a young age you were either dissecting worms or mentally testing social issues in political situations. You can write well and may find yourself in some type of media position, perhaps as a journalist or photographer. Although art is a real pull for you, the camera would be more your style as it captures your analytical ability. You very well could develop your talents and handle both sides of the camera well: behind it, directing motion pictures, or in front, acting in a film.

Fear and doubt inhibit you at times, but you can rise above these things. You like to help those in need. Independent, yet gentle and kind, you are drawn to the security of a stable relationship. Would-be mates are attracted by your magnetism, but you often discount possibilities because of some underlying fear. Remain open-minded.

You set high standards, not only for yourself, but also for others. In rising to meet these top standards, there will be falls, yet you find you easily pick yourself up and dust yourself off. Not having sufficient patience and understanding of your mate raises much more conflict, but when you learn to do so, the rewards are great.

✶ ✶ ✶

MAY 23 GEMINI • The twins of the zodiac

May 21 at 4:00 A.M. to June 21 at 12:00 P.M. • NUMEROLOGY 5

Possessions and Desires . . .

Gem: Topaz—This is an excellent gift to be exchanged between very loyal friends.
Flower: Water Lily—Your motives are always for the best.
Astral Color, Color Need, Apparel Color: Your Astral Color is Red, which enhances passion, power, excitement, and strength. Violet in your environment keeps you empathetic towards others. In your wardrobe, Coral brings you a brilliant and sharp appearance.
Fragrance: You should flood your living space with the scent of distilled floral bouquet or freshly cut wood. This will give your ever-curious mind a rest from its constant search for new experiences.
Tree: Apple—You are creative, full of joy, and nearly magical. You bring happiness.
Instruments: Viola, trumpet
Composer: Liszt
Bird: Flamingo—This beautiful, gregarious bird is always careful of its enemy. It is also a caretaker of the young who tries to keep everyone happy.
Symbol: Triangle—You have the right combination of abilities.

Harmonious Health and Nutrition . . .

Health Scent: Peach—This scent may balance your good qualities so that they equal your charm.
Favorable Foods: Parsnips, oranges, wholewheat bread, molasses, eggs

What's Lucky . . .

Lucky Numbers: 5, 9, 10, 23
Best Months: April and August
Best Day of the Week: Wednesday
Best Month Days: 5, 4, 23
Lucky Charms: A rabbit's foot or a white candle.
Harmonious Signs for Relationships and Partnerships: Aquarius and Libra

Spiritual Guides . . .

Star: Al Divah—Those with this star could feel that they are mistreated by relatives.
Angel: Ambriel—This angel governs travel and transportation, particularly over water, and helps to create love and good communication.
Guardian Angel: Plavwell—This angel gives power and strength to one's presence.
Spiritual Stone: Chrysoprasus—This stone aids in relaxation.

✷ JUDITH'S INSIGHT ✷

You like to play the role of hero/heroine, whether it is on the screen or in real life. Perhaps you most enjoy writing about heroic people. Analytical by nature, you could become overcritical unless, of course, you are that well-paid, published critic. Versatility abounds when it comes to your career—you can do anything from editing or writing the books to performing on stage or screen. You will be involved with literature or publishing or heading a media company. As long as you have pen and paper, you will be successful.

You find mates perhaps too early in life. You're independent in almost every aspect of your life—except your emotional ties. Love affairs are frequent, and you can be moody when it comes to showing affection. Once you have loved people in your life, your loyalty and devotion make it difficult for your significant other to sever the ties.

Family members play you like a fine violin, but you allow it. Having children involved in your life, in one way or another, is of great importance to you. The fun and spontaneity in your relationships enable you to maintain them easily. When it comes to real intimacy, these relationships require more work, as you tend to shy away. Lucky when it comes to earning money, you will have opportunities to do so in many different capacities throughout your life. You particularly desire beautiful things—even if you don't realize it. This may be expressed in a well-manicured lawn or the fine suits you wear. Eventually you feel more balanced, and harmony finds you in later years.

★ ★ ★

MAY 24

GEMINI • The twins of the zodiac

May 21 at 4:00 A.M. to June 21 at 12:00 P.M. • NUMEROLOGY 6

Possessions and Desires . . .

Gem: Topaz—This is an excellent gift to be exchanged between very loyal friends.

Flower: Aconite—You need to work on liking people more.

Astral Color, Color Need, Apparel Color: Your Astral Color is Red, which enhances passion, excitement, and strength. Violet in your environment keeps you empathetic toward others. In your wardrobe, Green is your power color for overcoming obstacles.

Fragrance: You should flood your living space with the scent of distilled floral bouquet or freshly cut wood. This will give your ever-curious mind a rest from its constant search for new experiences.

Tree: Palm—You tend to be very healthy and creative.

Instruments: Tambourine, lyre

Composer: Schubert

Bird: Goldfinch—there are forty-four different species of finches which vary greatly. This can sometimes be the most charming of birds. These gentle creatures can be very moody in unsettled weather.

Symbol: Crescent—You are more likely to be influenced by the phases of the moon. Your easygoing manner leads you to peaceful situations.

Harmonious Health and Nutrition . . .

Health Scent: Orange Blossom—This scent may balance your body, mind, and soul.

Favorable Foods: Cabbage, huckleberries, whole-wheat bread, buttermilk

What's Lucky . . .

Lucky Numbers: 5, 6, 9, 12
Best Months: April and August
Best Day of the Week: Wednesday
Best Month Days: 6, 15, 24
Lucky Charms: A religious token or card from any religion.
Harmonious Signs for Relationships and Partnerships: Aquarius and Libra

Spiritual Guides . . .

Star: Al Henah—Those born under this star are easily wounded.

Angel: Ambriel—This angel governs travel and transportation, particularly over water, and helps to create love and good communication.

Guardian Angel: Michael—"Who is like God."

Spiritual Stone: Chrysoprasus—This stone aids in relaxation.

✳ JUDITH'S INSIGHT ✳

You enjoy writing, especially about issues of a mysterious nature. You love music, art, and the sciences. You could find yourself drawn to a career in science. Generally, you have a lot of enthusiasm about which direction you take in life, but occasionally you are stifled when your environment is no longer stimulating and comfortable. Small annoyances from people bother you more than you think, but the atmosphere at the moment has much to do with it. Watch out for those who drink too much around you.

Lighthearted and sympathetic, you yearn for love, and when you find it, you appreciate how much being loved means to you. You reap what you sow and cultivate great relationships with current friends, while maintaining friendships from childhood. Relationships continue to emerge as you get older. Family occupies a large role in your life, especially your father or another male—be aware that this could be a vulnerable situation for you. Your enthusiasm can make you appear intense in relationships. All in all, you will have an understanding mate and will learn to keep the balance.

As for your career, make sure you gravitate toward putting your thoughts on paper. If you are a caretaker, for example, a nurse, doctor, therapist, or psychologist, keep that pen handy and maintain a journal. This will not only assist you in ousting emotions so that they have no place to hide, but give you a basis for perhaps a literary piece. It may not seem creative, but becoming a detective or investigator could bring out things in you that you don't realize are there. You can be shrewd when needed, and this, too, supports your aspirations. You prefer working alone, but you recognize that team work can be more advantageous. You circulate with people in high positions and sometimes are intrigued by them. As time passes, you'll be at the top.

MAY 25 GEMINI • The twins of the zodiac

May 21 at 4:00 A.M. to June 21 at 12:00 P.M. • NUMEROLOGY 7

Possessions and Desires . . .

Gem: Ruby—This stone may lead you to energy, friendship, and happiness.

Flower: Rhubarb—You may love to give advice, but you are not apt to take it.

Astral Color, Color Needs, Apparel Color: Your Astral Color is Red, which enhances passion, excitement, and strength. Violet in your environment keeps you empathetic toward others. In your wardrobe, Wine gives you energy.

Fragrance: You should flood your living space with the scent of distilled floral bouquet or freshly cut wood. This will give your ever-curious mind a rest from its constant search for new experiences.

Tree: Sycamore—Yours is the ability to love, communicate honestly with others, and have lasting relationships.

Instrument: Harp

Composers: Gluck, Brahms

Bird: Skylark—This handsome bird is beautiful when it sings. It always whistles as it works.

Symbol: Heart—You are enthusiastic, empathetic, and full of generosity and love.

Harmonious Health and Nutrition . . .

Health Scent: Jasmine—This scent may make you more easygoing when you are stressed.

Favorable Foods: Prunes, whole-wheat bread, molasses, goat's milk

What's Lucky . . .

Lucky Numbers: 5, 7, 9, 14

Best Months: April and August

Best Day of the Week: Wednesday

Best Month Days: 6, 15, 24

Lucky Charm: An old key.

Harmonious Signs for Relationships and Partnerships: Aquarius and Libra

Spiritual Guides . . .

Star: Al Divah—Those with this star could feel that they are mistreated by relatives.

Angel: Ambriel—This angel governs travel and transportation, particularly over water, and helps to create love and good communication.

Guardian Angel: Raphael—This angel attends to all of your needs when you are looking for guidance.

Spiritual Stone: Chrysoprasus—This stone aids in relaxation.

✶ JUDITH'S INSIGHT ✶

You are at times impractical; your fondness for pleasure attracts you to sports, entertainment, and amusements. One of these areas may be a great place to work: in the movies, entertaining people on stage, or on the athletic field. You do anything to entertain others and enjoy yourself. You switch easily from having a good time to being more serious. You also long for knowledge and may have many years of education or take classes in different fields for your own enjoyment. Be cautious about getting sidetracked and leaving things undone. Even if you don't attend classes, you will make the effort to learn by observing others.

You are basically content and free from anxieties. Sympathetic at times, you can also be demanding. You enjoy being generous, but you fear being taken advantage of. When you feel comfortable and believe you are receiving, you give more freely. Your skepticism of others' generosity fades with the years. With family members, you swing back and forth from closeness and security to feeling insecure, which, at times, creates distance.

Despite your intuition and good sense, you allow people into your life too quickly and may give too much credence to what they say. Trust your instincts—your first impression is most often right. You are critical at times, and your analytical side could foster a career in computers, working from your home or office. You may find that two careers surface simultaneously. You're capable of doing both, but one will most likely become a hobby. You feel complete with a partner in harmonious situations, be it marriage, partnership, or friendship. Stay active—loneliness may bring about depression. Not to say there isn't harmony in being alone. You just prefer to hold hands through life.

✶ ✶ ✶

MAY 26
GEMINI • The twins of the zodiac
May 21 at 4:00 A.M. to June 21 at 12:00 P.M. • NUMEROLOGY 8

Possessions and Desires . . .

Gem: Topaz—This is an excellent gift to be exchanged between very loyal friends.

Flower: Phlox—You may go along with the crowd more than could be good for you.

Astral Color, Color Need, Apparel Color: Your Astral Color is Red, which enhances passion, excitement, and strength. Violet in your environment keeps you empathetic toward others. In your wardrobe, Coral brings you a brilliant and sharp appearance.

Fragrance: You should flood your living space with the scent of distilled floral bouquet or freshly cut wood. This will give your ever-curious mind a rest from its constant search for new experiences.

Tree: Pine—Your relationships tend to be balanced, both emotionally and mentally.

Instrument: Cello

Composer: Mozart

Bird: Bobolink—This charming singer is equally good as a soloist or a member of an orchestra. It is a very romantic bird, useful as an insect destroyer, and elegant, with beautiful feathers, and always pleasant to have around.

Symbol: Wings—You are the source of balance in your world—this will bring you contentment.

Harmonious Health and Nutrition . . .

Health Scent: Almond—This scent may revitalize you and open you to greater possibilities.

Favorable Foods: Kale, grapes, whole-wheat bread, eggs

What's Lucky . . .

Lucky Numbers: 5, 8, 9, 16

Best Months: April and August

Best Day of the Week: Wednesday

Best Month Days: 8, 17, 26

Lucky Charm: Red ribbon in your wallet or doorway.

Harmonious Signs for Relationships and Partnerships: Aquarius and Libra

Spiritual Guides . . .

Star: Al Henah—Those born under this star are easily wounded.

Angel: Ambriel—This angel governs travel and transportation, particularly over water, and helps to create love and good communication

Guardian Angel: Seraphim—An angel that brings love, light, and passion.

Spiritual Stone: Chrysoprasus—This stone aids in relaxation.

✴ JUDITH'S INSIGHT ✴

You appreciate the finer things in life. You like Paris, the carnival, and springtime. You have extreme likes and dislikes. Strong and confident as you leave the house, you are easily discouraged and arrive home depressed and unmotivated. You could live two different lives, and no one would know it. You always wish you were someplace else. Easily distracted, you switch from project to project. If channeled properly, your drive could further a successful life's work. You will probably seek multiple educational degrees or vocational skills. Just about any job in education would be a number one choice.

Keep a journal, and you'll see progress. You will be pleasantly surprised how good a writer you are. Keep track, too, of your dreams—you feel comfortably connected to them. Your fear of publicity curbs your need to be known and heard. One way or another you seek to contribute to others; if not on stage, perhaps, through your writing. With your distinctive voice, you may have the opportunity to write song lyrics, and record the songs as well! If singing is not a career, you should join your local choir or other choral group.

Balancing the scales is learning about yourself while including family and loved ones. Childhood friends support you. You may have many careers before you find a balance in your mid-forties, but the trip along the way is more than satisfactory. You know how to have a good time by leaving your mind at home. When things become overwhelming, you recognize you must turn off your mind for a while.

★ ★ ★

MAY 27

GEMINI • The twins of the zodiac

May 21 at 4:00 A.M. to June 21 at 12:00 P.M. • NUMEROLOGY 9

Possessions and Desires . . .

Gem: Topaz—This is an excellent gift to be exchanged between very loyal friends.

Flower: Meadowsweet—You should guard against thinking that there is no purpose to whatever challenge the universe gives you.

Astral Color, Color Need, Apparel Color: Your Astral Color is Red, which enhances passion, excitement, and strength. Violet in your environment keeps you empathetic toward others. In your wardrobe, Coral brings you a brilliant and sharp appearance.

Fragrance: You should flood your living space with the scent of distilled floral bouquet or freshly cut wood. This will give your ever-curious mind a rest from its constant search for new experiences.

Tree: Holly—Beware that you are not carried away by your passionate nature. The only way to grow is to be open to new experiences..

Instruments: Violin, tympanum

Composer: Gluck

Bird: Mockingbird—the most proficient minstrel in the world's orchestra; graceful and enthusiastic.

Symbol: Anchor—This tranquil symbol signifies stability and strength, and stands for strong commitments in relationships.

Harmonious Health and Nutrition . . .

Health Scent: Lavender—This scent might lead others to trust you and make you patient.

Favorable Foods: Cucumbers, oranges, whole-wheat bread, cottage cheese

What's Lucky . . .

Lucky Numbers: 5, 9, 18, 27

Best Months: April and August

Best Day of the Week: Wednesday

Best Month Days: 9, 18, 27

Lucky Charms: A U.S. coin or a bill of any amount from the year you were born.

Harmonious Signs for Relationships and Partnerships: Aquarius and Libra

Spiritual Guides . . .

Star: Al Divah—Those with this star could feel that they are mistreated by relatives.

Angel: Ambriel—This angel governs travel and transportation, particularly over water, and helps to create love and good communication.

Guardian Angel: Gabriel—"God is my strength."

Spiritual Stone: Chrysoprasus—This stone aids in relaxation.

✶ JUDITH'S INSIGHT ✶

Your intuition and active mind form a strong desire for the mystical and the unknown. Your niche may be in psychic work or another spiritual field. Your practical side, however, creates contradiction, unless you write about it. You have talent for organization, and you desire conquest on a large scale. The ability to acquire wealth and power is yours, but watch out for unnecessary spending. You find power exciting and thrive on conflict. You'd do well on a debating team or in the political arena. Legal contests will present themselves. Be careful that you're not on the losing side. Be on guard for feeling out of control and overreacting.

In love, you lean toward obsessiveness or possessiveness. Demonstrate the affection you want others to. Think less and act more. You have more of a romantic mind than a romantic heart. In younger years, you are flirtatious. Luck in love comes in your thirties. If you marry earlier, you may fear you've chosen the wrong person or have years of dispute, but all gets resolved if that's what you want.

There is no undertaking too large for you, but your overzealous style may cause career downfalls. Fear not, most things work out. As for family, you assume enough responsibility to feel consumed. You may move away—not necessarily to create distance from the emotional drain—circumstances may simply bring this about. Don't fight it. You may choose a strong mate, and then find that strength and vitality are too much for you. In time, there will be balance and harmony. Financially, you do reasonably well. You accumulate many possessions to reassure yourself of your wealth and stability, but you must learn to share and to develop your generosity.

✶ ✶ ✶

MAY 28 GEMINI • The twins of the zodiac

May 21 at 4:00 A.M. to June 21 at 12:00 P.M. • NUMEROLOGY 1

Possessions and Desires . . .

Gem: Turquoise—This stone may help you find material wealth.

Flower: Oleander—You tend to hope more for peace than happiness.

Astral Color, Color Need, Apparel Color: Your Astral Color is Red, which enhances passion, excitement, and strength. Violet in your environment keeps you empathetic toward others. In your wardrobe, Wine gives you energy.

Fragrance: You should flood your living space with the scent of distilled floral bouquet or freshly cut wood. This will give your ever-curious mind a rest from its constant search for new experiences.

Tree: Walnut—You are unusually helpful and always looking for constant changes in your life.

Instruments: Oboe, flute, clarinet, piano, French horn, organ, piccolo

Composer: Böhm

Bird: Hummingbird—This bird is delicate and graceful. It can remain still for hours, then suddenly dart off and be as busy as a bee.

Symbol: Crown—the universal sign of dignity.

Harmonious Health and Nutrition . . .

Health Scent: Strawberry—Soothing by nature, the strawberry promotes self-esteem and encourages love.

Favorable Foods: Beets, cherries, whole-wheat bread, goat's milk

What's Lucky . . .

Lucky Numbers: 1, 5, 9, 10
Best Months: April and August
Best Day of the Week: Wednesday
Best Month Days: 1, 10, 19, 28
Lucky Charm: A new penny in your shoe.
Harmonious Signs for Relationships and Partnerships: Aquarius and Libra

Spiritual Guides . . .

Star: Al Henah—Those born under this star are easily wounded.

Angel: Ambriel—This angel governs travel and transportation, particularly over water, and helps to create love and good communication.

Guardian Angel: Malachi—"Messenger of Jehovah."

Spiritual Stone: Chrysoprasus—This stone aids in relaxation.

✳ JUDITH'S INSIGHT ✳

Creative, original and self-reliant, you are also impractical at times. You love your independence, but sometimes have to recognize your need for others. You should learn to develop your sensitivities and let people in. Build on your artistic capabilities in a career, be it photographer, artist, decorator, architect, or builder. You should follow your inclination toward the larger visions in life. When you do, you achieve. Although you seem strong and ambitious, self-esteem is sometimes low, which is the source of most of your problems. You dislike being alone and possess a driving need to always be with that special someone.

You have little patience for slow career advancement. You much prefer to simply be placed at the top. This is an immature outlook and could leave you perched at the top with little to offer. You crave recognition from friends and family. The more they stroke, the more you respond. Likewise, people get in with you with honey, not vinegar. Success awaits you, but you must make it happen. Whether your spot is in theater, fashion or beauty, you have a style all your own. The fashion industry really beckons, and you could do well. You are drawn to creative pursuits, but sometimes cannot draw on your own creativity. Be patient here until you get to a powerful situation.

Recognize that you alone don't always have to bear all the burdens. Extend your hand, take from others, and share the weight. In time, as you cultivate your sense of partnership, be it a love relationship, work, or play, you achieve harmony.

✳ ✳ ✳

MAY 29 GEMINI • The twins of the zodiac

May 21 at 4:00 A.M. to June 21 at 12:00 P.M. • NUMEROLOGY 2

Possessions and Desires . . .

Gem: Sapphire—This gem may help you find forgiveness from those you've wronged.

Flower: French Marigold—You may need to learn to trust those you love and get over being so jealous.

Astral Color, Color Need, Apparel Color: Your Astral Color is Red, which enhances passion, excitement, and strength. Violet in your environment keeps you empathetic toward others. In your wardrobe, Green is your power color for overcoming obstacles.

Fragrance: You should flood your living space with the scent of distilled floral bouquet or freshly cut wood. This will give your ever-curious mind a rest from its constant search for new experiences.

Tree: Maple—You have great stability and flashes of intuition.

Instruments: Pipe organ, cymbal, drum

Composers: Handel, Johann Sebastian Bach

Bird: Cuckoo—a good flyer and very seldom a quitter. Some cuckoos tend to think they favor lonely isolation, but what they really yearn for is a family relationship.

Symbol: Cross—the symbol of self-sacrifice and reconciliation.

Harmonious Health and Nutrition . . .

Health Scent: Apple—You are creative, full of joy, and nearly magical. You bring happiness.

Favorable Foods: Cabbage, huckleberries, whole-wheat bread, margarine

What's Lucky . . .

Lucky Numbers: 1, 5, 9, 11
Best Months: April and August
Best Day of the Week: Wednesday
Best Month Days: 2, 11, 20, 29
Lucky Charms: Two 50-cent pieces. Give someone else one of them.
Harmonious Signs for Relationships and Partnerships: Aquarius and Libra

Spiritual Guides . . .

Star: Al Henah—Those born under this star are easily wounded.

Angel: Ambriel—This angel governs travel and transportation, particularly over water, and helps to create love and good communication.

Guardian angel: St. John—The guardian that brings simplicity to all that is complicated.

Spiritual Stone: Chrysoprasus—This stone aids in relaxation.

✶ JUDITH'S INSIGHT ✶

It is easier for you to stick to something than to make changes in your life. You may dwell on your purpose in life, yet your lack of adventurousness keeps you where you are. Determined and dedicated, you prefer being on one ladder until you reach the top. It may feel like you're taking the long road. Family members are too important to you; you're often overly responsible for family and sometimes feel underappreciated. Others may see you as a drifting rebel rather than the solid rock that you are. You seem to deal with conflict on one level or another, on a daily basis. Learn to recognize you are not here to solve everyone's difficulties. Your frankness gets you in trouble, particularly with those who don't know you well. You are witty and charming. Consider writing about what goes on around you.

Relationships appear to be slow to develop at first; you tend to rush things. Be patient—you do better in time as you and your mate grow together and overcome the trouble spots. You push away those you love when angry. When you do devote yourself to someone, you give 110 percent. As long as your partner accepts your romanticism, your relationship has no limits. Stubbornness can be your greatest flaw. When you find yourself complaining, stop and listen. Others may complain about the same things about you. Your sympathetic side allows you to commiserate with others and may lead to a public, humanitarian career, as in a state hospital, school or medical institution, or perhaps making laws to improve life for the unfortunate. Creating boundaries for yourself, as well as others, will be very, very important. Once you learn to do this, you no longer need to go overboard in your emotional, physical, or professional life; the balance will contribute much to your happiness.

✶ ✶ ✶

MAY 30

GEMINI • The twins of the zodiac

May 21 at 4:00 A.M. to June 21 at 12:00 P.M. • NUMEROLOGY 3

Possessions and Desires . . .

Gem: Topaz—This is an excellent gift to be exchanged between very loyal friends.

Flower: Carolina Rose—You could fear losing yourself in love.

Astral Color, Color Need, Apparel Color: Your Astral Color is Red, which enhances passion, excitement, and strength. Violet in your environment keeps you empathetic toward others. In your wardrobe, Green is your power color for overcoming obstacles.

Fragrance: You should flood your living space with the scent of distilled floral bouquet or freshly cut wood. This will give your ever-curious mind a rest from its constant search for new experiences.

Tree: Elm—You have willpower, strength, and the ability to stand alone.

Instrument: Trombone

Composers: Verdi, Mendelssohn, Schumann

Bird: Swan—Regarded as royal and sacred, this bird has the protective nature of a mother, and can become a furious fighter in the defense of its young.

Symbol: Wreath—You have been crowned with a special personality. You are strong but extremely compassionate.

Harmonious Health and Nutrition . . .

Health Scent: Rose—This scent will lead you to passionate thoughts and make you feel warm inside.

Favorable Foods: Celery, peaches, whole-wheat bread, cottage cheese

What's Lucky . . .

Lucky Numbers: 3, 5, 6, 9
Best Months: April and August
Best Day of the Week: Wednesday
Best Month Days: 3, 12, 21, 30
Lucky Charm: A pen that someone else has already used.

Harmonious Signs for Relationships and Partnerships: Aquarius and Libra

Spiritual Guides . . .

Star: Al Henah—Those born under this star are easily wounded.

Angel: Ambriel—This angel governs travel and transportation, particularly over water, and helps to create love and good communication.

Guardian Angel: Johiel—This angel is a protector of all those with a humble heart.

Spiritual Stone: Chrysoprasus—This stone aids in relaxation.

✴ JUDITH'S INSIGHT ✴

You are enthusiastic, energetic, and ambitious. You can adapt to nearly any work scenario and efficiently accomplish it. There are no holds barred when it comes to your work. Contradiction may exist in your personality—you can be best friend or worst enemy to another. Compassionate and kind, you attract love mates easily. Be wary that you don't make commitments before you are ready. Once you commit, you are generally loyal, but you love to flirt. If you reassure your partner that the flirting is harmless, you'll fare better in the relationship. You are consistent and tolerant; it is difficult for you to let go. You can be the best child or the worst, the best parent or the worst, all in the same day. You're a bundle of contradictions, but your unfailing loyalty outweighs the conflict. Full of pride, you value beautiful things, and you're willing to work for them. A well-rounded environment makes you happiest. Since you're always looking for a new challenge, more than one career beckons. Accept this as you will grow in strength with each accomplishment. Reporter, critic, reviewer, musician, and artist are all good careers for you. Since you have such a talent with dress and style, you may even find a career in designing clothing.

You thrive among people who are warm and witty, and friendships come easily to you. You like leaving your door ajar, but be careful of unworthy persons who may walk in seeking to take advantage.

✴ ✴ ✴

MAY 31   GEMINI • The twins of the zodiac
May 21 at 4:00 A.M. to June 21 at 12:00 P.M. • NUMEROLOGY 4

Possessions and Desires . . .

Gem: Emerald—Those who carry this stone tend to be lucky in love.
Flower: Pink—Your boldness may take you far.
Astral Color, Color Need, Apparel Color: Your Astral Color is Red, which enhances passion, excitement, and strength. Violet in your environment keeps you empathetic toward others. In your wardrobe, Coral brings you a brilliant and sharp appearance.
Fragrance: You should flood your living space with the scent of distilled floral bouquet or freshly cut wood. This will give your ever-curious mind a rest from its constant search for new experiences.
Tree: Cherry—You will find yourself faced with constant new emotional awakenings.
Instruments: Bass, clarinet
Composers: Haydn, Wagner
Bird: Killdeer—This bird is usually found consorting with other species, and can adapt to any environment.
Symbol: Star—You are full of inner brightness and will stand out in any crowd. You will be seen as special.

Harmonious Health and Nutrition . . .

Health Scent: Vanilla—This scent will fill you with a feeling of cleanliness and stability.
Favorable Foods: Celery, mulberry, whole-wheat bread, buttermilk

What's Lucky . . .

Lucky Numbers: 4, 5, 8, 9
Best Months: April and August
Best Day of the Week: Wednesday
Best Month Days: 4, 13, 22, and 31
Lucky Charm: A piece of material cut from something in your home.
Harmonious Signs for Relationships and Partnerships: Aquarius and Libra

Spiritual Guides . . .

Star: Al Divah—Those with this star could feel that they are mistreated by relatives.
Angel: Ambriel—This angel governs travel and transportation, particularly over water, and helps to create love and good communication.
Guardian Angel: St. John—This angel simplifies that which is complicated.
Spiritual Stone: Chrysoprasus—This stone aids in relaxation.

✷ JUDITH'S INSIGHT ✷

You must develop tact. When you master being more diplomatic, you will have it made. You can sometimes be overly frank, despite veiling your frankness in a subtle way. Learning finesse will be your number one hurdle. Mostly satisfied with yourself, you can be critical of others, although most often with good reason. Others may view you as conceited; you do have a high regard for yourself. If you have low self-esteem, the last thing you would do is let anybody else know.

Fond of your family and friends and eager to spend time with them, you put on a party in a matter of minutes. You work at enhancing your charm and augmenting your natural beauty, but this is done subtly. With regard to spending and investing your money, you are quite cautious, although willing to spend on yourself and family members. You respect others' boundaries and create your own. You could be a great reporter, critic, reviewer, publisher, writer, musician, or artist. As well as you work on your own, you also do well with others—except in situations where others get the credit.

Owning your own home and property is definitely important—you will have both. You tend to allow your mate freedom without letting it be known just how closely you're watching. As you mature, you relax more and are less intense; as a result, you enjoy life much more than ever before, and likewise, others enjoy you more.

✷ ✷ ✷

JUNE

JUNE 1   GEMINI • The twins of the zodiac
May 21 at 4:00 A.M. to June 21 at 12:00 P.M. • NUMEROLOGY 1

Possessions and Desires . . .

Gem: Turquoise—This stone may help you find material wealth.

Flower: Marjoram—You tend to blush easily.

Astral Color, Color Need, Apparel Color: Your Astral Color is Red, which enhances passion, excitement, and strength. Violet in your environment keeps you empathetic toward others. In your wardrobe, Wine gives you energy.

Fragrance: You should flood your living space with the scent of distilled floral bouquet or freshly cut wood. This will give your ever-curious mind a rest from its constant search for new experiences.

Tree: Walnut—You are unusually helpful and always looking for constant changes in your life.

Instruments: Oboe, flute, clarinet, piano, French horn, organ, piccolo

Composer: Böhm

Bird: Bird of paradise—the "bird of the gods." You will shine and love extraordinary circumstances.

Symbol: Crown—the universal sign of dignity.

Harmonious Health and Nutrition . . .

Health Scent: Strawberry—Soothing by nature, the strawberry promotes self-esteem and encourages love.

Favorable Foods: Beets, apricots, whole-wheat bread, margarine

What's Lucky . . .

Lucky Numbers: 5, 9, 11
Best Months: April and August
Best Day of the Week: Wednesday
Best Month Days: 1, 10, 19, 28
Lucky Charm: A new penny in your shoe.

Harmonious Signs for Relationships and Partnerships: Aquarius and Libra

Spiritual Guides . . .

Star: Al Henah—Those born under this star are easily wounded.

Angel: Ambriel—This angel governs travel and transportation, particularly over water, and helps to create love and good communication.

Guardian Angel: Malachi—"Messenger of Jehovah."

Spiritual Stone: Chrysoprasus—This stone aids in relaxation.

✴ JUDITH'S INSIGHT ✴

"Fascinating" is a good word to describe you. You are also exceptionally kindhearted, hopeful, insightful, and full of enthusiasm. Your loving instinct allows you to nurture those around you, causing them to admire you. Your desire to please others will make you an adoring partner in love. You tend to hide your flirtatious side, allowing only a chosen few in.

You'll have more than one career in creative fields—perhaps art or writing. Expect to work with books, paper, and pencil: reading, writing, or possibly drawing. With your ability, you are capable of handling more than one job at a time. You can be torn between different directions in your life and at times may feel frustrated. When you put your efforts into a project, the results should be positive.

Some think of you as brilliant. Don't be discouraged when you hit those pitfalls that seem to come out of nowhere. You tend to spring right back with no problem.

✴ ✴ ✴

JUNE 2　GEMINI • The twins of the zodiac
May 21 at 4:00 A.M. to June 21 at 12:00 P.M. • NUMEROLOGY 2

Possessions and Desires . . .

Gem: Sapphire—This gem may help you find forgiveness from those you've wronged.
Flower: Double Red Pink—Your life will be full of love and affection.
Astral Color, Color Need, Apparel Color: Your Astral Color is Red, which enhances passion, excitement, and strength. Violet in your environment keeps you empathetic toward others. In your wardrobe, Green gives you confidence.
Fragrance: You should flood your living space with the scent of distilled floral bouquet or freshly cut wood. This will give your ever-curious mind a rest from its constant search for new experiences.
Tree: Maple—You have great stability and flashes of intuition.
Instruments: Pipe organ, cymbal, drum
Composers: Handel, Johann Sebastian Bach
Bird: Stork—Turkish bird, held in high esteem the world over. This bird is intelligent but may have strange tendencies.
Symbol: Cross—the symbol of self-sacrifice and reconciliation.

Harmonious Health and Nutrition . . .

Health Scent: Apple—You are creative, full of joy, and nearly magical. You bring happiness.
Favorable Foods: Peas, grapes, whole-wheat bread, eggs

What's Lucky . . .

Lucky Numbers: 9, 5, 11
Best Months: April and August
Best Day of the Week: Wednesday
Best Month Days: 2, 11, 20, 29

Lucky Charms: Two 50-cent pieces. Give someone else one of them.
Harmonious Signs for Relationships and Partnerships: Aquarius and Libra

Spiritual Guides . . .

Star: Al Divah—Those with this star could feel that they are mistreated by relatives.
Angel: Ambriel—This angel governs travel and transportation, particularly over water, and helps to create love and good communication.
Guardian Angel: St. John—This angel simplifies that which is complicated.
Spiritual Stone: Chrysoprasus—This stone aids in relaxation.

✳ JUDITH'S INSIGHT ✳

Your inventive ways can bring you a lot of new beginnings in your life. You are the one who gets there first. You love literature, history, and books. Somewhere along the way, you search to make history yourself. You have a sharp mind and an overwhelming intelligence, which will make you work hard to get to the top.

When it comes to love, be wary of your fickle side. Finding that special someone may take some time. You are warmhearted and receptive, which is beneficial to all relationships and partnerships. Look for the one with whom you feel harmony.

When it comes to understanding all sides of an issue, you outdo yourself. You would make a great debater. Professor, historian, inventor, or publisher—none of these careers is out of your reach. It wouldn't be surprising if you found a career in computers; you could be a leader in either hardware or software.

Remember the word *choices*, because you will have a life full of them.

✳ ✳ ✳

JUNE 3 GEMINI • The twins of the zodiac

May 21 at 4:00 A.M. to June 21 at 12:00 P.M. • NUMEROLOGY 3

Possessions and Desires . . .

Gem: Ruby—This stone may lead you to energy, friendship, and happiness.

Flower: Yellow Pink—Be careful what you refuse isn't what you will desire above all at a later time.

Astral Color, Color Need, Apparel Color: Your Astral Color is Red, which enhances passion, excitement, and strength. Violet in your environment keeps you empathetic toward others. In your wardrobe, Coral brings you a brilliant and sharp appearance.

Fragrance: You should flood your living space with the scent of distilled floral bouquet or freshly cut wood. This will give your ever-curious mind a rest from its constant search for new experiences.

Tree: Elm—You have willpower, strength, and the ability to stand alone.

Instrument: Trombone

Composers: Verdi, Mendelssohn, Schumann

Bird: Swan—Regarded as royal and sacred, this bird has the protective nature of a mother, and can become a furious fighter in the defense of its young.

Symbol: Wreath—You have been crowned with a special personality. You are strong but extremely compassionate.

Harmonious Health and Nutrition . . .

Health Scent: Rose—This scent will lead you to passionate thoughts and make you feel warm inside.

Favorable Foods: Beets, prunes, whole-wheat bread, molasses, cottage cheese

What's Lucky . . .

Lucky Numbers: 3, 5, 9
Best Months: April and August
Best Day of the Week: Wednesday
Best Month Days: 3, 12, 21, 30

Lucky Charm: A pen that someone else has already used.

Harmonious Signs for Relationships and Partnerships: Aquarius and Libra

Spiritual Guides . . .

Star: Al Henah—Those born under this star are easily wounded.

Angel: Ambriel—This angel governs travel and transportation, particularly over water, and helps to create love and good communication.

Guardian Angel: Johiel—This angel is a protector of all those with a humble heart.

Spiritual Stone: Chrysoprasus—This stone aids in relaxation.

✳ JUDITH'S INSIGHT ✳

You are cunning and smooth. These aspects of your personality, along with your charm and wit, will help bring you just about everything in life you could want. You know how to use these gifts to your advantage.

Fortunate in love, it may take someone hopelessly devoted to put up with you and your mood swings. Keeping you satisfied will be your partner's biggest challenge. As long as you can enjoy your freedom, friends, and many social contacts, you will be fine. The more invitations, the better.

Ambition is one of your strongest qualities, and you use it well. You will work hard to get to the top, while experiencing your share of downfalls. Lower your standards a bit. In the end, you are likely to have multiple successes. You do well either owning your own company or, on a larger scale, being the head of an organization or president of a company. Any skill you care to develop will only improve with time. You may fancy a position in government, whether it be a municipal, state, or federal job.

You make friends easily enough, but you try to dominate the crowd. Force yourself to hold back; one way or another you become the leader.

★ ★ ★

JUNE 4 GEMINI • The twins of the zodiac
May 21 at 4:00 A.M. to June 21 at 12:00 P.M. • NUMEROLOGY 4

Possessions and Desires . . .

Gem: Emerald—Those who carry this stone tend to be lucky in love.
Flower: Daily Rose—Many people will wish they were as happy as you.
Astral Color, Color Need, Apparel Color: Your Astral Color is Red, which enhances passion, excitement, and strength. Violet in your environment keeps you empathetic toward others. In your wardrobe, Wine gives you energy.
Fragrance: You should flood your living space with the scent of distilled floral bouquet or freshly cut wood. This will give your ever-curious mind a rest from its constant search for new experiences.
Tree: Cherry—You will find yourself faced with constant new emotional awakenings.
Instruments: Bass, clarinet
Composers: Haydn, Wagner
Bird: Robin—the most sociable of all birds, with the ability to create quick friendships. It also can easily adapt to any home. When it wants something, it has the tendency to try to snatch it.
Symbol: Star—You are full of inner brightness and will stand out in any crowd. You will be seen as special.

Harmonious Health and Nutrition . . .

Health Scent: Vanilla—this scent will fill you with a feeling of cleanliness and stability.
Favorable Foods: Celery, whole-wheat bread, molasses, eggs

What's Lucky . . .

Lucky Numbers: 5, 9, 22
Best Months: April and August
Best Day of the Week: Wednesday
Best Month Days: 4, 13, 22, 31
Lucky Charm: A piece of material cut from something in your home.

Harmonious Signs for Relationships and Partnerships: Aquarius and Libra

Spiritual Guides . . .

Star: Al Henah—Those born under this star are easily wounded.
Angel: Ambriel—This angel governs travel and transportation, particularly over water, and helps to create love and good communication.
Guardian Angel: Uriel—This angel brings the light of God's guidance.
Spiritual Stone: Chrysoprasus—This stone aids in relaxation.

✷ JUDITH'S INSIGHT ✷

You think you're smart, and you are, but your strong intuition is your major gift. You have an investigative nature and present a challenge to others around you. The unknown fascinates you; those around you find *you* fascinating.

You are likely to have unusual relationships or to be drawn to unusual individuals. Making commitments will be the great challenge for you. Family may think of you as a rebel; others might say the black sheep. You simply march to the beat of a different drummer and love it when others notice.

Without question, you would succeed at undercover work. You love the exotic, thrills, and adventure. It would not be surprising if you had all of them. Many different careers present possibilities to you, as long as you are using your creativity. Somewhere along the way, try picking up a pen and paper—whether it is working on designing contracts or signing them. The greater the challenge, the better. Any kind of investigative or police work should appeal to you as well.

Friends think of you often, but your flamboyant style may sometimes make them uneasy. Still, your kind ways and warm heart keep people in your life. Be careful that your erratic tendencies don't discourage them. Stop beating yourself up when things don't move quickly enough—you'll just end up with a lot of bruises.

✷ ✷ ✷

JUNE 5 GEMINI • The twins of the zodiac
May 21 at 4:00 A.M. to June 21 at 12:00 P.M. • NUMEROLOGY 5

Possessions and Desires . . .

Gem: Sardius—this stone could give the wearer unusual insights into his or her own heart.
Flower: Lancaster Rose—Many people may be envious of your cheerful nature.
Astral Color, Color Need, Apparel Color: Your Astral Color is Red, which enhances passion, excitement, and strength. Violet in your environment keeps you empathetic toward others. In your wardrobe, Green gives you confidence.
Fragrance: You should flood your living space with the scent of distilled floral bouquet or freshly cut wood. This will give your ever-curious mind a rest from its constant search for new experiences.
Tree: Apple—You are creative, full of joy, and nearly magical. You bring happiness.
Instruments: Viola, trumpet
Composer: Liszt
Bird: Flamingo—This beautiful, gregarious bird is always careful of its enemy. It is also a caretaker of the young who tries to keep everyone happy.
Symbol: Triangle—You have the right combination of abilities.

Harmonious Health and Nutrition . . .

Health Scent: Peach—This scent may balance your good qualities so that they equal your charm.
Favorable Foods: Parsnips, prunes, whole-wheat bread, molasses, margarine

What's Lucky . . .

Lucky Numbers: 5, 9, 23
Best Months: April and August
Best Day of the Week: Wednesday
Best Month Days: 4, 5, 23
Lucky Charms: A rabbit's foot or a white candle.
Harmonious Signs for Relationships and Partnerships: Aquarius and Libra

Spiritual Guides . . .

Star: Al Divah—Those with this star could feel that they are mistreated by relatives.
Angel: Ambriel—This angel governs travel and transportation, particularly over water, and helps to create love and good communication.
Guardian Angel: Plavwell—This angel gives power and strength to one's presence.
Spiritual Stone: Chrysoprasus—This stone aids in relaxation.

✷ JUDITH'S INSIGHT ✷

Your keen intelligence and resourcefulness make you very much a live one. You are energetic and enthusiastic; everything around you fascinates and intrigues you. Your love of travel should lead you to visit a lot of exotic places or, at the very least, to create an exotic environment. Your suitcase is always packed.

Falling in love and keeping it will be your greatest challenge. You waffle and brood and keep yourself from being totally devoted. When it comes to love, try to get out of your own way. It's easier to blame others than to take responsibility for your own actions. In due time you find balance, once you're in a relationship for a considerable amount of time. Have no fear, you eventually find someone who is patient with you.

In any working environment, you have the talent to make yourself shine. Consider a career in entertainment, writing, publishing, or computer graphics. You might own a resort hotel or hold a job in that industry. Talented as you are, you may find yourself hunting and hunting. Before you know it, you may find yourself on stage. Have faith—not only will you find yourself at some time connected to the theater or arts, but you may be the one doing the writing. Or you could be involved in astronomy, astrology, or art. Make sure your career brings you many challenges.

You are a risk taker and won't be happy unless there are challenges. From jumping out of an airplane to climbing the tallest mountain—you always take the risk.

✷ ✷ ✷

JUNE 6 GEMINI • The twins of the zodiac
May 21 at 4:00 A.M. to June 21 at 12:00 P.M. • NUMEROLOGY 6

Possessions and Desires . . .

Gem: Topaz—This is an excellent gift to be exchanged between very loyal friends.
Flower: Thorn Apple—You may not be above fibbing to win the heart of the one you want.
Astral Color, Color Need, Apparel Color: Your Astral Color is Red, which enhances passion, excitement, and strength. Violet in your environment keeps you empathetic toward others. In your wardrobe, Coral brings you a brilliant and sharp appearance.
Fragrance: You should flood your living space with the scent of distilled floral bouquet or freshly cut wood. This will give your ever-curious mind a rest from its constant search for new experiences.
Tree: Palm—You tend to be very healthy and creative.
Instruments: Tambourine, lyre
Composer: Schubert
Bird: Falcon—an expert hunter. When well-trained, it can adapt to many tasks and is usually obedient.
Symbol: Crescent—You are more likely to be influenced by the phases of the moon. Your easygoing manner leads you to peaceful situations.

Harmonious Health and Nutrition . . .

Health Scent: Orange Blossom—This scent may balance your body, mind, and soul.
Favorable Foods: Red raspberries, whole-wheat bread, molasses, cottage cheese

What's Lucky . . .

Lucky Numbers: 5, 9, 24
Best Months: April and August
Best Day of the Week: Wednesday
Best Month Days: 6, 15, 24

Lucky Charms: A religious token or card from any religion.
Harmonious Signs for Relationships and Partnerships: Aquarius and Libra

Spiritual Guides . . .

Star: Al Henah—Those born under this star are easily wounded.
Angel: Ambriel—This angel governs travel and transportation, particularly over water, and helps to create love and good communication.
Guardian Angel: Michael—"Who is like God."
Spiritual Stone: Chrysoprasus—This stone aids in relaxation.

✶ JUDITH'S INSIGHT ✶

You have a strong, magnetic personality and a hand to bring you whatever you wish for. Others may see you as lucky. Your charm and wit enhance your career, especially if you choose politics. You are more devoted and loyal than most people think. When it comes to romance, your style is subtle. This is most attractive, particularly to your mate, who must be a powerhouse. At times, you might lack flexibility in your relationship. Look before you leap. Otherwise, in love, you could experience some heartache. Keep both feet on the ground. As a lover, you are deep and emotional in all your thoughts. The problem here is that you are afraid to let others know who you really are. If a mate takes the time to know you in a relationship and removes those bricks one by one, eventually you will find happiness.

It will seem as if money just falls into your lap, and at some point or another it does. But consider the possibility that you could invent, create, or design architecture that will bring you fame. As a salesperson, you'll be the one who lands the largest contract in company history. No matter what career you choose you'll eventually be wealthy.

✶ ✶ ✶

JUNE 7 GEMINI • The twins of the zodiac
May 21 at 4:00 A.M. to June 21 at 12:00 P.M. • NUMEROLOGY 7

Possessions and Desires . . .

Gem: Ruby—This stone may lead you to energy, friendship, and happiness.

Flower: Red Tulip—You will hear many open declarations of love in your life.

Astral Color, Color Need, Apparel Color: Your Astral Color is Red, which enhances passion, excitement, and strength. Violet in your environment keeps you empathetic toward others. In your wardrobe, Green gives you confidence.

Fragrance: You should flood your living space with the scent of distilled floral bouquet or freshly cut wood. This will give your ever-curious mind a rest from its constant search for new experiences.

Tree: Sycamore—Yours is the ability to love, communicate honestly with others, and have lasting relationships.

Instrument: Harp

Composers: Gluck, Brahms

Bird: Goldfinch—there are forty-four different species of finches which vary greatly. This can sometimes be the most charming of birds. These gentle creatures can be very moody in unsettled weather.

Symbol: Heart—You are enthusiastic, empathetic, and full of generosity and love.

Harmonious Health and Nutrition . . .

Health Scent: Jasmine—This scent may make you more easygoing when you are stressed.

Favorable Foods: Lettuce, apricots, whole-wheat bread, molasses, buttermilk

What's Lucky . . .

Lucky Numbers: 5, 7, 9
Best Months: April and August
Best Day of the Week: Wednesday
Best Month Days: 6, 15, 24

Lucky Charm: An old key.
Harmonious Signs for Relationships and Partnerships: Aquarius and Libra

Spiritual Guides . . .

Star: Al Henah—Those born under this star are easily wounded.

Angel: Ambriel—This angel governs travel and transportation, particularly over water, and helps to create love and good communication.

Guardian Angel: Raphael—This angel attends to all of your needs when you are looking for guidance.

Spiritual Stone: Chrysoprasus—This stone aids in relaxation.

✦ JUDITH'S INSIGHT ✦

You are profound in your thinking—dwelling on things that occupy your mind. If only you could just turn it off. This constant thinking could be great for work and bad for love or emotional circumstances. Your mind never shutting down often leads you on an emotional roller coaster ride. People seem to overwhelm you, though it just may be your mood. Work on calming techniques. Keep yourself from getting overwrought and burned out because you don't like to say No.

Extremely loyal on the one hand, you do have a tendency to flirt. In fact at times you may even want to do more than flirt. You adore your family, but you will create situations in life that give you distance. You provide a sense of power to others around you and may be the comfort zone for your friends and family.

You will go back and forth with your career. A career in writing would be comfortable for you. Although it may take years for you to recognize your talent, your imagination could transform any boring story. You may find yourself in multiple careers or taking on multiple jobs—one for structure, the other for love.

Order pleases you both at home and in your relationships. Write about it in a play or script. With your talent, you may just be published.

✦ ✦ ✦

JUNE 8
GEMINI • The twins of the zodiac
May 21 at 4:00 A.M. to June 21 at 12:00 P.M. • NUMEROLOGY 8

Possessions and Desires . . .

Gem: Chrysolite—This gem may help you clear your mind of sadness and worry.

Flower: Variegated Tulip—You usually see the beauty in things that others miss.

Astral Color, Color Need, Apparel Color: Your Astral Color is Red, which enhances passion, excitement, and strength. Violet in your environment keeps you empathetic toward others. In your wardrobe, Wine gives you energy.

Fragrance: You should flood your living space with the scent of distilled floral bouquet or freshly cut wood. This will give your ever-curious mind a rest from its constant search for new experiences.

Tree: Pine—Your relationships tend to be balanced, both emotionally and mentally.

Instrument: Cello

Composer: Mozart

Bird: Lark—known for the beauty of its song, which is sometimes very unusual. It is also credited with extraordinary intelligence.

Symbol: Wings—You are the source of balance in your world—this will bring you contentment.

Harmonious Health and Nutrition . . .

Health Scent: Almond—This scent may revitalize you and open you to greater possibilities.

Favorable Foods: Peas, prunes, whole-wheat bread, molasses, eggs

What's Lucky . . .

Lucky Numbers: 5, 8, 9
Best Months: April and August
Best Day of the Week: Wednesday
Best Month Days: 8, 17, 26
Lucky Charm: Red ribbon in your wallet or doorway.
Harmonious Signs for Relationships and Partnerships: Aquarius and Libra

Spiritual Guides . . .

Star: Al Henah—Those born under this star are easily wounded.

Angel: Ambriel—This angel governs travel and transportation, particularly over water, and helps to create love and good communication.

Guardian Angel: Seraphim—An angel that brings love, light, and passion.

Spiritual Stone: Chrysoprasus—This stone aids in relaxation.

✷ JUDITH'S INSIGHT ✷

Quite the observer, you take in just about everything that is humanly possible—all at once. You are deep, thoughtful, and charming. Life for you may not be easy because you take on too much at one time. Give yourself a break. You reject restrictions of any kind and thrive on your independence.

Since you've been misunderstood for most of your life, you may eventually find a relationship with a soul mate who understands you. Hopefully you will be single at the time. Be patient—finding the right mate takes some time. Be cautious because you could have trouble with your neighbors. Others may seem as if they are tracking you and following what you are doing.

Your philosophical nature will probably put you in serious literary work, science, or mathematics. Somewhere along the way you may even have a desire for architecture. Your strong spiritual sense may draw you to learn more about mysticism. A teacher or counselor by nature, be selective about who and what you listen to. Be especially careful about taking things too seriously.

You are a dear friend with a select few close companions with whom you find balance and harmony and total security. Eventually you do seem to find that harmony in friendships and relationships gets easier, and you tend not to be so scattered with your emotions.

✷ ✷ ✷

JUNE 9

GEMINI • The twins of the zodiac

May 21 at 4:00 A.M. to June 21 at 12:00 P.M. • NUMEROLOGY 9

Possessions and Desires . . .

Gem: Topaz—This is an excellent gift to be exchanged between very loyal friends.

Flower: Thyme—You tend not to be happy unless you are very active.

Astral Color, Color Need, Apparel Color: Your Astral Color is Red, which enhances passion, excitement, and strength. Violet in your environment keeps you empathetic toward others. In your wardrobe, Coral brings you a brilliant and sharp appearance.

Fragrance: You should flood your living space with the scent of distilled floral bouquet or freshly cut wood. This will give your ever-curious mind a rest from its constant search for new experiences.

Tree: Holly—Beware that you are not carried away by your passionate nature. The only way to grow is to be open to new experiences.

Instruments: Violin, tympanum

Composer: Gluck

Bird: Mockingbird—the most proficient minstrel in the world's orchestra; graceful and enthusiastic.

Symbol: Anchor—This tranquil symbol signifies stability and strength, and stands for strong commitments in relationships.

Harmonious Health and Nutrition . . .

Health Scent: Lavender—This scent might lead others to trust you and make you patient.

Favorable Foods: Cabbage, bananas, whole-wheat bread, molasses, cottage cheese

What's Lucky . . .

Lucky Numbers: 5, 9, 36
Best Months: April and August
Best Day of the Week: Wednesday
Best Month Days: 9, 18, 27

Lucky Charms: A U.S. coin or a bill of any amount from the year you were born.

Harmonious Signs for Relationships and Partnerships: Aquarius and Libra

Spiritual Guides . . .

Star: Al Henah—Those born under this star are easily wounded.

Angel: Ambriel—This angel governs travel and transportation, particularly over water, and helps to create love and good communication.

Guardian Angel: Gabriel—"God is my strength."

Spiritual Stone: Chrysoprasus—This stone aids in relaxation.

✱ JUDITH'S INSIGHT ✱

Your combination of intelligence, wit, charm, shrewdness, and attractiveness are a handful, and so are you. With your high energy, any career is possible. You will accomplish much in your lifetime because you're good at everything you try.

More flirtatious than loyal? Not really. You're more loyal and devoted, though others may beg to differ. You want a secure relationship but love to be recognized. Many opportunities for love affairs present themselves. It is likely you'll turn away more than you take on, at least in your later years. Otherwise, you may create unnecessary headaches for yourself.

Success will knock at your door rather often. From head of the class to head of the corporation, you are a born leader, and life will take you places. You clear obstacles and hurdles like a professional athlete. Be sure to exercise caution when it comes to legal issues, unless, of course, you choose to be an attorney and spend your life in the courtroom. One way or the other, legal issues appear throughout your life.

Your love of words and gift with them makes you a terrific conversationalist. This could actually be your greatest asset.

✱ ✱ ✱

JUNE 10 GEMINI • The twins of the zodiac
May 21 at 4:00 A.M. to June 21 at 12:00 P.M. • NUMEROLOGY 1

Possessions and Desires . . .

Gem: Agate—This stone may promote health and lead you to a long life.

Flower: Pomegranate—You may find that a little foolishness can be a lot of fun.

Astral Color, Color Need, Apparel Color: Your Astral Color is Red, which enhances passion, excitement, and strength. Violet in your environment keeps you empathetic toward others. In your wardrobe, Green gives you confidence.

Fragrance: You should flood your living space with the scent of distilled floral bouquet or freshly cut wood. This will give your ever-curious mind a rest from its constant search for new experiences.

Tree: Walnut—You are unusually helpful and always looking for constant changes in your life.

Instruments: Oboe, flute, clarinet, piano, French horn, organ, piccolo

Composer: Böhm

Bird: Bird of paradise—the "bird of the gods." You will shine and love extraordinary circumstances.

Symbol: Crown—the universal sign of dignity.

Harmonious Health and Nutrition . . .

Health Scent: Strawberry—Soothing by nature, the strawberry promotes self-esteem and encourages love.

Favorable Foods: Radishes, grapes, whole-wheat bread, molasses, goat's milk

What's Lucky . . .

Lucky Numbers: 5, 9, 10
Best Months: April and August
Best Day of the Week: Wednesday
Best Month Days: 1, 10, 19, 28
Lucky Charm: A new penny in your shoe.
Harmonious Signs for Relationships and Partnerships: Aquarius and Libra

Spiritual Guides . . .

Star: Al Henah—Those born under this star are easily wounded.

Angel: Ambriel—This angel governs travel and transportation, particularly over water, and helps to create love and good communication.

Guardian Angel: Malachi—"Messenger of Jehovah."

Spiritual Stone: Chrysoprasus—This stone aids in relaxation.

✷ JUDITH'S INSIGHT ✷

"Fascinating" could describe you. You have a good heart, and you lend a helping hand whenever you can. Did you know you have psychic abilities? It's no surprise that you may back away from that. A strong sense of independence and enthusiasm and a positive attitude will bring others to you. You love to be loved, and you become the nurturer whether you want to or not.

You do tend to have luck with friends because your natural instinct is to give a lot. Your loving instincts do allow you to have harmony in your family. At times, siblings could cause conflict, but you do tend to have decent relationships with them at one time or another.

Expect the unexpected when it comes to work. Multiple careers await you. You have the ability to do more than one career and may choose to do so. Expect to work with paper, whether it is writing, reading, or arithmetic. But no matter what the job, you always put your all into it. There may be jobs that tend to bring out your brilliance: professor, head of the college, or top sales rep, it doesn't matter; you will find that you will get to the top.

Don't get discouraged when you hit the puddles in a rainstorm and get splashed, because you will be able to overcome just about any and every obstacle that lands in your path. It takes time for things to happen. You do tend to find love and laughter as you get older.

✷ ✷ ✷

JUNE 11　GEMINI • The twins of the zodiac
May 21 at 4:00 A.M. to June 21 at 12:00 P.M. • NUMEROLOGY 2

Possessions and Desires . . .

Gem: Sapphire—This gem may help you find forgiveness from those you've wronged.
Flower: Black Poplar—You are courageous in the face of strife.
Astral Color, Color Need, Apparel Color: Your Astral Color is Red, which enhances passion, excitement, and strength. Violet in your environment keeps you empathetic toward others. In your wardrobe, Wine gives you energy.
Fragrance: You should flood your living space with the scent of distilled floral bouquet or freshly cut wood. This will give your ever-curious mind a rest from its constant search for new experiences.
Tree: Maple—You have great stability and flashes of intuition.
Instruments: Pipe organ, cymbal, drum
Composers: Handel, Johann Sebastian Bach
Bird: Stork—Turkish bird, held in high esteem the world over. This bird is intelligent but may have strange tendencies.
Symbol: Cross—the symbol of self-sacrifice and reconciliation.

Harmonious Health and Nutrition . . .

Health Scent: Apple—You are creative, full of joy, and nearly magical. You bring happiness.
Favorable Foods: Brussels sprouts, blackberries, whole wheat, peanuts, cottage cheese

What's Lucky . . .

Lucky Numbers: 2, 5, 9
Best Months: April and August
Best Day of the Week: Wednesday
Best Month Days: 2, 11, 20, 29
Lucky Charms: Two 50-cent pieces. Give someone else one of them.

Harmonious Signs for Relationships and Partnerships: Aquarius and Libra

Spiritual Guides . . .

Star: Al Divah—Those with this star could feel that they are mistreated by relatives.
Angel: Ambriel—This angel governs travel and transportation, particularly over water, and helps to create love and good communication.
Guardian Angel: St. John—This angel simplifies that which is complicated.
Spiritual Stone: Chrysoprasus—This stone aids in relaxation.

✶ JUDITH'S INSIGHT ✶

You have a keen understanding and tend to look closely at people. Where can you usually be found? At the center of attention! You are intrigued with literature, history, and books. Somewhere along the way you may even make a little history yourself. Quite the inventor, you create a lot of new beginnings, whether you father or you bear a lot of children. New beginnings will be important in your life.

You're an inspiration to everyone around you. When it comes to love, you go through some stages of indecisiveness or whimsy. You're generally better with a mate, but make sure you don't settle for the wrong one just for companionship. Be patient. Your kindness and gentleness are enhanced when in a relationship.

Your sharp mind and deep intelligence would make you a great attorney, county leader, political leader, or publisher. Your great communication skills could help you do wonders with computers or media jobs.

Remember, you will experience a lot of quick changes and detours. Expect the unexpected. You may have a strong desire to travel and could be interested in somebody who is from another country; you may have an opportunity to move out of the country somewhere along the way.

✶ ✶ ✶

JUNE 12   GEMINI • The twins of the zodiac
May 21 at 4:00 A.M. to June 21 at 12:00 P.M. • NUMEROLOGY 3

Possessions and Desires . . .

Gem: Ruby—This stone may lead you to energy, friendship, and happiness.
Flower: Prickly Pear—You are sometimes too quick to make fun of the shortcomings of others.
Astral Color, Color Need, Apparel Color: Your Astral Color is Red, which enhances passion, excitement, and strength. Violet in your environment keeps you empathetic toward others. In your wardrobe, Coral brings you a brilliant and sharp appearance.
Fragrance: You should flood your living space with the scent of distilled floral bouquet or freshly cut wood. This will give your ever-curious mind a rest from its constant search for new experiences.
Tree: Elm—You have willpower, strength, and the ability to stand alone.
Instrument: Trombone
Composers: Verdi, Mendelssohn, Schumann
Bird: Swan—Regarded as royal and sacred, this bird has the protective nature of a mother, and can become a furious fighter in the defense of its young.
Symbol: Wreath—You have been crowned with a special personality. You are strong but extremely compassionate.

Harmonious Health and Nutrition . . .

Health Scent: Rose—This scent will lead you to passionate thoughts and make you feel warm inside.
Favorable Foods: Cauliflower, peaches, rye, peanuts, buttermilk

What's Lucky . . .

Lucky Numbers: 3, 5, 9
Best Months: April and August
Best Day of the Week: Wednesday
Best Month Days: 3, 12, 21, 30
Lucky Charm: A pen that someone else has already used.

Harmonious Signs for Relationships and Partnerships: Aquarius and Libra

Spiritual Guides . . .

Star: Al Henah—Those born under this star are easily wounded.
Angel: Ambriel—This angel governs travel and transportation, particularly over water, and helps to create love and good communication.
Guardian Angel: Johiel—This angel is a protector of all those with a humble heart.
Spiritual Stone: Chrysoprasus—This stone aids in relaxation.

✶ JUDITH'S INSIGHT ✶

You know how to get what you want. Some call you a smooth operator, but because you are genuinely kindhearted and warm, people are willing to do what you want. You make new friends easily and keep old friends for decades. It's not that you're dominating, but people simply allow you to take control. One way or another, you become the leader of the pack.

You are mostly lucky in love; if a relationship does fail, another is forming right around the corner. You definitely can be more secure at work than with love. At times you can be moody and try to blame it on your partner. Keep in mind that the hardest task for you is recognizing your multidimensional personality.

You're more likely to succeed than not. You will do well in whatever job you choose, whether you work in or with an organization or large company. Your skills, whether they be mechanical or mental, operate on a grand scale. A position in government wouldn't be surprising.

You love a good party and respond to any social invitation—the more social, the better. Whether it be fishing, hunting, playing racquetball or tennis—it is not so much the sport, but the desire for the interaction with other people that attracts you.

You can be demanding, and sooner or later you get what you want. Have no fear, somewhere along the way you learn to give more than you get.

✶ ✶ ✶

JUNE 13   GEMINI • The twins of the zodiac
May 21 at 4:00 A.M. to June 21 at 12:00 P.M. • NUMEROLOGY 4

Possessions and Desires . . .

Gem: Emerald—Those who carry this stone tend to be lucky in love.

Flower: Potato Blossom—You should discover that what you give to others is really a gift to yourself.

Astral Color, Color Need, Apparel Color: Your Astral Color is Red, which enhances passion, excitement, and strength. Violet in your environment keeps you empathetic toward others. In your wardrobe, Green gives you confidence.

Fragrance: You should flood your living space with the scent of distilled floral bouquet or freshly cut wood. This will give your ever-curious mind a rest from its constant search for new experiences.

Tree: Cherry—You will find yourself faced with constant new emotional awakenings.

Instruments: Bass, clarinet

Composers: Haydn, Wagner

Bird: Lark—These birds are known for the beauty of their song which is sometimes very unusual. It is also credited with having extraordinary intelligence.

Symbol: Star—You are full of inner brightness and will stand out in any crowd. You will be seen as special.

Harmonious Health and Nutrition . . .

Health Scent: Vanilla—this scent will fill you with a feeling of cleanliness and stability.

Favorable Foods: Watercress, prunes, whole wheat, almonds, cottage cheese

What's Lucky . . .

Lucky Numbers: 4, 5, 13
Best Months: April and August
Best Day of the Week: Wednesday
Best Month Days: 4, 13, 22, 31
Lucky Charm: A piece of material cut from something in your home.

Harmonious Signs for Relationships and Partnerships: Aquarius and Libra

Spiritual Guides . . .

Star: Al Henah—Those born under this star are easily wounded.

Angel: Ambriel—This angel governs travel and transportation, particularly over water, and helps to create love and good communication.

Guardian Angel: St. John—This angel simplifies that which is complicated.

Spiritual Stone: Chrysoprasus—This stone aids in relaxation.

✳ JUDITH'S INSIGHT ✳

You are a born adventurer; if it isn't exotic, thrilling, or challenging, you don't want to go. You are extremely strong and intuitive, and you have a keen intellect and a strong, unusual mind. Likewise, relationships with unique people attract and draw you in. Commitments themselves will be a great challenge for you. You tend to keep close to your family, but maybe you're seen as the rebel every so often. You're a bit eccentric, and your living environment may be considered different or out of the realm of the ordinary.

Because of your investigative nature, you may find yourself digging through the dirt at a young age. Career possibilities may include being a rocket scientist, creating a television story, writing a script, or starring in the most popular film. Whether or not you write or direct doesn't matter; you will tend to have two or three jobs.

You like a challenge and, at the same time, you present a challenge. Fascinated with yourself, you create scenarios in which you even compete with yourself! But your impatience can pose problems. You are willful, determined, shrewd, and penetrating, and so you can be read as harsh at times. But your depth and kind and loving nature will eventually allow others to see you as you are—warm and sensitive.

✳ ✳ ✳

JUNE 14

GEMINI • The twins of the zodiac

May 21 at 4:00 A.M. to June 21 at 12:00 P.M. • NUMEROLOGY 5

Possessions and Desires . . .

Gem: Sardius—this stone could give the wearer unusual insights into his or her own heart.

Flower: Mountain Peak—Your aspirations tend to carry you where you wish to go.

Fragrance: You should flood your living space with the scent of distilled floral bouquet or freshly cut wood. This will give your ever-curious mind a rest from its constant search for new experiences.

Astral Color, Color Need, Apparel Color: Your Astral Color is Red, which enhances passion, excitement, and strength. Violet in your environment keeps you empathetic toward others. In your wardrobe, Wine gives you energy.

Tree: Apple—You are creative, full of joy, and nearly magical. You bring happiness.

Instruments: Viola, trumpet

Composer: Liszt

Bird: Flamingo—This beautiful, gregarious bird is always careful of its enemy. It is also a caretaker of the young who tries to keep everyone happy.

Symbol: Triangle—You have the right combination of abilities.

Harmonious Health and Nutrition . . .

Health Scent: Peach—This scent may balance your good qualities so that they equal your charm.

Favorable Foods: String beans, raspberries, rye, beechnuts, pressed cheese

What's Lucky . . .

Lucky Numbers: 5, 9, 14

Best Months: April and August

Best Day of the Week: Wednesday

Best Month Days: 4, 5, 23

Lucky Charms: A rabbit's foot or a white candle.

Harmonious Signs for Relationships and Partnerships: Aquarius and Libra

Spiritual Guides . . .

Star: Al Henah—Those born under this star are easily wounded.

Angel: Ambriel—This angel governs travel and transportation, particularly over water, and helps to create love and good communication.

Guardian Angel: Plavwell—This angel gives power and strength to one's presence.

Spiritual Stone: Chrysoprasus—This stone aids in relaxation.

✳ JUDITH'S INSIGHT ✳

You can be very tight with money, then suddenly show extreme generosity, especially when it comes to a gift for a friend. You're a good, loyal friend, and can be trusted with a secret. Energetic, enthusiastic, and very much alive, you are intrigued by others as much as they are by you.

When there is a crisis, you can be more warm-hearted than usual. You are loving, kind, and imaginative. However, your need for independence could isolate you. While in a relationship, learn to demonstrate how much you need closeness. You tend to behave as if it's not that important. This could be your greatest downfall. Allow your emotional side to be as directed as your working one, and you will find much more harmony in your life.

You are hard-working, intelligent, and resourceful; your career goals could range from computer graphics to writing or publishing. Somewhere along the way, you may make multiple career changes in the space of a year. Keep looking for the right fit. Inevitably, you lean toward using your creativity. You have a flare for the dramatic, in addition to a keen attraction to research, science, or mathematics. You could succeed in astronomy, astrology, or designing of any kind. Many chances to change your job and your residence present themselves along the way. You are a risk taker and could be the one air ballooning, power shooting or, perhaps, running for public office.

✶ ✶ ✶

JUNE 15

GEMINI • The twins of the zodiac

May 21 at 4:00 A.M. to June 21 at 12:00 P.M. • NUMEROLOGY 6

Possessions and Desires . . .

Gem: Topaz—This is an excellent gift to be exchanged between very loyal friends.
Flower: Wild Plum—You tend to love with the heat of a forest fire.
Fragrance: You should flood your living space with the scent of distilled floral bouquet or freshly cut wood. This will give your ever-curious mind a rest from its constant search for new experiences.
Astral Color, Color Need, Apparel Color: Your Astral Color is Red, which enhances passion, excitement, and strength. Violet in your environment keeps you empathetic toward others. In your wardrobe, Coral brings you a brilliant and sharp appearance.
Tree: Palm—You tend to be very healthy and creative.
Instruments: Tambourine, lyre
Composer: Schubert
Bird: Lark—known for the beauty of its song, which is sometimes very unusual. It is also credited with extraordinary intelligence.
Symbol: Crescent—You are more likely to be influenced by the phases of the moon. Your easygoing manner leads you to peaceful situations.

Harmonious Health and Nutrition . . .

Health Scent: Orange Blossom—This scent may balance your body, mind, and soul.
Favorable Foods: Cauliflower, peaches, whole wheat, nuts, buttermilk

What's Lucky . . .

Lucky Numbers: 5, 6, 9
Best Months: April and August
Best Day of the Week: Wednesday
Best Month Days: 6, 15, 24
Lucky Charms: A religious token or card from any religion.

Harmonious Signs for Relationships and Partnerships: Aquarius and Libra

Spiritual Guides . . .

Star: Al Divah—Those with this star could feel that they are mistreated by relatives.
Angel: Ambriel—This angel governs travel and transportation, particularly over water, and helps to create love and good communication.
Guardian Angel: Michael—"Who is like God."
Spiritual Stone: Chrysoprasus—This stone aids in relaxation.

✴ JUDITH'S INSIGHT ✴

You have a strong magnetic personality that brings you what you wish for in this lifetime. Your charm and good sense of humor get you through many a tight spot. No matter what anybody else says about you, you're faithful and loyal, and you consider doing whatever it takes to make others happy.

Your subtle style is most attractive, and you make a devoted mate. When it comes to romance, you like challenge and require a little spontaneity. Be more open in relationships, and try not to put up so many roadblocks. Your flirtatious ways are alluring, and you need and will choose a mate who takes the time to understand you.

Remember to keep both feet on the ground when it comes to work, because you may do three jobs at once. Although you may be one to rock the boat at work, you're dependable and seen as a hard worker. You catch on to things quickly and have no problem doing many things at once. Many hidden talents come out when you are older, especially in sports or creative talents. You may start off as an attorney who then becomes a golf pro, or perhaps a football player who turns into a sportscaster. You should have several careers, but you like diversification.

Eventually you could come across windfalls in your life, or maybe you'll invent or create something that generates a lot of money for you. Financially, you take what you have and do very well with it.

✴ ✴ ✴

JUNE 16

GEMINI • The twins of the zodiac

May 21 at 4:00 A.M. to June 21 at 12:00 P.M. • NUMEROLOGY 7

Possessions and Desires . . .

Gem: Agate—This stone may promote health and lead you to a long life.
Flower: Fly Orchis—You tend not to have a problem admitting when you have made a mistake.
Fragrance: You should flood your living space with the scent of distilled floral bouquet or freshly cut wood. This will give your ever-curious mind a rest from its constant search for new experiences.
Astral Color, Color Need, Apparel Color: Your Astral Color is Red, which enhances passion, excitement, and strength. Violet in your environment keeps you empathetic toward others. In your wardrobe, Green gives you confidence.
Tree: Sycamore—Yours is the ability to love, communicate honestly with others, and have lasting relationships.
Instrument: Harp
Composers: Gluck, Brahms
Bird: Skylark—This handsome bird is beautiful when it sings. It always whistles as it works.
Symbol: Heart—You are enthusiastic, empathetic, and full of generosity and love.

Harmonious Health and Nutrition . . .

Health Scent: Jasmine—This scent may make you more easygoing when you are stressed.
Favorable Foods: Cabbage, prunes, rye, peanuts, eggs

What's Lucky . . .

Lucky Numbers: 5, 7, 9
Best Months: April and August
Best Day of the Week: Wednesday
Best Month Days: 6, 15, 2
Lucky Charm: An old key.
Harmonious Signs for Relationships and Partnerships: Aquarius and Libra

Spiritual Guides . . .

Star: Al Henah—Those born under this star are easily wounded.
Angel: Ambriel—This angel governs travel and transportation, particularly over water, and helps to create love and good communication.
Guardian Angel: Raphael—This angel attends to all of your needs when you are looking for guidance.
Spiritual Stone: Chrysoprasus—This stone aids in relaxation.

✴ JUDITH'S INSIGHT ✴

You are profound in your thinking and would make an excellent writer. Unfortunately, your mind doesn't turn off easily, so you dwell on things entirely too much. You see life through rose-colored glasses, yet you analyze things to death. Overwhelming hurdles will present themselves, and you handle them with remarkable ease. Learn to check your criticism of others; this could trip you up. At the same time, try being a little less self-doubting and hard on yourself.

You learn the value of friendship early on, and as you mature, this feeling deepens. You are quite loyal. Someone you're attracted to may consider you a friend. Don't feel cast aside. This is a great compliment. Inevitably you find harmony in love.

At times you pull away from the family, either emotionally or physically. You provide a strong sense of power to those around you and will be a comfort zone for friends and family. Expect a tidy home—you value order! You enjoy the luxuries of life, and you find a way to make your home quite comfortable.

It may take time to recognize your true talents. Your wonderfully creative nature makes you impractical in business. You have the capabilities for a career as a musician or poet. Bookkeeper, cashier, accountant, literary agent, editor, confidential clerk, or psychologist would make a nice fit.

Foreign things intrigue you and inspire you to travel. Living in a foreign country or with a family of another culture awakens a strong connection to another time.

✴ ✴ ✴

JUNE 17

GEMINI • The twins of the zodiac

May 21 at 4:00 A.M. to June 21 at 12:00 P.M. • NUMEROLOGY 8

Possessions and Desires . . .

Gem: Chrysolite—This gem may help you clear your mind of sadness and worry.
Flower: Palm—You may know much success in life.
Fragrance: You should flood your living space with the scent of distilled floral bouquet or freshly cut wood. This will give your ever-curious mind a rest from its constant search for new experiences.
Astral Color, Color Need, Apparel Color: Your Astral Color is Red, which enhances passion, excitement, and strength. Violet in your environment keeps you empathetic toward others. In your wardrobe, Wine gives you energy.
Tree: Pine—Your relationships tend to be balanced, both emotionally and mentally.
Instrument: Cello
Composer: Mozart
Bird: Lark—known for the beauty of their song, which is sometimes very unusual. It is also credited with extraordinary intelligence.
Symbol: Wings—You are the source of balance in your world—this will bring you contentment.

Harmonious Health and Nutrition . . .

Health Scent: Almond—This scent may revitalize you and open you to greater possibilities.
Favorable Foods: Peas, pineapple, whole wheat, almonds, cottage cheese

What's Lucky . . .

Lucky Numbers: 5, 7, 8
Best Months: April and August
Best Day of the Week: Wednesday
Best Month Days: 8, 17, 26
Lucky Charm: Red ribbon in your wallet or doorway.
Harmonious Signs for Relationships and Partnerships: Aquarius and Libra

Spiritual Guides . . .

Star: Al Henah—Those born under this star are easily wounded.
Angel: Ambriel—This angel governs travel and transportation, particularly over water, and helps to create love and good communication.
Guardian Angel: Seraphim—An angel that brings love, light, and passion.
Spiritual Stone: Chrysoprasus—This stone aids in relaxation.

✳ JUDITH'S INSIGHT ✳

You have a nurturing, sympathetic, and generous nature. You take in everything. You're often in deep thought, and you tend to analyze everything. Your surroundings are quite important, and you like them comfortable and homey. You appreciate nice things, but that's not what makes you tick. It is more important for you to give than take for yourself, although this may not be the case in your early years.

The worst thing that could happen is having restrictions placed on you. This could be a problem when cultivating a relationship. The mate who provides you with a sense of freedom and trust could be the perfect match. Although you're a dear friend to those close to you, intimate friendships are few and far between. You probably only have a handful of dear friends throughout life, and usually you've known them since childhood.

Your signature personality trait is your willingness to take on responsibility. Life will be easier once you learn to resist the urge to take on the responsibilities of others. You have a philosophical nature and could wind up with a literary career—or with something in science or mathematics. In this technological age, you might also find yourself the head of a computer or New Age environmental company. The unknown and mystical intrigues you. You can sometimes be misunderstood and don't like to explain yourself to others.

The older you get, the less pressure you put on yourself, and your life tends to forge ahead with less stress.

✳ ✳ ✳

JUNE 18 GEMINI • The twins of the zodiac
May 21 at 4:00 A.M. to June 21 at 12:00 P.M. • NUMEROLOGY 9

Possessions and Desires . . .

Gem: Topaz—This is an excellent gift to be exchanged between very loyal friends.
Flower: Mustard—No one is fooled when you try to act indifferent.
Astral Color, Color Need, Apparel Color: Your Astral Color is Red, which enhances passion, excitement, and strength. Violet is your environment, keeps you empathetic toward others. In your wardrobe, Coral brings you a brilliant and sharp appearance.
Fragrance: You should flood your living space with the scent of distilled floral bouquet or freshly cut wood. This will give your ever-curious mind a rest from its constant search for new experiences.
Tree: Holly—Beware that you are not carried away by your passionate nature. The only way to grow is to be open to new experiences.
Instruments: Violin, tympanum
Composer: Gluck
Bird: Mockingbird—the most proficient minstrel in the world's orchestra; graceful and enthusiastic.
Symbol: Anchor—This tranquil symbol signifies stability and strength, and stands for strong commitments in relationships.

Harmonious Health and Nutrition . . .

Health Scent: Lavender—This scent might lead others to trust you and make you patient.
Favorable Foods: Beans, strawberries, rye, walnuts, buttermilk

What's Lucky . . .

Lucky Numbers: 5, 9, 18
Best Months: April and August
Best Day of the Week: Wednesday
Best Month Days: 9, 18, 27
Lucky Charms: A U.S. coin or a bill of any amount from the year you were born.

Harmonious Signs for Relationships and Partnerships: Aquarius and Libra

Spiritual Guides . . .

Star: Al Henah—Those born under this star are easily wounded.
Angel: Ambriel—This angel governs travel and transportation, particularly over water, and helps to create love and good communication.
Guardian Angel: Gabriel—"God is my strength."
Spiritual Stone: Chrysoprasus—This stone aids in relaxation.

✳ JUDITH'S INSIGHT ✳

Because you're charming, attractive, and alluring, you have no problem finding a mate. You are highly energetic and a willing participant in just about any sport. Inspired by challenge, you're one of those rare people who can do just about anything. Watch out for intense relationships—they can zap your energy. You need to allow yourself more patience for things to come to fruition, in their own time frame.

Keeping the balance with family will be much easier for you than keeping the balance in a love relationship. Family members understand you better and, therefore, have more patience. You tend toward extremes: you can give one hundred percent or be cold and completely isolate yourself from others. This may pose problems when it comes to maintaining long-term relationships. A lot of your emotional conflict will be fear-based—fear of what you really want, and fear of not getting it.

Be cautious that your interaction with the law finds you on the right side. You have to watch out for times where you will have problems with the IRS or just incur a lot of legal problems or situations. Unless, of course, you find yourself working for them. You may have a career, with reading, writing, or arithmetic, but not necessarily as a teacher. You will be surrounded by books or magazines at one time or another.

★ ★ ★

JUNE 19
GEMINI • The twins of the zodiac
May 21 at 4:00 A.M. to June 21 at 12:00 P.M. • NUMEROLOGY 1

Possessions and Desires . . .

Gem: Agate—This stone may promote health and lead you to a long life.

Flower: Mulberry Tree—You may be considered very wise by your peers.

Astral Color, Color Need, Apparel Color: Your Astral Color is Red, enhancing passion, excitement, and strength. Violet in your environment keeps you empathetic toward others. In your wardrobe, Green gives you confidence.

Fragrance: You should flood your living space with the scent of distilled floral bouquet or freshly cut wood. This will give your ever-curious mind a rest from its constant search for new experiences.

Tree: Walnut—You are unusually helpful and always looking for constant changes in your life.

Instruments: Oboe, flute, clarinet, piano, French horn, organ, piccolo

Composer: Böhm

Bird: Bird of Paradise—the "birds of the Gods." You will shine and love extraordinary circumstances.

Symbol: Crown—the universal sign of dignity.

Harmonious Health and Nutrition . . .

Health Scent: Strawberry—Soothing by nature, the strawberry promotes self-esteem and encourages love.

Favorable Foods: Brussels sprouts, raspberries, whole wheat, beechnuts, pressed cheese

What's Lucky . . .

Lucky Numbers: 5, 9, 10
Best Months: April and August
Best Day of the Week: Wednesday
Best Month Days: 1, 10, 19, 28
Lucky Charm: A new penny in your shoe.
Harmonious Signs for Relationships and Partnerships: Aquarius and Libra

Spiritual Guides . . .

Star: Al Henah—Those born under this star are easily wounded.

Angel: Ambriel—This angel governs travel and transportation, particularly over water, and helps to create love and good communication.

Guardian Angel: Malachi—"Messenger of Jehovah."

Spiritual Stone: Chrysoprasus—This stone aids in relaxation.

✶ JUDITH'S INSIGHT ✶

You are exceptional, kindhearted, hopeful, insightful, and full of enthusiasm. But you tend to waver when a decision is warranted, whether it be in your career or in your relationships. Feeling as if you're at a crossroads is a frequent theme throughout your life. Being torn in many different directions can be frustrating, but when you put your efforts into something and have direction, there is nothing that can stop you.

Your loving instincts provide nurturing beyond compare. You are a devoted friend and one of the most responsible family members; people respect you for your stamina and ability to carry things out. Because people depend on you, you tend to take on too much responsibility—whether you want to or not. Avoid feeling trapped by friends and family by saying No once in a while. It's healthy to go through stages of seclusion, but you dwell on things entirely too much and too long.

At some point in your life, your work will involve pen and paper, whether it be writing, sketching, or creating contracts. You might be a teacher or even a salesperson for a paper company.

Your mind is brilliant and your strong suit. Don't get discouraged when you encounter pitfalls—you are probably going to have to run an obstacle course here and there. Have no fear, not only do you get back on the horse, you learn to ride in the right direction.

✶ ✶ ✶

JUNE 20　GEMINI • The twins of the zodiac
May 21 at 4:00 A.M. to June 21 at 12:00 P.M. • NUMEROLOGY 2

Possessions and Desires . . .

Gem: Sapphire—This gem may help you find forgiveness from those you've wronged.
Flower: Black Mulberry—You will hold onto all of your childhood friends.
Astral Color, Color Need, Apparel Color: Your Astral Color is Red, which enhances passion, excitement, and strength. Violet in your environment keeps you empathetic toward others. In your wardrobe, Wine gives you energy.
Fragrance: You should flood your living space with the scent of distilled floral bouquet or freshly cut wood. This will give your ever-curious mind a rest from its constant search for new experiences.
Tree: Maple—You have great stability and flashes of intuition.
Instruments: Pipe organ, cymbal, drum
Composers: Handel, Johann Sebastian Bach
Bird: Cuckoo—a good flyer and very seldom a quitter. Some cuckoos tend to think they favor lonely isolation, but what they really yearn for is a family relationship.
Symbol: Cross—the symbol of self-sacrifice and reconciliation.

Harmonious Health and Nutrition . . .

Health Scent: Apple—You are creative, full of joy, and nearly magical. You bring happiness.
Favorable Foods: Watercress, peaches, rye, beechnuts, eggs

What's Lucky . . .

Lucky Numbers: 2, 5, 9
Best Months: April and August
Best Day of the Week: Wednesday
Best Month Days: 2, 11, 20, 29
Lucky Charms: Two 50-cent pieces. Give someone else one of them.

Harmonious Signs for Relationships and Partnerships: Aquarius and Libra

Spiritual Guides . . .

Star: Al Divah—Those with this star could feel that they are mistreated by relatives.
Angel: Ambriel—This angel governs travel and transportation, particularly over water, and helps to create love and good communication.
Guardian Angel: St. John—This angel simplifies that which is complicated.
Spiritual Stone: Chrysoprasus—This stone aids in relaxation.

✱ JUDITH'S INSIGHT ✱

You are loving and generous to a fault. You educate others on the art of giving. Kindness will allow you more happiness than you might otherwise believe. Remember the word *choices* because you will have plenty—especially in love. You can be quite fickle in love. Inevitably and later in life, you find peace and a long-lasting relationship and will do anything to make it work. Astute and receptive to the outside world, you don't seem to be as highly evolved when it comes to your own emotions. You are, unfortunately, drawn to someone who doesn't understand you.

Your healthy imagination may actually help your career choices. Whether you are putting things together for your children or working in the media or advertising, somewhere along the way your creativity will enhance your job. You may be on stage, but you're more likely to take a role in the writing process. You are sharp and intelligent, and education or preparing educational materials seem to play a role in your life. You may also have an interest in history, science, or research. If you don't, you could be rallying the community and fighting for the rights of neighbors and friends, the underdog and yourself. Learn to recognize and appreciate your humanitarianism.

Financially, you need to keep the balance until the time money and your generosity go hand in hand. Ultimately you will be financially secure.

✱ ✱ ✱

JUNE 21

GEMINI • The twins of the zodiac

May 21 at 4:00 A.M. to June 21 at 12:00 P.M. • NUMEROLOGY 3

Possessions and Desires . . .

Gem: Ruby—This stone may lead you to energy, friendship, and happiness.

Flower: Peony—You may find yourself being too forgiving when others hurt you.

Astral Color, Color Need, Apparel Color: Your Astral Color is Green, which gives you confidence. Green in your environment enhances your luck, because you will feel secure. In your wardrobe, Brown gives you confidence and a sharp look.

Fragrance: You should flood your living space with the scent of distilled floral bouquet or freshly cut wood. This will give your ever-curious mind a rest from its constant search for new experiences.

Tree: Elm—You have willpower, strength, and the ability to stand alone.

Instrument: Trombone

Composers: Verdi, Mendelssohn, Schumann

Bird: Swan—Regarded as royal and sacred, this bird has the protective nature of a mother, and can become a furious fighter in the defense of its young.

Symbol: Wreath—You have been crowned with a special personality. You are strong but extremely compassionate.

Harmonious Health and Nutrition . . .

Health Scent: Rose—This scent will lead you to passionate thoughts and make you feel warm inside.

Favorable Foods: Celery, grapes, rye, almonds, buttermilk

What's Lucky . . .

Lucky Numbers: 3, 5, 9

Best Months: April and August

Best Day of the Week: Wednesday

Best Month Days: 3, 12, 21, and 30

Lucky Charm: A pen that someone else has already used.

Harmonious Signs for Relationships and Partnerships: Aquarius and Libra

Spiritual Guides . . .

Star: Al Henah—Those born under this star are easily wounded.

Angel: Ambriel—This angel governs travel and transportation, particularly over water, and helps to create love and good communication.

Guardian Angel: Johiel—This angel is a protector of all those with a humble heart.

Spiritual Stone: Chrysoprasus—This stone aids in relaxation.

✶ JUDITH'S INSIGHT ✶

You are cunning and smooth, charming and funny; your sense of humor can get you through any tough situation. You may endure battles in relationships before you find harmony. It has a lot to do with you. As you get older, you change remarkably and have more patience and consideration for your partner. But keeping yourself satisfied will be a bit of a task when it comes to love. You need a lot of freedom, social invitations, and friends to keep you satisfied. You will be called selfish at times because you demand a lot, want a lot, and get a lot. Have no fear, for your turn will come to give back, and this is where you learn one of life's greatest lessons. An epiphany of sorts will be your teacher, and from then on, you undergo considerable change and give more than you receive.

You do well in your own business or working for a larger company—the bigger the better. With your organizational skills, there aren't many jobs you can't handle. It wouldn't be surprising for you to end up in a government position. At some point in your life, you may take a position where a uniform is required. You may have a job where frequent travel is involved. All in all, you do have a successful career.

You make friends quite easily and try to dominate the crowd. When you're not vying for control, the power is usually handed right over to you. One way or another you are placed in a powerful position.

✶ ✶ ✶

JUNE 22   CANCER • The waves of the moon of the zodiac
June 21 at 12:00 P.M. to July 22 at 11:00 P.M. • NUMEROLOGY 4

Possessions and Desires . . .

Gem: Sapphire—This gem may help you find forgiveness from those you've wronged.
Flower: Passionflower—Religion tends to be a very important factor in your life.
Astral Color, Color Need, Apparel Color: Your Astral Color is Green, which gives you confidence. Green in your environment enhances your luck, because you will feel secure. In your wardrobe, Silver is very stimulating for you.
Fragrance: You will be calmed by the scent of fresh linen dried in the breeze or wild orchids.
Tree: Cherry—You will find yourself faced with constant new emotional awakenings.
Instruments: Bass, clarinet
Composers: Haydn, Wagner
Bird: Killdeer—This bird is usually found consorting with other species, and can adapt to any environment.
Symbol: Star—You are full of inner brightness and will stand out in any crowd. You will be seen as special.

Harmonious Health and Nutrition . . .

Health Scent: Vanilla—This scent will fill you with a feeling of cleanliness and stability.
Favorable Foods: Lentils, bananas, sugar, chicken, eggs

What's Lucky . . .

Lucky Numbers: 3, 4, 7
Best Months: February and September
Best Day of the Week: Monday
Best Month Days: 4, 13, 22, 31
Lucky Charm: A piece of material cut from something in your home.

Harmonious Signs for Relationships and Partnerships: Pisces, Scorpio, and Taurus

Spiritual Guides . . .

Star: Al Nethra—Those with this star are treasured as friends.
Angel: Muriel—This angel aids us during times of emotional stress.
Guardian Angel: St. John—This angel simplifies that which is complicated.
Spiritual Stone: Chrysoprasus—This stone aids in relaxation.

✶ JUDITH'S INSIGHT ✶

You are a challenge to others and quite fascinating even to yourself. Bouts with self-doubt and low self-esteem could possibly be your greatest downfall. Because of your strong personality, people don't always realize how sensitive you are and can actually expect too much of you. Watch that this doesn't pull you down at times. You tend to stand secure even though your personality can be overwhelming.

You are likely to have unusual relationships or be drawn to a unique person. You may also desire to live in unusual situations or maybe choose a mate who is foreign born. Family may see you as a rebel or the black sheep. You are quite eccentric, and you love every minute of it. The more conversation pieces you have around you, the better. As you get older you tend to become more family oriented, and you make take a 180-degree turn to the more conservative. Later, a more structured family environment will appeal to you.

You will undertake many challenges and love the exotic, the thrilling, and the adventurous. Tap into your strong intuition more often. You could be a psychic, an astrologer, investigator, or detective. With your love of work, you can have a very successful career; you just need patience to get there.

✶ ✶ ✶

JUNE 23
CANCER • The waves of the moon of the zodiac

June 21 at 12:00 P.M. to July 22 at 11:00 P.M. • NUMEROLOGY 5

Possessions and Desires . . .

Gem: Sardius—This stone could give the wearer unusual insights into his or her own heart.

Flower: Pasqueflower—You tend to not ask other people to give you what you need.

Astral Color, Color Need, Apparel Color: Your Astral Color is Green, which gives you confidence. Green in your environment enhances your luck, because you will feel secure. In your wardrobe, Brown gives you confidence and a sharp appearance.

Fragrance: You will be calmed by the scent of fresh linen dried in the breeze or wild orchids.

Tree: Apple—You are creative, full of joy, and nearly magical. You bring happiness.

Instruments: Viola, trumpet

Composer: Liszt

Bird: Cuckoo—a good flyer and very seldom a quitter. Some cuckoos tend to think they favor lonely isolation, but what they really yearn for is a family relationship.

Symbol: Triangle—You have the right combination of abilities.

Harmonious Health and Nutrition . . .

Health Scent: Peach—This scent may balance your good qualities so that they equal your charm.

Favorable Foods: Beets, strawberries, honey, oysters, pressed cheese

What's Lucky . . .

Lucky Numbers: 3, 5, 7
Best Months: February and September
Best Day of the Week: Monday
Best Month Days: 4, 5, 23
Lucky Charms: A rabbit's foot or a white candle
Harmonious Signs for Relationships and Partnerships: Pisces, Scorpio, and Taurus

Spiritual Guides . . .

Star: Al Nethra—Those with this star are treasured as friends.

Angel: Muriel—This angel aids us during times of emotional stress.

Guardian Angel: Plavwell—This angel gives power and strength to one's presence.

Spiritual Stone: Jacinth—Holding this stone could aid in memory retention.

✴ JUDITH'S INSIGHT ✴

Some may call you a showoff, and you display yourself and your home like museum pieces. Things of beauty and taste appeal to you. Your energy and enthusiasm are addictive, so your name appears first on the invitation list. You have many hidden talents, and you might be in your mid-thirties before you figure out what you really want to do.

One big downfall is your impatience with those not as quick as you. When it comes to love, you are totally devoted to one mate, even if it lasts only a week or two. You find it easier to blame others than to take responsibility for problems. After forty, though, you tend to balance that.

It is most likely that you will have more than one job. A career in entertaining, writing, publishing, or computer graphics could please you. With your restlessness, it wouldn't be surprising if you were in a job with many changes or more than one title.

You have a strong desire to travel on a constant basis. Your suitcase should always be ready and packed. Or, since you are a risk taker, you could parachute out of planes. You are intrigued by the unusual and unknown, like astrology or psychology. You may come up with some of your own theories on life. Consider psychology as a possibility. You take on life and use every minute of your time to enjoy it. But, watch out for less active times—this could send you into a depression. So when you're feeling low, all you have to do is get your engine started again.

✴ ✴ ✴

JUNE 24 CANCER • The waves of the moon of the zodiac
June 21 at 12:00 P.M. to July 22 at 11:00 P.M. • NUMEROLOGY 6

Possessions and Desires . . .

Gem: Topaz—This is an excellent gift to be exchanged between very loyal friends.
Flower: Hemp—You may need to just accept that the universe will always have its own way.
Astral Color, Color Need, Apparel Color: Your Astral Color is Green, which gives you confidence. Green in your environment enhances your luck, because you will feel secure. In your wardrobe, Silver is very stimulating for you.
Fragrance: You will be calmed by the scent of fresh linen dried in the breeze or wild orchids.
Tree: Palm—You tend to be very healthy and creative.
Instruments: Tambourine, lyre
Composer: Schubert
Bird: Goldfinch—There are forty-four different species of finches which vary greatly. This can sometimes be the most charming bird. These gentle creatures can be very moody in unsettled weather.
Symbol: Crescent—You are more likely to be influenced by the phases of the moon. Your easygoing manner leads you to peaceful situations.

Harmonious Health and Nutrition . . .

Health Scent: Orange Blossom—This scent may balance your body, mind, and soul.
Favorable Foods: Carrots, grapes, sugar, liver, buttermilk

What's Lucky . . .

Lucky Numbers: 3, 6, 7
Best Months: February and September
Best Day of the Week: Monday
Best Month Days: 6, 15, 24
Lucky Charms: A religious token or card from any religion.

Harmonious Signs for Relationships and Partnerships: Pisces, Scorpio, and Taurus

Spiritual Guides . . .

Star: Al Terpha—The people born under this star are often delivered from trouble by luck.
Angel: Muriel—This angel aids us during times of emotional stress.
Guardian Angel: Michael—"Who is like God."
Spiritual Stone: Jacinth—Holding this stone could aid in memory retention.

✷ JUDITH'S INSIGHT ✷

There isn't anything you can't do. You are a great talker and avid reader. Seldom do you go into a deep conversation you can't handle. You seem pretty certain about how to get over the obstacles that inevitably come in your way. Eventually you learn to accept criticism, although at first you can be quite defensive.

When it comes to finding a mate, look before you leap. You have a tendency to jump in without really knowing the other person. Your worst heartaches come from not thinking before you speak. As a lover, you are deep and emotional. The problem is very few people ever get to see that. Too bad you're afraid to let others in, especially since you crave intimacy most. Your subtle style is most attractive, but your mate must be a powerhouse when it comes to romance. If that person doesn't appreciate spontaneity, they may never put a smile on your face. Don't worry, you fare quite well in your love life and other relationships. Work to send out more receptive signals. Harmony and happiness tend to come when you decide you're ready.

Although you like a challenge, from time to time you could just stop something in the middle and decide you want something else. It will seem as if money just falls into your lap. It is also very possible that you will create something and bring yourself to significant wealth.

✷ ✷ ✷

JUNE 25 CANCER • The waves of the moon of the zodiac
June 21 at 12:00 P.M. to July 22 at 11:00 A.M. • NUMEROLOGY 7

Possessions and Desires . . .

Gem: Ruby—This stone may lead you to energy, friendship, and happiness.

Flower: Hollyhock—You don't mind working for the security you want from life.

Astral Color, Color Need, Apparel Color: Your Astral Color is Green, which gives confidence. Green in your environment enhances your luck, because you will feel secure. In your wardrobe, Brown gives confidence and a sharp look.

Fragrance: You will be calmed by the scent of fresh linen dried in the breeze or wild orchids.

Tree: Sycamore—Yours is the ability to love, communicate honestly with others, and have lasting relationships.

Instrument: Harp

Composers: Gluck, Brahms

Bird: Skylark—This handsome bird is beautiful when it sings. It always whistles as it works.

Symbol: Heart—You are enthusiastic, empathetic, and full of generosity and love.

Harmonious Health and Nutrition . . .

Health Scent: Jasmine—This scent may make you more easygoing when you are stressed.

Favorable Foods: Spinach, bananas, sugar, salmon, eggs

What's Lucky . . .

Lucky Numbers: 3, 7, 25
Best Months: February and September
Best Day of the Week: Monday
Best Month Days: 6, 15, 24
Lucky Charm: An old key.

Harmonious Signs for Relationships and Partnerships: Pisces, Scorpio, and Taurus

Spiritual Guides . . .

Star: Al Nethra—Those with this star are treasured as friends.

Angel: Muriel—This angel aids us during times of emotional stress.

Guardian Angel: Ralphael—This angel attends to all of your needs when you are looking for guidance.

Spiritual Stone: Jacinth—Holding this stone could aid in memory retention.

✶ JUDITH'S INSIGHT ✶

You are kind, gentle, sweet, and nurturing. You love your home to look neat and tidy. Highly sensitive, you can be quick on the defense as well as on the offense. When people are nice to you, you are at your best; and the nicer they are, the nicer you are in return. You can be secretive, and sometimes a bit flirtatious and even promiscuous. Try to relax that mind: you dwell on things far too long. That is okay for work, but unhealthy emotionally. Your tendency is to be extremely loyal.

You are a comfort zone for your friends and family, but you don't know how to say No. Keep yourself from getting worked up when it comes to love. Use your sense of humor as much as you want, and then use it some more.

You are profound in your thinking; a career in writing would be a nice fit for you. Although it may take you years to recognize all your talents, your number one talent is your imagination. Family members remind you from time to time how inventive you were as a child. You may go back and forth with careers until your thirties; then you will, without a doubt, find the right path and follow it to the end of the rainbow.

✶ ✶ ✶

JUNE 26 CANCER • The waves of the moon of the zodiac
June 21 at 12:00 P.M. to July 22 at 11:00 P.M. • NUMEROLOGY 8

Possessions and Desires . . .

Gem: Chrysolite—This gem may help you clear your mind of sadness and worry.
Flower: Sweet Scabiosa—That which you love tends to be what you see as genuine.
Astral Color, Color Need, Apparel Color: Your Astral Color is Green, which gives you confidence. Green in your environment enhances your luck, because you will feel secure. In your wardrobe, Brown gives you confidence and a sharp appearance.
Fragrance: You will be calmed by the scent of fresh linen dried in the breeze or wild orchids.
Tree: Pine—Your relationships tend to be balanced, both emotionally and mentally.
Instrument: Cello
Composer: Mozart
Bird: Bobolink—This charming singer is equally good as a soloist or a member of an orchestra. It is a very romantic bird, most useful as an insect destroyer, and elegant, with beautiful feathers, and always pleasant to have around.
Symbol: Wings—You are the source of balance in your world—this will bring you contentment.

Harmonious Health and Nutrition . . .

Health Scent: Almond—This scent may revitalize you and open you to greater possibilities.
Favorable Foods: Okra, apples, honey, chicken, buttermilk

What's Lucky . . .

Lucky Numbers: 3, 7, 8
Best Months: February and September
Best Day of the Week: Monday
Best Month Days: 8, 17, 26
Lucky Charm: Red ribbon in your wallet or doorway.
Harmonious Signs for Relationships and Partnerships: Pisces, Scorpio, and Taurus

Spiritual Guides . . .

Star: Al Nethra—Those with this star are treasured as friends.
Angel: Muriel—This angel aids us during times of emotional stress.
Guardian Angel: Seraphim—An angel that brings love, light, and passion.
Spiritual Stone: Jacinth—Holding this stone could aid in memory retention.

✳ JUDITH'S INSIGHT ✳

Although you're charming and giving, you can be too serious. You don't miss much: you take it in, store it, and review it like a movie. You can be misunderstood and considered intense. Few people really get to know that mind of yours. You rarely speak without something concrete to say. Every once in a while you have a tendency to go overboard either with spending or partying. Your small circle of friends from childhood will stick with your almost forever.

It may take work for a mate to please you. Your serious soul locks others out. You may find life uneasy at times, and others may see you as a lonely heart looking for a place to connect. Certain special people bring out your terrific sense of humor. And you're better with a partner than alone.

For you there aren't enough hours in a day. Remember not to bite off more than you can chew. This is yet another way you overdo it. When it comes to family ties, you keep them. Family for you could also be close, dear friends or even former lovers. You're a free bird who needs a secure nest where you can always come in for a landing and feel safe. So although you may have one appearance, you really are someone else.

You love to teach and instruct and are a wealth of information, not only from books but your own philosophies of life. You would make a great teacher, professor, or instructor. You can even do well with emotional counseling, guidance counseling, or nurturing of any kind. Not to say that you are not smart enough to be the head of the company—that side of you exists as well. Of course, you would be the boss with a heart.

✳ ✳ ✳

JUNE 27

CANCER • The waves of the moon of the zodiac

June 21 at 12:00 P.M. to July 22 at 11:00 P.M. • NUMEROLOGY 9

Possessions and Desires . . .

Gem: Sapphire—This gem may help you find forgiveness from those you've wronged.
Flower: Schinus—You may find much peace in actively practicing your chosen religion.
Astral Color, Color Need, Apparel Color: Your Astral Color is Green, which gives you confidence. Green in your environment enhances your luck, because you will feel secure. In your wardrobe, Silver is very stimulating for you.
Fragrance: You will be calmed by the scent of fresh linen dried in the breeze or wild orchids.
Tree: Holly—Beware that you are not carried away by your passionate nature. The only way to grow is to be open to new experiences.
Instruments: Violin, tympanum
Composer: Gluck
Bird: Mockingbird—the most proficient minstrel in the world's orchestra; graceful and enthusiastic.
Symbol: Anchor—This tranquil symbol signifies stability and strength, and stands for strong commitments in relationships.

Harmonious Health and Nutrition . . .

Health Scents: Lavender—This scent might lead others to trust you and make you patient.
Favorable Foods: Cucumbers, cherries, sugar, oysters, pressed cheese

What's Lucky . . .

Lucky Numbers: 3, 7, 9
Best Month: February and September
Best Day of the Week: Monday
Best Month Days: 9, 18, 27
Lucky Charm: A U.S. coin or a bill of any amount from the year you were born.
Harmonious Signs for Relationships and Partnerships: Pisces, Scorpio, and Taurus

Spiritual Guides . . .

Star: Al Terpha—The people born under this star are often delivered from trouble by luck.
Angel: Muriel—This angel aids us during times of emotional stress.
Guardian Angel: Gabriel—"God is my strength."
Spiritual Stone: Jacinth—Holding this stone could aid in memory retention.

✴ JUDITH'S INSIGHT ✴

You are the truest and most loyal of friends. A combination of intelligence and wit makes you charming, shrewd, and attractive. You really are a great conversationalist, though others may see you as quiet. Your gift with words may be your greatest asset, although your kind advice and good heart are the cornerstones of your makeup.

Your search for love may not be complete until you are a little older. And be careful when you find it—that's when the challenges really begin. A nurturing soul, you really do love your domestic side. Somewhere along the way, you learn to recognize this.

You do tend to be more creative than you think, and, as you get older, you may put that creativity to work—painting, writing, or building sand castles. You may find work as caregiver in a hospital. A career in publishing, as an editor or a writer, may present itself to you. Success will knock at your door often, and you will have chances to move. Make sure that you are not in a stagnant situation. In time you could be head of a corporation or wind up in your own business or assisting your mate in his or hers.

A few legal issues may arise, or you may just work for attorneys. You encounter an obstacle or two, but you hurdle them like a master athlete. The older you get, the better you become. As you get older when it comes to work, your tendency is to stay in one place for the security it provides.

✴ ✴ ✴

Possessions and Desires . . .

Gem: Emerald—Those who carry this stone tend to be lucky in love.

Flower: Snapdragon—Be careful to get the facts before assuming you know another's intentions.

Astral Color, Color Need, Apparel Color: Your Astral Color is Green, which gives you confidence. Green in your environment enhances your luck, because you will feel secure. In your wardrobe, Brown gives you confidence and a sharp look.

Fragrance: You will be calmed by the scent of fresh linen dried in the breeze or wild orchids.

Tree: Walnut—You are unusually helpful and always looking for new beginnings.

Instruments: Oboe, flute, clarinet, piano, French horn, organ, piccolo

Composer: Böhm

Bird: Bird of Paradise—the "bird of the Gods." You will shine and love extraordinary form.

Symbol: Crown—the universal sign of dignity.

Harmonious Health and Nutrition . . .

Health Scent: Strawberry—Soothing by nature, the strawberry promotes self-esteem and encourages love.

Favorable Foods: Carrots, figs, honey, liver, eggs

What's Lucky . . .

Lucky Numbers: 3, 7, 10
Best Months: February and September
Best Day of the Week: Monday
Best Month Days: 1, 10, 19, 28
Lucky Charm: A new penny in your shoe.
Harmonious Signs for Relationships and Partnerships: Pisces, Scorpio, and Taurus

Spiritual Guides . . .

Star: Al Nethra—Those with this star are treasured as friends.

Angel: Muriel—This angel aids us during times of emotional stress.

Guardian Angel: Malachi—"Messenger of Jehovah."

Spiritual Stone: Jacinth—Holding this stone could aid in memory retention.

✶ JUDITH'S INSIGHT ✶

You're essentially kindhearted and nice to others. You're definitely one who is interested in material things. You will have a lot of things, from a beautiful home to a nice car to attractive clothes. You are sympathetic and kind in spite of your changeable mood. When it comes to friendship, you are true and loyal. You consider gossip an art and may be intrigued by what others have to say. In financial matters you can be rather intractable, not outwardly generous with others, because a lot of the time you spend your money on yourself.

In love, allow doors and windows to open. You tend to be too closed-minded. Give yourself a chance to find the right mate, otherwise you may be doing double duty and amid a lot of conflict. A triangle of some sort is quite possible. Family matters do have an important role in your life.

It would be very surprising if you weren't intrigued by the art of poetry and love. If you are male, you may find that these things play a valuable role in your life. You are quite artistic or will be attracted to the arts and to beauty. You can be anything from an upholsterer to a decorator or a sculptor. Your nurturing side may lead you to medicine and helping others.

Don't be discouraged when you hit curves in the road, because you will have many. As time goes on, you get used to them and master them like a professional race car driver. If you have a car, it may be a valuable asset to you and something you treat like a child.

✶ ✶ ✶

JUNE 29　CANCER • The waves of the moon of the zodiac
June 21 at 12:00 P.M. to July 22 at 11:00 P.M. • NUMEROLOGY 2

Possessions and Desires . . .

Gem: Sapphire—This gem may help you find forgiveness from those you've wronged.
Flower: Saint Johnswort—Be careful not to let superstitions rule your life.
Astral Color, Color Need, Apparel Color: Your Astral Color is Green, which gives you confidence. Green in your environment enhances your luck, because you will feel secure. In your wardrobe, Silver is stimulating for you.
Fragrance: You will be calmed by the scent of fresh linen dried in the breeze or wild orchids.
Tree: Maple—You have both great stability and flashes of intuition.
Instruments: Pipe organ, cymbal, drum
Composers: Handel, Johann Sebastian Bach
Bird: Cuckoo—a good flyer and very seldom a quitter. Some cuckoos tend to think they favor lonely isolation, but what they really yearn for is a family relationship.
Symbol: Cross—the symbol of self-sacrifice and reconciliation.

Harmonious Health and Nutrition . . .

Health Scent: Apple—You are creative, full of joy, and nearly magical. You bring happiness.
Favorable Foods: Lima beans, cherries, sugar, salmon, buttermilk

What's Lucky . . .

Lucky Numbers: 3, 7, 11
Best Months: February and September
Best Day of the Week: Monday
Best Month Days: 2, 11, 20, 29
Lucky Charms: Two 50-cent pieces. Give someone else one of them.

Harmonious Signs for Relationships and Partnerships: Pisces, Scorpio, and Taurus

Spiritual Guides . . .

Star: Al Nethra—Those with this star are treasured as friends.
Angel: Muriel—This angel aids us during times of emotional stress.
Guardian Angel: Uriel—This angel brings the light of God's guidance.
Spiritual Stone: Jacinth—Holding this stone could aid in memory retention.

✶ JUDITH'S INSIGHT ✶

Beginnings are important to you, and you will thrive on change. You welcome new things—new love, a new house, new clothes, new furniture. When it comes to love, you weave a tangled web. Expect the unexpected, especially in your twenties. As you get older you become less erratic, and your chances of finding a mate improve. When you do, look for some security. Warmhearted and kind, you do put up barricades when it comes to relationships. Sometimes you listen with only one ear. Your life will be full of choices over and over again.

As far as career is concerned, it is doubtful that you will pick one early in life and stick with it. If you do, however, somewhere along the way you will either hold a second career or take up a hobby that will consume most of your time. Your love of literature, history, and books will present itself; you may even make a little history yourself. You do have a sharp mind and an overwhelming intelligence that may lead you to become a professor, historian, writer, inventor, or publisher. The way the world is going today, you may be a leader in hardware or software in computers.

✶ ✶ ✶

JUNE 30 CANCER • The waves of the moon of the zodiac
June 21 at 12:00 P.M. to July 22 at 11:00 P.M. • NUMEROLOGY 3

Possessions and Desires . . .

Gem: Sapphire—This gem may help you find forgiveness from those you've wronged.
Flower: Sunflower—You should be adored by the one that you love.
Astral Color, Color Need, Apparel Color: Your Astral Color is Green, which gives you confidence. Green in your environment enhances your luck, because you will feel secure. In your wardrobe, Brown gives you confidence and a sharp appearance.
Fragrance: You will be calmed by the scent of fresh linen dried in the breeze or wild orchids.
Tree: Elm—You have willpower, strength, and the ability to stand alone.
Instrument: Trombone
Composers: Verdi, Mendelssohn, Schumann
Bird: Swan—Regarded as royal and sacred, this bird has the protective nature of a mother, and can become a furious fighter in the defense of its young.
Symbol: Wreath—You have been crowned with a special personality. You are strong but extremely compassionate.

Harmonious Health and Nutrition . . .

Health Scent: Rose—This scent will lead you to passionate thoughts and make you feel warm inside.
Favorable Foods: String beans, gooseberries, honey, chicken, pressed cheese

What's Lucky . . .

Lucky Numbers: 3, 7, 30
Best Months: February and September
Best Day of the Week: Monday
Best Month Days: 3, 12, 21, 30
Lucky Charm: A pen that someone else has already used.

Harmonious Signs for Relationships and Partnerships: Pisces, Scorpio, and Taurus

Spiritual Guides . . .

Star: Al Nethra—Those with this star are treasured as friends.
Angel: Muriel—This angel aids us during times of emotional stress.
Guardian Angel: Johiel—This angel is a protector of all those with a humble heart.
Spiritual Stone: Jacinth—Holding this stone could aid in memory retention.

✶ JUDITH'S INSIGHT ✶

Your personality will bring you just about anything you want in life. You have wit, charm, and a sense of humor. Cunning and smooth, you have loads of self-reliance and love to rule. You make friends easily but dominate the crowd. You are a social butterfly and need a lot of friends. The more social invitations, the better.

You emerge as a leader early on. You are fortunate in love, and relationships fall at your feet. Unfortunately, being with the wrong person will cause you to get into many a rut. Take your time in choosing the right partner. In order for someone to keep you satisfied, they have to know you well enough to provide the freedom you require. Trust is vital in your relationship.

You would do well owning your own company, but if you work for a large company, the larger it is, the better. Your excellent organizational skills are superb in any office situation. It wouldn't be surprising if you decide on a career working in government—municipal or otherwise. You are quite a handy person and do have a knack for mechanical things. Fast things (like cars) intrigue you, and you seek out all kinds of challenges.

You can be considered a handful because you demand a lot. You are here to live life to the fullest.

✶ ✶ ✶

JULY

JULY 1 CANCER • The waves of the moon of the zodiac
June 21 at 12:00 P.M. to July 22 at 11:00 P.M. • NUMEROLOGY 1

Possessions and Desires . . .

Gem: Emerald—Those who carry this stone tend to be lucky in love.

Flower: Sycamore—You may have a strong curiosity about everything around you.

Astral Color, Color Need, Apparel Color: Your Astral Color is Green, which gives you confidence. Green in your environment enhances your luck, because you will feel secure. In your wardrobe, Silver is a stimulating color for you.

Fragrance: You will be calmed by the scent of fresh linen dried in the breeze or wild orchids.

Tree: Walnut—You are unusually helpful and always looking for constant changes in your life.

Instruments: Oboe, flute, clarinet, piano, French horn, organ, piccolo

Composer: Böhm

Bird: Cuckoo—A good flyer and very seldom a quitter. Many seem more independent than they actually are. Yearn for more nurturing than one would expect.

Symbol: Crown—the universal sign of dignity.

Harmonious Health and Nutrition . . .

Health Scent: Strawberry—Soothing by nature, the strawberry promotes self-esteem and encourages love.

Favorable Foods: Parsley, honey, oysters, buttermilk

What's Lucky . . .

Lucky Numbers: 3, 7, 11
Best Months: February and September.
Best Day of the Week: Monday
Best Month Days: 1, 10, 19, 28

Lucky Charm: A new penny in your shoe.
Harmonious Signs for Relationships and Partnerships: Pisces, Scorpio, and Taurus

Spiritual Guides . . .

Star: Al Nethra—Those with this star are treasured as friends.

Angel: Muriel—This angel aids us during times of emotional stress.

Guardian Angel: Malachi—"Messenger of Jehovah."

Spiritual Stone: Jacinth—Holding this stone could aid in memory retention.

✶ JUDITH'S INSIGHT ✶

You are kind, loving, loyal, and true. You are a great humanitarian and giving will be very important to you. It will be more important for you to give than receive. You are so attached to your home and family sometimes it will seem hard for you to make decisions without considering everybody's happiness. It is more likely than not that you will find harmony in loving relationships. Children and marriage could play a large role in your life at one time or another.

Your nurturing side will probably lead you into a profession as a doctor, nurse, or medical assistant. It wouldn't be surprising if, somewhere along the way, you were brought to the public eye with whatever career you choose. You are independent and can adapt to changes very easily. You are fond of theater and drama, and you may have a career in that field. There is a good chance you will attain wealth.

You have a great love for the unknown and are intrigued by mysterious environments. Strange things happen to you. You may even be a bit psychic. Your life will probably be quite unpredictable.

✶ ✶ ✶

JULY 2

CANCER • The waves of the moon of the zodiac

June 21 at 12:00 P.M. to July 22 at 11:00 P.M. • NUMEROLOGY 2

Possessions and Desires . . .

Gem: Sapphire—This gem may help you find forgiveness from those you've wronged.

Flower: Xanthium—You sometimes are rude without meaning to be.

Astral Color, Color Need, Apparel Color: Your Astral Color is Green, which gives you confidence. Green in your environment enhances your luck, because you will feel secure. In your wardrobe, Brown gives you confidence and a sharp look.

Fragrance: You will be calmed by the scent of fresh linen dried in the breeze or wild orchids.

Tree: Maple—You have both great stability and flashes of intuition.

Instruments: Pipe organ, cymbal, drum

Composers: Handel, Johann Sebastian Bach

Bird: Stork—Turkish bird, held in high esteem the world over. This bird is intelligent but may have strange tendencies.

Symbol: Cross—the symbol of self-sacrifice and reconciliation.

Harmonious Health and Nutrition . . .

Health Scent: Apple—You are creative, full of joy, and nearly magical. You bring happiness.

Favorable Foods: Cabbage, grapefruit, whole oats, molasses, cottage cheese

What's Lucky . . .

Lucky Numbers: 2, 3, 7

Best Months: February and September

Best Day of the Week: Monday

Best Month Days: 2, 11, 20, 29

Lucky Charms: Two 50-cent pieces. Give someone else one of them.

Harmonious Signs for Relationships and Partnerships: Pisces, Scorpio, and Taurus

Spiritual Guides . . .

Star: Al Nethra—Those with this star are treasured as friends.

Angel: Muriel—This angel aids us during times of emotional stress.

Guardian Angel: Uriel—This angel brings the light of God's guidance.

Spiritual Stone: Jacinth—Holding this stone could aid in memory retention.

✸ JUDITH'S INSIGHT ✸

You show much persistence and consistency through your life. You are as stable as the day is long. You always show good judgment in whatever you do. You conscience is very strong. You can be moody, neat as a pin, strong as an ox, and cranky as a crab. You can be bothered by things in your environment because of your sensitive nature.

Your tendency is to do better with relationships than not. Your home is important, even if it is the garage. You have a strong determination. Not only do you create a successful career for yourself, you look to enhance the success of other people, especially those with whom you have a friendship or relationship. Your career could be in a counseling or homemaking environment. You could also be anything from a carpenter to chiropractor. Whatever you do, you will nurture and serve those around you.

You like to create drama in life. Travel will be important to you, but you'll be luckier on sea or surrounded by water. You are inspired by anything you do around water. If you want to write, do it near a lake. Your more romantic and sentimental times will be better when you are surrounded by water. If you are feeling low and need to stimulate yourself, walk along the beach, and look for answers in the waves.

★ ★ ★

JULY 3
CANCER • The waves of the moon of the zodiac
June 21 at 12:00 P.M. to July 22 at 11:00 P.M. • NUMEROLOGY 3

Possessions and Desires . . .

Gem: Emerald—Those who carry this stone tend to be lucky in love.
Flower: Wood Sorrel—You may mother those you care for.
Astral Color, Color Need, Apparel Color: Your Astral Color is Green, which gives you confidence. Green in your environment enhances your luck, because you will feel secure. In your wardrobe, Silver is a stimulating color for you.
Fragrance: You will be calmed by the scent of fresh linen dried in the breeze or wild orchids.
Tree: Elm—You have willpower, strength, and the ability to stand alone.
Instrument: Trombone
Composers: Verdi, Mendelssohn, Schumann
Bird: Stork—Turkish bird, held in high esteem the world over. This bird is intelligent but may have strange tendencies.
Symbol: Wreath—You have been crowned with a special personality. You are strong but extremely compassionate.

Harmonious Health and Nutrition . . .

Health Scent: Rose—This scent will lead you to passionate thoughts and make you feel warm inside.
Favorable Foods: Cauliflower, peaches, caraway, honey, salmon, eggs

What's Lucky . . .

Lucky Numbers: 3, 7, 21
Best Months: February and September
Best Day of the Week: Monday
Best Month Days: 3, 12, 21, 30
Lucky Charm: A pen that someone else has already used.

Harmonious Signs for Relationships and Partnerships: Pisces, Scorpio, and Taurus

Spiritual Guides . . .

Star: Al Nethra—Those with this star are treasured as friends.
Angel: Muriel—This angel aids us during times of emotional stress.
Guardian Angel: Johiel—This angel is a protector of all those with a humble heart.
Spiritual Stone: Jacinth—Holding this stone could aid in memory retention.

✶ JUDITH'S INSIGHT ✶

You are intelligent and intuitive and sometimes too logical for your own good. You do tend to have strong opinions. Yet, usually you speak only when you really have something to say. Others in your life may think you are serious by nature, but you are just shy. You may not truly realize your independent nature.

You want a happy home and do what you must to make it happen. The challenge for you is keeping from doing too much for others; whether it be furniture that has to be moved or a neighbor in need of a helping hand, you are always there to help.

You may desire a career in the health field, which means that you could eventually be the head of a facility or perhaps the owner. You would be a successful entrepeneur. You do lean toward a public life at one time or another. It won't be surprising if your name is in print at some point. Though it does take some time for you to find your niche, you will be quite successful in whatever you choose.

Your home is most important to you, especially living with a long term mate. Just don't make this decision hastily. You will be the one who does it all to keep your relationship going, friends or lovers. When others don't return the same energies, you will take all you can, but eventually leave. If affections and devotion are returned, you can live happily ever after.

★ ★ ★

JULY 4 CANCER • The waves of the moon of the zodiac
June 21 at 12:00 P.M. to July 22 at 11:00 P.M. • NUMEROLOGY 4

Possessions and Desires . . .

Gem: Sapphire—This gem may help you find forgiveness from those you've wronged.
Flower: Water willow: Patience is hard for you, but you will learn it along the way.
Astral Color, Color Need, Apparel Color: Your Astral Color is Green, which gives you confidence. Green in your environment enhances your luck, because you will feel secure. In your wardrobe, Brown gives you confidence and a sharp look.
Fragrance: You will be calmed by the scent of fresh linen dried in the breeze or wild orchids.
Tree: Cherry—You will find yourself faced with constant new emotional awakenings.
Instruments: Bass, clarinet
Composers: Haydn, Wagner
Bird: Stork—Turkish bird, held in high esteem the world over. This bird is intelligent but may have strange tendencies.
Symbol: Star—You are full of inner brightness and will stand out in any crowd. You will be seen as special.

Harmonious Health and Nutrition . . .

Health Scent: Vanilla—This scent will fill you with a feeling of cleanliness and stability.
Favorable Foods: Celery, black figs, whole oats, molasses, oysters, cream

What's Lucky . . .

Lucky Numbers: 3, 4, 7
Best Months: February and September
Best Day of the Week: Monday
Best Month Days: 4, 13, 22, 31
Lucky Charm: A piece of material cut from something in your home.

Harmonious Signs for Relationships and Partnerships: Pisces, Scorpio, and Taurus

Spiritual Guides . . .

Star: Al Nethra—Those with this star are treasured friends.
Angel: Muriel—This angel aids us during times of emotional stress.
Guardian Angel: Uriel—This angel brings the light of God's guidance.
Spiritual Stone: Jacinth—Holding this stone could aid in memory retention

✶ JUDITH'S INSIGHT ✶

You are exceptionally sensitive and have a warm heart that could heat the world. You surround yourself with loads of people, yet you seem lonely. Many strange, unusual things occur throughout your life. Believe it or not, these experiences will enhance your life, though at the time they may seem devastating. Later on, you will have learned from them.

It is extremely easy for you to make friends, although you allow relationships to drift away. You blame others for not being there when it is you who pushes them away. What you feel is not necessarily what you show, and this could create problems.

You could be a great doctor, lawyer, or teacher. You could be successful working in film or theater. No matter what career you eventually become active in, with time you will rise almost to the top—it would be quite surprising if you didn't.

You tend to stand apart from the crowd. You have a strong sense of loyalty, not only to your family, but to your country. You tend to be the one that lends the helping hand.

✶ ✶ ✶

JULY 5

CANCER • The waves of the moon of the zodiac

June 21 at 12:00 P.M. to July 22 at 11:00 P.M. • NUMEROLOGY 5

Possessions and Desires . . .

Gem: Emerald—Those who carry this stone tend to be lucky in love.

Flower: Crown of Roses—You will be recognized as a very moral person.

Astral Color, Color Need, Apparel Color: Your Astral Color is Green, which gives you confidence. Green in your environment enhances your luck, because you will feel secure. In your wardrobe, Silver is a stimulating color for you.

Fragrance: You will be calmed by the scent of fresh linen dried in the breeze or wild orchids.

Tree: Apple—You are creative, full of joy, and nearly magical. You bring happiness.

Instruments: Viola, trumpet

Composer: Liszt

Bird: Cuckoo—a good flyer and very seldom a quitter. Some cuckoos tend to think they favor lonely isolation, but what they really yearn for is a family relationship.

Symbol: Triangle—You have the right combination of abilities.

Harmonious Health and Nutrition . . .

Health Scent: Peach—This scent may balance your good qualities so that they equal your charm.

Favorable Foods: Beets, watermelon, caraway, salmon, buttermilk

What's Lucky . . .

Lucky Numbers: 3, 5, 7

Best Months: February and September

Best Day of the Week: Monday

Best Month Days: 4, 5, 23

Lucky Charms: A rabbit's foot or a white candle.

Harmonious Signs for Relationships and Partnerships: Pisces, Scorpio, and Taurus

Spiritual Guides . . .

Star: Al Nethra—Those with this star are treasured as friends.

Angel: Muriel—This angel aids us during times of emotional stress.

Guardian Angel: Plavwell—The guardian that gives power and strength to one's presence.

Spiritual Stone: Jacinth—Holding this stone could aid in memory retention.

✷ JUDITH'S INSIGHT ✷

Don't judge your whole life by your childhood. You may feel as if you will never be happy, but you will. Stop fulfilling your own negative prophecies and start thinking more positively. Your sound mind and sharp intellect will lead you down a path of strong learning and teaching. Your confidence does waver, however, and you may have trouble with your self-esteem. But when your kind heart and deep soul become evident, life is bound to be better for you. Others may take advantage of you because of your kind and sympathetic nature. Yes, you are warm and sensitive, but when things don't go your way you can be cold and removed.

As kind and giving as you are, your communication skills need some work. Friends never realize what they mean to you unless you tell them. Relationships will bring you the most happiness and your greatest sadness, not necessarily from the same people. It may seem as if it takes forever to find the perfect love, but you must remain patient—in time there is balance. Security is almost more important to you than romance, so pay attention to your choices. Learn to not force issues. You don't always need to be right.

Charming personality that you have, you would work well with people. Your nuturing attitude makes it easy for you to do anything from homemaker to caretaker. You would do well working with children. But you would do well as a counselor, whether it is a guidance counselor or psychiatrist.

✷ ✷ ✷

JULY 6
CANCER • The waves of the moon of the zodiac
June 21 at 12:00 P.M. to July 22 at 11:00 P.M. • NUMEROLOGY 6

Possessions and Desires . . .

Gem: Sapphire—This gem may help you find forgiveness from those you've wronged.
Flower: White Rosebud—The lessons you learned in your early youth never cease to be of use.
Astral Color, Color Need, Apparel Color: Your Astral Color is Green, which gives you confidence. Green in your environment enhances your luck, because you will feel secure. In your wardrobe, Brown gives you confidence and a sharp look.
Fragrance: You will be calmed by the scent of fresh linen dried in the breeze or wild orchids.
Tree: Palm—You tend to be very healthy and creative.
Instruments: Tambourine, lyre
Composer: Schubert
Bird: Goldfinch—These gentle creatures can seem moody, especially in unsettled weather.
Symbol: Crescent—You are more likely to be influenced by the phases of the moon. Your easygoing manner leads you to peaceful situations.

Harmonious Health and Nutrition . . .

Health Scent: Orange Blossom—This scent may balance your body, mind, and soul.
Favorable Foods: Cauliflower, oranges, honey, oysters, eggs

What's Lucky . . .

Lucky Numbers: 3, 6, 7
Best Months: February and September
Best Day of the Week: Monday
Best Month Days: 6, 15, 24
Lucky Charms: A religious token or card from any religion.

Harmonious Signs for Relationships and Partnerships: Pisces, Scorpio, and Taurus

Spiritual Guides . . .

Star: Al Nethra—Those with this star are treasured as friends.
Angel: Muriel—This angel aids us during times of emotional stress.
Guardian Angel: Michael—"Who is like God."
Spiritual Stone: Jacinth—Holding this stone could aid in memory retention.

✶ JUDITH'S INSIGHT ✶

Your kind heart will lead you down the right path and help you find everything you want. You sometimes view things through rose-colored glasses. Your magnetic personality will take you anywhere you want to go. With your magical charisma, life appears to be quite easy. You are a quality-of-life person with honorable charm. Be careful to keep that cranky, crab side under control.

You tend to protect yourself when it comes to intimacy. Your strong love and devotion for your family will bring harmony and happiness. You do get intense without realizing it, and it may be hard for others to make that clear to you.

You have a great determination. With your powerful ambition you will go far, but it does take you many tries to get there. You tend to advance in careers such as teaching, counseling, law, building, government, and politics.

You tend to carry the problems of the world on your shoulders. Just remember to shrug them off every once in a while and let unwanted pressures fade.

★ ★ ★

JULY 7   CANCER • The waves of the moon of the zodiac
June 21 at 12:00 P.M. to July 22 at 11:00 P.M. • NUMEROLOGY 7

Possessions and Desires . . .

Gem: Sapphire—This gem may help you find forgiveness from those you've wronged.
Flower: Red Rosebud—Love brings only little disappointments.
Astral Color, Color Need, Apparel Color: Your Astral Color is Green, which gives you confidence. Green in your environment enhances your luck, because you will feel secure. In your wardrobe, Silver is a stimulating color for you.
Fragrance: You will be calmed by the scent of fresh linen dried in the breeze or wild orchids.
Tree: Sycamore—Yours is the ability to love, communicate honestly with others, and have lasting relationships.
Instrument: Harp
Composers: Gluck, Brahms
Bird: Warbling Parakeet—the most beautiful of all birds, known as the love bird. It does seem to have the powers of imitation.
Symbol: Heart—You are enthusiastic, empathetic, and full of generosity and love.

Harmonious Health and Nutrition . . .

Health Scent: Jasmine—This scent may make you more easygoing when you are stressed.
Favorable Foods: Turnips, caraway, molasses, salmon, cottage cheese

What's Lucky . . .

Lucky Numbers: 3, 7, 25
Best Months: February and September
Best Day of the Week: Monday
Best Month Days: 6, 15, 24
Lucky Charm: An old key.

Harmonious Signs for Relationships and Partnerships: Pisces, Scorpio, and Taurus

Spiritual Guides . . .

Star: Al Nethra—Those with this star are treasured as friends.
Angel: Muriel—This angel aids us during times of emotional stress.
Guardian Angel: Raphael—This angel attends to all of your needs when you are looking for guidance.
Spiritual Stone: Jacinth—Holding this stone could aid in memory retention.

✶ JUDITH'S INSIGHT ✶

You have a great sense of humor, along with strong loyalties and devotion. You are just and fair in your regard and feeling for others. You have only the best intentions, even if others aren't receptive to your advice when you offer it. You are capable of overcoming just about any condition.

You give your all, and gladly, especially when it comes to your family. In turn, they will do anything for you. You hit many obstacles and emotional hurdles, which makes you and your immediate family draw close. Love is a challenge at times, but you are the devoted mate who really does try to make your partner happy. Even though you may be settled in a relationship, you may look for another mate, only to realize that you could not find anyone better.

You are much more creative than you give yourself credit for. You accomplish more than you think. No matter what job you take, responsibility is no challenge. You are a delightful, well-organized, and faithful employee. When it comes to hard work, devotion, and loyalty, you win hands down.

You may have a bout with the legal system or with the law. It wouldn't be too serious an issue.

✶ ✶ ✶

JULY 8 CANCER • The waves of the moon of the zodiac
June 21 at 12:00 P.M. to July 22 at 11:00 P.M. • NUMEROLOGY 8

Possessions and Desires . . .

Gem: Emerald—Those who carry this stone tend to be lucky in love.
Flower: White Rose—The lessons you learned in your early youth never cease to be of use.
Astral Color, Color Need, Apparel Color: Your Astral Color is Green, which gives you confidence. Green in your environment enhances your luck, because you will feel secure. In your wardrobe, Brown gives you confidence and a sharp look.
Fragrance: You will be calmed by the scent of fresh linen dried in the breeze or wild orchids.
Tree: Pine—Your relationships tend to be balanced, both emotionally and mentally.
Instrument: Cello
Composer: Mozart
Bird: Bobolink—This charming singer is equally good as a soloist or a member of an orchestra. It is a very romantic bird, most useful as an insect destroyer, and elegant, with beautiful feathers, and always pleasant to have around.
Symbol: Wings—You are the source of balance in your world. This will bring you contentment.

Harmonious Health and Nutrition . . .

Health Scent: Almond—This scent may revitalize you and open you to greater possibilities.
Favorable Foods: Cabbage, whole oats, honey, oysters, cream

What's Lucky . . .

Lucky Numbers: 3, 7, 8
Best Months: February and September
Best Day of the Week: Monday
Best Month Days: 8, 17, 26
Lucky Charm: Red ribbon in your wallet or doorway.
Harmonious Signs for Relationships and Partnerships: Pisces, Scorpio, and Taurus

Spiritual Guides . . .

Star: Al Nethra—Those with this star are treasured as friends.
Angel: Muriel—This angel aids us during times of emotional stress.
Guardian Angel: Seraphim—An angel that brings love, light and passion.
Spiritual Stone: Jacinth—Holding this stone could aid in memory retention.

✶ JUDITH'S INSIGHT ✶

You are very sensitive and try to be stronger than you are. You take life a bit too seriously. You can be ego-driven and strong-minded, and your aims may be high. As you mature, you learn to be quite charitable and generous. Believe it or not, after your forties, life gets easier for you.

You want love and security in your family. In time, you will find the perfect mate. Unfortunately, you have to have patience and faith in order for things to become more harmonious. You go out of your way for friends and family and sometimes feel like nobody understands. A beautiful home and a structured family are nevertheless important to you. If you settle down by the beach or the sea, you may feel more relaxed and happy.

A perfectionist at work, you would make a great builder, designer, artist, writer, teacher, or poet. Whatever you create, you devote time and talent to it. Allow your knowledge to grow and, in time, good things only tend to get greater.

Financially, you have to watch out and expect the unexpected, although at times you may have a few windfalls, which just tend to accumulate. Just remember, not everyone around you is a psychic, and it would be better for you to communicate than think that life is written as a script. Take the time to not only be kind but to have an open mind.

✶ ✶ ✶

JULY 9   CANCER • The waves of the moon of the zodiac
June 21 at 12:00 P.M. to July 22 at 11:00 P.M. • NUMEROLOGY 9

Possessions and Desires . . .

Gem: Sapphire—This gem may help you find forgiveness from those you've wronged.
Flower: Wild Rose—You tend to love with the heat of a forest fire.
Astral Color, Color Need, Apparel Color: Your Astral Color is Green, which gives you confidence. Green in your environment enhances your luck, because you will feel secure. In your wardrobe, Silver is a stimulating color for you.
Fragrance: You will be calmed by the scent of fresh linen dried in the breeze or wild orchids.
Tree: Holly—Beware that you are not carried away by your passionate nature. The only way to grow is to be open to new experiences.
Instruments: Violin, tympanum
Composer: Gluck
Bird: Mockingbird—the most proficient minstrel in the world's orchestra; graceful and enthusiastic.
Symbol: Anchor—This tranquil symbol signifies stability and strength, and stands for strong commitments in relationships.

Harmonious Health and Nutrition . . .

Health Scent: Lavender—This scent might lead others to trust you and make you patient.
Favorable Foods: Cauliflower, dates, caraway, salmon, eggs

What's Lucky . . .

Lucky Numbers: 3, 7, 9
Best Months: February and September
Best Day of the Week: Monday
Best Month Days: 9, 18, 27
Lucky Charms: A U.S. coin or a bill of any amount from the year you were born.
Harmonious Signs for Relationships and Partnerships: Pisces, Scorpio, and Taurus

Spiritual Guides . . .

Star: Al Nethra—Those with this star are treasured as friends.
Angel: Muriel—This angel aids us during times of emotional stress.
Guardian Angel: Gabriel—"God is my strength."
Spiritual Stone: Jacinth—Holding this stone could aid in memory retention.

✳ JUDITH'S INSIGHT ✳

A true original, you're daring and fearless in just about everything you do. You have a legal mind—inventive, imaginative, and not very easily discouraged. You aim high, and you certainly are able to reach those heights. You have much more control of yourself than you recognize. You are capable of much self-sacrifice in your life, and you are more a giver than a taker. You pass through much mental suffering with few complaints. You may find yourself in unique and unfortunate situations, but you tend to get through these challenges unscathed.

You are a good friend to many because you are conscientious about what and how others feel. Your intuitive nature allows you inner knowledge. Listen to yourself more. Love is overwhelming around you—your family members adore you. But it takes time to find the right mate, even though you may think you have found someone special early in life. Challenges exist not only in work but in your love life.

You do many things in the blink of an eye. You will find success in any career you choose, whether it's lawyer, psychic, counselor, actor, writer, or restaurateur.

You walk away from things when you feel nobody is listening. You will travel on many streets and paths and down many highways. You will definitely leave your mark, no matter what the situation, and you never really understand just how much you affect other people.

✳ ✳ ✳

JULY 10 CANCER • The waves of the moon of the zodiac

June 21 at 12:00 P.M. to July 22 at 11:00 P.M. • NUMEROLOGY 1

Possessions and Desires . . .

Gem: Emerald—Those who carry this stone tend to be lucky in love.
Flower: Fig Tree—Whatever you do you tend to do a lot.
Astral Color, Color Need, Apparel Color: Your Astral Color is Green, which gives you confidence. Green in your environment enhances your luck, because you will feel secure. In your wardrobe, Brown gives you confidence and a sharp look.
Fragrance: You will be calmed by the scent of fresh linen dried in the breeze or wild orchids.
Tree: Walnut—You are unusually helpful and always looking for new beginnings.
Instruments: Oboe, flute, clarinet, piano, French horn, organ, piccolo
Composer: Böhm
Bird: Hummingbird—This bird is delicate and graceful. It can remain still for hours, then dart off and be as busy as a bee.
Symbol: Crown—the universal sign of dignity.

Harmonious Health and Nutrition . . .

Health Scent: Strawberry—Soothing by nature, the strawberry promotes self-esteem and encourages love.
Favorable Foods: Asparagus, lemons, whole oats, molasses, oysters, buttermilk

What's Lucky . . .

Lucky Numbers: 3, 7, 10
Best Months: February and September
Best Day of the Week: Monday
Best Month Days: 1, 10, 19, 28
Lucky Charm: A new penny in your shoe.

Harmonious Signs for Relationships and Partnerships: Pisces, Scorpio, and Taurus

Spiritual Guides . . .

Star: Al Nethra—Those with this star are treasured as friends.
Angel: Muriel—This angel aids us during times of emotional stress.
Guardian Angel: Malachi—"Messenger of Jehovah."
Spiritual Stone: Jacinth—Holding this stone could aid in memory retention.

✷ JUDITH'S INSIGHT ✷

At times, you wear your heart on your sleeve, but other times you hide it. You may go through a lot of changes; expect the unexpected. You tend to be somewhat fearful, in spite of the fact that you appear very secure and always seem like you know what you're doing. A great humanitarian, you will always try to imagine what you can do for other people.

At heart, you have very strong values, and family means a lot to you. Your kind and loyal nature brings you closer to your home and family. Although you are independent, you shy away from too much change.

You have a great love for the unknown and for mysterious environments. It also wouldn't be surprising for you to be involved in the arts, theater, or drama. You may succeed as a lawyer or doctor. You can sell all right—as long as the buyer comes to you.

You have a good chance of gaining wealth and may not want to live in ways that let other people know about it. Your dress will be modest and simple, and your home will be decorated with fine furniture and antiques.

✷ ✷ ✷

JULY 11

CANCER • The waves of the moon of the zodiac

June 21 at 12:00 P.M. to July 22 at 11:00 P.M. • NUMEROLOGY 2

Possessions and Desires . . .

Gem: Sapphire—This gem may help you find forgiveness from those you've wronged.

Flower: Angelica—You will be an inspiration for those you allow to know you.

Astral Color, Color Need, Apparel Color: Your Astral Color is Green, which gives you confidence. Green in your environment enhances your luck, because you will feel secure. In your wardrobe, Silver is a stimulating color for you.

Fragrance: You will be calmed by the scent of fresh linen dried in the breeze or wild orchids.

Tree: Maple—You have both great stability and flashes of intuition.

Instruments: Pipe organ, cymbal, drum

Composers: Handel, Johann Sebastian Bach

Bird: Cuckoo—a good flyer and very seldom a quitter. Some cuckoos tend to think they favor lonely isolation, but what they really yearn for is a family relationship.

Symbol: Cross—the symbol of self-sacrifice and reconciliation.

Harmonious Health and Nutrition . . .

Health Scent: Apple—You are creative, full of joy, and nearly magical. You bring happiness.

Favorable Foods: Kale, watermelon, caraway, salmon, cream

What's Lucky . . .

Lucky Numbers: 2, 3, 7

Best Months: February and September

Best Day of the Week: Monday

Best Month Days: 2, 11, 20, 29

Lucky Charms: Two 50-cent pieces. Give someone else one of them.

Harmonious Signs for Relationships and Partnerships: Pisces, Scorpio, and Taurus

Spiritual Guides . . .

Star: Al Nethra—Those with this star are treasured as friends.

Angel: Muriel—This angel aids us during times of emotional stress.

Guardian Angel: St. John—This angel simplifies that which is complicated.

Spiritual Stone: Jacinth—Holding this stone could aid in memory retention.

✳ JUDITH'S INSIGHT ✳

You are gentle, sympathetic, thoughtful, determined, and interested in other human beings. Most may view you as moody. You show much persistence and consistency throughout your life and exercise good judgment. You are as stable as the day is long. You always have good intentions, almost to a fault. Others may misunderstand or take offense at that. You have a lot of success with relationships, partners, and your own social environment. Once you get a friend, you never seem to have to let go. You have some strong ties to home life.

You could have a successful career as a doctor, counselor, chiropractor, even carpenter. No matter what you do, you lean toward nurturing others. You have a conscientious side and a good bedside manner. Because of your sensitivity and strong intuitive qualities, you tend to be very aware of the atmosphere and surroundings. Of course, your tendency is to always want to do better than yesterday, and you could be overly ambitious. At times you create drama.

You look for inspiration in everything. Travel will be important . . . more so as you age. You need to be around water, whether it is living, working, or playing. It would be very surprising if water sports would not appeal to you. When you are feeling low and need to stimulate yourself, take yourself for a walk along the beach or a swim in the pool, and if all else fails, drink some water.

★ ★ ★

JULY 12   CANCER • The waves of the moon of the zodiac
June 21 at 12:00 P.M. to July 22 at 11:00 P.M. • NUMEROLOGY 3

Possessions and Desires . . .

Gem: Sapphire—This gem may help you find forgiveness from those you've wronged.

Flower: Basil—Be careful that the things you hate don't distract you from living a full life.

Astral Color, Color Need, Apparel Color: Your Astral Color is Green, which gives you confidence. Green in your environment enhances your luck, because you will feel secure. In your wardrobe, Brown gives you confidence and a sharp look.

Fragrance: You will be calmed by the scent of fresh linen dried in the breeze or wild orchids.

Tree: Elm—You have willpower, strength, and the ability to stand alone.

Instrument: Trombone

Composers: Verdi, Mendelssohn, Schumann

Bird: Swan—Regarded as royal and sacred, this bird has the protective nature of a mother, and can become a furious fighter in the defense of its young.

Symbol: Wreath—You have been crowned with a special personality. You are strong but extremely compassionate.

Harmonious Health and Nutrition . . .

Health Scent: Rose—This scent will lead you to passionate thoughts and make you feel warm inside.

Favorable Foods: Onions, oranges, whole oats, honey, cottage cheese

What's Lucky . . .

Lucky Numbers: 3, 4, 7
Best Months: February and September
Best Day of the Week: Monday
Best Month Days: 3, 12, 21, 30
Lucky Charm: A pen that someone else has already used.
Harmonious Signs for Relationships and Partnerships: Pisces, Scorpio, and Taurus

Spiritual Guides . . .

Star: Al Nethra—Those with this star are treasured as friends.

Angel: Muriel—This angel aids us during times of emotional stress.

Guardian Angel: Johiel—This angel is a protector of all those with a humble heart.

Spiritual Stone: Jacinth—Holding this stone could aid in memory retention.

✳ JUDITH'S INSIGHT ✳

You are a quiet person and a deep thinker. As a general rule, you tend to have a bit of a hot temper and act on impulse. You are somewhat critical by nature and can get yourself involved in big, crucial problems. Your judgments aren't always the best, even though you have a good heart and act with good intentions. You can be the great humanitarian and want to offer a helping hand. However, you don't always know how to show this side of yourself. You tend to live in a world of your own and like it that way. Although you dislike being needy, you do tend to rely on other people a great deal. You're intelligent and intuitive but somewhat illogical at times. You have to learn to think before you speak and wait until you really have something to say.

You love your home and try to make it beautiful and harmonious, but you tend to weave many tangled webs. You aim high and are quite capable; however, as responsible as you are, you're always the last one out of bed. You accomplish much more in your later life than you do in earlier years, and you do veer off the track at times. Once you get out of your own way, you will become quite successful.

You may jump around in careers and look for something that offers adventure and spontaneity. Unfortunately, you need to be around something with more security. Watch out for bouts with the law or legal issues that may arise around you. It may be that you choose a legal career: attorney, judge, or police officer. You tend to lead an erratic life, and one way or another you will be in the public eye and in the newspaper. The publicity will, hopefully, be good. Eventually you find harmony and stop creating obstacles for yourself.

✳ ✳ ✳

JULY 13   CANCER • The waves of the moon of the zodiac
June 21 at 12:00 P.M. to July 22 at 11:00 P.M. • NUMEROLOGY 4

Possessions and Desires . . .

Gem: Emerald—Those who carry this stone tend to be lucky in love.
Flower: Daffodil—You may need to strengthen your self-regard.
Astral Color, Color Need, Apparel Color: Your Astral Color is Green, which gives you confidence. Green in your environment enhances your luck, because you will feel secure. In your wardrobe, Silver is a stimulating color for you.
Fragrance: You will be calmed by the scent of fresh linen dried in the breeze or wild orchids.
Tree: Cherry—You will find yourself faced with constant new emotional awakenings.
Instruments: Bass, clarinet
Composers: Haydn, Wagner
Bird: Killdeer—This bird is usually found consorting with other species, and can adapt to any environment.
Symbol: Star—You are full of inner brightness and will stand out in any crowd. You will be seen as special.

Harmonious Health and Nutrition . . .

Health Scent: Vanilla—This scent will fill you with a feeling of cleanliness and stability.
Favorable Foods: Celery, peaches, caraway, salmon, buttermilk

What's Lucky . . .

Lucky Numbers: 3, 7, 13
Best Months: February and September
Best Day of the Week: Monday
Best Month Days: 4, 13, 22, 31
Lucky Charm: A piece of material cut from something in your home.

Harmonious Signs for Relationships and Partnerships: Pisces, Scorpio, and Taurus

Spiritual Guides . . .

Star: Al Nethra—Those with this star are treasured as friends.
Angel: Muriel—This angel aids us during times of emotional stress.
Guardian Angel: Uriel—This angel brings the light of God's guidance.
Spiritual Stone: Jacinth—Holding this stone could aid in memory retention.

✷ JUDITH'S INSIGHT ✷

You are exceptionally sensitive, have a warm heart, and, if you had the chance, would do a lot for the world. You dwell too long on things. You have hidden talents and experience many strange circumstances. But believe it or not, these experiences eventually enhance your life.

It is extremely easy for you to make friends, although you push people away. What you want and what you say are two different things. This can be your downfall. You tend to blame others when things don't go your way, but you are a loyal and always helpful friend and would do anything for those you care about. Family can be overwhelming and overzealous and at times create conflict for you.

With your energy, there is no reason why you cannot accomplish many things in your lifetime. Unfortunately what you really want out of life takes time. The second part of your life will bring you closer to what you want. Watch that you don't make the wrong choices just because the choices are there. You would be a great doctor, lawyer, or teacher, but your aim eventually may be more in theater or film. No matter what career you eventually choose, somewhere along the way that actor in you comes out. You need to stand out in a crowd and, in due time, you will.

✷ ✷ ✷

JULY 14 CANCER • The waves of the moon of the zodiac
June 21 at 12:00 P.M. to July 22 at 11:00 P.M. • NUMEROLOGY 5

Possessions and Desires . . .

Gem: Sapphire—This gem may help you find forgiveness from those you've wronged.
Flower: Bay—You are serene even when those about you are awash in chaos.
Astral Color, Color Need, Apparel Color: Your Astral Color is Green, which gives you confidence. Green in your environment enhances your luck, because you will feel secure. In your wardrobe, Brown gives you confidence and a sharp look.
Fragrance: You will be calmed by the scent of fresh linen dried in the breeze or wild orchids.
Tree: Apple—You are creative, full of joy, and nearly magical. You bring happiness.
Instruments: Viola, trumpet
Composer: Liszt
Bird: Flamingo—This beautiful, gregarious bird is always cautious of its enemy. It is also a caretaker of the young who tries to keep everyone happy.
Symbol: Triangle—You have the right combination of abilities.

Harmonious Health and Nutrition . . .

Health Scent: Peach—This scent may balance your good qualities so they equal your charm.
Favorable Foods: Cauliflower, blackberries, whole oats, honey, cottage cheese

What's Lucky . . .

Lucky Numbers: 3, 5, 7
Best Months: February and September
Best Day of the Week: Monday
Best Month Days: 4, 5, 23
Lucky Charms: A rabbit's foot or a white candle.
Harmonious Signs for Relationships and Partnerships: Pisces, Scorpio, and Taurus

Spiritual Guides . . .

Star: Al Nethra—Those with this star are treasured as friends.
Angel: Muriel—This angel aids us during times of emotional stress.
Guardian Angel: Plavwell—The guardian that gives power and strength to one's presence.
Spiritual Stone: Jacinth—Holding this stone could aid in memory retention.

✴ JUDITH'S INSIGHT ✴

You can be taken advantage of because of your sensitivity, kindness, and sympathetic nature. Friends really never do know what they mean to you, because as kind and as giving as you are, you lack the communication skills to be that intimate. Your confidence does waver from time to time, and you go through periods of low self-esteem. But, it seems to others as if you have a very strong ego.

Your domestic, loving, and sympathetic nature may lead you to think that no matter what you do, you would make a perfect mother, father, or nanny. You seem to have great discipline. Don't judge your entire life by your early years, which may contain many unhappy moments. The relationships that bring you the most happiness also tend to bring you the most pain. Whether it is your mother or father, you tend to go through many challenges with parents. As a parent, if you become one, you go through your own challenges with your children. You do tend to have an open-door policy with your home, but unfortunately that never leaves you quiet time, and you need that to keep your balance.

You do best in careers where you are allowed freedom and are nurtured. You would do very well as a doctor, lawyer, clerk, inventor, promoter, or publicity agent. But with your kindness and your sweetness, you may want to work with children. Money does seem to roll in and roll out. You like to live well.

✶ ✶ ✶

JULY 15   CANCER • The waves of the moon of the zodiac
June 21 at 12:00 P.M. to July 22 at 11:00 P.M. • NUMEROLOGY 6

Possessions and Desires . . .

Gem: Sapphire—This gem may help you find forgiveness from those you've wronged.
Flower: Belladonna—You may find you treasure the times you spend in silence.
Astral Color, Color Need, Apparel Color: Your Astral Color is Green, which gives you confidence. Green in your environment enhances your luck, because you will feel secure. In your wardrobe, Silver is a stimulating color for you.
Fragrance: You will be calmed by the scent of fresh linen dried in the breeze or wild orchids.
Tree: Palm—You tend to be very healthy and creative.
Instruments: Tambourine, lyre
Composer: Schubert
Bird: Falcon—an expert hunter. When well-trained, it can adapt to many tasks and is usually obedient.
Symbol: Crescent—You are more likely to be influenced by the phases of the moon. Your easygoing manner leads you to peaceful situations.

Harmonious Health and Nutrition . . .

Health Scent: Orange Blossom—This scent may balance your body, mind, and soul.
Favorable Foods: Asparagus, cranberries, molasses, eggs

What's Lucky . . .

Lucky Numbers: 3, 7, 15
Best Months: February and September
Best Day of the Week: Monday
Best Month Days: 6, 15, 24
Lucky Charms: A religious token or card from any religion.
Harmonious Signs for Relationships and Partnerships: Pisces, Scorpio, and Taurus

Spiritual Guides . . .

Star: Al Nethra—Those with this star are treasured as friends.
Angel: Muriel—This angel aids us during times of emotional stress.
Guardian Angel: Michael—"Who is like God."
Spiritual Stone: Jacinth—Holding this stone could aid in memory retention.

✷ JUDITH'S INSIGHT ✷

You have a magical charisma and a sense of devotion to those around you that tends to make anyone you know always feel at home. You wear your heart on your sleeve. You never seem to let anybody else down; you never seem to turn a deaf ear; you always seem to have an open mind. You are respected and honored by those who know you. Your magnetic personality will bring you right down the path of life and get you where you want to go.

You protect yourself when it comes to intimacy with others, and you won't allow too many people to get close. Your domestic nature may afford you a perfect manicured lawn, an impeccable home, or a hand-designed kitchen that you made yourself. You can go through a hard time when it comes to finding a mate. Potential mates may see you as a more cranky person than you really are. Not to say that you are always unhappy, but the crab does seem to rear its head.

With your powerful ambitions, you tend to go far in any job. You would make a great trader, salesperson, lawyer, or professional of any kind. Your great devotion and determination help advance you in your career. You have no problem with taking on the responsibilities of others and may find yourself doing other people's work to make their lives easier. Remember to not bite off more than you can chew. You may become depressed in your middle years if you don't relax and have a little more fun.

✷ ✷ ✷

JULY 16　CANCER • The waves of the moon of the zodiac
June 21 at 12:00 P.M. to July 22 at 11:00 P.M. • NUMEROLOGY 7

Possessions and Desires . . .

Gem: Emerald—Those who carry this stone tend to be lucky in love.
Flower: Harebell—If you give into feeling sad you may forget what happiness is like.
Astral Color, Color Need, Apparel Color: Your Astral Color is Green, which gives you confidence. Green in your environment enhances your luck, because you will feel secure. In your wardrobe, Brown gives you confidence and a sharp look.
Fragrance: You will be calmed by the scent of fresh linen dried in the breeze or wild orchids.
Tree: Sycamore—Yours is the ability to love, communicate honestly with others, and have lasting relationships.
Instrument: Harp
Composers: Gluck, Brahms
Bird: Skylark—This handsome bird is beautiful when it sings. It always whistles as it works.
Symbol: Heart—You are enthusiastic, empathetic, and full of generosity and love.

Harmonious Health and Nutrition . . .

Health Scent: Jasmine—This scent may make you more easygoing when you are stressed.
Favorable Foods: Watercress, black figs, honey, oysters, cream

What's Lucky . . .

Lucky Numbers: 3, 7, 16
Best Months: February and September.
Best Day of the Week: Monday
Best Month Days: 6, 15, 24
Lucky Charm: An old key.
Harmonious Signs for Relationships and Partnerships: Pisces, Scorpio, and Taurus

Spiritual Guides . . .

Star: Al Nethra—Those with this star are treasured as friends.
Angel: Muriel—This angel aids us during times of emotional stress.
Guardian Angel: Raphael—This angel attends to all of your needs when you are looking for guidance.
Spiritual Stone: Jacinth—Holding this stone could aid in memory retention.

✳ JUDITH'S INSIGHT ✳

You are commanding, self-willed, and capable of great poise. You attract people very easily. Others may rely on your advice because you tend to see things quite clearly. You are a loyal soul and you like to help others. You can be defensive and argumentative, if need be. You can either love very strongly or hate very strongly, depending on the situation. You would make a great debater because you do see both sides of an issue clearly.

You are devoted to family members and their needs. You will do just about anything to help others overcome obstacles. Love at times tends to be a bit of a challenge, but you do bring a devoted mate into your life. Just remember, not all things come in the same package. It may take time for your mate to commit or even for you to commit. You may have a relationship that goes back and forth for years. Inevitably you may have the romance of your dreams, and this is what will really make you happy.

No job is too big or too small. You tend to handle responsibility as if it is no challenge at all. The more responsibility you're given, the more diligent and organized you become. Even as a employee, you're the one everyone looks to talk to. You start off all right financially, but there are times when money, or lack of it, can become stressful. Eventually you do get the balance, and you will be given a helping hand. Say thank you and give back when things do get better.

✳ ✳ ✳

JULY 17 CANCER • The waves of the moon of the zodiac
June 21 at 12:00 P.M. to July 22 at 11:00 P.M. • NUMEROLOGY 8

Possessions and Desires . . .

Gem: Sapphire—This gem may help you find forgiveness from those you've wronged.
Flower: Bilberry—You are generous to a fault.
Astral Color, Color Need, Apparel Color: Your Astral Color is Green, which gives you confidence. Green in your environment enhances your luck, because you will feel secure. In your wardrobe, Silver is a stimulating color for you.
Fragrance: You will be calmed by the scent of fresh linen dried in the breeze or wild orchids.
Tree: Pine—Your relationships tend to be balanced, both emotionally and mentally.
Instrument: Cello
Composer: Mozart
Bird: Bobolink—This charming singer is equally good as a soloist or a member of an orchestra. It is a very romantic bird, most useful as an insect destroyer, and elegant, with beautiful feathers, and always pleasant to have around.
Symbol: Wings—You are the source of balance in your world—this will bring you contentment.

Harmonious Health and Nutrition . . .

Health Scent: Almond—This scent may revitalize you and open you to greater possibilities.
Favorable Foods: Onions, watermelon, whole oats, cottage cheese

What's Lucky . . .

Lucky Numbers: 3, 7, 8
Best Months: February and September
Best Day of the Week: Monday
Best Month Days: 8, 17, 26
Lucky Charm: Red ribbon in your wallet or doorway.

Harmonious Signs for Relationships and Partnerships: Pisces, Scorpio, and Taurus

Spiritual Guides . . .

Star: Al Nethra—Those with this star are treasured as friends.
Angel: Muriel—This angel aids us during times of emotional stress.
Guardian Angel: Seraphim—An angel that brings love, light, and passion.
Spiritual Stone: Jacinth—Holding this stone could aid in memory retention.

✴ JUDITH'S INSIGHT ✴

You are quite sensitive and you have a desire to make the world a better place. You are fully aware of what it takes to make change, and you have no problem with working hard. You like things your own way, and if your efforts benefit others or yourself, that's all that matters. You hate the sin, and you love the sinner. You can be considered indifferent and cold when it comes to relationships, because you tend to be a bit fearful. Your sensitivity can go a long way. You may find that friends come and go in life, but never really that far. There may be more than one mate in your life. Depending on what kind of life you lead, this could be good or bad.

You could be a bit of a perfectionist when it comes to work and may be frustrated when it comes to working with other people. Be careful about your frustration. You could be a great counselor or advisor because of your kind soul, but you require a lot of physical activity for a career to be best for you. You would do well in any physical activity, whether it be sports or a job that requires mechanical or physical ability. You have a lot of energy. The more it is used up, the better.

JULY 18 CANCER • The waves of the moon of the zodiac
June 21 at 12:00 P.M. to July 22 at 11:00 P.M. • NUMEROLOGY 9

Possessions and Desires . . .

Gem: Emerald—Those who carry this stone tend to be lucky in love.
Flower: Bittersweet—You only wish to hear or tell the absolute truth.
Astral Color, Color Need, Apparel Color: Your Astral Color is Green, which gives you confidence. Green in your environment enhances your luck, because you will feel secure. In your wardrobe, Brown gives you confidence and a sharp look.
Fragrance: You will be calmed by the scent of fresh linen dried in the breeze or wild orchids.
Tree: Holly—Beware that you are not carried away by your passionate nature. The only way to grow is to be open to new experiences.
Instruments: Violin, tympanum
Composer: Gluck
Bird: Mockingbird—the most proficient minstrel in the world's orchestra; graceful and enthusiastic.
Symbol: Anchor—This tranquil symbol signifies stability and strength, and stands for strong commitments in relationships.

Harmonious Health and Nutrition . . .

Health Scent: Lavender—This scent might lead others to trust you and make you patient.
Favorable Foods: Cabbage, lemons, molasses, salmon, eggs

What's Lucky . . .

Lucky Numbers: 3, 7, 9
Best Months: February and September
Best Day of the Week: Monday
Best Month Days: 9, 18, 27
Lucky Charms: A U.S. coin or a bill of any amount from the year you were born.

Harmonious Signs for Relationships and Partnerships: Pisces, Scorpio, and Taurus

Spiritual Guides . . .

Star: Al Nethra—Those with this star are treasured as friends.
Angel: Muriel—This angel aids us during times of emotional stress.
Guardian Angel: Gabriel—"God is my strength."
Spiritual Stone: Jacinth—Holding this stone could aid in memory retention.

✶ JUDITH'S INSIGHT ✶

You love the good times—to just enjoy. Whether you know it or not, you have a burning desire to sacrifice yourself and help other people. You may have to overcome your share of obstacles. You pass through much mental suffering quietly and with few complaints. Your intuitive nature allows you a great deal of time to listen to yourself. You go through periods of sadness, but you are a survivor and get through them all.

You make a great parent. You have a loving home and kind heart and are very sensible and sensitive. You are original and daring and fearless in just about anything you do. You are creative and not easily discouraged. Your aims in life are high and you certainly possess the capabilities to achieve them. You eat challenges for breakfast, and it wouldn't be surprising if you had more than one career. There will be opportunities early, but be patient and don't choose the wrong one. You accomplish a lot because you set a lot of goals. You could be a psychologist, lawyer, owner of a restaurant, or laborer. It takes more time for you to find the right love, and if you exercise patience, you will have great success.

You will walk down many roadways and meet many people. Every road you travel on you will travel on twice. Remember that.

✶ ✶ ✶

JULY 19   CANCER • The waves of the moon of the zodiac
June 21 at 12:00 P.M. to July 22 at 11:00 P.M. • NUMEROLOGY 1

Possessions and Desires . . .

Gem: Sapphire—This gem may help you find forgiveness from those you've wronged.

Flower: Blackberry—You have as much energy as the sun.

Astral Color, Color Need, Apparel Color: Your Astral Color is Green, which gives you confidence. Green in your environmental enhances your luck, because you will feel secure. In your wardrobe, Silver is a stimulating color for you.

Fragrance: You will be calmed by the scent of fresh linen dried in the breeze or wild orchids.

Tree: Walnut—You are unusually helpful and always looking for new beginnings.

Instruments: Oboe, flute, clarinet, piano, French horn, organ, and piccolo

Composer: Böhm

Bird: Bird of Paradise—the "bird of the Gods." You will shine and love extraordinary circumstances.

Symbol: Crown—the universal sign of dignity.

Harmonious Health and Nutrition . . .

Health Scent: Strawberry—Soothing by nature, the strawberry promotes self-esteem and encourages love.

Favorable Foods: Parsley, dates, honey, oysters, cream

What's Lucky . . .

Lucky Numbers: 3, 7, 19
Best Months: February and September
Best Day of the Week: Monday
Best Month Days: 1, 10, 19, 28
Lucky Charm: A new penny in your shoe.
Harmonious Signs for Relationships and Partnerships: Pisces, Scorpio, and Taurus

Spiritual Guides . . .

Star: Al Nethra—Those with this star are treasured as friends.

Angel: Muriel—This angel aids us during times of emotional stress.

Guardian Angel: Malachi—"Messenger of Jehovah."

Spiritual Stone: Jacinth—Holding this stone could aid in memory retention.

✳ JUDITH'S INSIGHT ✳

You are kind and levelheaded. It will be a challenge to keep your dependency and independence in balance. You do tend to go through many strange circumstances in your lifetime and may even have a psychic encounter. You are a bit unpredictable, and you like it that way. You love to have a good time; the more invitations, the better.

You are attached to home and family and will work hard to keep your relationships stable. You can be a little self-sacrificing and may give up a little to keep harmony at home. Your nurturing side will inevitably bring you a family. Whether you have children of your own, adopt, or marry someone with children, it would be very surprising if children were not in your life.

You have strong values and morals. They may be threatened at times. Being the humanitarian that you are, it would not be surprising if you either worked as a volunteer or in a caretaking environment. You have a great love for the unknown and the mysterious. It may be that you'll become a detective or work in the theater or on a TV drama.

There is a good chance that you will have great wealth, either by lucrative investments or by inheriting money. You may live a little more simply than your bank account allows.

✳ ✳ ✳

JULY 20

CANCER • The waves of the moon of the zodiac

June 21 at 12:00 P.M. to July 22 at 11:00 P.M. • NUMEROLOGY 2

Possessions and Desires . . .

Gem: Emerald—Those who carry this stone tend to be lucky in love.

Flower: Bulrush—Be discreet in your dealing with others.

Astral Color, Color Need, Apparel Color: Your Astral Color is Green, which gives you confidence. Green in your environment enhances your luck, because you will feel secure. In your wardrobe, Brown gives you confidence and a sharp look.

Fragrance: You will be calmed by the scent of fresh linen dried in the breeze or wild orchids.

Tree: Maple—You have both great stability and flashes of intuition.

Instruments: Pipe organ, cymbal, drum

Composers: Handel, Johann Sebastian Bach

Bird: Cuckoo—a good flyer and very seldom a quitter. Some cuckoos tend to think they favor lonely isolation, but what they really yearn for is a family relationship.

Symbol: Cross—the symbol of self-sacrifice and reconciliation.

Harmonious Health and Nutrition . . .

Health Scent: Apple—You are creative, full of joy, and nearly magical. You bring happiness.

Favorable Foods: Beets, oranges, whole oats, salmon, eggs

What's Lucky . . .

Lucky Numbers: 3, 7, 20

Best Months: February and September

Best Day of the Week: Monday

Best Month Days: 2, 11, 20, 29

Lucky Charms: Two 50-cent pieces. Give someone else one of them.

Harmonious Signs for Relationships and Partnerships: Pisces, Scorpio, and Taurus

Spiritual Guides . . .

Star: Al Nethra—Those with this star are treasured as friends.

Angel: Muriel—This angel aids us during times of emotional stress.

Guardian Angel: St. Thomas—This angel brings affection from others and encourages you in all that you do.

Spiritual Stone: Jacinth—Holding this stone could aid in memory retention.

✷ JUDITH'S INSIGHT ✷

You can be quite inquisitive. You're also secretive and don't like to let anybody know what you're up to. Most people won't recognize this because of your open appearance and consistently caring nature. You have a kind heart and are considerate, yet you can be very moody. You tend to do better with relationships than not and work hard to keep them happy. You want to maintain friendships throughout your life. You do like stability, and it would be surprising for you not to live in the same home for a long time. You can be very neat and yet very disorganized at the same time. Your home is important, whether it's a garage, basement, palace, or attic.

Careerwise, you may have your hands in more than one pot. You could be a counselor, chiropractor, or carpenter. You have a bit of a creative mind and may desire to invent something. If you would like to be a creator or writer, you will probably find that you are more inspired when you are looking at the water. You are determined to be successful. No matter what the job is, you tend to rise to the top quickly, get bored, and then make a change.

Most of the romantic and sentimental times throughout your life will probably just coincidentally happen near the beach. When you are feeling low and look for a little stimulation or energy, find a beach and take a walk, or drink a pitcher of water. Travel will become important to you later in life. Choose places near water.

✷ ✷ ✷

JULY 21
CANCER • The waves of the moon of the zodiac
June 21 at 12:00 P.M. to July 22 at 11:00 P.M. • NUMEROLOGY 3

Possessions and Desires . . .

Gem: Sapphire—This gem may help you find forgiveness from those you've wronged.
Flower: Canterbury Bell—You tend to constantly seek approval from those around you.
Astral Color, Color Need, Apparel Color: Your Astral Color is Green, which gives you confidence. Green in your environment enhances your luck, because you will feel secure. In your wardrobe, Silver is a stimulating color for you.
Fragrance: You will be calmed by the scent of fresh linen dried in the breeze or wild orchids.
Tree: Elm—You have willpower, strength, and the ability to stand alone.
Instrument: Trombone
Composers: Verdi, Mendelssohn, Schumann
Bird: Cuckoo—a good flyer and very seldom a quitter. Some cuckoos tend to think they favor lonely isolation, but what they really yearn for is a family relationship.
Symbol: Wreath—You have been crowned with a special personality. You are strong but extremely compassionate.

Harmonious Health and Nutrition . . .

Health Scent: Rose—This scent will lead you to passionate thoughts and make you feel warm inside.
Favorable Foods: Turnips, huckleberry, caraway, oysters, buttermilk

What's Lucky . . .

Lucky Numbers: 3, 7, 21
Best Months: February and September
Best Day of the Week: Monday
Best Month Days: 3, 12, 21, 30
Lucky Charm: A pen that someone else has already used.
Harmonious Signs for Relationships and Partnerships: Pisces, Scorpio, and Taurus

Spiritual Guides . . .

Star: Al Nethra—Those with this star are treasured as friends.
Angel: Muriel—This angel aids us during times of emotional stress.
Guardian Angel: Johiel—This angel is a protector of all those with a humble heart.
Spiritual Stone: Jacinth—Holding this stone could aid in memory retention.

✷ JUDITH'S INSIGHT ✷

You live in a world of your own, and other people don't necessarily know this about you. You seem more outgoing than you are, and your nature is fearless and courageous. You like your quiet time, and are quite sentimental about any gifts or anything that you do in life. You are a bit of a daydreamer. You create your own story in your own mind on a day-to-day basis. You are naturally intelligent, intuitive, and quite logical. You speak with an impeccable vocabulary and usually have something very intelligent to say.

You want a happy home, and eventually you find it. The challenge for you will be to find harmony with your mate. Eventually you do. Watch out for relationship choices because you can be fickle at times. You can be overwhelmed by friends and family and by the tasks you tend to take on. Simply put, you do too much for others.

You want to lend a helping hand, but sometimes you go overboard. You will be quite successful in whatever you choose, but should put yourself in an energetic environment. You would do very well as an entrepreneur or in business—although, your creativity won't necessarily be used there. The best thing for you would be to create something and go into business on your own. You lean toward the public or publicity at one time or another—hopefully for the good and not the bad. A born politician, you can be charming and witty, and you can win people over to your side. People will be drawn to you one way or another and will want to do what you ask.

✷ ✷ ✷

JULY 22   CANCER • The waves of the moon of the zodiac
June 21 at 12:00 P.M. to July 22 at 11:00 P.M. • NUMEROLOGY 4

Possessions and Desires . . .

Gem: Emerald—Those who carry this stone tend to be lucky in love.
Flower: Celandine—Your happiness tends to occur later in life.
Astral Color, Color Need, Apparel Color: Your Astral Color is Green, which gives you confidence. Green in your environment enhances your luck, because you will feel secure. In your wardrobe, Brown gives you confidence and a sharp look.
Fragrance: You will be calmed by the scent of fresh linen dried in the breeze or wild orchids.
Tree: Cherry—You will find yourself faced with constant new emotional awakenings.
Instruments: Bass, clarinet
Composers: Haydn, Wagner
Bird: Stork—Turkish bird, held in high esteem the world over. This bird is intelligent but may have strange tendencies.
Symbol: Star—You are full of inner brightness and will stand out in any crowd. You will be seen as special.

Harmonious Health and Nutrition . . .

Health Scent: Vanilla—This scent will fill you with a feeling of cleanliness and stability.
Favorable Foods: Cauliflower, dates, molasses, salmon, cottage cheese

What's Lucky . . .

Lucky Numbers: 3, 4, 7
Best Months: February and September
Best Day of the Week: Monday
Best Month Days: 4, 13, 22, 31
Lucky Charm: A piece of material cut from something in your home.
Harmonious Signs for Relationships and Partnerships: Pisces, Scorpio, and Taurus

Spiritual Guides . . .

Star: Al Nethra—Those with this star are treasured as friends.
Angel: Muriel—This angel aids us during times of emotional stress.
Guardian Angel: Uriel—This angel brings the light of God's guidance.
Spiritual Stone: Jacinth—Holding this stone could aid in memory retention.

✶ JUDITH'S INSIGHT ✶

You fit into almost any situation with ease. You are full of life and activity, and your energy levels are boundless. Failures do not suit you—you have no time for negativity. You tend to procrastinate, but inevitably you rise to the occasion. You are exceptionally sensitive and have a warm heart. You do tend to be lonely sometimes and others may see you as a lost puppy.

It is extremely easy for you to make friends, but you must watch out for losing old friends. This, undoubtedly, is your worst shortcoming. You will share anything you have with your friends and family and do have many true and loving friends when you put a lot of energy into it. You can waver with love and find yourself chasing someone only to find it is not necessarily what you want.

You are not really fickle, but others may see you this way. Sometimes you look for the stage, screen, or limelight. Whether you become president of the PTA, run for town council, or appear in the local newspaper, somewhere or other notoriety will find you. You could be a great doctor, lawyer, teacher, even actor. You do have many wonderful talents, although you tend to be a bit scattered in the early part of your life. As you get older, you get more centered, and instead of feeling disillusioned by life, you follow your chosen path and get where you want to go.

✶ ✶ ✶

JULY 23 LEO • The heart of the zodiac

July 22 at 11:00 P.M. to August 23 at 6:00 A.M. • NUMEROLOGY 5

Possessions and Desires . . .

Gem: Diamond—This stone is thought to encourage harmony in relationships and gives strength to the troubled.

Flower: Indian Plum—You may find that the process of going without is more fun than the having.

Astral Color, Color Need, Apparel Color: Your Astral Color is Red, which enhances passion, power, excitement, and strength. Orange in your environment gives you confidence. In your wardrobe, Green is your power color for overcoming obstacles.

Fragrance: Surround yourself with the most romantic flowers you can find such as roses, lilies, and violets. The lavish scents will give an added boost to your natural enthusiasm.

Tree: Apple—You are creative, full of joy, and nearly magical. You bring happiness.

Instruments: Viola, trumpet

Composer: Liszt

Bird: Skylark—This handsome bird is beautiful when it sings. It always whistles as it works.

Symbol: Triangle—You have the right combination of abilities.

Harmonious Health and Nutrition . . .

Health Scent: Peach—This scent may balance your good qualities so that they equal your charm.

Favorable Foods: Watercress, raspberries, barley, red meat

What's Lucky . . .

Lucky Numbers: 5, 14, 23

Best Months: January and October

Best Day of the Week: Sunday

Best Month Days: 4, 5, 23

Lucky Charms: A rabbit's foot or a white candle.

Harmonious Signs for Relationships and Partnerships: Sagittarius and Aries

Spiritual Guides . . .

Star: Al Zubra—Those with this star fear punishment they don't deserve.

Angel: Verchiel—This angel enhances our ability to enjoy what life offers and gives much luck in legal dealings.

Guardian Angel: Plavwell—The guardian that gives power and strength to one's presence.

Spiritual Stone: Amethyst—This stone is thought to be a mood stabilizer and balances the emotions.

✶ JUDITH'S INSIGHT ✶

Your heart alone can set the world on fire. You love with ease, and your character is naturally sensational. You always look for something new and for the good in everything. You demand absolute honesty and faithfulness in others, and you give nothing less. Generous to a fault, you don't judge people, and you don't like being judged. You tend to be warm and sensitive, but you can be selfish and hung up on what is important to you. There aren't many obstacles you cannot overcome. You have a strong mind, an especially strong body, and an ego to match. Your self-esteem, however, wavers when things do go wrong in your life. Have no fear, the train will derail, but eventually you get back on track.

You go through a lot of emotional situations as a child; but fear not, your future is better. Friends really never truly realize what they have until you are gone. Relationships give you happiness, but you bring more happiness to others than they to you. It may seem life is taking forever to bring you harmony in love. Be patient—the more romance, the better you respond. Someone you trust and honor who can feed your ego is your perfect mate, and once you find that person, you'll stay.

You would do well in any career. A born leader, you can be head designer or head of the company. You are a teacher in your own right. You can start in the mailroom and work your way right up to the top of a company. There aren't many things you won't be good at.

✶ ✶ ✶

JULY 24　LEO • The heart of the zodiac

July 22 at 11:00 P.M. to August 23 at 6:00 A.M. • NUMEROLOGY 6

Possessions and Desires . . .

Gem: Agate—This stone may promote health and lead you to a long life.

Flower: White Lilac—You may keep the wisdom of childhood all your life.

Astral Color, Color Need, Apparel Color: Your Astral Color is Red, which enhances passion, power, excitement, and strength. Orange in your environment gives you confidence. In your wardrobe, Plum brings out the best in your looks.

Fragrance: Surround yourself with the most romantic flowers you can find such as roses, lilies, and violets. The lavish scents will give an added boost to your natural enthusiasm.

Tree: Palm—You tend to be very healthy and creative.

Instruments: Tambourine, lyre

Composer: Schubert

Bird: Lark—known for the beauty of its song, which is sometimes very unusual. It is also credited with extraordinary intelligence.

Symbol: Crescent—You are more likely to be influenced by the phases of the moon. Your easygoing manner leads you to peaceful situations.

Harmonious Health and Nutrition . . .

Health Scent: Orange Blossom—Balances the mind, body, and soul.

Favorable Foods: Radishes, lemons, whole oats, buttermilk

What's Lucky . . .

Lucky Numbers: 8, 15, 42

Best Months: January and October

Best Day of the Week: Sunday

Best Month Days: 6, 15, 24

Lucky Charms: A religious token or card from any religion.

Harmonious Signs for Relationships and Partnerships: Sagittarius and Aries

Spiritual Guides . . .

Star: Al Serpha—Those with this star know how special life can be.

Angel: Verchiel—This angel enhances our ability to enjoy what life offers and gives much luck in legal dealings.

Guardian Angel: Michael—"Who is like God."

Spiritual Stone: Amethyst—This stone is thought to be a mood stabilizer and balances the emotions.

✳ JUDITH'S INSIGHT ✳

No matter how you come into this life, you will soar to the top. You may enter the up elevator, but at times you will reach obstacles, like the doors getting jammed. You may find yourself back on the first floor only to begin your rise all over again. You could bear the world's problems; just make sure you have a place for your own. Pride is important to you, and you may hold on to things longer than you should. You have a great gift of turning your life around. Cranky when you're younger, as you get older you tend to be a little more sentimental and bring out your caring heart.

You love and heat intensely. Your accurate memory is long-lasting. You will stick by a friend and never forget a favor. Through thick or thin, you give and give and always put your best foot forward. You have a strong presence and a powerful mind. Ambition will take you where you want to go. Opportunities will present themselves, and you can go from one extreme to another. Friendships will be deep and may even help you advance in your careers. You tend to get what you give, as most people don't.

You are a powerful figure, and at times you may intimidate others. Your random acts of kindness will put you ahead in life, so keep doing the right thing, and when you are at the top, you don't have to worry about falling back down.

When you're in a long term relationship, you're looking for the exit door or searching avidly for the perfect mate.

Careers you would excel in are: dress designer and personal shopper. If you're interested in film, you could find yourself in the wardrobe department. School plays a role whether you are a perpetual student or professor.

JULY 25　LEO • The heart of the zodiac

July 22 at 11:00 P.M. to August 23 at 6:00 A.M. • NUMEROLOGY 7

Possessions and Desires . . .

Gem: Ruby—This stone may lead you to energy, friendship, and happiness.

Flower: Lilac—You tend to let your own horn become a very rusty instrument; a loud toot now and again couldn't hurt.

Astral Color, Color Need, Apparel Color: Your Astral Color is Red, which enhances passion, power, excitement, and strength. Orange in your environment gives you confidence. In your wardrobe, Purple reflects your giving personality and brings you luck.

Fragrance: Surround yourself with the most romantic flowers you can find such as roses, lilies, and violets. The lavish scents will give an added boost to your natural enthusiasm.

Tree: Sycamore—Yours is the ability to love, communicate honestly with others, and have lasting relationships.

Instrument: Harp

Composers: Gluck, Brahms

Bird: Skylark—This handsome bird is beautiful when it sings. It always whistles as it works.

Symbol: Heart—You are enthusiastic, empathetic, and full of generosity and love.

Harmonious Health and Nutrition . . .

Health Scent: Jasmine—This scent may make you more easygoing when you are stressed.

Favorable Foods: Cabbage, grapefruit, caraway seeds, red meat

What's Lucky . . .

Lucky Numbers: 7, 14, 34

Best Months: January and October

Best Day of the Week: Sunday

Best Month Days: 6, 15, 24

Lucky Charm: An old key.

Harmonious Signs for Relationships and Partnerships: Sagittarius and Aries

Spiritual Guides . . .

Star: Al Gieba—The lucky born with this star are treated like royalty.

Angel: Verchiel—This angel enhances our ability to enjoy what life offers and gives much luck in legal dealings.

Guardian Angel: Raphael—This angel attends to all of your needs when you are looking for guidance.

Spiritual Stone: Amethyst—This stone is thought to be a mood stabilizer and balances the emotions.

✴ JUDITH'S INSIGHT ✴

You are sympathetic and kind and have an intensely loving nature. Your smile can bring great warmth to others. Honorable, strong and loyal, you have only the best intentions with regard to other people's feelings and would do anything for them. Other people see you better than you see yourself. You are a responsible soul, and no challenge is too great as long as you are doing for others.

You are capable of overcoming just about any condition, especially when it comes to family. You give your all and gladly. Family will do anything for you because of your devotion to them. You will overcome obstacles and emotional hurdles and create happiness and harmony for yourself. At times love is a challenge; you tend to choose powerful mates, and at times there could be intense struggles.

You are much more creative than you think. You can be well-organized when it comes to work, and you would make a loyal employee. If you are the employer, you tend to be open to the emotional needs of others. Financially, you endure peaks and valleys, and at times you feel like you'll never make it. Eventually, there is a balance, and later on in life you will be in fine financial shape.

You are a good humanitarian, and you lend a helping hand to whomever needs it. You are as good as the other guy, and you just need to have as much faith in yourself as you do in others.

Leadership qualities could make you a supervisor in any career. Human resources, computer programming, and clinical psychology may be some of the careers that you excel at; not to mention a schoolteacher or television producer.

✴ ✴ ✴

JULY 26 LEO • The heart of the zodiac
July 22 at 11:00 P.M. to August 23 at 6:00 A.M. • NUMEROLOGY 8

Possessions and Desires . . .

Gem: Diamond—This stone is thought to encourage harmony in relationships and gives strength to the troubled.

Flower: Magnolia—You have a great love of nature.

Astral Color, Color Need, Apparel Color: Your Astral Color is Red, which enhances passion, power, excitement, and strength. Orange in your environment gives you confidence. In your wardrobe, Green is your power color for overcoming obstacles.

Fragrance: Surround yourself with the most romantic flowers you can find such as roses, lilies, and violets. The lavish scents will give an added boost to your natural enthusiasm.

Tree: Pine—Your relationships tend to be harmonious, both emotionally and mentally.

Instrument: Cello

Composer: Mozart

Bird: Bobolink—This charming singer is equally good as a soloist or a member of an orchestra. It is a very romantic bird, most useful as an insect destroyer, and elegant, with beautiful feathers, and always pleasant to have around.

Symbol: Wings—You are the source of balance in your world—this will bring you contentment.

Harmonious Health and Nutrition . . .

Health Scent: Almond—This scent may revitalize you and open you to greater possibilities.

Favorable Foods: Green lima beans, sour plums, rice bran, buttermilk

What's Lucky . . .

Lucky Numbers: 8, 17, 26
Best Months: January and October
Best Day of the Week: Sunday
Best Month Days: 8, 17, 26
Lucky Charm: Red ribbon in your wallet or doorway.
Harmonious Signs for Relationships and Partnerships: Sagittarius and Aries

Spiritual Guides . . .

Star: Al Zubra—Those with this star fear punishment they don't deserve.

Angel: Verchiel—This angel enhances our ability to enjoy what life offers and gives much luck in legal dealings.

Guardian Angel: Seraphim—An angel that brings love, light and passion.

Spiritual Stone: Amethyst—This stone is thought to be a mood stabilizer and balances the emotions.

✶ JUDITH'S INSIGHT ✶

You are a loving, sensitive, and giving person, inclined to be poetic and musical. Because of your sensitivity, you must try to be stronger. Keeping emotional balance will be your great challenge. Your aim is high, and you wish the best for others. When it comes to love, you want nothing more than to settle down. Unfortunately, there are times when commitments will require work. Be patient. With a lot of love, timing, and perseverance, your home will eventually be just the way you want it.

You seem to amaze people with your ability to juggle many things. You can be a perfectionist, not only when it comes to your home and family, but when it comes to how you look in public. You're quite vain, and you may even look to alter your appearance. It would be very surprising if you didn't have a desire to create or invent something. You know how to do everything, and you love bargains. You can be anything from artist to writer, teacher to poet. Besides your career, a hobby may take a lot of your time. Your keen sense of knowledge allows you to do any job with ease. Responsibility does not scare you. You can be motivated by a new job.

You will be great with money and generous with your friends. You like the act of giving and expect others to recognize you for it. You also like the occasional pat on the back. Your communication skills could use polishing—your bark is worse than your bite. Somewhat impractical, you can get into battles over principles and might be considered stubborn. You are indeed a good person—don't take life so seriously.

✶ ✶ ✶

JULY 27
LEO • The heart of the zodiac
July 22 at 11:00 P.M. to August 23 at 6:00 A.M. • NUMEROLOGY 9

Possessions and Desires . . .

Gem: Ruby—This stone may lead you to energy, friendship, and happiness.

Flower: Saxifrage—You may need too much affection from others because you don't care enough for yourself.

Astral Color, Color Need, Apparel Color: Your Astral Color is Red, which enhances passion, power, excitement, and strength. Orange in your environment gives you confidence. In your wardrobe, Plum brings out the best in your looks.

Fragrance: Surround yourself with the most romantic flowers you can find such as roses, lilies, and violets. The lavish scents will give an added boost to your natural enthusiasm.

Tree: Holly—Beware that you are not carried away by your passionate nature. The only way to grow is to be open to new experiences.

Instruments: Violin, tympanum

Composer: Gluck

Bird: Mockingbird—the most proficient minstrel in the world's orchestra; graceful and enthusiastic.

Symbol: Anchor—This tranquil symbol signifies stability and strength, and stands for strong commitments in relationships.

Harmonious Health and Nutrition . . .

Health Scent: Lavender—This scent might lead others to trust you and make you patient.

Favorable Foods: Cucumbers, limes, barley, red meat

What's Lucky . . .

Lucky Numbers: 7, 17, 27
Best Months: January and October
Best Day of the Week: Sunday
Best Month Days: 9, 18, 27
Lucky Charms: A U.S. coin or a bill of any amount from the year you were born.

Harmonious Signs for Relationships and Partnerships: Sagittarius and Aries

Spiritual Guides . . .

Star: Al Gieba—The lucky born with this star are treated like royalty.

Angel: Verchiel—This angel enhances our ability to enjoy what life offers and gives much luck in legal dealings.

Guardian Angel: Gabriel—"God is my strength."

Spiritual Stone: Amethyst—This stone is thought to be a mood stabilizer and balances the emotions.

✴ JUDITH'S INSIGHT ✴

You are an original. Daring in thought, fearless, and determined in just about anything you do, you have lofty goals. You are capable of accomplishing just about anything you set out to. Born independent, you only become more so as you get older. You are enjoyable, bright, cheerful, and sensitive. In later years, your more altruistic qualities will present themselves. You have a grand mind and intellect. Some unique and unfortunate things will happen in your life, but you survive them. You pass through mental suffering quietly and without complaints. Your intuitive nature makes you aware of others, and you know how to put yourself in their shoes. Because of this sensitivity, you are a good friend.

It will take time for you to find the right love, but you will. You may push the right one away a couple of times before realizing who you have. There will be many challenges, and you can conquer not just one but maybe all. Challenges exist in your love life and also in your work and career. Your past always pops up in your future. You can be a counselor, psychologist, psychic, writer, or restaurant owner.

You have an inner knowledge that will take you far beyond the ordinary places. You accomplish a lot because you set out to do a lot.

✴ ✴ ✴

JULY 28

LEO • The heart of the zodiac

July 22 at 11:00 P.M. to August 23 at 6:00 A.M. • NUMEROLOGY 1

Possessions and Desires . . .

Gem: Ruby—This stone may lead you to energy, friendship, and happiness.

Flower: Money Plant—You are sometimes too honest.

Astral Color, Color Need, Apparel Color: Your Astral Color is Red, which enhances passion, power, excitement, and strength. Orange in your environment gives you confidence. In your wardrobe, Purple reflects your giving personality and brings you luck.

Fragrance: Surround yourself with the most romantic flowers you can find such as roses, lilies, and violets. The lavish scents will give an added boost to your natural enthusiasm.

Tree: Walnut—You are unusually helpful and always looking for constant changes in your life.

Instruments: Oboe, flute, clarinet, piano, French horn, organ, piccolo

Composer: Böhm

Bird: Bird of Paradise—the "bird of the Gods." You will shine and love extraordinary form.

Symbol: Crown—the universal sign of dignity.

Harmonious Health and Nutrition . . .

Health Scent: Strawberry—Soothing by nature, the strawberry promotes self-esteem and encourages love.

Favorable Foods: Brussels sprouts, sour cherries, caraway seeds, buttermilk

What's Lucky . . .

Lucky Numbers: 2, 8, 10
Best Months: January and October
Best Day of the Week: Sunday
Best Month Days: 1, 10, 19, 28

Lucky Charm: A new penny in your shoe.
Harmonious Signs for Relationships and Partnerships: Sagittarius and Aries

Spiritual Guides . . .

Star: Al Zubra—Those with this star fear punishment they don't deserve.

Angel: Verchiel—This angel enhances our ability to enjoy what life offers and gives much luck in legal dealings.

Guardian Angel: Malachi—"Messenger of Jehovah."

Spiritual Stone: Amethyst—This stone is thought to be a mood stabilizer and balances the emotions.

✶ JUDITH'S INSIGHT ✶

You will become a good humanitarian. You may have a bit of psychic ability. You have a great love for the unknown and will thrive on mysterious environments.

Your kind, loving, and loyal nature will allow you happiness at home with family and friends. You are so attached to home and family that sometimes it will be difficult for you to make decisions without considering everybody else's happiness and well-being while leaving your own behind. Children and marriage play a large part in your life and may be a place where decisions are made with your heart.

You have a love of the arts: theater, drama, and music. This may lead you to a career, but your nurturing side will probably lead you to a profession in health care. Somewhere along the way you may be in the public eye or have a bit of notoriety.

You will do very well with financial investments. You may not always want others to recognize the money you have.

✶ ✶ ✶

JULY 29   LEO • The heart of the zodiac
July 22 at 11:00 P.M. to August 23 at 6:00 A.M. • NUMEROLOGY 2

Possessions and Desires . . .

Gem: Agate—This stone may promote health and lead you to a long life.

Flower: Verbena—You may feel that your life is in some way enchanted.

Astral Color, Color Need, Apparel Color: Your Astral Color is Red, which enhances passion, power, excitement, and strength. Orange in your environment gives you confidence. In your wardrobe, Green is your power color for overcoming obstacles.

Fragrance: Surround yourself with the most romantic flowers you can find such as roses, lilies, and violets. The lavish scents will give an added boost to your natural enthusiasm.

Tree: Holly—Beware that you are not carried away by your passionate nature. The only way to grow is to be open to new experiences.

Instruments: Violin, tympanum

Composer: Gluck

Bird: Goldfinch—These gentle creatures can seem moody, especially in unsettled weather.

Symbol: Anchor—This tranquil symbol signifies stability and strength, and stands for strong commitments in relationships.

Harmonious Health and Nutrition . . .

Health Scent: Lavender—This scent might lead others to trust you and make you patient.

Favorable Foods: Radishes, pomegranates, barley, red meat

What's Lucky . . .

Lucky Numbers: 2, 11, 22
Best Months: January and October
Best Day of the Week: Sunday
Best Month Days: 9, 18, 27
Lucky Charms: A U.S. coin or a bill of any amount from the year you were born.
Harmonious Signs for Relationships and Partnerships: Sagittarius and Aries

Spiritual Guides . . .

Star: Al Zubra—Those with this star fear punishment they don't deserve.

Angel: Verchiel—This angel enhances our ability to enjoy what life offers and gives much luck in legal dealings.

Guardian Angel: Gabriel—"God is my strength."

Spiritual Stone: Amethyst—This stone is thought to be a mood stabilizer and balances the emotions.

✳ JUDITH'S INSIGHT ✳

You are capable of attaining anything you set your mind to. You're almost too enthusiastic and energetic for some people, and they may misinterpret this behavior and view you as showy. You could do very well in sports and may be recognized at some point in your life for your athletic abilities. You have an idealistic, curious mind.

You're giving and loving, and you have a strong sense of responsibility when it comes to the family. Whether you are the oldest, the youngest, or in the middle, you're the one everybody turns to. Family is very important to you, and it would be unusual if you didn't have your own. Whether you do or not, children and family values have heavy influence over you, and you lend your heart out a whole lot.

Travel is important to you, and at some point in your life you may be inspired by someone or something foreign or the desire to live abroad. If you write, you may even choose an exotic atmosphere for stimulation. You are fond of singing, and you look for an occupation or occasion where you can do so. You will always have a strong desire to be successful, although for years you may not know exactly what you'll be successful at. Keep believing, because you will do very well and bring yourself into the public eye (even if it is on a municipal board or the PTA).

The vitality you possess is there for a reason. In your earlier years, you may seem like the rebel and the one who fights for the underdog. You do better financially after your forties.

✳ ✳ ✳

Possessions and Desires . . .

Gem: Ruby—This stone may lead you to energy, friendship, and happiness.

Flower: Patagonian (mint)—You may have very strong scruples.

Astral Color, Color Need, Apparel Color: Your Astral Color is Red, which enhances passion, power, excitement, and strength. Orange in your environment gives you confidence. In your wardrobe, Purple reflects your giving personality and brings you luck.

Fragrance: Surround yourself with the most romantic flowers you can find such as roses, lilies, and violets. The lavish scents will give an added boost to your natural enthusiasm.

Tree: Holly—Beware that you are not carried away by your passionate nature. The only way to grow is to be open to new experiences.

Instruments: Violin, tympanum

Composer: Gluck

Bird: Stork—Turkish bird, held in high esteem the world over. This bird is intelligent but may have strange tendencies.

Symbol: Wreath—You have been crowned with a special personality. You are strong but extremely compassionate.

Harmonious Health and Nutrition . . .

Health Scent: Lavender—This scent might lead others to trust you and make you patient.

Favorable Foods: Cabbage, grapefruit, caraway seeds, buttermilk

What's Lucky . . .

Lucky Numbers: 3, 12, 21

Best Months: January and October

Best Day of the Week: Sunday

Best Month Days: 9, 18, 27

Lucky Charms: A U.S. coin or a bill of any amount from the year you were born.

Harmonious Signs for Relationships and Partnerships: Sagittarius and Aries

Spiritual Guides . . .

Star: Al Gieba—The lucky born with this star are treated like royalty.

Angel: Verchiel—This angel enhances our ability to enjoy what life offers and gives much luck in legal dealings.

Guardian Angel: Gabriel—"God is my strength."

Spiritual Stone: Amethyst—This stone is thought to be a mood stabilizer and balances the emotions.

✶ JUDITH'S INSIGHT ✶

You tend to lend a helping hand to others around you, only they may not necessarily take it so readily. Sometimes you can be misunderstood because you can be such a giver. Material things could be important to you. You have a style all your own and enjoy life in the comfort zone.

A late bloomer when it comes to love, you can be overwhelmed by family and friends because you put yourself out for everyone else. Be sure to save time for yourself and a partner, otherwise you may become resentful.

Careerwise, you can fit into just about any situation. If you cook, you will shine. If you are on stage, you will be the star. If you are a lawyer, you win cases. No matter what you do, you will rise to the top. In the beginning your aims may be low, but as you grow, aim higher. Your ambition will be there, but sometimes it could use a jolt. Your enthusiasm could be knocked down by negativity from others around you. Remember to turn a deaf ear to anything negative. You would do well as an entrepreneur. That does not mean that your caretaking personality won't lead to the health field. You might become a successful doctor or an administrator of a hospital.

You do tend to lean towards the public or publicity, so at some point or another you may find your name in the news.

✶ ✶ ✶

JULY 31 LEO • The heart of the zodiac

July 22 at 11:00 P.M. to August 23 at 6:00 A.M. • NUMEROLOGY 4

Possessions and Desires . . .

Gem: Agate—This stone may promote health and lead you to a long life.

Flower: Osier—You tend to be very frank in your opinions.

Astral Color, Color Need, Apparel Color: Your Astral Color is Red, which enhances passion, power, excitement, and strength. Orange in your environment gives you confidence. In your wardrobe, Plum brings out the best in your looks.

Fragrance: Surround yourself with the most romantic flowers you can find such as roses, lilies, and violets. The lavish scents will give an added boost to your natural enthusiasm.

Tree: Cherry—You will find yourself faced with constant new emotional awakenings.

Instruments: Bass, clarinet

Composers: Haydn, Wagner

Bird: Skylark—This handsome bird is beautiful when it sings. It always whistles as it works.

Symbol: Star—You are full of inner brightness and will stand out in any crowd. You will be seen as special.

Harmonious Health and Nutrition . . .

Health Scent: Vanilla—This scent will fill you with a feeling of cleanliness and stability.

Favorable Foods: Cabbage, grapefruit, caraway seeds, buttermilk

What's Lucky . . .

Lucky Numbers: 4, 13, 24

Best Months: January and October

Best Day of the Week: Sunday

Best Month Days: 4, 13, 22, 31

Lucky Charm: A piece of material cut from something in your home.

Harmonious Signs for Relationships and Partnerships: Sagittarius and Aries

Spiritual Guides . . .

Star: Al Gieba—The lucky born with this star are treated like royalty.

Angel: Verchiel—This angel enhances our ability to enjoy what life offers and gives much luck in legal dealings.

Guardian Angel: Uriel—This angel brings the light of God's guidance.

Spiritual Stone: Amethyst—This stone is thought to be a mood stabilizer and balances the emotions.

✶ JUDITH'S INSIGHT ✶

You are exceptionally sensitive and have quite a heart. You tend to have too much pride for your own good. You are as loyal as the day is long, and you are an honorable friend. You want to stop bad things from happening, not only to yourself; you sometimes stand in the way so bad things don't happen to other people. You do have unusual experiences throughout your life, but you eventually handle them and recognize that they did enhance your life. You could take a tragedy and turn it into a major motion picture. You need a sense of independence in what you are doing and to not allow yourself to get bored.

Your energies will dwindle if you are not emotionally fed. You go through a lot of entanglements, and you tend to blame others when things go wrong. Just remember, don't stand in your own way, and don't stand in others' way of helping you.

It is extremely easy for you to make friends, although you do have to watch out for falling into periods of feeling sorry for yourself. You can be your own worst enemy. You can also allow relationships to drift apart because you are waiting to see who calls first and can't bring yourself to pick up the phone.

You could be a great doctor, lawyer, teacher; just about anything you want, you can do. You have extraordinary power, energy, and perseverance.

✶ ✶ ✶

AUGUST

AUGUST 1   LEO • The heart of the zodiac

July 22 at 11:00 P.M. to August 23 at 6:00 A.M. • NUMEROLOGY 1

Possessions and Desires . . .

Gem: Ruby—This stone may lead you to energy, friendship, and happiness.

Flower: Burgundy Rose—You often don't realize just how much love you carry inside.

Astral Color, Color Need, Apparel Color: Your Astral Color is Red, which enhances passion, power, excitement, and strength. Orange in your environment gives you confidence. In your wardrobe, Purple reflects your giving personality and brings you luck.

Fragrance: Surround yourself with the most romantic flowers you can find such as roses, lilies, and violets. The lavish scents will give an added boost to your natural enthusiasm.

Tree: Walnut—You are unusually helpful and aways looking for new beginnings.

Instruments: Oboe, flute, clarinet, piano, French horn, organ, piccolo

Composer: Böhm

Bird: Cuckoo—A good flyer and very seldom a quitter. Many seem more independent than they actually are; yearn for more nurturing than one would expect.

Symbol: Crown—the universal sign of dignity.

Harmonious Health and Nutrition . . .

Health Scent: Strawberry—Soothing by nature, the strawberry promotes self-esteem and encourages love.

Favorable Foods: Spinach, apples, whole oats, red meat

What's Lucky . . .

Lucky Numbers: 1, 2, 17
Best Months: January and October
Best Day of the Week: Sunday
Best Month Days: 1, 10, 19, 28
Lucky Charm: A new penny in your shoe.

Harmonious Signs for Relationships and Partnerships: Sagittarius and Aries

Spiritual Guides . . .

Star: Al Gieba—The lucky born with this star are treated like royalty.

Angel: Verchiel—This angel enhances our ability to enjoy what life offers and gives much luck in legal dealings.

Guardian Angel: Malachi—"Messenger of Jehovah."

Spiritual Stone: Amethyst—This stone is thought to be a mood stabilizer and balances the emotions.

✶ JUDITH'S INSIGHT ✶

Because you're energetic and enthusiastic, everyone always wants to be around you. You are exceptionally loyal to family and friends. Your desire for love will bring it right to you; just be sure to keep your eyes open. It may take some time to meet the right person. Your mate should understand your need for romance and spontaneity, otherwise a struggle could arise.

Your strong business instincts may result in many opportunities coming your way. There aren't too many jobs you can't tackle. One way or the other, you will take on the role of caretaker, whether with your own children, your parents, or work. Several careers, from nursing to music to performing, are all possibilities for you. You may have more than one career, and it may take time to find out exactly what you want to do.

You like a neat and tidy home and enjoy changes around your environment. New things, whether it be furniture, clothing or housing, delight you. Because of your curious nature, you cannot resist the temptation to see what everyone else is up to. Don't be surprised if you take on too much at times. You may have a tendency to burn out. Regardless of career, it is highly likely that you will take on a hobby or two. Find something that suits you, and remember to enjoy the fun things in life.

✶ ✶ ✶

AUGUST 2

LEO • The heart of the zodiac

July 22 at 11:00 P.M. to August 23 at 6:00 A.M. • NUMEROLOGY 2

Possessions and Desires . . .

Gem: Ruby—This stone may lead you to energy, friendship, and happiness.

Flower: Damask Rose—You seem to have an inner glow that warms other people's hearts.

Astral Color, Color Need, Apparel Color: Your Astral Color is Red, which enhances passion, power, excitement, and strength. Orange in your environment gives you confidence. In your wardrobe, Green is your power color for overcoming obstacles.

Fragrance: Surround yourself with the most romantic flowers you can find such as roses, lilies, and violets. The lavish scents will give an added boost to your natural enthusiasm.

Tree: Maple—You have both great stability and flashes of intuition.

Instruments: Pipe organ, cymbal, drum

Composers: Handel, Johann Sebastian Bach

Bird: Skylark—This handsome bird is beautiful when it sings. It always whistles as it works.

Symbol: Cross—the symbol of self-sacrifice and reconciliation.

Harmonious Health and Nutrition . . .

Health Scent: Apple—You are creative, full of joy, and nearly magical. You bring happiness.

Favorable Foods: Cabbage, limes, barley, red meat, buttermilk

What's Lucky . . .

Lucky Numbers: 2, 8, 28
Best Months: January and October
Best Day of the Week: Sunday
Best Month Days: 2, 11, 20, 29
Lucky Charms: Two 50-cent pieces. Give someone else one of them.
Harmonious Signs for Relationships and Partnerships: Sagittarius and Aries

Spiritual Guides . . .

Star: Al Zubra—Those with this star fear punishment they don't deserve.

Angel: Verchiel—This angel enhances our ability to enjoy what life offers and gives much luck in legal dealings.

Guardian Angel: Uriel—This angel brings the light of God's guidance.

Spiritual Stone: Amethyst—This stone is thought to be a mood stabilizer and balances the emotions.

✷ JUDITH'S INSIGHT ✷

Original, daring, and fearless in all your actions, you uplift those around you mentally and socially. People trust in you and have confidence in you. Your personality alone will bring you advancement in life one way or the other. Opportunities present themselves seemingly out of nowhere.

With a flair for the dramatic, you are likely to be drawn to the arts, literature, music, theater, and film. Your natural talent in these areas can enhance any career choice. Your gift of gab and your skill with words and communicating could make you a good preacher, teacher, writer, poet, publisher, or editor.

You have good intuition and a great memory. With your style, you will have no trouble attracting a mate. In love, you may find yourself with too many rather than too few choices. Pick the right mate for the right reasons. You are magnanimous and broad-minded, and very few people don't like you. Steer clear of entanglements when it comes to friendship.

Work comes easily, but you may actually have to "work" at play! Without the proper time to enjoy yourself, you have a tendency to get cranky and even depressed. Take as much time for yourself as you do for others. Watch out for family matters that drain your energy.

✷ ✷ ✷

AUGUST 3　LEO • The heart of the zodiac

July 22 at 11:00 P.M. to August 23 at 6:00 A.M. • NUMEROLOGY 3

Possessions and Desires . . .

Gem: Agate—This stone may promote health and lead you to a long life.

Flower: Moss Rose—You tend to let those you love know how you feel.

Astral Color, Color Need, Apparel Color: Your Astral Color is Red, which enhances passion, power, excitement, and strength. Orange in your environment gives you confidence. In your wardrobe, Purple reflects your giving personality and brings you luck.

Fragrance: Surround yourself with the most romantic flowers you can find such as roses, lilies, and violets. The lavish scents will give an added boost to your natural enthusiasm.

Tree: Elm—You have willpower, strength, and the ability to stand alone.

Instrument: Trombone

Composers: Verdi, Mendelssohn, Schumann

Bird: Warbling Parakeet—the most beautiful of all birds, known as the love bird. It does seem to have the powers of imitation.

Symbol: Wreath—You have been crowned with a special personality. You are strong but extremely compassionate.

Harmonious Health and Nutrition . . .

Health Scent: Rose—This scent will lead you to passionate thoughts and make you feel warm inside.

Favorable Foods: Turnips, limes, rice bran, red meat, buttermilk

What's Lucky . . .

Lucky Numbers: 5, 23, 32

Best Months: January and October

Best Day of the Week: Sunday

Best Month Days: 3, 12, 21, 30

Lucky Charm: A pen that someone has already used.

Harmonious Signs for Relationships and Partnerships: Sagittarius and Aries

Spiritual Guides . . .

Star: Al Serpha—Those with this star know how special life can be.

Angel: Verchiel—This angel enhances our ability to enjoy what life offers and gives much luck in legal dealings.

Guardian Angel: Johiel—This angel is a protector of all those with a humble heart.

Spiritual Stone: Amethyst—This stone is thought to be a mood stabilizer and balances the emotions.

✷ JUDITH'S INSIGHT ✷

Ultraresponsible, you always know how to carry out every task you want to accomplish. At times you may lack enthusiasm, and this could pose problems for you. Be careful of feeling sorry for yourself and putting yourself into positions that you know perfectly well will make you unhappy. Take time with big decisions—you could rush into things at times.

Your intense mind will lead you into careers involving reading or writing, but your passion for design may lead you to the arts or some other creative endeavor. Look for hobbies that fully utilize your physical power. A career such as physical therapy, construction, or even waiting on tables could also work for you. Your nurturing side may lead to a career in counseling. Just learn to recognize when it's you that needs the counseling.

Legal matters of one kind or another will be important. It may be that you choose law enforcement or advocacy as your life's work. Make sure you stay on the right side of the law.

A good and loyal friend, you know how to keep a secret (particularly your own). Family plays a large role in your life. You may grow up adoring someone and, as you mature, recognize that this someone should instead adore you.

Your life's lesson is accepting balance. You love the fun and romance in a relationship, but when things get too serious, you want to run. Once you begin to practice balance in your life, you should be able to make better choices. Your work is cut out for you.

✷ ✷ ✷

AUGUST 4

LEO • The heart of the zodiac

July 22 at 11:00 P.M. to August 23 at 6:00 A.M. • NUMEROLOGY 4

Possessions and Desires . . .

Gem: Diamond—This stone is thought to encourage harmony in relationships and gives strength to the troubled.

Flower: Morning Glory—You have honest and open intentions.

Astral Color, Color Need, Apparel Color: Your Astral Color is Red, which enhances passion, power, excitement, and strength. Orange in your environment gives you confidence. In your wardrobe, Plum brings out the best in your looks.

Fragrance: Surround yourself with the most romantic flowers you can find such as roses, lilies, and violets. The lavish scents will give an added boost to your natural enthusiasm.

Tree: Cherry—You will find yourself faced with constant new emotional awakenings.

Instruments: Bass, clarinet

Composers: Haydn, Wagner

Bird: Skylark—This handsome bird is beautiful when it sings. It always whistles as it works.

Symbol: Star—You are full of inner brightness and will stand out in any crowd. You will be seen as special.

Harmonious Health and Nutrition . . .

Health Scent: Vanilla—This scent will fill you with a feeling of cleanliness and stability.

Favorable Foods: Savory, raspberries, rice bran, red meat, buttermilk

What's Lucky . . .

Lucky Numbers: 4, 8, 44

Best Months: January and October

Best Day of the Week: Sunday

Best Month Days: 4, 13, 22, 31

Lucky Charm: A piece of material cut from something in your home.

Harmonious Signs for Relationships and Partnerships: Sagittarius and Aries

Spiritual Guides . . .

Star: Al Gieba—The lucky born with this star are treated like royalty.

Angel: Verchiel—This angel enhances our ability to enjoy what life offers and gives much luck in legal dealings.

Guardian Angel: St. Thomas—This angel brings affection from others and encourages you in all that you do.

Spiritual Stone: Amethyst—This stone is thought to be a mood stabilizer and balances the emotions.

✴ JUDITH'S INSIGHT ✴

You have a desire to be heard one way or another, whether it be through music, art, or writing, and eventually, you will. Nothing less than all is enough for you. You give more than you take. The more glitz and light in your life, the better you like it. You can turn a small event into an ongoing affair. The unconventional and unique appeals to your sense of creativity. Some may see you as eccentric or strange.

Learn to be patient, especially in love relationships. In time, you will learn balance. It is much simpler to blame others than take responsibility for things running amok in a relationship. You give and give to a fault—it is by far your best attribute. But sometimes your partner may feel overwhelmed by your generosity.

Steer clear of addictions of any kind. You have a tendency to act compulsively when you try to ride both sides of the seesaw. As long as your work is rewarding, you will get the most out of life. If people are nice to you, you are at your best.

Watch closely those extremes! You can stand on the stage and be afraid no one sees you.

Some possible careers are: movie star, singer, director, writer, restaurateur, deli manager, chef, and magazine editor.

✴ ✴ ✴

AUGUST 5

LEO • The heart of the zodiac
July 22 at 11:00 P.M. to August 23 at 6:00 A.M. • NUMEROLOGY 5

Possessions and Desires . . .

Gem: Ruby—This stone may lead you to energy, friendship, and happiness.

Flower: Hundred-leaved Rose—You will have many reasons to be proud of yourself.

Astral Color, Color Need, Apparel Color: Your Astral Color is Red, which enhances passion, power, excitement, and strength. Orange in your environment gives you confidence. In your wardrobe, Green is your power color for overcoming obstacles.

Fragrance: Surround yourself with the most romantic flowers you can find such as roses, lilies, and violets. The lavish scents will give an added boost to your natural enthusiasm.

Tree: Apple—You are creative, full of joy, and nearly magical. You bring happiness.

Instruments: Viola, trumpet

Composer: Liszt

Bird: Skylark—This handsome bird is beautiful when it sings. It always whistles as it works.

Symbol: Triangle—You have the right combination of abilities.

Harmonious Health and Nutrition . . .

Health Scent: Peach—Balances your good qualities so that they equal your charm.

Favorable Foods: Watercress, oranges, caraway seeds, red meat, buttermilk

What's Lucky . . .

Lucky Numbers: 8, 9, 23
Best Months: January and October
Best Day of the Week: Sunday
Best Month Days: 4, 5, 23
Lucky Charms: A rabbit's foot or a white candle.
Harmonious Signs for Relationships and Partnerships: Sagittarius and Aries

Spiritual Guides . . .

Star: Al Zubra—Those with this star fear punishment they don't deserve.

Angel: Verchiel—This angel enhances our ability to enjoy what life offers and gives much luck in legal dealings.

Guardian Angel: Plavwell—The guardian that gives power and strength to one's presence.

Spiritual Stone: Amethyst—This stone is thought to be a mood stabilizer and balances the emotions.

✷ JUDITH'S INSIGHT ✷

Talented in many ways, you love to be entertained and have the energy to do it. Good times and parties are when you are at your best.

You love the law and may look for a career in it. Your energy is contagious, and even two jobs may not be enough. In all likelihood you'll take up a time-consuming hobby in addition to your life's work. Keep a close eye on the higher-ups on the job and work to make them happy. Be careful of your directness, particularly with family and friends. Some may ask you to back off, even when all you're trying to do is help.

Your flair for fashion leaves others breathless, so impeccable is your manner of dress. Perhaps a career in retail would satisfy you. Aspirations and goals are high, and you have the skill to achieve all of them. You may experience a pitfall or two, maybe as early as age twenty, but your resiliency is one of your finest qualities.

In love, you allow yourself just enough freedom to hang yourself. You crave attention too much and are a nonstop flirt. Flattery will get them everywhere, but you do see right through the phonies in life.

You'll need to keep one eye on the purse strings and one eye on those fingers that love to spend. More than once in your life, you will have to tighten up the budget. While you are certainly capable of living on a budget, if you didn't spend money, you probably wouldn't enjoy working so hard for it.

✷ ✷ ✷

AUGUST 6   LEO • The heart of the zodiac

July 22 at 11:00 P.M. to August 23 at 6:00 A.M. • NUMEROLOGY 6

Possessions and Desires . . .

Gem: Diamond—This stone is thought to encourage harmony in relationships and gives strength to the troubled.

Flower: Sardony—You tend to feel the universe has an ironic sense of humor.

Astral Color, Color Need, Apparel Color: Your Astral Color is Red, which enhances passion, power, excitement, and strength. Orange in your environment gives you confidence. In your wardrobe, Purple reflects your giving personality and brings you luck.

Fragrance: Surround yourself with the most romantic flowers you can find such as roses, lilies, and violets. The lavish scents will give an added boost to your natural enthusiasm.

Tree: Palm—You tend to be very healthy and creative.

Instruments: Tambourine, lyre

Composer: Schubert

Bird: Cuckoo—A good flyer and very seldom a quitter. Many seem more independent than they actually are; yearn for more nurturing than one would expect.

Symbol: Crescent—You are more likely to be influenced by the phases of the moon. Your easygoing manner leads you to peaceful situations.

Harmonious Health and Nutrition . . .

Health Scent: Orange Blossom—This scent may balance your body, mind, and soul.

Favorable Foods: Radishes, sour cherries, barley, red meat, buttermilk

What's Lucky . . .

Lucky Numbers: 8, 9, 42
Best Months: January and October
Best Day of the Week: Sunday
Best Month Days: 6, 15, 24
Lucky Charms: A religious token or card from any religion.

Harmonious Signs for Relationships and Partnerships: Sagittarius and Aries

Spiritual Guides . . .

Star: Al Serpha—This star makes special things happen in one's life.

Angel: Verchiel—This angel enhances our ability to enjoy what life offers and gives much luck in legal dealings.

Guardian Angel: Michael—"Who is like God."

Spiritual Stone: Amethyst—This stone is thought to be a mood stabilizer and balances the emotions.

✳ JUDITH'S INSIGHT ✳

Good things come to those who wait or to those who have the stamina to stand in line as long as you do. Sometimes it may seem your life is going nowhere or even moving backwards. Be patient; you'll get what you want.

As a young person, your judgment could get you into your share of trouble for things you don't do. As you mature, so do your choices. You love to party, and that could be a problem. Learn to exercise some balance. You do take life seriously sometimes, and perhaps your need to socialize somehow compensates for this. Mostly, others take pride in knowing you.

A pleasant surprise of money, an inheritance, or some other windfall comes into your life. Perhaps you invent a product that brings you a large sum of money.

It make take a lifetime (or seem that way) to find the perfect mate. You should work harder to keep things together and take a less aloof attitude when it comes to love. Many relationship opportunities will present themselves along the way, but you may have trouble choosing the right one. Take your time; even your loyalty has its limits.

Careers for you could be in politics, law, or firefighting. You are mechanically inclined and definitely have a flair for entertainment. Perhaps you may find yourself behind the curtain or cameras as a photographer, lighting technician, or stage hand. Somewhere along the way, the spotlight is there.

✳ ✳ ✳

AUGUST 7

LEO • The heart of the zodiac

July 22 at 11:00 P.M. to August 23 at 6:00 A.M. • NUMEROLOGY 7

Possessions and Desires . . .

Gem: Ruby—This stone may lead you to energy, friendship, and happiness.

Flower: Saint foil—Your emotions tend to be easily understood.

Astral Color, Color Need, Apparel Color: Your Astral Color is Red, which enhances passion, power, excitement, and strength. Orange in your environment gives you confidence. In your wardrobe, Plum brings out the best in your looks.

Fragrance: Surround yourself with the most romantic flowers you can find such as roses, lilies, and violets. The lavish scents will give an added boost to your natural enthusiasm.

Tree: Sycamore—Yours is the ability to love, communicate honestly with others, and have lasting relationships.

Instrument: Harp

Composers: Gluck, Brahms

Bird: Warbling Parakeet—The most beautiful of all birds, known as the love bird. It does seem to have the powers of imitation.

Symbol: Heart—You are enthusiastic, empathetic, and full of generosity and love.

Harmonious Health and Nutrition . . .

Health Scent: Jasmine—This scent may make you more easygoing when you are stressed.

Favorable Foods: Lima beans, lemons, whole oats, red meat, buttermilk

What's Lucky . . .

Lucky Numbers: 8, 9, 34
Best Months: January and October
Best Day of the Week: Sunday
Best Month Days: 6, 15, 24
Lucky Charm: An old key.

Harmonious Signs for Relationships and Partnerships: Sagittarius and Aries

Spiritual Guides . . .

Star: Al Serpha—This star makes special things happen in one's life.

Angel: Verchiel—This angel enhances our ability to enjoy what life offers and gives much luck in legal dealings.

Guardian Angel: Raphael—This angel attends to all of your needs when you are looking for guidance.

Spiritual Stone: Amethyst—This stone is thought to be a mood stabilizer and balances the emotions.

✴ JUDITH'S INSIGHT ✴

Boy, what a handful . . . that's how others describe you, and you love each and every minute of it. You are generous, energetic, and funny. No wonder everyone invites you to the party. You not only know how to have a good time, but you put on a good time for family and friends. Party planning or catering may be good career choices for you. The great organizer, you could also be head of an organization, nonprofit or otherwise. Business is the way to go for you, and you may have something to do with the health care industry.

Your love mate may enjoy your energy but wish you to slow down at times. Find a way to uncomplicate things for your own sake as well as your partner's. Keep your eyes focused on the road, because at times you feel like your life is changing so fast you can't hold on.

You are known to create havoc. Challenges in whatever you do will keep you awake at night. Dignified and stylish, you can be the envy of relatives and neighbors and even your devoted mate. Watch out for a tendency to demand too much from others. Very few possess the energy you have.

✴ ✴ ✴

AUGUST 8

LEO • The heart of the zodiac

July 22 at 11:00 P.M. to August 23 at 6:00 A.M. • NUMEROLOGY 8

Possessions and Desires . . .

Gem: Ruby—This stone may lead you to energy, friendship, and happiness.

Flower: Scabiosa—You will find that even the untidiest love affairs are important lessons on the way to a suitable one.

Astral Color, Color Need, Apparel Color: Your Astral Color is Red, which enhances passion, power, excitement, and strength. Orange in your environment gives you confidence. In your wardrobe, Purple reflects your giving personality and brings you luck.

Fragrance: Surround yourself with the most romantic flowers you can find such as roses, lilies, and violets. The lavish scents will give an added boost to your enthusiasm.

Tree: Pine—Your relationships tend to be harmonious, both emotionally and mentally.

Instrument: Cello

Composer: Mozart

Bird: Skylark—This handsome bird is beautiful when it sings. It always whistles as it works.

Symbol: Wings—You are the source of balance in your world—this will bring you contentment.

Harmonious Health and Nutrition . . .

Health Scents: Almond—This scent may revitalize you and open you to greater possibilities.

Favorable Foods: Cucumbers, limes, rice bran, red meat, buttermilk

What's Lucky . . .

Lucky Numbers: 8, 17, 26
Best Months: January and October
Best Day of the Week: Sunday
Best Month Days: 8, 17, 26
Lucky Charm: Red ribbon in your wallet or doorway

Harmonious Signs for Relationships and Partnerships: Sagittarius and Aries

Spiritual Guides . . .

Star: Al Serpha—This star makes special things happen in one's life.

Angel: Verchiel—This angel enhances our ability to enjoy what life offers and gives much luck in legal dealings.

Guardian Angel: Seraphim—An angel that brings love, light, and passion.

Spiritual Stone: Amethyst—This stone is thought to be a mood stabilizer and balances the emotions.

✴ JUDITH'S INSIGHT ✴

You may spend half your life trying to convince others of your way of thinking. Your persistence, consistency, and energy are unbeaten! You can be a contradiction at times, and you want to have a piece of everything. You'd be wise to learn to practice some balance in your life. As you mature and your self-esteem increases, you'll be better equipped to equalize things.

Your career is more important to you than you let on. As a youth, you have great expectations, and if everything goes along as planned, you'll be fine. If not, you could backslide and feel indifferent and drained of energy. Work in the public eye seems to be very lucky for you. Any profession that brings you into the limelight is where you belong. Around the age of forty, you may choose a completely different career track and be on the road to success.

Some people see you as unusual because of your attraction to the exotic. You like being noticed and wearing different things. Your love life may experience a lot of emotional peaks and valleys. Your family or friends may run you ragged emotionally as well. Recognize your need for a pat on the back every now and then for all the hard work you do. Without it, you lose enthusiasm and energy.

✴ ✴ ✴

AUGUST 9

LEO • The heart of the zodiac

July 22 at 11:00 P.M. to August 23 at 6:00 A.M. • NUMEROLOGY 9

Possessions and Desires . . .

Gem: Agate—This stone may promote health and lead you to a long life.

Flower: Witch Hazel—Be careful that you don't allow other people's troubles to overwhelm you.

Astral Color, Color Need, Apparel Color: Your Astral Color is Red, which enhances passion, power, excitement, and strength. Orange in your environment gives you confidence. In your wardrobe, Green is your power color for overcoming obstacles.

Fragrance: Surround yourself with the most romantic flowers you can find such as roses, lilies, and violets. The lavish scents will give an added boost to your enthusiasm.

Tree: Holly—Beware that you are not carried away by your passionate nature. The only way to grow is to be open to new experiences.

Instruments: Violin, tympanum

Composer: Gluck

Bird: Warbling Parakeet—The most beautiful of all birds, known as the love bird. It does seem to have the powers of imitation.

Symbol: Anchor—This tranquil symbol signifies stability and strength, and stands for strong commitments in relationships.

Harmonious Health and Nutrition . . .

Health Scent: Lavender—This scent might lead others to trust you and make you patient.

Favorable Foods: Turnips, sour cherries, barley, red meat, buttermilk

What's Lucky . . .

Lucky Numbers: 8, 9, 45

Best Months: January and October

Best Day of the Week: Sunday

Best Month Days: 9, 18, 27

Lucky Charms: A U.S. coin or a bill of any amount from the year you were born.

Harmonious Signs for Relationships and Partnerships: Sagittarius and Aries

Spiritual Guides . . .

Star: Al Zubra—Those with this star fear punishment they don't deserve.

Angel: Verchiel—This angel enhances our ability to enjoy what life offers and gives much luck in legal dealings.

Guardian Angel: Gabriel—"God is my strength."

Spiritual Stone: Amethyst—This stone is thought to be a mood stabilizer and balances the emotions.

✷ JUDITH'S INSIGHT ✷

You have determination, enthusiasm, and extravagance—you like to do things in a big way. You have great style, charm, and a terrific sense of humor. You love travel, music, and entertainment of any kind. You can be emotional, and with your sheer strength, that may confuse others. Inclined to have unusual relationships, you are lucky with friends and seem to hang onto them forever. Sometimes you might try turning off that mind of yours to give yourself a much-needed rest.

You have hidden talents that would let you thrive in a business setting, publishing, entertainment, or medicine. Watch your tendency to behave erratically—that energy can go both ways!

In love relationships, be cautious of feeling trapped once committed. Your ambition is strong and can dominate the other person, especially in the beginning. If they last more than three or four months, you tend to temper that better. Make sure your partner has the stamina to keep up with you.

Your impeccable taste and style may lead you to either a career or hobby in fine art.

✶ ✶ ✶

AUGUST 10 LEO • The heart of the zodiac

July 22 at 11:00 P.M. to August 23 at 6:00 A.M. • NUMEROLOGY 1

Possessions and Desires . . .

Gem: Ruby—This stone may lead you to energy, friendship, and happiness.

Flower: Whortleberry—You sometimes betray yourself without meaning to.

Astral Color, Color Need, Apparel Color: Your Astral color is Red, which enhances passion, power, excitement, and strength. Orange in your environment gives you confidence. In your wardrobe, Plum brings out the best in your looks.

Fragrance: Surround yourself with the most romantic flowers you can find such as roses, lilies, and violets. The lavish scents will give an added boost to your enthusiasm.

Tree: Walnut—You are unusually helpful and aways looking for new beginnings.

Instruments: Oboe, flute, clarinet, piano, French horn, organ, piccolo

Composer: Böhm

Bird: Cuckoo—A good flyer and very seldom a quitter. Many seem more independent than they actually are. They yearn for more nurturing than one would expect.

Symbol: Crown—the universal sign of dignity.

Harmonious Health and Nutrition . . .

Health Scent: Strawberry—soothing by nature, the strawberry promotes self-esteem and encourages love.

Favorable Foods: Spinach, grapefruit, whole oats, red meat, buttermilk

What's Lucky . . .

Lucky Numbers: 8, 9, 37
Best Months: January and October
Best Day of the Week: Sunday
Best Month Days: 1, 10, 19, 28

Lucky Charm: A new penny in your shoe.
Harmonious Signs for Relationships and Partnerships: Sagittarius and Aries

Spiritual Guides . . .

Star: Al Gieba—The lucky born with this star are treated like royalty.

Angel: Verchiel—This angel enhances our ability to enjoy what life offers and gives much luck in legal dealings.

Guardian Angel: Malachi—"Messenger of Jehovah."

Spiritual Stone: Amethyst—This stone is thought to be a mood stabilizer and balances the emotions.

✷ JUDITH'S INSIGHT ✷

Exceptionally loyal to friends and family, you have an overwhelming amount of energy. You love to be loved, and anything that will bring the attention around to you makes you happy. As long as your partner is able to bring romance and spontaneity to you, no one is a more loyal mate. If you wait until you're a little older before making that commitment, odds are you will find love that lasts and only gets better.

Somewhere along the way, you may have a desire to entertain. You could succeed in any line of work from theater business manager to car salesperson to lawyer. Remember these are all connected to performing! Stay in touch with your nurturing side as well. Teaching or nursing are both good job choices.

Whether cleaning out the garage, picking up your room, or rearranging the office, your intense energy always makes you eager to do something new. Be careful to measure that verve . . . others may be overwhelmed by it. You, too, may give in to depression simply because you think life lacks a constant stream of stimulation. New projects and beginnings help corral that awesome drive of yours.

✷ ✷ ✷

AUGUST 11
LEO • The heart of the zodiac
July 22 at 11:00 P.M. to August 23 at 6:00 A.M.. • NUMEROLOGY 2

Possessions and Desires . . .

Gem: Ruby—This stone may lead you to energy, friendship, and happiness.
Flower: Fireweed—You have an inner solidity that holds up those who rely on you.
Astral Color, Color Need, Apparel Color: Your Astral Color is Red, which enhances passion, power, excitement, and strength. Orange in your environment gives you confidence. In your wardrobe, Purple reflects your giving personality and brings you luck.
Fragrance: Surround yourself with the most romantic flowers you can find such as roses, lilies, and violets. The lavish scents will give an added boost to your enthusiasm.
Tree: Maple—You have both great stability and flashes of intuition.
Instruments: Pipe organ, cymbal, drum
Composers: Handel, Johann Sabastian Bach
Bird: Skylark—This handsome bird is beautiful when it sings. It always whistles as it works.
Symbol: Cross—the symbol of self-sacrifice and reconciliation.

Harmonious Health and Nutrition . . .

Health Scent: Apple—You are creative, full of joy, and nearly magical. You bring happiness.
Favorable Foods: Lima beans, raspberries, caraway seeds, red meat

What's Lucky . . .

Lucky Numbers: 8, 9, 22
Best Months: January and October
Best Day of the Week: Sunday
Best Month Days: 2, 11, 20, 29
Lucky Charms: Two 50-cent pieces. Give someone else one of them.
Harmonious Signs for Relationships and Partnerships: Sagittarius and Aries

Spiritual Guides . . .

Star: Al Gieba—The lucky born with this star are treated like royalty.
Angel: Verchiel—This angel enhances our ability to enjoy what life offers and gives much luck in legal dealings.
Guardian Angel: St. John—This angel simplifies that which is complicated.
Spiritual Stone: Amethyst—This stone is thought to be a mood stabilizer and balances the emotions.

✳ JUDITH'S INSIGHT ✳

Daring, fearless . . . sound familiar? You have the necessary confidence and personality to bring advancement into your life and into others'. People enjoy you and your natural way of communicating. Music, the dramatic arts, or writing: somewhere along the way, you words will be taken seriously. You are here to teach and learn. Your good intuition and memory make lots of choices available to you.

In love, you must be cautious when connecting with a mate. You tend to be overzealous when it comes to commitment. Happiness will come to you, especially in the area of family, where you gain most of your strength. As a youth, you may not be as aware of this.

As magnanimous as you are, you have a few enemies, particularly in the workplace. With friends and in social situations, however, you look for harmony as much as possible. Jobs will come easy to you because you are able to do so many different things. Titles don't mean much to you, although along the way, you do have the opportunity to take your place at the top. It's not necessary for you to go out of your way to make your presence known.

Financially, you'll do fine, and as you mature, you'll become more charitable with your money. Your charitable nature may make you seek an opportunity to raise money for nonprofit organizations. With your inventiveness, you may end up in careers such as computer programming, product development, or arts and crafts.

✳ ✳ ✳

AUGUST 12　LEO • The heart of the zodiac

July 22 at 11:00 P.M. to August 23 at 6:00 A.M. • NUMEROLOGY 3

Possessions and Desires . . .

Gem: Agate—This stone may promote health and lead you to a long life.

Flower: Vine—You will have happiness and laughter in your life.

Astral Color, Color Need, Apparel Color: Your Astral Color is Red, which enhances passion, power, excitement, and strength. Orange in your environment gives you confidence. In your wardrobe, Green is your power color for overcoming obstacles.

Fragrance: Surround yourself with the most romantic flowers you can find such as roses, lilies, and violets. The lavish scents will given an added boost to your enthusiasm.

Tree: Elm—You have willpower, strength, and the ability to stand alone.

Instrument: Trombone

Composers: Verdi, Mendelssohn, Schumann

Bird: Warbling Parakeet—the most beautiful of all birds, known as the love bird. It does seem to have the powers of imitation.

Symbol: Wreath—You have been crowned with a special personality. You are strong but extremely compassionate.

Harmonious Health and Nutrition . . .

Health Scent: Rose—This scent will lead you to passionate thoughts and make you feel warm inside.

Favorable Foods: Cucumbers, lemons, rice bran, red meat, buttermilk

What's Lucky . . .

Lucky Number: 3, 12, 21
Best Months: January and October
Best Day of the Week: Sunday
Best Month Days: 3, 12, 21, 30

Lucky Charm: A pen that someone else has already used.
Harmonious Signs for Relationships and Partnerships: Sagittarius and Aries

Spiritual Guides . . .

Star: Al Zubra—Those with this star fear punishment they don't deserve.

Angel: Verchiel—This angel enhances our ability to enjoy what life offers and gives much luck in legal dealings.

Guardian Angel: Johiel—This angel is a protector of all those with a humble heart.

Spiritual Stone: Amethyst—This stone is thought to be a mood stabilizer and balances the emotions.

✷ JUDITH'S INSIGHT ✷

Capable is your middle name. There isn't much that you don't like, and with your enthusiasm and energy, you go out of your way for others. If you did have a weakness, it would be your tendency to dwell on things too long. Don't think so much.

You are strong and able and can do anything from designing cabinets to building them. Try putting your verve into something physical, whether it be a sport (or a career in sports), physical therapy, or sports medicine. Around your mid-thirties, you begin a lifelong self-improvement journey. You could be a great counselor largely because you make such a good friend.

Law and authority are lucky for you, but you may have a lawsuit or two to contend with. Family plays a huge role in your life, but when it comes to relationships, you may have disagreements and feel misunderstood. You let others in only so far. Try being more patient.

As far as giving goes, you have a big heart. Watch our for the urge to give more than you have.

✷ ✷ ✷

AUGUST 13   LEO • The heart of the zodiac
July 22 at 11:00 P.M. to August 23 at 6:00 A.M. • NUMEROLOGY 4

Possessions and Desires . . .

Gem: Diamond—This stone is thought to encourage harmony in relationships and gives strength to the troubled.

Flower: Vetch—You may be a great person to have as a friend.

Astral Color, Color Need, Apparel Color: Your Astral Color is Red, which enhances passion, power, excitement, and strength. Orange in your environment gives you confidence. In your wardrobe, Plum brings out the best in your looks.

Fragrance: Surround yourself with the most romantic flowers you can find such as roses, lilies, and violets. The lavish scents will give an added boost to you enthusiasm.

Tree: Cherry—You will find yourself faced with constant new emotional awakenings.

Instruments: Bass, clarinet

Composers: Haydn, Wagner

Bird: Skylark—This handsome bird is beautiful when it sings. It always whistles as it works.

Symbol: Star—You are full of inner brightness and will stand out in any crowd. You will be seen as special.

Harmonious Health and Nutrition . . .

Health Scent: Vanilla—This scent will fill you with a feeling of cleanliness and stability.

Favorable Foods: Spinach, sour cherries, barley, red meat, buttermilk

What's Lucky . . .

Lucky Numbers: 4, 13, 31
Best Months: January and October
Best Day of the Week: Sunday
Best Month Days: 4, 13, 22, 31
Lucky Charm: A piece of material cut from something in your home.
Harmonious Signs for Relationships and Partnerships: Sagittarius and Aries

Spiritual Guides . . .

Star: Al Zubra—Those with this star fear punishment they don't deserve.

Angel: Verchiel—This angel enhances our ability to enjoy what life offers and gives much luck in legal dealings.

Guardian Angel: St. Thomas—This angel brings affection from others and encourages you in all that you do.

Spiritual Stone: Amethyst—This stone is thought to be a mood stabilizer and balances the emotions.

✶ JUDITH'S INSIGHT ✶

You always want what you can't have, and eventually you get it anyway. Drawn to music, acting, and writing, somewhere along the way, these will play a great role in your life. You give more than you take because it's easier to you that way. Some may see you as strange or eccentric, spiritual, or drawn to the underdog.

Patience is your life's lesson, particularly when it comes to love and family. This could be a setback. You're better with friends and social life than with intimate relationships, however much you desire to have one. Unfortunately, you want your partner to do all the work. You like to watch and see how much others are willing to put into a relationship first.

Watch out for addictions. You can be extreme at times . . . both at work and play. Try to listen more to your terrific intuition and less to what others may be saying. That's what intuition is for! When things get too out of balance, you can be depressed. It's not that you feel sorry for yourself, but you may throw a little pity party now and then. Try not to overdo things. Your tendency is to make things come to life with your positive attitude.

You need to find more than one career in your lifetime. You could do anything from building houses to decorating them. You have more leadership qualities than you think.

✶ ✶ ✶

AUGUST 14   LEO • The heart of the zodiac

July 22 at 11:00 P.M. to August 23 at 6:00 A.M. • NUMEROLOGY 5

Possessions and Desires . . .

Gem: Ruby—This stone may lead you to energy, friendship, and happiness.

Flower: Thrift—You usually have a very sympathetic nature.

Astral Color, Color Need, Apparel Color: Your Astral Color is Red, which enhances passion, power, excitement, and strength. Orange in your environment gives you confidence. In your wardrobe, Purple reflects your giving personality and brings you luck.

Fragrance: Surround yourself with the most romantic flowers you can find such as roses, lilies, and violets. The lavish scents will give an added boost to your enthusiasm.

Tree: Apple—You are creative, full of joy, and nearly magical. You bring happiness.

Instruments: Viola, trumpet

Composer: Liszt

Bird: Skylark—This handsome bird is beautiful when it sings. It always whistles as it works.

Symbol: Triangle—You have the right combination of abilities.

Harmonious Health and Nutrition . . .

Health Scent: Peach—Balances your good qualities so they equal your charm.

Favorable Foods: Turnips, oranges, caraway seeds, red meat, buttermilk

What's Lucky . . .

Lucky Numbers: 5, 15, 32
Best Months: January and October
Best Day of the Week: Sunday
Best Month Days: 4, 5, 23
Lucky Charms: A rabbit's foot or a white candle.
Harmonious Signs for Relationships and Partnerships: Sagittarius and Aries

Spiritual Guides . . .

Star: Al Serpha—This star makes special things happen in one's life.

Angel: Verchiel—This angel enhances our ability to enjoy what life offers and gives much luck in legal dealings.

Guardian angel: Plavwell—The guardian that gives power and strength to one's presence.

Spiritual Stone: Amethyst—This stone is thought to be a mood stabilizer and balances the emotions.

✶ JUDITH'S INSIGHT ✶

You are talented in many ways, and your energy can outlast all those around you. Entertainment, sports, or any kind of physical job would work wonderfully for you. You crave entertainment somewhere along the way; you love fun and games, no matter how daring, adventurous, or exciting.

Your love of justice may lead you to a career in law. You are interested in the unknown, and people thrive on your energy and inclination toward the exotic. Socially, you can be quite popular. Travel and outdoor sports should appeal to you.

Watch out for your fiery temper; people sometimes let you down, especially in love relationships. When you feel secure, you can pour on the affection. Otherwise, you might be shy and pessimistic.

Aim high—you're assertive enough to accomplish a lot. There may be two or three jobs over the course of your life, or you just may wear so many hats that it seems that way. Good executive abilities and communication skills may guide you to a job in the media.

Lots of your energy goes into keeping things neat, and this could drive others (especially those living with you) a bit crazy. This may completely reverse itself at some time, and the clutter may build for years!

★ ★ ★

AUGUST 15

LEO • The heart of the zodiac

July 22 at 11:00 P.M. to August 23 at 6:00 A.M. • NUMEROLOGY 6

Possessions and Desires . . .

Gem: Diamond—This stone is thought to encourage harmony in relationships and gives strength to the troubled.

Flower: Throatwort—Your best gifts are often neglected.

Astral Color, Color Need, Apparel Color: Your Astral Color is Red, which enhances passion, power, excitement, and strength. Orange in your environment gives you confidence. In your wardrobe, Green is your power color for overcoming obstacles.

Fragrance: Surround yourself with the most romantic flowers you can find such as roses, lilies, and violets. The lavish scents will give an added boost to your enthusiasm.

Tree: Palm—You tend to be very healthy and creative.

Instruments: Tambourine, lyre

Composer: Schubert

Bird: Skylark—This handsome bird is beautiful when it sings. It always whistles as it works.

Symbol: Crescent—You are more likely to be influenced by the phases of the moon. Your easygoing manner leads you to peaceful situations.

Harmonious Health and Nutrition . . .

Health Scent: Orange Blossom—This scent may balance your body, mind, and soul.

Favorable Foods: Radishes, figs, whole oats, red meat, buttermilk

What's Lucky . . .

Lucky Numbers: 6, 9, 32

Best Months: January and October

Best Day of the Week: Sunday

Best Month Days: 6, 15, 24

Lucky Charms: A religious token or card from any religion.

Harmonious Signs for Relationships and Partnerships: Sagittarius and Aries

Spiritual Guides . . .

Star: Al Serpha—This star makes special things happen in one's life.

Angel: Verchiel—This angel enhances our ability to enjoy what life offers and gives much luck in legal dealings.

Guardian Angel: Michael—"Who is like God."

Spiritual Stone: Amethyst—This stone is thought to be a mood stabilizer and balances the emotions.

✴ JUDITH'S INSIGHT ✴

You are an inspiration to all your friends. Most of the time you can melt ice with your love and tenderness, but watch out for that fiery temper that surfaces from time to time. You have no problem demonstrating devotion to your family and friends. You must learn to be patient.

You can be either energetic or downright lazy, depending on the situation. When things are going your way, your stamina runs high. If you get knocked down a bit, however, you could lean toward depression, and you keep this to yourself. A party person at heart, you need to exercise some moderation with food, drink, and spending. Most of the time, you're aware of what makes you and those around you happy. Your family will be high priority either early in life or later on. Because of your ability to inspire others, people feel that need and want you around.

As smart as you are and as strong as your ego is, you do experience bouts of low self-esteem every once in awhile. Watch out for being misguided in love relationships—you may choose the wrong kind of person in your hurry to settle down. Take your time in looking for the right someone. You tend to want a high-maintenance individual (like yourself!).

As far as career goes, you are naturally mechanically inclined and have a flair for computers, drawing, graphics, and camera work. If you don't go into photography as your life's work, take it up as a hobby. You will come into money, whether you win the lottery or inherit a significant sum.

Keep your head high and watch your emotional gauge. Balance for you is key.

✴ ✴ ✴

AUGUST 16 LEO • The heart of the zodiac

July 22 at 11:00 P.M. to August 23 at 6:00 A.M. • NUMEROLOGY 7

Possessions and Desires . . .

Gem: Ruby—This stone may lead you to energy, friendship, and happiness.
Flower: Butterfly Orchid—You tend to be a very happy person.
Astral Color, Color Need, Apparel Color: Your Astral Color is Red, which enhances passion, power, excitement, and strength. Orange in your environment gives you confidence. In your wardrobe, Plum brings out the best in your looks.
Fragrance: Surround yourself with the most romantic flowers you can find such as roses, lilies, and violets. The lavish scents will give an added boost to your enthusiasm.
Tree: Sycamore—Yours is the ability to love, communicate honestly with others, and have lasting relationships.
Instrument: Harp
Composer: Brahms
Bird: Skylark—This handsome bird is beautiful when it sings. It always whistles as it works.
Symbol: Heart—You are enthusiastic, empathetic, and full of generosity and love.

Harmonious Health and Nutrition . . .

Health Scent: Jasmine—This scent may make you more easygoing when you are stressed.
Favorable Foods: Radishes, figs, whole oats, red meat, buttermilk

What's Lucky . . .

Lucky Numbers: 8, 9, 61
Best Months: January and October
Best Day of the Week: Sunday
Best Month Days: 6, 15, 24
Lucky Charm: An old key.
Harmonious Signs for Relationships and Partnerships: Sagittarius and Aries

Spiritual Guides . . .

Star: Al Zubra—Those with this star fear punishment they don't deserve.
Angel: Verchiel—This angel enhances our ability to enjoy what life offers and gives much luck in legal dealings.
Guardian Angel: Raphael—This angel attends to all of your needs when you are looking for guidance.
Spiritual Stone: Amethyst—This stone is thought to be a mood stabilizer and balances the emotions.

✶ JUDITH'S INSIGHT ✶

Others may see you as a handful, but you are actually very kind, funny, and generous. Born with the gift to entertain, you make a great host, party planner, or caterer. You may even go into the entertainment business. But if you choose a more "serious" profession, such as law, you will give impassioned speeches and presentations. Regardless of what career you choose, there will have to be some thrill or notoriety involved.

You tend to want a "good time" and don't always understand when things go wrong in love relationships. This could be problematic, and a lot of the time, you're the source of the complications. It upsets you when your mate changes moods. When your partner is easygoing, you enjoy that; but if things get tough, you head for the hills. Try and keep yourself centered. Put yourself in your mate's shoes; you may be a bit more understanding.

Not everyone is born with such high intellect as you. Your instincts and intuition are natural, and you should try to follow them. More often than not, they're right on the money. Smart as you are, you will need to find a career that provides enough challenge to interest you. Your life's lesson: practice patience.

✶ ✶ ✶

AUGUST 17   LEO • The heart of the zodiac

July 22 at 11:00 P.M. to August 23 at 6:00 A.M. • NUMEROLOGY 8

Possessions and Desires . . .

Gem: Ruby—This stone may lead you to energy, friendship, and happiness.

Flower: Pear—You may express your affections too frequently.

Astral Color, Color Need, Apparel Color: Your Astral Color is Red, which enhances passion, power, excitement, and strength. Orange in your environment gives you confidence. In your wardrobe, Purple reflects your giving personality and brings you luck.

Fragrance: Surround yourself with the most romantic flowers you can find such as roses, lilies, and violets. The lavish scents will give an added boost to your enthusiasm.

Tree: Pine—Your relationships tend to be harmonious, both emotionally and mentally.

Instrument: Cello

Composer: Mozart

Bird: Skylark—This handsome bird is beautiful when it sings. It always whistles as it works.

Symbol: Wings—You are the source of balance in your world—this will bring you contentment.

Harmonious Health and Nutrition . . .

Health Scent: Almond—This scent may revitalize you and open you to greater possibilities.

Favorable Foods: Cabbage, sour plums, barley, red meat, buttermilk

What's Lucky . . .

Lucky Numbers: 8, 17, 22
Best Months: January and October
Best Day of the Week: Sunday
Best Month Days: 8, 17, 26
Lucky Charm: Red ribbon in your wallet or doorway
Harmonious Signs for Relationships and Partnerships: Sagittarius and Aries

Spiritual Guides . . .

Star: Al Gieba—The lucky born with this star are treated like royalty.

Angel: Verchiel—This angel enhances our ability to enjoy what life offers and gives much luck in legal dealings.

Guardian Angel: Seraphim—An angel that brings love, light, and passion.

Spiritual Stone: Amethyst—This stone is thought to be a mood stabilizer and balances the emotions.

✴ JUDITH'S INSIGHT ✴

Consistent and persistent . . . you could win awards! You have a strong mind and strong views and spend a great deal of time trying to convince others of your way of thinking. You are impulsive, intuitive, and (at times) authoritative; should you give up on school, your natural intelligence more than makes up for it. You're highly energetic, but look for ways to corral that verve. You're better off when you're in control.

When it comes to love, because you're so giving, people could take advantage of you. Often they see your strength, but you may hide how much you really take on. You are loyal in every way, and your family, friends, and lovers all tend to lean on you. Be careful of emotional obstacles that could cause you heartache.

Career is more important to you than you think, and you may wind up later in life at a job you only dreamed of as a youth. You may take on a hobby and, later on, make it your career. Someone you know may help you land a job. People like you, and things seem like they're handed to you. .Be sure to get the recognition you deserve for the work you do.

From clergyperson to salesperson, business manager to teacher, no matter what job you do, it must have a creative or artistic outlet of some kind.

★ ★ ★

AUGUST 18

LEO • The heart of the zodiac

July 22 at 11:00 P.M to August 23 at 6:00 A.M. • NUMEROLOGY 9

Possessions and Desires . . .

Gem: Ruby—This stone may lead you to energy, friendship, and happiness.

Flower: Blue Periwinkle—You are in harmony with nature.

Astral Color, Color Need, Apparel Color: Your Astral Color is Red, which enhances passion, power, excitement, and strength. Orange in your environment gives you confidence. In your wardrobe, Green is your power color for overcoming obstacles.

Fragrance: Surround yourself with the most romantic flowers you can find such as roses, lilies, and violets. The lavish scents will give an added boost to your enthusiasm.

Tree: Holly—Beware that you are not carried away by your passionate nature. The only way to grow is to be open to new experiences.

Instruments: Violin, tympanum

Composer: Gluck

Bird: Skylark—This handsome bird is beautiful when it sings. It always whistles as it works.

Symbol: Heart—You are enthusiastic, empathetic, and full of generosity and love.

Harmonious Health and Nutrition . . .

Health Scent: Lavender—This scent might lead others to trust you and make you patient.

Favorable Foods: Watercress, apples, rice bran, red meat, buttermilk

What's Lucky . . .

Lucky Numbers: 8, 9, 99
Best Months: January and October
Best Day of the Week: Sunday
Best Month Days: 9, 18, 27
Lucky Charm: A U.S. coin or a bill of any amount from the year you were born.

Harmonious Signs for Relationships and Partnerships: Sagittarius and Aries

Spiritual Guides . . .

Star: Al Gieba—The lucky born with this star are treated like royalty.

Angel: Verchiel—This angel enhances our ability to enjoy what life offers and gives much luck in legal dealings.

Guardian Angel: Gabriel—"God is my strength."

Spiritual Stone: Amethyst—This stone is thought to be a mood stabilizer and balances the emotions.

✷ JUDITH'S INSIGHT ✷

You have style, charm, and a great sense of humor. You tend to look for the unusual and may be drawn to exotic things or perhaps live in another country. You may simply create an atmosphere that stands out as different from everybody else's. Get used to extravagance! You love it and grow into it as you mature.

Some see you as eccentric and strange, though this is not the case. You like unusual things around you; you dare to be different. You're one of those gifted people who succeed at almost everything they try. Watch your energy levels—they could be erratic and drive people crazy. In love, you go through many flirtations and affairs of the heart because you tend to fall in love with your friends. Avoid feelings of entrapment in relationships by waiting until later to settle down. Your ambition makes you a controller, and this can get in the way, especially during intimacy.

Fine things in life appeal to you. You love the theater, arts, and travel. High-quality taste may bring high-quality desires. Somewhere along the way, you do take your chances with others around the world by traveling.

The perfect career would be in the theater, but that may not come to you.

✷ ✷ ✷

AUGUST 19

LEO • The heart of the zodiac

July 22 at 11:00 P.M. to August 23 at 6:00 A.M. • NUMEROLOGY 1

Possessions and Desires . . .

Gem: Agate—This stone may promote health and lead you to a long life.

Flower: Pimpernel—You usually like a life of constant change.

Astral Color, Color Need, Apparel Color: Your Astral Color is Red, which enhances passion, power, excitement, and strength. Orange in your environment gives you confidence. In your wardrobe, Plum brings out the best in your looks.

Fragrance: Surround yourself with the most romantic flowers you can find such as roses, lilies, and violets. The lavish scents will give an added boost to your enthusiasm.

Tree: Walnut—You are unusually helpful and aways looking for new beginnings.

Instruments: Oboe, flute, clarinet, piano, French horn, organ, piccolo

Composer: Böhm

Bird: Warbling Parakeet—the most beautiful of all birds, known as the love bird. It does seem to have the powers of imitation.

Symbol: Crown—the universal sign of dignity.

Harmonious Health and Nutrition . . .

Health Scent: Strawberry—Soothing by nature, the strawberry promotes self-esteem and encourages love.

Favorable Foods: Spinach, grapefruit, whole oats, red meat, buttermilk

What's Lucky . . .

Lucky Numbers: 8, 9, 91
Best Months: January and October
Best Day of the Week: Sunday
Best Month Days: 1, 10, 19, 28
Lucky Charm: A new penny in your shoe.

Harmonious Signs for Relationships and Partnerships: Sagittarius and Aries

Spiritual Guides . . .

Star: Al Gieba—The lucky born with this star are treated like royalty.

Angel: Verchiel—This angel enhances our ability to enjoy what life offers and gives much luck in legal dealings.

Guardian Angel: Malachi—"Messenger of Jehovah."

Spiritual Stone: Amethyst—This stone is thought to be a mood stabilizer and balances the emotions.

✶ JUDITH'S INSIGHT ✶

Versatility is your middle name. Few tasks exist that you cannot tackle and master. You always look for symmetry in your life, and organization to you spells H-A-R-M-O-N-Y. Your life is neatly arranged. Your passions run to the extreme, and you push yourself to your physical limits. Watch out for exhaustion causing health problems.

You are capable of seeing the talent in others, and sports or coaching should interest you. You are likely to be a workaholic, but then "extreme" is a theme throughout your life. Be careful of overindulging in any area. Quite the shopper, you look for oddities and unusual things. Your job may satisfy your appetite for the unconventional.

Your desire for love brings out the best in you, though it may take time to find that special someone. You may have to kiss a few toads, but when you least expect it and stop trying, you'll turn around one day and notice the perfect partner who was there all along. Romance and spontaneity must be important to your spouse.

Your life's lesson: take time to stop and smell the roses. Living near the water may inspire you.

✶ ✶ ✶

AUGUST 20

LEO • The heart of the zodiac

July 22 at 11:00 P.M. to August 23 at 6:00 A.M. • NUMEROLOGY 2

Possessions and Desires . . .

Gem: Ruby—This stone may lead you to energy, friendship, and happiness.

Flower: Crowfoot—You may want to try to be more grateful to others for their generosity.

Astral Color, Color Need, Apparel Color: Your Astral Color is Red, which enhances passion, power, excitement, and strength. Orange in your environment gives you confidence. In your wardrobe, Purple reflects your giving personality and brings you luck.

Fragrance: Surround yourself with the most romantic flowers you can find such as roses, lilies, and violets. The lavish scents will give an added boost to your enthusiasm.

Tree: Maple—You have both great stability and flashes of intuition.

Instruments: Pipe organ, cymbal, drum

Composers: Handel, Johann Sebastian Bach

Bird: Skylark—This handsome bird is beautiful when it sings. It always whistles as it works.

Symbol: Cross—the symbol of self-sacrifice and reconciliation.

Harmonious Health and Nutrition . . .

Health Scent: Apple—You are creative, full of joy, and nearly magical. You bring happiness.

Favorable Foods: Lima beans, pomegranates, rice bran, red meat, buttermilk

What's Lucky . . .

Lucky Numbers: 2, 8, 9
Best Months: January and October
Best Day of the Week: Sunday
Best Month Days: 2, 11, 20, 29

Lucky Charms: Two 50-cent pieces. Give someone else one of them.

Harmonious Signs for Relationships and Partnerships: Sagittarius and Aries

Spiritual Guides . . .

Star: Al Serpha—This star makes special things happen in one's life.

Angel: Verchiel—This angel enhances our ability to enjoy what life offers and gives much luck in legal dealings.

Guardian Angel: St. John—This angel simplifies that which is complicated.

Spiritual Stone: Amethyst—This stone is thought to be a mood stabilizer and balances the emotions.

✳ JUDITH'S INSIGHT ✳

Brilliant and capable, you could do anything you set your mind to. A bit extreme at times, check your tendencies to spend too much, give too much, eat too much . . . get the picture? Socially, others find you inspiring, and somewhere along the way, opportunities will present themselves through your many friends.

Drawn to art, music, literature, or drama, you love the theater and movies. A terrific communicator, you may find in yourself a desire to write a book, a play, or perhaps a newspaper article. Learn to trust your intuition more—yours is exceptional. Your personality is magnanimous, attracting others to you. Be careful who you let into your life. When it comes to relationships, people expect you to have few faults. Surprise—you are not perfect, and you know it. However, this may be difficult for others to accept. In love and in business, you work better with a partner. Take your time choosing the right ones.

✶ ✶ ✶

AUGUST 21

LEO • The heart of the zodiac

July 22 at 11:00 P.M. to August 23 at 6:00 A.M. • NUMEROLOGY 3

Possessions and Desires . . .

Gem: Ruby—This stone may lead you to energy, friendship, and happiness.

Flower: Cuckooflower—Your passions run as hot as a candle flame and are just as easily extinguished.

Astral Color, Color Need, Apparel Color: Your Astral Color is Red, which enhances passion, power, excitement, and strength. Orange in your environment gives you confidence. In your wardrobe, Green is your power color for overcoming obstacles.

Fragrance: Surround yourself with the most romantic flowers you can find such as roses, lilies, and violets. The lavish scents will give an added boost to your enthusiasm.

Tree: Elm—You have willpower, strength, and the ability to stand alone.

Instrument: Trombone

Composers: Verdi, Mendelssohn, Schumann

Bird: Skylark—This handsome bird is beautiful when it sings. It always whistles as it works.

Symbol: Wreath—You have been crowned with a special personality. You are strong but extremely compassionate.

Harmonious Health and Nutrition . . .

Health Scent: Rose—This scent will lead you to passionate thoughts and make you feel warm inside.

Favorable Foods: Sprouts, black figs, barley, red meat, buttermilk

What's Lucky . . .

Lucky Numbers: 8, 9, 12
Best Months: January and October
Best Day of the Week: Sunday

Best Month Days: 3, 12, 21, 30
Lucky Charm: A pen that someone else has already used.
Harmonious Signs for Relationships and Partnerships: Sagittarius and Aries

Spiritual Guides . . .

Star: Al Zubra—Those with this star fear punishment they don't deserve.

Angel: Verchiel—This angel enhances our ability to enjoy what life offers and gives much luck in legal dealings.

Guardian Angel: St. Thomas—This angel brings affection from others and encourages you in all that you do.

Spiritual Stone: Amethyst—This stone is thought to be a mood stabilizer and balances the emotions.

✶ JUDITH'S INSIGHT ✶

Whether you're the boss or not, you should be. You are a highly responsive person who can take on tons of responsibility. People recognize this, so they tend to heap it on. Fortunately, you can take it, but taking on too much at one time will drain your enthusiasm. Watch out for feeling sorry for yourself. You may be pushed into a corner, feel trapped, and then complain about it. Whether it's in love, at work, or with your family, learn to ease up on yourself and listen to your inner voice. Saying No is not the end of the world.

You are a great friend and could enjoy a counseling career, such as law or therapy. Because you accomplish everything you try, you may have more than one career in your lifetime. Anything to do with investigating or research finds you breathless with excitement. Look for careers that exploit this inclination.

Family plays a large role in your life. There, too, you must watch out for extremes.

✶ ✶ ✶

AUGUST 22   LEO • The heart of the zodiac

July 22 at 11:00 P.M. to August 23 at 6:00 A.M. • NUMEROLOGY 4

Possessions and Desires . . .

Gem: Agate—This stone may promote health and lead you to a long life.

Flower: Currant—You should guard against spending too much time feeling depressed.

Astral Color, Color Need, Apparel Color: Your Astral Color is Red, which enhances passion, power, excitement, and strength. Orange in your environment gives you confidence. In your wardrobe, Plum brings out the best in your looks.

Fragrance: Surround yourself with the most romantic flowers you can find such as roses, lilies, and violets. The lavish scents will give an added boost to your enthusiasm.

Tree: Cherry—You will find yourself faced with constant new emotional awakenings.

Instruments: Bass, clarinet

Composers: Haydn, Wagner

Bird: Skylark—This handsome bird is beautiful when it sings. It always whistles as it works.

Symbol: Star—You are full of inner brightness and will stand out in any crowd. You will be seen as special.

Harmonious Health and Nutrition . . .

Health Scent: Vanilla—This scent will fill you with a feeling of cleanliness and stability.

Favorable Foods: Cabbage, raspberries, barley, red meat, buttermilk

What's Lucky . . .

Lucky Numbers: 8, 9, 32
Best Months: January and October
Best Day of the Week: Sunday

Best Month Days: 4, 13, 22, 31
Lucky Charm: A piece of material cut from something in your home.
Harmonious Signs for Relationships and Partnerships: Sagittarius and Aries

Spiritual Guides . . .

Star: Al Serpha—This star makes special things happen in one's life.

Angel: Verchiel—This angel enhances our ability to enjoy what life offers and gives much luck in legal dealings.

Guardian Angel: Uriel—This angel brings the light of God's guidance.

Spiritual Stone: Amethyst—This stone is thought to be a mood stabilizer and balances the emotions.

✶ JUDITH'S INSIGHT ✶

You live by the seat of your pants and love it. Everything you try is a breeze. You accept help only when you are able to give too. Love means everything to you, and you're willing to work at your relationship. Your mate must champion you and your undertakings, and a sense of humor is mandatory. As long as your partner understands you, your love life will flourish.

Reading and writing don't seem to interest you as much as an uncanny knack for details. Sometimes coworkers misinterpret your giving acts. Even friends can misunderstand you—they don't always appreciate your sunny, selfless disposition.

Material possessions are important to you, and you surround yourself with things. Make sure you don't clutter yourself right out of your room.

✶ ✶ ✶

AUGUST 23 LEO • The heart of the zodiac
August 23 at 6:00 A.M. to September 23 at 3:00 A.M. • NUMEROLOGY 5

Possessions and Desires . . .

Gem: Ruby—This stone may lead you to energy, friendship, and happiness.
Flower: Daffodil—You may need to strengthen your self-regard.
Astral Color, Color Need, Apparel Color: Your Astral Color is Red, which enhances passion, power, excitement, and strength. Orange in your environment gives you confidence. In your wardrobe, Purple reflects your giving personality and brings you luck.
Fragrance: Surround yourself with the most romantic flowers you can find such as roses, lilies, and violets. The lavish scents will give an added boost to your enthusiasm.
Tree: Apple—You are creative, full of joy, and nearly magical. You bring happiness.
Instruments: Viola, trumpet
Composer: Liszt
Bird: Warbling Parakeet—the most beautiful of all birds, know as the love bird. It does seem to have the powers of imitation.
Symbol: Triangle—You have the right combination of abilities.

Harmonious Health and Nutrition . . .

Health Scent: Peach—This scent may balance your good qualities so that they equal your charm.
Favorable Foods: Cucumbers, limes, whole oats, red meat, buttermilk

What's Lucky . . .

Lucky Numbers: 8, 9, 32
Best Months: January and October
Best Day of the Week: Sunday
Best Month Days: 5, 4, 23
Lucky Charms: A rabbit's foot or a white candle.
Harmonious Signs for Relationships and Partnerships: Sagittarius and Aries

Spiritual Guides . . .

Star: Al Serpha—This star makes special things happen in one's life.
Angel: Verchiel—This angel enhances our ability to enjoy what life offers and gives much luck in legal dealings.
Guardian Angel: St. Thomas—This angel brings affection from others and encourages you in all that you do.
Spiritual Stone: Amethyst—This stone is thought to be a mood stabilizer and balances the emotions.

✴ JUDITH'S INSIGHT ✴

Get out of your own way. You have talent and energy enough for two. You love to entertain and be entertained. So long as you're the center of attention, things are just fine by you. This may take you a lifetime to recognize. You have a strong devotion toward family, though they may misunderstand your actions at times.

You dress impeccably and have a flair for fashion. Look for a career in retail or the beauty industry. Even if you don't work in the beauty business, you always look like you do. High aims and aspirations lead you into great responsibility.

When it comes to love, allow yourself just enough freedom. You bring on attention and flattery, but you spot the phonies a mile away. You may have a volatile relationship, but you are mostly devoted to your spouse or partner, and you would do anything to keep things from coming apart. You make a great friend as well.

Be sure to keep an eye on finances—sometimes you give away more than you should. For some reason, you may be secretive about money, always hiding something away for a rainy day. Life's hurdles will present themselves, but you take them on and clear them like a trained athlete.

✶ ✶ ✶

AUGUST 24
VIRGO • The festivities and celebrations of the zodiac
August 23 at 6:00 A.M. to September 23 at 3:00 A.M. • NUMEROLOGY 6

Possessions and Desires . . .

Gem: Jasper—This stone could grant the bearer protection from sadness.
Flower: Dahlia—You may crave stability in all situations.
Astral Color, Color Need, Apparel Color: Your Astral Color is Navy Blue—the color of style and refinement. Violet in your environment keeps you empathetic toward others. In your wardrobe, Green is your power color for overcoming obstacles.
Fragrance: Try never to mix scents. Purchase your products all from the same company so your environment will be clean and harmonious.
Tree: Palm—You tend to be very healthy and creative.
Instruments: Tambourine, lyre
Composer: Schubert
Bird: Stork—Turkish bird, held in high esteem the world over. This bird is intelligent but may have strange tendencies.
Symbol: Crescent—You are more likely to be influenced by the phases of the moon. Your easygoing manner leads you to peaceful situations.

Harmonious Health and Nutrition . . .

Health Scent: Orange Blossom—This scent may balance your body, mind, and soul.
Favorable Foods: Asparagus, strawberries, molasses, beef, cottage cheese

What's Lucky . . .

Lucky Numbers: 3, 5, 42
Best Months: February and November
Best Day of the Week: Wednesday
Best Month Days: 6, 15, 24

Lucky Charms: A religious token or card from any religion.
Harmonious Signs for Relationships and Partnerships: Capricorn and Taurus

Spiritual Guides . . .

Star: Al Awa—Those with this star are often objects of others' desire.
Angel: Hamaliel—This angel governs logic and shows us what is real. His lessons in personal ethics always improve our karma.
Guardian Angel: Michael—"Who is like God."
Spiritual Stone: Jasper—This stone may soothe bruised emotions.

✷ JUDITH'S INSIGHT ✷

If you would just learn patience, everything will come to your door. Be sure to recognize when someone is knocking. One step at a time, especially in love, is the best approach for you. People are devoted to you, and half the time you don't even know it. Try to take the time to enjoy yourself more; otherwise your negativity can get the best of you.

Your very good mind makes you hungry for knowledge. An avid reader and traveler, you should think less about trying things and just try them. Sometimes you think yourself right out of an idea. You are a great worker; it takes a lot to tire you out. You'd make a good writer or communicator of some kind. Politics and, yes, firefighting may tempt you. Again, you may spend too much time thinking about career and not enough time doing what you really want.

Your sweet soul makes you an understanding parent and good partner. Sometimes you play too hard in love and don't always reveal your inner thoughts. Try using those terrific communication skills in your relationship. Your partner will appreciate it.

✷ ✷ ✷

AUGUST 25   VIRGO • The festivities and celebrations of the zodiac
August 23 at 6:00 A.M. to September 23 at 3:00 A.M. • NUMEROLOGY 7

Possessions and Desires . . .

Gem: Hyacinth—This stone might aid the memory.

Flower: Sweet Flag—If you don't follow your own sense of honor don't expect to ever be honored.

Astral Color, Color Need, Apparel Color: Your Astral Color is Navy Blue—the color of style and refinement. Violet in your environment keeps you empathetic toward others. In your wardrobe, Light Blue gives you strength and determination.

Fragrance: Try never to mix scents. Purchase your products all from the same company so your environment will be clean and harmonious.

Tree: Sycamore—Yours is the ability to love, communicate honestly with others, and have lasting relationships.

Instrument: Harp

Composers: Gluck, Brahms

Bird: Killdeer—This bird is usually found consorting with other species, and can adapt to any environment.

Symbol: Heart—You are enthusiastic, empathetic, and full of generosity and love.

Harmonious Health and Nutrition . . .

Health Scent: Jasmine—This scent may make you more easygoing when you are stressed.

Favorable Foods: Peas, huckleberries, chocolate, oysters, eggs

What's Lucky . . .

Lucky Numbers: 3, 5, 26
Best Months: February and November
Best Day of the Week: Wednesday
Best Month Days: 6, 15, 24

Lucky Charm: An old key.
Harmonious Signs for Relationships and Partnerships: Capricorn and Taurus

Spiritual Guides . . .

Star: Sumak al Azel—Those with this star are called upon to serve.

Angel: Hamaliel—This angel governs logic and shows us what is real. His lessons in personal ethics always improve our karma.

Guardian Angel: Raphael—This angel attends to all of your needs when you are looking for guidance.

Spiritual Stone: Jasper—This stone may soothe bruised emotions.

✳ JUDITH'S INSIGHT ✳

Anyone who is as generous, funny, and energetic as you is bound to be a handful at times. You know how to party and have a good time. With that, there's this shy side, though most people see you as the comedian. You may want to attempt a career in entertainment, if not on stage, then on the business end. You may attempt writing a screenplay.

Your instincts seem good, and although your heart may say one thing, your levelheaded reason keeps you from making mistakes. It may take time for find that special someone. When you recognize love, your heart is open and you let it in. That is not to say you won't have your share of headaches. The friends and family who give you the most devotion are the ones you give back to. You need only a few close friends around you, and that seems to work fine.

Life's ups and downs don't seem to dampen your stylish approach to things. A class act, really, you will have your share of opportunities, but it may take a long time before you recognize what they are.

✷ ✷ ✷

AUGUST 26

VIRGO • The festivities and celebrations of the zodiac

August 23 at 6:00 A.M. to September 23 at 3:00 A.M. • NUMEROLOGY 8

Possessions and Desires . . .

Gem: Jasper—This stone could grant the bearer protection from sadness.

Flower: Everlasting—What you love you tend to love forever.

Astral Color, Color Need, Apparel Color: Your Astral Color is Navy Blue—the color of style and refinement. Violet in your environment keeps you empathetic toward others. In your wardrobe, Green is your power color for overcoming obstacles.

Fragrance: Look for those classic scents that give you the feeling of freshness and sparkling clean, scents containing jasmine, ylang ylang, and roses.

Tree: Pine—Your relationships tend to be harmonious, both emotionally and mentally.

Instrument: Cello

Composer: Mozart

Bird: Cuckoo—A good flyer and very seldom a quitter. Many seem more independent than they actually are; yearn for more nurturing than one would expect.

Symbol: Wings—You are the source of balance in your world—this will bring you contentment.

Harmonious Health and Nutrition . . .

Health Scent: Almond—This scent may revitalize you and open you to greater possibilities.

Favorable Foods: Peas, huckleberries, chocolate, oysters, eggs

What's Lucky . . .

Lucky Numbers: 3, 5, 62

Best Months: February and November

Best Day of the Week: Wednesday

Best Month Days: 8, 17, 26

Lucky Charm: Red ribbon in your wallet or doorway.

Harmonious Signs for Relationships and Partnerships: Capricorn and Taurus

Spiritual Guides . . .

Star: Al Awa—Those with this star are often objects of others' desire.

Angel: Hamaliel—This angel governs logic and shows us what is real. His lessons in personal ethics always improve our karma.

Guardian Angel: Seraphim—An angel that brings love, light, and passion.

Spiritual Stone: Jasper—This stone may soothe bruised emotions.

✳ JUDITH'S INSIGHT ✳

You are never at a loss for words; it would be surprising were you not to do something with language. Conscientious to a fault, you get irritated with opinionated, controlling people. Somehow you put people at ease, make a good friend, and certainly know how to keep a secret.

You're far-sighted and intuitive, even psychic, and would do well with anything involving books, publishing, editing, or writing. No matter what the job, business will be good to you. Your flair for detail may lead you to designing, whether it be flower arrangements or landscapes. Science is another possibility. Searching for answers and mystery fascinate you. Computers may interest you.

Sometimes you can be too fussy with people and should learn to give out those necessary pats on the back. You don't necessarily need the spotlight, but you could be the one in charge of directing it.

✳ ✳ ✳

Possessions and Desires . . .

Gem: Jasper—This stone could grant the bearer protection from sadness.

Flower: Filbert—You may constantly find yourself reconnecting with those you care about.

Astral Color, Color Need, Apparel Color: Your Astral Color is Navy Blue—the color of style and refinement. Violet in your environment keeps you empathetic toward others. In your wardrobe, Light Blue gives you strength and determination.

Fragrance: Look for those classic scents that give you the feeling of freshness and sparkling clean scents containing jasmine, ylang ylang, and roses.

Tree: Holly—Beware that you are not carried away by your passionate nature. The only way to grow is to be open to new experiences.

Instruments: Violin, tympanum

Composer: Gluck

Bird: Goldfinch—These gentle creatures can seem moody, especially in unsettled weather.

Symbol: Anchor—This tranquil symbol signifies stability and strength, and stands for strong commitments in relationships.

Harmonious Health and Nutrition . . .

Health Scent: Strawberry—Soothing by nature, the strawberry promotes self-esteem and encourages love.

Favorable Foods: Mushrooms, pineapple, raw sugar, liver, buttermilk

What's Lucky . . .

Lucky Numbers: 3, 5, 28

Best Months: February and November

Best Day of the Week: Wednesday

Best Month Days: 9, 18, 27

Lucky Charms: A U.S. coin or a bill of any amount from the year you were born.

Harmonious Signs for Relationships and Partnerships: Capricorn and Taurus

Spiritual Guides . . .

Star: Al Awa—Those with this star are often objects of others' desire.

Angel: Hamaliel—This angel governs logic and shows us what is real. His lessons in personal ethics always improve our karma.

Guardian Angel: Gabriel—"God is my strength."

Spiritual Stone: Jasper—This stone may soothe bruised emotions.

✶ JUDITH'S INSIGHT ✶

Fond of travel, a lover of music, you are a fine judge of paintings and recognize good work. You could be an art critic. Determination and extravagance seem to polarize you. You're extremely emotional, but others see you as strong. You're drawn to unusual relationships, so a long-distance love affair may work for you. Maintaining friendships comes easily to you—you seem to hang on to them forever. In love relationships, however, once you've made that commitment, you have a tendency to feel trapped. Your ambitious nature requires a good deal of freedom. Unless your mate knows this and respects it, problems could arise.

You're a classy, sharp dresser and look rich in the way you present yourself (even if you're not). Sometimes you get anxious because you think too much and overstep your mark, but this is all self-inflicted and can be worked on.

✶ ✶ ✶

AUGUST 28

VIRGO • The festivities and celebrations of the zodiac

August 23 at 6:00 A.M. to September 23 at 3:00 A.M. • NUMEROLOGY 1

Possessions and Desires . . .

Gem: Jasper—This stone could grant the bearer protection from sadness.

Flower: Flax—You are comfortable letting the universe guide you where it wants you to go.

Astral Color, Color Need, Apparel Color: Your Astral Color is Navy Blue—the color of style and refinement. Violet in your environment keeps you empathetic toward others. In your wardrobe, Green is your power color for overcoming obstacles.

Fragrance: Look for those classic scents that give you the feeling of freshness and sparkling clean scents containing jasmine, ylang ylang, and roses.

Tree: Walnut—You are unusually helpful and always looking for constant changes in your life.

Instruments: Oboe, flute, clarinet, piano, French horn, organ, piccolo

Composer: Böhm

Bird: Robin—the most sociable of all birds, with the ability to create quick friendships. It also can easily adapt to any home. When it wants something, it has the tendency to try to snatch it.

Symbol: Crown—the universal sign of dignity.

Harmonious Health and Nutrition . . .

Health Scent: Strawberry—Soothing by nature, the strawberry promotes self-esteem and encourages love.

Favorable Foods: Turnips, cranberries, molasses, beef, goat's milk

What's Lucky . . .

Lucky Numbers: 3, 5, 10
Best Months: February and November
Best Day of the Week: Wednesday
Best Month Days: 1, 10, 19, 28

Lucky Charm: A new penny in your shoe.
Harmonious Signs for Relationships and Partnerships: Capricorn and Taurus

Spiritual Guides . . .

Star: Sumak al Azel—Those with this star are called upon to serve.

Angel: Hamaliel—This angel governs logic and shows us what is real. His lessons in personal ethics always improve our karma.

Guardian Angel: Malachi—"Messenger of Jehovah."

Spiritual Stone: Jasper—This stone may soothe bruised emotions.

✷ JUDITH'S INSIGHT ✷

Your versatility makes you desirable. A lover of music and art, you have a lot of energy and a terrific mind, even if you may not have the degree to back it up. Striving for the more materialistic things in life or dealing with the sadder issues of life will drain you of all of your energies. You can go from compassion and advocacy for the downtrodden to cocktail parties with the rich and famous with equal contentment. Your energy and enthusiasm will take you places. A more loyal friend or family loved one is difficult to find.

Your deep desire for love will bring it right to you. Sometimes, however, your choices are made with blinders on. The need for romance is strong, and you require lots of spontaneity.

You are a classic workaholic; a nine to five job is fine, but you may devote yourself to other endeavors three times more. Journalism and publishing as well as music and theater all appeal to your creative nature. There will be very few jobs you take on that you don't master, if any.

Your energy levels and drive toward perfection usually take you in a positive direction.

✷ ✷ ✷

AUGUST 29

VIRGO • The festivities and celebrations of the zodiac

August 23 at 6:00 A.M. to September 23 at 3:00 A.M. • NUMEROLOGY 2

Possessions and Desires . . .

Gem: Hyacinth—This stone might aid the memory.

Flower: Flower-of-an-hour—You usually see the beauty in the smallest things that others tend to overlook.

Astral Color, Color Need, Apparel Color: Your Astral Color is Navy Blue—the color of style and refinement. Violet in your environment keeps you empathetic toward others. In your wardrobe, Light Blue gives you strength and determination.

Fragrance: Look for those classic scents that give you the feeling of freshness and sparkling clean scents containing jasmine, ylang ylang, and roses.

Tree: Maple—You have both great stability and flashes of intuition.

Instruments: Pipe organ, cymbal, drum

Composers: Handel, Johann Sebastian Bach

Bird: Stork—Turkish bird, held in high esteem the world over. This bird is intelligent but may have strange tendencies.

Symbol: Cross—the symbol of self-sacrifice and reconciliation.

Harmonious Health and Nutrition . . .

Health Scents: Apple—You are creative, full of joy, and nearly magical. You bring happiness.

Favorable Foods: Celery, strawberry, chocolate, chicken, cottage cheese

What's Lucky . . .

Lucky Numbers: 3, 5, 11

Best Months: February and November

Best Day of the Week: Wednesday

Best Month Days: 2, 11, 20, 29

Lucky Charms: Two 50-cent pieces. Give someone else one of them.

Harmonious Signs for Relationships and Partnerships: Capricorn and Taurus

Spiritual Guides . . .

Star: Al Awa—Those with this star are often objects of others' desire.

Angel: Hamaliel—This angel governs logic and shows us what is real. His lessons in personal ethics always improve our karma.

Guardian Angel: St. Thomas—This angel brings affection from others and encourages you in all that you do.

Spiritual Stone: Jasper—This stone may soothe bruised emotions.

✶ JUDITH'S INSIGHT ✶

Others see you as living in your own world—that's how original you are. Daring and fearless, adventure colors all your actions. Your personality alone will bring advancement into your life. Others are inspired just being around you. Career opportunities will fall at your feet.

Attention from prospective lovers comes easily. Your appearance is neat and distinguished. It takes you time to warm up to someone in order for you to feel comfortable. You demonstrate affection only when others show theirs for you.

You are drawn to a meticulous environment, whether it be work, school, or home life. A career as a builder or in an artistic field should appeal to you, so fond are you of the arts. Don't rule out a career that has something to do with water. Writing and journalism are both possibilities for you. Jobs always seem to come your way.

As unselfish and broad-minded as you are, almost everyone likes you. Your family is more proud of you than you believe. The biggest success comes with family and friends, with a business a close second.

✶ ✶ ✶

AUGUST 30 VIRGO • The festivities and celebrations of the zodiac

August 23 at 6:00 A.M. to September 23 at 3:00 A.M. • NUMEROLOGY 3

Possessions and Desires . . .

Gem: Jasper—This stone could grant the bearer protection from sadness.

Flower: Flowering Reed—You allow the universe to be your guide when it comes to finding happiness.

Astral Color, Color Need, Apparel Color: Your Astral Color is Navy Blue—the color of style and refinement. Violet in your environment keeps you empathetic toward others. In your wardrobe, Green is your power color for overcoming obstacles.

Fragrance: Look for those classic scents that give you the feeling of freshness and sparkling clean, scents containing Jasmine, ylang ylang, and roses.

Tree: Elm—You have willpower, strength, and the ability to stand alone.

Instrument: Trombone

Composers: Verdi, Mendelssohn, Schumann

Bird: Stork—Turkish bird, held in high esteem the world over. This bird is intelligent but may have strange tendencies.

Symbol: Wreath—You have been crowned with a special personality. You are strong but extremely compassionate.

Harmonious Health and Nutrition . . .

Health Scent: Rose—This scent will lead you to passionate thoughts and make you feel warm inside.

Favorable Foods: Sorrel, raspberries, raw sugar, fish, eggs

What's Lucky . . .

Lucky Numbers: 3, 5, 30
Best Months: February and November
Best Day of the Week: Wednesday

Best Month Days: 3, 12, 21, 30
Lucky Charm: A pen that someone else has already used.
Harmonious Signs for Relationships and Partnerships: Capricorn and Taurus

Spiritual Guides . . .

Star: Sumak al Azel—Those with this star are called upon to serve.

Angel: Hamaliel—This angel governs logic and shows us what is real. His lessons in personal ethics always improve our karma.

Guardian Angel: Johiel—This angel is a protector of all those with a humble heart.

Spiritual Stone: Jasper—This stone may soothe bruised emotions.

✳ JUDITH'S INSIGHT ✳

As responsible as you are, be careful of others taking advantage of you. You get more jobs than you know what to do with because everyone sees you as so capable. It may take time for your career to evolve. An intensely strong mind may lead you to research or writing or working with small, fine things. You have the physical presence to be an athlete or a physical therapist or both.

Overindulgence will be a problem for you. You will be tempted to do things you know are wrong for you. Try to resist those impulses.

A dear friend, you know how to keep a secret. You may enjoy practicing law or a career in law enforcement because of this tight-lipped quality. A bout or two with the law could shake things up. Make sure you are on the right side.

Family and romances are all fulfilling to you. Just try to be patient and don't rush into things. Everything can't happen overnight.

✳ ✳ ✳

AUGUST 31
VIRGO • The festivities and celebrations of the zodiac
August 23 at 6:00 A.M. to September 23 at 3:00 A.M. • NUMEROLOGY 4

Possessions and Desires ...

Gem: Emerald—Those who carry this stone tend to be lucky in love.
Flower: Foxglove—You may need to learn that sincerity will get you farther than empty flattery.
Astral Color, Color Need, Apparel Color: Your Astral Color is Navy Blue—the color of style and refinement. Violet in your environment keeps you empathetic toward others. In your wardrobe, Light Blue gives you strength and determination.
Fragrance: Try never to mix scents. Purchase your products all from the same company so your environment will be clean and harmonious.
Tree: Cherry—You will find yourself faced with constant new emotional awakenings.
Instruments: Bass, clarinet
Composers: Haydn, Wagner
Bird: Killdeer—This bird is usually found consorting with other species, and can adapt to any environment.
Symbol: Star—You are full of inner brightness and will stand out in any crowd. You will be seen as special.

Harmonious Health and Nutrition ...

Health Scent: Vanilla—This scent will fill you with a feeling of cleanliness and stability.
Favorable Foods: Brussels sprouts, prunes, molasses, liver, buttermilk

What's Lucky ...

Lucky Numbers: 3, 4, 5
Best Months: February and November
Best Day of the Week: Wednesday
Best Month Days: 4, 13, 22, 31
Lucky Charm: A piece of material cut from something in your home.

Harmonious Signs for Relationships and Partnerships: Capricorn and Taurus

Spiritual Guides ...

Star: Al Awa—Those with this star are often objects of others' desire.
Angel: Hamaliel—This angel governs logic and shows us what is real. His lessons in personal ethics always improve our karma.
Guardian Angel: Uriel—This angel brings the light of God's guidance.
Spiritual Stone: Jasper—This stone may soothe bruised emotions.

✶ JUDITH'S INSIGHT ✶

You want to be seen and heard, and you just might have your way. Most likely, it will be through writing of some kind or, possibly, music. You give your all, no matter what—you don't know any other way. Drawn to unusual places and people, you may travel a bit or even live abroad at one point in your life.

Patience and patience . . . that's the key in love. Sometimes you doubt another's affection simply because they have their mind on other things. You want and need a secure relationship, and someday you realize it's you who needs to feel secure in yourself. Giving too much or too little can overwhelm you and your partner. Shyness may be a problem for you at the beginning of a relationship.

Be careful to check your tendencies to overdo it, whether it be work or play. You are known to go to extremes, both good and bad. You may have to clear a few hurdles in your work life before you can relax and really perform, which you eventually do and do well. Later in your life is better—the second half of your life really takes off once you learn to stop taking things so personally.

✶ ✶ ✶

SEPTEMBER

SEPTEMBER 1 VIRGO • The festivities and celebrations of the zodiac
August 23 at 6:00 A.M. to September 23 at 3:00 A.M. • NUMEROLOGY 1

Possessions and Desires . . .

Gem: Jasper—This stone could grant the bearer protection from sadness.

Flower: Fumitory—You may spend too much time complaining about what can't be altered.

Astral Color, Color Need, Apparel Color: Your Astral Color is Navy Blue—the color of style and refinement. Violet in your environment keeps you empathetic toward others. In your wardrobe, Green is your power color for overcoming obstacles.

Fragrance: Look for those classic scents that give you the feeling of fresh and sparkling clean, scents containing jasmine, ylang ylang, and roses.

Tree: Cherry—You will find yourself faced with constant new emotional awakenings.

Instruments: Bass, clarinet

Composers: Haydn, Wagner

Bird: Stork—Turkish bird, held in high esteem the world over. This bird is intelligent but may have strange tendencies.

Symbol: Star—You are full of inner brightness and will stand out in any crowd. You will be seen as special.

Harmonious Health and Nutrition . . .

Health Scent: Strawberry—Soothing by nature, the strawberry promotes self-esteem and encourages love.

Favorable Foods: Watercress, raspberries, raw sugar, chicken, goat's milk

What's Lucky . . .

Lucky Numbers: 1, 3, 5
Best Months: February and November
Best Day of the Week: Wednesday
Best Month Days: 4, 13, 22, 31
Lucky Charm: A new penny in your shoe.

Harmonious Signs for Relationships and Partnerships: Capricorn and Taurus

Spiritual Guides . . .

Star: Al Awa—Those with this star are often objects of others' desire.

Angel: Hamaliel—This angel governs logic and shows us what is real. His lessons in personal ethics always improve our karma.

Guardian Angel: Malachi—"Messenger of Jehovah."

Spiritual Stone: Jasper—This stone may soothe bruised emotions.

✴ JUDITH'S INSIGHT ✴

You have unbelievable concentration as well as a well-balanced mind. You are mechanically inclined. You might be annoying to those around you because you constantly need everything in perfect order. You make friends easily, but some will pull away due to your frankness and impatience. It is possible to be *too* honest. You are loyal, comforting, and always there for your friends in their time of need.

You would do well in government jobs related to accounting. Maybe you could work for the IRS. If the word *audit* gives you chills, consider a career as a chef or restaurateur. Your impeccable organizational skills could be put to good use in acting, writing, directing, and, definitely, editing. You love to sing, though you may not be very good at it.

As you get older, losing your looks would be something you take very seriously. You are capital *V* Vain. When you're in love, you can be cloying because you look to your relationships to provide you with self-esteem—you need *constant* reassurance. You are loyal and faithful to your mate but overthink the union to the point your spouse will wonder if you have nothing but doubts. Realize your brain is way too active, and relax!

Financially, you do well and enjoy great success.

✴ ✴ ✴

SEPTEMBER 2

VIRGO • The festivities and celebrations of the zodiac

August 23 at 6:00 A.M. to September 23 at 3:00 A.M. • NUMEROLOGY 2

Possessions and Desires . . .

Gem: Jasper—This stone could grant the bearer protection from sadness.

Flower: Helenium—You may need to learn that letting tears go washes away the hurt more quickly than holding them in.

Astral Color, Color Need, Apparel Color: Your Astral Color is Navy Blue—the color of style and refinement. Violet in your environment keeps you empathetic toward others. In your wardrobe, Light Blue gives you strength and determination.

Fragrance: Look for those classic scents that give you the feeling of fresh and sparkling clean, scents containing jasmine, ylang ylang, and roses.

Tree: Maple—You have both great stability and flashes of intuition.

Instruments: Pipe organ, cymbal, drum

Composers: Handel, Johann Sebastian Bach

Bird: Goldfinch—These gentle creatures can seem moody, especially in unsettled weather.

Symbol: Cross—the symbol of self-sacrifice and reconciliation.

Harmonious Health and Nutrition . . .

Health Scent: Apple—A vivacious scent encouraging energy. Will help you to be more creative, intuitive, and positive.

Favorable Foods: Turnips, cherries, chocolate, beef, cottage cheese

What's Lucky . . .

Lucky Numbers: 3, 5, 11

Best Months: February and November

Best Day of the Week: Wednesday

Best Month Days: 2, 11, 20, 29

Lucky Charms: Two 50-cent pieces. Give someone else one of them.

Harmonious Signs for Relationships and Partnerships: Capricorn and Taurus

Spiritual Guides . . .

Star: Al Awa—Those with this star are often objects of others' desire.

Angel: Hamaliel—This angel governs logic and shows us what is real. His lessons in personal ethics always improve our karma.

Guardian Angel: St. John—This angel simplifies that which is complicated.

Spiritual Stone: Jasper—This stone may soothe bruised emotions.

✶ JUDITH'S INSIGHT ✶

You are trustworthy and conscientious in whatever you do, be it work, home life, or play. It's likely that you will work in a job that utilizes your mind, but you could be a professional athlete. The best of both worlds would be employment where you can sweat while you think and still be paid for it. You have a lifelong insatiable love of learning. It's too bad library cards don't accumulate frequent flyer miles! You soak knowledge up like a sponge. A strong desire for travel only enhances your thirst for knowledge. You are so curious you catch yourself eavesdropping on conversations in restaurants, on the bus, or at parties.

Temperamentally suited to work with nature, you'd make a very happy flower arranger, designer, gardener, or landscaper. Otherwise you may find yourself working with waterways, the ocean, or even—believe it or not—vitamins! (You're talented in science and chemistry.) Your sharp mind may lead you to consider journalism, editing, proofreading, or anchoring the evening news.

Your frankness could threaten many friendships. Aim at being less judgmental and feeling superior to others. Learn to notice how words affect people and measure your meaning against their interpretation. You can control this if you recognize it, for you are as loyal as they come. You enjoy fast responses to your romantic overtures, but when it comes to you and love, slower is better. If you're impatient, you had better formulate a quick escape route.

The person you believe in most should be you. Listen to your insights more often.

SEPTEMBER 3 VIRGO • The festivities and celebrations of the zodiac
August 23 at 6:00 A.M. to September 23 at 3:00 A.M. • NUMEROLOGY 3

Possessions and Desires . . .

Gem: Jasper—This stone could grant the bearer protection from sadness.

Flower: Hepatica—You tend to have enough self-confidence to fight your way through what you get yourself into.

Astral Color, Color Need, Apparel Color: Your Astral Color is Navy Blue—the color of style and refinement. Violet in your environment keeps you empathetic toward others. In your wardrobe, Green is your power color for overcoming obstacles.

Fragrance: Look for those classic scents that give you the feeling of fresh and sparkling clean, scents containing jasmine, ylang ylang, and roses.

Tree: Elm—You have willpower, strength, and the ability to stand alone.

Instrument: Trombone

Composers: Verdi, Mendelssohn, Schumann

Bird: Killdeer—This bird is usually found consorting with other species, and can adapt to any environment.

Symbol: Star—You are full of inner brightness and will stand out in any crowd. You will be seen as special.

Harmonious Health and Nutrition . . .

Health Scent: Rose—This scent will lead you to passionate thoughts and make you feel warm inside.

Favorable Foods: Peas, strawberry, molasses, liver, eggs

What's Lucky . . .

Lucky Numbers: 3, 5, 21
Best Months: February and November
Best Day of the Week: Wednesday
Best Month Days: 3, 12, 21, 30
Lucky Charm: A pen that someone else has already used.

Harmonious Signs for Relationships and Partnerships: Capricorn and Taurus

Spiritual Guides . . .

Star: Al Awa—Those with this star are often objects of others' desire.

Angel: Hamaliel—This angel governs logic and shows us what is real. His lessons in personal ethics always improve our karma.

Guardian Angel: Johiel—This angel is a protector of all those with a humble heart.

Spiritual Stone: Jasper—This stone may soothe bruised emotions.

✶ JUDITH'S INSIGHT ✶

You are excellent with details and designs. Though you may not have much interest in it, you could be a great decorator. Anything related to architecture, movie set design, engineering, or computer programming should appeal to you. It is imperative that you find a job that will send you home mentally exhausted, or your home life could be chaos.

You love constant change not only with your furniture but your body. New glasses, different hairstyle—the list is endless. Romance is another area where you always want something new. You may have at least one very important relationship that you choose to leave, later regret leaving, and then can never get back. You want stability, but you run from it like the wind.

As long as things are stimulating, you won't be bored. You know you have the ability to do just about anything. The reason every one calls you pushy and impatient is because, well, you are. You just don't suffer fools well. When you need to be, you can be kind, open-minded, and nurturing. If you take time to notice that other people have lives too, your heart goes out to them.

With very little effort but a lot of focus you can control any situation and effect change in your world. You can make things happen.

✶ ✶ ✶

SEPTEMBER 4 VIRGO • The festivities and celebrations of the zodiac

August 23 at 6:00 A.M. to September 23 at 3:00 A.M. • NUMEROLOGY 4

Possessions and Desires . . .

Gem: Jasper—This stone could grant the bearer protection from sadness.

Flower: Hoya—You may carve your place in the world through your sharp wits and hard work.

Astral Color, Color Need, Apparel Color: Your Astral Color is Navy Blue—the color of style and refinement. Violet in your environment keeps you empathetic towards others. In your wardrobe, Light Blue, gives you strength and determination.

Fragrance: Look for those classic scents that give you the feeling of fresh and sparkling clean, scents containing jasmine, ylang ylang, and roses.

Tree: Cherry—You will find yourself faced with constant new emotional awakenings.

Instruments: Bass, clarinet

Composers: Haydn, Wagner

Bird: Cuckoo—A good flyer and very seldom a quitter. Many seem more independent than they actually are; yearn for more nurturing than one would expect.

Symbol: Star—You are full of inner brightness and will stand out in any crowd. You will be seen as special.

Harmonious Health and Nutrition . . .

Health Scent: Vanilla—This scent will fill you with a feeling of cleanliness and stability.

Favorable Foods: Parsnips, peaches, raw sugar, fish, goat's milk

What's Lucky . . .

Lucky Numbers: 3, 5, 22
Best Months: February and November
Best Day of the Week: Wednesday
Best Month Days: 4, 13, 22, 31
Lucky Charm: A piece of material cut from something in your home.
Harmonious Signs for Relationships and Partnerships: Capricorn and Taurus

Spiritual Guides . . .

Star: Al Awa—Those with this star are often objects of others' desire.

Angel: Hamaliel—This angel governs logic and shows us what is real. His lessons in personal ethics always improve our karma.

Guardian Angel: St. Thomas—This angel brings affection from others and encourages you in all that you do.

Spiritual Stone: Jasper—This stone may soothe bruised emotions.

★ JUDITH'S INSIGHT ★

No matter how large the crowd, you stand out. Solid, sensible and headstrong, under many layers of ego, you have a golden vein of kindness and always wear your heart on your sleeve. Your intentions may be good, but you must be cautious in selecting your methods. Sometimes your actions will be grossly misunderstood.

You may be so fascinated by all the opportunities for employment that you can't find anything to do. Multiple talents and determination are usually gifts, not curses. There are very few jobs you can't do; your skills and abilities make you well suited to be a builder, clockmaker, artist, engineer, or teacher. Your love of finding fault can also lead you into a career as a theater critic or even government troubleshooter. You could also be a counselor, mediator, or designer.

You'll make an excellent parent once you're completely past the "me" stage in your life. There is no doubt that you can be selfish to an extreme. You can't become a well-rounded human being if you think the world revolves around you. You enjoy helping others with their problems, but are limited when it comes to keeping promises. Give others time to forgive you. Your style is *yours;* nobody understands it or would be caught dead doing it, but they all admire your moves anyway. You like unusual things and may be drawn to out-of-the ordinary people, those like no one else on the planet. Among the wildly different you manage to fit in.

★ ★ ★

SEPTEMBER 5 VIRGO • The festivities and celebrations of the zodiac
August 23 at 6:00 A.M. to September 23 at 3:00 A.M. • NUMEROLOGY 5

Possessions and Desires . . .

Gem: Jasper—This stone could grant the bearer protection from sadness.

Flower: Mimosa—You may be too sensitive to criticism.

Astral Color, Color Need, Apparel Color: Your Astral Color is Navy Blue—the color of style and refinement. Violet in your environment keeps you empathetic toward others. In your wardrobe, Green is your power color for overcoming obstacles.

Fragrance: Look for those classic scents that give you the feeling of fresh and sparkling clean, scents containing jasmine, ylang ylang, and roses.

Tree: Apple—You are creative, full of joy, and nearly magical. You bring happiness.

Instruments: Viola, trumpet

Composer: Liszt

Bird: Robin—the most sociable of all birds, with the ability to create quick friendships. It also can easily adapt to any home. When it wants something, it has the tendency to try to snatch it.

Symbol: Triangle—You have the right combination of abilities.

Harmonious Health and Nutrition . . .

Health Scent: Peach—This scent may balance your good qualities so that they equal your charm.

Favorable Foods: Parsley, prunes, molasses, chicken, buttermilk

What's Lucky . . .

Lucky Numbers: 3, 5, 23

Best Months: February and November

Best Day of the Week: Wednesday

Best Month Days: 4, 5, 23

Lucky Charms: A rabbit's foot or a white candle.

Harmonious Signs for Relationships and Partnerships: Capricorn and Taurus

Spiritual Guides . . .

Star: Al Awa—Those with this star are often objects of others' desire.

Angel: Hamaliel—This angel governs logic and shows us what is real. His lessons in personal ethics always improve our karma.

Guardian Angel: Plavwell—The guardian that gives power and strength to one's presence.

Spiritual Stone: Jasper—This stone may soothe bruised emotions.

✶ JUDITH'S INSIGHT ✶

Versatility is your greatest asset. Happiest doing many things at once, you're busy holding down the fort and propping up the sky. This creates a very interesting problem. Others feel free to burden you because you appear to be so capable. You are often disappointed, wishing others would rise to your high standards. The person who fails you the most is you because you expect altogether too much of yourself.

You have a kind heart but can be hotheaded and complaining at times. The complaining part can trip you up. You love changes and may need to make many of them in your life: new clothes, new cars; you trade things in easily.

The yellow caution flag is waving when it comes to relationships. Romantic ties remain difficult for you. Committing to one for you may be more objectionable than having your teeth pulled. Getting you to decide to get married, live together, or even go on a second date will make your prospects crazy. After taking the dreaded plunge, you happily bond to your family with bands of steel. Once you're in, you give yourself totally to your spouse and children.

Loyal and dependable, you're the one that family and friends call when they need advice or help. A great listener, your wide-open ear even takes in strangers. Friends of friends you haven't even met call you because they've heard how understanding you can be. Unfortunately, because you can resent this, you're prone to mood swings and can easily snap at people with the least provocation.

In your career you will be the great communicator as a writer, director, telephone operator, computer analyst, and film critic.

✶ ✶ ✶

SEPTEMBER 6 VIRGO • The festivities and celebrations of the zodiac
August 23 at 6:00 A.M. to September 23 at 3:00 A.M. • NUMEROLOGY 6

Possessions and Desires . . .

Gem: Jasper—This stone could grant the bearer protection from sadness.

Flower: Iris—You are the one with an open ear for your friends.

Astral Color, Color Need, Apparel Color: Your Astral Color is Navy Blue—the color of style and refinement. Violet in your environment keeps you empathetic toward others. In your wardrobe, Light Blue gives you strength and determination.

Fragrance: Look for those classic scents that give you the feeling of fresh and sparkling clean, scents containing jasmine, ylang ylang, and roses.

Tree: Palm—You tend to be very healthy and creative.

Instruments: Tambourine, lyre

Composer: Schubert

Bird: Killdeer—This bird is usually found consorting with other species, and can adapt to any environment.

Symbol: Star—You are full of inner brightness and will stand out in any crowd. You will be seen as special.

Harmonious Health and Nutrition . . .

Health Scent: Orange Blossom—This scent may balance your mind, body, and soul.

Favorable Foods: Swiss chard, black figs, chocolate, beef, cottage cheese

What's Lucky . . .

Lucky Numbers: 3, 5, 42

Best Months: February and November

Best Day of the Week: Wednesday

Best Month Days: 6, 15, 24

Lucky Charms: A religious token or card from any religion.

Harmonious Signs for Relationships and Partnerships: Capricorn and Taurus

Spiritual Guides . . .

Star: Sumak al Azel—Those with this star are called upon to serve.

Angel: Hamaliel—This angel governs logic and shows us what is real. His lessons in personal ethics always improve our karma.

Guardian Angel: Michael—"Who is like God."

Spiritual Stone: Jasper—This stone may soothe bruised emotions.

✶ JUDITH'S INSIGHT ✶

You have a good head on your shoulders and learned to be very responsible at an early age. You have limitless sympathy for your fellow human beings. You enjoy helping others even though you complain that people take advantage of you. Sometimes you feel like a fish out of water, and because of drastic living changes, you never really settle in at the new place. It may be a different state or country, or perhaps the neighborhood has completely altered. You yearn for travel to exotic places but never seem to get around to it. Life seems boring without frequent challenges.

When it comes to relationships, you always secretly wish your mate was more romantic. At the same time, you'd die if anyone found out how mushy you are. You love freedom and adventure, so keep this in mind. You may experience a whirlwind courtship followed by a hasty marriage. Not too much later you may regret not giving the matter more thought and time.

Work for you must be stable and provide enough room to explore your creative side. This flair for innovation should translate into a career at a museum, theater, apparel design firm, or fragrance manufacturer. If you feel your urge to nurture is stronger, you may desire employment as a doctor, teacher, or day care provider. You are more likely to do many things because of your strong ambition and determination. Your lesson in life is learning patience. If it feels like your whole life is spent standing in line waiting for your share, you're correct. But look at it this way: you're in the right line for success. Just after you turn fifty you shoot to the top of your field—farther than you ever expected.

✶ ✶ ✶

SEPTEMBER 7 VIRGO • The festivities and celebrations of the zodiac
August 23 at 6:00 A.M. to September 23 at 3:00 A.M. • NUMEROLOGY 7

Possessions and Desires . . .

Gem: Hyacinth—This stone might aid the memory.

Flower: Madder—You have a lot of attention being paid to you.

Astral Color, Color Need, Apparel Color: Your Astral Color is Navy Blue—the color of style and refinement. Violet in your environment keeps you empathetic toward others. In your wardrobe, Green is your power color for overcoming obstacles.

Fragrance: Look for those classic scents that give you the feeling of fresh and sparkling clean, scents containing jasmine, ylang ylang, and roses.

Tree: Pine—Your relationships tend to be harmonious, both emotionally and mentally.

Instrument: Cello

Composer: Mozart

Bird: Stork—Turkish bird, held in high esteem the world over. This bird is intelligent but may have strange tendencies.

Symbol: Wings—You are the source of balance in your world—this will bring you contentment.

Harmonious Health and Nutrition . . .

Health Scent: Almond—This scent may revitalize you and open you to greater possibilities.

Favorable Foods: Radishes, raspberries, chocolate, oysters, buttermilk

What's Lucky . . .

Lucky Numbers: 3, 5, 44

Best Months: February and November

Best Day of the Week: Wednesday

Best Month Days: 8, 17, 26

Lucky Charm: An old key.

Harmonious Signs for Relationships and Partnerships: Capricorn and Taurus

Spiritual Guides . . .

Star: Al Awa—Those with this star are often objects of others' desire.

Angel: Hamaliel—This angel governs logic and shows us what is real. His lessons in personal ethics always improve our karma.

Guardian Angel: Seraphim—An angel that brings love, light, and passion.

Spiritual Stone: Jasper—This stone may soothe bruised emotions.

✶ JUDITH'S INSIGHT ✶

Optimistic, steady, determined, and both mentally and physically capable, you can expect many accomplishments in life because you allow nothing to stand in your way. You may have years that seem excruciating to live through, but later on you will remember them as not so bad. Although you like to think of yourself as liberal, you have a strong conservative streak that refuses to be buried.

Make sure your surroundings are in order. You go ballistic when you put something on the table and later find it's disappeared. Many things that you see as a reflection of you, like clothes, house, garage, attic, or car, must be in perfect condition, even if they're twenty years old. You like a stable home and family, but you have to be the one that keeps it that way.

Love will be what you make it; luckily you're the one in control. If you ever lose what you see as your due authority, you become very upset. Your family can always rely on you in spite of how much heartache they sometimes give in return. Don't be blinded to your pushy and possessive nature.

When you decide to do things, you tend to overdo them. You have great organizational skills, but may have trouble balancing everyday demands made on you. Try not to overreact to daily pressures. A physical job that makes use of your strength may appeal to you. You are nurturing and probably attracted to careers in medicine; you would make an excellent emergency room nurse or plastic surgeon.

★ ★ ★

SEPTEMBER 8
VIRGO • The festivities and celebrations of the zodiac
August 23 at 6:00 A.M. to September 23 at 3:00 A.M. • NUMEROLOGY 8

Possessions and Desires . . .

Gem: Emerald—Those who carry this stone tend to be lucky in love.

Flower: Monkshood—You may wish you lived in times of great chivalry.

Astral Color, Color Need, Apparel Color: Your Astral Color is Navy Blue—the color of style and refinement. Violet in your environment keeps you empathetic toward others. In your wardrobe, Light Blue gives you strength and determination.

Fragrance: Look for those classic scents that give you the feeling of fresh and sparkling clean, scents containing jasmine, ylang ylang, and roses.

Tree: Holly—Beware that you are not carried away by your passionate nature. The only way to grow is to be open to new experiences.

Instruments: Violin, tympanum

Composer: Gluck

Bird: Goldfinch—These gentle creatures can seem moody, especially in unsettled weather.

Symbol: Star—You are full of inner brightness and will stand out in any crowd. You will be seen as special.

Harmonious Health and Nutrition . . .

Health Scent: Lavender—This scent might lead others to trust you and make you patient.

Favorable Foods: Sorrel, huckleberries, raw sugar, chicken, cottage cheese

What's Lucky . . .

Lucky Numbers: 3, 5, 36

Best Months: February and November

Best Day of the Week: Wednesday

Best Month Days: 9, 18, 27

Lucky Charm: Red ribbon in your wallet or doorway

Harmonious Signs for Relationships and Partnerships: Capricorn and Taurus

Spiritual Guides . . .

Star: Al Awa—Those with this star are often objects of others' desire.

Angel: Hamaliel—This angel governs logic and shows us what is real. His lessons in personal ethics always improve our karma.

Guardian Angel: Gabriel—"God is my strength."

Spiritual Stone: Jasper—This stone may soothe bruised emotions.

✶ JUDITH'S INSIGHT ✶

You're a terrific person! Given your many abilities, you're on the express elevator right up to the top. You are intelligent and know how to make the most of your challenging personality. You are wise beyond your years; people are drawn to your way of thinking. Please remember that energy is a flow that you have to keep in motion. When it comes to your work, home, or play, don't ever impede your own momentum.

Some say you're nosy—you see it as a healthy curiosity and thirst for knowledge. You may want to get paid for this quality. Work as an investigator, research scientist, paralegal, or creative director may find you. You are a dependable employer; your crew soon learns how to keep you happy. When your employees disappoint you, though, sometimes you may be so grouchy that you frighten yourself.

You desire constant change and attention in romance. Find a mate who takes life as seriously as you, or you'll be very frustrated much of the time. You have a dry wit and great sense of humor, but use them sparingly. Your family may subject you to lots of pressure, and you tend to "adopt" your friends. Remember to create reasonable boundaries, or other people will press you beneath the weight of their need.

Give yourself some slack every now and then. You are a stylish perfectionist who is seldom satisfied. Lighten up! Leave the dishes in the sink or let the grass grow if it means getting more enjoyment out of today.

✶ ✶ ✶

Possessions and Desires . . .

Gem: Jasper—This stone could grant the bearer protection from sadness.

Flower: Monkshood—You may wish you lived in times of great chivalry.

Astral Color, Color Need, Apparel Color: Your Astral Color is Navy Blue—the color of style and refinement. Violet in your environment keeps you empathetic toward others. In your wardrobe, Green is your power color for overcoming obstacles.

Fragrance: Look for those classic scents that give you the feeling of fresh and sparkling clean, scents containing jasmine, ylang ylang, and roses.

Tree: Holly—Beware that you are not carried away by your passionate nature. The only way to grow is to be open to new experiences.

Instruments: Violin, tympanum

Composer: Gluck

Bird: Robin—the most sociable of all birds, with the ability to create quick friendships. It also can easily adapt to any home. When it wants something, it has the tendency to try to snatch it.

Symbol: Anchor—This tranquil symbol signifies stability and strength, and stands for strong commitments in relationships.

Harmonious Health and Nutrition . . .

Health Scent: Lavender—This scent might lead others to trust you and make you patient.

Favorable Foods: Parsnips, cherries, molasses, brains, eggs

What's Lucky . . .

Lucky Numbers: 3, 5, 81

Best Months: February and November

Best Day of the Week: Wednesday

Best Month Days: 9, 18, 27

Lucky Charms: A U.S. coin or a bill of any amount from the year you were born.

Harmonious Signs for Relationships and Partnerships: Capricorn and Taurus

Spiritual Guides . . .

Star: Al Awa—Those with this star are often objects of others' desire.

Angel: Hamaliel—This angel governs logic and shows us what is real. His lessons in personal ethics always improve our karma.

Guardian Angel: Gabriel—"God is my strength."

Spiritual Stone: Jasper—This stone may soothe bruised emotions.

✱ JUDITH'S INSIGHT ✱

If you could muster enough belief in yourself, you would be the perfect athlete. People stare at you for one reason or another. It goes beyond your well-groomed outer appearance. Was that you on the cover of that fashion or news magazine? You would love it if you could find a job where they paid you for ideas. You'd be a millionaire ten times over! However, the next time you go to work you know you'll be doing something physical. For example, you could be a personal trainer.

Romance for you takes energy. You can be loyal to the right someone, but until then, you're a shameless flirt who dashes in and out of relationships. Use your own insights to write or create a book like this. Your intuition is one of your strongest assets. Right now this may be a dream, but a great work waits inside. One day you will let it out.

You are passionate when you speak or write, molding feelings into strong sentences. People around you know you understand their meaning. You would make an excellent counselor. Listen closely for opportunity to tap you out a coded message concerning a second or third career. You could be someone who has "postal worker" on the bottom of your résumé and "best-selling author" at the top.

Okay, some see you as a know-it-all; so what if it's true? Learn to give others only what they can handle of your wisdom. This is particularly good advice when dealing with your spouse or the constant stream of *I told you so's* could be the grounds for your divorce. Surprisingly, you may be happier if you jump into things without thinking them through completely.

✱ ✱ ✱

SEPTEMBER 10 VIRGO • The festivities and celebrations of the zodiac
August 23 at 6:00 A.M. to September 23 at 3:00 A.M. • NUMEROLOGY 1

Possessions and Desires . . .

Gem: Jasper—This stone could grant the bearer protection from sadness.

Flower: Tear Drop—You are happier when you are patient.

Astral Color, Color Need, Apparel Color: Your Astral Color is Navy Blue—the color of style and refinement. Violet in your environment keeps you empathetic toward others. In your wardrobe, Light Blue gives you strength and determination.

Fragrance: Look for those classic scents that give you the feeling of fresh and sparkling clean, scents containing jasmine, ylang ylang, and roses.

Tree: Walnut—You are unusually helpful and always looking for constant changes in your life.

Instruments: Oboe, flute, clarinet, piano, French horn, organ, piccolo

Composer: Böhm

Bird: Cuckoo—A good flyer and very seldom a quitter. Many seem more independent than they actually are; yearn for more nurturing than one would expect.

Symbol: Crown—the universal sign of dignity.

Harmonious Health and Nutrition . . .

Health Scent: Strawberry—Soothing by nature, the strawberry promotes self-esteem and encourages love.

Favorable Foods: Turnips, black figs, raw sugar, barley, buttermilk

What's Lucky . . .

Lucky Numbers: 3, 5, 28
Best Months: February and November
Best Day of the Week: Wednesday
Best Month Days: 1, 10, 19, 28
Lucky Charm: A new penny in your shoe
Harmonious Signs for Relationships and Partnerships: Capricorn and Taurus

Spiritual Guides . . .

Star: Al Awa—Those with this star are often objects of others' desire.

Angel: Hamaliel—This angel governs logic and shows us what is real. His lessons in personal ethics always improve our karma.

Guardian Angel: Malachi—"Messenger of Jehovah."

Spiritual Stone: Jasper—This stone may soothe bruised emotions.

✶ JUDITH'S INSIGHT ✶

You have mind like a laser light. There is nothing your executive abilities can't handle. You have a well-balanced intellect and a well-rounded personality. If you don't earn your living by thinking, you're likely to work at jobs that require mechanical or technical skills. You only need to put your hands on a failing device to get it to work better than the designer intended.

Kind and giving, you readily make friends. Acquaintances, however, may blanch at your cutting and hurtful remarks. When your friends need you, you are loyal and comforting in the beginning, but you lack patience if they don't recover as quickly as you would.

Government or accounting positions look good. Your taste and organizational skills may be better suited for the fashion industry. Sing out your love for music, but limit it to the shower. You may be better off as the person who comes up with the lyrics.

When the first gray hairs and facial lines appear, you overreact. Spending money you may not have won't impress people for long or bring back your youth. Use that well-developed sense of humor to help you relax and accept normal changes.

Relationships come easily to you. However, once you enter into one, the thrill usually leaves. Small things about your mate irritate you. Make sure you really get to know your partner before you marry. The more adjusting you do before the bond, the less friction there will be after. Choose a partner for other reasons than how cute you two look together in photos.

★ ★ ★

SEPTEMBER 11

VIRGO • The festivities and celebrations of the zodiac

August 23 at 6:00 A.M. to September 23 at 3:00 A.M. • NUMEROLOGY 2

Possessions and Desires . . .

Gem: Jasper—This stone could grant the bearer protection from sadness.

Flower: Cranberry—You may need to learn the only cure for heartache is to accept the bitter with the sweet.

Astral Color, Color Need, Apparel Color: Your Astral Color is Navy Blue—the color of style and refinement. Violet in your environment keeps you empathetic toward others. In your wardrobe, Green is your power color for overcoming obstacles.

Fragrance: Look for those classic scents that give you the feeling of fresh and sparkling clean, scents containing jasmine, ylang ylang, and roses.

Tree: Maple—You have both great stability and flashes of intuition.

Instruments: Pipe organ, cymbal, drum

Composers: Handel, Johann Sebastian Bach

Bird: Killdeer—This bird is usually found consorting with other species, and can adapt to any environment.

Symbol: Cross—the symbol of self-sacrifice and reconciliation.

Harmonious Health and Nutrition . . .

Health Scent: Apple—A vivacious scent encouraging energy. Will help you to be more creative, intuitive and positive.

Favorable Foods: Mushrooms, cranberries, chocolate, liver, cottage cheese

What's Lucky . . .

Lucky Numbers: 2, 3, 5
Best Months: February and November
Best Day of the Week: Wednesday
Best Month Days: 2, 11, 20, 29
Lucky Charms: Two 50-cent pieces. Give someone else one of them.

Harmonious Signs for Relationships and Partnerships: Capricorn and Taurus

Spiritual Guides . . .

Star: Al Awa—Those with this star are often objects of others' desire.

Angel: Hamaliel—This angel governs logic and shows us what is real. His lessons in personal ethics always improve our karma.

Guardian Angel: St. John—This angel simplifies that which is complicated.

Spiritual Stone: Jasper—This stone may soothe bruised emotions.

✷ JUDITH'S INSIGHT ✷

You are a faithful and ardent mate, and your scrupulous and principled approach to life is award-winning. Once committed to a task, you dedicate yourself to it. Your biggest hindrance is your overactive mind. A high achiever, you sometimes go overboard in setting impossible goals.

As you mature, you learn to drink up knowledge. You're most comfortable in a natural setting, and would choose to relax sitting by a pond or picnicking in the woods, roasting marshmallows over a campfire. These opportunities are rare, but with proper planning you fit them into your busy lifestyle.

You may work for the government in the sciences, perhaps chemistry, but you may supplement your income through journalism, editing, or proofreading. Your unrehearsed and outspoken responses get you into trouble at times, and you could lose a friend by speaking harshly. Put more energy into the rewarding relationships, and let the unworkable ones go. Beware of quick responses and look before you leap.

LIsten to your inner self. It's time to believe in yourself more than you do. There's nothing to be feared from your own insight. You are a genuinely good person and a caring soul. It will take time for you to recognize this. Other people already do.

✷ ✷ ✷

279

SEPTEMBER 12

VIRGO • The festivities and celebrations of the zodiac

August 23 at 6:00 A.M. to September 23 at 3:00 A.M. • NUMEROLOGY 3

Possessions and Desires . . .

Gem: Jasper—This stone could grant the bearer protection from sadness.

Flower: Jonquil—Your affections tend to be readily returned.

Astral Color, Color Need, Apparel Color: Your Astral Color is Navy Blue—the color of style and refinement. Violet in your environment keeps you empathetic toward others. In your wardrobe, Light Blue gives you strength and determination.

Fragrance: Look for those classic scents that give you the feeling of fresh and sparkling clean, scents containing jasmine, ylang ylang, and roses.

Tree: Elm—You have willpower, strength, and the ability to stand alone.

Instrument: Trombone

Composers: Verdi, Mendelssohn, Schumann

Bird: Cuckoo—A good flyer and very seldom a quitter. Many seem more independent than they actually are; yearn for more nurturing than one would expect.

Symbol: Wreath—You have been crowned with a special personality. You are strong but extremely compassionate.

Harmonious Health and Nutrition . . .

Health Scent: Rose—This scent will lead you to passionate thoughts and make you feel warm inside.

Favorable Foods: Brussels sprouts, pineapple, chocolate, chicken, buttermilk

What's Lucky . . .

Lucky Numbers: 3, 5, 66

Best Months: February and November

Best Day of the Week: Wednesday

Best Month Days: 3, 12, 21, 30

Lucky Charm: A pen that someone else has already used.

Harmonious Signs for Relationships and Partnerships: Capricorn and Taurus

Spiritual Guides . . .

Star: Al Awa—Those with this star are often objects of others' desire.

Angel: Hamaliel—This angel governs logic and shows us what is real. His lessons in personal ethics always improve our karma.

Guardian Angel: Johiel—This angel is a protector of all those with a humble heart.

Spiritual Stone: Jasper—This stone may soothe bruised emotions.

✶ _JUDITH'S INSIGHT_ ✶

Your splendid mind is just one of your great qualities. When a situation calls for good judgment, smart advice, or clever decisions, you're _the_ person to ask. Much of the time, you're right. You can be expected to resolve disputes honestly, firmly, clearly, and without prejudice. You remember thousands of details and are skilled at planning. Good jobs for you are computer programmer, architect, set designer, or engineer. You should also explore law or a related career. Change excites you in your earlier years.

You won't find it difficult making friends. People struggle to get closer to you because of your attractive personality and good looks. Getting stuck in one place frightens you, but a more stable life offers a peace you've never known. You're a sweetheart when things are going your way: affectionate and caring to those around you. When misunderstandings occur, however, your stubborn temperament emerges.

Determined and assertive, you set clear goals. Huge obstacles seem to suddenly drop out of the sky, usually landing on your head. For a while you're dazed, but when the dust settles, you get right back on track. Others can count on you for comfort. Why are you surprised when your abruptness is met with disaster?

There are so many jobs you can see yourself doing that choosing the best is daunting. Eventually you discover the secret to your own happiness is to have more than one. You may work nine to five for someone else and turn a favorite hobby into a moneymaking sideline.

You have no trouble finding mates. Staying happy with them may be a problem. You have a habit of being too critical, but you will grow out of that. When you do, love tends to turn into a fairytale of love.

SEPTEMBER 13 VIRGO • The festivities and celebrations of the zodiac
August 23 at 6:00 A.M. to September 23 at 3:00 A.M. • NUMEROLOGY 4

Possessions and Desires . . .

Gem: Hyacinth—This stone might aid the memory.

Flower: Love-in-a-mist—Your emotions usually are an unknown land you need to explore.

Astral Color, Color Need, Apparel Color: Your Astral Color is Navy Blue—the color of style and refinement. Violet in your environment keeps you empathetic toward others. In your wardrobe, Green is your power color for overcoming obstacles.

Fragrance: Look for those classic scents that give you the feeling of fresh and sparkling clean, scents containing jasmine, ylang ylang, and roses.

Tree: Cherry—You will find yourself faced with constant new emotional awakenings.

Instruments: Bass, clarinet

Composers: Haydn, Wagner

Bird: Stork—Turkish bird, held in high esteem the world over. This bird is intelligent but may have strange tendencies.

Symbol: Star—You are full of inner brightness and will stand out in any crowd. You will be seen as special.

Harmonious Health and Nutrition . . .

Health Scent: Vanilla—This scent will fill you with a feeling of cleanliness and stability.

Favorable Foods: Celery, cranberries, raw sugar, liver, cottage cheese

What's Lucky . . .

Lucky Numbers: 3, 5, 67

Best Months: February and November

Best Day of the Week: Wednesday

Best Month Days: 4, 13, 22, 31

Lucky Charm: A piece of material cut from something in your home.

Harmonious Signs for Relationships and Partnerships: Capricorn and Taurus

Spiritual Guides . . .

Star: Al Awa—Those with this star are often objects of others' desire.

Angel: Hamaliel—This angel governs logic and shows us what is real. His lessons in personal ethics always improve our karma.

Guardian Angel: Uriel—This angel brings the light of God's guidance.

Spiritual Stone: Jasper—This stone may soothe bruised emotions.

✷ JUDITH'S INSIGHT ✷

You have a powerful body that you keep in great shape. Stop worrying that people are out to get you. If you wait until you get older to find courage, you may miss out on much. Try not to wince when people want to get close to you. You have an impressive mind and good judgment. You're honest and usually correct. You are unique and most likely a star athlete.

What you end up doing will shock some. Your secret desires are marketable skills. Some examples of work you'd be good at include building trades, clockmaking, law, journalism, writing, inventing, or the merchant marine.

You make a excellent parent once you get over your self-absorbed phase. Unresolved childhood fears need sorting out. Getting older means growing up. You are amiable enough and lucky in love. You may have to choose between two or more wonderful partners who have an equal hold on your affections.

For you, a promise made is a promise kept. With your unusual style that yields surprising results, you enjoy exotic art. As you learn more of life's lessons, you work to help those who are less fortunate. Many different types of people are drawn to you. Your eclectic group of friends all regard you highly.

✷ ✷ ✷

SEPTEMBER 14 VIRGO • The festivities and celebrations of the zodiac
August 23 at 6:00 A.M. to September 23 at 3:00 A.M. • NUMEROLOGY 5

Possessions and Desires . . .

Gem: Emerald—Those who carry this stone tend to be lucky in love.

Flower: Acacia—You will have more than your share of close friends in your life.

Astral Color, Color Need, Apparel Color: Your Astral Color is Navy Blue—the color of style and refinement. Violet in your environment keeps you empathetic toward others. In your wardrobe, Light Blue gives you strength and determination.

Fragrance: Look for those classic scents that give you the feeling of fresh and sparkling clean, scents containing jasmine, ylang ylang, and roses.

Tree: Apple—You are creative, full of joy, and nearly magical. You bring happiness.

Instruments: Viola, trumpet

Composer: Liszt

Bird: Goldfinch—These gentle creatures can seem moody, especially in unsettled weather.

Symbol: Triangle—You have the right combination of abilities.

Harmonious Health and Nutrition . . .

Health Scent: Peach—This scent may balance your good qualities so that they equal your charm.

Favorable Foods: Endive, black figs, chocolate, beef, goat's milk

What's Lucky . . .

Lucky Numbers: 3, 5, 14
Best Months: February and November
Best Day of the Week: Wednesday
Best Month Days: 4, 5, 23
Lucky Charms: A rabbit's foot or a white candle.
Harmonious Signs for Relationships and Partnerships: Capricorn and Taurus

Spiritual Guides . . .

Star: Al Awa—Those with this star are often objects of others' desire.

Angel: Hamaliel—This angel governs logic and shows us what is real. His lessons in personal ethics always improve our karma.

Guardian Angel: Plavwell—The guardian that gives power and strength to one's presence.

Spiritual Stone: Jasper—This stone may soothe bruised emotions

✳ JUDITH'S INSIGHT ✳

You are kindhearted and hotheaded. Once the bills are paid, you can be generous. You may live in two places, probably owning a vacation home or living in the suburbs with an apartment in the city. If you aren't moving every year, you are always getting different furniture. Even when you're new in town, your address book is packed. You need constant variety in cars, clothes, and friends.

There's a flashing yellow warning light when it comes to you and relationships. Those who have dated you can only wonder what they did to make you so completely avoid them afterward. They didn't know you were fussy, finicky, and fickle. You make some commitments along the way, but they usually don't last. If you do manage to find a partner who is as comfortable with change as you, you can be a faithful spouse. It will seem like you are both married to different people every month.

Employers love you; you're trustworthy, capable, and reliable. You are witty and fun to be with. Your soul desires a deep connection with religion or a spiritual movement. Beware of losing yourself in a cult. You can be a legal clerk, freelance magazine writer, telemarketer, scientist, or research assistant. No matter what type of company issues the checks, they tend to be big ones. Cash seems to fall out of the sky and into your pockets. Expect to be very secure by middle age.

✳ ✳ ✳

SEPTEMBER 15 VIRGO • The festivities and celebrations of the zodiac
August 23 at 6:00 A.M. to September 23 at 3:00 A.M. • NUMEROLOGY 6

Possessions and Desires . . .

Gem: Jasper—This stone could grant the bearer protection from sadness.

Flower: Rose Acacia—You tend to want to surround yourself with elegant things.

Astral Color, Color Need, Apparel Color: Your Astral Color is Navy Blue—the color of style and refinement. Violet in your environment keeps you empathetic toward others. In your wardrobe, Green is your power color for overcoming obstacles.

Fragrance: Look for those classic scents that give you the feeling of fresh and sparkling clean, scents containing jasmine, ylang ylang, and roses.

Tree: Palm—You tend to be very healthy and creative.

Instruments: Tambourine, lyre

Composer: Schubert

Bird: Cuckoo—A good flyer and very seldom a quitter. Many seem more independent than they actually are; yearn for more nurturing than one would expect.

Symbol: Crescent—You are more likely to be influenced by the phases of the moon. Your easygoing manner leads you to peaceful situations.

Harmonious Health and Nutrition . . .

Health Scent: Orange Blossom—This scent may balance your body, mind, and soul.

Favorable Foods: Watercress, cranberries, molasses, liver, eggs

What's Lucky . . .

Lucky Numbers: 3, 5, 6

Best Months: February and November

Best Day of the Week: Wednesday

Best Month Days: 6, 15, 24

Lucky Charms: A religious token or card from any religion.

Harmonious Signs for Relationships and Partnerships: Capricorn and Taurus

Spiritual Guides . . .

Star: Al Awa—Those with this star are often objects of others' desire.

Angel: Hamaliel—This angel governs logic and shows us what is real. His lessons in personal ethics always improve our karma.

Guardian Angel: Michael—"Who is like God."

Spiritual Stone: Jasper—This stone may soothe bruised emotions.

✷ JUDITH'S INSIGHT ✷

The world dumped itself on your shoulders at a very young age. Through it all, you learned to keep your head held high. You're never without three or four strays who look to you for assistance. They could be either animals or people. Your hobby could be helping people; you have time for little else. You are a ball of energy and as funny as a comic. You have talents that can be used in business; maybe you should start your own.

You seem to like doing things the hard way. You are lonely and wish with all your heart to have someone special. You attract needy people with your cloying personality. You usually find a solid commitment with a kindred spirit who loves you without making you feel drained.

You think too much and should seek a career that will keep your mind occupied. You would do very well as a law professor, court clerk, gossip columnist, or host of a radio call-in show.

You are always involved in volunteer activities. Everyone else on the PTA knows who to ask to bake eight dozen cookies at the last minute and chaperone the fifth-grade dance. Later in life you may make time for sports. You might pick golf because the space around you feels immense.

Most people enjoy when life is easy. You only have gears for uphill and are uncomfortable on downward slopes. Heaven forbid you should coast: something would snap. You are selflessly kind, which is rare, and you are one of the universe's gifts to the world.

✷ ✷ ✷

SEPTEMBER 16
VIRGO • The festivities and celebrations of the zodiac
August 23 at 6:00 A.M. to September 23 at 3:00 A.M. • NUMEROLOGY 7

Possessions and Desires . . .

Gem: Emerald—Those who carry this stone tend to be lucky in love.

Flower: Adonis Flos—You spend too much time dwelling on past hurts.

Astral Color, Color Need, Apparel Color: Your Astral Color is Navy Blue—the color of style and refinement. Violet in your environment keeps you empathetic toward others. In your wardrobe, Light Blue gives you strength and determination.

Fragrance: Look for those classic scents that give you the feeling of fresh and sparkling clean, scents containing jasmine, ylang ylang, and roses.

Tree: Sycamore—Yours is the ability to love, communicate honestly with others, and have lasting relationships.

Instrument: Harp

Composers: Gluck, Brahms

Bird: Killdeer—This bird is usually found consorting with other species, and can adapt to any environment.

Symbol: Heart—You are enthusiastic, empathetic, and full of generosity and love.

Harmonious Health and Nutrition . . .

Health Scent: Jasmine—This scent may make you more easygoing when you are stressed.

Favorable Foods: Parsnips, raspberries, raw sugar, oysters, cottage cheese

What's Lucky . . .

Lucky Numbers: 3, 5, 7
Best Months: February and November
Best Day of the Week: Wednesday
Best Month Days: 6, 15, 24
Lucky Charm: An old key.
Harmonious Signs for Relationships and Partnerships: Capricorn and Taurus

Spiritual Guides . . .

Star: Sumak al Azel—Those with this star are called upon to serve.

Angel: Hamaliel—This angel governs logic and shows us what is real. His lessons in personal ethics always improve our karma.

Guardian Angel: Raphael—This angel attends to all of your needs when you are looking for guidance.

Spiritual Stone: Jasper—This stone may soothe bruised emotions.

✴ JUDITH'S INSIGHT ✴

You are physically and mentally powerful; life is going to be an endless stream of accomplishments. You want to champion liberal causes, but your conservative friends make so much sense you guiltily agree with them. You like to have a place for everything and everything in its place. Others may see you as obsessively tidy, both on the job and in your appearance. Your hair always looks perfect. You put your outfits together with great flair.

Known for creating harmony out of chaos, you should consider a career in movies behind the scenes: as art director, set decorator, costume designer, or wardrobe person. If you're not ready for the big time, you may want to volunteer for a community theatrical company.

Pushy and possessive by nature, you can't stand to see things done in a half-baked manner. Keeping the balance in everyday life is sometimes difficult for you because you are very meticulous. Things simply must be a certain way, which you see as the right or only way.

You may raise the levels of stress for yourself and those around you. The warning whistle blows on the pressure-cooker when you try to enter into relationships. You are so set in your ways that you may experience difficulty finding a person who can understand you. You probably won't deviate much from the mental picture you have in your head of the proper mate. Eventually you will find your other half, but it may take longer than you hoped. This extended search will teach you your most-needed life lesson: patience. As usual, everything comes together for you.

✴ ✴ ✴

SEPTEMBER 17 VIRGO • The festivities and celebrations of the zodiac
August 23 at 6:00 A.M. to September 23 at 3:00 A.M. • NUMEROLOGY 8

Possessions and Desires . . .

Gem: Jasper—This stone could grant the bearer protection from sadness.

Flower: Box (tree)—You have a very dry sense of humor and are not very outgoing.

Astral Color, Color Need, Apparel Color: Your Astral Color is Navy Blue—the color of style and refinement. Violet in your environment keeps you empathetic toward others. In your wardrobe, Green is your power color for overcoming obstacles.

Fragrance: Look for those classic scents that gives you the feeling of fresh and sparkling clean, scents containing jasmine, ylang ylang, and roses.

Tree: Pine—Your relationships tend to be harmonious, both emotionally and mentally.

Instrument: Cello

Composer: Mozart

Bird: Goldfinch—These gentle creatures can seem moody, especially in unsettled weather.

Symbol: Wings—You are the source of balance in your world—this will bring you contentment.

Harmonious Health and Nutrition . . .

Health Scent: Almond—This scent may revitalize you and open you to greater possibilities.

Favorable Foods: Asparagus, cranberries, chocolate, chicken, goat's milk

What's Lucky . . .

Lucky Numbers: 3, 5, 8

Best Months: February and November

Best Day of the Week: Wednesday

Best Month Days: 8, 17, 26

Lucky Charm: Red ribbon in your wallet or doorway

Harmonious Signs for Relationships and Partnerships: Capricorn and Taurus

Spiritual Guides . . .

Star: Caphir—People born under this star catch what they chase.

Angel: Hamaliel—This angel governs logic and shows us what is real. His lessons in personal ethics always improve our karma.

Guardian Angel: Seraphim—An angel that brings love, light, and passion.

Spiritual Stone: Jasper—This stone may soothe bruised emotions.

✳ JUDITH'S INSIGHT ✳

Intelligent and charismatic, you are always willing to lend a helping hand. You always want to learn new things. Your career choices reflect this, as you are inclined to work as a researcher, investigator, scientist, paralegal, or attorney.

You are a most dependable employee if the workplace is one that you enjoy. Your intuitive tendencies can be thrown off if your environment is not right. You are wise beyond your years. A very serious person, you should seek a mate who won't expect you to be too frivolous. Not to say you can't have a good time, but you need to ponder situations and are very calm emotionally. Any spouse of yours has to understand all sides of you.

Even if you know you're right most of the time, don't offer advice too often to family and friends. Sometimes they should learn lessons on their own, and they may become dependent on your telling them what to do. Hard feelings may arise. You like things to be perfect; you tastefully create your own world. Learn that nothing is perfect, and even perfect chaos sometimes can be a higher order.

You insist on harmony in all things: career, love, friends, your home, and family. Financially, it may take time for you to feel secure. You will learn that security is sometimes not what you have accumulated monetarily but what you have gained emotionally.

✶ ✶ ✶

SEPTEMBER 18 VIRGO • The festivities and celebrations of the zodiac
August 23 at 6:00 A.M. to September 23 at 3:00 A.M. • NUMEROLOGY 9

Possessions and Desires . . .

Gem: Jasper—This stone could grant the bearer protection from sadness.
Flower: Buttercup—You have more than the angels protecting you.
Astral Color, Color Need, Apparel Color: Your Astral Color is Navy Blue—the color of style and refinement. Violet in your environment keeps you empathetic toward others. In your wardrobe, Light Blue gives you strength and determination.
Fragrance: Look for those classic scents that give you the feeling of fresh and sparkling clean, scents containing jasmine, ylang ylang, and roses.
Tree: Holly—Beware that you are not carried away by your passionate nature. The only way to grow is to be open to new experiences.
Instruments: Violin, tympanum
Composer: Gluck
Bird: Robin—the most sociable of all birds, with the ability to create quick friendships. It also can easily adapt to any home. When it wants something, it has the tendency to try to snatch it.
Symbol: Anchor—This tranquil symbol signifies stability and strength, and stands for strong commitments in relationships.

Harmonious Health and Nutrition . . .

Health Scent: Lavender—This scent might lead others to trust you and make you patient.
Favorable Foods: Endive, strawberries, raw sugar, liver, eggs

What's Lucky . . .

Lucky Numbers: 3, 5, 81
Best Months: February and November
Best Day of the Week: Wednesday
Best Month Days: 9, 18, 27
Lucky Charms: A U.S. coin or a bill of any amount from the year you were born.
Harmonious Signs for Relationships and Partnerships: Capricorn and Taurus

Spiritual Guides . . .

Star: Al Awa—Those with this star are often objects of others' desire.
Angel: Hamaliel—This angel governs logic and shows us what is real. His lessons in personal ethics always improve our karma.
Guardian Angel: Gabriel—"God is my strength."
Spiritual Stone: Jasper—This stone may soothe bruised emotions.

✶ JUDITH'S INSIGHT ✶

A natural athlete, you are so energetic, you can't find enough ways to release it. You would be good at anything that requires a physically fit body. You have the knack for doing things quite well, and others think everything comes very easily to you.

You probably prefer to work at a job where you can use your mind. Your outward appearance may lead you into a career such as modeling, acting, or consulting in the beauty and glamour trade. You do have a good head on your shoulders, but you may have more success in life by showing off those shoulders.

Your passionate nature leads to large, mostly good, changes in your life. It may take you time to recognize this asset. You are a very wise person, and other people could benefit from what you know naturally. Your philosophy of life has the potential to open doors for others by giving them powerful insights and by teaching them kindness and understanding. If you have no desire to write or give speeches, you should at least keep a journal of your dreams, thoughts, and feelings. This emotional diary could be the basis of a completely different career from the one you are currently in. You may be considered a know-it-all because you're right most of the time. You must learn that some people don't always recognize wisdom, especially when it comes in such a good-looking package.

Playfully affectionate at times, you make a loyal mate in a committed relationship. Recognize the pressures you sometimes put on people because of your obsession with order. Relax your standards to a level that makes those around you comfortable.

✶ ✶ ✶

Possessions and Desires . . .

Gem: Jasper—This stone could grant the bearer protection from sadness.

Flower: Cabbage—You tend to focus too much on what's in it for you.

Astral Color, Color Need, Apparel Color: Your Astral Color is Navy Blue—the color of style and refinement. Violet in your environment keeps you empathetic toward others. In your wardrobe, Green is your power color for overcoming obstacles.

Fragrance: Look for those classic scents that give you the feeling of fresh and sparkling clean, scents containing jasmine, ylang ylang, and roses.

Tree: Walnut—You are unusually helpful and always looking for constant changes in your life.

Instruments: Oboe, flute, clarinet, piano, French horn, organ, piccolo

Composer: Böhm

Bird: Killdeer—This bird is usually found consorting with other species, and can adapt to any environment.

Symbol: Crown—the universal sign of dignity.

Harmonious Health and Nutrition . . .

Health Scent: Strawberry—Soothing by nature, the strawberry promotes self-esteem and encourages love.

Favorable Foods: Parsley, black figs, molasses, chicken, goat's milk

What's Lucky . . .

Lucky Numbers: 3, 5, 19

Best Months: February and November

Best Day of the Week: Wednesday

Best Month Days: 10, 19, 28

Lucky Charm: A new penny in your shoe.

Harmonious Signs for Relationships and Partnerships: Capricorn and Taurus

Spiritual Guides . . .

Star: Sumak al Azel—Those with this star are called upon to serve.

Angel: Hamaliel—This angel governs logic and shows us what is real. His lessons in personal ethics always improve our karma.

Guardian Angel: Malachi—"Messenger of Jehovah."

Spiritual Stone: Jasper—This stone may soothe bruised emotions.

✴ JUDITH'S INSIGHT ✴

You are truthful and conscientious, almost pure, by nature. Others fail to see the real you and think of you as prudish. They mistake your intensity for coldness. Cautious when it comes to getting close to people, you constantly evaluate and reevaluate situations before you act. You can be a pain in the neck because you do everything by the book.

You make friends easily, but some take offense at your honesty and directness. Most people can't face the whole truth. A loyal and comforting friend, nobody is more dependable than you. You will succeed if you decide to work in jobs involving money such as a government clerk, banker, accountant, or cashier.

An avid reader, you feel that it's impossible to study too much. You never stop taking classes and will make a great scholar. Be sure to save some time to have fun. Your love of music may lead to a career there. You might not be able to sing but would make a fine songwriter.

The older you get, the more important your appearance will become. Vanity could be your weakness. You may have a strong desire to travel. You were the kid sitting over a microscope or taking apart a computer. Your attraction to nature may lead you into hobbies like flower arranging, gardening, and environmental activism.

When it comes to relationships, strong emotions make you uncomfortable and guarded. The more affection you receive, the happier you are. You wait for others to approach you. Be cautious about pushing others away. You must follow your intuition.

✴ ✴ ✴

SEPTEMBER 20

VIRGO • The festivities and celebrations of the zodiac

August 23 at 6:00 A.M. to September 23 at 3:00 A.M. • NUMEROLOGY 2

Possessions and Desires . . .

Gem: Hyacinth—This stone might aid the memory.

Flower: China Pink—It takes time, but your wishes do come true.

Astral Color, Color Need, Apparel Colors: Your Astral Color is Navy Blue—the color of style and refinement. Violet in your environment keeps you empathetic toward others. In your wardrobe, Light Blue gives you strength and determination.

Fragrance: Look for those classic scents that give you the feeling of fresh and sparkling clean, scents containing jasmine, ylang ylang, and roses.

Tree: Maple—You have both great stability and flashes of intuition.

Instruments: Pipe organ, cymbal, drum

Composers: Handel, Johann Sebastian Bach

Bird: Cuckoo—A good flyer and very seldom a quitter. Many seem more independent than they actually are; yearn for more nurturing than one would expect.

Symbol: Cross—the symbol of self-sacrifice and reconciliation.

Harmonious Health and Nutrition . . .

Health Scent: Apple—A vivacious scent encouraging energy. Will help you to be more creative, intuitive and positive.

Favorable Foods: Celery, huckleberries, molasses, beef, buttermilk

What's Lucky . . .

Lucky Numbers: 3, 5, 20
Best Months: February and November
Best Day of the Week: Wednesday
Best Month Days: 2, 11, 20, 29

Lucky Charms: Two 50-cent pieces. Give someone else one of them.

Harmonious Signs for Relationships and Partnerships: Capricorn and Taurus

Spiritual Guides . . .

Star: Al Awa—Those with this star are often objects of others' desire.

Angel: Hamaliel—This angel governs logic and shows us what is real. His lessons in personal ethics always improve our karma.

Guardian Angel: Uriel—This angel brings the light of God's guidance.

Spiritual Stone: Jasper—This stone may soothe bruised emotions.

✴ JUDITH'S INSIGHT ✴

Many may see you as shy, but you love being noticed. In love, you long for stability and security. You go out of your way to understand others, and you should look for a partner who could understand you. Take time selecting that special someone. Later in life you learn that love is not always neat and orderly the way you would like it.

You have an eye for fine things and are drawn to excitement of any kind. The older you get, the more confident and determined you seem. You seek adventure in your own way. Your love of nature and the unusual should make you a great camper, and you may have the desire to climb mountains or sail around the world.

Plan a career in journalism, research, or law. You would make an excellent paralegal. Because of your love of travel and nature, anthropology fascinates you. Stay out of other people's way, and at the same time, be careful not to trip over your own feet.

As much as you explore the world and all it has to offer, it will be your home that is your palace.

✴ ✴ ✴

Possessions and Desires . . .

Gem: Jasper—This stone could grant the bearer protection from sadness.

Flower: Cornflower—You have an abundance of inner riches.

Astral Color, Color Need, Apparel Color: Your Astral Color is Navy Blue—the color of style and refinement. Violet in your environment keeps you empathetic toward others. In your wardrobe, Green is your power color for overcoming obstacles.

Fragrance: Look for those classic scents that give you the feeling of fresh and sparkling clean, scents containing jasmine, ylang ylang, and roses.

Tree: Elm—You have willpower, strength, and the ability to stand alone.

Instrument: Trombone

Composers: Verdi, Mendelssohn, Schumann

Bird: Killdeer—This bird is usually found consorting with other species, and can adapt to any environment.

Symbol: Wreath—You have been crowned with a special personality. You are strong but extremely compassionate.

Harmonious Health and Nutrition . . .

Health Scent: Rose—This scent will lead you to passionate thoughts and make you feel warm inside.

Favorable Foods: Swiss chard, pineapple, raw sugar, liver, buttermilk

What's Lucky . . .

Lucky Numbers: 3, 5, 12
Best Months: February and November
Best Day of the Week: Wednesday
Best Month Days: 3, 12, 21, 30

Lucky Charm: A pen that someone else has already used.

Harmonious Signs for Relationships and Partnerships: Capricorn and Taurus

Spiritual Guides . . .

Star: Caphir—People born under this star catch what they chase.

Angel: Hamaliel—This angel governs logic and shows us what is real. His lessons in personal ethics always improve our karma.

Guardian Angel: Johiel—This angel is a protector of all those with a humble heart.

Spiritual Stone: Jasper—This stone may soothe bruised emotions.

✶ JUDITH'S INSIGHT ✶

Intrigued with any knowledge you can drink up, you make the perfect student, even if you never expand your formal education. You have more hidden talent than you know. You may seem egotistical and have bouts of low self-esteem.

Your polite charm attracts others to you. Unfortunately, you should avoid some of them. You always look great and are really a very tender soul. Avoid falling victim to your moods and appearing cranky.

Your ability to have all your ducks in a row at times makes it easy for you to adapt to most working environments, especially those in accounting, law, journalism, or business. Even if it's counting change, you have a knack with numbers. As a general rule, you love money, and it wouldn't be surprising for your career to be centered on it.

Impeccable taste in style and fashion, you love being dressed in a sharp suit or outfit. A born critic, you take on that role even when no one asks. Lucky in love, you have a certain sweetness and charm that attracts prospective partners to you. Your lesson in life: learn when to walk and when to run.

✶ ✶ ✶

Possessions and Desires . . .

Gem: Emerald—Those who carry this stone tend to be lucky in love.

Flower: Primrose—You will never lose sight of the simple pleasures of childhood.

Astral Color, Color Need, Apparel Color: Your Astral Color is Navy Blue—the color of style and refinement. Violet in your environment keeps you empathetic toward others. In your wardrobe, Light Blue gives you strength and determination.

Fragrance: Look for those classic scents that give you the feeling of fresh and sparkling clean, scents containing jasmine, ylang ylang, and roses.

Tree: Cherry—You will find yourself faced with constant new emotional awakenings.

Instruments: Bass, clarinet

Composers: Haydn, Wagner

Bird: Goldfinch—These gentle creatures can seem moody, especially in unsettled weather.

Symbol: Star—You are full of inner brightness and will stand out in any crowd. You will be seen as special.

Harmonious Health and Nutrition . . .

Health Scent: Vanilla—This scent will fill you with a feeling of cleanliness and stability.

Favorable Foods: Endive, raspberries, chocolate, chicken, cottage cheese

What's Lucky . . .

Lucky Numbers: 3, 5, 44

Best Months: February and November

Best Day of the Week: Wednesday

Best Month Days: 4, 13, 22, 31

Lucky Charm: A piece of material cut from something in your home.

Harmonious Signs for Relationships and Partnerships: Capricorn and Taurus

Spiritual Guides . . .

Star: Al Awa—Those with this star are often objects of others' desire.

Angel: Hamaliel—This angel governs logic and shows us what is real. His lessons in personal ethics always improve our karma.

Guardian Angel: St. Thomas—This angel brings affection from others and encourages you in all that you do.

Spiritual Stone: Jasper—This stone may soothe bruised emotions.

✳ JUDITH'S INSIGHT ✳

You stand out in a crowd. Strong, sensible, and a bit headstrong, you must be cautious about how people are perceiving you. Sometimes it may not be enough to mean well. You have many talents, and your determination takes you places. The possibilities are endless.

You are creative to some degree and may do very well in theater, engineering, teaching, or government. You make an excellent parent because you're so good to your own. Learn to conquer the urge toward self-centeredness. There is no doubt you'll have stages in your life when your own needs will blind you to the needs of others.

In relationships of any kind, you will be the more eager to please and easygoing. You need things to have rules and follow an established order. You should always agree to find a balance acceptable for everyone involved. Your word is law. You are just as good at making promises as following them through.

Known for your different style in doing things, you like unique art and insist on a very well-organized home. Your living arrangements, relationships, and family are very important to you. You can take things very seriously. You are a sensitive soul and subject yourself to way more stress than you should. When you begin to feel overwhelmed, step back and free your thoughts before you lose perspective.

✶ ✶ ✶

SEPTEMBER 23 VIRGO • The festivities and celebrations of the zodiac
August 23 at 6:00 A.M. to September 23 at 3:00 A.M. • NUMEROLOGY 5

Possessions and Desires . . .

Gem: Jasper—This stone could grant the bearer protection from sadness.

Flower: Ivy Spig—You may spend so much time trying to please others that you forget to take care of you.

Astral Color, Color Need, Apparel Color: Your Astral Color is Crimson, which reflects your ability to nurture. Yellow in your environment stimulates and exhilarates you. In your wardrobe, Brown brings you stability.

Fragrance: Look for those classic scents that give you the feeling of fresh and sparkling clean, scents containing jasmine, ylang ylang, and roses.

Tree: Apple—You are creative, full of joy, and nearly magical. You bring happiness.

Instruments: Viola, trumpet

Composer: Liszt

Bird: Stork—Turkish bird, held in high esteem the world over. This bird is intelligent but may have strange tendencies.

Symbol: Triangle—You have the right combination of abilities.

Harmonious Health and Nutrition . . .

Health Scent: Peach—This scent may balance your good qualities so that they equal your charm.

Favorable Foods: Watercress, raspberries, molasses, beef, cottage cheese

What's Lucky . . .

Lucky Numbers: 3, 5, 32
Best Months: February and November
Best Day of the Week: Wednesday
Best Month Days: 4, 5, 23
Lucky Charms: A rabbit's foot or a white candle.
Harmonious Signs for Relationships and Partnerships: Capricorn and Taurus

Spiritual Guides . . .

Star: Al Awa—Those with this star are often objects of others' desire.

Angel: Hamaliel—This angel governs logic and shows us what is real. His lessons in personal ethics always improve our karma.

Guardian Angel: Plavwell—The guardian that gives power and strength to one's presence.

Spiritual Stone: Jasper—This stone may soothe bruised emotions.

✶ JUDITH'S INSIGHT ✶

You have a kind heart and a warm soul combined with a hair-trigger temper. A quality person who has a strong desire for success, you love frequent changes, especially in your home. You can never get your furniture quite the way you want, and you rearrange rooms on a regular basis. A frequent shopper, you express who you are through your manner of dress. Every day you have a completely different style of clothing. Versatility is a recurring theme throughout your life.

Extremely flexible, you're capable of handling just about any predicament and command respect from others. You would do well in the legal profession. Your methodical and organized mind lends itself to research. You do tend to overanalyze at times, which results in your taking things too seriously. Balance and harmony are key. Usually, you get what you want, but not without expending a lot of effort.

Listen to that little voice inside your head more often. You were blessed with fine instincts for a reason.

No challenge is too great for you, and you'll have many to meet. You could be offered many career opportunities because of the quality of your work. At some time, you may want to write a book that could be published. Some of your work may make you famous. While you are struggling so to get ahead and keep up with the neighbors, be sure to take time to love and laugh. You are a person who thrives on work but still needs to fit in some enjoyment. Otherwise, what's the point of working so hard?

You put a lot of energy into everything you do including romance and love relationships. But you are one who needs a lot of attention. Keep this in mind when picking a mate.

✶ ✶ ✶

SEPTEMBER 24

LIBRA • The scales of justice

September 23 at 3:00 A.M. to October 23 at 12:00 P.M. • NUMEROLOGY 6

Possessions and Desires . . .

Gem: Diamond—This stone is thought to encourage harmony in relationships and gives strength to the troubled.

Flower: Cress—You like to be in control of your world.

Astral Color, Color Need, Apparel Color: Your Astral color is Crimson, which reflects your ability to nurture. Yellow in your environment stimulates and exhilarates you. In your wardrobe, Brown brings you stability.

Fragrance: Pick scents that are soft and not overwhelming, like eclectic mixtures of wildflowers.

Tree: Palm—You tend to be very healthy and creative.

Instruments: Tambourine, lyre

Composer: Schubert

Bird: Goldfinch—there are no less than forty-four species of the finch, from the dull and inviting, to the extraordinarily active and exquisite. This can sometimes be the most charming bird. These gentle creatures can be very shy in unsettled weather.

Symbol: Crescent—You are more likely to be influenced by the phases of the moon. Your easygoing manner leads you to peaceful situations.

Harmonious Health and Nutrition . . .

Health Scent: Orange Blossom—This scent may balance your body, mind, and soul.

Favorable Foods: Radishes, watermelon, wholewheat bread, walnuts

What's Lucky . . .

Lucky Numbers: 6, 9
Best Months: August and December
Best Day of the Week: Friday
Best Month Days: 6, 15, 24
Lucky Charms: A religious token or card from any religion.

Harmonious Signs for Relationships and Partnerships: Aquarius and Gemini

Spiritual Guides . . .

Star: Al Icliel—This is the star for those who easily submit to authority.

Angel: Zuriel—This angel lends us the power to find balance when we desperately need it.

Guardian Angel: Michael—"Who is like God."

Spiritual Stone: Sapphire—The stone of serenity and prosperity.

✷ JUDITH'S INSIGHT ✷

You have a great head on your shoulders, but you take responsibility too seriously. Why must you worry about everyone else's problems? Your family and friends are extremely important to you. But you often focus your intense concentration on problems for so long, you may miss the big picture.

You love drama in relationships. Stability and loyalty are equally important. Sometimes you like to stir the emotional pot and keep your partner on his or her toes. Usually you give love only after having received it. You yearn for freedom and adventure, but must have the security of knowing someone waits at home for you. Keep all this in mind when you choose a mate; you might forget and pick an unsuitable, inflexible partner.

No matter what career you choose, you'll earn a good living. Your early years will be steady and calm, but age loosens your thirst for freedom and spontaneity after a mild midlife crisis. You may work for one place faithfully for twenty years and then suddenly quit.

You have a creative way of nurturing and will do well as a teacher, day care provider, or doctor. Your love of art and fashion may lead you to a museum, an apparel or fragrance manufacturer, or the theater. It is most likely that you will have more than one career in your lifetime.

A good friend, you must check your temper at times. You are genuine, well-organized, and well-prepared in all your dealings. The more stable you can make your environment, the more settled you find your emotions.

✶ ✶ ✶

SEPTEMBER 25

LIBRA • The scales of justice

September 23 at 3:00 A.M. to October 23 at 12:00 P.M. • NUMEROLOGY 7

Possessions and Desires . . .

Gem: Agate—This stone may promote health and lead you to a long life.
Flower: Crocus—You love it when your home is in harmony.
Astral Color, Color Need, Apparel Color: Your Astral color is Crimson, which reflects your ability to nurture. Yellow in your environment stimulates and exhilarates you. In your wardrobe, Rose gives you balance and harmony.
Fragrance: Pick scents that are soft and not overwhelming, like eclectic mixtures of wildflowers.
Tree: Sycamore—The ability to have love, communicate with others, and have lasting relationships.
Instrument: Cello
Composers: Gluck, Brahms
Bird: Skylark—This handsome bird is beautiful when it sings. It always whistles while it works.
Symbol: Heart—You are enthusiastic, empathetic, and full of generosity and love.

Harmonious Health and Nutrition . . .

Health Scent: Jasmine—This scent may make you more easygoing when you are stressed.
Favorable Foods: Asparagus, prunes, wholewheat bread, Brazil nuts

What's Lucky . . .

Lucky Numbers: 6, 9
Best Months: August and December
Best Day of the Week: Friday
Best Month Days: 6, 15, 24
Lucky Charm: An old key.
Harmonious Signs for Relationships and Partnerships: Aquarius and Gemini

Spiritual Guides . . .

Star: Al Zubena—Those with this star often seek and find redemption.
Angel: Zuriel—This angel lends us the power to find balance when we desperately need it.
Guardian Angel: Raphael—This angel attends to all of your needs when you are looking for guidance.
Spiritual Stone: Sapphire—the stone of serenity and prosperity.

✶ JUDITH'S INSIGHT ✶

Positive, strong, and determined—both physically and mentally—you will accomplish much in life. Family and friends rely on you. Some expect you to meet all their needs. Make sure you don't take on more than you should. Relationships will be difficult because you want predictability at all times, as if you were following a script. It's impossible to live life with no surprises, and you'd be better off accepting the unexpected.

You have a pushy nature and need to be in control of your own life. Try to balance this by choosing your challenges, or everyday life will be very strenuous for you. You are too organized and prone to losing the big picture in an ocean of detail.

You are a snappy dresser and love it when people comment—which they often do—on your impeccable taste. There are several careers that you should find appealing. You would make a great nurse, computer analyst, actor, builder, or artist. What a range! There are so many different and competing sides to your personality, you do best if you use your abundant energy to further your ambitions. This is the key to unlocking your potential.

You are considerate, smart, and sweet. You are liberal minded, and there will be times in life you'll have so much freedom you'll feel uncomfortable. Stability and boundaries are needed much more than you realize.

✶ ✶ ✶

SEPTEMBER 26

LIBRA • The scales of justice

September 23 at 3:00 A.M. to October 23 at 12:00 P.M. • NUMEROLOGY 8

Possessions and Desires . . .

Gem: Chrysolite—This gem may help you clear your mind of sadness and worry.
Flower: Dock—You tend to be a very patient person.
Astral Color, Color Need, Apparel Color: Your Astral Color is Crimson, which reflects your ability to nurture. Yellow in your environment stimulates and exhilarates you. In your wardrobe, Brown brings you stability.
Fragrance: Pick scents that are soft and not overwhelming, like eclectic mixtures of wildflowers.
Tree: Pine—Your relationships tend to be harmonious, both emotionally and mentally.
Instrument: Cello
Composer: Mozart
Bird: Bobolink—This charming singer is equally good as a soloist or a member of an orchestra. It is a very romantic bird, most useful as an insect destroyer, and elegant, with beautiful feathers, and always pleasant to have around.
Symbol: Wings—You are the source of balance in your world—this will bring you contentment.

Harmonious Health and Nutrition . . .

Health Scent: Almond—This scent may revitalize you and open you to greater possibilities.
Favorable Foods: Carrots, bananas, whole-wheat bread, walnuts

What's Lucky . . .

Lucky Numbers: 6, 9
Best Months: August and December
Best Day of the Week: Friday
Best Month Days: 8, 17, 26
Lucky Charm: Red ribbon in your wallet or doorway.
Harmonious signs for Relationships and Partnerships: Aquarius and Gemini

Spiritual Guides . . .

Star: Al Zubena—Those with this star often seek and find redemption.
Angel: Zuriel—This angel lends us the power to find balance when we desperately need it.
Guardian Angel: Seraphim—An angel that brings love, light, and passion.
Spiritual Stone: Sapphire—the stone of serenity and prosperity.

✴ *JUDITH'S INSIGHT* ✴

An excellent student with fantastic grades, you are on a lifelong hunt for knowledge. You'd be a terrific investigator, researcher, scientist, and participant in any way in the legal profession. Try to put your other, creative side to good use even in jobs that require rigid adherence to set rules. Unless you have something to say, you don't speak. People like the sound of your voice.

You are a responsible employee, but may want to be as independent as possible. It wouldn't be surprising if you were gifted musically or if music played an important role in your life. You could be a creative director for a recording company or write music at some point in your life. You are a super executive and have no problem solving many puzzling business problems.

Your desire for constant change may help you at work, but it doesn't in relationships. Remember that energy is a flow that works best in a circuit; pick a mate who will send back what you give him or her. You're very affectionate and need that special someone to give you hugs, kisses, and sweet smiles every single day. Your family and friends will feel that they need to give you constant advice and may turn surly if you don't follow their suggestions. Don't feel pressured away from living your own life. You can be too much the perfectionist. Try to relax and leave the vacuuming and the gardening until tomorrow when you're more rested. Take time today to enjoy life more. You deserve it.

★ ★ ★

SEPTEMBER 27
LIBRA • The scales of justice
September 23 at 3:00 A.M. to October 23 at 12:00 P.M. • NUMEROLOGY 9

Possessions and Desires . . .

Gem: Beryl—This gem could be good for meditation and concentration.
Flower: Dandelion—You can be very in tune with the universe and have a strong intuition.
Astral Color, Color Need, Apparel Color: Your Astral Color is Crimson, which reflects your ability to nurture. Yellow in your environment stimulates and exhilarates you. In your wardrobe, Rose gives you balance and harmony.
Fragrance: Pick scents that are soft and not overwhelming, like eclectic mixtures of wildflowers.
Tree: Holly—Beware that you are not carried away by your passionate nature. The only way to grow is to be open to new experiences.
Instruments: Violin, tympanum
Composer: Gluck
Bird: Mockingbird—the most proficient minstrel in the world's orchestra; graceful and enthusiastic.
Symbol: Anchor—This tranquil symbol signifies stability and strength, and stands for strong commitments in relationships.

Harmonious Health and Nutrition . . .

Health Scent: Lavender—This scent might lead others to trust you and make you patient.
Favorable Foods: Celery, plums, whole-wheat bread, peanuts

What's Lucky . . .

Lucky Numbers: 6, 9
Best Months: August and December
Best Day of the Week: Friday
Best Month Days: 9, 18, 27
Lucky Charms: A U.S. coin or a bill of any amount from the year you were born.

Harmonious Signs for Relationships and Partnerships: Aquarius and Gemini

Spiritual Guides . . .

Star: Al Icliel—This is the star of those who easily submit to authority.
Angel: Zuriel—This angel lends us the power to find balance when we desperately need it.
Guardian Angel: Gabriel—"God is my strength."
Spiritual Stone: Sapphire—the stone of serenity and prosperity.

✶ JUDITH'S INSIGHT ✶

You want to be known for your mind, but a beauty like you stands out from the crowd like an ink spot on white carpeting. Learn to deal with admiration and attention—it will follow you all your life. Just don't let it go to your head that others are always fawning over you.

You could be a writer or philosopher because of your words of wisdom. In the game of life, this is your strong suit. You have a passionate personality that speaks volumes, and if you wanted to, you could have a career in professional sports.

People really enjoy your company and fall for your charm with the force of gravity. You may have a reputation of being conceited about how much you know. Though you offer many good opinions, those around may prefer you to keep your words of wisdom to yourself. Even if you're usually right, coming from you it's unwelcome.

Don't close any doors to possible careers because you don't really know what direction you want your life to take later on. Family and friends adore you for your amiable demeanor, and you have no problem keeping active friendships. Look for the best in everybody, and don't be forced to choose between groups of bickering friends.

✶ ✶ ✶

SEPTEMBER 28 LIBRA • The scales of justice
September 23 at 3:00 A.M. to October 23 at 12:00 P.M. • NUMEROLOGY 1

Possessions and Desires . . .

Gem: Diamond—This stone is thought to encourage harmony in relationships and gives strength to the troubled.

Flower: Gooseberry—You may spend so much time waiting for something better to happen that you miss what is good about your life.

Astral Color, Color Need, Apparel Color: Your Astral color is Crimson, which reflects your ability to nurture. Yellow in your environment stimulates and exhilarates you. In your wardrobe, Brown brings you stability.

Fragrance: Pick scents that are soft and not overwhelming, like eclectic mixtures of wildflowers.

Tree: Walnut—You are unusually helpful and always looking for constant changes in your life.

Instrument: Clarinet

Composer: Böhm

Bird: Hummingbird—This bird is delicate and graceful. It can remain still for hours, then dart off and be as busy as a bee.

Symbol: Crown—the universal sign of dignity.

Harmonious Health and Nutrition . . .

Health Scent: Strawberry—Soothing by nature, the strawberry promotes self-esteem and encourages love.

Favorable Foods: Corn, raspberries, whole-wheat bread, walnuts

What's Lucky . . .

Lucky Numbers: 6, 9
Best Months: August and December
Best Day of the Week: Friday
Best Month Days: 1, 10, 19
Lucky Charm: A new penny in your shoe.
Harmonious Signs for Relationships and Partnerships: Aquarius and Gemini

Spiritual Guides . . .

Star: Al Zubena—Those with this star often seek and find redemption.

Angel: Zuriel—This angel lends us the power to find balance when we desperately need it.

Guardian Angel: Malachi—"Messenger of Jehovah."

Spiritual Stone: Sapphire—the stone of serenity and prosperity.

✶ JUDITH'S INSIGHT ✶

Your mind is your greatest asset. With great focus and a well-rounded mind, you are equally good at cooking and changing the oil or tuning up the car. You would find success in employment in national or local government. Tax accounting would be a perfect career for you. Since you are such a great cook, you would make an excellent chef or restaurateur. Your refined taste and organizational skills are marketable. You won't have difficulty initiating and completing projects. Your love of work and long hours pay off down the road. Watch out for jealous coworkers. Your seemingly perfect ways can annoy others.

Making new friends is useful because you may lose some along the way with your bluntness. You need to learn patience and tact with others, particularly when they are in need of consolation. Should you decide to be a physician or nurse, you'll need to work on your bedside manner.

You're fond of music and may enjoy singing. Someone close to you could be heavily involved in music. As you get older you may develop an understanding that life isn't as serious as you previously believed. For you, looser is better.

You are romantically guarded; whoever wants to storm the castle you built around your heart had better be very patient. This is not necessarily a bad thing, it's just that relationships take time for you. You may meet many different types before you discover your perfect soul mate in a surprising situation. You are loyal and faithful when you finally make a commitment.

✶ ✶ ✶

SEPTEMBER 29

LIBRA • The scales of justice

September 23 at 3:00 A.M. to October 23 at 12:00 P.M. • NUMEROLOGY 2

Possessions and Desires . . .

Gem: Chrysolite—This gem may help you clear your mind of sadness and worry.

Flower: Guelderrose—You open up when you feel emotional warmth.

Astral Color, Color Need, Apparel Color: Your Astral Color is Crimson, which reflects your ability to nurture. Yellow in your environment stimulates and exhilarates you. In your wardrobe, Rose gives you balance and harmony.

Fragrance: Pick scents that are soft and not overwhelming, like eclectic mixtures of wildflowers.

Tree: Maple—You have great stability and flashes of intuition.

Instrument: Pipe organ

Composers: Handel, Johann Sebastian Bach

Bird: Stork—Storks have a strange type of intelligence that is easily misunderstood. The stork is known to have a pleasing nature.

Symbol: Cross—the symbol of self-sacrifice and reconciliation.

Harmonious Health and Nutrition . . .

Health Scent: Apple—You are creative and full of joy, and nearly magical. You bring happiness.

Favorable Foods: Peas, prunes, whole-wheat bread, almonds

What's Lucky . . .

Lucky Numbers: 6, 9

Best Months: August and December

Best Day of the Week: Friday

Best Month Days: 2, 11, 20

Lucky Charms: Two 50-cent pieces. Give someone else one of them.

Harmonious Signs for Relationships and Partnerships: Aquarius and Gemini

Spiritual Guides . . .

Star: Al Icliel—This is the star of those who easily submit to authority.

Angel: Zuriel—This angel lends us the power to find balance when we desperately need it.

Guardian Angel: St. John—This angel simplifies that which is complicated.

Spiritual Stone: Sapphire—the stone of serenity and prosperity.

✷ JUDITH'S INSIGHT ✷

You do whatever needs to be done in the exact manner it should be done. You are pleasant to deal with and happy just to be alive. Sports will play a role in your life, if only as a hobby. You are intrigued by how things work and what people who have come before have felt and thought. One of your most cherished goals is to extensively travel the country or the world.

You will probably be a bit headstrong at times. A career connected with nature is perfect—you so love the outdoors. Gardening, flower arranging, and being near rivers and other waterways also appeal to your senses. You might live on or near the sea and love it. Follow your interest in science and chemistry. You may have ambitions of becoming a doctor.

Your frank and judgmental nature could cost you a friend or two when you are younger. Fortunately, the years teach you to be a little more balanced in what you say. You may seem cold to some people, but that's only because you're so shy. To know you is to love you, and there aren't many as loyal as you. Relationships take time for you, and you don't feel settled unless you're part of a couple. Friendships, relationships, or partners always add something vital and necessary to your life. You will learn to listen to yourself more because your self-esteem grows as you get older.

You can be your own worst enemy and need to relax and enjoy life. You have psychic abilities and really do know the right direction to take. Listen to your heart: all the answers you need are deep in your soul.

✷ ✷ ✷

SEPTEMBER 30

LIBRA • The scales of justice

September 23 at 3:00 A.M. to October 23 at 12:00 P.M. • NUMEROLOGY 3

Possessions and Desires . . .

Gem: Ruby—This stone may lead you to energy, friendship, and happiness.

Flower: Bluebell—You are steadfast and constant in your emotions.

Astral Color, Color Need, Apparel Color: Your Astral Color is Crimson, which reflects your ability to nurture. Yellow in your environment stimulates and exhilarates you. In your wardrobe, Brown brings you stability.

Fragrance: Pick scents that are soft and not overwhelming, like eclectic mixtures of wildflowers.

Tree: Elm—You have willpower, strength, and the ability to stand alone.

Instrument: Trombone

Composers: Verdi, Mendelssohn, Schumann

Bird: Swan—Regarded as royal and sacred, this bird has the protective nature of a mother, and can become a furious fighter in the defense of its young.

Symbol: Wreath—You have been crowned with a special personality. You are strong but extremely compassionate.

Harmonious Health and Nutrition . . .

Health Scent: Rose—This scent will lead you to passionate thoughts and make you feel warm inside.

Favorable Foods: Spinach, cherries, wholewheat bread, peanuts

What's Lucky . . .

Lucky Numbers: 6, 9

Best Months: August and December

Best Day of the Week: Friday

Best Month Days: 3, 12, 21

Lucky Charm: A pen that someone else has already used.

Harmonious Signs for Relationships and Partnerships: Aquarius and Gemini

Spiritual Guides . . .

Star: Al Icliel—This is the star of those who easily submit to authority.

Angel: Zuriel—This angel lends us the power to find balance when we desperately need it.

Guardian Angel: Johiel—This angel is a protector of all those with a humble heart.

Spiritual Stone: Sapphire—the stone of serenity and prosperity.

✳ JUDITH'S INSIGHT ✳

You welcome change and love to rearrange things. Your home is your place of security. Very good at juggling thousands of small details and talented in design, you would be a good architect, set designer, engineer, project manager, or computer programmer.

You are fascinated with the process of learning, and nothing escapes your interest. Extremely good at math, you may find job satisfaction working with accounting or numbers. You have a strong physical presence that others feed off. You accomplish more in one hour than most can in a day. You make things happen.

Watch out for your arrogance. People need patience from you most. Kind and open-minded with those close to you, you can also be compassionate and caring to strangers. You may become famous through your humanitarian efforts.

When it comes to romance, you know right away who you want but can never have him or her right away. Things take time, especially a relationship to last a lifetime. Your life's lesson is to wait with grace and balance.

Order and neatness are a must, but you don't want to be the one who keeps it that way. You are a good person who would do well to understand that others don't think or rush into situations as quickly as you. Use your intuition. You know the right answers are inside you, but they usually seem too good to be true. You can be a success at work if you choose to make the effort and are patient. Remember to always be flexible, and you will get where you want to go.

★ ★ ★

OCTOBER

OCTOBER 1   LIBRA • The scales of justice
September 23 at 3:00 A.M. to October 23 at 12:00 P.M.   •   NUMEROLOGY 1

Possessions and Desires . . .

Gem: Turquoise—This stone might help you find material gain.

Flower: Horse Chestnut—You may thirst for the good things in life.

Astral Color, Color Need, Apparel Color: Your Astral Color is Crimson, which reflects your ability to nurture. Yellow in your environment stimulates and exhilarates you. In your wardrobe, Rose gives you balance and harmony.

Fragrance: Pick scents that are soft and not over-whelming, like eclectic mixtures of wildflowers.

Tree: Walnut—You are unusually helpful and always looking for constant changes in your life.

Instrument: Organ

Composer: Böhm

Bird: Dove—the bird of hope during strife. It coos its song even in the dark of night.

Symbol: Crown—the universal sign of dignity.

Harmonious Health and Nutrition . . .

Health Scent: Strawberry—Soothing by nature, the strawberry promote self-esteem and encourages love

Favorable Foods: Asparagus, bananas, whole-wheat bread, almonds

What's Lucky . . .

Lucky Numbers: 6, 9
Best Months: August and December
Best Day of the Week: Friday
Best Month Days: 1, 10, 19
Lucky Charm: A new penny in your shoe.
Harmonious Signs for Relationships and Partnerships: Aquarius and Gemini

Spiritual Guides . . .

Star: Al Icliel—This is the star of those who easily submit to authority.

Angel: Zuriel—This angel lends us the power to find balance when we desperately need it.

Guardian Angel: Malachi—"Messenger of Jehovah."

Spiritual Stone: Sapphire—the stone of serenity and prosperity.

✴ JUDITH'S INSIGHT ✴

You never fear showing what you feel. You are a very emotional person. Your home is your kingdom, and you are most comfortable when in your own space. Your sunny disposition makes it easy for others to like you.

You would make a wonderful teacher or professor, but your options aren't limited to education. You have talent for mathematics, bookkeeping, and sales. You may lean toward a career using your creative ability or, perhaps, one in the legal profession. You could be a skilled craftsperson or mechanic. You have a way with words and the ability to make the complex seem clear to other people. You would be a great theater or book critic.

You can be quickly knocked off balance when emotionally overwhelmed. Your intensity may be more than you or others close to you can handle. You're giving and kindhearted, so others easily attach themselves to you. Be careful to temper your generosity, or you may become exhausted. Ninety percent of the time you're a sweetie, but when things don't go your way, you can be a bitter pill.

Protecting yourself by recognizing your limitations and needs will help you avoid many heartaches in your life. Although at times undoubtedly complicated, you are happiest in a long term relationship. You find comfort in being in a partnership.

★ ★ ★

OCTOBER 2 LIBRA • The scales of justice
September 23 at 3:00 A.M. to October 23 at 12:00 P.M. • NUMEROLOGY 2

Possessions and Desires . . .

Gem: Sapphire—This gem may help you find forgiveness from those you've wronged.
Flower: Juniper—You may spend too much time guarding yourself from imagined dangers.
Astral Color, Color Need, Apparel Color: Your Astral Color is Crimson, which reflects your ability to nurture. Yellow in your environment stimulates and exhilarates you. In your wardrobe, Brown brings you stability.
Fragrance: Pick scents that are soft and not overwhelming, like eclectic mixtures of wildflowers.
Tree: Maple—You have great stability and flashes of intuition.
Instrument: Cymbal
Composers: Handel, Johann Sebastian Bach
Bird: Cuckoo—a good flyer, and very seldom a quitter. Some cuckoos tend to think they favor lonely isolation, but what they really yearn for is a family relationship.
Symbol: Cross—the symbol of self-sacrifice and reconciliation.

Harmonious Health and Nutrition . . .

Health Scent: Apple—A vivacious scent encouraging energy. Will help you to be more creative, intuitive and positive.
Favorable Foods: Radishes, blackberries, whole-wheat bread, Brazil nuts

What's Lucky . . .

Lucky Numbers: 6, 9
Best Months: August and December
Best Day of the Week: Friday
Best Month Days: 2, 11, 20
Lucky Charms: Two 50-cent pieces. Give someone else one of them.
Harmonious Signs for Relationships and Partnerships: Aquarius and Gemini

Spiritual Guides . . .

Star: Al Zubena—Those with this star often seek and find redemption.
Angel: Zuriel—This angel lends us the power to find balance when we desperately need it.
Guardian Angel: St. John—This angel simplifies that which is complicated.
Spiritual Stone: Sapphire—the stone of serenity and prosperity.

✦ JUDITH'S INSIGHT ✦

Sincerity is your strongest characteristic. They say that nice guys finish last, and you prove them wrong. Your kindness and genuineness will bring you many good things throughout your life. Sometime around middle age or just after, you and one other person may decide to start a business. This person won't exactly be your equal, but they will still be vital to your success.

You need to be with someone in a close relationship to feel settled. You are cautious when it comes to finding love, as you should be. Finding a devoted mate may take years. Remember, don't sacrifice yourself just to have a partner. You may find that behavior brings you momentary happiness but in the long run yields only distress.

You would do well in jobs in government, engineering, or any highly structured industry. There's a side of you that yearns to be theatrical, even if it's in customer service, using humor to soothe people with complaints. You are a born communicator and will send the world a message whether as an artist or innovator. It is very important for you to find peace in the places you live and work. If the atmosphere around you is not conducive to your inner serenity, you will not succeed. You do better later in life when you don't feel the need to be so serious all the time. Most people get more fearful as they get older, but you're the reverse. Just remember to relax and laugh especially during low times. Just because balance is a difficult struggle for you doesn't mean that you can't eventually find it.

★ ★ ★

OCTOBER 3   LIBRA • The scales of justice

September 23 at 3:00 A.M. to October 23 at 12:00 P.M.   •   NUMEROLOGY 3

Possessions and Desires . . .

Gem: Ruby—This stone may lead you to energy, friendship, and happiness.

Flower: Wheat—You could end up very wealthy.

Astral Color, Color Need, Apparel Color: Your Astral Color is Crimson, which reflects your ability to nurture. Yellow in your environment stimulates and exhilarates you. In your wardrobe, Rose gives you balance and harmony.

Fragrance: Pick scents that are soft and not overwhelming, like eclectic mixtures of wildflowers.

Tree: Elm—You have willpower, strength, and the ability to stand alone.

Instrument: Trombone

Composers: Verdi, Mendelssohn, Schumann

Bird: Eagle—This bird is quick to use its powers of flight. It can see immeasurable distances in a single glance, and can sometimes appear to be indifferent.

Symbol: Wreath—You have been crowned with a special personality. You are strong but extremely compassionate.

Harmonious Health and Nutrition . . .

Health Scent: Rose—This scent will lead you to passionate thoughts and make you warm.

Favorable Foods: Spinach, peaches, wholewheat bread, walnuts

What's Lucky . . .

Lucky Numbers: 6, 9

Best Months: August and December

Best Day of the Week: Friday

Best Month Days: 3, 12, 21

Lucky Charm: A pen that someone else has already used.

Harmonious Signs for Relationships and Partnerships: Aquarius and Gemini

Spiritual Guides . . .

Star: Al Zubena—Those with this star often seek and find redemption.

Angel: Zuriel—This angel lends us the power to find balance when we desperately need it.

Guardian Angel: Johiel—This angel is a protector of all those with a humble heart.

Spiritual Stone: Sapphire—the stone of serenity and prosperity.

✶ JUDITH'S INSIGHT ✶

You love justice, so don't be surprised to find yourself in a courthouse often during your life. If you don't choose to enter the legal profession, you may have many dealings with it, usually having to do with important documents like contracts, financial reports, or stocks and bonds. It's up to you whether you're a champion of the underdog or the underdog yourself. You would also make a great mediator, psychologist, or philosopher. You understand the secrets that lie beneath what others see. You will understand life more clearly than most people could ever hope to imagine.

You have good friends because you know relationships take work, and you're a willing, devoted friend. You find mates quite easily, and this could be beneficial if you go about it properly. Others will strive to bring you happiness, not only emotionally, but financially. You have an alluring charm and wit.

You will be successful; your career will be very important to you after you turn thirty. In your late forties, after a brief midlife crisis, you may change jobs and work in a completely different, perhaps artistic field. The real you always rises to the top.

You are great with children, either your own or those close to you. Anything you do around young people brings luck. You will make a huge difference in a lot of lives, but you may not always understand just how much your efforts mean.

✶ ✶ ✶

OCTOBER 4   LIBRA • The scales of justice

September 23 at 3:00 A.M. to October 23 at 12:00 P.M. • NUMEROLOGY 4

Possessions and Desires . . .

Gem: Emerald—Those who carry this stone tend to be lucky in love.
Flower: Venus's Looking Glass—You are more comfortable using flattery than frankness.
Astral Color, Color Need, Apparel Color: Your Astral Color is Crimson, which reflects your ability to nurture. Yellow in your environment stimulates and exhilarates you. In your wardrobe, Brown brings you stability.
Fragrance: Pick scents that are soft and not overwhelming, like eclectic mixtures of wildflowers.
Tree: Cherry—You will find yourself faced with constant new emotional awakenings.
Instrument: Bass
Composers: Haydn, Wagner
Bird: Robin—the most sociable of all birds, with the ability to create quick friendships. It also can easily adapt to any home. When it wants something, it has the tendency to try to snatch it.
Symbol: Star—You are full of inner brightness and will stand out in any crowd. You will be seen as special.

Harmonious Health and Nutrition . . .

Health Scent: Vanilla—This scent will fill you with a feeling of cleanliness and stability.
Favorable Foods: Carrots, prunes, whole-wheat bread, peanuts

What's Lucky . . .

Lucky Numbers: 6, 9
Best Months: August and December
Best Day of the Week: Friday
Best Month Days: 4, 13, 22
Lucky Charm: A piece of material cut from something in your home.

Harmonious Signs for Relationships and Partnerships: Aquarius and Gemini

Spiritual Guides . . .

Star: Al Icliel—This is the star of those who easily submit to authority.
Angel: Zuriel—This angel lends us the power to find balance when we desperately need it.
Guardian Angel: Uriel—This angel brings the light of God's guidance.
Spiritual Stone: Sapphire—the stone of serenity and prosperity.

✶ *JUDITH'S INSIGHT* ✶

Here today, gone tomorrow is how you operate. It would be surprising to find you settled for more than a minute. You are a little erratic and drawn to unusual surroundings and people. The only thing you'll be patient about is working toward a lasting relationship. You are self-sacrificing or feel you are. In love matches, you tend to be a jellyfish that does what your mate dictates. Deep down you want a lot from a mate and need even more.

You can be contrary and change your mind way too often. Very close friends and family are important to you, but you push people away, which creates tension at work or social gatherings. Unfortunately, you only need to show up to have others drawn to you. You would prefer to be a professional athlete more than the work you wind up doing. Watch out for silly injuries, as you may be accident prone.

You can do any job you choose. Since you are drawn to the peculiar, you may be employed in a career that is a strange smattering of many fields. If you don't work at multiple jobs, you wear several hats at once. You would be successful doing scientific, legal, or other research.

You will be well-known for your cultural, religious, or political contributions.

✶ ✶ ✶

OCTOBER 5   LIBRA • The scales of justice
September 23 at 3:00 A.M. to October 23 at 12:00 P.M. • NUMEROLOGY 5

Possessions and Desires . . .

Gem: Sardius—This stone could give the wearer unusual insights into his or her own heart.
Flower: Turnip—You tend to greatly enjoy helping others.
Astral Color, Color Need, Apparel Color: Your Astral Color is Crimson, which reflects your ability to nurture. Yellow in your environment stimulates and exhilarates you. In your wardrobe, Rose gives you balance and harmony.
Fragrance: Pick scents that are soft and not overwhelming, like eclectic mixtures of wildflowers.
Tree: Apple—You are creative, full of joy, and nearly magical. You bring happiness.
Instrument: Trumpet
Composer: Liszt
Bird: Flamingo—This beautiful, gregarious bird is always careful of its enemy. It is also a caretaker of the young and tries to keep everyone happy.
Symbol: Triangle—You have the right combination of abilities.

Harmonious Health and Nutrition . . .

Health Scent: Peach—This scent may balance your good qualities so that they equal your charm.
Favorable Foods: Tomatoes, watermelon, wholewheat bread, almonds

What's Lucky . . .

Lucky Numbers: 6, 9
Best Months: August and December
Best Day of the Week: Friday
Best Month Days: 4, 5, 23
Lucky Charms: A rabbit's foot or a white candle.
Harmonious Signs for Relationships and Partnerships: Aquarius and Gemini

Spiritual Guides . . .

Star: Al Zubena—Those with this star often seek and find redemption.
Angel: Zuriel—This angel lends us the power to find balance when we desperately need it.
Guardian Angel: Plavwell—The guardian that gives power and strength to one's presence.
Spiritual Stone: Sapphire—the stone of serenity and prosperity.

✶ JUDITH'S INSIGHT ✶

You are highly compassionate and have no problem showing it. You love to have a good time and will do anything to smile on another's face. You have refined taste, a sharp mind, and a love of intellectual pursuits. Mentally graced with a little something extra, whether it be a high IQ, psychic abilities, extreme common sense, or all three, you are very special. Because you get so much done every day, you will accomplish much during your life. Combined with your other gifts, your patience and kindness allow you many fine opportunities to succeed. Only you can select your goals—no one else has the vision to see that far. You should make history in one way or another.

You go out of your way for everybody, even if it means sacrificing yourself. However, you are prone to be overly practical and levelheaded when it comes to romance and close relationships. You need to turn off the clattering of your computerlike mind for a moment so you can hear the symphony that your heart is playing. Choosing a mate to spend your life with isn't like buying a car or house. For one thing, there is *never* a resale value.

You always give and sacrifice without asking for your needs to be met. You may have more heartache than anyone should be forced to bear. You can adapt to almost any situation. You don't just go with the flow, you enhance it.

✶ ✶ ✶

OCTOBER 6

LIBRA • The scales of justice

September 23 at 3:00 A.M. to October 23 at 12:00 P.M. • NUMEROLOGY 6

Possessions and Desires . . .

Gem: Topaz—This is an excellent gift to be exchanged between very loyal friends.

Flower: Tuberose—You might find that you can't enjoy yourself unless there is a dash of danger.

Astral Color, Color Need, Apparel Color: Your Astral Color is Crimson, which reflects your ability to nurture. Yellow in your environment stimulates and exhilarates you. In your wardrobe, Brown brings you stability.

Fragrance: Pick scents that are soft and not overwhelming, like eclectic mixtures of wildflowers.

Tree: Palm—You tend to be very healthy and creative.

Instrument: Lyre

Composer: Schubert

Bird: Falcon—An expert hunter. When well-trained, it can adapt to many tasks and is usually obedient.

Symbol: Crescent—You are more likely to be influenced by the phases of the moon. Your easygoing manner leads you to peaceful situations.

Harmonious Health and Nutrition . . .

Health Scent: Orange Blossom—This scent may balance your body, mind, and soul.

Favorable Foods: Lettuce, prunes, whole-wheat bread, walnuts

What's Lucky . . .

Lucky Numbers: 6, 9

Best Months: August and December

Best Day of the Week: Friday

Best Month Days: 6, 15, 24

Lucky Charms: A religious token or card from any religion.

Harmonious Signs for Relationships and Partnerships: Aquarius and Gemini

Spiritual Guides . . .

Star: Al Icliel—This is the star of those who easily submit to authority.

Angel: Zuriel—This angel lends us the power to find balance when we desperately need it.

Guardian Angel: Michael—"Who is like God."

Spiritual Stone: Sapphire—the stone of serenity and prosperity.

✴ JUDITH'S INSIGHT ✴

You appreciate the art world, and maybe one day it will appreciate you. You see the world with an artist's eye. Creativity may be one of your strongest traits. You are very self-reliant except when it comes to love, where you find yourself adrift in a leaky emotional rowboat surrounded by a sea of need. Intimate relationships will mean everything to you, and you will do just about anything to find a secure partner. You don't have to be so anxious; your magnetic personality will attract a soul mate to you, but it will be difficult at first for the two of you to figure out how to adjust your powerful energies.

You have survived many disappointments; it sometimes seems that you avoid life's pitfalls just to wind up in the pits. You seem to thrive on adversity and laugh off even the greatest sorrow with style. Entertainment is important to you. You will be passionately fond of some form of the performing arts. You will be either a movie buff, music collector, or actor in a local play. You also love to celebrate living the good life by hosting frequent parties. You will be in the public eye in one way or another, whether you are the head of the PTA or the ringleader of your friends.

Your friends stay friends for life. You only lose friends when they leave this earth. But even then, they will be by your side as guardian angels. As you get older, you'll recognize everybody you meet changes you in some significant way. You are very persuasive, and others may consider you stubborn. This could be a positive thing for the most part but an obstacle in relationships. You are loyal to everyone, even if trusts are betrayed. Some see you as a rebel without a cause. Later in your life you just may find your cause.

✴ ✴ ✴

OCTOBER 7 LIBRA • The scales of justice

September 23 at 3:00 A.M. to October 23 at 12:00 P.M. • NUMEROLOGY 7

Possessions and Desires . . .

Gem: Sapphire—This stone may help you find forgiveness from those you wronged.

Flower: Traveler's Joy—You usually can't be happy unless you first feel safe.

Astral Color, Color Need, Apparel Color: Your Astral Color is Crimson, which reflects your ability to nurture. Yellow in your environment stimulates and exhilarates you. In your wardrobe, Rose gives you balance and harmony.

Fragrance: Pick scents that are soft and not overwhelming, like eclectic mixtures of wildflowers.

Tree: Sycamore—Yours is the ability to love, communicate honestly with others, and have lasting relationships.

Instrument: Harp

Composers: Gluck, Brahms.

Bird: Warbling Parakeet—the most beautiful of all birds, known as the love bird. It does seem to have the powers of imitation.

Symbol: Heart—You are enthusiastic, empathetic, and full of generosity and love.

Harmonious Health and Nutrition . . .

Health Scent: Jasmine—This scent may make you more easygoing when you are stressed.

Favorable Foods: Tomatoes, prunes, wholewheat bread, almonds

What's Lucky . . .

Lucky Numbers: 6, 9

Best Months: August and December

Best Day of the Week: Friday

Best Month Days: 6, 15, 24

Lucky Charm: An old key.

Harmonious Signs for Relationships and Partnerships: Aquarius and Gemini

Spiritual Guides . . .

Star: Al Zubena—Those with this star often seek and find redemption.

Angel: Zuriel—This angel lends us the power to find balance when we desperately need it.

Guardian Angel: Raphael—This angel attends to all of your needs when you are looking for guidance.

Spiritual Stone: Sapphire—the stone of serenity and prosperity.

✶ JUDITH'S INSIGHT ✶

You are ready, willing, and able to help others whenever they need you. You always like to be the good guy. You're ambitious and energetic and can be successful in out-of-the-ordinary professions. You have a tendency to dominate in all situations, usually because everyone recognizes you're the person who deserves to be in charge. You can easily see the way out of any predicament.

In every job you do, you will be the troubleshooter. If something doesn't work, gets stuck, or becomes lost or hopelessly tangled, you are the one everyone expects to solve the problem. You will develop a fondness for the fine arts and are energized by being with groups of people.

Your family and close friends give you a heaping portion of heartaches and heartburn. After tempers cool, you are the one who patches up the holes and makes everything all better.

You will have a strongly intense love relationship at least once in your life. Love and being attached are the most important things to you. Just remember to stop thinking and start doing—it's the only way to get to where you want. Never allow your fears to choke off your ability to be happy. Allow yourself the time it takes for everything to come into your life. You have patience for others; you just need patience when it comes to you.

Some careers that you may excel at: lawyer, investigator, a president or vice president of a large corporation, real estate, philosopher, writer, and doctor.

✶ ✶ ✶

OCTOBER 8 LIBRA • The scales of justice

September 23 at 3:00 A.M. to October 23 at 12:00 P.M. • NUMEROLOGY 8

Possessions and Desires . . .

Gem: Chrysolite—This gem may help you clear your mind of sadness and worry.
Flower: Tamarisk—You may get a secret thrill from tales of outlaws.
Astral Color, Color Need, Apparel Color: Your Astral Color is Crimson, which reflects your ability to nurture. Yellow in your environment stimulates and exhilarates you. In your wardrobe, Brown brings you stability.
Fragrance: Pick scents that are soft and not overwhelming, like eclectic mixtures of wildflowers.
Tree: Pine—Your relationships tend to be harmonious, both emotionally and mentally.
Instrument: Cello
Composer: Mozart
Bird: Bobolink—This charming singer is equally good as a soloist or a member of an orchestra. It is a very romantic bird, most useful as an insect destroyer, and elegant, with beautiful feathers, and is always pleasant to have around.
Symbol: Wings—You are the source of balance in your world—this will bring you contentment.

Harmonious Health and Nutrition . . .

Health Scent: Almond—This scent may revitalize you and open you to greater possibilities.
Favorable Foods: Lettuce, blackberries, wholewheat bread, Brazil nuts

What's Lucky . . .

Lucky Numbers: 6, 9
Best Months: August and December
Best Day of the Week: Friday
Best Month Days: 8, 17, 26
Lucky Charm: Red ribbon in your wallet or doorway.
Harmonious Signs for Relationships and Partnerships: Aquarius and Gemini

Spiritual Guides . . .

Star: Al Zubena—Those with this star often seek and find redemption.
Angel: Zuriel—This angel lends us the power to find balance when we desperately need it.
Guardian Angel: Seraphim—An angel that brings love, light, and passion.
Spiritual Stone: Sapphire—the stone of serenity and prosperity.

✴ _JUDITH'S INSIGHT_ ✴

You can take life much too seriously, especially when young. You are prone to feeling far more pressure than the situation warrants. Other people aren't the ones who are causing you to feel so much stress; the guilty party is wearing your sneakers.

You're charming and understanding; this wins you attention every time. You tend to bore easily, especially when looking for that special someone to love. It'll be much easier for you to find a job than a spouse. You are very gifted when it comes to the qualities employers look for. You may aspire to become a musician, artist, teacher, lawyer, or designer. You are original and can be considered an innovative person. Somehow great ideas always find you right when you need them. You will work well with others because you enjoy their company.

Your family is a source of grief for you. They seem to leap from one crisis to another. You and your spouse may often feel like the only sane people trapped in an asylum because of the crazy life the two of you lead. You have the nasty habit of creating difficulties for yourself without meaning to.

You should be very wealthy for at least part of your life. Opportunities don't just knock, they blow your door off the hinges. Just remember that it never hurts to save money when you have it for possible times of hardship.

You'll find that the more you try to focus on what's best in others, the more you'll like yourself.

✴ ✴ ✴

Possessions and Desires . . .

Gem: Beryl—This gem could be good for meditation and concentration.
Flower: Celandine—Your happiness tends to occur later in life.
Astral Color, Color Need, Apparel Color: Your Astral Color is Crimson, which reflects your ability to nurture. Yellow in your environment stimulates and exhilarates you. In your wardrobe, Rose gives you balance and harmony.
Fragrance: Pick scents that are soft and not overwhelming, like eclectic mixtures of wildflowers.
Tree: Holly—Beware that you are not carried away by your passionate nature. The only way to grow is to be open to new experiences.
Instruments: Violin, tympanum
Composer: Gluck
Bird: Mockingbird—the most proficient minstrel in the world's orchestra; graceful and enthusiastic.
Symbol: Anchor—This tranquil symbol signifies stability and strength, and stands for strong commitments in relationships.

Harmonious Health and Nutrition . . .

Health Scent: Lavender—This scent might lead others to trust you and make you patient.
Favorable Foods: Carrots, peaches, whole-wheat bread, walnuts

What's Lucky . . .

Lucky Numbers: 6, 9, 18
Best Months: August and December
Best Day of the Week: Friday
Best Month Days: 9, 18, 27
Lucky Charms: A U.S. coin or a bill of any amount from the year you were born.

Harmonious Signs for Relationships and Partnerships: Aquarius and Gemini

Spiritual Guides . . .

Star: Al Icliel—This is the star of those who easily submit to authority.
Angel: Zuriel—This angel lends us the power to find balance when we desperately need it.
Guardian Angel: Gabriel—"God is my strength."
Spiritual Stone: Sapphire—the stone of serenity and prosperity.

✴ JUDITH'S INSIGHT ✴

For you there is no middle ground. You are equally ready to either smile or punch your way out of any situation. Honor is very important to you. You are a natural lawyer, debater, or critic. You would also make a much-sought-after surgeon. You are easily amused; with a comfy chair and a good book, you can be quite happy. You love learning new things. You are a born leader who will earn and deserve a position of authority.

Finding a mate should be a piece of cake. You must be careful not to hold on to all you catch, as some will cause you nothing but the worst kind of trouble. You have to keep your eyes, ears, and mind very open. You may have a large number of relationships.

You have a style that's all your own, and you tend to be very independent. Others see you as a loner, but you see yourself as a member of a fun group you have yet to find. It will be your life's work to fully integrate your personality. You are kindhearted, but your head is running the show. A warm soul like yours is filled with compassion, but you believe that others should learn to take care of themselves. Your good habits multiply to drive out the bad as you get older, and you become a much happier person.

Put yourself in the middle of your own life; wallflowers don't get to grow.

✴ ✴ ✴

OCTOBER 10 LIBRA • The scales of justice
September 23 at 3:00 A.M. to October 23 at 12:00 P.M. • NUMEROLOGY 1

Possessions and Desires . . .

Gem: Opal—Holding this stone may help you discover enough hope to go on.
Flower: Stock—You tend to love what you love all your life.
Astral Color, Color Need, Apparel Color: Your Astral Color is Crimson, which reflects your ability to nurture. Yellow in your environment stimulates and exhilarates you. In your wardrobe, Brown brings you stability.
Fragrance: Pick scents that are soft and not overwhelming, like eclectic mixtures of wildflowers.
Tree: Walnut—You are unusually helpful and always looking for constant changes in your life.
Instruments: French horn, organ, violin
Composer: Böhm
Bird: Bird of Paradise—the "birds of the Gods." You will shine and love extraordinary circumstances.
Symbol: Crown—the universal sign of dignity.

Harmonious Health and Nutrition . . .

Health Scent: Strawberry—Soothing by nature, the strawberry promotes self-esteem and encourages love.
Favorable Foods: Corn, prunes, whole-wheat bread, almonds

What's Lucky . . .

Lucky Numbers: 6, 9
Best Months: August and December
Best Day of the Week: Friday
Best Month Days: 1, 10, 19
Lucky Charm: A new penny in your shoe.
Harmonious Signs for Relationships and Partnerships: Aquarius and Gemini

Spiritual Guides . . .

Star: Al Zubena—Those with this star often seek and find redemption.
Angel: Zuriel—This angel lends us the power to find balance when we desperately need it.
Guardian Angel: Malachi—"Messenger of Jehovah."
Spiritual Stone: Sapphire—the stone of serenity and prosperity.

✷ JUDITH'S INSIGHT ✷

They say that the love of money is the root of all evil, but it's not that for you. Money to you is just a way to keep score; it doesn't mean much more than that. It seems that it's always flowing in a steady stream headed your way. This is good because you love to win. You're happiest at home and never really comfortable anywhere else. If anything disturbs the security you feel there, you will become dangerously restless. Your natural optimism makes it easy for you to cultivate both friends and lovers.

You'd make a wonderful grade school teacher but are more likely to work in a tightly structured environment because you crave financial security. Government, law, publishing, or other communications-related careers will probably suit you. You may wish to be employed as a skilled craftsperson or work with machines.

You are prone to losing yourself in your relationships and not always for the better. You need to maintain your balance when dealing with those you love. You overanalyze and magnify a small fight into a disaster and then at the end of the day forget that anything happened. When you learn to be less self-centered and opinionated, you will enjoy social interactions more. You are open to the point of bluntness. This works in business but can be a problem when it comes to love.

✷ ✷ ✷

Possessions and Desires . . .

Gem: Opal—Holding this stone may help you discover enough hope to go on.

Flower: Black-eyed Susan—You never stop struggling to overcome your troubles.

Astral Color, Color Need, Apparel Color: Your Astral Color is Crimson, which reflects your ability to nurture. Yellow in your environment stimulates and exhilarates you. In your wardrobe, Rose gives you balance and harmony.

Fragrance: Pick scents that are soft and not overwhelming, like eclectic mixtures of wildflowers.

Tree: Maple—You have great stability and flashes of intuition.

Instrument: Drum

Composers: Handel, Johann Sebastian Bach

Bird: Stork—Turkish bird, held in high esteem the world over. This bird is intelligent but may have strange tendencies.

Symbol: Cross—the symbol of self-sacrifice and reconciliation.

Harmonious Health and Nutrition . . .

Health Scent: Apple—A vivacious scent encouraging energy. Will help you to be more creative, intuitive, and positive.

Favorable Foods: Radishes, watermelon, whole-wheat bread, peanuts

What's Lucky . . .

Lucky Numbers: 6, 9
Best Months: August and December
Best Day of the Week: Friday
Best Month Days: 2, 11, 20
Lucky Charms: Two 50-cent pieces. Give someone else one of them.
Harmonious Signs for Relationships and Partnerships: Aquarius and Gemini

Spiritual Guides . . .

Star: Al Zubena—Those with this star often seek and find redemption.

Angel: Zuriel—This angel lends us the power to find balance when we desperately need it.

Guardian Angel: St. John—This angel simplifies that which is complicated.

Spiritual Stone: Sapphire—the stone of serenity and prosperity.

★ JUDITH'S INSIGHT ★

Kindness and sincerity are your greatest attributes. They say nice guys finish last, but you disprove them by finishing first and way ahead of the pack. When you help others, you bring out the best both in yourself and in everyone involved. Some say you make too many sacrifices, but you get more out of giving than the effort you expend.

You are happier in a partnership or relationship than on your own. You fear going through life alone without the love you need. You may commit to several unusual, hard-to-explain relationships during your lifetime. You are independent and dependent at the same time. You find enjoyment and security doing things as a part of a group.

You could be a musician, artist, teacher, or lawyer. You will never work in a job that lacks a clearly defined structure. Chaos makes you anxious. Even something as simple as an open window in the winter or unpainted ceilings can make you restless and moody. The more you feel connected to your working space, the better your productivity.

You are thorough in anything you do, true and loyal to friends, and quite conscientious. You fight to the end for your beliefs. You have your whole life mapped out, especially when it comes to career. You are like an artist who scraps things many times before making them perfectly. Everything you do will have a finished, well-thought-out quality to it.

★ ★ ★

OCTOBER 12

LIBRA • The scales of justice

September 23 at 3:00 A.M. to October 23 at 12:00 P.M. • NUMEROLOGY 3

Possessions and Desires . . .

Gem: Ruby—This stone may lead you to energy, friendship, and happiness.

Flower: Mundi Rose—If variety is the spice of life, yours is never mild.

Astral Color, Color Need, Apparel Color: Your Astral Color is Crimson, which reflects your ability to nurture. Yellow in your environment stimulates and exhilarates you. In your wardrobe, Brown brings you stability.

Fragrance: Pick scents that are soft and not overwhelming, like eclectic mixtures of wildflowers.

Tree: Elm—You have willpower, strength, and the ability to stand alone.

Instrument: Trombone

Composers: Verdi, Mendelssohn, Schumann

Bird: Eagle—This bird is quick to use its powers of flight. It can see immeasurable distances in a single glance, and can sometimes appear to be indifferent.

Symbol: Wreath—You have been crowned with a special personality. You are strong but extremely compassionate.

Harmonious Health and Nutrition . . .

Health Scent: Rose—This scent will lead you to passionate thoughts and make you feel warm inside.

Favorable Foods: Lentils, black figs, whole-wheat bread, almonds

What's Lucky . . .

Lucky Numbers: 6, 9
Best Months: August and December
Best Day of the Week: Friday
Best Month Days: 3, 12, 21
Lucky Charm: A pen that someone else has already used.
Harmonious Signs for Relationships and Partnerships: Aquarius and Gemini

Spiritual Guides . . .

Star: Al Zubena—Those with this star often seek and find redemption.

Angel: Zuriel—This angel lends us the power to find balance when we desperately need it.

Guardian Angel: Johiel—This angel is a protector of all those with a humble heart.

Spiritual Stone: Sapphire—the stone of serenity and prosperity.

✶ JUDITH'S INSIGHT ✶

Everything you love, you love deeply. Even the simplest things interest you. The smallest gestures are extremely important to you. You can be sentimental at heart, but you balance out the mush with a very clear and bright mind. You always understand the larger ramifications and would make an excellent author, counselor, or teacher. Your desire to learn what no one else knows may make you a scientist or surgeon. You have good friends because you work hard at maintaining connections. Nothing really comes easy to you in life, but you stubbornly keep practicing.

You have been blessed with charm, wit, and a devoted nature. You are more a giver than a taker. You have at least one great success you will remember and be well-known, respected, and admired for. You crave order and rules, both in your personal life and on the job.

Certain contracts or legal papers will be very important to you. There is every indication that you will do very well in the legal profession. More often than not you will come out on top when involved in trials. You're a winner, and your luck rubs off on others. You are generous with money. Just remember that you are here to make a difference—in large ways and small.

You like having a partner and you are usually in one relationship or another. Not every relationship will be what you want it to be, but you find yourself being more secure in having a mate than not.

✶ ✶ ✶

OCTOBER 13 LIBRA • The scales of justice

September 23 at 3:00 A.M. to October 23 at 12:00 P.M. • NUMEROLOGY 4

Possessions and Desires . . .

Gem: Emerald—Those who carry this stone tend to be lucky in love.

Flower: Red Rose—love shouldn't disappoint you for any length of time.

Astral Color, Color Need, Apparel Color: Your Astral Color is Crimson, which reflects your ability to nurture. Yellow in your environment stimulates and exhilarates you. In your wardrobe, Rose gives you balance and harmony.

Fragrance: Pick scents that are soft and not overwhelming, like eclectic mixtures of wildflowers.

Tree: Cherry—You will find yourself faced with constant new emotional awakenings.

Instruments: Clarinet, French Horn, piano

Composers: Haydn, Wagner

Bird: Killdeer—This bird is usually found consorting with other species, and can adapt to any environment.

Symbol: Star—You are full of inner brightness and will stand out in any crowd. You will be seen as special.

Harmonious Health and Nutrition . . .

Health Scent: Vanilla—This scent will fill you with a feeling of cleanliness and stability.

Favorable Foods: Asparagus, raspberries, whole-wheat bread, almonds

What's Lucky . . .

Lucky Numbers: 6, 9

Best Months: August and December

Best Day of the Week: Friday

Best Month Days: 4, 13, 22

Lucky Charm: A piece of material cut from something in your home.

Harmonious Signs for Relationships and Partnerships: Aquarius and Gemini

Spiritual Guides . . .

Star: Al Zubena—Those with this star often seek and find redemption.

Angel: Zuriel—This angel lends us the power to find balance when we desperately need it.

Guardian Angel: Uriel—This angel brings the light of God's guidance.

Spiritual Stone: Sapphire—the stone of serenity and prosperity.

✷ JUDITH'S INSIGHT ✷

You have mechanical abilities and can easily fix broken things. You are very original and will leave your mark on the world. You don't always have the time and energy you need in order to accomplish all your dreams. You know this but still won't give up the battle.

Home is extremely important, especially how it looks to others. You are overly giving in order to have a relationship that lasts. Your partner will expect you to sacrifice for him or her and then resent you for it. You will usually pick a difficult mate who has a more powerful personality. It's always your time, patience, and efforts that keep the marriage steady. At some point your partner may realize what you mean to him or her, allowing you to feel more satisfaction in love.

You learn early that acquiring things does not necessarily guarantee happiness. Family and friends are important to you. You keep people at arm's length, which leads to tension. It's easier to be distant than admit you have feelings that might hurt someone you care about.

You may love dangerous sports but tend to be a little accident prone. You should be all right if you are smart enough to be cautious. Good at everything, you would make a great salesperson, computer programmer, musician, or teacher. You have a dramatic flair, and your work belongs on stage, whether you are the actor or playwright. Your confidence takes you far. You are patient to a point but become frustrated once you reach your limits. Learn to stay grounded and continue waiting for what you need, and all will come to you.

✷ ✷ ✷

OCTOBER 14   LIBRA • The scales of justice
September 23 at 3:00 A.M. to October 23 at 12:00 P.M. • NUMEROLOGY 5

Possessions and Desires . . .

Gem: Sardius—This stone could give the wearer unusual insights into his or her own heart.

Flower: China Rose—You could fall into the trap of thinking that something new is necessarily more beautiful than what you have.

Astral Color, Color Need, Apparel Color: Your Astral Color is Crimson, which reflects your ability to nurture. Yellow in your environment stimulates and exhilarates you. In your wardrobe, Brown brings you stability.

Fragrance: Pick scents that are soft and not overwhelming, like eclectic mixtures of wildflowers.

Tree: Apple—You are creative, full of joy, and nearly magical. You bring happiness.

Instrument: Viola

Composer: Liszt

Bird: Flamingo—This beautiful, gregarious bird is always careful of its enemy. It is also a caretaker of the young, and tries to keep everyone happy.

Symbol; Triangle—You have the right combination of abilities.

Harmonious Health and Nutrition . . .

Health Scent: Peach—This scent may balance your good qualities so that they equal your charm.

Favorable Foods: Spinach, cherries, wholewheat bread, Brazil nuts

What's Lucky . . .

Lucky Numbers: 6, 9

Best Months: August and December

Best Day of the Week: Friday

Best Month Days: 4, 5, 23

Lucky Charms: A rabbit's foot or a white candle.

Harmonious Signs for Relationships and Partnerships: Aquarius and Gemini

Spiritual Guides . . .

Star: Al Zubena—Those with this star often seek and find redemption.

Angel: Zuriel—This angel lends us the power to find balance when we desperately need it.

Guardian Angel: Plavwell—The guardian that gives power and strength to ones presence.

Spiritual Stone: Sapphire—the stone of serenity and prosperity.

✴ *JUDITH'S INSIGHT* ✴

Family is very important to you. You need complete freedom, yet crave a stable, committed home and family life. This could be a bit of a contradiction, but at times in your life you will feel like you are receiving the best of both worlds.

Work is tremendously difficult, but somehow you manage. There will be endless delays and pressures before you eventually get where you want. You love nature and need to be around flowers, trees, and running brooks for inspiration. You would do very well as an environmental lawyer or someone fighting for the rights of animals or children.

With your patience, kindness, and intelligence, you will contribute much at work. Strong compassion, a love of life, and a unique vision will make you very successful and maybe even famous. Others are very surprised when you become moody and cranky. Work to manage your levels of frustration, understimulation, and insecurity.

Romance and intimate relationships are extremely important to you. Be sure to choose someone who is openly, physically affectionate. You need to touch and be touched frequently. You connect with your soul mate only after sacrificing logic on Cupid's altar. Who you marry isn't anyone you would have chosen using your head.

You love to travel, entertain, and be entertained; you may throw large parties, rub elbows with performers, or direct a local theatrical production.

✴ ✴ ✴

OCTOBER 15   LIBRA • The scales of justice
September 23 at 3:00 A.M. to October 23 at 12:00 P.M. • NUMEROLOGY 6

Possessions and Desires . . .

Gem: Diamond—This stone is thought to encourage harmony in relationships and gives strength to the troubled.

Flower: Raspberry—You will find you are here for a multiple purpose.

Astral Color, Color Need, Apparel Color: Your Astral Color is Crimson, which reflects your ability to nurture. Yellow in your environment stimulates and exhilarates you. In your wardrobe, Rose gives you balance and harmony.

Fragrance: Pick scents that are soft and not overwhelming, like eclectic mixtures of wildflowers.

Tree: Palm—You tend to be very healthy and creative.

Instrument: Tambourine

Composer: Schubert

Bird: Lark—known for the beauty of its song, which is sometimes very unusual. It is also credited with extraordinary intelligence.

Symbol: Crescent—You are more likely to be influenced by the phases of the moon. Your easygoing manner leads you to peaceful situations

Harmonious Health and Nutrition . . .

Health Scent: Orange Blossom—This scent may balance your body, mind, and soul.

Favorable Foods: Kale, peaches, whole-wheat bread, walnuts

What's Lucky . . .

Lucky Numbers: 6, 9

Best Months: August and December

Best Day of the Week: Friday

Best Month Days: 6, 15, 24

Lucky Charms: A religious token or card from any religion.

Harmonious Signs for Relationships and Partnerships: Aquarius and Gemini

Spiritual Guides . . .

Star: Al Icliel—This is the star of those who easily submit to authority.

Angel: Zuriel—This angel lends us the power to find balance when we desperately need it.

Guardian Angel: Michael—"Who is like God."

Spiritual Stone: Sapphire—the stone of serenity and prosperity.

✴ JUDITH'S INSIGHT ✴

Your fine art appreciation may lead you to some sort of recognition for your contributions. Your refined taste draws you to the stage, concert hall, or movie studio.

Your seem so independent, people don't realize how needy you are. You have to get very close to someone before you can bring yourself to reveal your insecurities. Relationships with friends, lovers, and family mean everything to you. You have a strong magnetic personality and may find your mate at work. As much as you like challenges on the job, you loathe them in love. You want spontaneity, desire, fun, and romance—love at first sight, butterflies. You believe that true love won't ever be work. You're very lucky because love usually finds you this way.

It may be through your work or hobbies, but you should become famous. You will do well when employed as an attorney, scientist, teacher, author, or coach. You keep in contact with childhood friends; no one that you care for leaves your life for very long. You are so giving that many people see you as guardian angel.

You encounter lots of disappointments. They tend to hit unexpectedly. Fortunately, you recover quickly. Just as surprising, you may come into a sizable windfall. You might have to endure with your usual grace a number of small or chronic medical problems. You refuse to close the door on whatever life offers, and this will bring you many pleasant changes.

✴ ✴ ✴

OCTOBER 16 LIBRA • The scales of justice
September 23 at 3:00 A.M. to October 23 at 12:00 P.M. • NUMEROLOGY 7

Possessions and Desires . . .

Gem: Agate—This stone may promote health and lead you to a long life.

Flower: Split Reed—If something feels wrong to you it usually is.

Astral Color, Color Need, Apparel Color: Your Astral Color is Crimson, which reflects your ability to nurture. Yellow in your environment stimulates and exhilarates you. In your wardrobe, Brown brings you stability.

Fragrance: Pick scents that are soft and not overwhelming, like eclectic mixtures of wildflowers.

Tree: Sycamore—Yours is the ability to love, communicate honestly with others, and have lasting relationships.

Instruments: Harp, violin, cello

Composers: Gluck, Brahms

Bird: Skylark—This handsome bird is beautiful when it sings. It always whistles as it works.

Symbol: Heart—You are enthusiastic, empathetic, and full of generosity and love.

Harmonious Health and Nutrition . . .

Health Scent: Jasmine—This scent may make you more easygoing when you are stressed.

Favorable Foods: Swiss chard, prunes, whole-wheat bread, peanuts

What's Lucky . . .

Lucky Numbers: 6, 9

Best Months: August and December

Best Day of the Week: Friday

Best Month Days: 6, 15, 24

Lucky Charm: An old key

Harmonious Signs for Relationships and Partnerships: Aquarius and Gemini

Spiritual Guides . . .

Star: Al Zubena—Those with this star often seek and find redemption.

Angel: Zuriel—This angel lends us the power to find balance when we desperately need it.

Guardian Angel: Raphael—This angel attends to all of your needs when you are looking for guidance.

Spiritual Stone: Sapphire—the stone of serenity and prosperity.

✶ *JUDITH'S INSIGHT* ✶

You are always eager to assist, and often under-appreciated; those you help may not even take the time to say thank you. You're ambitious and energetic as long as you believe in yourself. You can be successful in very odd ways. You are criticized for being domineering, but it's usually because someone hands you the reins, then complains that you have them. You have great intentions, but don't always see the big picture. You have a giving heart, but need to watch around you for what the outcome may be.

You should find employment as a troubleshooter. You were born to solve problems, large and small. You are a people person who gains energy just from being with others.

Unfortunately, love for you means heartache. After a long, dusty trail your tattered heart will find a soul mate who adores you and gives you the world. It make take you a while to accept their love because you fear your own happiness. You can complicate some situations to the point where you're unable to come to a decision. Sometimes it's impossible to please everyone.

Work on bringing some order to your scattered thoughts and get on the road to where you want to be.

✶ ✶ ✶

OCTOBER 17 LIBRA • The scales of justice

September 23 at 3:00 A.M. to October 23 at 12:00 P.M. • NUMEROLOGY 8

Possessions and Desires . . .

Gem: Chrysolite—This gem may help you clear your mind of sadness and worry.

Flower: Single Reed—You usually have a natural sense of rhythm.

Astral Color, Color Need, Apparel Color: Your Astral Color is Crimson, which reflects your ability to nurture. Yellow in your environment stimulates and exhilarates you. In your wardrobe, Rose gives you balance and harmony.

Fragrance: Pick scents that are soft and not overwhelming, like eclectic mixtures of wildflowers.

Tree: Pine—Your relationships tend to be harmonious, both emotionally and mentally.

Instrument: Cello

Composer: Mozart

Bird: Bobolink—This charming singer is equally good as a soloist or a member of an orchestra. It is a very romantic bird, most useful as an insect destroyer, and elegant, with beautiful feathers, and always pleasant to have around.

Symbol: Wings—You are the source of balance in your world—this will bring you contentment.

Harmonious Health and Nutrition . . .

Health Scent: Almond—This scent may revitalize you and open you to greater possibilities.

Favorable Foods: Peas, raspberries, whole-wheat bread, almonds

What's Lucky . . .

Lucky Numbers: 6, 9

Best Months: August and December

Best Day of the Week: Friday

Best Month Days: 8, 17, 26

Lucky Charm: Red ribbon in your wallet or doorway.

Harmonious Signs for Relationships and Partnerships: Aquarius and Gemini

Spiritual Guides . . .

Star: Al Zubena—Those with this star often seek and find redemption.

Angel: Zuriel—This angel lends us the power to find balance when we desperately need it.

Guardian Angel: Seraphim—An angel that brings love, light, and passion.

Spiritual Stone: Sapphire—the stone of serenity and prosperity.

✷ JUDITH'S INSIGHT ✷

You are very unbalanced and tend to live your life in a rut in order to give yourself a semblance of security. You hate to choose sides because you don't like to surrender any possibilities. You blame everyone else for the enormous stress you place on yourself. You will be quite wealthy not through work but by money falling in your lap. You could be lucky with the lottery, pick the right stock, or win at gambling.

Family and friends are likely to call on you for every crisis, and you are always there for them. At some point you will find this too overwhelming and may suddenly move far away to escape. You hold the wild cards of charm and understanding in your hand; when you play them, they win for you the attention and love that you need and deserve. You get bored easily, so it may take you some time to settle on a mate who can hold your attention. You like a clean, warm environment and a harmonious home. You always give in, but you never give up on love.

It won't be hard for you to find a career, but staying in just one may prove quite difficult. You aspire to be a renowned musician, artist, or acting teacher, but are more likely to be a manager or agent. You're an excellent idea person with entrepreneurial capabilities. You define yourself through your work, so it's difficult for you to be satisfied unless you have a career you think has sufficient status. Your energy, individuality, and ability to work with others outweigh your lack of focus.

✶ ✶ ✶

OCTOBER 18
LIBRA • The scales of justice
September 23 at 3:00 A.M. to October 23 at 12:00 P.M. • NUMEROLOGY 9

Possessions and Desires . . .

Gem: Beryl—This gem could be good for meditation and concentration.

Flower: Rhododendron—You have the ability to be a winner, at just about everything.

Astral Color, Color Need, Apparel Color: Your Astral Color is Crimson, which reflects your ability to nurture. Yellow in your environment stimulates and exhilarates you. In your wardrobe, Brown brings you stability.

Fragrance: Pick scents that are soft and not overwhelming, like eclectic mixtures of wildflowers.

Tree: Holly—Beware that you are not carried away by your passionate nature. The only way to grow is to be open to new experiences.

Instruments: Violin, tympnum

Composer: Gluck

Bird: Mockingbird—the most proficient minstrel in the world's orchestra; graceful and enthusiastic.

Symbol: Anchor—This tranquil symbol signifies stability and strength, and stands for strong commitments in relationships.

Harmonious Health and Nutrition . . .

Health Scent: Lavender—This scent might lead others to trust you and make you patient.

Favorable Foods: Tomatoes, strawberries, whole-wheat bread, Brazil nuts

What's Lucky . . .

Lucky Numbers: 6, 9

Best Months: August and December

Best Day of the Week: Friday

Best Month Days: 9, 18, 27

Lucky Charm: A U.S. coin or a bill of any amount from the year you were born.

Harmonious Signs for Relationships and Partnerships: Aquarius and Gemini

Spiritual Guides . . .

Star: Al Icliel—This is the star of those who easily submit to authority.

Angel: Zuriel—This angel lends us the power to find balance when we desperately need it.

Guardian Angel: Gabriel—"God is my strength."

Spiritual Stone: Sapphire—the stone of serenity and prosperity.

✶ *JUDITH'S INSIGHT* ✶

You are a born leader and always will be in charge. No matter what the situation, you excel; you are the most ardent lover and vicious fighter. Your kind heart and warmth will convince others to defend you. You highly value honor and will struggle tooth-and-nail for not only yours but for others'. You are completely loyal to all that love you.

You would make a great debater because you can clearly see both sides of any issue. It will be difficult for you to narrow your choices when picking a career, as so much interests you. You would make a wonderful surgeon. No matter what career you choose, eventually you'll hold a position of responsibility and authority. You may even be publicly recognized and become very famous.

Looking for a mate may require some time and patience, though you seem to attract all the wrong ones quite easily. Be sure you understand exactly what you need from a love relationship, because mistakes in this area could be costly. The appearance of your home is very important to you. Not to say that you're too materialistic, but you do have a powerful desire to be surrounded by the finer things in life.

You will be well known for your unique style, especially as you get older.

★ ★ ★

318

OCTOBER 19

LIBRA • THE LIONS

September 23 at 3:00 A.M. to October 23 at 12:00 P.M. • NUMEROLOGY 1

Possessions and Desires . . .

Gem: Agate—This stone may promote health and lead you to a long life.

Flower: Austrian Rose—You are artistic and drawn to beauty.

Astral Color, Color Need, Apparel Color: Your Astral Color is Crimson, which reflects your ability to nurture. Yellow in your environment stimulates and exhilarates you. In your wardrobe, Rose gives you balance and harmony.

Fragrance: Pick scents that are soft and not overwhelming, like eclectic mixtures of wildflowers.

Tree: Walnut—You are unusually helpful and always looking for constant changes in your life.

Instruments: Piccolo, violin, flute

Composer: Böhm

Bird: Hummingbird—This bird is delicate and graceful. It can remain still for hours, then be as busy as a bee.

Symbol: Crown—the universal sign of dignity.

Harmonious Health and Nutrition . . .

Health Scent: Strawberry—soothing by nature, the strawberry promotes self-esteem and encourages love.

Favorable Foods: Kale, cherries, whole-wheat bread, peanuts

What's Lucky . . .

Lucky Numbers: 6, 9

Best Months: August and December

Best Day of the Week: Friday

Best Month Days: 1, 10, 19

Lucky Charm: A new penny in your shoe

Harmonious Signs for Relationships and Partnerships: Aquarius and Gemini

Spiritual Guides . . .

Star: Al Zubena—Those with this star often seek and find redemption.

Angel: Zuriel—This angel lends us the power to find balance when we desperately need it.

Guardian Angel: Malachi—"Messenger of Jehovah."

Spiritual Stone: Sapphire—the stone of serenity and prosperity.

✱ JUDITH'S INSIGHT ✱

You are the type who suffers in silence for a long time before eventually coming into your own. Everyone has disappointments, but you feel yours more keenly than most. Because you never feel secure, you struggle to create a safe environment for everybody around you. Your home is very, very important to you. You're at your best there. If you have the opportunity to work from home, it will suit you splendidly.

You tend to make relationships last a long time, and those who leave your life usually return to it down the road. You would make a wonderful teacher, professor, scientist, chemist, or researcher. You have great skill with operating and repairing all types of machines—from cars to computers.

You get overwhelmed by other's emotions, so love can be hard for you. Intimacy quickly tosses you out of balance. Very few people will be able to tell what you are feeling. It would be preferable for you to marry a mind-reader or a very empathic mate, because you lack basic communication skills. Your kindhearted nature will bring many people into your life, but only a very few will be truly close to you. You are prone to pushing people away because your fear-driven coldness leads them to think you are incapable of caring. You are like the sun with planets in orbit around you. The lighthearted, laughing side of you lures people in while your anxieties keep them forever at arm's length.

✱ ✱ ✱

319

OCTOBER 20 LIBRA • The scales of justice

September 23 at 3:00 A.M. to October 23 at 12:00 P.M. • NUMEROLOGY 2

Possessions and Desires . . .

Gem: Sapphire—This gem may help you find forgiveness from those you've wronged.

Flower: Rose Campion—You tend to think that real love needs to be earned.

Astral Color, Color Need, Apparel Color: Your Astral Color is Crimson, which reflects your ability to nurture. Yellow in your environment stimulates and exhilarates you. In your wardrobe, Rose gives you balance and harmony.

Fragrance: Pick scents that are soft and not overwhelming, like eclectic mixtures of wildflowers.

Tree: Maple—You have great stability and flashes of intuition.

Instrument: Pipe organ, guitar

Composers: Handel, Johann Sebastian Bach

Bird: Cuckoo—a good flyer, and very seldom a quitter. Some cuckoos tend to think they favor lonely isolation, but what they really yearn for is a family relationship.

Symbol: Cross—the symbol of self-sacrifice and reconciliation.

Harmonious Health and Nutrition . . .

Health Scent: Apple—A vivacious scent encouraging energy. Will help you to be more creative, intuitive and positive.

Favorable Foods: Asparagus, peaches, whole-wheat bread, walnuts

What's Lucky . . .

Lucky Numbers: 6, 9
Best Months: August and December
Best Day of the Week: Friday
Best Month Days: 2, 11, 20
Lucky Charms: Two 50-cent pieces. Give someone else one of them.
Harmonious Signs for Relationships and Partnerships: Aquarius and Gemini

Spiritual Guides . . .

Star: Al Zubena—Those with this star often seek and find redemption.

Angel: Zuriel—This angel lends us the power to find balance when we desperately need it.

Guardian Angel: St. John—This angel simplifies that which is complicated.

Spiritual Stone: Sapphire—the stone of serenity and prosperity.

✳ JUDITH'S INSIGHT ✳

How you look to others means everything to you; even the crease in your pants must be absolutely perfect. You are more comfortable in relationships and partnerships than on your own. You need a sounding board and support to succeed. You could still run your own business or find yourself in positions of control, but it's much easier if you have help than if you have to do everything yourself.

You have great organizational skills and will do very well with money and finance. You can make a dollar go a long, long way. It's crucial for you to find peace and order in the environment in which you live. Even your garage is in perfect shape.

You're emotionally cool when younger. The distance becomes a problem for you as you get older. You struggle to allow laughter and love into your heart. You spend your life trying to protect yourself, only to recognize that you are your own worst enemy. You need people more than you know. Your family is extremely important. No sacrifice is too great to keep them all together. Accomplishing this may sometimes be a struggle.

You would make a great teacher, artist, designer, preacher, or counselor. You listen well and don't respond unless you really have something worthwhile to say.

✶ ✶ ✶

OCTOBER 21 LIBRA • The scales of justice
September 23 at 3:00 A.M. to October 23 at 12:00 P.M. • NUMEROLOGY 3

Possessions and Desires . . .

Gem: Ruby—This stone may lead you to energy, friendship, and happiness.
Flower: Buttercup—You become more and more graceful with age.
Astral Color, Color Need, Apparel Color: Your Astral Color is Crimson, which reflects your ability to nurture. Yellow in your environment stimulates and exhilarates you. In your wardrobe, Brown brings you stability.
Fragrance: Pick scents that are soft and not over-whelming, like eclectic mixtures of wildflowers.
Tree: Elm—You have willpower, strength, and the ability to stand alone.
Instrument: Trombone
Composers: Verdi, Mendelssohn, Schumann
Bird: Swan—Regarded as royal and sacred, this bird has the protective nature of a mother, and can become a furious fighter in the defense of its young.
Symbol: Wreath—You have been crowned with a special personality. You are strong but extremely compassionate.

Harmonious Health and Nutrition . . .

Health Scent: Rose—This scent will lead you to passionate thoughts and make you feel warm inside.
Favorable Foods: Carrots, bananas, whole-wheat bread, almonds

What's Lucky . . .

Lucky Numbers: 6, 9
Best Months: August and December
Best Day of the Week: Friday
Best Month Days: 3, 12, 21
Lucky Charm: A pen that someone else has already used.
Harmonious Signs for Relationships and Partnerships: Aquarius and Gemini

Spiritual Guides . . .

Star: Al Icliel—This is the star of those who easily submit to authority.
Angel: Zuriel—This angel lends us the power to find balance when we desperately need it.
Guardian Angel: Johiel—This angel is a protector of all those with a humble heart.
Spiritual Stone: Sapphire—the stone of serenity and prosperity.

✶ JUDITH'S INSIGHT ✶

You feel responsible for the whole world and think every burden rests on your shoulders. You know you need others, but always feel that you must struggle alone. You don't understand that reaching out for a partner's hand doesn't make you weak. Later in life you learn that accepting aid from people doesn't mean that you have to agree with everything they do. To need is to be human.

You have many good friends because you work hard to keep them. Your uncertainty makes you appear secretive. Often you will forget the many nice things you've done for others. You have a fantastic sense of humor, but at times are afraid to laugh. Letting go will be one of the great challenges of your life.

You will be successful in more ways than one; your ambition will never let you quit short of your goals. Because you're so loyal, people go out of their way for you. You love law and order; it would be very surprising if both weren't important factors in your life. You or someone close to you—maybe a spouse, child, or parent—are heavily involved with legal papers in some way.

You do tend to have luck with a buck and may have the opportunity to turn that single into a huge pile. You are naturally giving and, thankfully, as you get older you become more caring and sharing.

Some careers for you: parent, child care provider, therapist. writer, C.E.O. of a company, critic, chef, or hotel manager.

✶ ✶ ✶

OCTOBER 22 LIBRA • The scales of justice

September 23 at 3:00 A.M. to October 23 at 12:00 P.M. • NUMEROLOGY 4

Possessions and Desires . . .

Gem: Emerald—Those who carry this stone tend to be lucky in love.

Flower: Red Primrose—Your best gifts are often overlooked even by you.

Astral Color, Color Need, Apparel Color: Your Astral Color is Crimson, which reflects your ability to nurture. Yellow in your environment stimulates and exhilarates you. In your wardrobe, Rose gives you balance and harmony.

Fragrance: Pick scents that are soft and not over-whelming, like eclectic mixtures of wildflowers.

Tree: Cherry—You will find yourself faced with constant new emotional awakenings.

Instruments: Bass, clarinet

Composers: Haydn, Wagner

Bird: Robin—the most sociable of all birds, with the ability to create quick friendships. It also can easily adapt to any home. When it wants something, it has the tendency to try to snatch it.

Symbol: Star—You are full of inner brightness and will stand out in any crowd. You will be seen as special.

Harmonious Health and Nutrition . . .

Health Scent: Vanilla—This scent will fill you with a feeling of cleanliness and stability.

Favorable Foods: Spinach, peaches, whole-wheat bread, peanuts

What's Lucky . . .

Lucky Numbers: 6, 9

Best Months: August and December

Best Day of the Week: Friday

Best Month Days: 4, 13, 22

Lucky Charm: A piece of material cut from something in your home.

Harmonious Signs for Relationships and Partnerships: Aquarius and Gemini

Spiritual Guides . . .

Star: Al Zubena—Those with this star often seek and find redemption.

Angel: Zuriel—This angel lends us the power to find balance when we desperately need it.

Guardian Angel: Uriel—This angel brings the light of God's guidance.

Spiritual Stone: Sapphire—the stone of serenity and prosperity.

✶ JUDITH'S INSIGHT ✶

You have an attractive personality that draws everything you wish to you with the force of gravity. Stand still and watch your career, money, and spouse come rushing your way. You are a little eccentric and are partial to unusual people, situations, and surroundings.

Just because you can pull in what you need doesn't mean you can keep it without expending any energy. This is particularly true when it comes to a lasting relationship. Love will not be easy for you until you get older because your fears loom larger than your desires. As you get older, you will experience a love that will force you to give of yourself in order to keep it. It's very difficult for you to give emotionally, so you compensate with material gifts. Friends and families are important to you, but you push them away. You run away from the slightest unpleasantness instead of seeking to solve the situation.

You will do very well in sports or any activity where you work up a sweat. If you're not a professional athlete, you will be a passionate amateur. You can do just about any job available, so long as it's something you favor. When your energy is flowing you, can make the most difficult task seem like a cakewalk.

You tend to be well known and respected for your contributions.

Some careers for you: lawyer, guidance counselor, nutritionist, doctor, paralegal, or chemist.

★ ★ ★

OCTOBER 23   SCORPIO • The resourceful one of the zodiac

October 23 at 12:00 P.M. to November 22 at 5:00 A.M. • NUMEROLOGY 5

Possessions and Desires . . .

Gems: Sardius—This stone could give the wearer unusual insights into his or her own heart.

Flower: Polyanthus—You may need to learn that everything you are proud to have earned was only what the universe chose to give you.

Astral Color, Color Need, Apparel Color: Your Astral Color is Crimson, which reflects your ability to nurture. Yellow in your environment stimulates and exhilarates you. In your wardrobe, Brown brings you stability.

Fragrance: Buy pots of cinnabar or other scents from the sunny mediterranean or Orient. You are the most passionate sign of the zodiac, and your fragrance must be as unpredictable as you are.

Tree: Apple—You are creative, full of joy, and nearly magical. You bring happiness.

Instrument: Trumpet

Composer: Liszt

Bird: Flamingo—This beautiful, gregarious bird is always careful of its enemy. It is also a caretaker of the young and tries to keep everyone happy.

Symbol: Triangle—You have the right combination of abilities.

Harmonious Health and Nutrition . . .

Health Scent: Peach—This scent may balance your good qualities so that they equal your charm.

Favorable Foods: Asparagus, raspberries, whole-wheat bread, Brazil nuts

What's Lucky . . .

Lucky Numbers: 6, 9

Best Months: August and December

Best Day of the Week: Friday

Best Month Days: 4, 5, 23

Lucky Charm: A pen that someone else has already used.

Harmonious Signs for Relationships and Partnerships: Aquarius and Gemini

Spiritual Guides . . .

Star: Al Icliel—This is the star of those who easily submit to authority.

Angel: Zuriel—This angel lends us the power to find balance when we desperately need it.

Guardian Angel: Plavwell—The guardian that gives power and strength to one's presence.

Spiritual Stone: Sapphire—the stone of serenity and prosperity

✶ JUDITH'S INSIGHT ✶

You are very compassionate and have no problem showing it, though you sometimes lose interest unless you feel committed to a cause. You love adventure, even vicariously through a book or a movie. You crave constant stimulation and expect to live an exciting adventure every day.

Relationships can be contentious if your partner doesn't share or understand your need for thrill-seeking. An imprudent union with a quiet partner will lead to severe problems that will definitely end with two broken hearts. It's like pulling teeth to get you either into or out of a relationship. You have a rich emotional life but sometimes forget to be sensible.

Your patience, kindness, and intelligence will present you many opportunities to succeed. Your love of challenging, new experiences will often distract you from your goals. You make history in one way or another. You would like to be more practical and level-headed than you are. You love to learn and are equally fascinated by science fiction and history. Something that happened in the distant past will play a very big role in your life, though you may not notice how right away. When in doubt, follow your heart rather than your head.

Some careers for you could be: philosopher, chef, investigator, graphic artist, or troubleshooter.

✶ ✶ ✶

OCTOBER 24

SCORPIO • The resourceful one of the zodiac

October 23 at 12:00 P.M. to November 22 at 5:00 A.M. • NUMEROLOGY 6

Possessions and Desires . . .

Gems: Topaz—This is an excellent gift to be exchanged between very loyal friends.

Flower: Plane—People think you're very bright.

Astral Color, Color Need, Apparel Color: Your Astral Color is Crimson, which reflects your ability to nurture. Yellow in your environment stimulates and exhilarates you. In your wardrobe, Rose gives you balance and harmony.

Fragrance: Buy pots of cinnabar or other scents from the sunny Mediterranean or Orient. You are the most passionate sign of the zodiac, and your fragrance must be as unpredictable as you are.

Trees: Palm—You tend to be very healthy and creative.

Instruments: Tambourine, lyre

Composer: Schubert

Bird: Goldfinch—There are no less than forty-four species of the finch, from the dull and inviting, the extraordinarily active and exquisite. These gentle creatures can be very shy in unsettled weather.

Symbol: Triangle—You have the right combination of abilities.

Harmonious Health and Nutrition . . .

Health Scent: Orange Blossom—This scent may balance your body, mind, and soul.

Favorable Foods: Cabbage, strawberries, barley, beef, pressed cheese

What's Lucky . . .

Lucky Numbers: 2, 4

Best Months: January and July

Best Day of the Week: Tuesday

Best Month Days: 4, 5, 23

Lucky Charms: A religious token or card from any religion.

Harmonious Signs for Relationships and Partnerships: Cancer and Pisces

Spiritual Guides . . .

Star: Al Kalb—Those with this star are often delightful.

Angel: Ambriel—This angel governs travel and transportation, particularly over water, and helps to create love and good communication.

Guardian Angel: Michael—"Who is like God."

Spiritual Stone: Chalcedony—This stone might help when taking long trips, especially by car.

✷ JUDITH'S INSIGHT ✷

Your suspicious nature should lead you into law enforcement, auditing, or insurance investigation, although your artistic talents may put you on stage or into a gallery. You go through more emotions in an hour than most people experience in a lifetime. Your independent nature fools others into believing you aren't as needy as you are. You aren't usually a taker, but rarely are you a giver. You remain very cynical and skeptical. Disappointments come and go, and you dwell on them far too long. Learn to enjoy the moment and not take life so seriously.

While walking life's tightrope you try to balance your heavy insecurities with your massive ego. When you fall off, it's usually into a deep, self-centered depression. You frequently fail to notice all the possibilities available to you. You are a very good friend, but one who's waiting for the other shoe to drop. People must prove themselves to you over and over again, and still you expect disappointment. You have to learn that trust doesn't just sprout spontaneously; it has to be grown from seed. You think the world owes you something and are never satisfied with what you have. You never allow yourself to forget, forgive, or get over the wounds of childhood.

You are lucky with money, which is good, because you like to gamble and fail to remember the lessons of losing. As you get older you finally surmount your ingrained cynicism and learn that you are a very caring person.

★ ★ ★

OCTOBER 25
SCORPIO • The resourceful one of the zodiac
October 23 at 12:00 P.M. to November 22 at 5:00 A.M. • NUMEROLOGY 7

Possessions and Desires . . .

Gem: Agate—This stone may promote health and lead you to a long life.
Flower: Indian Pink—The things you dislike greatly in your youth could be the passions of your later years.
Astral Color, Color Need, Apparel Color: Your Astral Color is Black, the color of protection, birth, and beginnings. Red in your environment gives you energy and stamina. In your wardrobe, Green is your power color for overcoming obstacles.
Fragrance: Buy pots of cinnabar or other scents from the sunny Mediterranean or Orient. You are the most passionate sign of the zodiac, and your fragrance must be as unpredictable as you are.
Tree: Sycamore—Yours is the ability to love, communicate honestly with others, and have lasting relationships.
Instruments: Viola, trumpet
Composer: Liszt
Bird: Skylark—This handsome bird is beautiful when it sings. It always whistles while it works.
Symbol: Heart—You are enthusiastic, empathetic, and full of generosity and love.

Harmonious Health and Nutrition . . .

Health Scent: Jasmine—This scent may make you more easygoing when you are stressed.
Favorable Foods: Celery, blackberries, oats, chicken, eggs

What's Lucky . . .

Lucky Numbers: 2, 4
Best Months: January and July
Best Day of the Week: Tuesday
Best Month Days: 6, 15, 24
Lucky Charm: An old key.
Harmonious Signs for Relationships and Partnerships: Cancer and Pisces

Spiritual Guides . . .

Star: Al Kalb—Those with this star are often delightful.
Angel: Ambriel—This angel governs travel and transportation, particularly over water, and helps to create love and good communication.
Guardian Angel: Raphael—This angel attends to all of your needs when you are looking for guidance.
Spiritual Stone: Chalcedon—This stone might help when taking long trips, especially by car.

✶ JUDITH'S INSIGHT ✶

You don't get as much from life as you should because you tend to live in your head. You are given to extremes. You need to use your imagination as it was intended—find creative ways in which to support yourself. You talk the talk, but you lack the energy to walk the walk. You can be successful in extraordinary ways.

You have a passive-aggressive personality and try to dominate in all circumstances. You won't hold the steering wheel, but you can't seem to let the driver go where he or she will. You want to get to the top, but would rather whine than work to get there. You are a fine problem-solver with excellent ideas, opinions, and advice that could be useful to any field that employs you. You just have a huge blind spot when you look in the mirror.

You make a good parent or would do very well with children, even as a teacher. Later in life you may find yourself back in school learning a different career, or else the profession you choose requires many years of study. You would be successful as a lecturer, military commander, or highly specialized physician.

You have many heartaches and disappointments early in life, and these form obstacles to mature relationships. You tend surround yourself with those you know will disappoint you because it's all you expect. Stop thinking so much and resolve to do something. Once you find your direction, you'll finally arrive at your desired destination.

✶ ✶ ✶

OCTOBER 26

SCORPIO • The resourceful one of the zodiac

October 23 at 12:00 P.M. to November 22 at 5:00 A.M. • NUMEROLOGY 8

Possessions and Desires . . .

Gem: Chrysolite—This gem may help you clear your mind of sadness and worry.

Flower: Larch—You may find your audacity can lead you to folly.

Astral Color, Color Need, Apparel Color: Your Astral Color is Black, the color of protection, birth, and beginnings. Red in your environment gives you energy and stamina. In your wardrobe, Wine gives you energy.

Fragrance: Buy pots of cinnabar or other scents from the sunny Mediterranean or Orient. You are the most passionate sign of the zodiac, and your fragrance must be as unpredictable as you are.

Tree: Pine—Your relationships tend to be harmonious, both emotionally and mentally.

Instruments: Viola, trumpet

Composer: Beethoven

Bird: Bobolink—This charming singer is equally good as a soloist or a member of an orchestra. It is a very romantic bird, most useful as an insect destroyer, and elegant, with beautiful feathers, and always pleasant to have around.

Symbol: Wings—You are the source of balance in your world—this will bring you contentment.

Harmonious Health and Nutrition . . .

Health Scent: Almond—This scent may revitalize you and open you to greater possibilities.

Favorable Foods: Carrots, cranberries, rye crisp, fresh oysters, buttermilk

What's Lucky . . .

Lucky Numbers: 2, 4

Best Months: January and July

Best Day of the Week: Tuesday

Best Month Days: 4, 5, 23

Lucky Charm: Red ribbon in your wallet or doorway.

Harmonious Signs for Relationships and Partnerships: Cancer and Pisces

Spiritual Guides . . .

Star: Al Shaula—People who are born with this star are careful to avoid being cruel.

Angel: Ambriel—This angel governs travel and transportation, particularly over water, and helps to create love and good communication.

Guardian Angel: Seraphim—An angel that brings love, light, and passion.

Spiritual Stone: Chalcedon—This stone might help when taking long trips, especially by car.

✷ JUDITH'S INSIGHT ✷

You tend to take on more burdens than you can carry and are far too serious while hauling them. You are overconscientious without knowing it. You doubt your own capabilities and lack self-esteem. Your off-center wit and charm are often misconstrued as egotism. You're very understanding of others but fail miserably to gauge the bone-crushing amount of pressure you place on yourself.

You think romance is boring and so may delay looking for the right mate until all the good ones are taken. Somewhere along the way, you will surprise yourself by becoming a leader, or maybe you will suddenly realize that everyone has been following you all along. You have a caring heart shivering in the shadows cast by your ever-pondering mind. You are much more intelligent than you let on. When you're older, you'll be more comfortable showing off your mental talents.

You very much need to be a part of a family. If you don't get this feeling from those who are blood relations, you seek it from very close friends. You should become quite wealthy in this lifetime, if for no other reason than that you hold your coins so tightly the presidents scream.

Some careers for you: executive chef, hotel manager, head of securities. You have excellent mechanical and physical capabilities. You are unbelievably meticulous in nature.

✷ ✷ ✷

OCTOBER 27

SCORPIO • The resourceful one of the zodiac

October 23 at 12:00 P.M. to November 22 at 5:00 A.M. • NUMEROLOGY 9

Possessions and Desires . . .

Gem: Beryl—This gem could be good for meditation and concentration.

Flower: Peppermint—Others should flock to you for warmth.

Astral Color, Color Need, Apparel Color: Your Astral Color is Black, the color of protection, birth, and beginnings. Red in your environment gives you energy and stamina. In your wardrobe, Tan gives you balance and harmony.

Fragrance: Buy pots of cinnabar or other scents from the sunny Mediterranean or Orient. You are the most passionate sign of the zodiac, and your fragrance must be as unpredictable as you are.

Tree: Holly—Beware that you are not carried away by your passionate nature. The only way to grow is to be open to new experiences.

Instruments: Viola, trumpet

Composer: Liszt

Bird: Mockingbird—the most proficient minstrel in all the world's orchestra; graceful and enthusiastic.

Symbol: Anchor—This tranquil symbol signifies stability and strength, and stands for strong commitments in relationships.

Harmonious Health and Nutrition . . .

Health Scent: Lavender—This scent might lead others to trust you and make you patient.

Favorable Foods: Spinach, watermelon, oats, beef, pressed cheese

What's Lucky . . .

Lucky Numbers: 2, 4

Best Months: January and July

Best Day of the Week: Tuesday

Best Month Days: 9, 18, 27

Lucky Charm: A U.S. coin or a bill of any amount from the year you were born.

Harmonious Signs for Relationships and Partnerships: Cancer and Pisces

Spiritual Guides . . .

Star: Al Kalb—Those with this star are often delightful.

Angel: Ambriel—This angel governs travel and transportation, particularly over water, and helps to create love and good communication.

Guardian Angel: Gabriel—"God is my strength."

Spiritual Stone: Chalcedon—This stone might help when taking long trips, especially by car.

✶ JUDITH'S INSIGHT ✶

Your secretive nature may keep others from ever really knowing the real you. You like to protect yourself unnecessarily. You are the perfect "fun" date: adventurous, energetic, and totally entertaining. Your gifts of eloquence, humor, style and charm are so alluring that attracting a mate is easy as pie, but keeping relationships may be tough for you.

The natural careers for you would be lawyer, surgeon, chemist, or clergyperson. You are witty, well-spoken, affable, clever, and curious, all of which ensure that you're rarely bored. It is very important for you to be considered successful—you need to be noticed. You seek recognition in more than one career and in your hobbies. You are authoritative and likely to gain respect and responsibility. Local, state, and national politics interest you. Very often, you volunteer to lead the PTA or local charity organization.

You can be fearful that others will discover how spiritual you are. What you feel the most strongly you conceal the most completely. Family and friends are important to you for the affection that they can give you. Most of the time, you're surrounded by many people and are a devoted friend, child, parent, spouse, or sibling.

✶ ✶ ✶

OCTOBER 28
SCORPIO • The resourceful one of the zodiac
October 23 at 12:00 P.M. to November 22 at 5:00 A.M. • NUMEROLOGY 1

Possessions and Desires . . .

Gem: Agate—This stone may promote health and lead you to a long life.

Flower: Osmunda—You tend to be a happy dreamer.

Astral Color, Color Need, Apparel Color: Your Astral Color is Black, the color of protection, birth and beginnings. Red in your environment gives you energy and stamina. In your wardrobe, Green is your power color for overcoming obstacles.

Fragrance: Buy pots of cinnabar or other scents from the sunny Mediterranean or Orient. You are the most passionate sign of the zodiac, and your fragrance must be as unpredictable as you are.

Tree: Walnut—You are unusually helpful and always looking for constant changes in your life.

Instruments: Oboe, flute, clarinet, piano, French horn, organ, piccolo

Composer: Böhm

Bird: Bird of Paradise—the "bird of the Gods." You will shine and love extraordinary circumstances.

Symbol: Crown—the universal sign of dignity.

Harmonious Health and Nutrition . . .

Health Scent: Strawberry—Soothing by nature, the strawberry promotes self-esteem and encourages love.

Favorable Foods: Cabbage, apple, barley, salmon, eggs

What's Lucky . . .

Lucky Numbers: 2, 4
Best Months: January and July
Best Day of the Week: Tuesday
Best Month Days: 4, 5, 23
Lucky Charm: A new penny in your shoe.
Harmonious Signs for Relationships and Partnerships: Cancer and Pisces

Spiritual Guides . . .

Star: Al Kalb—Those with this star are often delightful.

Angel: Ambriel—This angel governs travel and transportation, particularly over water, and helps to create love and good communication.

Guardian Angel: Plavwell—The guardian that gives power and strength to one's presence.

Spiritual Stone: Chalcedon—This stone might help when taking long trips, especially by car.

✷ JUDITH'S INSIGHT ✷

You have the need to dig deeply into everything. Getting to the bottom of things is your specialty, and you pursue it in careers such as scientist, chemist, astronomer, astrologer, paralegal, or inventor. For you, solving problems is as important and natural as breathing. You love to read history and are likely to make it.

You have no problem catching the hearts of others—deciding the next step in relationships, however, will always seem crippling. You simultaneously fear and yearn for a solid commitment. You are far too difficult for even you to figure out. You tend to look for problems even when none exist, but you refuse to be honest about your concerns. You tend to run from conflict. You need calm and peace so much that you force others to keep silent when open discussion would be more healing.

You change your mind on major issues three times a day. Your home is your castle, and you will always feel more secure when there. Your optimism makes it easy for others to believe that things will get better in time. You are too intense and easily overwhelmed by sentiment. Your kindhearted generosity will complicate your life in ways you can't imagine. You readily agree to help, but often don't follow through. Eventually, you will be a huge success in more than one area. You may accomplish more in one lifetime than most do in several.

✷ ✷ ✷

OCTOBER 29
SCORPIO • The resourceful one of the zodiac

October 23 at 12:00 P.M. to November 22 at 5:00 A.M. • NUMEROLOGY 2

Possessions and Desires . . .

Gem: Sapphire—This gem may help you find forgiveness from those you've wronged.

Flower: Oxeye—You usually are extremely patient.

Astral Color, Color Need, Apparel Color: Your Astral Color is Black, the color of protection, birth, and beginnings. Red in your environment gives you energy and stamina. In your wardrobe, Wine gives you energy.

Fragrance: Buy pots of cinnabar or other scents from the sunny Mediterranean or Orient. You are the most passionate sign of the zodiac, and your fragrance must be as unpredictable as you are.

Tree: Maple—You have great stability and flashes of intuition.

Instruments: Viola, trumpet

Composer: Beethoven

Bird: Stork—Turkish bird, held in high esteem the world over. This bird is intelligent but may have strange tendencies.

Symbol: Cross—the symbol of self-sacrifice and reconciliation.

Harmonious Health and Nutrition . . .

Health Scent: Apple—A vivacious scent encouraging energy. Will help you to be more creative, intuitive and positive.

Favorable Foods: Celery, raspberry, oats, beef, buttermilk

What's Lucky . . .

Lucky Numbers: 2, 4

Best Months: January and July

Best Day of the Week: Tuesday

Best Month Days: 2, 11, 20

Lucky Charms: Two 50-cent pieces. Give someone else one of them.

Harmonious Signs for Relationships and Partnerships: Cancer and Pisces

Spiritual Guides . . .

Star: Al Shaula—People who are born with this star are careful to avoid being cruel.

Angel: Ambriel—This angel governs travel and transportation, particularly over water, and helps to create love and good communication.

Guardian Angel: St. John—This angel simplifies that which is complicated.

Spiritual Stone: Chalcedon—This stone might help when taking long trips, especially by car.

✶ JUDITH'S INSIGHT ✶

Being caring, considerate, and compassionate will get you in the kind of trouble most people pray for. You will be overwhelmed by offers and opportunities in work, friendships, and relationships. People will go well out of their way just to be near your sensitivity and charm. "Popular" doesn't begin to describe it.

You do better at work where you have partners. Remember to select the right ones. You may want be on your own, thinking you should be more independent, but you will be lonely. You need someone you feel close enough to share with—whether it be an assistant, mentor, or office best buddy. Others think money is more important to you than it really is. If you become wealthy, as you should, they will finally understand you value it only as a tool to help others.

If you sacrifice too much for love, you'll only end up miserable. You are a slavishly devoted mate whose efforts are largely ignored. You have many troubles from those you love, but time will send you the perfect match. You are always searching for romance, though sometimes in horribly wrong places.

Your best careers are in government, engineering, acting, or communications. You may come up with an innovation or two that make you rich. It is very important for you to feel peace in your surroundings. Where you work and live will be the deciding factor in your success. As you get older the chains of seriousness fall away, so you can run with laughter and love to your special destiny.

✶ ✶ ✶

OCTOBER 30

SCORPIO • The resourceful one of the zodiac

October 23 at 12:00 P.M. to November 22 at 5:00 A.M. • NUMEROLOGY 3

Possessions and Desires . . .

Gem: Ruby—This stone may lead you to energy, friendship, and happiness.

Flower: Parsley—You tend to see life as one long, continuous party.

Astral Color, Color Need, Apparel Color: Your Astral Color is Black, the color of protection, birth, and beginnings. Red in your environment gives you energy and stamina. In your wardrobe, Tan gives you balance and harmony.

Fragrance: Buy pots of cinnabar or other scents from the sunny Mediterranean or Orient. You are the most passionate sign of the zodiac, and your fragrance must be as unpredictable as you are.

Tree: Elm—You have willpower, strength, and the ability to stand alone.

Instruments: Viola, trumpet

Composer: Liszt

Bird: Eagle—This bird is quick to use its powers of flight. It can see immeasurable distances in a single glance, and can sometimes appear to be indifferent.

Symbol: Wreath—You have been crowned with a special personality. You are strong but extremely compassionate.

Harmonious Health and Nutrition . . .

Health Scent: Rose—This scent will lead you to passionate thoughts and make you feel warm inside.

Favorable Foods: Mushrooms, black figs, barley, fresh oysters, pressed cheese

What's Lucky . . .

Lucky Numbers: 2, 4
Best Months: January and July
Best Day of the Week: Tuesday
Best Month Days: 4, 5, 23
Lucky Charm: A pen that someone else has already used.

Harmonious Signs for Relationships and Partnerships: Cancer and Pisces

Spiritual Guides . . .

Star: Al Kalb—Those with this star are often delightful.

Angel: Ambriel—This angel governs travel and transportation, particularly over water, and helps to create love and good communication.

Guardian Angel: Johiel—This angel is a protector of all those with a humble heart.

Spiritual Stone: Chalcedon—This stone might help when taking long trips, especially by car.

✷ JUDITH'S INSIGHT ✷

You love justice and fight hard for a principle you believe in. You would make a great mediator, psychologist, or advocate. You clearly understand both sides of complex issues and strive to comprehend even the opinions you don't agree with. You keep your friends for life. You find happiness in close relationships. Although you receive much heartache and disappointment from romance, you accept what life offers. You always work diligently at making things better. You're charming, devoted, and easy to love. You probably have difficulties with your siblings if you have them. It may seem that your family has neglected you in some way.

You will be successful because of your powerful vision and unstoppable attitude. If you are an entrepreneur, you may have two or three businesses fail before you succeed. In any career, years will go by before you're recognized for your talents. Don't worry if it seems like you're going downhill; you are just picking up speed. You will learn something important from every job you take.

You could do well in stocks, bonds, or anything to do with paper money. You remain optimistic because you know that eventually most things go your way. If you fully trust your intuition, you'll make better choices in life. You add balance to your environment with great organizational, intellectual, and creative skill. You possess the willingness to work very hard for what you want.

✶ ✶ ✶

OCTOBER 31

SCORPIO • The resourceful one of the zodiac

October 23 at 12:00 P.M. to November 22 at 5:00 A.M. • NUMEROLOGY 4

Possessions and Desires . . .

Gem: Emerald—Those who carry this stone tend to be lucky in love.

Flower: Common Nettle—You tend to work well with others.

Astral Color, Color Need, Apparel Color: Your Astral Color is Black, the color of protection, birth, and beginnings. Red in your environment gives you energy and stamina. In your wardrobe, green is your power color for overcoming obstacles.

Fragrance: Buy pots of cinnabar or other scents from the sunny Mediterranean or Orient. You are the most passionate sign of the zodiac, and your fragrance must be as unpredictable as you are.

Tree: Cherry—You will find yourself faced with constant new emotional awakenings..

Instruments: Bass, clarinet

Composers: Haydn, Wagner

Bird: Robin—the most sociable of all birds, with the ability to create quick friendships. It also can be easily adapt to any home. When it wants something, it has the tendency to try to snatch it.

Symbol: Star—You are full of inner brightness and will stand out in any crowd. You will be seen as special.

Harmonious Health and Nutrition . . .

Health Scent: Vanilla—This scent will fill you with a feeling of cleanliness and stability.

Favorable Foods: Tomatoes, pineapple, rye crisps, salmon, buttermilk

What's Lucky . . .

Lucky Numbers: 2, 4
Best Months: January and July
Best Day of the Week: Tuesday
Best Month Days: 4, 5, 23
Lucky Charm: A piece of material cut from something in your home.

Harmonious Signs for Relationships and Partnerships: Cancer and Pisces

Spiritual Guides . . .

Star: Al Shaula—People who are born with this star are careful to avoid being cruel.

Angel: Ambriel—This angel governs travel and transportation, particularly over water, and helps to create love and good communication.

Guardian Angel: Uriel—This angel brings the light of God's guidance.

Spiritual Stone: Chalcedon—This stone might help when taking long trips, especially by car.

✶ JUDITH'S INSIGHT ✶

Everybody around you will feel nurtured by you in one way or another. Your low self-esteem worsens as you get older, so you should decide to conquer it now. You see education as a tool to help yourself and others. You may not get all that you learn from books; instead, you may graduate with honors from the school of hard knocks.

You're lucky in love and have secure relationships. Love whoever you want, but be yourself. You start life being very dependent on others and only later discover your own inner strength. That's why so many others depend on you. However, someone as loyal and devoted as you usually isn't such a good flirt.

You may become more involved in strenuous physical activities such as long-distance running as you get older. Don't overdo it, or you'll be plagued by injuries. Seek jobs in which you can continually grow in knowledge and responsibility. You would do well as a nurse, researcher, teacher, or child care provider. You may even want to write or work on either side of a camera at one point. You might pursue law if you thought you could champion the rights of the downtrodden.

Some type of fame finds you in this lifetime; your name will be printed in books, though maybe in small print.

✶ ✶ ✶

NOVEMBER

NOVEMBER 1

SCORPIO • The resourceful one of the zodiac

October 23 at 12:00 P.M. to November 22 at 5:00 A.M. • NUMEROLOGY 1

Possessions and Desires . . .

Gem: Turquoise—This stone might help you find material wealth.

Flower: Nasturtium—You have a strong love of your country.

Astral Color, Color Need, Apparel Color: Your Astral Color is Black, the color of protection, birth, and beginnings. Red in your environment gives you energy and stamina. In your wardrobe, Wine gives you energy.

Fragrance: Buy pots of cinnabar or other scents from the sunny Mediterranean or Orient. You are the most passionate sign of the zodiac, and your fragrance must be as unpredictable as you are.

Tree: Walnut—You are unusually helpful and always looking for constant changes in your life.

Instruments: Oboe, flute, clarinet, piano, French horn, organ, piccolo

Composer: Böhm

Bird: Bird of paradise—"the bird of the gods." You will shine and love extraordinary circumstances.

Symbol: Crown—the universal sign of dignity.

Harmonious Health and Nutrition . . .

Health Scent: Strawberry—Soothing by nature, the strawberry promotes self-esteem and encourages love.

Favorable Foods: Carrots, black figs, barley, beef, buttermilk

What's Lucky . . .

Lucky Numbers: 2, 4
Best Months: January and July
Best Day of the Week: Tuesday
Best Month Days: 4, 5, 23
Lucky Charm: A new penny in your shoe.

Harmonious Signs for Relationships and Partnerships: Cancer and Pisces

Spiritual Guides . . .

Star: Al Kalb—Those with this star are often delightful.

Angel: Ambriel—This angel governs travel and transportation, particularly over water, and helps to create love and good communication.

Guardian Angel: Plavwell—The guardian that gives power and strength to one's presence.

Spiritual Stone: Chalcedon—This stone might help when taking long trips, especially by car.

✷ JUDITH'S INSIGHT ✷

With your boundless energy and exceptionally powerful presence, others around you sense your zest for life. You are creative in every sense of the word, and your good ideas and imagination bring success. You are observant by nature and would make a great critic. There will definitely be success in a government job; your opinions would be extremely well received. You have many strong feelings, and when you express them, people listen.

Your keen wit and sense of humor naturally attract people. If you feel neglected in your love life, you may become sarcastic. Although you're bighearted and forgiving, you can be moody at times. You dwell on things too long when angered and need to be more resilient. On the whole, you will do well in life because you work hard at being a good person. Watch out for disillusionment. It could be difficult for you to make a comeback after experiencing disappointments.

You tend to find love, but just remember, for you it's "the more you give, the more you get." You are too practical at times and need to be more emotionally involved in what is going on around you.

✷ ✷ ✷

NOVEMBER 2

SCORPIO • The resourceful one of the zodiac

October 23 at 12:00 P.M. to November 22 at 5:00 A.M. • NUMEROLOGY 2

Possessions and Desires . . .

Gem: Sapphire—This gem may help you find forgiveness from those you've wronged.

Flower: Mountain ash—You tend to be very prudent in your business.

Astral Color, Color Need, Apparel Color: Your Astral Color is Black, the color of protection, birth, and beginnings. Red in your environment gives you energy and stamina. In your wardrobe, Tan gives you balance and harmony.

Fragrance: Buy pots of cinnabar or other scents from the sunny Mediterranean or Orient. You are the most passionate sign of the zodiac, and your fragrance must be as unpredictable as you are.

Tree: Maple—You have great stability and flashes of intuition.

Instruments: Pipe organ, cymbal, drum

Composers: Handel, Johann Sebastian Bach

Bird: Cuckoo—a good flyer, and very seldom a quitter. Some cuckoos tend to think they favor lonely isolation, but what they really yearn for is a family relationship.

Symbol: Cross—the symbol of self-sacrifice and reconciliation.

Harmonious Health and Nutrition . . .

Health Scent: Apple—A vivacious scent encouraging energy. Will help you to be more creative, intuitive and positive.

Favorable Foods: Mushrooms, cranberries, barley, fresh oysters, buttermilk

What's Lucky . . .

Lucky Numbers: 2, 4

Best Months: January and July

Best Day of the Week: Tuesday

Best Month Days: 2, 11, 20

Lucky Charms: Two 50-cent pieces. Give someone else one of them.

Harmonious Signs for Relationships . and Partnerships: Cancer and Pisces

Spiritual Guides . . .

Star: Al Shaula—People born with this star are careful to avoid being cruel.

Angel: Ambriel—This angel governs travel and transportation, particularly over water, and helps to create love and good communication.

Guardian Angel: St. Thomas—This angel brings affection from others and encourages you in all that you do.

Spiritual Stone: Chalcedon—This stone might help when taking long trips, especially by car.

★ JUDITH'S INSIGHT ★

You can be the most frustrating human being on the planet. It may take a rocket scientist to figure you out simply because it's too scary for you to let others know who you really are. If you can keep your emotions from getting in the way, your abundant talent, energy, and imagination will help you succeed in your chosen career. You prefer to be your own boss and don't function well when others tell you what to do.

Your fearless and meticulous nature combined with your interest in the sciences would make you a great surgeon. Strong principles and a defense-oriented personality will lead you into a courtroom, either as a judge or as a lawyer fighting the good fight, usually championing the underdog. You have a strong physical and mental presence. You love challenging occupations, but you can coast on your luck as a stockbroker or market analyst. You are charged and raring to go, and never, ever need new batteries.

Relationships are more difficult for you because you choose the unusual and desire the unconventional. What can you expect from a person who finds the pursuit of material possessions so darn intriguing? You have the key to your own happiness when it comes to finding a mate. You make things as complicated or as simple as you decide.

You will get what you give in life; maybe this is the lesson you're here to learn.

★ ★ ★

NOVEMBER 3 SCORPIO • The resourceful one of the zodiac

October 23 at 12:00 P.M. to November 22 at 5:00 A.M. • NUMEROLOGY 3

Possessions and Desires . . .

Gem: Ruby—This stone may lead you to energy, friendship, and happiness.

Flower: Mugwort—Happiness will be waiting for you to realize you already have it.

Astral Color, Color Need, Apparel Color: Your Astral Color is Black, the color of protection, birth, and beginnings. Red in your environment gives you energy and stamina. In your wardrobe, Green is your power color for overcoming obstacles.

Fragrance: Buy pots of cinnabar or other scents from the sunny Mediterranean or Orient. You are the most passionate sign of the zodiac, and your fragrance must be as unpredictable as you are.

Tree: Elm—You have willpower, strength, and the ability to stand alone.

Instrument: Trombone

Composers: Verdi, Mendelssohn, Schumann

Bird: Swan—Regarded as royal and sacred, this bird has the protective nature of a mother, and can become a furious fighter in the defense of its own.

Symbol: Wreath—You have been crowned with a special personality. You are strong but extremely compassionate.

Harmonious Health and Nutrition . . .

Health Scent: Rose—This scent will lead you to passionate thoughts and make you feel warm inside.

Favorable Foods: Okra, lemon, barley, salmon, eggs

What's Lucky . . .

Lucky Numbers: 2, 4
Best Months: January and July
Best Day of the Week: Tuesday
Best Month Days: 4, 5, 23
Lucky Charm: A pen that someone else has already used.

Harmonious Signs for Relationships and Partnerships: Cancer and Pisces

Spiritual Guides . . .

Star: Al Kalb—Those with this star are often delightful.

Angel: Ambriel—This angel governs travel and transportation, particularly over water, and helps to create love and good communication.

Guardian Angel: St. Thomas—This angel brings affection from others and encourages you in all that you do.

Spiritual Stone: Chalcedon—This stone might help when taking long trips, especially by car.

✷ JUDITH'S INSIGHT ✷

You're quite the challenging person and love being that way. You can't wait to travel the entire wide world and soak up all the knowledge, experiences, and excitement every corner has to offer. You would make a great journalist, photographer, or researcher. After you've traveled, seek work in government, business or other endeavors that require someone dependable. You have original ideas and are creative, but you tend to rely more on your organizational and administrative skills.

Romance depends on you. When you finally decide to be happy, you'll work at it until you make it happen. Before you're ready, prospective suitors find you a messy battlefield. Unfortunately, the person who must bear the real brunt of your combative nature is you.

You tend to be generous when you have money in your pocket. When cash is low, you give freely of your time and energy. You're very sympathetic and charitable to those people you favor, but if you feel disrespect or disloyalty, you can become overly defensive and arrogant.

Remember, you're the traveler: whether you do it early or late in life, you're sure to find a way to cram in as much as you can from the universe around you.

✷ ✷ ✷

NOVEMBER 4

SCORPIO • The resourceful one of the zodiac

October 23 at 12:00 P.M. to November 22 at 5:00 A.M. • NUMEROLOGY 4

Possessions and Desires . . .

Gem: Emerald—Those who carry this stone tend to be lucky in love.

Flower: Mushroom—You may need to learn to trust more those who care for you.

Astral Color, Color Need, Apparel Color: Your Astral Color is Black, the color of protection, birth, and beginnings. Red in your environment gives you energy and stamina. In your wardrobe, Wine gives you energy.

Fragrance: Buy pots of cinnabar or other scents from the sunny Mediterranean or Orient. You are the most passionate sign of the zodiac, and your fragrance must be as unpredictable as you are.

Tree: Cherry—You will find yourself faced with constant new emotional awakenings.

Instruments: Bass, clarinet

Composers: Haydn, Wagner

Bird: Kildeer—This common bird is usually found consorting with other species, and can adapt to any environment.

Symbol: Star—You are full of inner brightness and will stand out in any crowd. You will be seen as special.

Harmonious Health and Nutrition . . .

Health Scent: Vanilla—This scent will fill you with a feeling of cleanliness and stability.

Favorable Foods: Cabbage, blackberries, oats, fresh oysters, buttermilk

What's Lucky . . .

Lucky Numbers: 2, 4
Best Months: January and July
Best Day of the Week: Tuesday
Best Month Days: 4, 13, 22
Lucky Charm: A piece of material cut from something in your home.
Harmonious Signs for Relationships and Partnerships: Cancer and Pisces

Spiritual Guides . . .

Star: Al Kalb—Those with this star are often delightful.

Angel: Ambriel—This angel governs travel and transportation, particularly over water, and helps to create love and good communication.

Guardian Angel: Uriel—This angel brings the light of God's guidance.

Spiritual Stone: Chalcedon—This stone might help when taking long trips, especially by car.

✴ JUDITH'S INSIGHT ✴

Why do you feel like the underdog? Without enthusiasm for achieving your goals and finding new resolve, disappointments usually take awhile to pass. Having taken on adult responsibilities at an early age makes you feel old. Your self-esteem wavers during your younger years, but as you grow older and connect with your mate, harmony and happiness blossom. You don't realize how special you are. A kind heart, an active mind, strong values, and a vibrant imagination contribute to your uniqueness. Every day you face numerous contradictions in how you see yourself, and while you sort things out, life keeps presenting you bigger challenges. You are the dutiful child, spouse, student, parent, or worker—no matter what your role in life, you take it seriously.

Focus less on the contents of your wallet or bank account as the measure of your success. You're well-rounded and have so many different talents, you could have difficulty choosing one career. You could have a career in politics or music or you could even be a brain surgeon. You will develop a great desire to accomplish many things and may achieve them as you get older. Your strong need for justice makes you want to help underdogs, either as a public defender or an advocate for children.

You have so many uncommon gifts that finding the best way to use them takes time. Your first lesson: be patient with yourself.

✴ ✴ ✴

NOVEMBER 5

SCORPIO • The resourceful one of the zodiac

October 23 at 12:00 P.M. to November 22 at 5:00 A.M. • NUMEROLOGY 5

Possessions and Desires . . .

Gem: Sardius—This stone could give the wearer unusual insights into his or her own heart.

Flower: Mimosa—You may be too sensitive to criticism.

Astral Color, Color Need, Apparel Color: Your Astral Color is Black, the color of protection, birth, and beginnings. Red in your environment gives you energy and stamina. In your wardrobe, Tan gives you balance and harmony.

Fragrance: Buy pots of cinnabar or other scents from the sunny Mediterranean or Orient. You are the most passionate sign of the zodiac, and your fragrance must be as unpredictable as you are.

Tree: Apple—You are creative, full of joy, and nearly magical. You bring happiness.

Instruments: Viola, trumpet

Composer: Liszt

Bird: Flamingo—This beautiful, gregarious bird is always careful of its enemy. It is also a caretaker of the young and tries to keep everyone happy.

Symbol: Triangle—You have the right combination of abilities.

Harmonious Health and Nutrition . . .

Health Scent: Peach—This scent may balance your good qualities so that they equal your charm.

Favorable Foods: Asparagus, cranberries, barley, beef, pressed cheese

What's Lucky . . .

Lucky Numbers: 2, 4

Best Months: January and July

Best Day of the Week: Tuesday

Best Month Days: 4, 5, 23

Lucky Charms: A rabbit's foot or a white candle

Harmonious Signs for Relationships and Partnerships: Cancer and Pisces

Spiritual Guides . . .

Star: Al Shaula—People born with this star are careful to avoid being cruel.

Angel: Ambriel—This angel governs travel and transportation, particularly over water, and helps to create love and good communication.

Guardian Angel: Plavwell—The guardian that gives power and strength to one's presence.

Spiritual Stone: Chalcedon—This stone might help when taking long trips, especially by car.

✷ JUDITH'S INSIGHT ✷

Organization is your strong suit, but you're talented in many other ways. You have a deep love and understanding of acting and nature. Your energy keeps you from knowing whether you're coming or going. Hint: Usually you're doing both.

Look for careers relating to art or beauty. Tell prospective employers you can be trained to do just about anything—you won't be lying. You have strong imagination and unflagging stamina. You are gifted, especially in situations that require intelligence. Expect to be frustrated when faced with stagnation. You need to be constantly learning.

Cupid could prove a challenging adversary in this lifetime. Many times through the years, your love life will suddenly swing from happy to bleak and back again. Understand that you become bored easily with your mate—although you're always or continuously loyal. Selecting a mate too early in life may trap you in a union that will bring you grief, though you cannot leave. The later you get married, the better your chances at happiness. There are lessons you must first learn when it comes to love, relationships, and family. Beware of the times when any or all of these overwhelm you.

You need your friends, and connections remain close for many years. Try not to second-guess yourself. If you learn patience and stability while focusing on what you're really looking for, you won't be so anxious all the time.

★ ★ ★

NOVEMBER 6 SCORPIO • The resourceful one of the zodiac
October 23 at 12:00 P.M. to November 22 at 5:00 A.M. • NUMEROLOGY 6

Possessions and Desires . . .

Gem: Topaz—This is an excellent gift to be exchanged between very loyal friends.

Flower: Mandrake—You may tend to let your fears hold you back from enjoying life.

Astral Color, Color Need, Apparel Color: Your Astral Color is Black, the color of protection, birth, and beginnings. Red in your environment gives you energy and stamina. In your wardrobe, Green is your power color for overcoming obstacles.

Fragrance: Buy pots of cinnabar or other scents from the sunny Mediterranean or Orient. You are the most passionate sign of the zodiac, and your fragrance must be as unpredictable as you are.

Tree: Palm—You tend to be very healthy and creative.

Instruments: Tambourine, lyre

Composer: Schubert

Bird: Falcon—an expert hunter. When well-trained, it can adapt to many tasks and is usually obedient.

Symbol: Crescent—You are more likely to be influenced by the phases of the moon. Your easygoing manner leads you to peaceful situations.

Harmonious Health and Nutrition . . .

Health Scent: Orange Blossom—This scent may balance your body, mind, and soul.

Favorable Foods: Corn, watermelon, barley, fresh oysters, eggs

What's Lucky . . .

Lucky Numbers: 2, 4
Best Months: January and July
Best Day of the Week: Tuesday
Best Month Days: 6, 14, 24
Lucky Charms: A religious token or card from any religion.
Harmonious Signs for Relationships and Partnerships: Cancer and Pisces

Spiritual Guides . . .

Star: Al Shaula—People born with this star are careful to avoid being cruel.

Angel: Ambriel—This angel governs travel and transportation, particularly over water, and helps to create love and good communication.

Guardian Angel: Michael—"Who is like God."

Spiritual Stone: Chalcedon—This stone might help when taking long trips, especially by car.

✳ JUDITH'S INSIGHT ✳

You are lovable by nature, but a nuclear physicist couldn't explain yourself to you or others. Besides your extreme moods, you feel the need to keep your feelings secret until you've sorted them out. Why don't you think of asking for help? The added trouble is, on the surface, you don't seem all that complex. You can be a cheerful social butterfly or icy cold and distant, as the whim strikes you. Calling you a challenge is an understatement.

Do you want to be a philosopher, writer, electrician, government agent, lawyer, nurse, or doctor? Any of these suit you. You have a strong mind, resolute heart, and powerful energies. The right opportunities may take time to find, but when you're not looking, you discover yourself standing in the middle of exactly the right job.

Be kind to the person who eventually captures your heart. You offer them a formidable task. Maintaining a relationship with you takes a lot of energy. Keep the desire fresh, or you run the risk of taking it for granted and unwittingly tearing down all that has been built. Even though you're very kind, loving, and altogether affectionate, you require extra attention because you're so unsure of yourself and what makes you happy.

Look forward to the time when you finally discover your missing balance; the passing of time teaches you respect for yourself.

✳ ✳ ✳

Possessions and Desires . . .

Gem: Emerald—This gem is thought to aid in soothing the connection between the desires of the soul with those of the body

Flower: Marvel-of-Peru—You tend to think that the brave are foolish.

Astral Color, Color Need, Apparel Color: Your Astral Color is Black, the color of protection, birth, and beginnings. Red in your environment gives you energy and stamina. In your wardrobe, Wine gives you energy.

Fragrance: Buy pots of cinnabar or other scents from the sunny Mediterranean or Orient. You are the most passionate sign of the zodiac, and your fragrance must be as unpredictable as you are.

Tree: Sycamore—Yours is the ability to love, communicate honestly with others, and have lasting relationships.

Instrument: Harp

Composers: Gluck, Brahms

Bird: Warbling Parakeet—the most beautiful of all birds, it is known as the love bird. It does seem to have the powers of imitation.

Symbol: Heart—You are enthusiastic, empathetic, and full of generosity and love.

Harmonious Health and Nutrition . . .

Health Scent: Jasmine—This scent may make you more easygoing when you are stressed.

Favorable Foods: Cauliflower, cranberries, barley, salmon, buttermilk

What's Lucky . . .

Lucky Numbers: 2, 4

Best Months: January and July

Best Day of the Week: Tuesday

Best Month Days: 4, 5, 23

Lucky Charm: An old key.

Harmonious Signs for Relationships and Partnerships: Cancer and Pisces

Spiritual Guides . . .

Star: Al Kalb—Those with this star are often delightful.

Angel: Ambriel—This angel governs travel and transportation, particularly over water, and helps to create love and good communication.

Guardian Angel: Raphael—This angel attends to all of your needs when you are looking for guidance.

Spiritual Stone: Chalcedon—This stone might help when taking long trips, especially by car.

✶ JUDITH'S INSIGHT ✶

If persistence and consistency count in this world, you will have all the success and happiness you'll ever need. A natural intelligence enables you to write and follow a personal book of rules you'll rely on all your life. Your sensitivity may help or hinder or both. You don't seem as passionate as you are. Family and other attachments might trip you up. It will sometimes take hard work just to keep your emotional car on the road. Try to develop relationships based on harmony.

You will do well if you decide to become a scientist, chemist, critic, philosopher, or jurist. You are quite the thinker; while that's a good thing sometimes, you don't know how to shut off your mind when necessary. You are a hard worker who is prone to overanalyzing. Unfortunately, you add way too much imagination to your rumination. This is good if you were writing a book, but not necessarily when trying to maintain a family or a relationship. At times you harm yourself by mixing in your insecurities and fear with your confidence. On a good day, spilled milk gets cleaned up. On a bad one, it could be destructive.

Keep your emotions in balance, and all you desire can be yours. It sounds like a fortune cookie, but really it's your life.

✶ ✶ ✶

NOVEMBER 8 SCORPIO • The resourceful one of the zodiac

October 23 at 12:00 P.M. to November 22 at 5:00 A.M. • NUMEROLOGY 8

Possessions and Desires . . .

Gem: Chrysolite—This gem may help you clear your mind of sadness and worry.
Flower: Lupine—You usually are very imaginative.
Astral Color, Color Need, Apparel Color: Your Astral Color is Black, the color of protection, birth, and beginnings. Red in your environment gives you energy and stamina. In your wardrobe, Tan gives you balance and harmony.
Fragrance: Buy pots of cinnabar or other scents from the sunny Mediterranean or Orient. You are the most passionate sign of the zodiac, and your fragrance must be as unpredictable as you are.
Tree: Pine—Your relationships tend to be harmonious, both emotionally and mentally.
Instrument: Cello
Composer: Mozart
Bird: Bobolink—This charming singer is equally good as a soloist or a member of an orchestra. It is a very romantic bird, useful as an insect destroyer, and elegant, with beautiful feathers, and always pleasant to have around.
Symbol: Wings—You are the source of balance in your world—this will bring you contentment.

Harmonious Health and Nutrition . . .

Health Scent: Almond—This scent may revitalize you and open you to greater possibilities.
Favorable Foods: Asparagus, strawberries, rye crisp, chicken, eggs

What's Lucky . . .

Lucky Numbers: 2, 4
Best Months: January and July
Best Day of the Week: Tuesday
Best Month Days: 4, 5, 23
Lucky Charm: Red ribbon in your wallet or doorway.
Harmonious Signs for Relationships and Partnerships: Cancer and Pisces

Spiritual Guides . . .

Star: Al Kalb—Those with this star are often delightful.
Angel: Ambriel—This angel governs travel and transportation, particularly over water, and helps to create love and good communication.
Guardian Angel: Seraphim—An angel that brings love, light, and passion.
Spiritual Stone: Chalcedon—This stone might help you keep things together when you feel frayed.

✷ JUDITH'S INSIGHT ✷

You are wonderful at planning and scheming. With your gift for organization, it's a snap for you to put together parties, events, even businesses. Impeccably stylish, you do things your own way. Your love of learning makes you a great student. With just a pen you can turn a piece of paper into a flower to fool a butterfly. Your gift for understanding others is balanced by your cluelessness when it comes to yourself. Those who don't know you see harmony and patience; however, your close friends and family experience how difficult you can be. In relationships, you love a good challenge, so why would your lover expect smooth sailing? All you're trying to do is balance your natural cynicism toward relationships with a lifelong quest for perfect love. As you get older, curbing that skepticism gets easier, so your head lets your heart discover its intended home. If you choose a mate too early in life, expect a lot of bickering before you learn to smooth out the bumpy patches on the road to serenity.

As with romance, success on the job finds you later rather than sooner. You may move from career to career, but all are likely to center around some kind of design or creation. Theater and entertainment may spark your interest, particularly in comedy. As long as you find a job that provides constant applause, your ego is satisfied. Constantly seeking growth, you crave approval and acknowledgment of your many talents. Yours is a life of new beginnings always brimming with fire, energy, and enthusiasm.

✷ ✷ ✷

NOVEMBER 9

SCORPIO • The resourceful one of the zodiac

October 23 at 12:00 P.M. to November 22 at 5:00 A.M. • NUMEROLOGY 9

Possessions and Desires . . .

Gem: Beryl—This gem could be good for meditation and concentration.

Flower: Lotus—Be careful you don't raise barriers between yourself and what you truly love.

Astral Color, Color Need, Apparel Color: Your Astral Color is Black, the color of protection, birth, and beginnings. Red in your environment gives you energy and stamina. In your wardrobe, Green is your power color for overcoming obstacles.

Fragrance: Buy pots of cinnabar or other scents from the sunny Mediterranean or Orient. You are the most passionate sign of the zodiac, and your fragrance must be as unpredictable as you are.

Tree: Holly—Beware that you are not carried away by your passionate nature. The only way to grow is to be open to new experiences.

Instruments: Violin, tympanum

Composer: Gluck

Bird: Mockingbird—the most proficient minstrel in the world's orchestra; graceful and enthusiastic.

Symbol: Anchor—This tranquil symbol signifies stability and strength, and stands for strong commitments in relationships.

Harmonious Health and Nutrition . . .

Health Scent: Lavender—This scent might lead others to trust you and make you patient.

Favorable Foods: Cabbage, black figs, oats, salmon, pressed cheese

What's Lucky . . .

Lucky Numbers: 2, 4

Best Months: January and July

Best Day of the Week: Tuesday

Best Month Days: 9, 18, 27

Lucky Charm: A U. S. coin or a bill of any amount from the year you were born.

Harmonious Signs for Relationships and Partnerships: Cancer and Pisces

Spiritual Guides . . .

Star: Al Shaula—People born with this star are careful to avoid being cruel.

Angel: Ambriel—This angel governs travel and transportation, particularly over water, and helps to create love and good communication.

Guardian Angel: Gabriel—"God is my strength."

Spiritual Stone: Chalcedon—This stone might help when taking long trips, especially by car.

✷ JUDITH'S INSIGHT ✷

You have a very adept mind for music or art. Be cautious when it comes to extremes in the area of self-confidence. Your ego may seem inflated to others because you lack self-esteem. This may trip you up and keep you from obtaining higher rewards in life, both with money and advancement.

Naturally secretive, you don't like showing off your accomplishments, but you do well with careers in the public eye. You tend to gravitate toward those who make you feel secure, which could be a problem. Other people may find you snobbish or gossipy and not trust you. Watch for signs of being misunderstood, especially if you want to be successful. Continuing to be defensive creates enemies out of nowhere.

When it comes to love, you're a more devoted mate than most, even in light of your flirtatious manner. Again, your charm and wit draws in that special person. Give more than you take by allowing others access to that heart of yours. Fight the urge to flee when asked your feelings. At the very least, admit your fear. Tell those you care about how much they mean to you. If you can accept the challenge, you can be happy.

Relax and enjoy being the sparkling, enchanting individual that everyone loves being around.

Some careers you may excel at are: psychologist, with your analytical side; lawyer; paralegal; realtor; musician; or entertainer.

✷ ✷ ✷

NOVEMBER 10
SCORPIO • The resourceful one of the zodiac

October 23 at 12:00 P.M. to November 22 at 5:00 A.M. • NUMEROLOGY 1

Possessions and Desires . . .

Gem: Agate—This stone may promote health and lead you to a long life.

Flower: Lotus—You have very little difficulty expressing your thoughts and feelings.

Astral Color, Color Need, Apparel Color: Your Astral Color is Black, the color of protection, birth, and beginnings. Red in your environment gives you energy and stamina. In your wardrobe, Wine gives you energy.

Fragrance: Buy pots of cinnabar or other scents from the sunny Mediterranean or Orient. You are the most passionate sign of the zodiac, and your fragrance must be as unpredictable as you are.

Tree: Walnut—You are unusually helpful and always looking for constant changes in your life.

Instruments: Oboe, flute, clarinet, piano, French horn, organ, piccolo

Composer: Böhm

Bird: Bird of paradise—the "bird of the gods." You will shine and love extraordinary circumstances.

Symbol: Crown—the universal sign of dignity.

Harmonious Health and Nutrition . . .

Health Scent: Strawberry—Soothing by nature, the strawberry promotes self-esteem and encourages love.

Favorable Foods: Celery, blackberries, barley, beef, eggs

What's Lucky . . .

Lucky Numbers: 2, 4
Best Months: January and July
Best Day of the Week: Tuesday
Best Month Days: 4, 5, 23
Lucky Charm: A new penny in your shoe

Harmonious Signs for Relationships and Partnerships: Cancer and Pisces

Spiritual Guides . . .

Star: Al Shaula—people born with this star are careful to avoid being cruel.

Angel: Ambriel—This angel governs travel and transportation, particularly over water, and helps to create love and good communication.

Guardian Angel: Malachi—"Messenger of Jehovah."

Spiritual Stone: Chalcedon—This stone might help when taking long trips, especially by car.

✳ JUDITH'S INSIGHT ✳

You make things happen, not only in your life, but in the lives of those around you. Challenges are important to you, though you may not realize how much. You are blessed with creativity and love to initiate new beginnings. Control your enthusiasm and exercise caution until you have all the facts. Your naiveté may allow you to be misled or cheated. Your moods swing dramatically from sunny optimism to bleak pessimism.

You need to be with a partner more than you care to admit. Choosy in love, you force the other to prove his or her emotions first. Watch out for too much of this or you may lose one or two people who really mean a lot. Overall, you'll be lucky with partnerships and have many good friends.

You may know some people in high places who will aid you in your career, though with your determined nature, you don't really need help. You may desire multiple jobs. Areas that would be good for you are music, philosophy, law, or design. Later on, you develop an interest in humanitarian or volunteer work.

Your life is a fight for your beliefs, and you have the sensitivity and energy to battle for causes of others, too.

✷ ✷ ✷

344

NOVEMBER 11 SCORPIO • The resourceful one of the zodiac

October 23 at 12:00 P.M. to November 22 at 5:00 A.M. • NUMEROLOGY 2

Possessions and Desires . . .

Gem: Sapphire—This gem may help you find forgiveness from those you've wronged.

Flower: Lotus Tree—You may have the blessing of effortless agreement between yourself and your friends.

Astral Color, Color Need, Apparel Color: Your Astral Color is Black, the color of protection, birth, and beginnings. Red in your environment gives you energy and stamina. In your wardrobe, Tan gives you balance and harmony.

Fragrance: Buy pots of cinnabar or other scents from the sunny Mediterranean or Orient. You are the most passionate sign of the zodiac, and your fragrance must be as unpredictable as you are.

Tree: Maple—You have great stability and flashes of intuition.

Instruments: Pipe organ, cymbal, drum

Composers: Handel, Johann Sebastian Bach

Bird: Stork—Storks have a strange type of intelligence that is easily misunderstood. The stork is known to have a pleasing nature.

Symbol: Cross—the symbol of self-sacrifice and reconciliation.

Harmonious Health and Nutrition . . .

Health Scent: Raspberry—This scent might bring you a feeling of harmony with the universe.

Favorable Foods: Dandelion, cranberries, barley, chicken, buttermilk

What's Lucky . . .

Lucky Numbers: 2, 4

Best Months: January and July

Best Day of the Week: Tuesday

Best Month Days: 4, 5, 23

Lucky Charms: Two 50-cent pieces. Give someone else one of them.

Harmonious Signs for Relationships and Partnerships: Cancer and Pisces

Spiritual Guides . . .

Star: Al Kalb—Those with this star are often delightful.

Angel: Ambriel—This angel governs travel and transportation, particularly over water, and helps to create love and good communication.

Guardian Angel: St. John—This angel simplifies that which is complicated.

Spiritual Stone: Chalcedon—This stone might help when taking long trips, especially by car.

✶ JUDITH'S INSIGHT ✶

You are talented, energetic, and bighearted, with a strong and sensible mind. Your imagination will allow you success if you can wait for your unconventional methods to work. When you're younger, try to resist your nasty habit of making all the wrong choices. You are too busy looking to ever find anything. Others may become frustrated with you as you seem to take the longest path possible.

You need to be in control, and work is best when you're the boss. You're meticulous and organized, so consider a career in medicine, as either a surgeon or researcher. You would also do well in the legal profession.

With your strong physical power, if you don't choose a career in professional sports, you should make them a hobby—at which you'll excel. You wake up charged every day and remain energized, as long as you get your way. Obstacles drain and depress you—you take everything too personally.

You're difficult to work with, and you can be a nightmare to love. Relationships will be the most complicated part of your life, and it's usually your fault. You clutch the key to your heart and often refuse to give it out. Eventually, you'll realize that the spiritual is more important than the material and discover all the joys a relationship can offer.

Keep your head up high and that abundant energy flowing; your life's lesson is to learn to work with others as you reach your destiny.

✶ ✶ ✶

NOVEMBER 12

SCORPIO • The resourceful one of the zodiac

October 23 at 12:00 P.M. to November 22 at 5:00 A.M. • NUMEROLOGY 3

Possessions and Desires . . .

Gem: Ruby—This stone may lead you to energy, friendship, and happiness.

Flower: Lichen—You tend to love being by yourself.

Astral Color, Color Need, Apparel Color: Your Astral Color is Black, the color of protection, birth, and beginnings. Red in your environment gives you energy and stamina. In your wardrobe, Green is your power color for overcoming obstacles.

Fragrance: Buy pots of cinnabar or other scents from the sunny Mediterranean or Orient. You are the most passionate sign of the zodiac, and your fragrance must be as unpredictable as you are.

Tree: Elm—You have willpower, strength, and the ability to stand alone.

Instrument: Trombone

Composers: Verdi, Mendelssohn, Schumann

Bird: Eagle—This bird is quick to use its powers of flight. It can see immeasurable distances in a single glance, and can sometimes appear to be indifferent.

Harmonious Health and Nutrition . . .

Health Scent: Rose—This scent will lead you to passionate thoughts and make you feel warm inside.

Favorable Foods: Asparagus, watermelon, oats, salmon, pressed cheese

What's Lucky . . .

Lucky Numbers: 2, 4
Best Months: January and July
Best Day of the Week: Tuesday
Best Month Days: 3, 12, 21
Lucky Charm: A pen that someone else has already used.

Harmonious Signs for Relationships and Partnerships: Cancer and Pisces

Spiritual Guides . . .

Star: Al Kalb—Those with this star are often delightful.

Angel: Ambriel—This angel governs travel and transportation, particularly over water, and helps to create love and good communication.

Guardian Angel: Johiel—This angel is a protector of all those with a humble heart.

Spiritual Stone: Chalcedon—This stone might help when taking long trips, especially by car.

✴ JUDITH'S INSIGHT ✴

You make things happen, get the ball rolling, and keep it in motion. You are born to be famous or at least well known. Your efforts with children will be acknowledged. You're destined to make a difference in the lives of those around you, and the experience will change you forever.

Your determination and passion allow you your pick of careers, though it may take you a long time to feel successful. Think about becoming a pediatrician, as it suits your caring nature and kind heart. You need not work with children, however, to leave an impression on them. They look up to you no matter what. Charm takes you far—all the way to the bank and maybe even the Senate.

Home environment and family mean everything to you. This feeling grows deeper as you mature. You cheerfully pull everybody onto the bandwagon and enlist their help in the work you do for others.

Your ambition enables you to travel the world and experience many different cultures. Always exploring the universe, you will discover it inside yourself.

You can be hard to get a commitment from when it comes to love, until you really become ready.

✴ ✴ ✴

NOVEMBER 13

SCORPIO • The resourceful one of the zodiac

October 23 at 12:00 P.M. to November 22 at 5:00 A.M. • NUMEROLOGY 4

Possessions and Desires . . .

Gem: Emerald—Those who carry this stone tend to be lucky in love.

Flower: Field Lily—You have great humility when greatness finds you.

Astral Color, Color Need, Apparel Color: Your Astral Color is Black, the color of protection, birth, and beginnings. Red in your environment gives you energy and stamina. In your wardrobe, Wine gives you energy.

Fragrance: Buy pots of cinnabar or other scents from the sunny Mediterranean or Orient. You are the most passionate sign of the zodiac, and your fragrance must be as unpredictable as you are.

Tree: Cherry—You will find yourself faced with constant new emotional awakenings.

Instruments: Bass, clarinet

Composers: Haydn, Wagner

Bird: Robin—the most sociable of all birds, with the ability to create quick friendships. It also can easily adapt to any home. When it wants something, it has the tendency to try to snatch it.

Symbol: Star—You are full of inner brightness and will stand out in any crowd. You will be seen as special.

Harmonious Health and Nutrition . . .

Health Scent: Vanilla—This scent will fill you with a feeling of cleanliness and stability.

Favorable Foods: Spinach, strawberries, rye crisps, fresh oysters, buttermilk

What's Lucky . . .

Lucky Numbers: 2, 4
Best Months: January and July
Best Day of the Week: Tuesday
Best Month Days: 4, 13, 22
Lucky Charm: A piece of material cut from something in your home.

Harmonious Signs for Relationships and Partnerships: Cancer and Pisces

Spiritual Guides . . .

Star: Al Shaula—People born with this star are careful to avoid being cruel.

Angel: Ambriel—This angel governs travel and transportation, particularly over water, and helps to create love and good communication.

Guardian Angel: Uriel—This angel brings the light of God's guidance.

Spiritual Stone: Chalcedon—This stone might help when taking long trips, especially by car.

✳ JUDITH'S INSIGHT ✳

You draw people in without their knowing why. Your appealing manner can persuade others to do whatever you want. Your great sense of humor can disappear if the joke is on you. You have a tendency toward selfishness but really do anything for anyone you can.

You crave challenge and desire the opportunity to travel and know all the world can offer. When you're searching for a mate, remember that you dislike feeling tied down. Make it clear from the start that you need freedom and independence, or the partnership will never work. The more confined you feel, the more you struggle to be free.

Keep this in mind as well when choosing a career. Look for one that offers freedom and constant stimulation. Being a free bird doesn't necessarily mean you don't depend on others. Oddly, you do well in jobs with clearly defined structure, like those in government. You may even find yourself working for a uniform company or wearing a uniform, say as a firefighter, cop, or member of the armed forces. No matter what career you choose, your good work ethic and strong intellect bring you success.

Follow your need to travel, if not in your physical world, then with your mind and your soul.

✳ ✳ ✳

NOVEMBER 14

SCORPIO • The resourceful one of the zodiac

October 23 at 12:00 P.M. to November 22 at 5:00 A.M. • NUMEROLOGY 5

Possessions and Desires . . .

Gem: Sardius—This stone could give the wearer unusual insights into his or her own heart.

Flower: Yellow Lily—You usually hate any hint of falsehood.

Astral Color, Color Need, Apparel Color: Your Astral Color is Black, the color of protection, births, and beginnings. Red in your environment gives you energy and stamina. In your wardrobe, Tan gives you balance and harmony.

Fragrance: Buy pots of cinnabar or other scents from the sunny Mediterranean or Orient. You are the most passionate sign of the zodiac, and your fragrance must be as unpredictable as you are.

Tree: Apple—You are creative, full of joy, and nearly magical. You bring happiness.

Instruments: Viola, trumpet

Composer: Liszt

Bird: Flamingo—This beautiful, gregarious bird is always careful of its enemy. It is also a caretaker of the young and tries to keep everyone happy.

Symbol: Triangle—You have the right combination of abilities.

Harmonious Health and Nutrition . . .

Health Scent: Peach—This scent may balance your good qualities so that they equal your charm.

Favorable Foods: Cauliflower, cranberries, barley, chicken, eggs

What's Lucky . . .

Lucky Numbers: 2, 4

Best Months: January and July

Best Day of the Week: Tuesday

Best Month Days: 4, 5, 23

Lucky Charm: A rabbit's foot or a white candle.

Harmonious Signs for Relationships and Partnerships: Cancer and Pisces

Spiritual Guides . . .

Star: Al Kalb—Those with this star are often delightful.

Angel: Ambriel—This angel governs travel and transportation, particularly over water, and helps to create love and good communication.

Guardian Angel: Plavwell—The guardian that gives power and strength to one's presence.

Spiritual Stone: Chalcedon—This stone might help when taking long trips, especially by car.

✶ *JUDITH'S INSIGHT* ✶

Your deep love for the arts and natural instincts should guide you to a career that takes advantage of your imagination. Your fine investigative abilities enable you to get to the truth. Some may see you as skeptical. Personality and the gift of gab take you far at work. You'd make an excellent salesperson or worker in the beauty industry. Highly charged and very good at combining different ideas to create an entirely new product, you could be equally comfortable working in marketing or boutiques or producing a show.

Romance is a source of frustration for you. You want fresh new beginnings and challenges. Marrying later in life proves better as you will have exhausted your emotional wanderlust. You make a better friend than lover. When you put yourself in a love relationship, you lose focus. As a friend, when you feel freedom from restrictions, you're wonderfully loyal.

Expect to find yourself flying off to one country after another. You were born to visit exotic places. A wild practical joker, you can be difficult to get along with. However, you usually host the parties and comfort others with encouragement and security. Keep your home neat . . . it is vital. If you don't decide to become a professional chef, your friends and family will benefit from your culinary skill.

✶ ✶ ✶

NOVEMBER 15

SCORPIO • The resourceful one of the zodiac

October 23 at 12:00 P.M. to November 22 at 5:00 A.M. • NUMEROLOGY 6

Possessions and Desires . . .

Gem: Topaz—This is an excellent gift to be exchanged between very loyal friends.

Flower: Laurestine—If you neglect your own needs you may end up very bitter.

Astral Color, Color Need, Apparel Color: Your Astral Color is Black, the color of protection, birth, and beginnings. Red in your environment gives you energy and stamina. In your wardrobe, Green is your power color for overcoming obstacles.

Fragrance: Buy pots of cinnabar or other scents from the sunny Mediterranean or Orient. You are the most passionate sign of the zodiac, and your frangrance must be as unpredictable as you are.

Tree: Palm—You tend to be very healthy and creative.

Instruments: Tambourine, lyre

Composer: Schubert

Bird: Lark—known for the beauty of its song, which is sometimes very unusual. It is also credited with extraordinary intelligence.

Symbol: Crescent—You are more likely to be influenced by the phases of the moon. Your easygoing manner leads you to peaceful situations

Harmonious Health and Nutrition . . .

Health Scent: Orange Blossom—This scent may balance your body, mind, and soul.

Favorable Foods: Cabbage, blackberries, oats, salmon, pressed cheese

What's Lucky . . .

Lucky Numbers: 2, 4

Best Months: January and July

Best Day of the Week: Tuesday

Best Month Days: 6, 15, 14

Lucky Charm: A religious token or card from any religion.

Harmonious Signs for Relationships and Partnerships: Cancer and Pisces

Spiritual Guides . . .

Star: Al Shaula—People born with this star are careful to avoid being cruel.

Angel: Ambriel—This angel governs travel and transportation, particularly over water, and helps to create love and good communication.

Guardian Angel: Michael—"Who is like God."

Spiritual Stone: Chalcedon—This stone might help when taking long trips, especially by car.

✷ JUDITH'S INSIGHT ✷

Strong tendencies toward the sciences may entice you to consider a career studying nature. You love time spent near bodies of water and recognize this as a source of calm and contentment. If ever you're flagging in courage or depressed, a quick aquatic visit will perk you right up. You should live near the sea, a river, a lake, or at the very least, a reservoir.

You make many friends and could keep them due to your generally truthful and trustworthy nature. But remember, a person who is too truthful and frank is hard for people to accept, so curb your need to be overly direct. You are a proud person with well-developed character; people respect you.

You are completely devoted in love, and as long as each romantic interlude lasts, you feel as if it's forever. The reasons for breakups will vary as much as the unconventional relationships you choose. You may carry on multiple relationships all at once.

You are versatile and capable of doing anything well; your strong mind and energetic body govern a giving soul. The right employment may take time to discover. Stop looking for it, and it will find you. For you, job satisfaction lies beyond a journey through some disappointment. Console yourself along the way. Inevitably, you'll find the career in which you'll be a success.

Some careers that you may excel at: musician, lawyer, chemist, doctor, or scientist.

✷ ✷ ✷

NOVEMBER 16

SCORPIO • The resourceful one of the zodiac

October 23 at 12:00 P.M. to November 22 at 5:00 A.M. • NUMEROLOGY 7

Possessions and Desires . . .

Gem: Agate—This stone may promote health and lead you to a long life.

Flower: Mountain Laurel—You will always have great ambitions concerning your life.

Astral Color, Color Need, Apparel Color: Your Astral Color is Black, the color of protection, birth, and beginnings. Red in your environment gives you energy and stamina. In your wardrobe, Wine gives you energy.

Fragrance: Buy pots of cinnabar or other scents from the sunny Mediterranean or Orient. You are the most passionate sign of the zodiac, and your fragrance must be as unpredictable as you are.

Tree: Sycamore—Yours is the ability to love, communicate honestly with others, and have lasting relationships.

Instrument: Harp

Composers: Gluck, Brahms

Bird: Skylark—This handsome bird is beautiful when it sings. It always whistles as it works.

Harmonious Health and Nutrition . . .

Health Scent: Jasmine—This scent may make you more easygoing when you are stressed.

Favorable Foods: Celery, black figs, rye crisps, beef, buttermilk

What's Lucky . . .

Lucky Numbers: 2, 4
Best Months: January and July
Best Day of the Week: Tuesday
Best Month Days: 4, 5, 23
Lucky Charm: An old key.
Harmonious Signs for Relationships and Partnerships: Cancer and Pisces

Spiritual Guides . . .

Star: Al Kalb—Those with this star are often delightful.

Angel: Ambriel—This angel governs travel and transportation, particularly over water, and helps to create love and good communication.

Guardian Angel: Raphael—This angel attends to all of your needs when you are looking for guidance.

Spiritual Stone: Chalcedon—This stone might help when taking long trips, especially by car.

✴ JUDITH'S INSIGHT ✴

If you can't succeed, nobody can. Loaded with determination and perseverance, you have all the basic tools needed to conquer the world. People want to help you because of your vibrant enthusiasm. They'll be anxious to take part in your many victories. You were born to lead, and your followers are aware of your strength and appreciate your sensitivity. Somewhere along the way, you may discover certain personality traits that need work. But as you do with all other difficult obstacles, given enough time, you find a way to overcome them.

Relationships can be a struggle. It may seem you'd be better off without one or that true love will never find you. Your perfect mate understands you and is capable of sticking it out.

You are here to accomplish much and probably won't rest until you do. Besides being a born leader, you are a teacher of life. A natural philosopher, you give great advice. You would make an excellent preacher, counselor, or motivational speaker. Your charm, wit, and energy will not quit. All you need is time to reach the forefront both in your chosen field and in life.

✴ ✴ ✴

NOVEMBER 17

SCORPIO • The resourceful one of the zodiac

October 23 at 12:00 P.M. to November 22 at 5:00 A.M. • NUMEROLOGY 8

Possessions and Desires . . .

Gem: Chrysolite—This gem may help you clear your mind of sadness and worry.

Flower: Laurel—You tend to find victory even in defeat.

Astral Color, Color Need, Apparel Color: Your Astral Color is Black, the color of protection, birth, and beginnings. Red in your environment gives you energy and stamina. In your wardrobe, Tan gives you balance and harmony.

Tree: Pine—Your relationships tend to be harmonious, both emotionally and mentally.

Instrument: Cello

Composer: Mozart

Bird: Bobolink—This charming singer is equally good as a soloist or a member of an orchestra. It is a very romantic bird, most useful as an insect destroyer, and elegant, with beautiful feathers, and always pleasant to have around.

Symbol: Wings—You are the source of balance in your world—This will bring you contentment.

Harmonious Health and Nutrition . . .

Health Scent: Almond—This scent may revitalize you and open you to greater possibilities.

Favorable Foods: Dandelion, blackberries, barley, salmon, eggs

What's Lucky . . .

Lucky Numbers: 2, 4

Best Months: January and July

Best Day of the Week: Tuesday

Best Month Days: 8, 17, 26

Lucky Charm: Red ribbon in your wallet or doorway.

Harmonious Signs for Relationships and Partnerships: Cancer and Pisces

Spiritual Guides . . .

Star: Al Kalb—Those with this star are often delightful.

Angel: Ambriel—This angel governs travel and transportation, particularly over water, and helps to create love and good communication.

Guardian Angel: Seraphim—An angel that brings love, light, and passion.

Spiritual Stone: Chalcedon—This stone might help when taking long trips, especially by car.

✴ JUDITH'S INSIGHT ✴

You have skill at organization, usually pulling things together by sheer force. Consider a career as a troubleshooter—your knack for handling difficult issues lends itself to problem solving. You do things your own way and cannot tolerate interference. While you can be a great student of life, many things don't seem to interest you. You are naturally artistic and yearn for a job that utilizes your creative side.

Your love of travel deepens as you mature. You feel safe and secure around large bodies of water. While you seek serenity, you are quick-minded and sometimes even quicker tempered. Your lesson in life: learn to deal with losses and difficulties.

Better as part of a family or fellowship than on your own, you sometimes rely on luck in making choices about the people in your life. Stability in matters of the heart may take time, but you stick it out until you find a mate who understands you. The life you build together will be worth the struggle.

When you least expect it, success will fall right into your lap. The taste of victory only increases your appetite for more challenge. You should pursue many differing fields. Who else has the skills to be a great designer, artist, or teacher, and could do equally well in the stock market, gambling, or even the theater?

Understand that you have an ego that needs to be fed. Be careful not to overdo it.

✴ ✴ ✴

NOVEMBER 18

SCORPIO • The resourceful one of the zodiac

October 23 at 12:00 P.M. to November 22 at 5:00 A.M. • NUMEROLOGY 9

Possessions and Desires . . .

Gem: Beryl—This gem could be good for meditation and concentration.

Flower: Houstonia—You are content with what the universe gives you.

Astral Color, Color Need, Apparel Color: Your Astral Color is Black, the color of protection, birth, and beginnings. Red in your environment gives you energy and stamina. In your wardrobe, Green is your power color for overcoming obstacles.

Fragrance: Buy pots of cinnabar or other scents from the sunny Mediterranean or Orient. You are the most passionate sign of the zodiac, and your fragrance must be as unpredictable as you are.

Tree: Holly—Beware that you are not carried away by your passionate nature. The only way to grow is to be open to new experiences.

Instruments: Violin, tympanum

Composer: Gluck

Bird: Mockingbird—the most proficient minstrel in the world's orchestra; graceful and enthusiastic.

Symbol: Anchor—This tranquil symbol signifies stability and strength, and stands for strong commitments in relationships.

Harmonious Health and Nutrition . . .

Health Scent: Lavender—This scent might lead others to trust you and make you patient.

Favorable Foods: Asparagus, cranberries, oats, fresh oysters, buttermilk

What's Lucky . . .

Lucky Numbers: 2, 4
Best Months: January and July
Best Day of the Week: Tuesday
Best Month Days: 4, 5, 23
Lucky Charm: A U.S. coin or a bill of any amount from the year you were born.

Harmonious Signs for Relationships and Partnerships: Cancer and Pisces

Spiritual Guides . . .

Star: Al Shaula—People born with this star are careful to avoid being cruel.

Angel: Ambriel—This angel governs travel and transportation, particularly over water, and helps to create love and good communication.

Guardian Angel: Gabriel—"God is my strength."

Spiritual Stone: Chalcedon—This stone might help when taking long trips, especially by car.

★ JUDITH'S INSIGHT ★

No matter what career you choose, the opportunity to work in the limelight will present itself. What begins as a bit part in your grade school play may lead to you starring in a major motion picture. Be aware of your emotional extremes—your self-confidence can ride high or drop down low. Your pocketbook is either completely empty or stuffed full.

You are naturally secretive, and this makes the search for a close relationship difficult. Others may see you as untruthful because you tend to keep your feelings to yourself.

You will excel in the field of public affairs or in a public company. Consider a career in government. You don't have to be a politician, but by no means should you consider it out of your reach. By being kinder to others you'll like yourself more and fare better in life. Try being as generous as you can. The older you get, the more giving you become. If you get lucky financially, try sharing the wealth.

Usually deep in thought, you don't always let others know what you're thinking. You are strongly intuitive and need to learn to trust your inner voice. If you don't, you'll eventually wish you had. You have great executive abilities and uncanny organizational skills.

Learn to go with what you know is true, and success will find you.

★ ★ ★

NOVEMBER 19

SCORPIO • The resourceful one of the zodiac

October 23 at 12:00 P.M. to November 22 at 5:00 A.M. • NUMEROLOGY 1

Possessions and Desires . . .

Gem: Turquoise—This stone might help you find material wealth.

Flower: Hornbeam—You may place more emphasis on how things look than how they really are.

Astral Color, Color Need, Apparel Color: Your Astral Color is Black, the color of protection, birth, and beginnings. Red in your environment gives you energy and stamina. In your wardrobe, Wine gives you energy.

Fragrance: Buy pots of cinnabar or other scents from the sunny Mediterranean or Orient. You are the most passionate sign of the zodiac, and your fragrance must be as unpredictable as you are.

Tree: Walnut—You are unusually helpful and always looking for constant changes in your life.

Instruments: Oboe, flute, clarinet, piano, French horn, organ, piccolo

Composer: Böhm

Bird: Bird of paradise—the "bird of the gods." You will shine and love extraordinary circumstances.

Symbol: Crown—the universal sign of dignity.

Harmonious Health and Nutrition . . .

Health Scent: Strawberry—soothing by nature, the strawberry promotes self-esteem and encourages love.

Favorable Foods: Cabbage, black figs, barley, salmon, eggs

What's Lucky . . .

Lucky Numbers: 2, 4
Best Months: January and July
Best Day of the Week: Tuesday
Best Month Days: 1, 10, 19
Lucky Charm: A new penny in your shoe.
Harmonious Signs for Relationships and Partnerships: Cancer and Pisces

Spiritual Guides . . .

Star: Al Shaula—People born with this star are careful to avoid being cruel.

Angel: Ambriel—This angel governs travel and transportation, particularly over water, and helps to create love and good communication.

Guardian Angel: Malachi—"Messenger of Jehovah."

Spiritual Stone: Chalcedon—This stone might help when taking long trips, especially by car.

✷ JUDITH'S INSIGHT ✷

Your exceptional power and energy just never quit. You glow like a long-lasting, superbright incandescent bulb. You are creative in every sense of the word; your ideas are usually the good ones. You are astute and observant by nature and would make an extraordinary critic. Although you may see it as common sense or natural intelligence, you rely heavily on intuition.

There is a job for you in government if you want it. Your opinions are well received, and you always win in debate. When you speak people really do listen. With your sense of humor and wit, everyone wants to stay part of the huge crowd that surrounds you.

You will have many friends, acquaintances, and lovers, and this is your choice. Watch out for a tendency for sarcasm—others may see you as moody. So long as the party is going your way and in your control, everything is fine by you. You can pout if you don't get your way. Try to find a better method to release that building before it gets the best of you. Try to swiftly deal with depression during difficult times in your life. You have a tendency to wallow for too long instead of going forward.

Depending on which road you take, you can accomplish as much or as little as you please.

✷ ✷ ✷

NOVEMBER 20

SCORPIO • The resourceful one of the zodiac

October 23 at 12:00 P.M. to November 22 at 5:00 A.M. • NUMEROLOGY 2

Possessions and Desires . . .

Gem: Sapphire—This gem may help you find forgiveness from those you've wronged.

Flower: Honeysuckle—You are generous and devoted.

Astral Color, Color Need, Apparel Color: Your Astral Color is Black, the color of protection, birth, and beginnings. Red in your environment gives you energy and stamina. In your wardrobe, Tan gives you balance and harmony.

Fragrance: Buy pots of cinnabar or other scents from the sunny Mediterranean or Orient. You are the most passionate sign of the zodiac, and your fragrance must be as unpredictable as you are.

Tree: Maple—You have great stability and flashes of intuition.

Instruments: Pipe organ, cymbal, drum

Composers: Handel, Johann Sebastian Bach

Bird: Stork—Turkish bird, held in high esteem the world over. This bird is intelligent but may have strange tendencies.

Symbol: Cross—The symbol of self-sacrifice and reconciliation.

Harmonious Health and Nutrition . . .

Health Scent: Raspberry—This scent might bring you a feeling of harmony with the universe.

Favorable Foods: Cauliflower, watermelon, oats, fresh oysters, pressed cheese

What's Lucky . . .

Lucky Numbers: 2, 4

Best Months: January and July

Best Day of the Week: Tuesday

Best Month Days: 2, 11, 20

Lucky Charms: Two 50-cent pieces. Give someone else one of them.

Harmonious Signs for Relationships and Partnerships: Cancer and Pisces

Spiritual Guides . . .

Star: Al Shaula—People born with this star are careful to avoid being cruel.

Angel: Ambriel—This angel governs travel and transportation, particularly over water, and helps to create love and good communication.

Guardian Angel: St. John—This angel simplifies that which is complicated.

Spiritual Stone: Chalcedon—This stone might help when taking long trips, especially by car.

✱ JUDITH'S INSIGHT ✱

You are talented and energetic with a vivid imagination. This alone could pave the way to success. Try to keep your emotional side from getting in the way. You'll do best as the boss—not only of yourself, but of your surroundings. Entertainment at home is important to you, as is an extremely tidy house. You need to feel secure at home. When things are unsettled with friends and family, you'll experience a great deal of pain. You prefer harmony around you, but you won't back away from standing up to a surly neighbor.

You may do well as an athlete and probably enjoy some physical activity every single day. You are interested in learning and will drink up knowledge whatever the source: movies, traveling, or books. You would do well as a stockbroker, analyst, or paralegal or in any career in which there is constant research.

Relationships can pose problems for you because you hang onto your heart. It is hard for you to let go once you fall in love. People must prove themselves to you before you can relax. Learn to let go. You're not holding on; you're holding yourself back.

Yes, life can be messy and complicated—jump in and get dirty.

✱ ✱ ✱

NOVEMBER 21

SCORPIO • The resourceful one of the zodiac

October 23 at 12:00 P.M. to November 22 at 5:00 A.M. • NUMEROLOGY 3

Possessions and Desires . . .

Gem: Ruby—This stone may lead you to energy, friendship, and happiness.

Flower: Hawkweed—You grasp the significance of events more quickly that those around you.

Astral Color, Color Need, Apparel Color: Your Astral Color is Black, the color of protection, birth, and beginnings. Red in your environment gives you energy and stamina. In your wardrobe, Green is your power color for overcoming obstacles.

Fragrance: Buy pots of cinnabar or other scents from the sunny Mediterranean or Orient. You are the most passionate sign of the zodiac, and your fragrance must be as unpredictable as you are.

Tree: Elm—You have willpower, strength, and the ability to stand alone.

Instrument: Trombone

Composers: Verdi, Mendelssohn, Schumann

Bird: Swan—Regarded as royal and sacred, this bird has the protective nature of a mother, and can become a furious fighter in the defense of its young.

Symbol: Wreath—This symbol is like the crown in having a special personality, but those with your mark also show lots of compassion for others.

Harmonious Health and Nutrition . . .

Health Scent: Rose—This scent will lead you to passionate thoughts and make you feel warm inside.

Favorable Foods: Cauliflower, watermelon, oats, fresh oysters, pressed cheese

What's Lucky . . .

Lucky Numbers: 2, 4
Best Months: January and July
Best Day of the Week: Tuesday
Best Month Days: 3, 12, 21
Lucky Charm: A pen that someone else has already used.

Harmonious Signs for Relationships and Partnerships: Cancer and Pisces

Spiritual Guides . . .

Star: Al Kalb—Those with this star are often delightful.

Angel: Ambriel—This angel governs travel and transportation, particularly over water, and helps to create love and good communication.

Guardian Angel: Johiel—This angel is a protector of all those with a humble heart.

Spiritual Stone: Chalcedon—This stone might help when taking long trips, especially by car.

★ JUDITH'S INSIGHT ★

World travel should appeal to you because of your perfect ease in any situation. You have a sort of sweetness about you, love to soak up knowledge, and do it very well. You experience exciting things nearly every day because it's in your nature to seek them out. Even if you don't actually move from place to place in ships and planes, some amount of your life will be spent seeking knowledge about other religions, foods, people, and cultures.

Your love life is up to you. First, decide you want to be happy. Your mind actually rules your heart. Try to understand that with most people, it's the other way around. A more combative or sensitive person would be difficult to find. Most of your fighting takes place within yourself. The trouble with this is you always lose.

You would do well employed in government or in jobs where you travel to new locations or environments constantly. For instance, transportation and travel industries should attract you. You act more independent than is really the case. As you mature, you learn to recognize how important friends and family are to you. Be as generous with money as you can afford to be. Your genuine love of people makes you sympathetic and charitable, even when finances are tight.

It is a diverse world, and it's all yours.

★ ★ ★

Possessions and Desires . . .

Gem: Emerald—Those who carry this stone tend to be lucky in love.

Flower: Gourd—You tend not to be happy unless you have an overabundance of what you want.

Astral Color, Color Need, Apparel Color: Your Astral Color is Red, the color of passion, power, excitement, and strength. Violet in your environment keeps you empathetic toward others. In your wardrobe, Purple reflects your giving personality and brings you luck.

Fragrance: You need to be bathed in exotic scents that will give your imagination room to roam. Experiment with imported incense and tinctures to show the world what a spirited individual you are.

Tree: Cherry—You will find yourself faced with constant new emotional awakenings.

Instruments: Bass, clarinet

Composers: Haydn, Wagner

Bird: Robin—The most sociable of all birds, with the ability to create quick friendships. It also can easily adapt to any home. When it wants something, it has the tendency to try to snatch it.

Symbol: Star—You are full of inner brightness and will stand out in any crowd. You will be seen as special.

Harmonious Health and Nutrition . . .

Health Scent: Vanilla—This scent will fill you with a feeling of cleanliness and stability.

Favorable Foods: Asparagus, cranberries, oats, salmon, buttermilk

What's Lucky . . .

Lucky Numbers: 5, 7

Best Months: February and June

Best Day of the Week: Thursday

Best Month Days: 4, 13, 22

Lucky Charm: A piece of material cut from something in your home.

Harmonious Signs for Relationships and Partnerships: Aries, Leo, Sagittarius

Spiritual Guides . . .

Star: Al Naim—Those with this star are often delightful.

Angel: Aduachiel—This angel governs the balance of elements—water, earth, fire, and air—and helps maintain a calm disposition.

Guardian Angel: Uriel—This angel brings the light of God's guidance.

Spiritual Stone: Emerald—This gem is thought to aid in smoothing the connection between the desires of the soul and those of the body.

✴ _JUDITH'S INSIGHT_ ✴

You often feel older than you are because of your well-developed sense of responsibility. An appealing inner charm steadily draws others to you. When you aks why people like you so much, they won't always be able to supply a reason. There's just that special something you possess.

You may feel misunderstood until you grow up and start recognizing how out of the ordinary you are. You are unique, with a kind heart and overactive mind, and you have strong values no matter what environment you grow up in.

You can lack tact, and your sense of humor can waver, especially if the joke is on you. Life is not going to be always easy. Luckily you have the strength to meet the challenges you'll face. It's very important for you to do what you consider is your duty. In every relationship, you'll fulfill what the other person expects, even to your own detriment.

Well-rounded and with many different talents, you don't fully recognize all your gifts until you're older. You may be strongly interested in electricity, music, or politics. Your firm convictions fuel the need to accomplish much in this life. You would do very well as a social worker or in another job as a force for true justice. You have the ability to communicate your ideas clearly, and your words often find their way into the heads and hearts of many.

✴ ✴ ✴

NOVEMBER 23
SAGITTARIUS • The adventurous one of the zodiac
November 22 at 5:00 A.M. to December 21 at 10:00 P.M. • NUMEROLOGY 5

Possessions and Desires . . .

Gem: Sardius—This stone could give the wearer unusual insights into his or her own heart.
Flower: Fuchsia—You tend to have good taste in what you wear and your surroundings.
Astral Color, Color Need, Apparel Color: Your Astral Color is Red, the color of passion, power, excitement, and strength. Violet in your environment will keep you empathetic toward others. In your wardrobe, Green is your power color for overcoming obstacles.
Fragrance: You need to be bathed in exotic scents that will give your imagination room to roam. Experiment with imported incense and tinctures to show the world what a spirited individual you are.
Tree: Apple—You are creative, full of joy, and nearly magical. You bring happiness.
Instruments: Viola, trumpet
Composer: Liszt
Bird: Flamingo—This beautiful, gregarious bird is always careful of its enemy. It is also a caretaker of the young and tries to keep everyone happy.
Symbol: Triangle—You have the right combination of abilities.

Harmonious Health and Nutrition . . .

Health Scent: Peach—This scent may balance your good qualities so that they equal your charm.
Favorable Foods: Cabbage, oranges, rice, pecans, chicken

What's Lucky . . .

Lucky Numbers: 5 & 7
Best Months: February and June
Best Day of the Week: Thursday
Best Month Days: 4, 5, 23
Lucky Charm: A rabbit's foot or a white candle.
Harmonious Signs for Relationships and Partnerships: Aries, Leo, Sagittarius

Spiritual Guides . . .

Star: Al Beldah—those with this star are sometimes the victims of hasty judgments.
Angel: Aduachiel—this angel governs the balance of elements—water, earth, fire, and air—and helps maintain a calm disposition.
Guardian Angel: Plavwell—The guardian that gives power and strength to one's presence.
Spiritual Stone: Emerald—This gem is thought to aid in smoothing the connection between the desires of the soul and those of the body.

✳ JUDITH'S INSIGHT ✳

Positive, fearless, and masterful, it's not enough for you to achieve success at work; you need recognition for your spectacular accomplishments with your family and hobbies. These strong traits can lead you to a public or political career. Even if this is not your way, you should someday find yourself in the public eye.

You'd make a great consultant or counselor. Unlike most, you can be your own best advocate and usually know what's best for you. Law and order appeal to you, and you might consider a career in that profession. You would excel as a soldier, teacher, or surgeon. Your desire for drama may lead you to come form of acting. A natural poet, you often create songs and, if you have the voice, sing them yourself.

Those you love may not always understand what you see as your purely good intentions. You want a relationship with a firm commitment, but one that allows a strong sense of freedom. Discipline yourself with your spouse and children, if you have them. You may become suspicious and jealous with your mate. Beware of acting overly demanding and rigid with those living around you. Remember, a heavy hand may lead to a heavy heart.

Your biggest challenge in life is to put to effective use the many skills and gifts you were born with. Hang onto the reins tightly because it is likely to be an eventful ride. Incorporate your love of travel into a life where you'll frequently visit very different places.

✳ ✳ ✳

357

NOVEMBER 24
SAGITTARIUS • The adventurous one of the zodiac

November 22 at 5:00 A.M. to December 21 at 10:00 P.M. • NUMEROLOGY 6

Possessions and Desires . . .

Gem: Topaz—This is an excellent gift to be exchanged between very loyal friends.

Flower: Dark Geranium—Allow yourself more freedom, when you yearn for it.

Astral Color, Color Need, Apparel Color: Your Astral Color is Red, the color of passion, power, excitement, and strength. Violet in your environment keeps you empathetic toward others. In your wardrobe, Green is your power color for overcoming obstacles.

Fragrance: You need to be bathed in exotic scents that will give your imagination room to roam. Experiment with imported incense and tinctures to show the world what a spirited individual you are.

Tree: Palm—You tend to be very healthy and creative.

Instruments: Tambourine, lyre

Composer: Schubert

Bird: Goldfinch—There are forty-four different species of finches which vary greatly. These gentle creatures can be very shy in unsettled weather.

Symbol: Crescent—You are more likely to be influenced by the phases of the moon. Your easygoing manner leads you to peaceful situations.

Harmonious Health and Nutrition . . .

Health Scent: Orange Blossom—This scent may balance your body, mind, and soul

Favorable Foods: Savory, apples, caraway seed, almond, chicken

What's Lucky . . .

Lucky Numbers: 5, 7
Best Months: February and June
Best Day of the Week: Thursday
Best Month Days: 6, 15, 24

Lucky Charm: A religious token or card from any religion.

Harmonious Signs for Relationships and Partnerships: Aries, Leo, Sagittarius

Spiritual Guides . . .

Star: Al Beldah—Those with this star are sometimes the victims of hasty judgments.

Angel: Aduachiel—This angel governs the balance of elements —water, earth, fire, and air—and helps maintain a calm disposition.

Guardian Angel: Michael—"Who is like God."

Spiritual Stone: Emerald—This gem is thought to aid in smoothing the connection between the desires of the soul and those of the body.

✴ JUDITH'S INSIGHT ✴

You are lovable by nature, and that quality softens your often demanding personality. Others may find you moody and complex. Although you can be quite the party animal at times, another side of you may be viewed as cold and aloof.

Because you want to do so many things, it may take you a while to get settled into a steady career. You'll plug away and chug along for years before a sudden opportunity arises leading to wealth or possibly fame.

You would do well in philosophy, writing, teaching, medicine, or law. These differing careers have one thing in common: they require strong persons who can control themselves and others. You accomplish the task with both charm and wit.

Romance is more than difficult for you. It would take a miracle for you to find somebody that wants to put up with your ever-changing desires. The other person can never be affectionate, kind, or loving enough to suit you. What's more, if your mate acts as thoughtlessly as you do sometimes, you're out the door. It doesn't have to be this way, but the only one who can change your destiny is you. If you want love in your life (and you do), you'll have to put your whole heart into it. It may take years for you to recognize this.

✴ ✴ ✴

NOVEMBER 25 SAGITTARIUS • The adventurous one of the zodiac

November 22 at 5:00 A.M. to December 21 at 10:00 P.M. • NUMEROLOGY 7

Possessions and Desires . . .

Gem: Ruby—This stone may lead you to energy, friendship, and happiness.

Flower: Nutmeg Geranium—What you let yourself expect will tend to be what you receive.

Astral Color, Color Need, Apparel Color: Your Astral Color is Red, the color of passion, power, excitement, and strength. Violet in your environment keeps you empathetic toward others. In your wardrobe, Purple reflects your giving personality and brings you luck.

Fragrance: You need to be bathed in exotic scents that will give your imagination room to roam. Experiment with imported incense and tinctures to show the world what a spirited individual you are.

Tree: Sycamore—Yours is the ability to love, communicate honestly with others, and have lasting relationships.

Instrument: Harp

Composers: Gluck, Brahms

Bird: Skylark—This handsome bird is beautiful when it sings. It always whistles as it works.

Symbol: Heart—You are enthusiastic, empathetic, and full of generosity and love

Harmonious Health and Nutrition . . .

Health Scent: Jasmine—This scent may make you more easygoing when you are stressed.

Favorable Foods: Greens, peaches, cereals, pecans, chicken

What's Lucky . . .

Lucky Numbers: 5, 7

Best Months: February and June

Best Day of the Week: Thursday

Best Month Days: 6, 15, 24

Lucky Charm: An old key.

Harmonious Signs for Relationships and Partnerships: Aries, Leo, Sagittarius

Spiritual Guides . . .

Star: Al Beldah—Those with this star are sometimes the victims of hasty judgments.

Angel: Aduachiel—This angel governs the balance of elements—water, earth, fire, and air—and helps maintain a calm disposition.

Guardian Angel: Raphael—This angel attends to all of your needs when you are looking for guidance.

Spiritual Stone: Emerald—This gem is thought to aid in smoothing the connection between the desires of the soul and those of the body.

✦ JUDITH'S INSIGHT ✦

You have more than enough power and passion for life to get all you want out of it. Give in. A career goal may include fun and frolic, but you need a challenge, too. You will work hard to be successful but are likely to be hindered or helped most by your environment. Try to keep where you are separate from who you are in your own mind. Don't let the excitement or boredom of the place control your emotions.

Your romantic soul makes you high maintenance when it comes to love and relationships. Of course, you're extremely kind, warm, and sensitive. Love for you is a forest fire whose flame seldom dies. Give your partner credit just for keeping up with you.

You can do just about anything you put your mind to except when it comes to making a quick decision. You analyze things to death, which will always interfere with your getting things done. Watch out for your mood swings hurting your cause. Many days, you may find all you'll do is argue with yourself.

You love to travel and may have the desire to visit exotic places. Your love of entertainment may lead you to a career in party planning, performing, or writing or as a critic. You're a person who clearly knows the difference between right and wrong, and there won't be a time in your life when you don't seek justice. You like helping the underdog, and it should be a comfort that you get out of life only as much as you put in.

★ ★ ★

NOVEMBER 26 SAGITTARIUS • The adventurous one of the zodiac
November 22 at 5:00 A.M. to December 21 at 10:00 P.M. • NUMEROLOGY 8

Possessions and Desires . . .

Gem: Chrysolite—This gem may help you clear your mind of sadness and worry.

Flower: Silver Leaf Geranium—You seem to remember all the tiny details.

Astral Color, Color Need, Apparel Color: Your Astral Color is Red, the color of passion, power, excitement, and strength. Violet in your environment will keep you empathetic toward others. In your wardrobe, Green is your power color for overcoming obstacles.

Fragrance: You need to be bathed in exotic scents that will give your imagination room to roam. Experiment with imported incense and tinctures to show the world what a spirited individual you are.

Tree: Pine—Your relationships tend to be harmonious, both emotionally and mentally.

Instrument: Cello

Composer: Mozart

Bird: Bobolink—This charming singer is equally good as a soloist or a member of an orchestra. It is a very romantic bird, useful as an insect destroyer, and elegant, with beautiful feathers, and always pleasant to have around.

Symbol: Wings—You are the source of balance in your world—this will bring you contentment.

Harmonious Health and Nutrition . . .

Health Scent: Almond—This scent may revitalize you and open you to greater possibilities.

Favorable Foods: Horseradish, grapes, rice, pecans, fish

What's Lucky . . .

Lucky Numbers: 5, 7
Best Months: February and June
Best Day of the Week: Thursday
Best Month Days: 8, 17, 26
Lucky Charm: Red ribbon in your wallet or doorway.

Harmonious Signs for Relationships and Partnerships: Aries, Leo, Sagittarius

Spiritual Guides . . .

Star: Al Naim—Those with this star are often delightful.

Angel: Aduachiel—this angel governs the balance of elements—water, earth, fire, and air—and helps maintain a calm disposition.

Guardian Angel: Seraphim—An angel that brings love, light, and passion.

Spiritual Stone: Emerald—This gem is thought to aid in smoothing the connection between the desires of the soul and those of the body.

✳ JUDITH'S INSIGHT ✳

Provided the subject is of interest, you make a great student. Your energy will bring you success, if you can manage to find a way to channel it. You are quick-minded and, unfortunately, sometimes quick-tempered. Though very serious while younger, as you get older you become the life of many parties.

Retail, particularly sales, may bring you success. You can talk anyone into buying anything. Your conversations are bright and interesting, and you have no fear of showing or receiving affection. Others feel close to you because of your naturally cheerful disposition. Consider making the most use of your gifts by opening your own business.

Relationships will be just a matter of finding the right method of convincing that special person you're the one. It's easy for you to meet people, so you should have many choices. Explore your love of travel—you are brimming with desire to delve into nature both close to you and far away.

You will feel secure around water and are invigorated by heights. You have a talent for innovation. The only restriction you'll ever feel is time. You're so busy that even if you live to be a hundred, there will be things you haven't gotten around to.

✳ ✳ ✳

NOVEMBER 27 SAGITTARIUS • The adventurous one of the zodiac
November 22 at 5:00 A.M. to December 21 at 10:00 P.M. • NUMEROLOGY 9

Possessions and Desires . . .

Gem: Beryl—This gem could be good for meditation and concentration.
Flower: Gentian—You are likely to live a blameless life.
Astral Color, Color Need, Apparel Color: Your Astral Color is Red, the color of passion, power, excitement, and strength. Violet in your environment will keep you empathetic toward others. In your wardrobe, Purple reflects your giving personality and brings you luck.
Fragrance: You need to be bathed in exotic scents that will give your imagination room to roam. Experiment with imported incense and tinctures to show the world what a spirited individual you are.
Tree: Holly—Beware that you are not carried away by your passionate nature. The only way to grow is to be open to new experiences.
Instruments: Violin, tympanum
Composer: Gluck
Bird: Mockingbird—the most proficient minstrel in the world's orchestra; graceful and enthusiastic.
Symbol: Anchor—This tranquil symbol signifies stability and strength, and stands for strong commitments in relationships.

Harmonious Health and Nutrition . . .

Health Scent: Lavender—This scent might lead others to trust you and make you patient.
Favorable Foods: Savory, prunes, bran, pecans, chicken

What's Lucky . . .

Lucky Numbers: 5, 7
Best Months: February and June
Best Day of the Week: Thursday
Best Month Days: 9, 18, 27
Lucky Charm: A U.S. coin or bill of any amount from the year you were born.

Harmonious Signs for Relationships and Partnerships: Aries, Leo, Sagittarius

Spiritual Guides . . .

Star: Al Beldah—Those with this star are sometimes the victims of hasty judgments.
Angel: Aduachiel—This angel governs the balance of elements—water, earth, fire, and air—and helps maintain a calm disposition.
Guardian Angel: Gabriel—"God is my strength."
Spiritual Stone: Emerald—This gem is thought to aid in smoothing the connection between the desires of the soul and those of the body.

✶ JUDITH'S INSIGHT ✶

You need plenty of excitement every day. The more pressure life gives you, the more you can get accomplished. While it's natural for you to feel stressed, you don't handle obstacles or interference very well. It's very important to you that your energies are directed in ways you consider proper. You have executive abilities and are highly skilled in organization.

Your family is a source of comfort and strength. Your inherited gifts might be either material things or your family's optimistic disposition. You love the finer things in life. Usually stylishly dressed, you are often noticed for your exquisite taste.

Not one to wear your emotions on your sleeve, you are naturally a bit secretive. Give all you can to relationships while in them. You adore making and receiving romantic gestures.

As long as you work with people, you'll do very well. You can be generous, and the more you do for others, the happier you are. Sometimes, however, you think too much. You may be troubled by regret, refusing to follow through on strong premonitions. You are well regarded by family and friends; somehow public recognition will follow you.

You have great counseling technique. Public relations, the media, any job in telecommunication or computers would suit you well.

✶ ✶ ✶

NOVEMBER 28 SAGITTARIUS • The adventurous one of the zodiac
November 22 at 5:00 A.M. to December 21 at 10:00 P.M. • NUMEROLOGY 1

Possessions and Desires . . .

Gem: Agate—This stone may promote health and lead you to a long life.

Flower: Gorse—You generally get along with everyone.

Astral Color, Color Need, Apparel Color: Your Astral Color is Red, the color of passion, power, excitement, and strength. Violet in your environment keeps you empathetic toward others. In your wardrobe, Green is your power color for overcoming obstacles.

Fragrance: You need to be bathed in exotic scents that will give your imagination room to roam. Experiment with imported incense and tinctures to show the world what a spirited individual you are.

Tree: Walnut—You are unusually helpful and always looking for constant changes in your life.

Instruments: Oboe, flute, clarinet, piano, French horn, organ, piccolo

Composer: Böhm

Bird: Bird of Paradise—the "bird of the Gods." You will shine and love extraordinary circumstances.

Symbol: Crown—the universal sign of dignity.

Harmonious Health and Nutrition . . .

Health Scent: Strawberry—Soothing by nature, the strawberry promotes self-esteem and encourages love.

Favorable Foods: Cabbage, apples, rice, almonds, fish

What's Lucky . . .

Lucky Numbers: 5, 7
Best Months: February and June
Best Day of the Week: Thursday
Best Month Days: 1, 10, 19

Lucky Charm: A new penny in your shoe.
Harmonious Signs for Relationships and Partnerships: Aries, Leo, Sagittarius

Spiritual Guides . . .

Star: Al Naim—Those with this star are often delightful.

Angel: Aduachiel—This angel governs the balance of elements—water, earth, fire, and air—and helps maintain a calm disposition.

Guardian Angel: Malachi—"Messenger of Jehovah."

Spiritual Stone: Emerald—This gem is thought to aid in smoothing the connection between the desires of the soul and those of the body.

✶ JUDITH'S INSIGHT ✶

You are fiery, determined, and generally quick in your actions. You're charming and physically fit and should have no problem cultivating relationships of any kind. You love to learn.

Your open-door policy to all possibilities only enhances your life. Be aware that your power and passion can intimidate other people. You will have intense enemies and deeply devoted friends. An iron will helps you on the job, though it's difficult admitting your mistakes. You can laugh at obstacles before and after you overcome them. A career either in acting, athletics, law, or state government could work for you.

You like to control those you love. This will cause problems with your partner and other family members. You may often be the cause of friction at home. Family is the primary focus of your life. If you choose to have them, your children and you will be very important to each other.

You do well at games of chance and may experience an occasional lucky streak. Keeping your wits about you can further the benefits of luck. Make sure you remain aware of what's going on around you.

✶ ✶ ✶

NOVEMBER 29 SAGITTARIUS • The adventurous one of the zodiac

November 22 at 5:00 A.M. to December 21 at 10:00 P.M. • NUMEROLOGY 2

Possessions and Desires . . .

Gem: Sapphire—This gem may help you find forgiveness from those you've wronged.

Flower: Goldilocks—You tend to always act like a young person.

Astral Color, Color Need, Apparel Color: Your Astral Color is Red, the color of passion, power, excitement, and strength. Violet in your environment will keep you empathetic toward others. In your wardrobe, Purple reflects your giving personality and brings you luck.

Fragrance: You need to be bathed in exotic scents that will give your imagination room to roam. Experiment with imported incense and tinctures to show the world what a spirited individual you are.

Tree: Maple—You have great stability and flashes of intuition.

Instruments: Pipe organ, cymbal, drum

Composers: Handel, Johann Sebastian Bach

Bird: Stork—Turkish bird, held in high esteem the world over. This bird is intelligent but may have strange tendencies.

Symbol: Cross—the symbol of self-sacrifice and reconciliation.

Harmonious Health and Nutrition . . .

Health Scent: Apple—A vivacious scent encouraging energy. Will help you to be more creative, intuitive and positive.

Favorable Foods: Horseradish, apricots, rice, pecans, chicken

What's Lucky . . .

Lucky Numbers: 5, 7
Best Months: February and June
Best Day of the Week: Thursday
Lucky Charms: Two 50-cent pieces. Give someone else one of them.

Harmonious Signs for Relationships and Partnerships: Aries, Leo, Sagittarius

Spiritual Guides . . .

Star: Al Beldah—Those with this star are sometimes the victims of hasty judgments.

Angel: Aduachiel—This angel governs the balance of elements—water, earth, fire, and air—and helps maintain a calm disposition.

Guardian Angel: St. John—This angel simplifies that which is complicated.

Spiritual Stone: Emerald—This gem is thought to aid in smoothing the connection between the desires of the soul and those of the body.

✶ JUDITH'S INSIGHT ✶

You love a good time. Quite the talker, you may do well in careers where you use your voice and mouth. Your vivid imagination and powerful energy sometimes frustrate other people. With the ability to turn disadvantage into success, you can make the best of just about any situation. It's better when you can be your own boss; any interference from others makes you cranky.

You do most things well but are easily flustered if sidetracked by problems. You are at your best in a party atmosphere. Your strong convictions may find you frequently defending others. You love to dig into things physically and mentally and so would be happy in employment involving research.

Your dominant concern is for those you love. Romance brings you great satisfaction and the most happiness. You're more giver than taker. Generous to a fault, you sacrifice anything and have energy to spare when working to make your family comfortable. It may take awhile to get over a disappointing love relationship.

Your passion to seek out the unusual, unknown, or international could find you seeking a career in the airline or travel industry. Wherever your particular road leads, you always want peace in the environment.

✶ ✶ ✶

NOVEMBER 30 SAGITTARIUS • The adventurous one of the zodiac
November 22 at 5:00 A.M. to December 21 at 10:00 P.M. • NUMEROLOGY 3

Possessions and Desires . . .

Gem: Ruby—This stone may lead you to energy, friendship, and happiness.

Flower: Goldenrod—You may spend so much time preparing for troubles you lose the joy of living.

Astral Color, Color Need, Apparel Color: Your Astral Color is Red, the color of passion, power, excitement, and strength. Violet in your environment keeps you empathetic toward others. In your wardrobe, Green is your power color for overcoming obstacles.

Fragrance: You need to be bathed in exotic scents that will give your imagination room to roam. Experiment with imported incense and tinctures to show the world what a spirited individual you are.

Tree: Elm—You have willpower, strength, and the ability to stand alone.

Instrument: Trombone

Composers: Verdi, Mendelssohn, Schumann

Bird: Eagle—This bird is quick to use its powers of flight. It can see immeasurable distances in a single glance, and can sometimes appear to be indifferent.

Symbol: Wreath—You have been crowned with a special personality. You are strong but extremely compassionate.

Harmonious Health and Nutrition . . .

Health Scent: Rose—This scent will lead you to passionate thoughts and make you feel warm inside.

Favorable Foods: Greens, prunes, cereals, pecans, fish

What's Lucky . . .

Lucky Numbers: 5, 7
Best Months: February and June
Best Day of the Week: Thursday
Best Month Days: 3, 12, 21

Lucky Charm: A pen that someone else has already used.

Harmonious Signs for Relationships and Partnerships: Aries, Leo, Sagittarius

Spiritual Guides . . .

Star: Al Beldah—Those with this star are sometimes the victims of hasty judgments.

Angel: Aduachiel—This angel governs the balance of elements—water, earth, fire, and air—and helps maintain a calm disposition.

Guardian Angel: Johiel—This angel is a protector of all those with a humble heart.

Spiritual Stone: Emerald—This gem is thought to aid in smoothing the connection between the desires of the soul and those of the body.

✦ JUDITH'S INSIGHT ✦

You always win and, therefore, have the most toys. You're playful and spontaneous, and you love to turn any situation into a party. You give of yourself, your time, your talent, and your money. Others depend on you for amusement, and you seldom let them down. People admire you for your worldview. Your presence is a gift all on its own.

You have no problem entering into relationships. Understand that you have so much energy that you may frighten some people. Once that special person gets to know you, they'll be ready for the commitment you so crave. Sleepyheads are not for you, and you avoid lazy types.

You waste no time and live life to its fullest. You're fun to be with, and you love to laugh. Be careful of your tendency to overdo things, both at work and play. Expect to succeed in careers that center around entertainment, hospitality, writing, reading, or children.

It may be likely that you'll have more than one career throughout your lifetime. You may have to take a job that pays the bills for awhile before landing your dream gig. You easily create bonds that become and remain true friendships forever.

✦ ✦ ✦

DECEMBER

DECEMBER 1 SAGITTARIUS • The adventurous one of the zodiac

November 22 at 5:00 A.M. to December 21 at 10:00 P.M. • NUMEROLOGY 1

Possessions and Desires . . .

Gem: Turquoise—This stone might help you find material wealth.

Flower: Scarlet Geranium—You are always generous with what you have to give.

Astral Color, Color Need, Apparel Color: Your Astral Color is Red, the color of passion, power, excitement, and strength. Violet in your environment keeps you empathetic toward others. In your wardrobe, Purple reflects your giving personality and brings you luck.

Fragrance: You need to be bathed in exotic scents that will give your imagination room to roam. Experiment with imported incense and tinctures to show the world what a spirited individual you are.

Tree: Walnut—You are unusually helpful and always looking for constant changes in your life.

Instruments: Oboe, flute, clarinet, piano, French horn, organ, piccolo

Composer: Böhm

Bird: Hummingbird—This bird is delicate and graceful. It can remain still for hours, then dart off and be as busy as a bee.

Symbol: Crown—the universal sign of dignity.

Harmonious Health and Nutrition . . .

Health Scent: Strawberry—Soothing by nature, the strawberry promotes self-esteem and encourages love.

Favorable Foods: Greens, black figs, unrefined cereals, almonds, chicken

What's Lucky . . .

Lucky Numbers: 5, 7
Best Months: February and June
Best Day of the Week: Thursday
Best Month Days: 1, 10, 19
Lucky Charm: A new penny in your shoe.

Harmonious Signs for Relationships and Partnerships: Aries, Leo, Sagittarius

Spiritual Guides . . .

Star: Al Naim—Those with this star are often delightful.

Angel: Aduachiel—this angel governs the balance of elements—water, earth, fire, and air—and helps maintain a calm disposition.

Guardian Angel: Malachi—"Messenger of Jehovah."

Spiritual Stone: Emerald—This gem is thought to aid in smoothing the connection between the desires of the soul and those of the body.

✦ JUDITH'S INSIGHT ✦

Energetic, enthusiastic, and determined, you would make the perfect athlete. Just about any sport should interest you. You can adapt yourself easily to different circumstances. Your name may even appear in the paper at one time or another, probably for being absolutely brilliant at something. You have plenty of self-confidence and should find your way no matter what obstacles you encounter.

A high-quality employee or employer, you create pleasant working conditions for your coworkers. You would do well as a musician, actor, athlete, or salesman. With your flair for design, you could do something in the fashion industry. A desire for travel may lead you to pursue flying. You are a natural when it comes to business and may be inclined to have your own eventually.

Love for you is a battle zone. You desperately want a commitment and will take more grief than you should to keep things together. Do not take your own advice when it comes to love. You need more romance than your selected mate can give. You love a fiery and passionate relationship and need constant spontaneity to keep your attention engaged. In return you offer fun and a kindhearted personality. Beware of getting exactly what you wish for; you could later regret who you end up with.

★ ★ ★

DECEMBER 2
SAGITTARIUS • The adventurous one of the zodiac

November 22 at 5:00 A.M. to December 21 at 10:00 P.M. • NUMEROLOGY 2

Possessions and Desires . . .

Gem: Sapphire—This gem may help you find forgiveness from those you've wronged.

Flower: Teasel—You may not like spending much time in crowds.

Astral Color, Color Need, Apparel Color: Your Astral Color is Red, the color of passion, power, excitement, and strength. Violet in your environment keeps you empathetic toward others. In your wardrobe, Green is your power color for overcoming obstacles.

Fragrance: You need to be bathed in exotic scents that will give your imagination room to roam. Experiment with imported incense and tinctures to show the world what a spirited individual you are.

Tree: Maple—You have great stability and flashes of intuition.

Instruments: Pipe organ, cymbal, drum

Composers: Handel, Johann Sebastian Bach

Bird: Cuckoo—A good flyer and very seldom a quitter. Many seem more independent than they actually are; yearn for more nurturing than one would expect.

Symbol: Cross—the symbol of self-sacrifice and reconciliation.

Harmonious Health and Nutrition . . .

Health Scent: Apple—You are creative, full of joy, and nearly magical. You bring happiness.

Favorable Foods: Cabbage, apples, rice, pecans, fish

What's Lucky . . .

Lucky Numbers: 5 7

Best Months: February and June

Best Day of the Week: Thursday

Best Month Days: 2, 11, 20

Lucky Charms: Two 50-cent pieces. Give someone else one of them.

Harmonious Signs for Relationships and Partnerships: Aries, Leo, Sagittarius

Spiritual Guides . . .

Star: Al Naim—Those with this star are often delightful.

Angel: Aduachiel—This angel governs the balance of elements—water, earth, fire, and air—and helps maintain a calm disposition.

Guardian Angel: St. Thomas—This angel brings affection from others and encourages you in all that you do.

Spiritual Stone: Emerald—This gem is thought to aid in smoothing the connection between the desires of the soul and those of the body.

✶ JUDITH'S INSIGHT ✶

Consistent, compassionate, persistent, and brave, you are not likely to turn off course because of any obstacles that occur. You are smart but can lack self-confidence. You live life more inside your head than others ever realize. You are always heard, even when silent.

Entertainment will play a strong role in your life, as will your love of fun. You aspire to a life of art or music. At the very least you'll become an avid moviegoer or collector of CDs. You love to travel and have the desire to circle the earth one way or another.

Family and children will be very important to you, and others will have to understand that your home relationships take priority over just about anything in your life. You don't tend to leave things too quickly, and you give your spouse all your attention. So long as you work to have all the ingredients going in, your relationships turn out wonderfully well.

You want very much to be successful, and while you are looking for it, it just might find you. Remember, square pegs don't fit into round holes. Your organizational skills may lead you down many paths in search of the perfect career. You would do well in government, law, travel, or entertainment. Medical matters take on strong meaning in your life, either as an employment or as volunteer work in a hospice.

✶ ✶ ✶

DECEMBER 3 SAGITTARIUS • The adventurous one of the zodiac

November 22 at 5:00 A.M. to December 21 at 10:00 P.M. • NUMEROLOGY 3

Possessions and Desires . . .

Gem: Ruby—This stone may lead you to energy, friendship, and happiness.

Flower: French Willow—You can be a person of simple tastes and have enough courage to seek out what is truly important.

Astral Color, Color Need, Apparel Color: Your Astral Color is Red, the color of passion, power, excitement, and strength. Violet in your environment keeps you empathetic toward others. In your wardrobe, Purple reflects your giving personality and brings you luck.

Fragrance: You need to be bathed in exotic scents that will give your imagination room to roam. Experiment with imported incense and tinctures to show the world what a spirited individual you are.

Tree: Elm—You have willpower, strength, and the ability to stand alone.

Instrument: Trombone

Composers: Verdi, Mendelssohn, Schumann

Bird: Swan—Regarded as royal and sacred, this bird has the protective nature of a mother, and can become a furious fighter in the defense of its own.

Symbol: Wreath—You have been crowned with a special personality. You are strong but extremely compassionate.

Harmonious Health and Nutrition . . .

Health Scent: Rose—This scent will lead you to passionate thoughts and make you feel warm inside.

Favorable Foods: Savory, peaches, bran, almonds, chicken

What's Lucky . . .

Lucky Numbers: 5, 7
Best Months: February and June
Best Day of the Week: Thursday
Best Month Days: 3, 12, 21, 30

Lucky Charm: A pen that someone else has already used.
Harmonious Signs for Relationships and Partnerships: Aries, Leo, Sagittarius

Spiritual Guides . . .

Star: Al Naim—Those with this star are often delightful.

Angel: Aduachiel—This angel governs the balance of elements—water, earth, fire, and air—and helps maintain a calm disposition.

Guardian Angel: Johiel—This angel is a protector of all those with a humble heart.

Spiritual Stone: Emerald—This gem is thought to aid in smoothing the connection between the desires of the soul and those of the body.

✷ JUDITH'S INSIGHT ✷

You are one charming pain in the neck. It would benefit you to learn that you can get more accomplished by keeping quiet. You can be kind and hard working, but you need to find your special niche in life before you achieve happiness.

Love will be tricky for you, as you're likely to be attracted to one very difficult person after another. The only way you'll be able to make a relationship work is by constantly feeding it loads of positive energy. Family is important to you, but you need to have an agreed-on amount of space or you'll end up feeling claustrophobic.

If you lead, you succeed. You're great at administration, but when people don't listen you get easily frustrated. Not only are you a good talker, you're a good listener. You would do well in politics and government, and you follow the letter of the law. You could also do well as a law or code enforcement officer.

You would also make an excellent builder, contractor, or designer. And if you haven't reached all your goals yet, pick up a paper and pen and spell out how you'll eventually succeed. Sometimes you have trouble getting started, but you should write, even if it's the local newspaper gossip column.

Life will be a constant learning experience for you. It may take time for you to find yourself, but it'll be worth the wait.

DECEMBER 4 SAGITTARIUS • The adventurous one of the zodiac
November 22 at 5:00 A.M. to December 21 at 10:00 P.M. • NUMEROLOGY 4

Possessions and Desires . . .

Gem: Emerald—Those who carry this stone tend to be lucky in love.
Flower: Fleur-de-lis—You may have a quick temper but are just as swift to show your affections.
Astral Color, Color Need, Apparel Color: Your Astral Color is Red, the color of passion, power, excitement, and strength. Violet in your environment will keep you empathetic toward others. In your wardrobe, Green is your power color for overcoming obstacles.
Fragrance: You need to be bathed in exotic scents that will give your imagination room to roam. Experiment with imported incense and tinctures to show the world what a spirited individual you are.
Tree: Cherry—You will find yourself faced with constant new emotional awakenings.
Instruments: Bass, clarinet
Composers: Haydn, Wagner
Bird: Killdeer—This bird is usually found consorting with other species, and can adapt to any environment.
Symbol: Star—You are full of inner brightness and will stand out in any crowd. You will be seen as special.

Harmonious Health and Nutrition . . .

Health Scent: Vanilla—This scent will fill you with a feeling of cleanliness and stability.
Favorable Foods: Dandelion, oranges, caraway seed, pecans, fish

What's Lucky . . .

Lucky Numbers: 5, 7
Best Months: February and June
Best Day of the Week: Thursday
Best Month Days: 4, 13, 22
Lucky Charm: A piece of material cut from something in your home.
Harmonious Signs for Relationships and Partnerships: Aries, Leo, Sagittarius

Spiritual Guides . . .

Star: Al Naim—Those with this star are often delightful.
Angel: Aduachiel—This angel governs the balance of elements—water, earth, fire, and air—and helps maintain a calm disposition.
Guardian Angel: Uriel—This angel brings the light of God's guidance.
Spiritual Stone: Emerald—This gem is thought to aid in smoothing the connection between the desires of the soul and those of the body.

✴ JUDITH'S INSIGHT ✴

You are very intelligent, highly motivated, spontaneous, and enthusiastic. You have a great imagination and are remarkable at handling people. Who could ask for more? You will probably live a very unconventional life. Drawn to the unique and unusual, you love to entertain and to be entertained.

Animals make you calm and happy. You may consider a career that involves animals. At one time or another, you may have a lot of pets. Just as rewarding for you is a career in jewelry, retail, manufacturing, or music. You have great physical qualities, high energy levels, and much skill when it comes to sports.

You have no problem maintaining friends because of your sincerity. Intimate relationships can be a little more difficult, and you may suffer through a few losers before you meet your true soul mate. Forget looking for fire; instead, look for someone who understands you.

You can be cautious and reserved when you don't feel comfortable and may try to pretend you're an altogether different person. Nothing bothers you more than disrespect and ingratitude. You are rigid when you want to be. Discipline can be very important to you. Be cautious when others try to corner you and keep you there.

You need to keep both feet on the ground because you have a tendency to make yourself restless or anxious.

✴ ✴ ✴

DECEMBER 5 SAGITTARIUS • The adventurous one of the zodiac
November 22 at 5:00 A.M. to December 21 at 10:00 P.M. • NUMEROLOGY 5

Possessions and Desires . . .

Gem: Sardius—This stone could give the wearer unusual insights into his or her own heart.
Flower: Fennel—You tend to be as strong as you need to be.
Astral Color, Color Need, Apparel Color: Your Astral Color is Red, the color of passion, power, excitement, and strength. Violet in your environment keeps you empathetic toward others. In your wardrobe, Purple reflects your giving personality and brings you luck.
Fragrance: You need to be bathed in exotic scents that will give your imagination room to roam. Experiment with imported incense and tinctures to show the world what a spirited individual you are.
Tree: Apple—You are creative, full of joy, and nearly magical. You bring happiness.
Instruments: Viola, trumpet
Composer: Liszt
Bird: Flamingo—This beautiful, gregarious bird is always careful of its enemy. It is also a caretaker of the young and tries to keep everyone happy.
Symbol: Triangle—You have the right combination of abilities.

Harmonious Health and Nutrition . . .

Health Scent: Peach—This scent may balance your good qualities so that they equal your charm.
Favorable Foods: Savory, grapes, bran, almonds, chicken

What's Lucky . . .

Lucky Numbers: 5, 7
Best Months: February and June
Best Day of the Week: Thursday
Best Month Days: 5, 4, 23
Lucky Charms: A rabbit's foot or a white candle.

Harmonious Signs for Relationships and Partnerships: Aries, Leo, Sagittarius

Spiritual Guides . . .

Star: Al Naim—Those with this star are often delightful.
Angel: Aduachiel—This angel governs the balance of elements—water, earth, fire, and air—and helps maintain a calm disposition.
Guardian Angel: Plavwell—The guardian that gives power and strength to one's presence.
Spiritual Stone: Sardonyx—This stone may cause people to be attracted to you.

✶ JUDITH'S INSIGHT ✶

You are interested in just about everything life has to offer. You're happiest creating a commotion or throwing a wild party. You know how to talk and get your point across. You are so filled with ideas that you could be an entrepreneur who starts up more than one business. You do well working with people and may be drawn to advertising, public relations, or even horse racing.

You have a style all your own. Direct your creative abilities toward fixing up your home and toward your career. Financially, you will reap rewards in unusual ways, and you won't necessarily have to work for all the money you receive.

Charm will bring relationships right to your door; your natural kindness will keep them there. You are always generous, not just with gifts but also affection. You are a pleasure to be around. There's a demanding side there, too, but in your case, the good outweighs the bad. Relationships do put you through a hoop or two, but you have enough stamina to end up where you want to be.

Follow your intuition once you recognize the voice inside.

✶ ✶ ✶

DECEMBER 6 SAGITTARIUS • The adventurous one of the zodiac

November 22 at 5:00 A.M. to December 21 at 10:00 P.M. • NUMEROLOGY 6

Possessions and Desires . . .

Gem: Topaz—This is an excellent gift to be exchanged between very loyal friends.

Flower: Dragon Plant—You are the strength for all of those around you.

Astral Color, Color Need, Apparel Color: Your Astral Color is Red, the color of passion, power, excitement, and strength. Violet in your environment will keep you empathetic toward others. In your wardrobe, Green is your power color for overcoming obstacles.

Fragrance: You need to be bathed in exotic scents that will give your imagination room to roam. Experiment with imported incense and tinctures to show the world what a spirited individual you are.

Tree: Palm—You tend to be very healthy and creative.

Instruments: Tambourine, lyre

Composer: Schubert

Bird: Falcon—an expert hunter. When well-trained, it can adapt to many tasks and is usually obedient.

Symbol: Crescent—You are more likely to be influenced by the phases of the moon. Your easygoing manner leads you to peaceful situations.

Harmonious Health and Nutrition . . .

Health Scent: Orange Blossom—This scent may balance your body, mind, and soul.

Favorable Foods: Horseradish, apples, rice, pecans, fish

What's Lucky . . .

Lucky Numbers: 5, 7
Best Months: February and June
Best Day of the Week: Thursday
Best Month Days: 6, 15, 24
Lucky Charm: A religious token or card from any religion.

Harmonious Signs for Relationships and Partnerships: Aries, Leo, Sagittarius

Spiritual Guides . . .

Star: Al Naim—Those with this star are often delightful.

Angel: Aduachiel—This angel governs the balance of elements—water, earth, fire, and air—and helps maintain a calm disposition.

Guardian Angel: Michael—"Who is like God."

Spiritual Stone: Emerald—This gem is thought to aid in smoothing the connection between the desires of the soul and those of the body.

✷ JUDITH'S INSIGHT ✷

You love to entertain and make the perfect host or hostess. You'd be clever to make a career out of this. Your friendly disposition makes it easy for you to meet and greet, and you very rarely feel out of place. In one form or another, you achieve success in the entertainment business, either as an owner or worker in a restaurant or club or as a choreographer or writer.

Your love of the outdoors and nature may lead to a career with horses. You love to gamble and must be careful this doesn't get you into some kind of trouble. Somewhere along the way, a dual income presents itself. You have two of everything; it seems as if doubles keep entering your life from a couple of directions.

There isn't a mean bone in your body, and you're a pleasure to be around. When it comes to love, you are attractive, strong, and energetic. Your positive energy and enthusiasm for life make others want to be around you, although at times you can have moments of stubbornness and mood swings.

Financial success comes to you through relationships as well as through your business. You can be very restless or very committed, depending on your partner. Somewhere along the way, finances begin to improve enough so you feel secure. Your generosity helps money come to you.

★ ★ ★

DECEMBER 7 SAGITTARIUS • The adventurous one of the zodiac
November 22 at 5:00 A.M. to December 21 at 10:00 P.M. • NUMEROLOGY 7

Possessions and Desires . . .

Gem: Agate—This stone may promote health and lead you to a long life.

Flower: Diomosa—You can be very shy around those you care for deeply.

Astral Color, Color Need, Apparel Color: Your Astral Color is Red, the color of passion, power, excitement, and strength. Violet in your environment keeps you empathetic toward others. In your wardrobe, Purple reflects your giving personality and brings you luck.

Fragrance: You need to be bathed in exotic scents that will give your imagination room to roam. Experiment with imported incense and tinctures to show the world what a spirited individual you are.

Tree: Sycamore—Yours is the ability to love, communicate honestly with others, and have lasting relationships.

Instrument: Harp

Composers: Gluck, Brahms

Bird: Warbling Parakeet—the most beautiful of all birds, known as the love bird. It does seem to have the powers of imitation.

Harmonious Health and Nutrition . . .

Health Scent: Jasmine—This scent may make you more easygoing when you are stressed.

Favorable Foods: Celery, grapes, caraway seed, pecans, chicken

What's Lucky . . .

Lucky Numbers: 5, 7
Best Months: February and June
Best Day of the Week: Thursday
Best Month Days: 6, 15, 24

Lucky Charm: An old key
Harmonious Signs for Relationships and Partnerships: Aries, Leo, Sagittarius

Spiritual Guides . . .

Star: Al Beldah—those with this star are sometimes the victims of hasty judgments.

Angel: Aduachiel—This angel governs the balance of elements—water, earth, fire, and air—and helps maintain a calm disposition.

Guardian Angel: Uriel—An individual archangel meaning: "the light of God."

Spiritual Stone: Emerald—This gem is thought to aid in smoothing the connection between the desires of the soul and those of the body

✷ JUDITH'S INSIGHT ✷

Dedicated to people in one way or another, you tend to be gentle, kind, outgoing, and always available. You are charming but don't necessarily lead a charmed life. Your share of heartaches will find you, but your stiff upper lip helps you maintain a good life.

You're fascinated with your surroundings and with light and would make an incredible painter and artist. So long as you don't lose yourself, you should spend some amount of time in your own world of imagination. You have a strong, determined mind when it comes to business and could do very well in accounting, finance, or the stock market. Here, too, your dreams will connect you to where you want to be.

When it comes to relationships, you are the ultimate romantic. Just make sure to take the chance and let your ideas flow. You can rise to any occasion and effect change to your environment with the best of them. No matter what you are doing, you know how to enjoy the moment. You are generous enough to give and smart enough to save. Your warm heart enables you to keep many close relationships.

✷ ✷ ✷

DECEMBER 8 SAGITTARIUS • The adventurous one of the zodiac

November 22 at 5:00 A.M. to December 21 at 10:00 P.M. • NUMEROLOGY 8

Possessions and Desires . . .

Gem: Chrysolite—This gem may help you clear your mind of sadness and worry.
Flower: Hollyhock—You can be very persuasive when you wish to be.
Astral Color, Color Need, Apparel Color: Your Astral Color is Red, the color of passion, power, excitement, and strength. Violet in your environment keeps you empathetic toward others. In your wardrobe, Green is your power color for overcoming obstacles.
Fragrance: You need to be bathed in exotic scents that will give your imagination room to roam. Experiment with imported incense and tinctures to show the world what a spirited individual you are.
Tree: Pine—Your relationships tend to be harmonious, both emotionally and mentally.
Instrument: Cello
Composer: Mozart
Bird: Bobolink—This charming singer is equally good as a soloist or a member of an orchestra. It is a very romantic bird, useful as an insect destroyer, and elegant, with beautiful feathers, and always pleasant to have around.
Symbol: Wings—You are the source of balance in your world—this will bring you contentment.

Harmonious Health and Nutrition . . .

Health Scent: Strawberry—Soothing by nature, the strawberry promotes self-esteem and encourages love.
Favorable Foods: Cabbage, peaches, unrefined cereals, pecans, fish

What's Lucky . . .

Lucky Numbers: 5, 7
Best Months: February and June
Best Day of the Week: Thursday
Best Month Days: 8, 17, 26

Lucky Charm: Red ribbon in your wallet or doorway.
Harmonious Signs for Relationships and Partnerships: Aries, Leo, and Sagittarius

Spiritual Guides . . .

Star: Al Naim—Those with this star are often delightful.
Angel: Aduachiel—this angel governs the balance of elements—water, earth, fire, and air—and helps maintain a calm disposition.
Guardian Angel: Seraphim—An angel that brings love, light, and passion.
Spiritual Stone: Emerald—This gem is thought to aid in smoothing the connection between the desires of the soul and those of the body.

✳ _JUDITH'S INSIGHT_ ✳

You'd make the best judge, lawyer, businessperson, or clergyperson. You have a genuine personality and can keep secrets and maintain loyalties. Your unflagging endurance would make you an excellent athlete. You love to learn and will soak up knowledge of any kind.

Your adult life will go more smoothly than your childhood because you need time to become at ease with yourself. You mature into a better person who enjoys life only after gaining wisdom. Remember periodically you need to clean the cobwebs of skepticism and the snakes of negativity out of your mind. You do find love because you give it so freely. You don't like to be criticized and crave attention; when choosing your life's partner, keep these traits in mind. You get what you receive in love and would be a terrific spouse for anyone except those who make you feel on edge.

If you handled rejection a little better, you could make a fantastic entertainer. You may experience some hard years of self-sacrifice, but you have many hidden talents and will do better as you mature. Guard your self-confidence through the tough times, expecting not just the good but the great ones to come.

✶ ✶ ✶

DECEMBER 9 SAGITTARIUS • The adventurous one of the zodiac
November 22 at 5:00 A.M. to December 21 at 10:00 P.M. • NUMEROLOGY 9

Possessions and Desires . . .

Gem: Beryl—This gem could be good for meditation and concentration.
Flower: Creeper—You may keep far too many things to yourself.
Astral Color, Color Need, Apparel Color: Your Astral Color is Red, the color of passion, power, excitement, and strength. Violet in your environment keeps you empathetic toward others. In your wardrobe, Purple reflects your giving personality and brings you luck.
Fragrance: You need to be bathed in exotic scents that will give your imagination room to roam. Experiment with imported incense and tinctures to show the world what a spirited individual you are.
Tree: Holly—Beware that you are not carried away by your passionate nature. The only way to grow is to be open to new experiences.
Instruments: Violin, tympanum
Composer: Gluck
Bird: Mockingbird—the most proficient minstrel in the world's orchestra; graceful and enthusiastic.
Symbol: Anchor—This tranquil symbol signifies stability and strength, and stands for strong commitments in relationships.

Harmonious Health and Nutrition . . .

Health Scent: Lavender—This scent might lead others to trust you and make you patient.
Favorable Foods: Horseradish, oranges, rice, almonds, chicken

What's Lucky . . .

Lucky Numbers: 5, 7
Best Months: February and June
Best Day of the Week: Thursday
Best Month Days: 9, 18, 27

Lucky Charms: A U.S. coin or bill of any amount from the year you were born.
Harmonious Signs for Relationships and Partnerships: Aries, Leo, Sagittarius

Spiritual Guides . . .

Star: Al Naim—Those with this star are often delightful.
Angel: Aduachiel—This angel governs the balance of elements—water, earth, fire, and air—and helps maintain a calm disposition.
Guardian Angel: Gabriel—"God is my strength."
Spiritual Stone: Emerald—This gem is thought to aid in smoothing the connection between the desires of the soul and those of the body.

✶ JUDITH'S INSIGHT ✶

Others see you as dependable, reliable, respectful, and capable of doing just about anything. You possess the drive to accomplish exactly what you want. You have great opinions on any number of topics. Yours is a matchless intellect.

Consider sports as a career. With your energy and enthusiasm you could be a success at any one you choose. You have the potential to really excel at the game of golf if not as a pro than as the most enthusiastic duffer on your local links. You're a born leader—everyone's pick to be head of the PTA.

You can be very generous to those you think are deserving. Otherwise, you tend to keep your money deep in your pockets. You will do well in relationships because of the effort you put into them. Seek out someone who understands you, because you don't always understand yourself. It takes time for you to figure out who you are; you'll know yourself better when you get older.

The outdoors encourages and motivates you. When you are feeling low, depressed, or achy, go outside, take a deep breath, and fill your lungs with fresh air. You get inspiration from your environment, so keep it clean and bright.

✶ ✶ ✶

Possessions and Desires . . .

Gem: Agate—This stone may promote health and lead you to a long life.

Flower: Coronilla—You will be successful if you can learn what you should truly wish for.

Astral Color, Color Need, Apparel Color: Your Astral Color is Red, the color of passion, power, excitement, and strength. Violet in your environment will keep you empathetic toward others. In your wardrobe, Green is your power color for overcoming obstacles.

Fragrance: You need to be bathed in exotic scents that will give your imagination room to roam. Experiment with imported incense and tinctures to show the world what a spirited individual you are.

Tree: Walnut—You are unusually helpful and always looking for constant changes in your life.

Instruments: Oboe, flute, clarinet, piano, French horn, organ, piccolo

Composer: Böhm

Bird: Bird of Paradise—the "bird of the Gods." You will shine and love extraordinary circumstances.

Symbol: Crown—the universal sign of dignity.

Harmonious Health and Nutrition . . .

Health Scent: Strawberry—Soothing by nature, the strawberry promotes self-esteem and encourages love.

Favorable Foods: Greens, apricots, rice, almonds, chicken

What's Lucky . . .

Lucky Numbers: 5, 7
Best Months: February and June
Best Day of the Week: Thursday
Best Month Days: 1, 10, 19
Lucky Charm: A new penny in your shoe.
Harmonious Signs for Relationships and Partnerships: Aries, Leo, Sagittarius

Spiritual Guides . . .

Star: Al Naim—Those with this star are often delightful.

Angel: Aduachiel—This angel governs the balance of elements—water, earth, fire, and air—and helps maintain a calm disposition.

Guardian Angel: Malachi—"Messenger of Jehovah."

Spiritual Stone: Emerald—This gem is thought to aid in smoothing the connection between the desires of the soul and those of the body.

✷ JUDITH'S INSIGHT ✷

Wise beyond your years, you have a natural intelligence that will take you anywhere you want to go. You are energetic and enthusiastic and get excited over the smallest things. You make a perfect athlete because you have strong will, steely desire, and great determination.

You should make a super parent. Even if you don't have children, people will want you to "adopt" theirs because you're so sympathetic and understanding. Family means everything to you.

You have plenty of self-confidence, but might not make use of it until you're older. You are not just a quality worker but at times a brilliant one. You will become recognized during your life for creativity and innovation. Expect something to be named for you. You know business naturally and have no qualms about hard work.

You're prone to loving drama more than your partner in relationships. Hopefully you can work off the energy on stage. You are a born comic or actor, though you fear it if you do recognize the talent. Your love life can be a battle because your biggest enemy is yourself. Making a commitment will be hard for you, but you stay almost indefinitely once it's made. Only years of misery will force you to make changes when things aren't working out. You don't believe in half measures and easily show your feelings.

Somewhere along the way you will pursue frequent travel, in either a career or ownership of property outside the borders of your state or country.

✷ ✷ ✷

DECEMBER 11 SAGITTARIUS • The adventurous one of the zodiac
November 22 at 5:00 A.M. to December 21 at 10:00 P.M. • NUMEROLOGY 2

Possessions and Desires . . .

Gem: Sapphire—This gem may help you find forgiveness from those you've wronged.
Flower: Cockle—You love to show your affection.
Astral Color, Color Need, Apparel Color: Your Astral Color is Red, the color of passion, power, excitement, and strength. Violet in your environment will keep you empathetic toward others. In your wardrobe, Purple reflects your giving personality and brings you luck.
Fragrance: You need to be bathed in exotic scents that will give your imagination room to roam. Experiment with imported incense and tinctures to show the world what a spirited individual you are.
Tree: Maple—You have great stability and flashes of intuition.
Instruments: Pipe organ, cymbal, drum
Composers: Handel, Johann Sebastian Bach
Bird: Stork—Turkish bird, held in high esteem the world over. This bird is intelligent but may have strange tendencies.
Symbol: Cross—the symbol of self-sacrifice and reconciliation.

Harmonious Health and Nutrition . . .

Health Scent: Apple—You are creative, full of joy, and nearly magical. You bring happiness.
Favorable Foods: Cabbage, oranges, caraway seed, pecans, fish

What's Lucky . . .

Lucky Numbers: 5, 7
Best Months: February and June
Best Day of the Week: Thursday
Best Month Days: 2, 11, 20
Lucky Charms: Two 50-cent pieces. Give someone else one of them.
Harmonious Signs for Relationships and Partnerships: Aries, Leo, Sagittarius

Spiritual Guides . . .

Star: Al Beldah—Those with this star are sometimes the victims of hasty judgments.
Angel: Aduachiel—This angel governs the balance of elements—water, earth, fire, and air—and helps maintain a calm disposition.
Guardian Angel: St. Thomas—This angel brings affection from others and encourages you in all that you do.
Spiritual Stone: Emerald—This gem is thought to aid in smoothing the connection between the desires of the soul and those of the body.

✷ JUDITH'S INSIGHT ✷

You want to take on the world and often do just that. You must be cautious of attempting too much all at once. You don't mind working hard as long as you're having fun. Once the play is gone from a situation, you will look for a change. This could be problematic when it comes to relationships. You'd never abandon your mate, but once the spark fades you could become cold and depressed.

Whether or not you recognize it, your heart is set on a life of merriment. Your aspirations lie in the arts. You may have to look for a more structured job to pay the bills. If this is the case, you'll get your entertainment from hobbies.

You have persistence and consistency and courage. Things don't usually stay stuck in the middle around you. Your environment is very important to you. You must live, work, and play in comfortable surroundings.

Your self-confidence will be challenged throughout your life. While you know where your heart lies and where your head is, keeping both organized may be a trial. You'd do well in careers having to do with government, travel, and entertainment. Whether in your day-to-day job or volunteer work, the medical field could also be very important to you.

You work hard at keeping things together and rarely lose friends because you take every relationship very seriously.

✷ ✷ ✷

DECEMBER 12 SAGITTARIUS • The adventurous one of the zodiac

November 22 at 5::00 A.M. to December 21 at 10:00 P.M. • NUMEROLOGY 3

Possessions and Desires . . .

Gem: Ruby—This stone may lead you to energy, friendship, and happiness.

Flower: Coriander—You often don't realize how special your talents are.

Astral Color, Color Need, Apparel Color: Your Astral Color is Red, the color of passion, power, excitement, and strength. Violet in your environment keeps you empathetic toward others. In your wardrobe, Green is your power color for overcoming obstacles.

Fragrance: You need to be bathed in exotic scents that will give your imagination room to roam. Experiment with imported incense and tinctures to show the world what a spirited individual you are.

Tree: Elm—You have willpower, strength, and the ability to stand alone.

Instrument: Trombone

Composers: Verdi, Mendelssohn, Schumann

Bird: Eagle—This bird is quick to use its powers of flight. It can see immeasurable distances in a single glance, and can sometimes appear to be indifferent.

Symbol: Wreath—You have been crowned with a special personality. You are strong but extremely compassionate.

Harmonious Health and Nutrition . . .

Health Scent: Rose—This scent will lead you to passionate thoughts and make you feel warm inside.

Favorable Foods: Leafy greens, apples, bran, almonds, chicken

What's Lucky . . .

Lucky Numbers: 5, 7
Best Months: February and June
Best Day of the Week: Thursday
Best Month Days: 3, 12, 21
Lucky Charm: A pen that someone else has already used.

Harmonious Signs for Relationships and Partnerships: Aries, Leo, Sagittarius

Spiritual guides . . .

Star: Al Naim—Those with this star are often delightful.

Angel: Aduachiel—This angel governs the balance of elements—water, earth, fire, and air—and helps maintain a calm disposition.

Guardian Angel: Johiel—This angel is a protector of all those with a humble heart.

Spiritual Stone: Emerald—This gem is thought to aid in smoothing the connection between the desires of the soul and those of the body.

✴ JUDITH'S INSIGHT ✴

Love will be one of your greatest challenges. You know you want it, but you live in complete fear of it. Once committed, you remain loyal, but until you cross the mental line into partnership, you fight it tooth and nail simply because the hope of happiness scares the pants off you. You are charming, yet people will not understand why you act the way you do.

It is important to you to be considered a success, and you are a born leader. You have great organizational skills and the gift of gab. You will do well in politics and government, construction, or outside sales—in short, jobs in which you can spend most of your time interacting with different kinds of people.

You follow the letter of the law and expect your neighbors to do the same. This tendency might stick you with a career as a petty bureaucrat. You would also make an excellent builder or designer in your work or hobbies. The desire to build things—whether it be model airplanes or birthday cakes—screams to come out.

You subject yourself to many emotional pitfalls. You can brood when things don't go your way. You are very good at giving advice but not so hot at taking it. You make a better talker than listener until you gain the wisdom necessary to balance the two.

✴ ✴ ✴

DECEMBER 13
SAGITTARIUS • The adventurous one of the zodiac
November 22 at 5:00 A.M. to December 21 at 10:00 P.M. • NUMEROLOGY 4

Possessions and Desires . . .

Gem: Emerald—Those who carry this stone tend to be lucky in love.
Flower: Citron—Be careful that your many gifts don't make you difficult to be around.
Astral Color, Color Need, Apparel Color: Your Astral Color is Red, the color of passion, power, excitement, and strength. Violet in your environment keeps you empathetic toward others. In your wardrobe, Purple reflects your giving personality and brings you luck.
Fragrance: You need to be bathed in exotic scents that will give your imagination room to roam. Experiment with imported incense and tinctures to show the world what a spirited individual you are.
Tree: Cherry—You will find yourself faced with constant new emotional awakenings.
Instruments: Bass, clarinet
Composers: Haydn, Wagner
Bird: Robin—The most sociable of all birds, with the ability to create quick friendships. It also can easily adapt to any home. When it wants something, it has the tendency to try to snatch it.
Symbol: Star—You are full of inner brightness and will stand out in any crowd. You will be seen as special.

Harmonious Health and Nutrition . . .

Health Scent: Vanilla—This scent will fill you with a feeling of cleanliness and stability.
Favorable Foods: Dandelion, oranges, rice, pecans, fish

What's Lucky . . .

Lucky Numbers: 5, 7
Best Months: February and June
Best Day of the Week: Thursday
Best Month Days: 4, 13, 22
Lucky Charm: A piece of material cut from something in your home.
Harmonious Signs for Relationships and Partnerships: Aries, Leo, Sagittarius

Spiritual Guides . . .

Star: Al Beldah—Those with this star are sometimes the victims of hasty judgments.
Angel: Aduachiel—This angel governs the balance of elements—water, earth, fire, and air—and helps maintain a calm disposition.
Guardian Angel: Uriel—This angel brings the light of God's guidance.
Spiritual Stone: Emerald—This gem is thought to aid in smoothing the connection between the desires of the soul and those of the body.

✷ JUDITH'S INSIGHT ✷

You must carefully avoid falling into ruts. A stale environment is the worst for you. You love to be challenged and always want more than you have. You have a way with people and words, and you can do a lot because you have a vivid imagination and don't recognize any obstacles until you've passed them. You're continually drawn to unique and unusual people and places and tend to lead an unconventional life.

You're creative in uncommon ways. Creativity isn't just writing or painting; it's a different way to recognize what's around you. You have brilliant ideas and can probably whip up a gourmet dinner with leftovers or make a go-cart out of junk from the back of the garage. You are highly intelligent and resourceful.

Making and maintaining friendships comes easily to you. Relationships can be trickier. You seem to think true love has to be a challenge. And you're very fussy, which doesn't help. Sooner or later you learn what's important.

You must be cautious, as you have a tendency to become overburdened to the point of explosion. Usually you have an even temperament, but every once in awhile you find the villain role attractive. You were born to help and, whether you realize it or not, to teach.

Keep yourself from being too anxious. Remember, the more stable your emotions, the easier your life becomes.

Some appealing careers: lecturer, historian, or professor. You might own a retail establishment or maybe even a restaurant.

✷ ✷ ✷

DECEMBER 14 SAGITTARIUS • The adventurous one of the zodiac
November 22 at 5:00 A.M. to December 21 at 10:00 P.M. • NUMEROLOGY 5

Possessions and Desires . . .

Gem: Sardius—This stone could give the wearer unusual insights into his or her own heart.
Flower: Coxcomb—Your complex personality can often bring you into conflict with others.
Astral Color, Color Need, Apparel Color: Your Astral Color is Red, the color of passion, power, excitement, and strength. Violet in your environment keeps you empathetic toward others. In your wardrobe, Green is your power color for overcoming obstacles.
Fragrance: You need to be bathed in exotic scents that will give your imagination room to roam. Experiment with imported incense and tinctures to show the world what a spirited individual you are.
Tree: Apple—You are creative, full of joy, and nearly magical. You bring happiness.
Instruments: Viola, trumpet
Composer: Liszt
Bird: Flamingo—This beautiful, gregarious bird is always careful of its enemy. It is also a caretaker of the young and tries to keep everyone happy.
Symbol: Triangle—You have the right combination of abilities.

Harmonious Health and Nutrition . . .

Health Scent: Peach—This scent may balance your good qualities so that they equal your charm.
Favorable Foods: Savory, grapes, bran, almonds, chicken

What's Lucky . . .

Lucky Numbers: 5, 7
Best Months: February and June
Best Day of the Week: Thursday
Best Month Days: 4, 5, 23
Lucky Charms: A rabbit's foot or a white candle.
Harmonious Signs for Relationships and Partnerships: Aries, Leo, Sagittarius

Spiritual Guides . . .

Star: Al Naim—Those with this star are often delightful.
Angel: Aduachiel—This angel governs the balance of elements—water, earth, fire, and air—and helps maintain a calm disposition.
Guardian Angel: Plavwell—The guardian that gives power and strength to one's presence.
Spiritual Stone: Emerald—This gem is thought to aid in smoothing the connection between the desires of the soul and those of the body.

✶ JUDITH'S INSIGHT ✶

You spend most of your life looking for the hurdles to jump over. The love and desire for challenge leads you to seek what most people fear. You're a gambler by nature, though not always with money. You are a collector of entertainment memorabilia, and this would be a great industry for you to work in. You would make a fine entrepreneur or toy maker.

Your high energies will lead you into becoming your own boss at one point or another. Sheer determination brings you success. You are shrewd and sharp in handling business situations. If you work for somebody else, you're sure to wind up being a leader, never a follower. You're filled with ideas and need a job with constant stimulation. You'd do well in anything in the media, public relations, or communications.

Your charm will bring relationships to your doorstep. Your natural kindness will keep people in your life for a very long time, and you always have a date. You're generous not only with gifts but also with your emotions.

Your good side should always outweigh your bad, though you can have a hot temper. Relationships will put you through a hoop here and there, but you have remarkable stamina. Financially you will reap rewards because of your knack for creativity. Follow your intuition whenever it leads you.

✶ ✶ ✶

DECEMBER 15 SAGITTARIUS • The adventurous one of the zodiac
November 22 at 5:00 A.M. to December 21 at 10:00 P.M. • NUMEROLOGY 6

Possessions and Desires . . .

Gem: Topaz—This is an excellent gift to be exchanged between very loyal friends

Flower: Coreopsis—You are nearly always very cheerful.

Astral Color, Color Need, Apparel Color: Your Astral Color is Red, the color of passion, power, excitement, and strength. Violet in your environment keeps you empathetic toward others. In your wardrobe, Purple reflects your giving personality and brings you luck.

Fragrance: You need to be bathed in exotic scents that will give your imagination room to roam. Experiment with imported incense and tinctures to show the world what a spirited individual you are.

Tree: Palm—You tend to be very healthy and creative.

Instruments: Tambourine, lyre

Composer: Schubert

Bird: Lark—known for the beauty of its song, which is sometimes very unusual. It is also credited with extraordinary intelligence.

Symbol: Crescent—You are more likely to be influenced by the phases of the moon. Your easygoing manner leads you to peaceful situations.

Harmonious Health and Nutrition . . .

Health Scent: Orange Blossom—This scent may balance your body, mind, and soul.

Favorable Foods: Celery, prunes, unrefined cereals, pecans, fish

What's Lucky . . .

Lucky Numbers: 5, 7

Best Months: February and June

Best Day of the Week: Thursday

Best Month Days: 6, 15, 24

Lucky Charm: A religious token or card from any religion.

Harmonious Signs for Relationships and Partnerships: Aries, Leo, Sagittarius

Spiritual Guides . . .

Star: Al Naim—Those with this star are often delightful.

Angel: Aduachiel—This angel governs the balance of elements—water, earth, fire, and air—and helps maintain a calm disposition.

Guardian Angel: Michael—"Who is like God."

Spiritual Stone: Emerald—This gem is thought to aid in smoothing the connection between the desires of the soul and those of the body.

✶ JUDITH'S INSIGHT ✶

Your friendly disposition makes it easy for you to enter into relationships. Friends and family are usually devoted to you because you treat them better than you treat yourself. Low self-esteem in childhood and adolescence could have a negative impact on your adulthood. If this is the case, you may want to take steps to understand the root causes. See someone who can give you good advice.

You make the perfect host or hostess and will gravitate to careers relating to entertainment, communications, or public relations. You are a people person and probably feel depressed if you are not constantly surrounded by activity and interaction with others. Your love of outdoors and nature leads you to enjoy hobbies that concern animals, children, and environmental causes.

Dual incomes pop up in your life at some point. It may not be until you are on social security, but you can confidently expect that it will happen. You may have to be very careful with money, but in your later years finances will improve.

There isn't a mean bone in your body. When it comes to love you're attracted to energetic people with strong personalities. Be very clear with prospective mates that they shouldn't try to dominate you. Life will present you with more than your share of obstacles, but you have the necessary strength to endure. Your ideas and abilities are all very good; you just have to learn to believe in yourself more.

✶ ✶ ✶

DECEMBER 16 SAGITTARIUS • The adventurous one of the zodiac

November 22 at 5:00 A.M. to December 21 at 10:00 P.M. • NUMEROLOGY 7

Possessions and Desires . . .

Gem: Ruby—This stone may lead you to energy, friendship, and happiness.

Flower: Rock Rose—Your love is usually very powerful.

Astral Color, Color Need, Apparel Color: Your Astral Color is Red, the color of passion, power, excitement, and strength. Violet in your environment keeps you empathetic toward others. In your wardrobe, Green is your power color for overcoming obstacles.

Fragrance: You need to be bathed in exotic scents that will give your imagination room to roam. Experiment with imported incense and tinctures to show the world what a spirited individual you are.

Tree: Sycamore—Yours is the ability to love, communicate honestly with others, and have lasting relationships.

Instrument: Harp

Composers: Gluck, Brahms

Bird: Skylark—This handsome bird is beautiful when it sings. It always whistles as it works.

Symbol: Heart—You are enthusiastic, empathetic, and full of generosity and love.

Harmonious Health and Nutrition . . .

Health Scent: Jasmine—This scent may make you more easygoing when you are stressed.

Favorable Foods: Horseradish, black figs, rice, almonds, chicken

What's Lucky . . .

Lucky Numbers: 5, 7
Best Months: February and June
Best Day of the Week: Thursday
Best Month Days: 6, 15, 24
Lucky Charm: An old key.
Harmonious Signs for Relationships and Partnerships: Aries, Leo, Sagittarius

Spiritual Guides . . .

Star: Al Beldah—Those with this star are sometimes the victims of hasty judgments.

Angel: Aduachiel—This angel governs the balance of elements—water, earth, fire, and air—and helps maintain a calm disposition.

Guardian Angel: Raphael—This angel attends to all of your needs when you are looking for guidance.

Spiritual Stone: Emerald—This gem is thought to aid in smoothing the connection between the desires of the soul and those of the body.

✦ JUDITH'S INSIGHT ✦

You are always charming but not always lucky. Life seems to constantly throw up roadblocks. Your profound imagination is your greatest blessing and worst curse; it's a powerful tool but one with two edges. Your intense inner focus often forces you to ignore those around you. You are determined to succeed at all costs, even if you lose a friendship or two on the way. You have a very clear opinion as to how your life should be. Your attitude is that if the real world sometimes doesn't always match your inner movie, why should you care; you don't spend much time there anyway.

You're kind and warmhearted and find delight in giving pleasure to those you care for. You can, however, appear cold to those whose gestures of affection make you uncomfortable. Because people find you intriguing, this could happen to you quite often. You have an idealized view of romance, so your relationships border on extreme passion. When you have to face the truth, you're prone to more than the usual number of heartaches. And you can't be alone for any length of time.

When things don't go your way, you pout. You are easily sucked into ditches and can never really overcome depression by yourself. Your energy supply comes from your environment or other people. You know how to enjoy life and are generous when you have resources to spare.

You would make an unbelievable casting agent or commercial photographer, so long as there was exotic travel. Antiques may be a hobby or career whether dealing with furniture or jewelry.

✦ ✦ ✦

DECEMBER 17
SAGITTARIUS • The adventurous one of the zodiac
November 22 at 5:00 A.M. to December 21 at 10:00 P.M. • NUMEROLOGY 8

Possessions and Desires . . .

Gem: Chrysolite—This gem may help you clear your mind of sadness and worry.

Flower: Chamomile—You don't spend enough time relaxing.

Astral Color, Color Need, Apparel Color: Your Astral Color is Red, the color of passion, power, excitement, and strength. Violet in your environment keeps you empathetic toward others. In your wardrobe, Purple reflects your giving personality and brings you luck.

Fragrance: You need to be bathed in exotic scents that will give your imagination room to roam. Experiment with imported incense and tinctures to show the world what a spirited individual you are.

Tree: Pine—Your relationships tend to be harmonious, both emotionally and mentally.

Instrument: Cello

Composer: Mozart

Bird: Bobolink—This charming singer is equally good as a soloist or a member of an orchestra. It is a very romantic bird, useful as an insect destroyer, and elegant, with beautiful feathers, and always pleasant to have around.

Symbol: Wings—You are the source of balance in your world—this will bring you contentment.

Harmonious Health and Nutrition . . .

Health Scent: Almond—This scent may revitalize you and open you to greater possibilities.

Favorable Foods: Greens, peaches, caraway seed, pecans, fish

What's Lucky . . .

Lucky Numbers: 5, 7
Best Months: February and June
Best Day of the Week: Thursday
Best Month Days: 8, 17, 26
Lucky Charm: Red ribbon in your wallet or doorway.

Harmonious Signs for Relationships and Partnerships: Aries, Leo, Sagittarius

Spiritual Guides . . .

Star: Al Naim—Those with this star are often delightful.

Angel: Aduachiel—This angel governs the balance of elements—water, earth, fire, and air—and helps maintain a calm disposition.

Guardian Angel: Seraphim—An angel that brings love, light, and passion.

Spiritual Stone: Emerald—This gem is thought to aid in smoothing the connection between the desires of the soul and those of the body.

✴ JUDITH'S INSIGHT ✴

Think of the world as a willing genie eagerly awaiting your wish. You approach life and learning with enthusiasm. Your childhood probably wasn't all it should have been. Don't worry: your adult years will more than make up for it. You want it all so much that your desire makes the very air around you sizzle.

Marriage is your natural state, but you need to be with someone who's willing to work with you on maintaining it. If by the third date you don't feel your prospective mate is capable of spontaneity, you know they probably aren't for you. Be sure to pick someone who doesn't get easily jealous, as you're a terrible flirt.

Along with a brighter personal life, your finances improve as you get older. You like to share that firsthand knowledge of life's pitfalls with others. You give unstintingly of your time and energy to worthwhile causes, usually through organized volunteer work.

The jobs you select early on will determine your success, so choose wisely. You'd like to become an entertainer of some kind, but shun the rejection that goes along with it. This is one area where your indomitable will may meet an immovable barrier.

Explore your natural gifts: understanding will come with time, but not without some soul-searching. Some people love justice and become judges. Others love kindness and become counselors. You, loving both, can take your pick.

✴ ✴ ✴

DECEMBER 18 SAGITTARIUS • The adventurous one of the zodiac

November 22 at 5:00 A.M. to December 21 at 10:00 P.M. • NUMEROLOGY 9

Possessions and Desires . . .

Gem: Beryl—This gem could be good for meditation and concentration.
Flower: Cedar of Lebanon—You are a truly honest person.
Astral Color, Color Need, Apparel Color: Your Astral Color is Red, the color of passion, power, excitement, and strength. Violet in your environment keeps you empathetic toward others. In your wardrobe, Green is your power color for overcoming obstacles.
Fragrance: You need to be bathed in exotic scents that will give your imagination room to roam. Experiment with imported incense and tinctures to show the world what a spirited individual you are.
Tree: Holly—Beware that you are not carried away by your passionate nature. The only way to grow is to be open to new experiences.
Instruments: Violin, tympanum
Composer: Gluck
Bird: Mockingbird—the most proficient minstrel in the world's orchestra; graceful and enthusiastic.
Symbol: Anchor—This tranquil symbol signifies stability and strength, and stands for strong commitments in relationships.

Harmonious Health and Nutrition . . .

Health Scent: Lavender—This scent might lead others to trust you and make you patient.
Favorable Foods: Savory, apricots, rice, almonds, chicken

What's Lucky . . .

Lucky Numbers: 5, 7
Best Months: February and June
Best Day of the Week: Thursday
Best Month Days: 9, 18, 27

Lucky Charms: A U.S. coin or bill of any amount from the year you were born.
Harmonious Signs for Relationships and Partnerships: Aries, Leo, Sagittarius

Spiritual Guides . . . .

Star: Al Naim—Those with this star are often delightful.
Angel: Aduachiel—This angel governs the balance of elements—water, earth, fire, and air—and helps maintain a calm disposition.
Guardian Angel: Gabriel—"God is my strength."
Spiritual Stone: Emerald—this gem is thought to aid in smoothing the connection between the desires of the soul and those of the body.

✶ JUDITH'S INSIGHT ✶

You seem to think the world exists just to wrestle with. There is no reason for you to believe otherwise, since you so often pin it to the mat. You were born to work hard, and you have more energy after accomplishing a difficult task than when you started. Reliable, responsible, and capable, you have the drive necessary to become an independent contractor or entrepreneur.

You adore adventure—the riskier the better. Sports or any activity where you could work up a good sweat should be attractive to you. You get a thrill out of fast cars in the fast lane, and even more so if the road is slick and the sky is dark. You are generous with those who truly need it, but scornful toward those who don't.

You're a good person in a relationship because you're so loyal and dependable. With the right person, you not only give what you get, you give more. Though more likely to have long, substantial relationships, you may be married more than once.

It takes time for you to figure out who you are. Expect to become more secure with yourself as you get older. You are likely to retire early and start your own business. Often the tiniest things give you the help you need when faced with difficulty. You crush obstacles that never should have existed in the first place.

✶ ✶ ✶

DECEMBER 19 SAGITTARIUS • The adventurous one of the zodiac
November 22 at 5:00 A.M. to December 21 at 10:00 P.M. • NUMEROLOGY 1

Possessions and Desires . . .

Gem: Turquoise—This stone may help you find material wealth.

Flower: Carnation—You can be too quick to refuse love or kindness.

Astral Color, Color Need, Apparel Color: Your Astral Color is Red, the color of passion, power, excitement, and strength. Violet in your environment keeps you empathetic toward others. In your wardrobe, Purple reflects your giving personality and brings you luck.

Fragrance: You need to be bathed in exotic scents that will give your imagination room to roam. Experiment with imported incense and tinctures to show the world what a spirited individual you are.

Tree: Walnut—You are unusually helpful and always looking for constant changes in your life.

Instruments: Oboe, flute, clarinet, piano, French horn, organ, piccolo

Composer: Böhm

Bird: Hummingbird—This bird is delicate and graceful. It can remain still for hours, then dart off and be as busy as a bee.

Symbol: Crown—the universal sign of dignity.

Harmonious Health and Nutrition . . .

Health Scent: Strawberry—Soothing by nature, the strawberry promotes self-esteem and encourages love.

Favorable Foods: Cabbage, apples, bran, pecans, fish

What's Lucky . . .

Lucky Numbers: 5, 7
Best Months: February and June
Best Day of the Week: Thursday
Best Month Days: 1, 10, 19
Lucky Charm: A new penny in your shoe.
Harmonious Signs for Relationships and Partnerships: Aries, Leo, Sagittarius

Spiritual Guides

Star: Al Naim—Those with this star are often delightful.

Angel: Aduachiel—This angel governs the balance of elements—water, earth, fire, and air—and helps maintain a calm disposition.

Guardian Angel: Malachi—"Messenger of Jehovah."

Spiritual Stone: Emerald—This gem is thought to aid in smoothing the connection between the desires of the soul and those of the body.

✴ JUDITH'S INSIGHT ✴

People know you're brilliant and won't be surprised when you accomplish something truly amazing and out of the ordinary. You are self-confident, enthusiastic, and generally trustworthy. A highly regarded employee, you never complain even when working conditions are terrible. You feel you're there to do the job, not to whine about it.

Expect to find enjoyment in being an actor, musician, salesperson, or any other career that offers the opportunity to make people smile. You have a strong desire to travel and may have many close relationships with people from all over the world. In business you care less about making money than contributing to the future of something you believe in.

Intimate relationships may be torture because you are too stubborn to give up on the unhealthy ones. Commitment and loyalty mean so much to you that quitting is never an option, so you are prone to experiencing real agony. It is crucial you really know everything you can about your mate before you tie the knot. You hear advice when it's given to you, but seldom take it until years later when your mind suddenly changes. You don't feel it's your place to give others your opinions.

A good soul with a kind heart and caring mind, your worst fault is that you might be violently emotional. Learning to control yourself is your key to being happy.

✶ ✶ ✶

DECEMBER 20

SAGITTARIUS • The adventurous one of the zodiac

November 22 at 5:00 A.M. to December 21 at 10:00 P.M. • NUMEROLOGY 2

Possessions and Desires . . .

Gem: Sapphire—This gem may help you find forgiveness from those you've wronged.

Flower: Cardinal Flower—You stand out from those who surround you.

Astral Color, Color Need, Apparel Color: Your Astral Color is Red, the color of passion, power, excitement, and strength. Violet in your environment keeps you empathetic toward others. In your wardrobe, Green is your power color for overcoming obstacles.

Fragrance: You need to be bathed in exotic scents that will give your imagination room to roam. Experiment with imported incense and tinctures to show the world what a spirited individual you are.

Tree: Maple—You have great stability and flashes of intuition.

Instruments: Pipe organ, cymbal, drum

Composers: Handel, Johann Sebastian Bach

Bird: Stork—Turkish bird, held in high esteem the world over. This bird is intelligent but may have strange tendencies.

Symbol: Cross—the symbol of self-sacrifice and reconciliation.

Harmonious Health and Nutrition . . .

Health Scent: Apple—You are creative, full of joy, and nearly magical. You bring happiness.

Favorable Foods: Celery, grapes, unrefined cereals, almonds, chicken

What's Lucky . . .

Lucky Numbers: 5, 7

Best Months: February and June

Best Day of the Week: Thursday

Best Month Days: 2, 11, 20

Lucky Charms: Two 50-cent pieces. Give someone else one of them.

Harmonious Signs for Relationships and Partnerships: Aries, Leo, Sagittarius

Spiritual Guides

Star: Al Beldah—Those with this star are sometimes the victims of hasty judgments.

Angel: Aduachiel—This angel governs the balance of elements—water, earth, fire, and air—and helps maintain a calm disposition.

Guardian Angel: St. Thomas—This angel brings affection from others and encourages you in all that you do.

Spiritual Stone: Emerald—This gem is thought to aid in smoothing the connection between the desires of the soul and those of the body.

✶ JUDITH'S INSIGHT ✶

You would make an incredible politician. You love to please people and crave attention. Athletics should feed your energy. Travel will work its way into your life somewhere along the way. Willing to travel on charter packages alone, you are likely to be found on a guided tour around the world.

You can be temperamental on occasion, but your personality is consistent, at least on the outside. When it comes to more intimate relationships, you will fight an uphill battle until you realize you really don't want to be alone. It may also take time for you to fall in love with being in love. It can be the biggest challenge of your life.

You love a bargain and shopping. You'd make a great personal shopper, purchasing agent, casting agent, or talent scout. A born hunter, you like to conquer with all your might, and when it comes to love, you will do it all. Money comes to those who wait, and wait and wait.

You have many tastes and even more hidden talents. Be as confident as you act. All will be fine.

✶ ✶ ✶

DECEMBER 21 SAGITTARIUS • The adventurous one of the zodiac
November 22 at 5:00 A.M. to December 21 at 10:00 P.M. • NUMEROLOGY 3

Possessions and Desires . . .

Gem: Ruby—This stone may lead you to energy, friendship, and happiness.
Flower: Japonica—You may realize that only you can free yourself of your emotional blocks.
Astral Color, Color Need, Apparel Color: Your Astral Color is Red, the color of passion, power, excitement, and strength. Violet in your environment keeps you empathetic toward others. In your wardrobe, Purple reflects your giving personality and brings you luck.
Fragrance: You need to be bathed in exotic scents that will give your imagination room to roam. Experiment with imported incense and tinctures to show the world what a spirited individual you are.
Tree: Maple—You have great stability and flashes of intuition.
Instrument: Trombone
Composers: Verdi, Mendelssohn, Schumann
Bird: Swan—Regarded as royal and sacred, this bird has the protective nature of a mother, and can become a furious fighters in the defense of its young.
Symbol: Wreath—You have been crowned with a special personality. You are strong but extremely compassionate.

Harmonious Health and Nutrition . . .

Health Scent: Rose—This scent will lead you to passionate thoughts and make you feel warm inside.
Favorable Foods: Leafy greens, black figs, rice, pecans, fish

What's Lucky . . .

Lucky Numbers: 5, 7
Best Months: February and June
Best Day of the Week: Thursday
Best Month Days: 3, 12, 21
Lucky Charm: A pen that someone else has already used.

Harmonious Signs for Relationships and Partnerships: Aries, Leo, Sagittarius

Spiritual Guides . . .

Star: Al Naim—Those with this star are often delightful.
Angel: Aduachiel—This angel governs the balance of elements—water, earth, fire, and air—and helps maintain a calm disposition.
Guardian Angel: Johiel—This angel is a protector of all those with a humble heart.
Spiritual Stone: Chalcedon—This stone might help when taking long trips, especially by car

✷ JUDITH'S INSIGHT ✷

You are in every way an original soul. Follow your heart and believe that the inner path created just for you will lead where you need to go. It often seems that everyone you know relies on you for strength. You're the one who calls to catch up first. You are eager to help others, but sometimes this trait will allow the unscrupulous to take advantage of you.

You need stability in your love life, although you prefer matters relating to bedroom activities to be a bit exotic. Moving makes you apprehensive, but on the other hand, you love to travel. You spend too much of your free time fixing up your house only to leave it behind! Stability is actually one of your prime goals. The places you live become your roots; pulling them up hurts.

Though home and relationships have to be settled and predictable, you seek work that can be downright dangerous. You take on risky projects and are more than capable of carrying them through. Taking on more than you can handle doesn't concern you because you still haven't found your limits. You are reliable, loyal, and dependable. Your positive attitude makes you a great employee, though you seem to be the only boss who could stand the strain of so daring a subordinate. Look at careers in manufacturing, art, fashion, decorating, entertainment, or communications. One or more of these could be hobbies.

You tend to bring the world to your neighborhood; you are pretty much a whole world all by yourself.

✶ ✶ ✶

DECEMBER 22
CAPRICORN • The goat of the zodiac

December 21 at 10:00 P.M. to January 21 at 3:00 A.M. • NUMEROLOGY 4

Possessions and Desires . . .

Gem: Moonstone—This gem could protect you from danger.

Flower: Petunia—You tend to be the last to realize your desires.

Astral Color, Color Need, Apparel Color: Your Astral Color is Brown, which helps keep you grounded and stable. Blue in your environment helps you avoid becoming listless and disorganized. In your wardrobe, Blue-Green enhances your luck, because you will feel secure.

Fragrance: You are stimulated by a combination of greens and flowers, such as white roses, jasmine, and greenery. They give you feelings of strength and security.

Tree: Cherry—You will find yourself faced with constant new emotional awakenings.

Instruments: Bass, clarinet

Composers: Haydn, Wagner

Bird: Hummingbird—This bird is delicate and graceful. It can remain still for hours, then dart off and be as busy as a bee.

Symbol: Star—You are full of inner brightness and will stand out in any crowd. You will be seen as special.

Harmonious Health and Nutrition . . .

Health Scent: Vanilla—This scent will fill you with a feeling of cleanliness and stability.

Favorable Foods: Cauliflower, prunes, whole wheat, walnuts, cottage cheese

What's Lucky . . .

Lucky Numbers: 1, 2, 8
Best Months: March and November
Best Day of the Week: Saturday
Best Month Days: 4, 13, 22, 31
Lucky Charm: A piece of material cut from something in your home.

Harmonious Signs for Relationships and Partnerships: Capricorn, Taurus, Virgo, and anyone born from July 27 to September 27.

Spiritual Guides . . .

Star: Vega—Those with this star can be warriors in search of victory, especially in legal situations.

Angel: Hanaeb—This angel shows us our worldly desires in order to give us strength when we are going through uncertainty.

Guardian Angel: Uriel—This angel brings the light of God's guidance.

Spiritual Stone: Sardonyx—This stone may cause people to be attracted to you.

✶ JUDITH'S INSIGHT ✶

You will be drawn to animals, and working with them brings you a happiness you never find in people or machines. You love horses in particular: their grace, power, freedom, and speed all speak to your soul with inexplicable eloquence. You might become either a veterinarian, trainer, or livestock farmer. At the very least you should own many pets. If this is the case, look for a career in businesses where you can be creative, like jewelry design, manufacturing, or music. In addition, you possess the strength and energy for athletic competition.

You have no problem maintaining lifelong friendships because you're sincere and steadfast. Expect to spend a long time searching for that special someone. This suits your cautious and reserved demeanor. You may take too long seeking perfection before you feel comfortable enough to commit to a love relationship. As long as you trust your partner, you are a loyal mate.

Nothing bothers you more than disrespect and lack of gratitude. You are rigid when you need to be. Self-discipline is extremely important to you. Avoid the tendency to get overanxious. You will shine at public functions because of your charismatic personality. People are attracted to you and don't always know why.

✶ ✶ ✶

DECEMBER 23

CAPRICORN • The goat of the zodiac

December 21 at 10:00 P.M. to January 21 at 3:00 A.M. • NUMEROLOGY 5

Possessions and Desires . . .

Gem: Moonstone—This gem could protect you from danger.

Flower: Bear's-breech—You will have luck with financial matters.

Astral Color, Color Need, Apparel Color: Your Astral Color is Brown helping to keep you grounded and stable. Have Blue in your environment to avoid becoming listless and disorganized. Your wardrobe should have Maroon, giving you confidence.

Fragrance: You are stimulated by a combination of greens and flowers, such as white roses, jasmine, and greenery. They give you feelings of elegance, strength and security.

Tree: Apple—You are creative, full of joy, and nearly magical. You bring happiness.

Instruments: Oboe, flute, clarinet, piano, French horn, organ, piccolo

Composer: Liszt

Bird: Hummingbird—This bird is delicate and graceful. It can remain still for hours, then dart off and be as busy as a bee.

Symbol: Triangle—You have the right combination of abilities.

Harmonious Health and Nutrition . . .

Health Scent: Peach—This scent may balance your good qualities so that they equal your charm.

Favorable Foods: Brussels sprouts, raspberries, rye, almonds, pressed cheese

What's Lucky . . .

Lucky Numbers: 1, 2, 8

Best Months: March and November

Best Day of the Week: Saturday

Best Month Days: 4, 5, 23

Lucky Charms: A rabbit's foot or a white candle.

Harmonious Signs for Relationships and Partnerships: Capricorn, Taurus, Virgo, and anyone born from July 27 to September 27.

Spiritual Guides . . .

Star: Vega—Those with this star can be warriors in search of victory, especially in legal situations.

Angel: Hanaeb—This angel shows us our worldly desires in order to give us strength when we are going through uncertainty.

Guardian Angel: Plavwell—The guardian that gives power and strength to one's presence.

Spiritual Stone: Sardonyx—This stone may cause people to be attracted to you.

✷ JUDITH'S INSIGHT ✷

You love to learn. You can understand the underlying circumstances of any situation easily. You see all the possible outcomes as clearly as if they had already happened and wisely choose among them. With a finely tuned mind, you know how to balance between the uncertainty of fire and steadfastness of earth. You are eager to seek out spontaneity and excitement as long as you have stability to return to at home.

There aren't many subjects that won't interest you. You could do especially well in law. An original worldview makes you a natural leader. Your warm wit and a broad sense of humor could take you into the limelight at one point or another. A job may await you in the field of communications. Your work life is so exciting that it seems like an endless stream of news bulletins. Your name belongs in flashing lights.

Charming and warm, you will have no problem finding and connecting with the right mate, although you don't see marriage as a source of excitement. You may neglect your family until later in life, and this causes friction. Because you spend so little time at home, your mate might consider the relationship dead. You will either end up changing your priorities or your address.

You do become a financial success in this lifetime. Expect your name to be remembered long after you leave this world behind.

★ ★ ★

DECEMBER 24

CAPRICORN • The goat of the zodiac

December 21 at 10:00 P.M. to January 21 at 3:00 A.M. • NUMEROLOGY 6

Possessions and Desires . . .

Gem: Moonstone—This gem could protect you from danger.

Flower: Chrysanthemum—You are drawn to what you know to be true.

Astral Color, Color Need, Apparel Color: Your Astral Color is Brown, which helps keep you grounded and stable. Blue in your environment helps you avoid becoming listless and disorganized. In your wardrobe, Maroon gives you confidence.

Fragrance: You are stimulated by a combination of greens and flowers, such as white roses, jasmine, and greenery. They give you feelings of elegance, strength, and security.

Tree: Palm—You tend to be healthy and creative.

Instruments: Tambourine, lyre

Composer: Schubert

Bird: Bird of Paradise—the "bird of the Gods." You will shine and love extraordinary circumstances.

Symbol: Anchor—This tranquil symbol signifies stability and strength, and stands for strong commitments in relationships.

Harmonious Health and Nutrition . . .

Health Scent: Orange Blossom—This scent may balance your body, mind, and soul.

Favorable Foods: Watercress, blackberries, whole wheat, beechnuts, eggs

What's Lucky . . .

Lucky Numbers: 1, 2, 8

Best Months: March and November

Best Day of the Week: Saturday

Best Month Days: 6, 15, 24

Lucky Charms: A religious token or card from any religion.

Harmonious Signs for Relationships and Partnerships: Capricorn, Taurus, Virgo, and anyone born from July 27 to September 27.

Spiritual Guides . . .

Star: Vega—Those with this star can be warriors in search of victory, especially in legal situations.

Angel: Hanaeb—This angel shows us our worldly desires in order to give us strength.

Guardian Angel: Michael—"Who is like God."

Spiritual Stone: Sardonyx—This stone may cause people to be attracted to you.

✶ *JUDITH'S INSIGHT* ✶

Everyone recognizes your charisma but you. Old-fashioned and conventional, you think boys will be boys, and girls are supposed to be young ladies. But that doesn't mean you stay that way your whole life. If you are a man you will lend yourself to your masculine pride. If you are a woman you will love a man who opens a door to a car, but never one that closes one on you in business.

You are so charming that you usually have several possible relationships running concurrently. Keeping your partners straight is your biggest romantic challenge. Unfortunately, when you find your perfect mate, he or she will hold this against you. It's just your luck to become smitten by the one person who stays away. You will come into your own; however, it takes you some time. Family and children are important to you. You desire passion, fun, and fantasy in the early years and comfortable stability as you get older.

You are your own worst enemy. Trying to control and dictate to others does not win and keep friends. You love to give advice and relish careers in counseling. You are independent and determined enough to be a great entrepreneur. You may find other possible employment opportunities in communications, bookkeeping, or teaching music.

Good things come to those who wait; sadly enough, you have yet to learn how.

✶ ✶ ✶

DECEMBER 25

CAPRICORN • The goat of the zodiac

December 21 at 10:00 P.M. to January 21 at 3:00 A.M. • NUMEROLOGY 7

Possessions and Desires . . .

Gem: Moonstone—This gem could protect you from danger.

Flower: Christmas Rose—You may need to find a natural way to tranquilize your anxiety.

Astral Color, Color Need, Apparel Color: Your Astral Color is Brown, which helps to keep you grounded and stable. Blue in your environment helps you avoid becoming listless and disorganized. In your wardrobe, Blue-Green enhances your luck and makes you feel secure.

Fragrance: You are stimulated by a combination of greens and flowers, such as white roses, jasmine and greenery. They give you feelings of elegance, strength, and security.

Tree: Sycamore—Yours is the ability to love, communicate honestly with others, and have lasting relationships.

Instrument: Harp

Composers: Gluck, Brahms

Bird: Hummingbird—This bird is delicate and graceful. It can remain still for hours, then dart off and be as busy as a bee.

Symbol: Heart—You are enthusiastic, empathetic, and full of generosity and love.

Harmonious Health and Nutrition . . .

Health Scent: Jasmine—This scent may make you more easygoing when you are stressed.

Favorable Foods: String beans, peaches, rye, peanuts, cottage cheese

What's Lucky . . .

Lucky Numbers: 1, 2, 8
Best Months: March and November
Best Day of the Week: Saturday
Best Month Days: 6, 15, 24
Lucky Charm: An old key.
Harmonious Signs for Relationships and Partnerships: Capricorn, Taurus, Virgo, and anyone born from July 27 to September 27.

Spiritual Guides . . .

Star: Vega—Those with this star can be warriors in search of victory, especially in legal situations.

Angel: Hanaeb—This angel shows us our worldly desires in order to give us strength when we are going through uncertainty.

Guardian Angel: Raphael—This angel attends to all of your needs when you are looking for guidance.

Spiritual Stone: Sardonyx—This stone may cause people to be attracted to you.

✳ JUDITH'S INSIGHT ✳

You are strong in your mind, body, and spirit, but at times weak when it comes to matters of the heart. Your tendency to meet obstacles head-on should be tempered with knowing how to avoid them. You are enthusiastic and generally a happy person. Full of energy, you can accomplish much in this life.

Only after you have experienced the worst kind of heartache will you find love. Learning to stand up for yourself in a relationship is a lesson you should master, the sooner the better. Eventually you find luck with a love match, and your mate will be very devoted. After all you go through to win that special person, be sure you take the time to maintain the relationship, or you might find yourself alone again.

You will do well in business and could create one from scratch. Two jobs may present themselves at the same time. You're prone to overwork, so be sure to take time to enjoy the life you've built for yourself.

You are better to others than you are to yourself. Low self-esteem early in life could cripple you emotionally unless you face and overcome it. You might consider seeking a professional to help you with this problem. Your sunny disposition makes it easy to form friendships. Always the perfect host or hostess, you would do very well in careers relating to entertainment or communications. You are a people person. Social interaction energizes you.

✳ ✳ ✳

DECEMBER 26
CAPRICORN • The goat of the zodiac

December 21 at 10:00 P.M. to January 21 at 3:00 A.M. • NUMEROLOGY 1

Possessions and Desires . . .

Gem: Moonstone—This gem could protect you from danger.

Flower: Balm of Gilead—You can be a cure for other people's depressions.

Astral Color, Color Need, Apparel Color: Your Astral Color is Brown, which helps to keep you grounded and stable. Blue in your environment helps you avoid becoming listless and disorganized. In your wardrobe, Maroon brings you confidence.

Fragrance: You are stimulated by a combination of greens and flowers such as white roses, jasmine, and greenery. They give you feelings of elegance, strength, and security.

Tree: Walnut—You are unusually helpful and aways looking for constant changes in your life.

Instruments: Oboe, flute, clarinet, piano, French horn, organ, piccolo

Composer: Böhm

Bird: Bird of paradise—the "birds of the gods." You will shine and love extraordinary circumstances.

Symbol: Crown—the universal sign of dignity.

Harmonious Health and Nutrition . . .

Health Scent: Strawberry—Soothing by nature, the strawberry promotes self-esteem and encourages love.

Favorable Foods: Asparagus, pineapples, whole wheat, beechnuts, buttermilk

What's Lucky . . .

Lucky Numbers: 1, 2, 8
Best Months: March and November
Best Day of the Week: Saturday
Best Month Days: 1, 10, 19, 28
Lucky Charm: A new penny in your shoe
Harmonious Signs for Relationships and Partnerships: Capricorn, Taurus, Virgo, and anyone born from July 27 to September 27.

Spiritual Guides . . .

Star: Vega—Those with this star can be warriors in search of victory, especially in legal situations.

Angel: Hanaeb—This angel shows us our worldly desires in order to give us strength when we are going through uncertainty.

Guardian Angel: Malachi—"Messenger of Jehovah."

Spiritual Stone: Sardonyx—This stone may cause people to be attracted to you.

✶ JUDITH'S INSIGHT ✶

The question you frequently hear is, How could someone so nice be so unlucky all the time? Your energy and drive surround you like a force field. You have a kind and gentle nature, although sometimes when nervous you treat people coldly.

You are fascinated with the world around you, and you can do anything once you decide what's best. It would be more satisfying for you to work outdoors. No matter what job you find yourself in, you realize that you are a born builder; whether the construction materials are stock portfolios, businesses, or the traditional bricks, mortar, and wood. And you always create something solid.

You fantasize more than you indulge in the romance life could offer you. If you can ever get what you feel out of your head and into practice, you will find a rapt audience of one in that special person. You are the most loyal and devoted mate that anybody could have. Where you live is ultra-important. You may not pay enough attention to your family until later in life. After a major life lesson, you become devoted to your home life.

You can handle what comes your way with aplomb and safely direct your own energies. At work you are a devoted servant, even if you're the boss. You are generous to those who are generous to you.

✶ ✶ ✶

DECEMBER 27

CAPRICORN • The goat of the zodiac

December 21 at 10:00 P.M. to January 21 at 3:00 A.M. • NUMEROLOGY 9

Possessions and Desires . . .

Gem: Moonstone—This gem could protect you from danger.

Flower: Ash Tree—The grandeur of the natural world fills you with awe and joy.

Astral Color, Color Need, Apparel Color: Your Astral Color is Brown, which helps to keep you grounded and stable. Blue in your environment helps you avoid becoming listless and disorganized. In your wardrobe, Maroon gives you confidence.

Fragrance: You are stimulated by a combination of greens and flowers, such as white roses, jasmine, and greenery. They give feelings of elegance, strength, and security.

Tree: Walnut—You are unusually helpful and always looking for constant changes in your life.

Instruments: Clarinet, piano, organ

Composer: Gluck

Bird: Hummingbird—This bird is delicate and graceful. It can remain still for hours, then dart off and be as busy as a bee.

Symbol: Anchor—This tranquil symbol signifies stability and strength, and stands for strong commitments in relationships.

Harmonious Health and Nutrition . . .

Health Scent: Lavender—This scent might lead others to trust you and make you patient.

Favorable Foods: Cauliflower, blackberries, rye, peanuts, cottage cheese

What's Lucky . . .

Lucky Numbers: 1, 2, 8
Best Months: March and November
Best Day of the Week: Saturday
Best Month Days: 9, 18, 27
Lucky Charms: A U.S. coin or a bill of any amount from the year you were born.

Harmonious Signs for Relationships and Partnerships: Capricorn, Taurus, Virgo, and anyone born from July 27 to September 27.

Spiritual Guides . . .

Star: Vega—Those with this star can be warriors in search of victory, expecially in legal situations.

Angel: Hanaeb—This angel shows us our worldly desires in order to give us strength when we are going through uncertainty.

Guardian Angel: Gabriel—"God is my strength."

Spiritual Stone: Sardonyx—This stone may cause people to be attracted to you.

✶ JUDITH'S INSIGHT ✶

You are capable, restless, and headstrong. When it comes to work, you're all business. Your fear that others may see you as weak causes you to be overly aggressive and abrupt. However, you aren't fooling anyone for long: everyone recognizes the soft, cuddly teddy bear that you really are. You would make a fine athlete, as you possess the energy, enthusiasm, and physical strength to endure. You may enjoy having several differing jobs at once.

You are more likely to find your spouse where you work and will probably have to kiss a lot of toads before discovering the one you overlooked was meant for you all along. Your wit and charm make you a very attractive catch, so luring others into your life won't be a problem. You are the most devoted person when it comes to home and family issues.

Learn to discover that you have many friends who prey on your good nature. They take full advantage of your unflagging loyalty. You put up with it because you are too stubborn to protect yourself. Even acquaintances find you to be generous and giving. After matters are settled, you still find yourself endlessly rethinking them. Your own success will surprise you.

You might become a businessperson of some kind or an entrepreneur. You would also make a good travel agent and travel coordinator.

✶ ✶ ✶

DECEMBER 28
CAPRICORN • The goat of the zodiac
December 21 at 10:00 P.M. to January 21 at 3:00 A.M. • NUMEROLOGY 1

Possessions and Desires . . .

Gem: Moonstone—This gem could protect you from danger.

Flower: Arbor Vitae—This is the flower of unchanging frendship.

Astral Color, Color Need, Apparel Color: Your Astral Color is Brown, which helps to keep you grounded and stable. Blue in your environment helps you avoid becoming listless and disorganized. In your wardrobe, Blue-Green enhances your luck and makes you feel secure.

Fragrance: You are stimulated by a combination of greens and flowers, such as white roses, jasmine, and greenery. They give you feelings of elegance, strength, and security.

Tree: Walnut—You are unusually helpful and always looking for constant changes in your life.

Instruments: Oboe, flute, clarinet, piano, French horn, organ, piccolo

Composer: Böhm

Bird: Hummingbird—This bird is delicate and graceful. It can remain still for hours, then dart off and be as busy as a bee.

Symbol: Crown—the universal sign of dignity.

Harmonious Health and Nutrition . . .

Health Scent: Strawberry—Soothing by nature, the strawberry promotes self-esteem and encourages love.

Favorable Foods: Lettuce, raspberries, whole wheat, walnuts, pressed cheese

What's Lucky . . .

Lucky Numbers: 1, 2, 8
Best Months: March and November
Best Day of the Week: Saturday
Best Month Days: 1, 10, 19, 28
Lucky Charm: A new penny in your shoe.
Harmonious Signs for Relationships and Partnerships: Capricorn, Taurus, Virgo, and anyone born from July 27 to September 27.

Spiritual Guides . . .

Star: Vega—Those with this star can be warriors in search of victory, especially in legal situations.

Angel: Hanaeb—This angel shows us our worldly desires in order to give us strength when we are going through uncertainty.

Guardian Angel: Malachi—"Messenger of Jehovah."

Spiritual Stone: Sardonyx—This stone may cause people to be attracted to you.

✷ JUDITH'S INSIGHT ✷

You can be really brilliant given the proper task. It is very likely that at some point in your life you will become well known. Your self-confidence will take you all the way to the bank and farther. Your work is always of the highest quality, and you rarely complain about tasks or working conditions. You are just as likely to end up digging ditches as holding a critical office position.

At some point in your life, you will happily find yourself on stage. The guitar may amuse your friends and lead to a career in music. People are drawn to you, and you do well working in jobs dealing with the public, such as customer service. You have a knack for art and could be a fine designer. Your love of travel may lead you to a career as an agent. A natural in business, you have no problem owning and operating your own or managing someone else's.

Your love life of peaks and valleys stabilizes once you decide you want a harmonious mate. Getting out of bad relationships can be nightmarish as a horror movie. You take advice well and are more than sensitive when other people are hurting.

You need to sharpen your communication skills. Amazing personal growth comes in your forties. Earlier on in life, you grab what you can. As you mature, however, you become just the opposite, giving beyond your means. People gravitate to you for your energy and enthusiasm.

✷ ✷ ✷

DECEMBER 29

CAPRICORN • The goat of the zodiac

December 21 at 10:00 P.M. to January 21 at 3:00 A.M. • **NUMEROLOGY 2**

Possessions and Desires . . .

Gem: Moonstone—This gem could protect you from danger.

Flower: Amaranth—You should have a very long life.

Astral Color, Color Need, Apparel Color: Your Astral Color is Brown, which helps to keep you grounded and stable. Blue in your environment helps you avoid becoming listless and disorganized. In your wardrobe, Maroon gives you confidence.

Fragrance: You are stimulated by a combination of greens and flowers, such as white roses, jasmine, and greenery. They give you feelings of elegance, strength, and security.

Tree: Maple—You have both great stability and flashes of intuition.

Instruments: Pipe organ, cymbal, drum

Composers: Handel, Johann Sebastian Bach

Bird: Hummingbird—This bird is delicate and graceful. It can remain still for hours, then dart off and be as busy as a bee.

Symbol: Crown—the universal sign of dignity.

Harmonious Health and Nutrition . . .

Health Scent: Strawberry—Soothing by nature, the strawberry promotes self-esteem and encourages love.

Favorable Foods: String beans, peaches, rye, almonds, cottage cheese

What's Lucky . . .

Lucky Numbers: 1, 2, 8
Best Months: March and November
Best Day of the Week: Saturday
Best Month Days: 2, 11, 20, 29
Lucky Charms: Two 50-cent pieces. Give someone else one of them.
Harmonious Signs for Relationships and Partnerships: Capricorn, Taurus, Virgo, and anyone born from July 27 to September 27.

Spiritual Guides . . .

Star: Vega—Those with this star can be warriors in search of victory, especially in legal situations.

Angel: Hanaeb—This angel shows us our worldly desires in order to give us strength when we are going through uncertainty.

Guardian Angel: Malachi—"Messenger of Jehovah."

Spiritual Stone: Sardonyx—This stone may cause people to be attracted to you.

✳ JUDITH'S INSIGHT ✳

You are persistent, consistent, brave, and not likely to turn off your chosen course because of obstacles. You endure *anything* to keep a commitment. When faced with unfamiliar circumstances, you become quiet and shy. You enjoy your version of entertainment when you make the time for it. Sadly, you tend to be a workaholic.

Though you'd like to work in the arts or music industries, it's highly likely that you find yourself in a cubicle working for a large company. You would do well as an attorney, as a teacher, or in business. You are thoughtful and have no problem showing emotion. You're convincing, smooth, and graceful in speech, which means you'd do nicely in politics or communications.

Some will consider you a worthy role model. You are loyal and possess a wicked sense of humor. Close companions always feel safe around you because you're fearless. Your spouse may even choose you for this particular quality. You are spirited and have a strong zest for life. You are capable of being somewhat reckless or headstrong. All in all, you are an extremely devoted friend and family member.

✱ ✱ ✱

DECEMBER 30

CAPRICORN • The goat of the zodiac

December 21 at 10:00 P.M. to January 21 at 3:00 A.M. • NUMEROLOGY 3

Possessions and Desires . . .

Gem: Moonstone—This gem could protect you from danger.

Flower: Ambrosia—Your love will tend to be returned.

Astral Color, Color Need, Apparel Color: Your Astral Color is Brown, helping to keep you grounded and stable. Have Blue in your environment to avoid becoming listless and disorganized. Your wardrobe should have Blue-Green, enhancing your luck, because you will feel secure.

Fragrance: You are stimulated by a combination of greens and flowers, such as white roses, jasmine, and greenery. They give you feelings of elegance, strength, and security.

Tree: Elm—You have willpower, strength, and the ability to stand alone.

Instrument: Trombone

Composers: Verdi, Mendelssohn, Schumann

Bird: Hummingbird—This bird is delicate and graceful. It can remain still for hours, then dart off and be as busy as a bee.

Symbol: Wreath—You have been crowned with a special personality. You are strong but extremely compassionate.

Harmonious Health and Nutrition . . .

Health Scent: Rose—This scent will lead you to passionate thoughts and make you feel warm inside.

Favorable Foods: Watercress, prunes, whole wheat, peanuts, pressed cheese

What's Lucky . . .

Lucky Numbers: 1, 2, 8

Best Months: March and November

Best Day of the Week: Saturday

Best Month Days: 3, 12, 21, 30

Lucky Charm: A pen that someone else has already used.

Harmonious Signs for Relationships and Partnerships: Capricorn, Taurus, Virgo, and anyone born from July 27 to September 27.

Spiritual Guides . . .

Star: Vega—Those with this star can be warriors in search of victory, especially in legal situations.

Angel: Hanaeb—This angel shows us our worldly desires in order to give us strength when we are going through uncertainty.

Guardian Angel: Johiel—This angel is a protector of all those who with a humble heart.

Spiritual Stone: Sardonyx—This stone may cause people to be attracted to you.

✷ JUDITH'S INSIGHT ✷

You're always thoughtful, and will do anything to improve someone else's day. Your charm and wit serve you well. As you get older, your love of challenge only increases. You may work for others while maintaining a business of your own on the side. You are more creative than you realize, and nothing delights you more than your own accomplishments.

You are mechanically inclined and should seek opportunities to work with your hands. A career in politics, government, or law enforcement should also mesh nicely with your skills. You could be a bit more flexible. You tend to rigidly follow the letter of the law without permitting exceptions.

A stable home life is so important that without it you wither emotionally. You have a clear sense of your personal values. Allow your intuition to be a sure and steady guide to success. It will take you there. Relationships are always easy because you make them so. You and your mate are devoted to each other—it would take a crane to pry you from each other's sides.

You have difficulty relaxing. As you get older, you feel more secure and let more of your personality develop in charming ways.

You will accomplish much if you can stop chasing down dead-end streets.

✸ ✸ ✸

DECEMBER 31

CAPRICORN • The goat of the zodiac

December 21 at 10:00 P.M. to January 21 at 3:00 A.M. • NUMEROLOGY 4

Possessions and Desires . . .

Gem: Moonstone—This gem might make you safer when you're nervous.

Flower: Apple Blossom—You will be famous even if it's just in your neighborhood.

Astral Color, Color Need, Apparel Color: Your Astral Color is Brown, which helps to keep you grounded and stable. Blue in your environment helps you avoid becoming listless and disorganized. In your wardrobe, Blue-Green enhances your luck and makes you feel secure.

Fragrance: You are stimulated by a combination of greens and flowers, such as white roses, jasmine, and greenery. They give you feelings of elegance, strength, and security.

Tree: Cherry—You will find yourself faced with constant new emotional awakenings.

Instruments: Bass, clarinet

Composers: Haydn, Wagner

Bird: Bird of paradise—the "bird of the gods." You will shine and love extraordinary circumstances.

Symbol: Star—You are full of inner brightness and will stand out in any crowd. You will be seen as special.

Harmonious Health and Nutrition . . .

Health Scent: Vanilla—This scent will fill you with a feeling of cleanliness and stability.

Favorable Foods: Asparagus, cherries, rye, beechnuts, eggs

What's Lucky . . .

Lucky Numbers: 1, 2, 8

Best Months: March and November

Best Day of the Week: Saturday

Best Month Days: 4, 13, 22, 31

Lucky Charm: A piece of material cut from something in your home.

Harmonious Signs for Relationships and Partnerships: Capricorn, Taurus, Virgo, and anyone born from July 27 to September 27.

Spiritual Guides . . .

Star: Vega—Those with this star can be warriors in search of victory, especially in legal situations.

Angel: Hanaeb—This angel shows us our worldly desires in order to give us strength when we are going through uncertainty.

Guardian Angel: Uriel—This angel brings the light of God's guidance.

Spiritual Stone: Sardonyx—This stone may cause people to be attracted to you.

✶ JUDITH'S INSIGHT ✶

You have executive abilities and are a born leader. You're highly intelligent and remarkable at handling people and events. Your vivid imagination may tempt you into an artistic career. Your executive ability, however, will surely land you in a business situation. You are drawn to unique, unusual, and exotic people and places. You love entertaining as much as being entertained. Anything that makes up the natural world interests you.

You may only be able to relax while outdoors, say, camping or fishing. Some may see you as a little narrow-minded and stubborn, but your thoughtfulness always redeems you. You will do well employed as a jeweler or retail manufacturer. You are a great athlete because of your high energy levels. Look for opportunity in this area.

Your sincerity makes you a popular friend. People don't just like you, they love you. On the other hand, romantically, plan on getting through many truly difficult years. Each failed relationship seems the same horrible event with a new unspeakable twist. The up side is that your experience ultimately makes you a devoted mate. You can be cautious and reserved and, when you choose to be, shy and introspective. Respect from you is earned, and ungrateful behavior deeply offends you.

You can be very disciplined and expect the same of those around you. You should fight the urge to be overanxious and keep both feet on the ground. You're too quick to lose your temper. Find a way to expend that extra energy in a positive way. In addition to your life's work, take on more than one hobby so that you always have something to do.

✶ ✶ ✶

RESOURCES

Our Fate and the Zodiac, Margaret Mayo. Brentano's, 1990.

Violets, Tennyson, D. Wolfe. Fiske & Co., Boston, 1898.

The Influence of the Stars, Rosa Baughan. Kegan, Paul Trench, Trubner & Co. Ltd., 1904

The Vibrations of Numbers, Mrs. L. Dow. Ballutti, Atlantic City, New Jersey, 1913.

Discourses from the Spirit World, Stephen Olin. Partridge and Butler, New York, 1853.

The Guide to Astrology, Raphael. W. Foulsham & Co., London, 1898.

A Practical Treatise of Astral Medicine and Therapeutics, Dr. M. Duz. W. Foulsham & Co., Paris, 1912.

The Philosophy of Numbers, Mrs. L. Dow. Ballutti, 1908.

The Astrologers Guide, Guido Bonatus. Jerom Cardan, Wm. C. Eldon Serjeant, London, 1886.

The Hindu Book of Astrology. The New York Magazine of Mysteries, 1908.

Astrology for All, Alan Leo, London, 1910.

A Manual of Astrology or the Book of the Stars. Thomas Tigg & Son, 1837.

Metaphysical Astrology, John Hazelrigg. Hermetric Publishing Company, 1917.

Asteophysic Principles, John Hazelrigg. Hermetric Publishing Company, 1917.

The Key of Destiny, F. Homer Curtis. E.P. Dutton, 1919.

The Occult Sciences, Arthur Edward Waite. Kegan, Paul Trench, Trubner & Co. Ltd., 1891.

The Book of Knowledge Children's Encyclopedia. The Grolier Society, 1918.

Sacred and Legendary Art, Mrs. Jameson. Longmans, Green & Co., London, 1870.

Sealed Book of Daniel Opened, William C. Thurman, 1867.

Number and Litten or Thirty-Two Paths of Wisdom, E.C.B. Peeke, 1908.

Ptolemy's Tetrabiblos, J.M. Ashmand, 1917.

The Guardian Angel, Oliver Wendell Holmes, 1895.

Mastery of Fate, C.D. Larson, The Progress Co., 1908.

Red-Letter Days, Gail Hamilton. Ticknor and Field, Boston, 1866.

Heliocentric Astrology and Solar Mentality, Yarmo Vedra. Holmes W. Morton, 1899.

The Birds Calendar, H. E. Parkhurst. Charles Scribner, 1894.

The Special Basis of Astrology, Joseph G. Dalton. McCoy Publishing, 1893.

The Book of Days, W & R Chambers. J.B. Lippincott & Co., 1864.

Practical Astrology, Comte C. de Saint-Germain. Laird & Lee Publishers, Chicago.

Astrology, M. M. MacGregor. The Penn Publishing Company, 1904.

Flower and Fruit, Jane H. Newell. Ginn & Company, 1896.

Stars of Destiny, Katherine Taylor Craig. E. P. Dutton & Company, New York, 1916.

Starlight, C. W. Leadbeater. Theosophical Publishing House, Adyar, Madras, India, 1917.

The Influence of the Stars, Rosa Baughan. George Redway, London, 1889.

Moon Lore, Rev. Timothy Harley, London, 1885.

The Influence of the Zodiac Upon Human Life, Eleanor Kirk, 1894.

The Viking Age, Paul B. Du Chaillu. Charles Scribner's Sons, 1889.

Flower Fables, Louisa May Alcott. Henry Altemus Company, Philadelphia, 1898.

The Living World, J. W. Buel. H. S. Smith, 1889.

Past, Present, and Future, J. White, Herald Publishing Association, Washington, D.C., 1909.